PRENTICE HALL WRITER'S SOLUTION

COPPER

SOURCEBOOK

ANNOTATED TEACHER'S EDITION

PRENTICE HALL
Simon & Schuster Education Group
A VIACOM COMPANY

Contents

Writer's Solution Sourcebook
Annotated Teacher's Edition

ISBN 0-13-834160-5

3 4 5 6 7 8 9 10 00 99 98 97

Acknowledgment
Grateful acknowledgement is given for permission to reuse the following audiovisual materials:
Chamber Theatre Productions Inc., Boston, MA. Filmed by Static and Motion
"Dr. Heidegger's Experiment" by Nathaniel Hawthorne. Adapted by Patricia H. Sankus; directed by Ingrid Sonnichsen. "The Tell-Tale Heart" by Edgar Allan Poe. Adapted by Ted Davis; directed by Patricia H. Sankus.

PRENTICE HALL
Simon & Schuster Education Group
A VIACOM COMPANY

Program Overview

Introducing the *Writer's Solution*

Writer's Solution is a complete print and technology program in writing instruction for your middle grades classroom. The program is designed to

- allow students to learn at their own pace.
- motivate student writing through its multimedia presentation.
- fit your curriculum through its flexibility.
- bring writers into your classroom to talk about writing.
- capitalize fully on the instructional power of technology while remaining easy to use.

In contrast to linear, textbook-driven traditional writing programs, the recursive nature of *Writer's Solution* mirrors the recursive nature of the writing process itself. Students do not progress in lock step through the program. Technology components can be used for a variety of instructional purposes, concentrating on particular areas and revisiting others as needed. The teaching philosophy behind *Writer's Solution* allows you to design an individual curriculum for each of your students to progress at his or her own pace.

This approach frees you to function as a "facilitator" who artfully guides students to learn from different resources and from each other. *Writer's Solution*'s resources and flexibility help you meet students' individual needs while managing a large class. For example, after the class begins a lesson on a type of writing, you can provide individualized attention as needed by assigning a particular tutorial to a student. However, because of the program's numerous innovations, we recommend that you carefully review the information that appears in the following pages. Here is some of what you will find:

- an overview of the program and its components
- answers to common questions about how to use the program
- information about integrating the language arts
- suggestions for addressing special needs
- complete scope and sequences for the major program components

Writer's Solution is structured for ease of use, meeting common objectives for effective writing. Instructional content is organized by nine "modes" of writing. Each mode corresponds to a tutorial in the *Writing Lab* CD-ROM, a chapter of the *Sourcebook*, and a featured writer segment on the *Writers at Work Videodisc*.

Writer's Solution Program Components

Writer's Solution is designed to be effective regardless of which components are available to you, or how often they are available. However, greater familiarity with each of them will maximize your instructional options.

- *Writers at Work Videodisc*

  This component allows you to bring writers into your classroom to talk about their writing and offer insights into how writing relates to their work and their lives. The writers represent particular kinds of writing; so your students will learn from poets, music critics, and even an aquarium director who writes about marine life. Each writer presents an introduction to a mode of writing, thoughts on how he or she approaches writing, and specific tips geared to the student writer. Use the barcodes found throughout this Annotated Teacher's Edition to play any section of the videodisc at any time, or simply use a standard remote control and follow the directions that appear on the screen.

- *Writing Lab* CD-ROM

  The *Writing Lab* provides comprehensive guided tutorials on nine modes of writing. Each tutorial provides thorough instruction via on-screen text, audio and video clips, and interactive features that coach students through the writing process. Students first learn about a type of writing through direct instruction and interactive Models From Literature. Then they progress through the stages of the writing process, saving their work in Prewriting Notes, a Writing Notebook, and an Activities Drawer.

  Students can use these same activities outside the context of a structured tutorial: They simply open the Writer's Tool Kit and begin writing. They work right in their on-line Writing Notebook, calling up interactive activities to help them as needed. These activities include graphic organizers, word bins, multimedia Inspirations for Writing, checklists, revision checkers, and more.

- *Language Lab* CD-ROM

  Engaging interactive lessons in language skills are grouped into twelve units on such topics as Building Paragraphs, Punctuation, Using Modifiers, and Styling Sentences. Like those in the *Writing Lab*, the lessons here do not demand that students proceed through them in linear fashion. Each lesson begins with a general introductory section and then moves on to three or four practice activities at graduated levels of difficulty, culminating in a writing or revising application. Students use friendly point-and-click mouse interactions and basic keyboarding skills to work through a lesson while media illustrate content, provide springboards for writing and revising activities, and sometimes serve simply as a reward. Each lesson is designed to be completed in a single class period, with practices that are either objective (a score can be taken) or open-ended, so that they can be printed out for evaluation.

- *Sourcebook*

  Students can continue working away from the computer with their print *Sourcebook*, tailored to the *Writing Lab* CD-ROM and *Writers at Work Videodisc* program. Additional Models From Literature and lessons on developing writing style provide students with extra support in refining their skills.

Writer's Solution Instructional Roadmap

There are many different ways you can make the components of *Writer's Solution* work together so that they work for you. The following is a suggested pathway for teaching, organized by the order in which you might use each component.

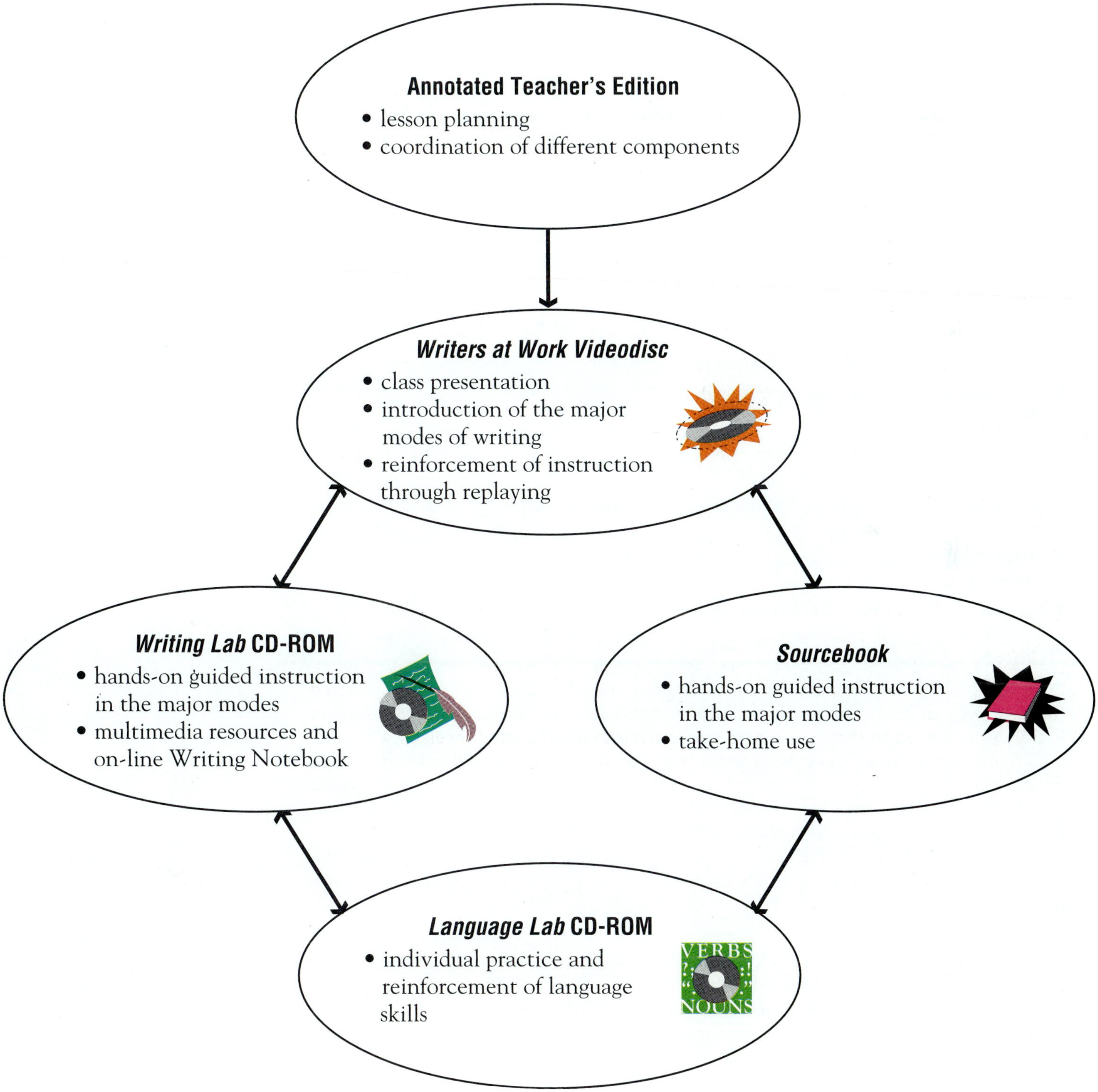

Instructional Purpose Guide

To stimulate learning by *activating prior knowledge* and *setting purpose:*
- *Writers at Work Videodisc*

To provide *direct instruction:*
- *Writing Lab* CD-ROM tutorials
- *Sourcebook* chapters
- Introduction sections of the *Language Lab* CD-ROM lessons

For additional *practice:*
- Writer's Tool Kit interactive exercises in the *Writing Lab* CD-ROM
- Language mechanics and usage practice activities in the *Language Lab* CD-ROM

For *remediation* as needed:
- Language mechanics and usage practice activities in the *Language Lab* CD-ROM

To provide a means of *extension/enrichment:*
- Group Discussions and Projects in the *Sourcebook*
- Group Discussions and Projects listed with the Inspirations for Writing in each *Writing Lab* CD-ROM lesson
- *Writers at Work Videodisc* with featured writer segments to stimulate discussion of real-world applications of writing
- Annotated Teacher's Edition notes on multimedia presentations and networking, and information on publishing and contest opportunities (pp. T17–T19)
- Annotated Teacher's Edition notes on Real-World Writing, Tech Prep, and Cultural and Cross-Curricular Connections

Using the Program

How to Use the *Sourcebook,* Annotated Teacher's Edition

At point of use, all relevant activities and features in each *Writer's Solution* component are called out. This enables you to plan lessons easily depending on time and classroom management issues. For instance, you may want to begin by playing the videodisc; the ATE will provide a summary of points raised by the featured writer and suggested questions that can be used to lead into a class discussion. In addition, a variety of notes throughout the ATE—Addressing Your Classroom Situation, Management Strategies, and Teaching Options—allow you to take full advantage of the flexible nature of the program.

The four-page interleaf that precedes each chapter provides sample lesson plans, connections to *Prentice Hall Literature, Copper,* and an at-a-glance overview of material found in each component. The side column annotations offer thematic, cross-curricular, and cultural connections as well as options for language acquisition/ESL, collaborative learning, and other teaching strategies.

Common Questions About Using *Writer's Solution* in the Language Arts Classroom:

How do the technology components of *Writer's Solution* affect my role as a teacher?

Teachers should be aware of several key points in using technology such as the *Writer's Solution* in a language arts classroom. The program is not self-paced in the old-fashioned CAI sense; the teacher is critical as facilitator. The recursive nature of this technology allows the teacher to individualize more effectively than ever before and create a more student-centered classroom through self-paced, individual, small and large group organization patterns.

The program components, particularly the *Sourcebook,* are different from a textbook; they are part of a recursive scope and sequence that requires teacher guidance of student progress. Students should take increasing responsibility for their progress through the program, but you will provide continual guidance and, initially perhaps, greater responsibility for "placing" a student in the appropriate component.

How can I use *Writer's Solution* to inspire student writing?

The components of *Writer's Solution* offer an array of interdisciplinary selections to aid students in mastering different types of writing. Selections are not only drawn from different content areas, but are embedded in interactive lessons that are rich with art, music, real author vignettes/segments, and multiple opportunities for student interaction with the material. All of this provides a springboard for student writing for a variety of purposes and audiences.

The components of *Writer's Solution* offer what will be difficult for you to supply any other way: a collection of high-quality material and activities from a variety of content areas and media that acts as a context and springboard for student thinking and writing, *for every lesson.*

How might I use each of the components, and how might they work together?

You have several student components to work with as well as the ATE, which provides an overview and guidance in the use of the student materials/components. You could begin lessons/units with brief intros from the Inspirations for Writing or the *Writers at Work Videodisc.* Or, have students begin working in the *Sourcebook,* and, as needed for additional practice or enrichment, go to the lessons in the *Writing Lab* or *Language Lab.* You can "assign" students to the *Language Lab* as needed (students can choose when to do this) during various stages in their writing process, editing and proofreading in particular.

You can require students to keep a writer's notebook as they progress through a variety of activities/stages in writing. Just as with a hard-copy notebook, you can read student-selected entries to verify that students are making regular/appropriate entries.

You can also easily integrate the use of the *Sourcebook* with the *Writing Lab.* In certain cases the *Sourcebook* may be the most accessible and therefore most regularly used component. It provides the foundation/organizational structure for using the other components. Because many teachers are novices at both using and managing technology, they may initially view the *Sourcebook* as a textbook. As they become more comfortable with the technology and receive staff development, they will venture further into this ATE and really use the ideas herein.

Common Questions About Tailoring *Writer's Solution* to Fit Different Classroom Situations

What do I do if I have only one day in the computer lab?

If you have only one day in the computer lab, you may want to devote the period to having students work through the Prewriting section of the tutorial in the *Writing Lab* CD-ROM for a single instructional purpose for the entire class. At the end of the period, have students print out their prewriting notes. They can then use these notes, along with the suggestions and instructions in the *Sourcebook,* to draft and revise their writing either in class or at home.

Conversely, you can have students work through the Prewriting phase in class or use the *Sourcebook* at home so that they may then be able to write their drafts on-line.

What do I do if I have a single computer in my classroom?

If access is limited to one computer per class, the two CD-ROMs can then function as support tools for individual students and groups of students who need extra guidance or practice, or as a means of extension by providing group and class projects and discussions.

What do I do if I have a single computer with a projection panel?

In this case, you will probably find it most effective to use *Writer's Solution* for class presentation. Work through the tutorial in the *Writing Lab* with your class, doing the Prewriting activities with your students and discussing the videos and interactive models that appear throughout the lesson. After you have walked through the entire lesson, students should be well prepared to write their drafts, using the suggestions and instruction in the *Sourcebook* for additional support.

If time and class size allow, you can have individual students come to the front of the class and work through activities such as Conflict Wheels. Make sure that all students have equal opportunity to demonstrate these activities for their peers.

The Inspirations for Writing are especially effective for whole-class instruction. You can browse through the Inspirations and writing topics with your students. Encourage them to take notes and to refer back to their notes to choose a writing topic.

What do I do if my classroom has a handful of computers?

If you have several computers in your classroom, you'll probably find it most effective to have students work in small groups to complete the "About . . ." and Choosing Your Topic sections of the tutorial in the *Writing Lab.* Students can then work individually, with or without a computer, to draft. You may then want to have students work in pairs to revise their work.

What do I do if I choose to assign a writing topic rather than using one of the writing options?

Any of the suggested lesson plans that can be found in the interleaf pages preceding each *Sourcebook* chapter in the Teacher's Edition will also work if you already have a writing topic in mind. Simply omit the Choosing a Topic phase from the lesson plan and have students work through the rest of the prewriting steps, such as Considering Audience and Purpose, before beginning to draft.

How Can I Best Use Technology in My Language Arts Classroom?

How can I take advantage of on-line resources?

In addition to the on-line publications listed on pages T17–T18, the vast resources available on the Internet can support student research by providing everything from NASA's latest space photos to tours of the White House.

- Kid's Web: http://www.npac.syr.edu/textbook/kidsweb/reference.html
- The World Wide Web's Virtual Library: http://info.cern.ch.hypertext/dataSources/[bySubject/]
- The Whole Internet Catalog: http://nearnet.gnn.com/gnn/wic/newrescat.toc.html
- NASA: http://newproducts.jpl.nasa.gov/
- The White House: http://www.whitehouse.gov/

What can I find in the *Writer's Solution User's Guide?*

Basic start-up procedures for both CD-ROMs; deciding where to begin; how to get on-line help; how to work through a lesson; sample activities/exercises to cover all the different kinds of controls; instructions for using the on-line Handbook.

What can I look forward to in future upgrades of *Writer's Solution?*

Upgrades to *Writer's Solution* in coming years will include an extensive electronic Teacher Management System that will allow you to control student progress more closely. A version for local area networks, with add-on applications for facilitating student communication between different computers, will allow for more on-line dialogue and group discussion.

Also in the future, students will be able to use Davidson's *Multimedia Workshop*, or a similar program, to produce multimedia presentations by importing any of the media—whether audio, video, photo, or art—from the *Writer's Solution* CD-ROMs.

If you have any suggestions for improvements to the program, please write to

Language Arts Editorial Director
Prentice Hall
1 Lake Street
Upper Saddle River, NJ 07458.

Integrating the Language Arts

Writer's Solution presents many unique opportunities to integrate the subdisciplines that together constitute today's language arts curriculum. Though extremely effective when used together, as can be seen on the chart on page T5, each component can stand alone as an effective support tool in areas other than writing instruction. For instance, the *Writers at Work Videodisc* for grade 6 can be used to stimulate or extend your class's study of noted writers such as Virginia Hamilton, Jane Yolen, Gary Soto, and Jean Craighead George—examples of whose writing can all be found in *Prentice Hall Literature, Copper.* Following are additional suggestions for how you might use *Writer's Solution* to integrate the language arts in your classroom.

Literature

The multimedia Inspirations for Writing can be found in any *Writing Lab* tutorial to help students choose a topic. Often these are excerpts—by way of film clips, animation, or audio recordings—from selections that can be found in *Prentice Hall Literature, Copper.* These Inspirations, with their high-interest format and appeal to different learning styles, can effectively spark student interest in literature in the following ways:

- *Students will want to read the entire selection.* For example, students intrigued by a brief film clip from *The Jungle Book* may be motivated to read the entire work.
- *Students will develop interest in a particular genre.* Browsing through the Inspirations may help to make an unfamiliar form such as haiku suddenly come alive. You can follow up by directing the student to additional literature selections in print form.
- *Students will explore thematic connections.* The Topic Ideas that accompany each Inspiration provide a powerful way for students to explore how and why a particular selection holds personal meaning for them. (See the complete listing of *Writer's Solution*'s themes on page T11.)
- *Students will want to read other selections by the same writer.* A reading of a poem by Nikki Giovanni can support a teaching unit on poetry by breathing life into literature. In addition, each Inspiration includes background information to help students learn more about the author and put the selection into historical and literary context.

Alternatively, you may want to explore the Inspirations once your class has already embarked on a literature unit. Students can then critically evaluate these excerpts from works by writers they are already studying. In addition, *Writer's Solution* contains many interactive Models from Literature that are not Inspirations but are used to help illustrate how professional writers meet the challenges of the writing process. The interleaf sections that precede each *Sourcebook* chapter can help you locate these links to literature so that you can include them in your lesson plans.

Finally, the Response to Literature chapter can be easily incorporated into your study of literature by having the entire class work through it or by directing individual students to the self-paced tutorial as needed.

Grammar and Mechanics

Teachers have found that one practical way in which students can develop a working knowledge of grammar is to start with writing and move into matters of grammar as such problems arise in the student's writing. The time to help students learn grammar is when they need help in revising the structure of their sentences. Working from the students' interests and needs, you can help them to see the relevance of grammatical instruction. Grammar, and mechanics as well, can become memorable for students only when they become relevant. And they become relevant as students edit and revise—that is, when student writers work at getting their words to reflect their thoughts accurately.

As students write, use their drafts as guideposts for which grammar concepts they need to master. You don't have to teach a concept or a structure formally. Presented in the context of the student's writing, the concept becomes a way to revise the sentence in question. You can present and reinforce these concepts either through teacher-student conferences, peer editing, or on-the-spot classroom discussion. *Writer's Solution* can function as a valuable resource for any of these strategies.

- Integrated grammar instruction is presented in the Proofreading section of each *Writing Lab* tutorial, as well as in the Developing Your Style section found in every *Sourcebook* chapter.
- The *Language Lab* CD-ROM. Comprehensive lessons in stylistic development and specific language skills are available here. Notes in the Annotated Teacher's Edition highlight relevant lessons at their point of use in each writing mode.
- The Annotated Teacher's Edition of the *Sourcebook* also connects writing to another valuable resource in grammar and mechanics instruction, Prentice Hall's popular *Writer's Companion.* Providing answers for students' most common questions about language skills and composition, the pertinent sections of this convenient handbook are cited both in the Developing Your Style section and the interleaf.

Further, by writing constantly, students develop what we might call the "writer's eye": They begin to read as writers. Those who read solely to gain information often pay little attention to the way in which ideas are phrased. The writer's eye helps students to become better peer editors and better editors of their own work. When students look at writing—their own or that of others—they soon discover that problems in the form or appearance of a piece of writing can seriously hinder communication. The form and structure of a sentence suddenly become important. Editing with a writer's eye, students first detect that something is amiss with a sentence. At this point, it does not take much to direct them toward the solution.

Vocabulary and the Construction of Meaning

Writer's Solution provides integrated vocabulary and comprehension instruction in the specific context of each writing mode and the multitude of genres it encompasses. For example, when studying the narrative form, students may become aware for the first time of the distinction between a *memoir* and an *autobiography*. Similarly, when working through the lesson on reports, students will learn researching strategies for locating information in library resources—in effect learning *how* to become familiar with new subject matter and its attendant vocabulary. In addition to these ways in which vocabulary is learned "indirectly," the following represent areas of more direct instruction in *Writer's Solution*.

- *Language Lab* lessons on Using Exact Nouns, Vivid and Precise Verbs, and Using Modifiers all serve to strengthen students' understanding of words in the context of sound writing.
- Interactive word bins in the *Writing Lab* allow students to enhance their vocabulary by including descriptive words, character traits, sensory words, and transition words into their writing.
- Annotated Models From Literature and other writing models in the *Writing Lab* and *Sourcebook* often draw attention to the reasons behind a writer's particular word choice.

In addition, cross-curricular and literature connections foster vocabulary building in the context of supporting student writing in these areas. As students talk about their writing, and writing in general, they develop a vocabulary for that discussion. Metalanguage leads to metacognition. Learning the lingo of any professional area—baseball, computers, biology, music—can be fun. Students enter the world of writing as they take command of the language needed to talk about writing and as they get more in touch with the experiences and interests that motivate them to write.

Speaking and Listening

Whether the setting is whole-class or private conference, *Writer's Solution* provides many opportunities for you to point out differences between the structures of written English and spoken English. These distinctions will help students develop critical speaking and listening skills that can be applied directly in the following ways.

- Group Discussions are presented throughout the *Writing Lab* and *Sourcebook* to support and extend instructional content.
- *Writers at Work Videodisc* segments allow for purposeful listening as well as providing the basis for meaningful follow-up discussion of the issues raised.
- Instruction on Considering Audience and Purpose is presented in three places—the *Writing Lab*, the *Sourcebook*, and the *Language Lab*—and serves to strengthen student speaking and listening skills.

Students usually need to move from the spoken idiom to the written language. This is one of the major advantages of returning to literature as often as possible, a strategy that *Writer's Solution* consistently makes use of. An active working knowledge of the vocabulary and structure of the language comes out of what is already being studied. What the student hears and reads ultimately comes out in his own language. The more reading and discussion that the student engages in, the more likely that new words and linguistic structures will begin to appear in the student's own writing. Linguistic osmosis is an important part of reading and hearing language.

Interdisciplinary Teaching

Writer's Solution represents an extremely powerful way of connecting language arts to the other disciplines. The *Writer's Solution* thematic organization of Topic Ideas and multimedia Inspirations for Writing supports interdisciplinary teaching by allowing you and your teaching team to build a unit from the ground up or to appropriate content to fit the curriculum you've already designed. The following are some resources for the interdisciplinary teacher.

Adapting Writing Modes to Other Disciplines

Instead of teaching such lessons as "Reports" or "Exposition: Giving Information" in isolation, meaningful writing purposes can spring directly from other disciplines. For instance, firsthand experimentation in the science classroom or original research conducted with the guidance of a social studies teacher can provide the material needed to produce quality work in the language arts setting. The *Writers at Work Videodisc* is especially helpful in illustrating how this approach works in everyday situations (e.g., by illuminating how an aquarium director combines scientific expertise and a solid grounding in the writing process to do her job).

Alternatively, *Writer's Solution* can simply be made available as a support tool to teachers in other disciplines on a more informal basis. For instance, the science teacher who notices the need for individualized reinforcement in writing lab reports can refer a student to the relevant *Writing Lab* tutorial. The CD-ROM itself can be kept in your school's computer lab so that it can be used by a variety of teachers.

Thematic Organization

The following represent the recurring themes of the *Writer's Solution* at the middle grades level:

- Knowing Yourself
- Turning Points
- Exploring the Past
- Decisions
- Humor and Fun
- Relationships
- Diversity
- Social Responsibility
- Goals/Achievements
- Nature
- Heroes
- Imagination

Cross-Curricular Connections

In addition to the more open-ended possibilities offered by the thematic approach, direct connections to other disciplines are made repeatedly in the Inspirations for Writing in the *Writing Lab*, in the side columns in the Annotated Teacher's Edition, and in the *Writers at Work Videodisc*.

Workplace Connection

Another way to approach interdisciplinary teaching is through workplace writing—non-literary writing that takes place in a real-world context. Students can learn about how writing is used in a variety of professions that correspond to subject areas they are currently studying or are interested in. Throughout *Writer's Solution* we have included workplace writing models such as book and media summaries and instructions for building and using a rain gauge. In addition, workplace writers such as police officer Charles Tsang, entertainment critic Kevin Powell, zoologist Deborah Behler, and ad copy writer Doug Raboy are supplemented by a bonus videodisc segment featuring Lucy Jones, devoted exclusively to practical writing.

The following are suggestions for teaching a guided lesson on practical writing using the videodisc as a springboard for class discussion and activities.

Writers at Work Videodisc: Practical Writing

Play frames 42460 to 51386

Segment 1: Lucy Jones on Practical Writing
Use the practical writing section of the videodisc featuring Brooklyn Botanic Garden vice president Lucy Jones as a springboard for a class discussion on practical writing. Play the segment in its entirety. Then, using the bar codes, replay portions of the videodisc piece and use them for class discussion and activities.

Play frames 43200 to 44474

Segment 2: Definition of Practical Writing
Lucy Jones is the vice president of education and information services at the Brooklyn Botanic Garden in Brooklyn, New York. To communicate with the public and with her co-workers, Jones uses various types of practical writing—writing that someone does in a real-life situation to convey or request information. Discuss with your students the definition of practical writing and the different types of practical writing mentioned in the video. Ask students to

brainstorm about various kinds of business letters, brochures, essay responses for test items, and memos they have seen. Examples include letters requesting information about a summer camp, brochures about new mountain bikes, essay responses to a social studies question, and memos explaining to corporate workers changes in company policy.

It's likely that most of your students have engaged in various kinds of practical writing. Have students share such examples with the class. Challenge students to name additional types of practical writing not mentioned in the video, such as invitations and contest entry forms. You might want to share examples of practical writing that you have done, such as letters requesting tickets to a play and complaints to a bank about an erroneous balance in a savings account.

Play frames 44583 to 46215

Segment 3: Writing Effective Letters

In this segment, Lucy Jones discusses one of the qualities of an effective letter that requests information: a narrow focus. Review with your students why Jones prefers receiving letters with specific requests. To illustrate the difficulty of responding to an unfocused letter, read aloud two letters requesting information, making sure that one of the letters is specific in its focus and one is general in nature. For example, one letter could ask NASA for *information about the mission of the latest space-shuttle launch*, while another could ask NASA for *information about any launches that have occurred at the Kennedy Space Center*. Ask volunteers to give a hypothetical response to each letter. Ask students which letter would be easier for a NASA official to respond to and why.

You might also want to make your students aware of the fact that letters requesting information or services of people—particularly of people in the business community—must be as brief as possible and get to the point quickly. Many people simply won't take the time to read a lengthy, rambling letter. Explore with your students possible reasons for this (a busy work schedule, etc.).

Play frames 46215 to 48384

Segment 4: Capturing the Reader's Attention

In this segment, Lucy Jones discusses the importance of capturing the reader's attention in a piece of practical writing. Whenever she writes a letter or a brochure, Jones wants to grab the reader's interest from the start. She wants to hook the reader right at the beginning so that he or she wants to read all that she has to say.

Jones mentions several ways to capture the reader's attention. For example, she places the most important information in a letter first, sometimes underlining or boldfacing material for emphasis. When designing a brochure, she includes a catchy title and imaginative artwork to attract the reader. Ask your students to brainstorm other ways to attract the reader's attention. Help students realize that an imaginative beginning can keep the reader riveted to a piece of writing. For example, a provocative question, a fascinating fact, or a startling anecdote can compel the reader to read on.

At this time, you might want to familiarize your students with the concept of a brochure. Emphasize that a brochure, or pamphlet, is a small printed piece that provides information about a specific topic, procedure, organization, corporation, or the like. In this video segment, Lucy Jones speaks about a brochure titled "City Kids Get Green," which she helped develop to publicize a junior flower show. Review with students how Jones made the brochure exciting, or *punched it up*.

Ask students to brainstorm about some of the typical subject matter that brochures deal with (features of new automobiles, descriptions of vacation resorts, instructions on water safety, etc.). Ask students about the purposes of brochures. Why are brochures written? (To inform, to promote or advertise, to explain, etc.)

Play frames 48535 to 50525

Segment 5: Considering Audience

Lucy Jones uses a simple but effective method to make sure her writing is tailored for its specific audience: She puts herself in the other person's shoes and asks questions that the other person would probably ask. Encourage your students to do the same when considering their audience.

To help your students practice Jones's technique for considering audience, write on the chalkboard some specific topics, such as "vegetable gardens," "basketball," and "chipmunks." Ask students what questions a seven-year-old might have on each topic. Then ask what questions an adult might have. Help students realize that what the intended audience wants to learn about a topic, as well as what that audience already knows about a topic, is crucial in determining what content, writing style, and type of language to use in a piece of practical writing.

Play frames 50540 to 51386

Segment 6: Revising

When Lucy Jones revises her work, she once again tries to experience her writing as her audience would. Ask your students to do the same when they revise. Help them to brainstorm about questions they can ask themselves, while revising their practical writing, whose answers can help them determine whether or not they are communicating what they intended to communicate to their audience. Possible questions include: *What is the main idea of my writing? Are there enough details or examples to make that idea clear to the reader? Is the type of language I use proper for my intended audience?*

Play frames 51389 to 51986

Segment 7: Using the Swiss Cheese Method

The "Swiss cheese method" is Lucy Jones's personal technique for combating writer's block. Whenever Jones is overwhelmed by the complexity or scope of a particular writing assignment, she simply pokes holes in the assignment by focusing on doing small pieces of it. Eventually, when all of the pieces are completed, Jones puts them all together to form the entire piece of writing. Discuss with the class the pluses and minuses of the "Swiss cheese method." Ask your students if they feel the technique is right for them. What other strategies for overcoming writer's block can your students recommend?

Play frames 51988 to 52725

Segment 8: The Importance of Proofreading

In this segment, Lucy Jones gives an important argument for conscientious proofreading that you might want to stress with your students. Jones states that whatever you write is a reflection of you. Indeed, a particular piece of writing, such as a business letter, is your introduction to someone and might be the only thing that a particular person will ever know about you. To ensure a stunning first—and perhaps *only*—impression, carefully check your writing for errors. Ask your students what they might think about the writer of a composition that is filled with careless mistakes.

Addressing Diverse Needs

The high-interest, self-paced, multimedia approach of *Writer's Solution* allows it to contribute greatly to the success of your students with special needs: ESL and Special Education students as well as those with different learning styles or "intelligences." In addition to delivering effective writing instruction, *Writer's Solution* provides valuable opportunities for these students in developing a broad range of social and communication skills.

Therefore, we suggest that you make copies of *Writer's Solution* available in a resource center or computer lab for other teachers to explore and perhaps use in contexts completely outside that of the language arts.

Language Acquisition and ESL Strategies

For both the ESL teacher and the language arts teacher who has occasional need for ESL materials, *Writer's Solution* provides a wide range of interactive features that can be repurposed for non-native speakers of English. On the other hand, it is important to keep in mind that *Writer's Solution* is primarily intended as a writing program for the English-speaking middle schooler; as such, it contains more resources for advanced ESL students than for those who may be challenged by its on-screen text and English-based navigational options.

The Annotated Teacher's Edition contains notes in every chapter that provide alternatives for ESL students based on whether they are at the basic, intermediate, or advanced level. The greatest strength of *Writer's Solution* in this area lies in the *Writing Lab* activities, which can be accessed throughout the tutorial or independently in the Writer's Tool Kit. For instance, the Choosing Your Topic section of the *Writing Lab* combines media with interactive graphics in the form of Brainstormers, Photo Storyboards, and Issues/Idea Wheels. The combination of text, graphics, and self-paced software features is a resource your ESL student is unlikely to encounter elsewhere. In addition, *Writer's Solution* contains the following features that may also be helpful to your ESL student:

- *Language Lab* practices. The different levels of practice are well suited to the different levels of ESL students in your classroom: You may wish to limit your basic-level students to the first practice, while your more advanced students may benefit from moving directly from the introduction to the writing/revising activity.
- *Language Lab* instructional feedback. While always text-based in nature, the feedback students receive as they make choices is frequently accompanied by media that should help get the point across for your basic-level students.

- Graphic organizers in the *Writing Lab*. These include Topic Webs, Cluster Diagrams, Timelines, Venn Diagrams, Story Maps, and Notecard Activities.
- The *Writing Lab* Word Bins activity can support the continued growth of your ESL students' vocabulary, used in context.
- *Writing Lab* text-based tools for writing. Advanced ESL students should benefit from activities such as self-interviews, Audience Profiles, checklists, K-W-L Charts, and revision checkers.
- *Writers at Work Videodisc*. Basic-level students who may be more comfortable with listening and speaking than with reading and writing should benefit from the author segments, which put instruction in the form of everyday speech.
- The Annotated Teacher's Edition of the *Sourcebook* provides a note at the start of the Guided Lesson to call out the specific features of the *Writing Lab* activities for that writing mode that can be adapted for use with your ESL students.

Addressing Learning Styles

The technology components of *Writer's Solution* are multisensory, specifically visual and auditory, thereby providing for different learning styles.

There are many ways a teacher can individualize instruction to address both student learning strengths and interests. The Annotated Teacher's Edition of the *Sourcebook* consistently provides specific suggestions for a variety of activities: individual, self-paced, small- and large-group.

In terms of the multiple intelligences identified by Howard Gardner, the *Writer's Solution* offers the learner who is:

- *linguistic:* opportunities to enrich word use through Prewriting activities; many revision points in the writing process; multiple ways in which to strengthen language skills (in both the Developing Your Style sections of the *Sourcebook* and the *Language Lab* CD-ROM lessons); many interactive writing models, including those by other student writers.
- *logical-mathematical and spatial:* the ability to move text and images easily in a variety of activities available in both the Writer's Tool Kit and the tutorials of the *Writing Lab*; to manipulate words and images to more closely align form and purpose.
- *musical:* audio components in *Writer's Solution* include many Inspirations for Writing in which music is integrated with images and text; in addition, audio annotations that accompany the writing models allow students to hear the step-by-step decisions that are made during the writing process.
- *bodily-kinesthetic:* ideas for creating multimedia products; suggestions for exploring the community made in the form of a Real-World Writing note in the Annotated Teacher's Edition of the *Sourcebook*; a multitude of meaningful and hands-on group and class activities and projects that accompany Topic Ideas in the *Writing Lab*.
- *interpersonal:* opportunities to engage in group and class projects and activities; opportunity to interact with the teacher as guide (student-centered) rather than lecturer (teacher-centered).
- *intrapersonal:* many opportunities to develop skill and comfort in self-reflection such as the Prewriting Notes and the Activities Drawer in the *Writing Lab* and the Reflecting on Your Writing section in the *Sourcebook*; an approach that fosters ability to work with others and to take responsibility for quality of work.

Using *Writer's Solution* With Your Special Education Students

Writer's Solution is an appropriate and useful tool for your special education students as well. Individualized instruction is critical for the learning success of those students who are challenged by emotional, behavioral, mental, and physical disabilities; *Writer's Solution* allows you to provide lessons that fit the learning style and particular needs of each student. In addition, *Writer's Solution* gives you the ability to track each learner's progress for assessment and evaluation of baseline skills and learning. Equally important, the multimedia format of sound, graphics, and text keeps learning fun and motivating for the special needs students, enabling them to access information and learn concepts in ways that are both appealing and make optimum use of their strengths.

Writer's Solution provides the following features that are especially important for special education students:

- Repetitive practice drills allow students to practice lower-level writing skills as many times as is necessary to acquire mastery.
- Immediate feedback in the form of pleasing graphics, sound, and written messages help to motivate the student and provide important reinforcement for learning.
- Students have the opportunity to work individually without the fear of negative peer comments, easing anxiety about "poor" or "failing" performance. The computer is a nonjudgmental facilitator in the learning process.
- The pleasing screen displays on the *Writing Lab* and *Language Lab* CD-ROM include both graphic cues in the form of icons and text labels—an important consideration for students with visual and reading difficulties. In addition, the point-and-click interface enables students to explore and experiment with *Writer's Solution* without memorizing commands or using the keyboard extensively.

- The writing process, from the germ of an idea to multiple revisions, is reflected in the *Writing Lab* lessons and tools. Special needs students need not worry about producing "perfect work" every time—they see that good writing is a developmental process that takes time and thought. The nature of the program allows them to create and revise with flexibility and ease.
- The *Writers at Work Videodisc* brings writers into the classroom, helping special needs students to see the value that an individual's unique experiences, culture, and point of view bring to the writing process.

Ideas for Using *Writer's Solution* With Special Education Students

Use *Writer's Solution* as you would any resource—review the student's IEP and select a lesson or activity geared toward the particular student's needs and abilities. The following suggestions may also be useful:

- Physically handicapped students may require special adaptation of the keyboard or monitor. Consult with your school's resource specialists or call a Macintosh representative for options.
- For students unfamiliar with computers, place stickers or other visual clues on the keyboard to help students discriminate commonly used keys and their functions. The Enter or Return key, the Delete key, the Shift key, and the Spacebar are good places to start.
- Navigation may be overwhelming for some students, especially at first. Construct linear lesson instructions for students to "go in" and "back out" of a lesson. Model the navigation, then have the student practice. Do the same for the various tools—for example, the on-line Writing Notebook. As the students become more comfortable with navigation and tools, they will take advantage of the intuitive interface and flexibility of the entire program.
- When using the *Language Lab* and *Writing Lab* CD-ROM, read on-line screen instructions aloud with students at the beginning of each lesson. Ask students to paraphrase the instructions to confirm their understanding. In addition, it may be useful to review words aloud in the Sensory Word Bins activity as well as for vocabulary-building exercises.
- As a group, read aloud the models in the *Writing Lab* CD-ROM and discuss the annotations. In addition, you may wish to use low-reading-level adaptations of classics (not provided with *Writer's Solution*) as models to supplement the program.
- Allow students to browse the Inspirations for Writing and select those that set their creative juices flowing. In a discussion with students, talk about why these particular images inspire them. Allow students to articulate their ideas aloud before they begin to write.

Assessment and Writer's Solution

An Interview With Dr. Sylvia Rendón

Sylvia Rendón, Ph.D., is currently a member of the Educational Technology Advisory Committee for the Texas Education Agency and is Program Coordinator for Humanities for the Tomball Independent School District in Tomball, Texas.

Prentice Hall: With all the possible ways of delivering instruction with *Writer's Solution*, many teachers will simply want to know "Where can I take grades?" What should these teachers know about the program?

Dr. Rendón: In the *Writing Lab* CD-ROM, students can print out copies of different drafts of the same piece of writing, and the teacher can grade for the types of revisions instead of grading only a final draft. Alternately, the teacher can get a process grade by looking at printouts of prewriting notes, drafts, checklists, and guidelines for peer revision. The teacher can take grades at various points in the *Language Lab* as well—for example, when students progress to a more difficult practice section that would show their deeper understanding of a concept or skill.

Prentice Hall: How will the three strategies of self, peer, and teacher assessment work with *Writer's Solution?*

Dr. Rendón: A student can self-assess using all her saved prewriting ideas or drafts; a student can also revisit any part of the Writing Lab to help in revising for content. Of course, a student can also print out any part of her writing process to put in a working portfolio and to review in a conference with peers or teacher.

Furthermore, the different features of *Writer's Solution* provide a variety of choices/options for assessing progress in both process and product. The group and class projects in the *Sourcebook* and *Writing Lab* provide opportunities for peers to assess each other's performance in process (e.g., the group process) as well as the actual writing produced.

Prentice Hall: How can *Writer's Solution* be used with portfolio assessment?

Dr. Rendón: The variety of individual and group activities will yield products that could go into a portfolio. A student has opportunities to refine products and to keep samples of a product in various stages of development, such as material from the Notepad and Activities Drawer, and *Language Lab* practices. In the *Writing Lab* a student can print out writing at any stage in the process, thereby allowing him to keep a working portfolio as well as a showcase portfolio.

Prentice Hall: What kind of new rubrics might teachers consider using in conjunction with *Writer's Solution?*

Dr. Rendón: What comes first to mind are reader-response rubrics designed for different types of text as well as rubrics to evaluate non-print products—for example, the presentations in the *Multimedia Workshop*. In addition, rubrics to evaluate process—for example, group decision making in the development of any group activities, projects, or presentations—will also be important. Of course, rubrics for self-assessment—How well did I do on activity X compared to the model or predetermined criteria?—will be important. For teachers who want to go further, a rubric that assesses the appropriateness of technology to a given task may be useful, though this could be an attribute/criterion in a broader rubric. The one constant is that any rubric used to assess student work must be shared with the student prior to her beginning an assignment, whether the teacher or student completes the rubric.

Prentice Hall: How might peer evaluation/cooperative learning work with *Writer's Solution?*

Dr. Rendón: For most writing assignments, students can work together through all stages of the process, including dividing up the drafting duties as well as the peer editing duties; and peer evaluation is part of all of this. Certainly Davidson's *Multimedia Workshop*, with which the two CD-ROMs have been developed to go hand in hand, provides an ideal context for students working together to create a product. In addition, a typical *Writing Lab* tutorial helps students with the peer revision through on-line tips, guidelines, checklists, and the like.

Prentice Hall: How can a teacher use performance-based assessment with *Writer's Solution?*

Dr. Rendón: Any activity, project, or presentation that requires students to apply skills in a meaningful context is performance-based instruction; therefore, it becomes apparent that *Writer's Solution* features provide opportunities for assessment of products at different stages of development. Again, the *Multimedia Workshop* offers opportunities for assessment of products in a variety of forms: print, visual, and so on.

Prentice Hall: How does *Writer's Solution* allow for more and richer opportunities in observation assessment?

Dr. Rendón: In addition to obtaining scores on objective practices, such as those in the *Language Lab*, the teacher and/or student can garner a wide range of "interactive" evidence of how well a student is progressing in a given type of writing. Process samples can be gathered by printing or directly observing a student working through on-line activities designed to support the writing process.

Prentice Hall: How might conferencing look different when using *Writer's Solution?*

Dr. Rendón: Students can conference with one another in front of the computer, revising throughout the conference; or students can make notes in the Writing Notebook as the conference progresses. Again, students can print out various drafts of a piece of writing to show progress and the teacher can better assess quality of students' revisions by viewing these drafts and discussing them in conference.

Prentice Hall: How does *Writer's Solution* provide assessment opportunities at the different levels of cognitive development?

Dr. Rendón: Lower levels of thinking such as knowledge and comprehension can be assessed through subjective practices that increase in difficulty. On the other hand, features like the Prewriting Notes help students move to higher levels of thinking as they evaluate ideas and synthesize information from a variety of sources, both non-print and textual.

The revision tools in *Writer's Solution* help students to apply language skills as they edit for language use. The prewriting and revision tools help students develop the ability to reflect on the content of their writing. The *Writing Lab* tools for peer revision help students evaluate their work against a set of criteria/guidelines. Also, as students engage in *Sourcebook*, Inspiration, and *Writing Lab* activities, they are continually evaluating their work in terms of form and content, as well as evaluating the way their groups work together.

Prentice Hall: Finally, how does *Writer's Solution* figure into the discussion of national standards in the language arts?

Dr. Rendón: *Writer's Solution* offers students the opportunity to meet three types of standards: content, performance, and delivery/opportunity to learn standards. Content is focused on the essential elements of effective writing; for example, the conventions of language are presented as tools for good writing, not in isolation. The content is aimed at giving students "power" in language arts; that is, they are being given content in language arts that they can actually use outside the school to make sense of their world.

In addition, *Writer's Solution* has performance standards for every type of writing that is covered. Students can perform at different levels of achievement, depending on the activity. For example, prewriting activities are not objectively scored because a student goes as far as he/she can. The objective practices, which assess knowledge-level thinking, can be graded, while the peer-revision activities have a different level of performance—"Is this clear? Can you follow my organization?" This is a much higher level of thinking and different level of performance.

In conclusion, it's important to note how *Writer's Solution* addresses the delivery standard in a variety of forms, addressing many learning styles in its multimedia approach. Every student has an opportunity to learn with *Writer's Solution* because it is so multidimensional.

Publications and Contests for Student Writing

Throughout *Writer's Solution,* students are challenged and inspired by reading the published work of peer writers. The possibility of recognition—and even reward—can be a strong motivator for student writers. The following publications frequently present student writing; others are devoted exclusively to the topic. Unless otherwise noted, each publication lists guidelines for writers and rules for submission in each issue.

CREATIVE KIDS
P. O. Box 8813
Waco, TX 76714-8813
Meant for elementary and middle school readers, *Creative Kids*—which is devoted solely to the work of "gifted, creative, and talented youngsters"—publishes creative writing, reviews, and other kinds of writing by writers ages 8–14.

LIFEPRINTS
Blindskills, Inc.
Box 5181
Salem, OR 97304
An international quarterly magazine, *Lifeprints* is especially interested in publishing personal-experience nonfiction by student writers, who may submit manuscript that is typed, on diskette, in Braille, or on audiocassette for the blind and visually impaired readership.

THE McGUFFEY WRITER
McGuffey Foundation School
5128 Westgate Drive
Oxford, OH 45056
Intended for readers ages 5–17, *The McGuffey Writer* is produced three times a year, and each issue is built upon a central theme. It publishes short stories, essays, poems, plays, and black-and-white artwork from students.

MERLYN'S PEN: THE NATIONAL MAGAZINES OF STUDENT WRITING
P. O. Box 1058
East Greenwich, RI 02818
Merlyn's Pen now publishes two editions—Intermediate (grades 7-10) and Senior (grades 11-12). Both invite "manuscripts that grip the readers' interest and stir the heart or mind," with an emphasis on the concerns of today's teenagers.

POETRY USA
2569 Maxwell Avenue
Oakland, CA 94123
Each issue of this quarterly newspaper includes "Young Poets Speak Out," a poetry feature for writers through the age of 18. Students are encouraged to study this periodical for a better understanding of the kind of poetry it publishes.

READ
c/o Weekly Reader Corporation
245 Long Hill Road
Middletown, CT 06457
Publishing at a seventh-to-ninth-grade reading level, each issue of *Read* includes "In Your Own Write," a feature devoted to student poetry. Interested students are urged to write for contest rules and guidelines.

SKIPPING STONES
P. O. Box 3939
Eugene, OR 97403
Writers through the age of 18 are especially encouraged to submit their writing—in any language—and artwork to this bimonthly multicultural magazine, which publishes work about personal interests and ethnic heritage as well as other kinds of writing.

STONE SOUP
Children's Art Foundation
P. O. Box 83
915 Cedar Street
Santa Cruz, CA 95063
Stone Soup accepts work from writers only through the age of 13. The magazine is of such high quality that it can be a valuable resource for any middle-school writing class. Editors Gerry Mandel and William Rubel admit "a preference for writing and art based on personal experiences and observations." Includes a teaching guide.

WRITING!
General Learning Corporation
60 Revere Drive
Northbrook, IL 60062-1563
Each issue of this classroom magazine for grades 7–12 includes one or more examples of student writing. The

pieces may be fiction, nonfiction, or poetry; however, all of the fiction that *Writing!* publishes comes from student writers. *Writing!* sponsors an annual writing contest to which students may submit prose or poetry that relates to the announced theme.

YOUNG AUTHOR'S MAGAZINE/THE MAGIC PENS
3015 Woodsdale Blvd.
Lincoln, NE 68502-5053
This classroom publication offers monthly issues (of *Young Author's Magazine*) and quarterly anthologies (of *The Magic Pens*) that are devoted to writing by students in grades K–12. Submissions may be in languages other than English (with Spanish, French, and Japanese appearing often); priority is given to submissions filed on e-mail, at this address:

yam@regulus.com

The publisher also sponsors The Write Course, a multicultural program with a focus on writing across the curriculum; teachers are encouraged to write for details.

On-Line Publications

- MidLink Magazine: The Electronic Magazine for Kids in the Middle Grades http://longwood.cs.ucf.edu/~Midlink/ A free, on-line World Wide Web project developed by and for middle school students. MidLink publishes (or posts) stories, poems, and projects contributed by individual students as well as by classes. Published or updated bimonthly, MidLink often has a seasonal theme along with more general topics, and all issues are available online for a year.
- KidPub http://en-garde.com/kidpub/intro.html Another free, on-line Web site. KidPub is a home page for readers and writers ages 8–13. Submissions of fiction and nonfiction are posted with brief notes describing the authors.
- Writers' Ink Roundtable. e-mail: WRITERS.INK Writers of any age who are subscribers to GEnie can submit manuscripts electronically; for further information, access page 440. This on-line association of writers includes an on-line magazine and several writing contests, including contests just for student writers. For information about how to subscribe to GEnie, call (800) 638-9636.

Contests

The following contests offer students the chance to be commended in print; in some cases, additional prizes are awarded. Contact each sponsoring organization for current submission rules.

ANNUAL POETRY CONTEST
National Federation of State Poetry Societies
3520 State Route 56
Mechanicsburg, OH 43044
This contest offers 50 categories of recognition for original unpublished poetry. Students should contact the NFSPS for guidelines about each category and should note that category #50 is devoted exclusively to student writing. There is no entry fee to submit a manuscript in this category (there is a $1 poem-entry fee in other categories), but an entrant may submit only one poem, no longer than 32 lines (deadline: March 15). Cash prizes are awarded, and the top poems in each category are published by the organization.

Teachers are also encouraged to contact their state chapter of the NFSPS for information about statewide writing competitions.

NATIONAL WRITTEN
& ILLUSTRATED BY . . . AWARDS
CONTEST FOR STUDENTS
Landmark Editions, Inc.
1402 Kansas Avenue
Kansas City, MO 64127
This is an annual book contest for students. Original illustrated books may be entered in one of three age categories: 6–9, 10–13, and 14–19 years of age. The winner in each category receives a publishing contract, is brought to Kansas City to meet with an editorial/design team, and earns royalties from the finished book.

Each entrant must be the illustrator (artwork or photography) as well as the writer of his or her book; the book itself must be between 16 and 24 pages long and must follow other specific guidelines, which are available from Landmark Editions, Inc.

PROGRAM TO RECOGNIZE EXCELLENCE
IN STUDENT LITERARY MAGAZINES
National Council of Teachers of English
1111 West Kenyon Road
Urbana, IL 61801-1096
This program sponsors excellence in middle school, junior high, and senior high student literary magazines; it is open to schools in the United States and Canada and to American schools abroad. There is a $25 entry fee. Each school may submit only one entry (deadline: July 1); state judges will decide the category in which it will be judged.

PROMISING YOUNG WRITERS PROGRAM
National Council of Teachers of English
1111 West Kenyon Road
Urbana, IL 61801-1096
Entrants in this contest, open to students in grade 8 only, must be selected by and entered through their schools (deadline: January 20). There is a $5 entry fee. State judges choose the entries that will go on to the national competition.

SCIENCE ESSAY AWARDS PROGRAM
General Learning Corporation

60 Revere Drive, Suite 200
Northbrook, IL 60062-1563
In this contest, co-sponsored by the DuPont Company, each entrant submits an essay of 600–1000 words, explaining the importance of the chosen science topic. There is a division for writers in grades 7–9; guidelines for each year's competition are available in October. The annual deadline is in January. Educational grants are awarded to the top three winners in each division, and cash prizes also are awarded to essays receiving honorable mention. In addition, the teacher who sponsors the top essay receives a cash award.

SEVENTEEN MAGAZINE
FICTION CONTEST
Seventeen Magazine
850 Third Avenue
New York, NY 10022
This contest looks for previously unpublished short stories (1500 to 3000 words long) from writers ages 13–21(deadline: April 30). Winning writers receive a cash prize, and their work may appear in *Seventeen*.

VERY SPECIAL ARTS
YOUNG PLAYWRIGHTS PROGRAM
Very Special Arts
Education Office
The John F. Kennedy Center
for the Performing Arts
Washington, DC 20566
This annual contest for young writers (ages 12–18, individuals or groups) recognizes the best original "script that incorporates some aspect of disability," and that script is produced at the John F. Kennedy Center for the Performing Arts Theater Lab. The deadline usually falls in mid-April.

PAUL A. WITTY OUTSTANDING
LITERATURE AWARD
International Reading Association
Special Interest Group for Reading
for Gifted and Creative Students
c/o Texas Christian University
P. O. Box 32925
Fort Worth, TX 76129
This international contest recognizes excellence in poetry (sets of five poems per entrant) and prose (single items of about 1000 words, maximum) in three age groups: elementary, middle school, and secondary. Each entry must be submitted by a sponsoring teacher (deadline: February 1). Cash prizes, certificates of merit, and other prizes are awarded.

THE YOUNG PLAYWRIGHTS FESTIVAL
NATIONAL PLAYWRITING COMPETITION
Young Playwrights Inc.
321 West 44th Street, Suite 906
New York, NY 10036
Young Playwrights Inc. invites scripts from individual students or student groups through age 18; its annual deadline is October 15. Winning plays are performed in an off-Broadway production; winners also receive a royalty and a year's membership in The Dramatists Guild. Furthermore, each entry receives a professional evaluation.

Special Resource

PRENTICE HALL ON THE INTERNET
Prentice Hall's World Wide Web site is one place students can publish their writing. Teachers or students can check the Language Arts section of our home page for writing contests, special events, forums, and other opportunities to publish on-line. Favorite authors of young adult literature also appear as guests on the Prentice Hall Web site. Students can e-mail authors for advice or to ask questions.

Scope and Sequence: The Writing Process

Videodisc Featured Writer	1 EXPRESSION Jane Yolen	2 DESCRIPTION Debbie Behler	3 NARRATION Virginia Hamilton	4 EXPOSITION: Giving Information Charles Tsang
Outcomes	Anecdote Personal journal entry Postcard message Personal letter Personal memoir	Remembrance Observation Description of people or places Description of an event or idea Stage Directions	Personal narrative Autobiographical incident Anecdote Firsthand biography Short story	Definition of several categories Classification of objects or concepts Summary of a true event or fictional story Synopsis of a media program Written instructions
About This Mode of Writing	About Expression Models of outcomes (above) Evaluation Checklist	About Description Models of outcomes (above) Evaluation Checklist	About Narration Models of outcomes (above) Evaluation Checklist	About Exposition That Gives Information Models of outcomes (above) Self-Evaluation Checklist
Prewriting Choosing a Topic	Choosing Your Topic Strategies for choosing a topic Cluster Wheel Personal Experience Timeline Marking a turning point Inspirations for expressive writing	Choosing Your Topic Strategies for choosing a topic Category Wheel Topics from your experience Describing an abstract idea Using unusual points of view Inspirations for description	Choosing Your Topic Strategies for choosing a topic Topic Wheels Using freewriting to discover your topic Photo Storyboard Writing from memory Turning fact into fiction Inspirations for narration	Choosing your topic Idea wheels Self-interview Strategies for choosing a topic Inspirations for exposition
Narrowing a Topic/Focusing Your Response		Narrowing your topic Evaluation Checklist for evaluating your topic Examples of narrowed topics Cluster Map		Narrowing your topic Checklists Examples of narrowed topics Topic Web Chain of Events charts Timeline Cluster Diagram
Considering Audience and Purpose	Considering audience and purpose Writing for a specific audience Audience Profile Examples of purposes Purpose Profile Understanding purpose	Considering audience and purpose Writing for different audiences Audience Profile Examples of possible purposes Choosing a purpose that fits your topic How audience and purpose are related Selecting appropriate details Audience and Purpose chart	Considering audience and purpose Writing for different audiences Audience Profile Examples of possible purposes Writing for a specific purpose Thinking about form	Considering audience and purpose Audience Profile Writing for different audiences Purpose Profile Writing for different purposes Identifying purpose
Gathering Details/ Developing Narrative Elements	Gathering details Feelings Word Bin Sunburst Diagram Using details to show emotions Using memory to choose details Creating a mood	Gathering sensory details Sensory Word Bin Detail Chart Choosing vivid details Using figurative language	Developing narrative elements Developing characters through dialogue and action Character Trait Word Bin Exploring setting Setting Word Bin Sunburst Diagram Using photos to choose a setting Gathering details for the plot Diagraming a story line Story Profile Unusual ways of developing narrative elements	Gathering Information Word Bin Using resources Using details Cluster Diagram Selecting important details Timeline Activity Gathering appropriate details Defining by what it is not

KEY: Writing Lab and Sourcebook Writing Lab Sourcebook

5 EXPOSITION: Making Connections	6 PERSUASION	7 REPORTS	8 CREATIVE WRITING	9 RESPONSE TO LITERATURE
Kevin Powell	Doug Raboy	Jean Craighead George	Gary Soto	Joseph Bruchac
Comparison and contrast of characters, places, events Written solution for a problem Short review	Written advice Written recommendation Advertisement Essay supporting an opinion	Biographical sketch I-search Non-literary book report Lab/experiment report Library research report	Song lyrics Poem Poem in a particular form Monologue Dialogue	Reader's response journal entry Letter to an author or character Response to a poem, drama, short story Review of a literary work
About Exposition That Makes Connections Models of outcomes (above) Self-Evaluation Checklist	About Persuasion Models of outcomes (above) Self-Evaluation Checklist	About Reports Models of outcomes (above) Self-Evaluation Checklists	About Creative Writing Models of outcomes (above) Self-Evaluation Checklists	About Response to Literature Models of outcomes (above) Self-Evaluation Checklist
Choosing your topic Topic Wheels Problem Wheel Product Evaluation Checklist Inspirations for exposition Strategies for choosing a topic	Choosing your topic Using newspaper headlines as a source for writing ideas Issues Wheel Interviewing yourself Taking a position on a national issue Inspirations for persuasion	Choosing your topic Idea Wheel Strategies for choosing a topic Selecting a challenging topic Inspirations for reports	Choosing your topic Strategies for choosing a topic Sunburst Diagram wheel Photo Storyboard Freewriting Taking a topic from science Inspirations for creative writing	Choosing your topic Choosing a literary work to respond to Idea Wheel Using a reader's response journal Freewriting Comparing two different works Inspirations for writing in response to literature
Narrowing your topic Checklist Cluster Diagram Examples of broad and narrow topics		Narrowing your topic Narrowing your topic with descriptive words Topic Web Examples of narrowed topics Asking who?, what?, when?, where?, why?		Focusing your response Examples of narrowed topics Topic Web
Considering audience and purpose Audience Profile Writing for different audiences Checklist for defining a purpose Writing for different purposes Surveying an audience	Considering audience and purpose Persuading different audiences Audience Profile Examples of purposes for persuasive writing Persuasive writing for different purposes Working with a partner or an opponent	Considering audience and purpose Audience Profile Writing for different audiences Identifying your purpose Writing for different purposes Purpose checklist Accomplishing your purpose Making your purpose clear	Considering audience and purpose Audience Profile Writing for different audiences Have a specific person in mind	Considering audience and purpose Audience Profile Writing for different audiences Identifying your purpose Examples of responding to literature for different purposes
Gathering details Venn Diagram Research outline Cluster Diagram Gathering opinions of experts	Gathering Evidence Distinguishing facts from opinions Pro-and-Con Notecard Activity Types of information Using research resources Researching current issues Taking a poll	Gathering information K-W-L chart Research strategy Using library resources Notetaking Notecard templates Help with focusing research Keeping a research log	Gathering details Chain of Events Image Word Bin Cluster Diagrams Using figurative language Character Trait Word Bin Using dialogue to show character traits Prop Word Bin Creating stage directions Checking your topic	Gathering details about a novel or short story, a poem, a drama Gathering details about plot, setting, characters, sound, meaning, stage directions, dialogue Chain of Events Considering similes and metaphors and the way a poem sounds Character personality profile Sunburst Diagram Freewriting Gathering details from your life

	1 EXPRESSION	2 DESCRIPTION	3 NARRATION	4 EXPOSITION: Giving Information
Organizing Details and Information		Organizing details spatially, chronologically, and in order of importance Topic Web Cluster diagram Chain of Events chart Outliner activity Trying an unusual organization		Organizing and ordering details spatially, chronologically, and in order of importance Cluster diagram Chain of events activity Using note cards
Drafting	Drafting Personal letter template Expressive Word Bin Getting started Journal entry	Drafting Transition Word Bin Getting started Describing without naming Sketching details	Drafting First- and third-person narratives Starting your narrative with character, action, or setting Connecting events Foreshadowing Transition Word Bin Getting started	Drafting definition, a summary, and written instructions Transition Word Bin Getting started
Revising and Editing	Revision Checklist Revision checker for sentence length Expressive Word Bin Peer review checklist and guidelines Reading your work aloud Varying sentence beginnings	Revision checker for vague adjectives Transition Word Bin Revision Hints Revision Checklist Featured senses Word Bin Peer review checklist and guidelines Working with a peer editor	Revision Checklist Revision checker for language variety Reading your draft aloud Peer review checklist and strategies	Revision Checklist Revision checker for transition words Removing unnecessary details Self-Evaluation Checklist Transition Word Bin Peer editing checklist and guidelines
Proofreading	About proofreading Proofreading Checklist Using capital letters correctly Identifying sentence fragments Revising and proofreading a journal	Proofreading Checklist Using adjectives and adverbs correctly	Proofreading Checklist Punctuating dialogue Making pronouns and antecedents agree	Proofreading Checklist Avoiding sentence fragments
Publishing and Presenting	Writing postcards and letters Making an audio or video recording Sharing with a large audience Other ways to share your work Reflecting on your writing Publishing around a theme	Reflecting on your writing Giving your description a title Suggestions for sharing with an audience Creating a booklet of many descriptions	Choosing a title Creating an audio tape Putting together a class anthology Creating chapters Sharing your narrative Reflecting on your writing	Creating a dictionary, an audio anthology of summaries, a class do-it-yourself magazine Sharing with a smaller audience Reflecting on your writing
Literature Model	"The Eagle and the Hummingbird" by Jane Yolen	"An Artichoke on Legs" by Jeanne K. Hanson and Deane Morrison	*The Bells of Christmas* by Virginia Hamilton	"My Life's Work: Crime Lab Scientist" by Jeff Saviano

KEY: Writing Lab and Sourcebook | Writing Lab | Sourcebook

5 EXPOSITION: Making Connections	6 PERSUASION	7 REPORTS	8 CREATIVE WRITING	9 RESPONSE TO LITERATURE
Organizing and ordering details point by point, subject by subject, in order of importance, and chronologically Different methods of organization Venn Diagram Chain of Events organizer	Organizing details Ordering by pros and cons and order of importance Using note cards Making a list	Grouping and ordering information spatially, chronologically, and in order of importance Branching organizer Keyhole organizer Timeline Notecard activity Going back to gather more information		
Drafting a comparison-and-contrast or problem-and-solution paper, and an evaluation Transition Word Bin Overcoming writer's block	Stating and supporting an argument Drafting introduction, body, and conclusion Avoiding faulty reasoning Transition Word Bin Strategies for beginning Attention-getting introductions Appealing to readers' emotions	Drafting the introduction, body, and conclusion Guidelines and models for quoting and citing sources Creating a bibliography Checklist to help draft the body of a report Transition Word Bin Crediting your sources Adding headings and concluding subheadings	Drafting a poem Using sound devices in poetry or song lyrics Writing dialogue or a monologue Stage directions Using similes Concrete Image Bin	Drafting the introduction, body, and conclusion Transition Word Bin Using quotations Getting started
Revision Checklist Removing unnecessary details Self-Evaluation Checklists Sentence variety checker Transition Word Bin Peer editing worksheet Peer Review checklist	Revision Checklist Adding supporting details Revision checker for sentence openers Peer review checklist Using persuasive words Read it twice Making a comment positive	Revision Checklist Transition Word Bin Revision checker for coherence Reading your report aloud Peer review checklist Using persuasive words Replacing informal language Eliminating unnecessary information Improving sentence variety	Revision Checklists Making dialogue sound realistic Replacing abstract words Reading your work aloud Revision checker for vague adjectives	Revision Checklist Revision checker for varied language Tips on revising from literary authors Peer review checklist and guidelines
Proofreading Checklist Correcting run-on sentences	Proofreading Checklist Using proper pronouns Revision checker for double comparisons	Proofreading Checklist Checking capitalization Using quotation marks	Proofreading checklists Checking use of possessive nouns	Proofreading Checklist Punctuating literary titles Using commas with items in a series
Creating guides to: activities, problem solving, evaluating products Sharing with a larger audience Reflecting on your writing How-to guide for your family	Presenting your composition as a speech Creating posters Creating a bulletin board display Reflecting on your writing	Create a table of contents, charts, graphs, or other visuals; a display or exhibit Sharing with a small audience Reflecting on your writing Conducting a critics' corner Publishing a mini-lesson	Holding a poetry festival Performing a scene Publishing for a small audience Reflecting on your writing	Titling your report and creating a cover Making a school library display Creating a class publication of literary reviews Audiotaping your response Videotaping your discussion of books Reflecting on your writing
"Dad Just Got Traded!" by Susan Fornoff	"All Together Now" by Barbara Jordan	"Pandas" by Gillian Standring	"Ode to Weightlifting" by Gary Soto	"The Circle of Blessing: Joy Harjo's 'Eagle Poem'" by Joseph Bruchac

Scope and Sequence: Language Skills

SKILL	LANGUAGE LAB UNIT OR SOURCEBOOK CHAPTER	LESSON NAME
action verbs	Choosing Words Using Verbs Narration	Vivid and Precise Verbs Using Verbs Using Vivid Verbs
adjectives	Choosing Words Using Modifiers Description	Vivid Adjectives and adverbs Adjective or Adverb? Using Modifiers Using Vivid Adjectives and Adverbs
adverbs	Choosing Words Using Modifiers Description	Vivid Adjectives and Adverbs Adjective or Adverb? Using Modifiers Using Vivid Adjectives and Adverbs
agreement, pronoun-antecedent	Using Pronouns	Pronouns and Antecedents
agreement, subject-verb	Subject-Verb Agreement	Agreement in Number Agreement With Compound Subjects Intervening Phrases
antecedents	Choosing Words Using Pronouns	Pronouns to Avoid Repetition Pronouns and Antecedents
apostrophes	Punctuation Using Pronouns Creative	Apostrophes and Hyphens Possessive Pronouns and Contractions Using Contractions
appositives	Using Pronouns	Special Problems with Pronouns
articles	Using Modifiers	Using Modifiers
audience, considering	Composing	Considering Audience and Purpose
bibliography	Reports	Citing Sources
choppy sentences	Styling Sentences	Combining Sentences
colons	Punctuation	Colons
commas	Punctuation Persuasion	Commas Using Commas
common nouns	Using Nouns	Using Nouns
compare/contrast order	Building Paragraphs	Transitional Words
complete sentences	Sentence Errors	Sentence Fragments
complex sentences	Persuasion	Varying Sentence Lengths
compound sentences	Sentence Errors Styling Sentences Exposition: Making Connections Persuasion	Run-on Sentences Combining Sentences Using Prepositions and Conjunctions Varying Sentence Lengths
compound subjects	Styling Sentences Subject-Verb Agreement Exposition: Giving Information	Combining Sentences Agreement With Compound Subjects Using Correct Subject-Verb Agreement

KEY: Language Lab Sourcebook: Developing Your Style lesson

SKILL	LANGUAGE LAB UNIT OR SOURCEBOOK CHAPTER	LESSON NAME
compound verbs	Styling Sentences	Combining Sentences
concluding sentences	Building Paragraphs	Concluding Sentence
conjunctions	Subject-Verb Agreement Using Modifiers	Agreement With Compound Subjects Forms of Comparison
contractions	Using Pronouns **Creative Writing**	Possessive Pronouns and Contractions **Using Contractions**
coordination	**Reports**	**Using Coordination and Subordination**
declarative sentences	Punctuation	End Marks
dialogue	Composing Punctuation	Writing Dialogue Quotation Marks
double comparisons	Using Modifiers	Forms of Comparison
double negatives	Using Modifiers	Avoiding Double Negatives
end marks	Punctuation	End Marks
exact nouns	Choosing Words **Exposition: Giving Information**	Exact Nouns **Exact Nouns**
exclamatory sentences	Punctuation	End Marks
footnotes	**Reports**	**Citing Sources**
formal language	Composing	Considering Audience and Purpose
forms of comparison	Using Modifiers **Exposition: Making Connections**	Forms of Comparison **Making Clear Comparisons**
hyphens	Punctuation	Apostrophes
imperative sentences	Punctuation	End Marks
independent clauses	**Exposition: Making Connections**	**Using Prepositions and Conjunctions**
informal language	Composing	Considering Audience and Purpose
interrogative sentences	Punctuation	End Marks
irregular verbs	Using Verbs	Principal Parts of Verbs
irrelevant sentences	Building Paragraphs	Unity in Paragraphs
linking verbs	Choosing Words Using Verbs **Narration**	Vivid and Precise Verbs Using Verbs **Using Vivid Verbs**
main idea	Building Paragraphs **Expression**	Main Idea and Topic Sentence **Unity in Paragraphs**
misplaced modifiers	Sentence Errors **Description**	Misplaced Modifiers **Avoiding Sentence Errors**

SKILL	LANGUAGE LAB UNIT OR SOURCEBOOK CHAPTER	LESSON NAME
modifiers	Using Modifiers Description	Adjective or Adverb? Forms of Comparison Using Modifiers Using Vivid Adjectives and Adverbs
narrowing a topic	Composing	Narrowing a Topic
nouns	Choosing Words Using nouns Exposition: Giving Information	Exact Nouns Using Nouns Using Exact Nouns
nouns of direct address	Punctuation	Commas
paragraphs	Building Paragraphs	Concluding Sentence Main Idea and Topic Sentence
parentheses	Reports	Citing Sources
periods	Punctuation	End Marks
phrases	Subject-Verb Agreement Exposition: Giving Information	Intervening Phrases Using Correct Subject-Verb Agreement
plural nouns	Using Nouns	Plural Nouns
point of view	Composing	Point of View
possessive nouns	Using Nouns	Possessive Nouns
possessive pronouns	Using Pronouns	Possessive Pronouns and Contractions Pronoun Case
prepositions	Exposition: Making Connections	Using Prepositions and Conjunctions
present tense	Using Verbs	Verb Tense
principal parts of verbs	Using Verbs	Principal Parts of Verbs
pronoun case	Using Pronouns	Pronoun Case Special Problems with Pronouns
pronouns	Choosing Words Using Pronouns Expression	Pronouns to Avoid Repetition Pronouns and Antecedents Pronoun Case Using Pronouns
proper nouns	Capitalization Using Nouns	Capitalization 2 Capitalization 3 Using Nouns
purpose for writing	Composing	Considering Audience and Purpose
quotation marks	Capitalization Punctuation Creative Writing Response to Literature	Capitalization in Sentences Quotation Marks Punctuating and Formatting Dialogue Using Quotation Marks and Underlining
run-on sentences	Sentence Errors Description	Run-on Sentences Avoiding Sentence Errors

KEY: Language Lab   Sourcebook: Developing Your Style lesson

SKILL	LANGUAGE LAB UNIT OR SOURCEBOOK CHAPTER	LESSON NAME
sensory details	Building Paragraphs	Supporting Sentences
sentence fragments	Sentence Errors **Description**	Sentence Fragments **Avoiding Sentence Errors**
simple sentences	Styling Sentences **Persuasion**	Correcting Stringy Sentences **Varying Sentence Lengths**
simple subjects	Subject-Verb Agreement **Exposition: Giving Information**	Agreement With Compound Subjects **Using Correct Subject-Verb Agreement**
singular nouns	Using Nouns	Plural Nouns
spatial order	Building Paragraphs	Transitional Words
stringy sentences	Styling Sentences	Correcting Stringy Sentences
subordination	**Reports**	**Using Coordination and Subordination**
supporting sentences	Building Paragraphs	Main Idea and Topic Sentence Supporting Sentences Unity in Paragraphs
time order	Building Paragraphs	Transitional Words
topic sentence	Building Paragraphs	Main Idea and Topic Sentence Unity in Paragraphs
transitional words	Building Paragraphs **Narration**	Transitional Words **Using Transitions**
unified paragraphs	Building Paragraphs	Unity in Paragraphs
verb phrases	Using Verbs	Using Verbs
verb tenses	Using Verbs	Verb Tense
verbs	Choosing Words Using Verbs	Vivid and Precise Verbs Using Verbs Verb tense
wordiness	Styling Sentences **Response to Literature**	Eliminating Unnecessary Words **Eliminating Unnecessary Words**

PRENTICE HALL WRITER'S SOLUTION

COPPER

SOURCE BOOK

PRENTICE HALL
Upper Saddle River, New Jersey
Needham, Massachusetts

ISBN 0-13-828773-2

2 3 4 5 6 7 8 9 10   00 99 98 97 96

PRENTICE HALL
Simon & Schuster Education Group
A VIACOM COMPANY

STAFF CREDITS

Editorial: Doug McCollum, Peter Gutierrez, Kelly Ackley, Amy Fleming, Jacqueline Regan, Richard Tortoriello, Elaine Goldman, Glenn E. Bell, Jim Jeglikowski

Marketing: Mollie Ledwith, Belinda Loh

Permissions: Doris Robinson

Design: AnnMarie Roselli, Kathryn Foot, Laura Bird, Gerry Schrenk

Media Resources: Suzi Myers, Martha Conway, Vickie Menanteaux, Melanie Jones

Production: Elizabeth Torjussen, Nancy Velthaus

Prepress Production: Kathryn Dix, Paula Massenaro, Carol Barbara

Print and Bind: Rhett Conklin, Matt McCabe

National Language Arts Consultants: Craig A. McGhee, Kathy Lewis, Karen Massey, Vennisa Travers, Gail Witt

Photo/Art Credits begin on page 310.

ACKNOWLEDGMENTS

Grateful acknowledgment is made to the following for permission to reprint copyrighted material:

Rhoda Blumberg
From *The Truth About Dragons* by Rhoda Blumberg. Copyright © 1980 by Rhoda Blumberg. Reprinted by permission of the author.

Georges Borchardt, Inc., for the Estate of John Gardner
From *Dragon, Dragon* by John Gardner. Copyright © 1975 by Boskydell Artists Ltd. Reprinted by permission of Georges Borchardt, Inc., for the Estate of John Gardner.

Joanne Bracco
From "Family Film Reviews." Permission granted by the author, Joanne Bracco. Reprinted from *Cinemascoop,* her monthly syndicated column originating in *San Francisco Peninsula Parent News* magazine Vol. 10. No. 2, copyright February 1994.

Curtis Brown Ltd.
From "The Eagle and the Hummingbird" by Jane Yolen. Copyright © 1985 by Jane Yolen. First appeared in *The Writer* magazine, March 1985, published by The Writer, Inc. Excerpt from "Virginia Hamilton" by Lee Bennett Hopkins. Copyright © 1972 by Lee Bennett Hopkins. First appeared in *The Horn Book Magazine,* December 1972, published by Horn Book Magazine. Reprinted by permission of Curtis Brown Ltd.

Bruchac, Joseph
From "The Circle of Blessing: Joy Harjo's 'Eagle Poem'" by Joseph Bruchac. Reprinted by permission of the author.

Carolrhoda Books, Inc.
From *Gorillas* by Paul Hermann Bürgel and Manfred Hartwig. Copyright 1989 by Kinderbuchverlag Reich Luzern AG, Lucerne, Switzerland. Adapted by Carolrhoda Books, Inc. Used by permission Carolrhoda Books, Inc. All rights reserved.

Clarion Books/Houghton Mifflin Company
Excerpts from *Lincoln: A Photobiography.* Copyright © 1987 by Russ Freedman. Reprinted by permission of Clarion Books/Houghton Mif Company. All rights reserved.

Jack Cope
From "Power," from *The Man Who Doubted and Other Stories* by Ja Cope. First published in 1967 by William Heinemann Ltd., London.

Crown Publishers, Inc.
From *Creature Design* by Carlo Rambaldi, from *Working in Hollywoo* Alexandra Brouwer and Thomas Lee Wright. Copyright © 1990 Alexandra Brouwer and Thomas Lee Wright. From *Nadja On My Way* Nadja Salerno-Sonnenberg. Copyright © 1989 by Nadja Saler Sonnenberg. Published by Crown Publishers, Inc.

Dell Books, a division of Bantam Doubleday Bell Publishing Group, Inc.
From "The Geese" by Richard Peck, from *Sounds and Silences: Poe For Now* by Richard Peck, Editor. Copyright © 1970, 1990 by Richa Peck. From "The Jacket" from *Small Faces* by Gary Soto. Copyri 1986 by Gary Soto. Used by permission of Dell Books, a division Bantam Doubleday Dell Publishing Group, Inc.

Enslow Publishers
From *Adventures with Atoms and Molecules: Chemistry Experiments Young People* by Robert C. Mebane and Thomas R. Rybolt. Reprinted permission of the publisher.

(Acknowledgments continue on page 309.)

ii

laster Teacher Editorial Board

Contributing Writers

iii

Table of Contents

iv

v

Chapter 4 *Exposition: Giving Information* 99

Chapter 5 *Exposition: Making Connections* 133

vi

Chapter 6 Persuasion

vii

Chapter 7 Reports 199

Chapter 8 Creative Writing 237

viii

1

Expression
Classroom Manager

Writer's Solution *Materials for Teaching Expression*

The *Writer's Solution* includes a wide range of materials for teaching expression. You can pick and choose from among these materials to create a lesson plan that suits your classroom needs, teaching style, and equipment situation. In the pages that follow, you'll find lesson plans suggesting some of the most effective ways of using these materials. You do not have to use all of the program components or all of its features to use it effectively. Just use what works for you. For a detailed description of each of the *Writer's Solution* components, see pages T4–T6.

Below is a detailed list of the *Writer's Solution* materials for Expression.

Writers at Work Videodisc

Featured Writer: Jane Yolen, Fiction Writer

Videodisc Segments

About Expression: Personal Portraits

Writing Tips: Varying Your Sentences; Trusting an Outside Eye

Interactive CD-ROMs

Writing Lab

Tutorial on Expression

About Expression
- Includes annotated Models From Literature and Evaluation Checklist

Choosing Your Topic
- Includes Inspirations for Expression and a video that provides writing ideas

Considering Audience and Purpose
- Includes video clips about identifying audience and writing purpose

Gathering Details
- Includes videos about using details and about creating a mood, and interactive instruction on using memory to choose details

Drafting
- Includes a video about a Virginia Woolf journal and one with Lucy Jones on overcoming writer's block, and a Student Model

Revising and Editing
- Includes videos with tips from Jane Yolen, a revision checker for sentence length, and Self-Evaluation and Peer Review Checklists

Proofreading
- Includes integrated grammar instruction on using capital letters, a Proofreading Checklist, and a Student Model

Publishing and Presenting
- Includes a writing model of a postcard and tips for making an audio or video recording

Writer's Tool Kit

Suggested Activities: Cluster Wheel; Personal Experience Timeline; Revising and Editing and Proofreading Checklists; Audience Profile; Purpose Statement Activity; Feelings Word Bin; Sunburst Diagram; Expressive Word Bin; Self-Evaluation Checklist.

Language Lab

Related Lessons: Vivid and Precise Verbs, Vivid and Precise Adjectives (Choosing Words unit); Unity in Paragraphs (Building Paragraphs unit); Considering Audience and Purpose (Composing unit); all lessons in Using Pronouns unit

Sourcebook

About Expression (pp. 4–10)

Guided Lesson on Expression (pp. 11–23)

Developing Your Style

Using Pronouns (p. 25)

Unity in Paragraphs (pp. 26–27)

Literature Model

"The Eagle and the Hummingbird" by Jane Yolen (pp. 28–29)

Below is a list of materials from Prentice Hall's student writing handbook that you can integrate with this lesson.

Writer's Companion

Mini-Lesson on Journal Writing, p. 99

Mini-Lesson on Personal Letter, p. 102

Mini-Lesson on Unity, Coherence, and Transitions, p. 62

Pronouns, p. 362

Action Verb, p. 283

Teaching Integrated Language Arts Using the Writer's Solution—*Starting With Literature*

Have students read and respond to personal journal entries, anecdotes, personal memoirs, personal letters, postcards, and other types of expressive writing. When discussing the selections, draw students' attention to elements of expression, such as including details that suit the audience and purpose for writing, using vivid language, including personal thoughts and feelings, and organizing the writing clearly. Point out that students can use the examples of expressive writing they read as models for writing their own expressive pieces. Lead into having students complete expressive writing assignments using the components of the *Writer's Solution.*

CONNECTIONS TO *PRENTICE HALL LITERATURE, COPPER,* SELECTIONS

Personal Journal/Anecdote/Personal Memoir	2E	3E
"The All-American Slurp," Lensey Namioka	■	▲
"The Drive-In Movies," Gary Soto	■	
"Belle Benchley: Zoo Director," Margery Facklam	■	
"Alone in the Nets," Arnold Adoff	■	▲
"Journey Home," Yoshiko Uchida	■	▲

Personal Letter/ Postcard	2E	3E
"Letter to the U. S. Government," Chief Seattle	■	▲
"Letter to Joan," C. S. Lewis	■	▲
"Letter to Scottie," F. Scott Fitzgerald	■	▲
"How to Write a Letter," Garrison Keillor	■	▲

You can use the *Writer's Solution* materials on expressive writing to support any of the following writing activities in *Prentice Hall Literature, Copper.*

CONNECTIONS TO *PRENTICE HALL LITERATURE, COPPER,* WRITING ACTIVITIES

Thinking and Writing Activities	2E	3E
Writing a Letter—Follows **"Auntie,"** Phillipa Pearce,	■	▲
"How to Write a Letter," Garrison Keillor,	■	▲
"Sea Songs," Myra Cohn Livingston,	■	▲
"The Living Kuan-yin," Carol Kendall and Yao-wen Li,	■	▲
and **"Letter to Scottie,"** F. Scott Fitzgerald		▲
Describing an Emotion—Follows **"The Sound of Summer Running,"** Ray Bradbury	■	▲
Writing a Diary Entry—Follows Chapter 6 of ***Tuck Everlasting***, Natalie Babbitt	■	▲
Writing an Anecdote—Follows **"Belle Benchley: Zoo Director,"** Margery Facklam	■	

■ **(2E)** *Prentice Hall Literature, Copper,* Second Edition

▲ **(3E)** *Prentice Hall Literature, Copper,* Paramount Edition

CONNECTIONS BETWEEN INSPIRATIONS FOR EXPRESSION AND *PRENTICE HALL LITERATURE*

You can use the multimedia Inspirations for Expression to motivate student reading as well as student writing. Many of the Inspirations are audio recordings or video adaptations of selections from *Prentice Hall Literature*, *Copper*. Have students work in small groups to look at and discuss an appropriate Inspiration before reading the corresponding selection. Then, after reading the selection, students can replay the Inspiration and select one of the accompanying topic ideas (see pp. 14–17). The following selections from *Prentice Hall Literature*, *Copper*, are included in the Inspirations for Expression:

- **"The All-American Slurp,"** Lensey Namioka
- **"Alone in the Nets,"** Arnold Adoff
- **"Journey Home,"** Yoshiko Uchida
- **"Letter to Scottie,"** F. Scott Fitzgerald
- **"How to Write a Letter,"** Garrison Keillor

Recommended Lesson Plan

The following lesson plan is recommended for providing students with thorough, comprehensive instructions in expressive writing. Because you may not have all the components of the *Writer's Solution* or may have limited access to equipment, the plan provides a number of options. Choose the options that best suit your teaching style and equipment situation. You may want to add a few days to the lesson plan to allow students time to publish their work and to hold conferences with students to discuss your assessment of their work.

FIVE-DAY LESSON PLAN	
Lesson Outcome:	**Each student writes a complete expressive piece.**
DAY 1	**Introduce your students to expressive writing.** Show the *Writers at Work Videodisc* segment featuring Jane Yolen. Use the segment as a springboard for class discussion or group activities.
DAY 2	**Have students choose a writing topic and plan their expressive piece.** OPTION 1 Have students work either individually or in small groups to look at About Expression and to choose a topic by browsing through the Inspirations for Expression. Then have students work individually to develop their ideas by completing the rest of the Prewriting stage of the tutorial on Expression. At the end of the period, have students print out their Prewriting notes. OPTION 2 Have students review the Descriptions From Literature in the About Expression section of the *Sourcebook*. Then have them choose from the topic suggestions and begin developing their expressive writing by completing the rest of the Prewriting stage of the Guided Lesson.
DAY 3	**Have students draft their expressive writing.** OPTION 1 Have students write their drafts on the computer following the instructions and using the activities provided in the Drafting section of the tutorial on Expression. Have students print out their expressive writing at the end of the period. OPTION 2 Have students write their drafts on paper following the instructions in the Guided Lesson (p. 20).
DAY 4	**Have students revise their expressive writing.** OPTION 1 Have students revise their expressive writing on the computer using the revision checkers, activities, and suggestions in the Revising and Editing section of the tutorial on Expression. OPTION 2 Have students revise their expressive writing following the suggestions in the Guided Lesson (pp. 21–22).

FIVE-DAY LESSON PLAN (continued)

DAY 5

Have students work in peer groups to make final revisions.
OPTION 1 Have pairs of students review each other's work following the guidelines in the peer revision section of the tutorial on Expression. The pairs should then hold conferences before each student makes final revisions. Students should then proofread and print out their final drafts.

OPTION 2 Have pairs of students review each other's work following the guidelines in the Guided Lesson. The pairs should then hold conferences before each student makes final revisions.

Condensed Lesson Plans

If you don't have a full week to devote to teaching expressive writing, you can use Three- or Four-Day Plans: Adapt the Five-Day Plan by having students learn about expression, choose a topic, and develop ideas for their expressive writing during Day 1. As in the Five-Day Plan, have students spend a day writing their drafts. For a Four-Day Plan, follow the last two days of the Five-Day Plan; for a Three-Day Plan, simply condense these two days into a single day of revision and forgo the option of working in peer groups.

TWO-DAY LESSON PLAN

Lesson Outcome: **Each student writes a complete expressive piece.**

DAY 1

Have students choose a topic and write their first drafts.
OPTION 1 Have students work in the open-ended environment in the *Writing Lab*. Working individually, students should choose a topic by browsing through the Inspirations for Expression. Then they should draft their expressive pieces in their on-line Notebooks using the available prewriting tools as needed.

OPTION 2 Using the suggestions and instructions in the *Sourcebook*, students should choose a topic and write a first draft of their expressive pieces.

DAY 2

Have students revise and edit their work.
OPTION 1 Have students revise on the computer using the tools, activities, and instructions in the tutorial on Expression.

OPTION 2 Have students revise their expressive writing following the suggestions in the *Sourcebook*.

If you have only one day to devote to teaching expressive writing, students can work individually in the open-ended environment in the *Writing Lab* by browsing through the Inspirations for Expression to choose a topic, using the prewriting tools as needed, and completing a quick-write draft of an expressive piece in their writing notebooks. Students may also use the *Sourcebook* to choose a topic and write a brief expressive piece.

Preparing to Teach

Lesson Objectives

Students will:

1. Choose a topic for expressive writing
2. Adapt writing to suit audience and purpose
3. Express a personal response to an event or idea
4. Use the proper form for journal entries and personal letters
5. Publish their finished work

Activating Prior Knowledge

Ask students to give examples of times they have written to capture their thoughts, feelings, or experiences. Students may say that they have kept diaries or journals; sent letters to authors, actors, or athletes they admire; or written postcards to friends describing summer vacation or travel experiences. Ask: *What kind of expressive writing—postcards or letters—do you enjoy writing more? Why? Which do you like to receive? Why?*

CHAPTER 1

Amanecer en la Montaña *(Dawn on the Mountain), 1949, Dr. Atl (Gerardo Murillo), Patrimonio de Jalisco*

Expression

> "Anything I've experienced can find its way into one of my stories."
>
> —Jane Yolen
> *Writer*

Humanities Note

The fine art, *Amanecer en la Montaña* ("Dawn on the Mountain"), is by Dr. Atl. Gerardo Murillo (1875–1964), a painter, poet, and author, took the name *Atl*, the Aztec word for "water," to show his pride in his Mexican American heritage.

Murillo made several trips to Europe to study art, but was committed to creating a true modern Mexican style of artistic expression. He invented a type of crayon made of pigment, resin, oil, and wax to use in his drawings and murals. Atl was a student, and eventually the director, of Mexico City's Academia de San Carlos. His work is known worldwide for its imposing views of the natural beauty of Mexico.

The deeply felt, surprisingly personal quality of this scene from nature lends itself well to an exploration of expressive writing. You might use the following questions as a basis for class discussion:

- What universal ideas, fables, or myths about dawn are expressed in this painting?
- What feelings or thoughts do you have when you watch the sun rise or set?

Addressing Your Classroom Situation

This chapter includes a variety of Models From Literature, writing topics, writing process strategies, and Student Models, along with two integrated skills lessons. Feel free to pick and choose from this material to create a customized lesson on expression that matches your classroom needs.

The following are some of the key features of the chapter:

- The chapter begins with a section introducing expression. This section includes thoughts about expression from writer Jane Yolen, Group Discussion questions, and Models From Literature for the following types of expression: personal memoir, anecdote, personal journal entry, personal letter, and postcard.
- The Prewriting section includes an assortment of idea-generating activities to help students choose a topic, along with some suggested topics from which they can select. This section also provides instruction, tips, and activities to help students consider their audience and purpose, and to choose details.
- The Drafting section addresses the issues of writing to express thoughts, ideas, and opinions, and also presents pointers for drafting.
- The Revising and Editing section focuses on reviewing drafts for ways to make ideas, emotions, and purpose more clear for the intended audience; choosing precise and vivid words; and making the writing more personal. It provides tips and checklists for self-revision, peer review, and for proofreading, as well as a student model to use to demonstrate revising techniques.
- The guided writing instruction is followed by a Student Model and then skills lessons on using pronouns and on unity in paragraphs. You may want to address these skills before students draft their expressive pieces, or you may prefer to focus on them during the revising/proofreading phase.
- The chapter ends with a Literature Model, *The Eagle and the Hummingbird*, a personal memoir by Jane Yolen.

Chapter Contents

About Expression

Guided Lesson

Student Model

Developing Your Style 1

Developing Your Style 2

Literature Model

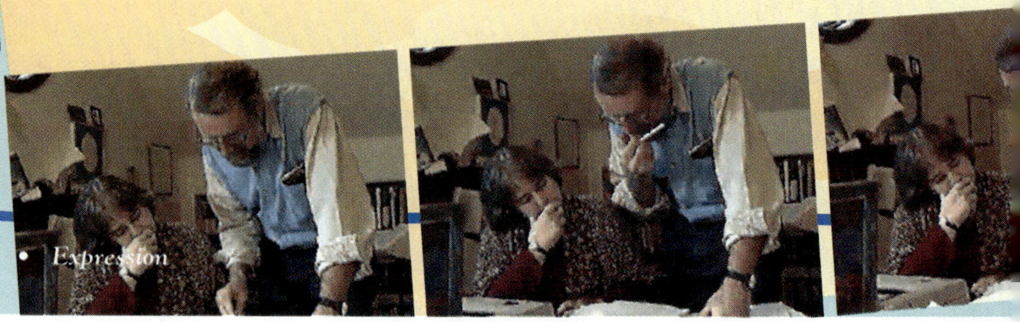

"You have an emotional response to everything. If you can think about your emotional response to a particular happening, you will make your writing much more alive."

"Even if you're writing an essay or a story or a poem, your feelings are going to slip in. Let them."

—Jane Yolen
Writer

"The most interesting journals and memoirs, like any good writing, are first of all keenly observant."

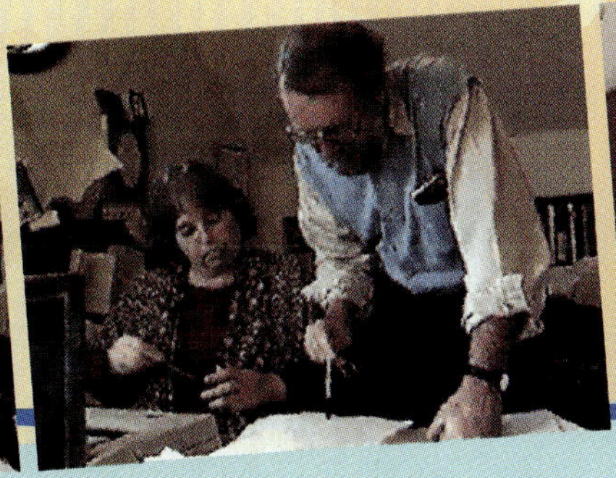

More About the Writer

Jane Yolen has written more than eighty books for children and young adults. She has a particular interest in the oral tradition—tales that have been passed along by storytellers from one generation to the next. She says that these tales lead to "the understanding of the deepest longings and most daring visions in humankind."

Jane Yolen has also said that she reads aloud every sentence she writes. You might ask students to explain why they think she uses this technique. Have them explain why they do or do not think it is a good practice.

Tech Prep Note

Point out that not only writers like Jane Yolen use expression. Workers in other fields write on the job. Teachers and administrators are often called upon to write anecdotes about students and colleagues. Ship officers and scientists at work on a project may keep journals. Doctors' offices send postcards to patients. Workers in other fields frequently contribute anecdotes to company or industry-wide publications. Ask: *Think about the adults you know and the jobs they have. How do they use expressive writing at work?*

Introducing Expressive Writing

About Expression

What Is Expression?

Expression is writing in which you share thoughts and feelings about events in your life. Whenever you use words to communicate your personal responses, you are writing expressively. Some expression is informal, such as personal journal entries and letters. Other forms of expression are meant to be published and are therefore more formal.

Group Discussion What kinds of clothes reflect your personality? What music appeals to you? With a group of classmates, discuss the ways in which you express yourself in daily life. Share examples of expression among group members. You may want to share with the group any songs or poems that you feel express your beliefs, opinions, and attitudes.

Teaching Options

There are a variety of ways you can introduce expressive writing using the components of the *Writer's Solution*:

- You can show the Expression segment from the *Writers at Work Videodisc*. Use this segment as a springboard for a class discussion on expression.
- You can have students work individually or in small groups to go through the About Expression section of the Expression tutorial in the *Writing Lab* CD-ROM.
- You can work through the About Expression section of the *Sourcebook* with the class.
- You can have students read the About Expression section of the *Sourcebook* before class starts so that, as a group, you can concentrate on the videodisc or CD-ROM lesson.

Sourcebook

Have students read aloud and discuss the About Expression section in the *Sourcebook*. Use the following questions to guide the discussion:

- How can you recognize expressive writing? Where might you find examples of it?
- What makes expressive writing interesting to the writer and the reader? What makes it important?
- How can expressive writing help you to discover more about yourself?
- What does expressive writing have in common with other kinds of writing? In what ways is it different?

Following the class discussion, divide your students into groups of three to five to engage in the Group Discussion (p. 4).

Writers at Work Videodisc

Use the Expression section of the videodisc, featuring writer Jane Yolen, as a springboard into a class discussion on expression. Play the chapter in its entirety, pausing as needed. Then feel free to use the barcodes to replay any segment to reinforce an important idea.

After students have viewed the video, have them take turns sharing their responses. Then move into a discussion of the writing techniques and personal insights that Yolen shares. Ask:

- Why do you think Jane Yolen emphasizes the emo-

How a Professional Writer Uses Expression

Most creative writers use expression in their work—whether creating a poem, story, or memoir. Jane Yolen, a popular fiction writer, uses expression both in her personal correspondence and in her fiction. In this excerpt from "Greyling," notice how Yolen conveys the emotional state of first the fisherman's wife and then the fisherman:

> "Each morning . . . the wife would say to the fisherman, 'You have your boat and your nets and your lines. But I have no baby to hold in my arms.' And again, in the evening, it was the same. She would weep and wail and rock the cradle that stood by the hearth. But year in and year out the cradle stayed empty.
>
> Now the fisherman was also sad that they had no child. But he kept his sorrow to himself so that his wife would not know his grief and thus double her own. Indeed, he would leave the hut each morning with a breath of song and return each night with a whistle on his lips. His nets were full but his heart was empty, yet he never told his wife."

How Expression Fits Into Your Life

More than any other form of writing, perhaps, expression results directly from what you as a person experience during your life. A sports victory, a triumph in math class, an argument with your best friend, or even your opinion of the school play can lead to expressive writing.

Although expressive writing can take many forms—from a journal or diary entry to a personal letter to a friend or relative—it provides a unique avenue of self-expression. Expressive writing gives you the opportunity to reveal through words the very essence of your personality.

tional content of writing? Do you agree that letting your feelings slip into something you are writing about makes for "a much more alive kind of writing," as Yolen contends? Explain.

- What do you think about Yolen's practice of keeping a file of writing ideas?

What kinds of things would you put in your own special file?

Play frames 322 to 9857

Writing Lab CD-ROM

The About Expression section of the tutorial on Expression includes the following options:

- **Author video** Students play a video to hear Jane Yolen's thoughts on expressive writing.
- **Interactive models of expressive writing** Students interact with literary models to hear insights about the elements of personal journal writing, anecdotes, personal memoirs, letters, and postcards.
- **Evaluation guidelines** These guidelines can be presented to students before they draft their expressive pieces to serve as a checklist to guide their writing. The guidelines can also be used for self-assessment after writing. If so, students can incorporate the ideas into a reflective piece they can choose to include in their portfolios.

Teaching Strategy

Discuss with students the idea that most creative writers use expression in their work. Ask students to describe the feelings expressed in the "Greyling" excerpt about the fisherman. Ask them to tell how this passage makes them feel.

Real-World Writing

Have students look for examples of expressive writing about local topics, such as efforts to lower crime or decrease noise, to begin a community garden, and so on. Help students identify people in your community who might write expressively on the topic.

As students share their findings, ask:

- In what ways do the writers use expression? How do they evoke feelings in their writing?
- How do the writers use details? How do you think they gathered the details?

Integrating Literature With Writing

Starting From Literature

You can use the models on pages 6–10 to illustrate the various elements of each type of expression. Or you can use the content or devices used in these pieces to inspire writing on any of the topics they address. For example, you can have students use their reactions to the powerful Filipovic excerpt on page 8 to write their own personal journal entry recalling a time when they felt fear and how they coped during the experience.

Clarification

Some students may be confused by all the different kinds of expressive writing presented here. For one thing, they might be confused by the distinction between anecdotes and personal memoirs. Guide them to appreciate that although each is a remembrance of a real event in the writer's life, anecdotes tend to be brief, are often humorous, and are about incidents that had less of an impact on the writer. Emphasize to students that whether they categorize their piece as an anecdote or a memoir, it should include precise and vivid details and should express their feelings.

Types of Expression

When will you use expression in your writing? Sometimes expression stands alone as a form of writing. Sometimes, however, expression is used in another type of writing. For instance, the author of a play may express his or her own feelings through the words of the characters. Following are a few types of writing that are likely to have an expressive emphasis.

1 Personal Memoir

- A memoir is a remembrance of a past event, usually one that has special meaning for the writer.
- A memoir includes specific details along with the writer's emotional response to the event.
- A personal memoir is written from the first-person point of view.

Model From Literature

In the following passage from "The Jacket," Gary Soto writes about an event from his childhood that made a lasting impression on him.

When I needed a new jacket and my mother asked what kind I wanted, I described something like bikers wear: black leather and silver studs with enough belts to hold down a small town. We were in the kitchen, steam on the windows from her cooking. She listened so long while stirring dinner that I thought she understood for sure the kind I wanted. The next day when I got home from school, I discovered draped on my bedpost a jacket the color of day-old guacamole. I threw my books on the bed and approached the jacket slowly, as if it were a stranger whose hand I had to shake. I touched the vinyl sleeve, the collar, and peeked at the mustard-colored lining.

Teaching From the Model

Guide students to analyze this excerpt from Gary Soto's "The Jacket," to understand the characteristics of a personal memoir:

- *It is a remembrance of an event of special significance in the writer's life.* This excerpt recalls a meaningful experience the writer had in which he learned that one cannot always get what one wants.
- *It includes specific details as well as the writer's emotional responses.* Soto describes both jackets in all their details, as well as the scene with his mother in the kitchen. He also explains his reaction upon seeing green vinyl instead of black leather.

Writing Strategy

Point out to students that personal memoirs are written using the first-person point of view. Discuss the distinction between first-person and third-person points of view, referring students to the Point of View lesson in the Composing unit of the *Language Lab*, as needed.

2 Anecdote

- An anecdote is a short, usually humorous, story about a real-life event.
- An anecdote is usually written in informal language.
- Many anecdotes contain an observation about life.

Model From Literature

This excerpt from *Childhood* by comedian Bill Cosby is an anecdote from his childhood. Notice how Cosby uses dialogue to help capture the humor and bring the episode to life.

When I was eleven, my job as a crossing guard gave me my first taste of romance: whenever a certain fetching female named Elaine reached the corner, I took personal charge of her trip.

"You may go now," I told her one morning, with a debonair smile and a sweep of my arm.

"But the light is red," she said.

"And so it is."

I had been too blinded by Elaine to see anything else.

"I could have gotten killed," she said.

And so she could, but she would have died for love.

Teaching From the Model

Guide students to understand the characteristics of this type of expression by reading and discussing the excerpt from *Childhood.*

- *It's an informal retelling of an event that really happened.* Cosby uses a conversational tone to retell the story of his "first taste of romance."
- *It's humorous.* Though there is an element of drama when Elaine says "I could have gotten killed," Cosby uses the incident to mock his own infatuation and romanticism by saying "she would have died for love."

Teaching Strategy

Since anecdotes are often most effective when spoken, invite interested students to share theirs within small groups. By presenting their anecdotes orally, students may gain some insight into how to write them more effectively. Remind students that Jane Yolen says she always reads her writing aloud.

Teaching From the Model

Guide students to recognize how this Zlata Filipovic excerpt is an example of a personal journal by calling attention to the following features:

- *It is dated.* The writer informs us that this entry was written on Saturday, May 2, 1992.
- *It describes an important realization.* Filipovic writes of her realization that the cellar, as horrible a place as it was, was saving the lives of her family.
- *The writer uses words and sentence fragments to express feelings.* Filipovic simply writes one word, "Horrible," to describe what it was like to hover in the darkness while shells pounded and glass shattered overhead.

Clarification

Talk with students about what it means to keep a journal, or private notebook, helping them to see its benefits as a way to remember key events, clarify feelings and ideas, outline plans, and try new writing skills. Point out that journals can be used to record thoughts and experiences, school-related observations and reflections, or an ongoing dialogue with a friend or teacher. You may wish also to talk over tips for keeping a journal.

3 Personal Journal Entry

- A personal journal is generally written for the writer alone.
- In a journal entry, a writer might use single words and sentence fragments to express feelings.
- Sometimes a writer will have important realizations while writing in a journal.
- Most journal entries are dated, which helps the writer locate thoughts and feelings at that time.

Model From Literature

This excerpt is from the journal of Zlata Filipovic, a young Bosnian girl who started keeping a journal in 1991 when she was ten years old. In the following passage, she describes her reaction to hiding in a cellar while Serbian shells bombarded her Eastern European city.

Saturday, 5/2/92

The cellar is ugly, dark, smelly. Mommy, who's terrified of mice, had two fears to cope with. The three of us were in the same corner as the other day. We listened to the pounding shells, the shooting, the thundering noise overhead. We even heard planes. At one moment I realized that this awful cellar was the only place that could save our lives. Suddenly, it started to look almost warm and nice. It was the only way we could defend ourselves against all this terrible shooting. We heard glass shattering in our street. Horrible. I put my fingers in my ears to block out the terrible sounds.

4 Personal Letter

- A personal letter usually contains the date, a salutation, a body, and a closing.
- It contains factual news as well as the writer's feelings and opinions.
- A personal letter is usually written in informal language.

Model From Literature

Author F. Scott Fitzgerald wrote the following passage in a letter to his daughter, who was away at summer camp.

Dear Pie,

I feel very strongly about you doing [your] duty. Would you give me a little more documentation about your reading in French?

. . . I think of you, and always pleasantly; but if you call me "Pappy" again I am going to take the White Cat out and beat his bottom hard, six times for every time you are impertinent. Do you react to that?

I will arrange the camp bill.

With dearest love, Daddy

Teaching From the Model

Guide students to analyze this excerpt to understand how it exemplifies the characteristics of a personal letter:

- *It contains a salutation, a body, and a closing.* Fitzgerald's letter to his daughter is written using the accepted personal letter format. It is likely that the actual letter included the date it was written.
- *It contains factual news as well as personal feelings.* Fitzgerald informs his daughter that he will pay the camp bill. He also lets her know that he doesn't appreciate the manner in which she has been addressing him.

Writers at Work Videodisc

Jane Yolen captures her feelings and experiences by writing personal letters to thirty friends and writers in which she "talks generally about how I see the world." Ask:

- How many people do you write to? What kinds of things do you write about?

Play frames 2215 to 3030

Teaching Strategy

Talk with students about the advantages of writing personal letters over making phone calls. Students may mention that it can be easier to express thoughts and feelings on paper than on the telephone. Others may point out that letters can get across exactly what you want to say, and that they can be read more than once.

Cross-Curricular Connection: *Literature*

Tell students that before people had telephones and e-mail, letter writing was a more widespread practice and the primary way people corresponded. Point out that people used to save their letters, and that some written by famous people are valuable today. Also point out that receiving letters was a cherished pastime, particularly since slower forms of transportation discouraged people from making long journeys.

Invite volunteers to bring old family letters to class to read aloud or to copy and distribute. Ask students to discuss common elements of these letters, such as descriptions of places and how the writer felt both physically and emotionally.

Exploring Related Literature

Suggest that students read the entire "Letter to Scottie" by F. Scott Fitzgerald, which can be found in *Prentice Hall Literature, Copper*.

Teaching From the Model

Guide students to analyze this message from E. B. White to understand the characteristics of a postcard:

- *It is brief and not of a private nature.* White has written only a few sentences, none of which requires privacy.
- *It can contain informal writing, as needed, to fit within a limited writing space.* White uses fragments—some without subjects, others without verbs—to keep his message brief.

Teaching Strategy

Invite students to bring in postcards they have received and are comfortable sharing with the class, to demonstrate the common parts and characteristics. The postcards can be read aloud, or quietly, and discussed by groups or pairs of students.

5 Postcard Message

- Writing a postcard is a way to send a brief message when there is no need for privacy.
- Sentence fragments are acceptable on a postcard, where space is tight and the writing style is informal.

Workplace Writing Model

In the following postcard message, written from Maine in 1943, author E. B. White addresses his secretary at *The New Yorker* magazine. As an experiment, he has asked her to mail him two identical letters—one sent via airmail and one by regular mail.

> White calling. The two letters arrived together, same mail, same bag, same morning. I enjoyed them both very much. See you soon.
>
> (I have always known that the airplane was essentially a slow poke. Fusses around too much at the start and finish. Flashy, but impractical.)

Language Acquisition/ ESL Teaching Strategy

The *Writing Lab* offers a series of options that can be easily adapted to meet the needs of your ESL students. For example:

- Your upper-basic and intermediate students will benefit from an audio example of a journal entry in the Drafting section. After listening to a student expressing her feelings, your students can discuss the characteristics of a journal-entry expression of emotions, beliefs, and reflections. Ask your students to write a journal for their own personal use. If, however, you wish to asses your students' progress in writing on a regular basis, you may consider using a dialogue journal. Each time the student makes an entry, the journal is turned in. You read the entry, writing a response and asking questions to stimulate the student, who then responds to you.

Guided Lesson

Now that you are more familiar with expressive writing, you're ready to begin developing your expression. This lesson will help guide you through the process of expressive writing. You may not want to start at the beginning of the lesson, however. Consider any ideas you have in mind for your expressive writing. Then use this chart to decide where to begin.

	START WITH
• If you **do not have a topic**	**Choosing Your Topic**
• If you already **have a topic but want to develop your ideas before you start to write**	**Gathering Details**
• If you already **have a topic and enough details to work with**	**Drafting**

Guiding Student Writing

Addressing Your Classroom Situation

- If you choose to assign topics or types of expression, allow time for students to narrow the topic to suit their interests or find an appealing focus to pursue.
- You may wish to have students write expressively in pairs. If so, brainstorm ways partners might collaborate usefully and fairly. One way, for example, for two students to write a postcard together is for one to show and discuss a picture postcard with the other, who then writes a message to go with it. Another way is for one student to respond in kind to the other's postcard. If two students wish to work together on an anecdote, one can verbally describe an incident to the other, who writes the anecdote, including all the vivid details.

- The Expressive Word Bin in the Drafting section can be adapted for use with your basic and intermediate ESL students. They can use the Expressive Word Bin to make their own lists of expressive words. Afterward, they can cut out pictures from magazines or draw pictures that demonstrate these feelings. The pictures and clippings are then posted on a wall in the classroom with the appropriate labels, such as *overwhelmed*, *exhausted*, *elated*. The students can then refer to this display when writing their drafts.
- The Considering Audience and Purpose section provides Student Models with audio annotations that can be used by your intermediate and advanced ESL students. Once the students have identified how the choice of audience affected the writing of the two samples, they then write their own postcard or personal memoir. Ask your intermediate ESL students to send a postcard to you at your school address. Ask your advanced ESL students to write a short personal memoir. Once in completed form, the memoirs can be put together in book form and read by the class or added to the class library.

Writing Lab CD-ROM

The Choosing Your Topic section of the tutorial on Expression includes the following options to help students come up with their own topics:

- **Video clip with ideas for writing** Students play a video to see pictures that can suggest writing topics from real life.
- **Cluster Wheel** Students use this tool to generate possible writing ideas.
- **Personal Experience Timeline** Students choose a period from their lives, map out key events on the timeline, then look through the timeline for possible writing topics.
- **Challenge activity** Students examine two literature models, one that is about a turning point and one that is an account of a lesson learned, to get ideas for writing.

Working individually or in small groups, students can experiment with these activities to find the ones that work best.

Writers at Work Videodisc

Play the videodisc segment in which Jane Yolen discusses where her writing topics come from. Ask:

- Do you think that personal experiences can be the source of expressive writing ideas, as Yolen contends? Explain. How else might you come up with topics?

Play frames 5360 to 6970

Prewriting

Choosing Your Topic

What feelings would you like to express? Decide on a form for your expression—a personal journal entry, a letter or postcard, or a memoir or anecdote. Then choose from a selection of suggested writing options (see pages 14–17) or experiment with the following strategies for coming up with a topic of your own.

If you're considering

. . . a personal journal entry:

CARRY A NOTEBOOK OR TAPE RECORDER AND RECORD YOUR THOUGHTS

Keep a notebook or tape recorder with you. When you see something interesting or unusual, take a few moments to record your thoughts. Also record any strong feelings you may experience in response to situations, such as winning a race, discovering a new ice cream flavor, or saving a stray kitten. Periodically review your notes to find writing ideas.

. . . a postcard message:

LOOK AT YOUR TOWN FROM A TOURIST'S VIEWPOINT

Imagine that you are seeing your town with fresh eyes. What points of interest would you show to a visitor? A new library? A skateboard pit? A statue of the founder of your town? Travel through your town with a camera and a notebook. Whenever you see something that would make a good postcard, take a picture of it or write notes about it. Review your photos and notes for possible writing ideas.

Teaching Strategy

Suggest to students that if they wish to keep a notebook for jotting down writing ideas, they should choose one small enough to carry around conveniently. Suggest that they pick one that appeals to them or decorate one as they like, so that they'll treat it with care and respect. In addition, to further encourage students to record their ideas and thoughts, suggest that they make entries using a favorite pen or pencil.

Addressing Ability Levels

You may wish to suggest to your **advanced students** that they consider writing a postcard to themselves from the perspective of someone they know, or as if written by a current celebrity or even a historical figure. For example a student could compose a postcard about your town today as if written by one of its founders.

. . . a personal memoir or anecdote:

Housecleaning for Topic Ideas

Sometimes worn-out ice skates or ballet slippers, an old Halloween costume, or your favorite teddy bear can bring to mind past experiences. Clean out your attic, basement, or closet to find reminders of your past. As you remember episodes, jot down a few notes about them. Then review your notes for possible writing ideas.

. . . a personal letter:

Group Activity

Share Ideas With Classmates

With a group of classmates, get together to discuss letters you've written or received. Talk about reasons for writing letters. For instance, you might write a letter to give news to a relative or family friend; to explain life in the United States to a pen pal in South America; to apologize to a friend after an argument. While your group brainstorms for different types of personal letters, take notes. Review those notes for possible writing ideas.

. . . a personal journal entry:

Group Activity

Reflect on Movies You've Seen

Has someone you know ever cried while watching a movie? Many movies evoke strong emotional responses in people. Sometimes an especially joyful or sad scene can bring viewers to tears. Which motion pictures have you responded to emotionally? List the titles of movies that have made you feel a strong emotion, such as happiness, sadness, or anger. Jot down the reasons for your emotional response. Later, review your notes for possible writing topics.

Language Acquisition/ ESL Teaching Strategy

The Group Activity can be modified for use by your intermediate and advanced ESL students. Ask your students to brainstorm the different kinds of letters that can be written. As a group, the students choose two of the letter types and group themselves accordingly in order to help each other list ideas for writing the letter. Encourage the students to discuss language use, word choice, and degree of formality.

The "Housecleaning for Topic Ideas" can be adapted to provide inspiration for your upper-basic and intermediate ESL students in thinking about a personal memoir or anecdote and to provide practice in employing past tenses. In a group discussion, ask your students to imagine that they're cleaning out a closet or attic. They can take notes on their memories, being sure to use the simple past tense—for example, *I found an old uniform, I saw my doll*—or the past continuous—for example, *I was thinking of my visit to my grandfather. We were traveling a lot that summer.* Based on these notes, the students can select a topic for writing.

Writing Lab CD-ROM

Using the Inspirations for Expression in the *Writing Lab* is an excellent way to stimulate creativity and to have students explore possible topics for expression. Students can browse through the Inspirations individually or in small groups. They can choose their own writing topics or you may prefer to assign topics.

The following is a list of the expression options included in the Inspirations, but not provided in the *Sourcebook*:

Personal Journal Entry About

- Life in a new country
- An older person
- Your qualities
- Casting an actor to play you
- Someone you remember
- Relating a painting to an event
- A scene in nature
- The spirit of competition
- A physical challenge
- Interpreting a quotation
- A response to a quotation

Anecdote Recalling

- A personal character trait
- A humorous incident
- The subject of a painting
- A humorous outdoor adventure
- A decision with humorous results

Personal Memoir About

- Sharing an activity
- A past experience
- A special experience
- Meeting someone
- How you see yourself
- A physical challenge

Inspirations for Expression

The following topics are suitable for expressive writing:

An Anecdote That Recalls a Humorous Situation

Like most people, you have probably had an experience that was awful at the time, but later you were able to see the humor in the situation. Write an entertaining anecdote about this experience that you could present orally. Include specific details.

A Personal Letter About a Victory

The boys in the photograph are examining medals they won in a soccer game. Think about competitions in which you experienced victory as a player or a spectator. What happened in the competition? How did you feel when you or your team won? Write a letter to a friend or a family member in which you tell about this exciting event.

A Thank-You Letter to a Friend

Thank-you letters are a polite way of acknowledging a gift from someone. Think of a real or imagined situation in which a person has given you a special gift or has helped you out in some extraordinary way. Then write a thank-you letter to him or her in which you express your feelings and thoughts about what this special gift meant to you.

A Postcard Message About an Exciting Vacation Experience

During summer vacation, people often try new, exciting sports—such as parasailing—or pursue favorite hobbies. What exciting things have you experienced while on vacation? Write a postcard message to a friend from a "vacation spot." You can write about a real experience or one that you make up. Use sensory images

Personal Letter

- To an important friend
- To a friend who needs help
- To cheer up someone
- About an exciting experience
- Explaining an exciting sport
- To someone from the past
- To someone you met briefly
- To a friend about defeat
- Of encouragement
- To a fictional character who has a poor self-image

Postcard Message

- To a friend
- Written during a jungle trip
- About an outdoor adventure

Caption

- About a painting's conflict
- For the painting *Shoe Series I*
- For a photograph

to help you express what is special and exciting about this vacation experience.

Postcard Message From a Photo Safari

Imagine that you are on a photo safari in a game park of East Africa. Your guide suddenly gathers you and your fellow travelers together and asks everyone to be still. As you look through your binoculars, you see a rhinoceros lumbering through the tall grass. Write a postcard message to a friend about this experience. Use precise words to capture the excitement of the event and to express your range of feelings.

A Personal Memoir About a Souvenir

A souvenir is an object that is saved as a reminder of an experience or an event. Think about the souvenirs you keep and the memories you attach to them. Write a personal memoir about one particular souvenir and the feelings it evokes in you. Use specific details to describe the memory.

A Personal Letter to a Special Person

Think about a person who is special to you. Write a letter to this person. Express your thoughts and feelings about him or her as well as details about past or present events. You don't have to mail this letter when you finish it, but you can if you wish.

An Anecdote About an Unusual Outcome

Sometimes things don't turn out the way you expected. For example, a sports upset, a winning raffle ticket, or a recipe that produces an exploding potato are all examples of unexpected events. Think of events in which you have been involved. Which of them had a surprising or humorous outcome? Write an anecdote, to be told orally, about that event.

Cultural Connection

Some students may choose to write a personal letter to a special person. Invite them to write to a figure they admire in their cultural community—for example, an artist, a writer, a politician, a social worker, a coach, a religious leader, or a teacher.

Addressing Ability Levels

Challenge your **more-advanced students** who choose to write an anecdote about an unusual outcome to write about an outcome that is yet to happen. They can choose an event that is just underway or not yet begun, and then write the anecdote as a prediction of the totally unexpected.

MORE *Inspirations* for Expression

A Postcard From a Beautiful Vacation Spot

Many people seek out beautiful settings for their vacations. What natural setting is most appealing to you? The Grand Canyon? Niagara Falls? The Ozarks? Choose a setting that you may have visited or one that you'd like to visit. Write a postcard about this place to a friend or a family member. If you have visited the place, try to recall how it made you feel. What did you do there and whom did you meet? If you've never been to the place, try to imagine what it would feel like to be there. Use vivid words to express your feelings and to describe the spot's natural beauty.

Group Project: Form an Imaginary Travel Club

With a group of classmates, look through an atlas or travel guide. Discuss the attractions of several countries. Then let each group member choose a country to "visit." After doing some research on that country, each group member should write three postcards as if they had been sent from that country. Display the finished postcards and appropriate illustrations on the bulletin board.

Group Project: Create a Display About Abraham Lincoln

Many people consider Abraham Lincoln to be one of the most important figures in American history. With a group of classmates, discuss Lincoln's skills as a writer, speechmaker, and statesman. Then each group member should write a brief essay expressing that person's thoughts and feelings about Abraham Lincoln. Work together with your classmates to create a display of your finished essays. Select illustrations and other graphics to display along with the finished essays.

A Personal Memoir About Meeting a Friend

Memoirs often include important events in a person's life—like sleeping through a test for which you had studied all night or meeting a friend through an unusual circumstance. Think about how you first met one of your friends. How did the situation come about? How did you feel about the person at first? Did it occur to you at the time that you would become friends? Write a personal memoir that tells about the experience. Include details and vivid language to bring that experience to life.

Thematic Connection: Knowing Yourself

Challenge students who choose to write a personal memoir about meeting a friend to consider writing the remembrance of the initial meeting as if from the perspective of the new friend. Alternately, you may wish to invite a pair of friends in the class to write a memoir about the experience of meeting one another, each writing as if from the other's point of view.

Thematic Connection: Humor

Challenge students who choose to write about a beautiful vacation spot to write the postcard to a family pet, either real or imagined. For example, a description of life among the bug, mice, and bird populations on a camping trip could be of consuming culinary interest to the family cat.

Writing Lab CD-ROM

The Inspirations for Expression also include the following Group Projects and Group Discussions. The Group Discussions encourage small groups of students to share their thoughts about an Inspiration and to generate possible writing topics. The Group Projects are structured activities in which students assume different roles.

Group Projects

- Making a greeting poster for new students
- Responding to Garrison Keillor by letter
- Creating a display about relationships between generations
- Creating a sports activity book
- Making an audio record of your lives and times
- Creating a collage about Abraham Lincoln
- Creating a travel booklet
- Creating a montage about foolish love
- Creating a sports picture book
- Creating a poster of modern proverbs

Group Discussions

- Discussing how to develop new character traits
- Naming candidates for the "Best Pair of Sneakers" award
- Discussing challenging sports activities
- Listing ideas about where beauty can be found

Shoe Series 1 *Marilee Whitehouse-Holm, Private Collection*

A Personal Memoir About a Favorite Article of Clothing

Perhaps the sneakers in the painting remind you of a pair of shoes or a piece of clothing that you can't bear to part with even though it's worn out. Think about a favorite article of clothing that has special meaning to you. Write a personal memoir that tells why you like it so much. Use vivid language to express your thoughts and feelings.

Cross-Curricular Connection: *Art*

Students who choose this topic idea may choose to write about a favorite work of art rather than a piece of clothing. For example, they can write about a painting that's been hanging in their house, an old photo they cherish, or even about the first time they saw a movie they've now seen many times.

Collaborative Learning

You may want to try the following if your class undertakes the Group Project dealing with Abraham Lincoln on page 16. Within each group, students can share the tasks of finding out about and responding to Lincoln's different skills. One or more students may wish to find examples of Lincoln's many effective uses of humorous anecdote to make his points and to defuse difficult situations. Another member of the group can collect and photocopy portraits of Lincoln as well as some of his letters and other writings to accompany the collage.

riting Lab CD-ROM

The Considering Audience and Purpose section includes the following options:

- **Video clip about considering one's audience** Students play a video to see and hear how the intended audience will affect the writer's choice of words and details.
- **Audience Profile activity** Students answer questions that help them focus on how best to write for their intended audience.
- **Audio-annotated Student Models** Students read a postcard and a personal memoir written for different audiences to hear about how the choice of audience affected the writing.
- **Video clip about purposes for writing** Students play the video, which has one segment showing boys rafting down the Colorado River and another showing a blues musician, to learn about some possible purposes for expressive writing.
- **Purpose Profile activity** Students respond to questions in order to help them define their writing purpose.
- **Interactive Instruction—tips for accomplishing a writing purpose** Students choose a general purpose most closely related to the one they have in mind to see suggestions for how best to accomplish that purpose.

Writers at Work Videodisc

Play the videodisc segment in which Jane Yolen talks about her two audiences, her circle of literate correspondents and future biographers. Ask:

- How can a biographer use a person's letters to find out more about that person?
- Why might someone want to read your letters in years to come? Whose letters, written in the past, have you read? How did you react to them?

Play frames 3030 to 3860

Prewriting

Considering Your Audience

Who are you writing for? Your audience may be yourself, one other person, or a large group of people. Think about how your audience will affect the language and details you use. If you're writing for yourself, for example, you might include personal feelings. But you would probably not include your most personal feelings when writing for your classmates. Emphasize details that you think would interest or appeal to your audience. Use these questions to help you write for your audience:

Questions for Considering Your Audience

- Is your audience's background similar to your own? If not, be sure to include basic details about your experience.
- What type of language best suits your audience? For close friends and family, use informal language. For larger groups or for adults, use more formal language.
- What is it about your subject that would appeal to your audience?

Considering Your Purpose

When writing an expressive essay for others, decide on a reason, or purpose, for putting your thoughts into words. For instance, when describing an awkward moment from your past, would you like your audience to laugh or would you prefer that they sympathize with you? To help find your specific purpose, answer the following questions:

Questions for Considering Your Purpose

- What thoughts and feelings do you want to communicate to your audience? Why do you want to share these thoughts and feelings?
- How do you want your audience to feel when they have finished reading your expressive writing? Why do you want them to feel that way?

Language Lab CD-ROM

If students need additional guidance in determining how best to deal with the issues of audience and purpose, you may want them to complete the Considering Audience and Purpose lesson in the Composing unit of the *Language Lab*.

Gathering Details

Before you begin drafting, take time to gather some details for your expressive writing. Details help bring your expressive writing to life. Whether you are writing about a particular issue or situation or about your thoughts and feelings, it is important to provide specific details.

To help you gather details, try looking through the Feelings Word Bin at right to come up with words that vividly express emotions.

FEELINGS WORD BIN

HAPPINESS	SADNESS	ANGER	FEAR
pleased	sorrowful	disgusted	fearful
merry	lonely	furious	nervous
cheerful	despairing	irritated	terrified
delighted	gloomy	annoyed	worried
excited	blue	enraged	dread
peaceful	depressed		alarmed
joyful			anxious
calm			

Another way to come up with expressive details is to create a Cluster Map. Write your topic in the center of a sheet of paper. Circle your topic. Then write down your thoughts, ideas, and opinions in the space surrounding your topic. Circle each item you write, then connect each item with a line to the topic. Refer to these details as you draft your expressive writing. Look at the example that follows:

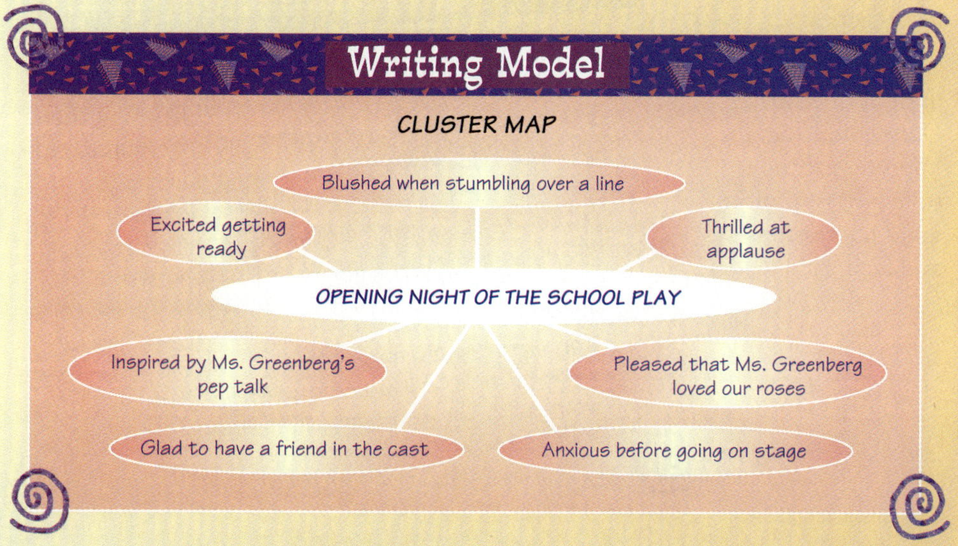

Writing Lab CD-ROM

The Gathering Details section includes the following options designed to help students gather details they can use to bring their expressive writing to life:

- **Video clip** Students play the video to learn ways to use details to help describe the experience they are writing about.
- **Feelings Word Bin activity** Students choose from a list of titles to see words that describe different emotions. They can use these words to capture emotions related to the experience they are describing in their expressions.
- **Sunburst Diagram activity** Students can use this graphic organizer to help them gather details related to their topic.
- **Interactive instruction in using emotional responses to gather details** Students see specific details related to feelings.
- **Interactive instruction in using memory to choose details** Students select events, such as a first dance class or an important test, to see feelings each might evoke. They choose the feelings to see descriptive details.
- **Video clip about how to express a mood** Students play a video to get suggestions for using details to create a particular mood.

Working individually or in small groups, students can experiment with these activities to find the ones that work best for them.

Writers at Work Videodisc

Play the videodisc segment in which Jane Yolen talks about the importance of being "keenly observant." Ask:

What can you say about the relationship between choosing details from what you see and hear and the emotional content of the event you are describing? Give an example from personal experience.

Play frames 919 to 2115

Teaching Strategy

Discuss how using sensory details can help bring writing to life. Brainstorm with the class a list of vivid verbs and modifiers that appeal to each of the five senses. Record the list and post it for future use. Invite students to add to the list as they think of new sensory words.

Drafting

As you begin drafting, focus on using language that clearly conveys the feelings you're trying to express. Remember to include details that are suitable for your audience. Also make sure you are sticking to the purpose you set for yourself. Look at the following tips for drafting:

Tips for Drafting

- Find a quiet, well-lit place to work. It might be a sunny room or just a quiet corner with a small table or desk. You may draft on paper or directly on a computer.
- Gather all your notes in one place. Also have any pictures, diagrams, or outlines that you might want to refer to as you draft.
- As you write, let your thoughts flow freely. Capture your feelings and reactions.
- Try to complete your draft in one sitting. During drafting, the important thing is to record your most vivid impressions and feelings.

Writing Model: Journal Entry

In this journal entry, notice how the writer clearly describes events and captures her feelings about them. Follow her example as you draft your own journal entry.

Yesterday everyone was talking about the terrible hurricane in Florida, so I volunteered to start a food drive. Tonight Rory and I are going to make posters asking everyone to donate canned food. Now that I've volunteered, I'm kind of nervous about the responsibility. What if we don't get enough food? Maybe I'll write a speech asking people to imagine that their house was wrecked by the hurricane. Just think: no refrigerator to raid!

Writing Lab CD-ROM

The Drafting section includes the following options:

- **Video clip of an example of expressive writing** Students play the video to hear how author Virginia Woolf expressed her innermost feelings in a description she wrote of a place she visited as a child.
- **Audio-annotated Student Model** Students read a draft of a personal letter. They can play an audio recording to hear explanations of choices the writer made.
- **Audio clip of a journal entry** Students play the audio to hear how one student describes events and captures her feelings about them in her journal entry.
- **Personal letter template** Students writing a personal letter use a format to help them organize their writing.
- **Expressive Word Bin** Students can do this activity to find useful words they can use to express their feelings.
- **Video clip about overcoming writer's block** Students play a video for tips on getting started from writer Lucy Jones.

Writers at Work Videodisc

Play the videodisc segment in which Jane Yolen talks about drafting. Ask:

- Why do you think Jane Yolen says that no one would want to read the first draft of one of her stories?
- What do you think about her approach to drafting? Do you think it would work to your advantage to follow her lead? Why?

Play frames 7011 to 7501

Writing Strategies

Discuss with students ways of hooking their readers right from the start, such as beginning with a sentence fragment.

Also discuss organization. Talk about the advantages of arranging details chronologically, spatially, or in order of importance. Then discuss how to use transitions to link ideas in each type of organization.

Teaching Strategy

Make it clear to students who intend to write journal entries that since they are writing exclusively for themselves, the confidentiality of their writing will be scrupulously observed to respect the privacy of their personal feelings.

Revising and Editing

FROM a WRITER

"The real writing is revising. Books aren't written; they're rewritten."

—Jane Yolen

Revising Your Work

Review your draft for ways to make your ideas and emotions clearer to your audience. You may want to reorganize some details or add precise, vivid words that better express your emotions. Use these questions to guide your review:

Revision Checklist

1. What can you do to appeal more strongly to your audience?
2. What can you do to make your purpose more clear?
3. How can you improve your word choice?
4. Have can you express your thoughts and feelings more accurately?

Having a Peer Review Your Work

You can get a fresh look at your expressive writing by using "an outside eye" when you read it over to yourself or by reviewing it with another person. Get together with a classmate and review each other's expressive writing. Use the following questions to guide your review:

Peer Review Checklist

1. Which parts of the writing did you like best? Why?
2. Which parts of the writing were not clear or needed more details?
3. Were the reasons for the feelings clear? If not, what suggestions do you have?
4. How can the organization plan of the writing be improved?

Writing Lab CD-ROM

The Revising and Editing section provides strategies for self-revision and peer revision. It includes the following options:

- **Video clip of a professional writer** Students play a video to hear tips on revising from Jane Yolen.
- **Self-Evaluation Checklist** Students answer questions to help them to evaluate their draft.
- **Revision checker for sentence length** Students use this tool to help vary the length of their sentences.
- **Audio-annotated Student Model** Students see and hear how another student has revised his letter.
- **Expressive Word Bin** Students use this device to replace any words that are vague, weak, or imprecise.
- **Interactive instruction in varying sentence beginnings** Students choose sentences to hear ideas for beginning sentences.
- **Video clip of a writer** Students play the video to find out what Jane Yolen says about having someone else review your work.
- **Peer Revision Checklist** Students get pointers to help them work with a peer editor.

Writers at Work Videodisc

Play the videodisc segment in which Jane Yolen talks about the revising process. Ask:

- What does Yolen mean when she says that "the real writing is in the revising"?
- How does Jane Yolen use peer review in her writing process? What advantages do you think she gets from having her husband and others read her work?

Play frames 7505 to 9324

Writers at Work Videodisc

Play the videodisc segment in which Jane Yolen talks about needing an "outside eye." Ask:

- Who might make a good outside eye for you? Why?

Have students discuss the pros and cons of peer review.

Also introduce the strategy of letting some time elapse between the drafting and revising stages in order to have a fresh perspective when revising.

Play frames 10965 to 11717

Student Model: Revised Draft

Following is the beginning of a personal letter written by Enoch Perez of Anson Jones Middle School in San Antonio, Texas. Notice how his revising techniques strengthened his expressive writing.

September 8, 19—

Dear Grandma,

On the way to your house just outside [of] San Diego, we ran into a [blinding] snow storm up in the mountain[s]. My dad told you about it, but I wanted you to know how we felt about it.

When we were going up the mountain, the weather was [comfortably] warm, ~~like~~ [as on] an early summer day. Our [old] truck didn't [seem to] want to climb up the mountain. When we were more than halfway up, it looked like rain. To our surprise, though, soon it began to snow.

Proofreading

After revising your work, check it carefully for errors in grammar, spelling, punctuation, and capitalization. This step is not so important in the writing you do for yourself, but you'll want to do it when writing for an audience. Use this checklist when you proofread your expressive writing:

Proofreading Checklist

1. Are all your sentences complete?
2. Does every sentence begin with a capital letter and end with the correct punctuation mark?
3. Did you use commas, end marks, and other punctuation marks correctly?
4. Did you check the spelling of any words you're not sure of?
5. Did you use pronouns correctly?

Writing Lab CD-ROM

The Revising and Editing section of the tutorial on Expression includes the following options:

- **Proofreading Checklist** This checklist presents questions similar to those provided in the *Sourcebook* (p. 22), with an additional reminder about indenting paragraphs.
- **Audio-annotated Student Model** Students can play an audio recording to hear an explanation of how the writer made proofreading corrections.
- **Interactive instruction on using capital letters and on making other proofreading changes** In the first activity, students choose sentences to see them capitalized correctly. In the second, they choose passages to get some insights about possible proofreading changes that would have improved one student's journal.

Working individually or in small groups, students can experiment with these activities to find the ones that work best.

Language Lab CD-ROM

Students who need more practice working with capitalization may benefit from working through the lessons in the Capitalization unit.

Teaching Strategy

You may find it useful to have students proofread with a different classmate than the one with whom they revised and edited their work. This way, students can have an "outside eye" to help detect errors that might have been missed earlier.

Establishing Assessment Criteria

As students begin revising their expressive writing, you might share with them the criteria you will use to evaluate their work. The following guidelines are included in the tutorial on expressive writing. You can use them as given, or modify them to suit your needs.

- Have you chosen an appropriate topic?
- Have you included details that suit your audience and purpose for writing?
- Does your writing include personal thoughts and feelings?
- Is your writing organized clearly?
- Did you use vivid languag to bring your writing to life?
- Is your writing free of errors in spelling, gramma and punctuation?

Publishing and Presenting

After you've proofread your writing, think about ways to share it with others. Here are some suggestions for sharing your expressive writing:

Read Your Work Aloud Get together with a small group of classmates and take turns reading your work aloud. You may wish to tape-record the readings and share them with an even larger group.

Display Your Work Gather appropriate photographs or pictures and display them along with your finished writing on a classroom bulletin board. Be sure to title your work.

Post Your Writing on an Electronic Bulletin Board Contact your school network administrator for information about electronic bulletin boards. Post your finished writing on a bulletin board for students in your grade.

Reflecting on Your Writing

What have you learned from the process of writing expressively? The following questions will help you reflect on your writing:

- What was your favorite part of writing expressively? What was your least favorite part?
- If you had to do it all over again, what would you do differently?
- What did you learn about yourself during this writing process?
- How can you apply what you've learned to other types of writing?

Portfolio Assessment

Have students write an evaluative statement that addresses some of the questions posed on page 23 of the *Sourcebook*. If students decide to include the completed expressive piece in their portfolio, they might attach this statement to it. Otherwise, the statement itself can go into the portfolio as a record of self-evaluation.

The following questions can be used to supplement the questions in the *Sourcebook*:

- What part of the expressive-writing process did I find most satisfying? Most challenging?
- Which type of expressive writing would I like to try next time? Why?
- In what ways is expressive writing like other kinds of writing I have done? How is it different?

After students have evaluated their work, confer with them to decide what to include in their portfolio. Students can select the completed piece and/or earlier drafts they think reflect growth and progress. Remind students to date all work.

Writing Lab CD-ROM

The Publishing and Presenting section includes the following options:

- **Tips for sharing expressive writing with many people** Students get the same three suggestions that are presented in the *Sourcebook*, page 23.
- **Writing Model of postcard form** Students choose parts of a postcard to learn more about each.
- **Making an audio or video recording** Students get tips for working as a group to record their expressions on an audio or video tape.
- **Interactive instruction for publishing around a theme** Students choose entries they wish to share with others and organize them around a theme, such as friendship or family.

The Multimedia Workshop

Students can use the templates in the Writing Workshop component of *The Multimedia Workshop* to word-process and present their final expressions. For instance, a student writing a postcard note might choose the greeting card template and embellish the presentation with clip art. Students who write an anecdote or memoir may wish to use the Scene Maker and Sequencer to create a video recording of their presentation. They can select music and sound effects to enhance their production.

Teaching From the Model

Draw students' attention to how Enoch Perez's letter includes the elements of expressive writing.

- *It includes the writer's personal thoughts and feelings.* Right from the start, Enoch tells his grandmother that the description will be from his own perspective. He describes how scared he was and why he acted as he did.
- *It uses vivid language and includes precise details.* In the second paragraph, Enoch uses comparisons and figurative language to paint a vivid picture of the ride up the mountain. In the last paragraph, the detail about ears popping gives one good indication of what the ride down the mountain was like.
- *It presents information suitable for the audience.* Enoch's grandmother is surely interested in her grandchild's view of the family's adventure.
- *It is well organized.* Enoch tells his story in chronological order. The events are easy to follow.

Technology Note: Networking

After your class has read the student model, they may be interested in sharing their own expressive writing efforts with students across the country via CompuServe, America Online, or the Internet by connecting to Prentice Hall's Internet home page. Look for special events, contests, as well as bulletin boards and pointers to student publications at http://www.phschool.com. One outcome of this exchange is that students all across the country can learn more about how their peers feel about similar problems and how they react to similar events in their lives. Your students may be surprised to discover how much they have in common with their peers around the country.

Student Model

Here is the complete, final draft of Enoch Perez's expressive writing.

Letter to Grandma

by Enoch Perez

September 8, 1995

Dear Grandma,

On the way to your house just outside of San Diego, we ran into a blinding snow storm up in the mountains. My dad told you about it, but I wanted you to know how we felt about it.

In the beginning of the letter, I stated directly that I wanted to tell my grandmother my version of the event that happened.

When we were going up the mountain, the weather was comfortably warm, as on an early summer day. Our old truck didn't seem to want to climb up the mountain. When we were more than halfway up, it looked like rain. To our surprise, though, it soon began to snow!

I used vivid adjectives and a comparison to describe how the day started out.

On the mountain we saw a police car crash into a big rock. Luis and Elena were scared, and I was too, but I was trying to act brave. We couldn't see the road. It also began to hail hard.

Here I revealed my true feelings to my grandmother.

As we were leaving the mountain, the weather was not as bad as at the peak of the mountain. It took a long time to get to the bottom. All the way down our ears popped. We didn't stop until we got to San Diego!

This detail will help the reader experience the descent from the mountain.

Love,
Enoch

Addressing Ability Levels

You may wish to challenge your **more-advanced students** to write a short passage that contains errors in pronoun use. Students can swap papers and make the necessary corrections and deletions.

Language Lab CD-ROM

For additional practice in using pronouns correctly, students can refer to the four lessons in the Using Pronouns unit.

Developing Your Style 1

Using Pronouns

How do you know what pronoun form to use when the pronoun is part of a group of words connected by *and* or *or*? Here are the rules:

- When a pronoun acts as the subject of a sentence or follows a linking verb, use a subject pronoun.
- When a pronoun follows an action verb, use an object pronoun.

Pronouns that act as the subject of a sentence take the subject case: *I, he, she, they, we*. Pronouns that receive the action of the verb take the object case: *me, him, her, them, us*.

You or I should chart a course back to Earth.

She and the captain are in charge on the bridge.

The captain rewarded the first mate and me.

Sometimes a noun comes right after a pronoun in a sentence. Some writers have a problem then in knowing which pronoun to use. You can test for the right pronoun by leaving out the noun.

We astronauts have to stick together. (We have to stick together.)

The captain ordered us pilots to land. (The captain ordered us to land.)

Practice Activities

1. Choose the correct pronoun for each sentence.
   a. My classmates and [I/me] watched the takeoff of the space shuttle.
   b. [Us/We] students were all interested in becoming astronauts.
   c. My brother and [I/me] sent away for information on NASA.
   d. The students most interested in science were Jake and [I/me].
   e. The space camp applications were sent to Meredith and [I/me].
2. Rewrite the following paragraph, correcting pronoun usage where necessary.

   My best friend and me want to become astronauts when we are older. There are many opportunities for we scientists in the future. Maybe someday all of us citizens will get licenses to drive our own spaceships!

25

Integrating Skills With Writing

Management Strategy

You can have students work through one or both of the skills lessons either before or after they write their expressions. If you use the lessons *before*, remind students to incorporate the techniques in their writing. If you address skills *after* students write their stories, have them include a section on "skills improvement" in the self-assessment document they prepare for their portfolios. The next time they write, their work can be evaluated in terms of their mastery of these skills.

You may want to give students these lessons as take-home assignments to be completed prior to the drafting, revising, or proofreading stages—wherever you see the greatest need. Or you may choose to assign the skills lessons only to those students whose drafts indicate a need for direct instruction in these particular skills.

Teaching Strategy

To connect the skills lessons to the students' writing, explain that one important feature of expressive writing or any writing is to make sure to use pronouns correctly. Then tell them that another key aspect of writing expressively is to write unified paragraphs—paragraphs containing only relevant sentences, each related clearly to one main idea.

Writer's Companion

To provide students with additional reinforcement in using pronouns, direct them to "Types of Pronouns (personal pronouns)" beginning on page 362, "Personal Pronoun Usage" on page 366, and to page 370 in the "Common Usage Problems" section.

Practice Activities: Suggested Answers

1. a. I
   b. We
   c. I
   d. I
   e. me
2. My best friend and I want to become astronauts when we are older. There are many opportunities for us scientists in the future. Maybe someday all of us citizens will get licenses to drive our own spaceships!

Teaching Strategies

Before students read about unified paragraphs and see the revised passage about comic strip characters, ask volunteers to tell what is confusing about the original passage and to suggest ways for making it more clear.

Review with students the meaning and typical placement of a topic sentence. Ask a student to tell the topic sentence of the example paragraph.

As needed, review the meaning of *irrelevant sentence*.

Clarification/Writing Strategy

You may wish to point out to students that sometimes when an irrelevant sentence is deleted from a paragraph, the sentences preceding or following it may need to be revised so that the paragraph makes sense or flows more smoothly.

Language Lab CD-ROM

To provide additional practice recognizing irrelevant sentences and writing unified paragraphs, refer students to the Unity in Paragraphs lesson in the Building Paragraphs unit.

Writer's Companion

To provide students with additional practice in writing unified paragraphs, direct them to "Unity, Coherence, and Transitions," starting on page 62.

Unity in Paragraphs

Why is the following paragraph confusing?

> Many comic strip characters show up in many places and have become well known to people all over the world. Drawings showing continuous action are as old as cave paintings. Characters such as Flash Gordon, Little Orphan Annie, and Snoopy have appeared on television, in movies, and in books. Some favorites have even been in parades!

The irrelevant sentence *Drawings showing continuous action are as old as cave paintings* makes the paragraph confusing because it does not support the main idea—that comic strip characters may appear in places other than in comic strips. With the irrelevant sentence eliminated, the resulting paragraph that follows is unified and easy to understand.

> Many comic strip characters show up in many places and have become well known to people all over the world. Characters such as Flash Gordon, Little Orphan Annie, and Snoopy have appeared on television, in movies, and in books. Some favorites have even been in parades!

A paragraph is said to be **unified** when all of its sentences relate to the main idea, which is usually stated in a topic sentence. Sentences that relate to the main idea are called **supporting sentences**, while sentences that don't relate are known as **irrelevant sentences**. Any irrelevant sentence must be deleted from a paragraph.

In the paragraph that follows on page 27, the topic sentence is underlined. Can you find the irrelevant sentence?

> Krazy Kat, dating from 1913, is considered one of the most creative comic strips of all time. Some comic strips tell continuous stories, while others consist of only a drawing or two. Critics give Krazy Kat artist George Herriman high marks for his artwork. They applaud his imaginative use of language.

The second sentence is irrelevant and should be deleted. When an irrelevant sentence is removed, some of the remaining sentences may have to be revised so that they flow smoothly together. In the following revised version of the paragraph about *Krazy Kat*, notice the underlined words that were added for smooth flow.

> Krazy Kat, dating from 1913, is considered one of the most creative comic strips of all time. For one thing, critics give Krazy Kat artist George Herriman high marks for his artwork. For another, they applaud his imaginative use of language.

Use the following guidelines to create unified paragraphs:

- Make sure that each sentence in your paragraph relates to or supports the main idea of the paragraph.
- Delete all sentences that do not relate to the main idea.
- When you delete an irrelevant sentence, revise the paragraph as needed so the remaining sentences flow smoothly.

Practice Activity

Revise each of the following paragraphs by deleting any irrelevant sentences and, if necessary, making further revisions for smooth sentence flow.

1. *The Flintstones* cartoon is popular with people of all ages. Even my mom remembers watching it when she was a kid. Recently, this cartoon was made into a feature film, which shows how popular these characters still are! Elizabeth Taylor played Wilma's mother.
2. My favorite cartoon character is Tweetie Bird. Scooby-doo is also great. Returning to Tweetie Bird, she manages to provoke the cat and never get caught. I also like her sense of humor and the way she talks: "I tought I taw a puddy tat. I did, I did taw a puddy tat!"

Language Acquisition/ ESL Teaching Strategy

Put your basic and intermediate ESL students into groups of two. Ask them to read the Practice Activity paragraphs together and identify their main ideas. They can then underline those sentences that support the main idea and cross out those that do not. When you're confident they understand the concept of a unified paragraph, ask them to write their own short paragraphs. The pairs can then exchange their paragraphs for correction. The students discuss which sentences support the main idea and those that are irrelevant.

Alternative Assessment

You may wish to invite students to write a paragraph that includes an irrelevant sentence. Students can swap papers and find and cross out the irrelevant sentence so that the paragraph is unified.

You might want to challenge your **more-advanced students** to write a paragraph that is not unified, including a sentence or two that will need revision once the irrelevant sentence is eliminated.

Practice Activity: Suggested Answers

Revised paragraphs may vary, but should resemble the following examples from which irrelevant sentences have been removed.

1. *The Flintstones* cartoon is popular with people of all ages. Even my mom remembers watching it when she was a kid. Recently, this cartoon was made into a feature film, which shows how popular these characters still are.
2. My favorite cartoon character is Tweetie Bird. I enjoy the way she manages to provoke the cat and never get caught. I also like her sense of humor and the way she talks: "I tought I taw a puddy tat. I did, I did taw a puddy tat!"

Integrating Literature With Writing

Management Strategy

You can have students read this model of expressive writing either before or after they have written their own expressive piece. If you choose to have them read it *before*, use it to draw their attention to techniques or ideas they can apply to their own writing. If you use it *after*, have students compare and contrast some of the elements of the piece with elements of their own expressive writing. Ask: *What can you learn from this excerpt that can help you the next time you write expressively?*

Activating Prior Knowledge

Invite students to tell anecdotes about times they felt a letdown rather than elation at the completion of something, or times when an actual event or product paled in comparison to the anticipation of it or the planning and efforts preceding it. Also invite students to share how they felt when an anticipated event or a finished product surpassed their expectations.

Purpose-Setting Questions

How do the elements of expression work to create a clear picture of the scene in and outside the writer's workroom? How do they enhance the description of the way the situation made the writer feel?

Reading Strategy

You can help guide reading by asking students to notice how Jane Yolen uses details, precise and vivid language, and comparisons in this memoir. When they finish reading, students can work as a whole class or in small discussion groups to compare their responses to the piece.

Teaching From the Model

- Discuss with students how Yolen writes this memoir from a first-person point of view. Talk about the effectiveness of this approach. Then ask students to tell how the writer uses images to reveal things about how and where she writes. You may wish to list responses on the chalkboard.
- Ask students to describe the mood of this piece and to explain how they think the writer is feeling as she nears the completion of her story. Ask them to identify the writing strategies Yolen uses to create the mood and to convey her feelings. Students should give examples to support all their ideas.
- Have students talk about how Yolen uses the image of an eagle to express how she feels when she is abou

Literature Model

In this personal memoir, Jane Yolen reveals the range of emotions she feels as she works on a story. Notice the images she uses to express what she is feeling.

The Eagle and the Hummingbird

by Jane Yolen

By using images of shadows, Yolen conveys a feeling of emptiness.

It is late afternoon. Outside my workroom window, shadows lengthen by the trees. My golden tomcat is prowling across the field. In my typewriter are the last lines of a story, and I have just typed the period that ends the work that I have held in my heart, in my head, and in my fingertips for the past few months. I should feel elated. Instead, I am struck by the growing dark shadows, the cat's fruitless search, and the day punctuated by a story's end.

Yolen lets the reader know exactly what she is feeling. It is important to express feelings honestly in a personal memoir.

All my stories end that way, with a small keening[1] note. Oh, I am glad enough to have done the work and finished within my self-imposed deadline. The images seem good enough. The sentences flow. There is a beginning, a middle, and a satisfying conclusion. Why then this letdown, this incomplete feeling, this sense of mourning?

This quotation from the American writer Edith Wharton expresses Yolen's own feelings. Using quotations that reveal your own feelings can strengthen your writing.

Something Edith Wharton once wrote always strikes me at this time: "I dream of an eagle, I give birth to a hummingbird."

When I begin a story, it is a great eagle of a tale. The strong pinions[2], the mighty wingbeat, the slashing beak and talons of my story will strike at my gut—I am sure of it—like Prometheus'[3] implacable fate. It is, in my first

imaginings, a story that will be the greatest ever written, will move the reader to laughter or tears, will bring about world understanding, universal brotherhood, and peace. *That* kind of writing.

And then I start to transplant the images in head and heart into black dots on a page. Perhaps I am just a poor translator. Words are never sharp enough to get at what it is I am dreaming. "Human language," wrote Flaubert, "is a cracked kettle on which we beat our tunes for bears to dance to when all the while we wish to move the stars to pity."

I try. Oh, I certainly try. I read my story aloud, trying to suck out the marrow from the dry bones of sentences. I polish, I rewrite, I close my eyes and snatch, like an incompetent fisherman, for that bright silver flash of word.

Sometimes I get very close to my eagle. Catch a few feathers of his tail. I suppose I can count on the fingers of two hands stories I have clothed in eagle feathers: "The Girl Who Cried Flowers," "The Lady and the Merman," "The White Seal Maid," "Brother Hart," "Greyling," "The Hundredth Dove." As it happens, they are not necessarily the ones critics have liked best or the ones that have been reprinted the most. One man's eagle is another's dove.

It is late afternoon. Outside my workroom, the lengthening shadows, like dark fingers, point away from me. The cat lies in wait by the door. A new story is teasing its way into my head, like a dark shadow, like a prowling cat. I again recall Edith Wharton's sentence— "I dream of an eagle. I give birth to a hummingbird"—but this time something different strikes me: It is not the dream that is important, but the birth. Where one ends, the other begins. The hummingbird is a bright little thing; it cannot be captured, and with almost defiant energy, it flies. How it flies!

---

1. keening (k n´ ing) *v.:* wailing (for the dead)

2. pinions (pin´ y§nz) *n.:* wings

3. Prometheus (pr m ´th §s): a figure from Greek mythology who steals fire from heaven and is punished by being chained forever to a rock. Each day, an eagle comes to eat his liver, which grows back each night.

Again Yolen uses a quotation—this time from the French novelist Flaubert—that captures her own feelings of disappointment

Yolen repeats the quotation from Wharton. Notice that this time she has a different response to it.

Language Acquisition/ ESL Teaching Strategy

Ask your advanced ESL students to identify the means by which Jane Yolen expresses her emotions in *The Eagle and the Hummingbird.* Working together, your students can develop a Cluster Diagram that can be used to organize the information. For example, the students may put *depression* or *letdown* at the center of the cluster and expand the diagram with such categories as *vocabulary*, *phrases*, and *quotations*, providing examples of how the author expresses her feelings. You should encourage your students to discuss the meaning of words and phrases, and to interpret the quotations.

Closure and Extension

To complete the lesson, you can ask students to sum up how this excerpt describing a writer's struggles exemplifies what they have learned about expressive writing.

Then invite students to share in small-group discussions or through brief journal entries what they have learned about themselves as writers and what points they would like to keep in mind for future writing efforts. Also ask what topics they would consider for future expressive writing. You might keep some of the topics in an idea file for later use.

to begin one of her stories. Ask them to explain how she uses the quote from the French novelist Flaubert to explain how she feels once she has begun writing.

- Ask students to describe how Yolen comes to feel about completing a story. Ask: *To Yolen, how is a new idea for writing more like a hummingbird than an eagle? How else might you use figurative language to describe her thinking?*

Thematic Connection: Knowing Yourself

Discuss with students how Yolen's mood and feelings seem to change during the passage. Invite them to recall a memorable, powerful, or significant event or period in their lives, during which time they experienced a change in attitude or feelings. Invite volunteers to tell or write about these experiences.

2

Description

Classroom Manager

Writer's Solution *Materials for Teaching Description*

The *Writer's Solution* includes a wide range of materials for teaching descriptive writing. You can pick and choose from among these materials to create a lesson plan that suits your classroom needs, teaching style, and equipment situation. In the pages that follow, you'll find lesson plans suggesting some of the most effective ways of using these materials. For an explanation of each of the components of the *Writer's Solution*, see pages T4–T6.

Below is a detailed list of the *Writer's Solution* materials for descriptive writing.

Writers at Work Videodisc

Featured Writer: Debbie Behler, Magazine Editor

Videodisc Segments

About Description

Using Precise Language

Using Sensory Language

Revising for Active Verbs

Interactive CD-ROMs

Writing Lab

Tutorial on Description

About Description
- Includes annotated Models From Literature and Evaluation Checklist

Choosing a Topic
- Includes Inspirations for Description and video clips about gathering ideas

Narrowing a Topic
- Includes a video clip of Debbie Behler's method

Considering Audience and Purpose
- Includes Audience Profile

Gathering Details
- Includes Featured Senses Bin and a video clip about vivid details used in a radio broadcast

Organizing Details
- Includes video clips that show how to organize details chronologically, spatially, and by order of importance

Drafting
- Includes a video tip from Debbie Behler and a Student Model

Revising and Editing
- Includes a video tip from Debbie Behler, two Word Bins, and a peer revision response sheet

Proofreading
- Includes integrated grammar instruction on using modifiers and a Student Model

Publishing and Presenting
- Includes a video clip of publishing options

Writer's Tool Kit

Suggested Activities: Inspirations for Description, Revising and Editing and Proofreading Checklists, Category Wheel, Cluster Map, Audience and Purpose Chart, Featured Senses Bin

Language Lab

Related Lessons: Exact Nouns, Vivid and Precise Verbs, Vivid Adjectives and Adverbs (Choosing Words unit); Considering Audience and Purpose (Composing unit); Using Modifiers, Adjective or Adverb? (Using Modifiers unit); Sentence Fragments, Run-on Sentences, Misplaced Modifiers (Sentence Errors unit)

Sourcebook

About Description (pp. 34–38)

Guided Lesson on descriptive writing (pp. 39–53)

Developing Your Style

Using Vivid Adjectives and Adverbs (pp. 55–56)

Avoiding Sentence Errors (pp. 57–58)

Literature Model

"An Artichoke on Legs" by Jeanne K. Hanson and Deane Morrison (p. 59)

Below is a list of materials from Prentice Hall's student writing handbook that you can integrate with this lesson.

Writer's Companion

Mini-Lesson on Biographical Sketch, p. 111

Mini-Lesson on Observation Report, p. 123

Adjectives, p. 284

Adverbs, p. 289

Teaching Integrated Language Arts Using *the* Writer's Solution—*Starting With Literature*

Have students read and respond to observations, descriptions of a person, descriptions of an idea, descriptions of an event, and other types of descriptive writing. In discussing the selections, draw students' attention to descriptive elements, such as using sensory details and precise language. Point out that students can use the descriptive writing they read as models for writing their own descriptive pieces. Lead into having students complete descriptive writing projects using the components of the *Writer's Solution.*

CONNECTIONS TO *PRENTICE HALL LITERATURE, COPPER,* SELECTIONS

Observation/Description of Person

	2E	3E
"Auntie," Philippa Pearce	■	▲
"The Scribe," Kristen Hunter	■	▲
"Eleven," Sandra Cisneros	■	▲
"Aaron's Gift," Myron Levoy	■	▲
"A Backwoods Boy," Russell Freedman	■	▲
From ***Between the Devil and the Sea***, Brenda A. Johnston	■	▲
"My Papa, Mark Twain," Susy Clemens	■	▲
"The Platoon System"(from ***A Girl From Yamhill***), Beverly Cleary	■	▲
"The Drive-In Movies," Gary Soto		▲

Description of Event/Description of Idea

	2E	3E
"Breaker's Bridge," Laurence Yep	■	▲
"The Circuit," Francisco Jimenez	■	▲
"The Stone," Lloyd Alexander	■	▲
"The All-American Slurp," Lensey Namioka	■	▲
"Power," Jack Cope	■	▲
"Space Stations of the Mind," Neil McAleer	■	▲
"The Strange Geometry of Stonehenge," Katherine B. Shippen	■	▲
Tuck Everlasting, Natalie Babbitt	■	▲
"The Hatchling Turtles," Jean Craighead George	■	▲

You can also use the *Writer's Solution* materials on description to guide students through writing activities in response to works of literature.

CONNECTIONS TO *PRENTICE HALL LITERATURE, COPPER,* WRITING ACTIVITIES

Thinking and Writing Activities

	2E	3E
Writing About an Experience at School—Follows **"Eleven,"** Sandra Cisneros	■	▲
Writing an Imaginary Travel Article—Follows **"Space Stations of the Mind,"** Neil McAleer	■	▲
Writing a Biographical Sketch—Follows **"A Backwoods Boy,"** Russell Freedman	■	▲
Writing a Biographical Narrative—Follows from ***Between the Devil and the Sea***, Brenda A. Johnston	■	▲
Writing a Character Sketch—Follows **"My Papa, Mark Twain,"** Susy Clemens	■	▲
Writing an Autobiographical Sketch—Follows **"The Platoon System,"** Beverly Cleary	■	▲
Writing a Descriptive Essay—Follows **"The Strange Geometry of Stonehenge,"** Katherine B. Shippen	■	▲
Describing a Natural Occurrence—Follows **"The Hatchling Turtles,"** Jean Craighead George	■	▲
Writing a Character Description—Follows **"Iduna and the Magic Apples,"** Marianna Mayer	■	▲
Responding to a Quotation—Follows ***Tuck Everlasting***, Natalie Babbitt	■	▲

Handbook of Writing About Literature/ Your Writing Process

	2E	3E
Writing Description—Includes activities and assignments	■	▲
Writing From Observation—Includes activities and assignments	■	▲
Writing to Explore a Content Area—Includes activities and assignments	■	▲

■ **(2E)** *Prentice Hall Literature, Copper,* Second Edition

▲ **(3E)** *Prentice Hall Literature, Copper,* Paramount Edition

CONNECTIONS BETWEEN INSPIRATIONS FOR DESCRIPTION AND *PRENTICE HALL LITERATURE, COPPER*

You can use the multimedia Inspirations for Description to motivate student reading as well as student writing. Many of the Inspirations are audio recordings or video adaptations of selections from *Prentice Hall Literature*, *Copper*. Have students work in small groups to look at and discuss an appropriate Inspiration before reading the corresponding selection. Then, after reading the selection, students can replay the Inspiration and select one of the accompanying Topic Ideas (pp. 42–45). The following selections from *Prentice Hall Literature*, *Copper*, are included in the Inspirations for Description:

- **"The Truth About Dragons,"** Rhoda Blumberg
- **"Abuelito Who,"** Sandra Cisneros
- ***Tuck Everlasting***, Natalie Babbitt
- **"The Strange Geometry of Stonehenge,"** Katherine B. Shippen

Recommended Lesson Plan

The following lesson plan is recommended for providing students with thorough, comprehensive instructions in descriptive writing. Because you may not have all the components of the *Writer's Solution* or may have limited access to equipment, the plan provides a number of options. Choose the options that best suit your teaching style and equipment situation. You may want to add a few days to the lesson plan to allow students time to publish their work and to hold conferences with students to discuss your assessment of their work.

FIVE-DAY LESSON PLAN	
Lesson Outcome:	**Each student writes a complete description.**
DAY 1	**Introduce your students to descriptive writing.** Show the *Writers at Work Videodisc* segment featuring Debbie Behler. Use the segment as a springboard for class discussion or group activities.
DAY 2	**Have students choose a writing topic and plan their descriptions.** OPTION 1 Have students work either individually or in small groups to look through the About Description section in the tutorial on Description and to choose a topic by browsing through the Inspirations for Description. Then have students work individually to develop their descriptions by completing the rest of the Prewriting stage of the tutorial on Description. At the end of the period, have students print out their Prewriting notes. OPTION 2 Have students review the descriptions in the Models From Literature in the About Description section of the *Sourcebook*. Then have them choose from the topic suggestions and begin developing their descriptions by completing the rest of the Prewriting stage of the Guided Lesson.
DAY 3	**Have students draft their descriptions.** OPTION 1 Have students write their drafts on the computer following the instructions and using the activities provided in the Drafting section of the tutorial on Description. Have students print out their descriptions at the end of the period. OPTION 2 Have students write their drafts on paper following the instructions in the Guided Lesson (pp. 39–53).

FIVE-DAY LESSON PLAN (continued)

DAY 4

Have students revise their descriptions.

OPTION 1 Have students revise their descriptions on the computer using the revision checkers, activities, and suggestions in the Revising and Editing section of the tutorial on Description.

OPTION 2 Have students revise their descriptions following the suggestions in the Guided Lesson (pp. 39–53).

DAY 5

Have students work in peer groups to make final revisions.

OPTION 1 Have pairs of students review each other's work following the guidelines in the peer revision section of the tutorial on Description. The pairs should then hold conferences before each student makes final revisions. Students should then proofread and print out their final drafts.

OPTION 2 Have pairs of students review each other's work following the guidelines in the Guided Lesson. The pairs should then hold conferences before each student makes final revisions.

Condensed Lesson Plans

Use the following lesson plans if you don't have a full week to devote to teaching description.

Four- and Three-Day Plans: Adapt the Five-Day Plan by having students learn about description, choose a topic, and develop ideas for their descriptions all during Day 1. As in the Five-Day Plan, have students spend a day writing their drafts. For a Four-Day Plan, follow the last two days of the Five-Day Plan; for a Three-Day Plan, simply condense these two days into a single day of revision and forgo the option of working in peer groups.

TWO-DAY LESSON PLAN

Lesson Outcome:	**Each student writes a complete description.**

DAY 1

Have students choose a topic and write their first drafts.

OPTION 1 Have students work in the open-ended environment in the *Writing Lab*. Working individually, students should choose a topic by browsing through the Inspirations for Description. Then they should write their descriptions in their on-line Notebooks using the available prewriting tools as needed.

OPTION 2 Using the suggestions and instructions in the *Sourcebook*, students should choose a topic and write a first draft of their descriptions.

DAY 2

Have students revise and edit their work.

OPTION 1 Have students revise on the computer using the tools, activities, and instructions in the tutorial on Description.

OPTION 2 Have students revise their descriptions following the suggestions in the *Sourcebook*.

Preparing to Teach

Lesson Objectives

Students will

1. Select an appropriate topic for description
2. Narrow the topic
3. Use precise language and sensory details
4. Choose and follow a logical organization for the description
5. Group related details around main ideas
6. Show connections between images and ideas
7. Revise work for content, organization, and style
8. Participate in peer review
9. Proofread for errors in spelling, grammar, and punctuation
10. Publish the finished composition

Activating Prior Knowledge

Ask students to cite examples of times they have written to describe something. Some may recall having written postcards or letters to friends or family members describing a trip, a summer vacation, a new neighborhood, or even a new friend. Ask: *How did you help your reader share the experience you were describing?*

CHAPTER 2

Tintern Abbey *J.M.W. Turner, British Museum*

Description

"The value of descriptive writing is that it brings the whole subject to the reader's attention."

—Deborah Behler
Zoologist and Wildlife Writer

Humanities Note

This painting, *Tintern Abbey*, is by J.M.W. Turner (1775–1851). Joseph Mallord William Turner was a premier British landscape painter. A precocious talent, Turner exhibited his first paintings at the age of fifteen. He subsequently studied at the Schools of the Royal Academy and took lessons from an architectural draftsman. Upon completion of his education, he toured England on foot, making watercolors of regional scenes.

The watercolor *Tintern Abbey* was painted during this early part of his career. The skilled depiction of the architectural elements in this painting reflect Turner's training. Romantic, pretty, and decorative, it appealed to the picture-buying public of his day.

Turner later developed his notable, almost abstract, approach to painting the light and atmosphere of a landscape. This later work was considered romantic, or more concerned with presenting a scene of beauty than one containing realistic detail. Use the following questions as the basis for class discussion to introduce description:

- How can you tell from this painting that Turner trained with an architectural draftsman?
- Describe Tintern Abbey, the place portrayed in Turner's painting. What words would you use to describe the style it is painted in?
- Think of a large structure you have visited. Describe the structure and what it feels like to be inside such a large interior.

Addressing Your Classroom Situation

This chapter includes a variety of Models From Literature, topic ideas, writing process strategies, and student models, along with two integrated skills lessons. Feel free to pick and choose from this material to create a customized lesson on descriptive writing that matches your classroom needs.

The following are some of the key features of the chapter:

- The chapter begins with a section introducing descriptive writing. This section includes thoughts about descriptive writing from writer Debbie Behler, group discussion questions, and Models From Literature models for the following three types of descriptive writing: observation, description of a person, description of an event.
- The Prewriting section includes an assortment of idea-generating activities to help students choose a type of descriptive writing, select a topic, and narrow the topic, along with some suggested topics from which they can select. This section provides instruction and activities to help students consider their audience and purpose, and to gather and organize details. A Cluster Map helps students to narrow topics. Writing Models guide them through other stages of the writing process.
- The Drafting section addresses the issues of how to begin a description and suggests a way to organize details by picturing the subject in a sketch, and then jotting down key words and details in appropriate places.
- The Revising and Editing section focuses on making sure that the description is as clear and precise as it can be.
- The guided writing instruction is followed by a Student Model and then skills lessons on using vivid adjectives and adverbs and on avoiding common sentence errors: run-on sentences, sentence fragments, and misplaced modifiers.
- The chapter ends with a complete Literature Model, an article entitled "An Artichoke on Legs," by Jeanne K. Hanson and Deane Morrison.

Chapter Contents

"Sensory language in descriptive writing is important because that's how people understand what's going on around them—what you see, what you hear, [what you] touch."

"Details bring . . . the situation to life."

—Deborah Behler
Zoologist and Wildlife Writer

"You don't want to lose your audience in long and involved sentences. . . . Make sure that each sentence moves the story along."

More About the Writer

Debbie Behler is an executive editor of a magazine and newsletter at the Bronx Zoo. Her job is to write descriptive pieces about the more than 4000 animals at the zoo. Behler observes the animals in their exhibits and does research to provide readers with more information than is provided at the exhibits.

Talk with your students about the kinds of details they think a zoologist might want to capture in a newsletter about the zoo's animals.

Tech Prep Note

Point out that not only nature writers like Debbie Behler use descriptive writing. Workers in other fields write descriptively on the job. Store owners write descriptive labels for products on their shelves and describe sales and other special store events. People working in human resources departments have to write descriptions of both jobs and qualified applicants. Hotel managers and innkeepers write to inform guests about local entertainment. Police officers write descriptions of suspected lawbreakers, crimes, and crime scenes. Ask: *Think about the adults you know and the jobs they have. How do they use their descriptive writing skills at work?*

Introducing Descriptive Writing

About Description

What Is Description?

Paintings and photographs allow people to capture images and share them with others. You can do the same thing with descriptive writing. Descriptive writing brings a person, an animal, a scene, or an experience to life for the readers. When you write a piece of description, you use words to capture how something looks, smells, tastes, feels, or sounds.

Group Discussion Take turns describing your favorite places, your favorite hobbies, or your favorite television shows. As you listen to one another, jot down details that help you picture what's being described. Share your notes with the rest of the group. Then discuss any details that would have made the description clearer.

34 • *Description*

Teaching Options

There are a variety of ways you can introduce descriptive writing using the components of the *Writer's Solution*:

- You can show the descriptive writing segment from the *Writers at Work Videodisc*. Use this segment as a springboard for a class discussion on descriptive writing.
- You can have students work individually or in small groups to go through the About Description section of the tutorial in the *Writing Lab* CD-ROM.
- You can work through the About Description section of the *Sourcebook* with the class.
- You can have students read the About Description section of the *Sourcebook* before class starts, so that as a group you can concentrate on the videodisc or CD-ROM lesson.

Sourcebook

Have students read aloud and discuss the About Description section in the *Sourcebook*. Use the following questions to guide the discussion:

- How can you recognize descriptive writing? Where might you find examples of it?
- Do you think different descriptions of the same topic are possible? Why?
- What makes descriptive writing important?

Following the class discussion, divide your students into groups of three to five to engage in the group discussion (p. 34).

Writers at Work Videodisc

Use the About Description section of the videodisc featuring writer Debbie Behler as a springboard into a class discussion on descriptive writing. Play the chapter in its entirety, pausing as needed. Then feel free to replay any segment to reinforce an important idea. Before you play the first segment, ask students to listen to what Debbie Behler says about descriptive writing.

After students have viewed the segment, have them take turns sharing their responses. Then move into a discussion of the writing techniques and personal insights that Behler shares. Ask:

- What does she say about the value of descriptive writing? How do her ideas apply to the writing she does?
- What does Behler say about where she gets her ideas for writing?

How a Professional Writer Uses Description

Just about every type of writer uses description—novelists, journalists, even comic book writers. Reporters might describe conditions in a country torn apart by war. An advertising executive might describe the look, taste, and smell of a new brand of yogurt. Debbie Behler, a writer who works at the Bronx Zoo in New York City, uses descriptive writing to capture how the animals look, act, and even smell. Here's what she has to say about descriptive writing and how it fits into her work:

> "Descriptive writing should explain and bring to life exactly what you're talking about. It makes it more personal and brings out some characteristic in the subject that's of interest to you and the reader. In the writing I do, I observe animals in their exhibits and see what their behavior is, see what they look like, and then try to create the picture of the animal in the wild—try to translate it into a form that a reader would understand."

How Description Fits Into Your Life

When was the last time you described a new band to a friend? On your walk home from school last week, did you describe to a friend any funny things that happened at school? Have you ever told your family what kind of sweater you'd like to get for your next birthday?

These are just a few of the many situations in which you would use description in your everyday life. When you describe something aloud, you probably use words, gestures, and body language to help paint a picture for your audience. When writing descriptively, however, you must rely on words alone to get your ideas across.

Play frames 11727 to 20482

Writing Lab CD-ROM

The About Description section of the tutorial includes the following options to help students understand what descriptive writing is:

- **Author video clip** Students play a video to hear Debbie Behler's thoughts about descriptive writing.
- **Interactive models of descriptive writing** Students interact with these models to gain insight into the elements of observations and descriptions.
- **Evaluation Checklist** These guidelines can be presented to students before they draft their descriptive pieces to serve as a checklist to guide their writing. The guidelines can also be used for self-assessment after writing.

Students can work individually or in small groups to complete the tutorial on descriptive writing. Or, if you have access to a projection panel, you can work through the About Description section with the entire class at once.

Writers at Work Videodisc

What does Debbie Behler mean when she says that descriptive writing should "bring to life" what the writer is describing?

Invite students to share experiences they have had describing animal behavior, such as that of a pet.

Play frames 12374 to 12921

Real-World Writing

Help students identify people in your community who write descriptively. These people might be music critics, food critics, tour guides, and environmental scientists.

Have students look for examples of descriptive writing in unexpected places, such as in store windows and in posters on buses and trains. As students share their findings, ask:

- How do the examples of descriptive writing that you've found create a picture for readers?
- What common features, if any, do you notice among the different descriptive writing pieces you've seen?

Integrating Literature With Writing

Starting From Literature

You can use the models on pages 36–38 to illustrate the various elements of each type of descriptive writing. Or you can use the content or devices used in these pieces to inspire writing on any of the topics they address. For example, have students use their reactions to the excerpt from "Jungle Journal" to write a description of a time they listened to sounds in nature, such as the chirps and noises made by birds, the scurrying about of squirrels and other small mammals, the chatter of crickets, or even the sounds made by the wind, trees, and streams.

Teaching From the Model

Guide students to recognize that the Lisa Jones excerpt is an example of the type of descriptive writing known as an *observation*:

- *It describes an aspect of nature the writer has witnessed over time.* The writer and her companions on the trek listened to the jungle sounds until the light faded completely.
- *It involves what the writer sees, hears, feels, smells, or tastes.* Jones appeals to the reader's senses when she describes the dripping forest she sees downstream, the thrush she hears from above, and the way the lemon ants taste.

Cross-Curricular Connection: *Science*

Some students might be interested in learning more about rain forests—such as the temperate rain forest that exists in the northwestern United States—and then writing descriptions of an imagined experience in one. Suggest that interested students find and watch a video about a rain forest to gather specific ideas and sensory details they can use in their descriptions.

Types of Description

Description can be part of a longer piece of writing or it can stand alone. For instance, in a short story about the adventures of a group of friends, there might be a descriptive passage about a surprise birthday party. On the other hand, a description of a wild animal might make up a complete article in a wildlife magazine. The following are a few of the types of writing likely to have a descriptive emphasis.

1 Observation

- In an observation, a writer describes something that he or she witnessed directly over a period of time.
- The writer reports what he or she sees, hears, feels, smells, or tastes.
- An observation is often about an aspect of nature or about a scientific event.

Model From Literature

In this passage from "Jungle Journal," environmentalist Lisa Jones describes her observations on a trek in a jungle in the South American country of Ecuador.

Far downstream, the forest is dripping after a huge downpour. We aren't walking however. We are standing in what could well be the world's most mosquito-ridden stretch of forest. We have listened for a long time to a nightingale thrush, whose song slowly descends, slows down, and fades to silence. Then we stop to eat some lemon ants, which really do taste like lemons. The light is dimming, and it is getting dark.

2 Description of a Person

- A description of a person may focus on physical appearance as well as on personality and achievements.
- It may be about a real-life person or about an imaginary one, such as a character in a novel or a play.
- A description may be used in formal introductions at awards banquets, in biographies, or in works of fiction.

Model From Literature

This is a passage from "The Drive-In Movies," a memoir by Gary Soto. Notice how Soto's skillful choice of words creates a vivid picture of his tired mother.

When she came out of the bedroom tying her robe, she yawned a hat-sized yawn and blinked red eyes at the weak brew of coffee I had fixed for her. I made her toast with strawberry jam spread to all the corners and set the three boxes of cereal in front of her. If she didn't care to eat cereal, she could always look at the back of the boxes as she drank her coffee.

Teaching From the Model

Guide students to understand the characteristics of this type of descriptive writing by reading and discussing the passage from Gary Soto's description:

- *It may focus on physical appearance*. In this passage from a story, Soto describes how the recently awakened person looked, how she was dressed, and what actions she took upon emerging exhausted from the bedroom.
- *It uses skillfully chosen words that bring the character to life*. Soto's description of the person's "hat-sized yawn" and how she "blinked red eyes" provides for the reader a vivid picture of the character.

Thematic Connection: Relationships

Have students think back to recall the first time they met someone they've come to know much better. Ask them to describe how that person looked to them and to share some of their initial impressions of the meeting. Students may choose to develop one of their remembrances as the topic for their description.

Exploring Related Literature

Students who choose this kind of descriptive writing may want to read "A Backwoods Boy," by Russell Freedman, which can be found in *Prentice Hall Literature, Copper*.

Cross-Curricular Connection: *Mathematics*

Challenge students to write or verbally give a brief description of a mathematical idea, as if to someone who is unfamiliar with it. For example, ask them to describe geometric concepts such as a circle, a line, a triangle, or a sphere. Or have them describe symmetry, tessellation, or congruence. Students can compare their descriptions with definitions in their math text or in a dictionary.

Teaching From the Model

Guide students to analyze this passage from "The Hatchling Turtles" to understand how it exemplifies a description of an event:

- *The event is recreated in vivid detail.* Point out how Jean Craighead George uses vivid verbs such as *lumbered, thumping, heaved,* and *flopped,* and adverbs such as *unsteadily* and *laboriously* to describe the action.
- *Most events are described in chronological order.* The demanding journey of the turtle as it crawls from the shore inland is described in time order, relating the animal's struggle in overcoming each obstacle in turn.

Writing Strategy

To help students appreciate the effectiveness of using precise language, have them free-write for a few minutes to describe an event they've recently witnessed. It can be, for example, a sporting event they watched on TV. Guide them to use the strategy many writers do—first write the passage, and then go back and replace verbs and modifiers they've chosen with others that are more precise and effective.

Clarification

Be sure students understand the distinction between a description of an event and a description of an observation. Guide them to appreciate that an observation, unlike an event, involves action that takes place over a period of time and is witnessed by an observer. Point out that observations are often about aspects of nature or science.

3 Description of an Event

- A description of an event can be real or it can be invented by the writer of a story.
- Most events are described in chronological, or time, order.
- Writers use vivid verbs and adverbs to describe actions and events.

Model From Literature

In this passage from "The Hatchling Turtles," Jean Craighead George describes the event of a green turtle coming ashore to lay its eggs. Notice the writer's creative choice of vivid verbs (*lumbered, crawled, heaved, flopped*) and adverbs (*unsteadily, laboriously*).

She lumbered ashore unsteadily, because the land felt strange and too firm under her feet. Dragging and pulling herself, she crawled to the top of the beach. She looked about, then went on, thumping laboriously over grass and sticks. She came to a log, heaved over it and flopped into the sand.

38 • *Description*

Exploring Related Literature

For additional examples of descriptive writing, invite students to read "The Hatchling Turtles," by Jean Craighead George, which can be found in its entirety in *Prentice Hall Literature, Copper.*

Language Acquisition/ ESL Teaching Strategy

The *Writing Lab* offers a series of options that can be easily adapted to meet the needs of your ESL students. For example:

- The Sensory Word Bin in the Gathering Details section can be adapted for use with your upper-basic and intermediate ESL students. Working in pairs, the students view the lists and choose one to study in greater detail. They then write sentences using the sensory images. You may wish to ask the pairs to make reference cards with photographs or drawings of

Guided Lesson

Now that you have learned what descriptive writing is, it's time to learn how to write descriptively. This lesson will help guide you through the process of writing your description. You don't have to start at the beginning, however. Think about your ideas for description. Then use this chart to decide where in the lesson to begin.

	START WITH
• If you **do not have a topic**	**Choosing Your Topic**
• If you already **have a general topic in mind** (animals, for example) **but need to focus on one aspect of it**	**Narrowing Your Topic**
• If you **have a narrow topic but don't know what words to use to describe it**	**Gathering Sensory Details**
• If you **have a topic and the details you'll use to describe it**	**Drafting**

Guiding Student Writing

Addressing Your Classroom Situation

- If you choose to assign topics or types of descriptive writing, allow time for students to narrow the topic to suit their interests or find an appealing focus to pursue.
- You may wish to have students work in pairs. If so, brainstorm ways partners might collaborate usefully and fairly. One way is for pairs to separate their chosen topic into parts so that one student describes a part using one kind of order and the other uses another. For example, to describe the turtle's journey inland, one might begin the piece by using a spatial order to describe the terrain and the impediments that awaited the turtle as it came ashore. The other could then complete the passage by describing the trip chronologically, focusing on how the creature made its way from the water's edge through the sand, then across the grass, and finally over it onto more sand.

the sensory images. Synonyms, phrases, and examples of descriptive sentences may be listed around the picture. The reference cards are then placed in a box for future use.

- Your basic ESL students will profit from an adaptation of the Chain of Events Chart in the Organizing Details section. In this option, students put events in chronological order. Ask your ESL students to describe orally the order of the events by using ordinal numbers—for example, *first, second, third.* Remind them that there are other words that help to show order—for example, *then, next, afterwards, finally*. If you wish, you may ask your students to put the chain of events in written form or to write their own chain of events.
- The Drafting section offers a video clip of a poet that can be adapted for use with your advanced ESL students. Not only will your students develop critical thinking skills, but they will also have an opportunity to engage in meaningful oral and written communication. After they have guessed the subject of Mary Austin's *Riddle*, ask them to write their own descriptive riddles to be interpreted by other students.

Writing Lab CD-ROM

The Choosing Your Topic section of the tutorial includes the following options to help students come up with their own topics:

- **Category Wheel Activity** In this activity, students "spin a wheel" to get combinations of words that may suggest writing topics.
- **Video about getting ideas from shopping** Students play the video and hear ways to get topic ideas while shopping in a favorite store.

Working individually or in small groups, students can experiment with these activities to find the ones that work best.

Writers at Work Videodisc

Play the videodisc segment in which Debbie Behler discusses her sources for topics. Behler says that she reads newspaper articles and scientific journals, and also gets timely ideas from watching television and listening to the radio. Ask:

- What do you think of her strategy? How else can she get up-to-date information about an animal?

Play frames 13535 to 14054

Prewriting

Choosing Your Topic

What would you like to describe? Any person, place, event, or object that interests you can make a good topic. You can choose from the selection of suggested writing options (see pages 42–45) or experiment with the following techniques to come up with your own topic.

If you're considering

. . . an observation:

TAKE A TRIP THROUGH TIME

Look through photograph albums for pictures of yourself, a friend, or a family member. Compare the earliest picture you can find of the subject with a picture as he or she appears today. Take notes on the changes you observe through the years. Has the person changed only a little or do you notice a dramatic change? Look through your notes to see if you have enough information for an observation.

. . . a description of a place:

LET TV BE YOUR GUIDE

Watch travel programs—or other programs set in interesting or imaginary places—on television. Take notes as you watch. What are the key features of each place? What makes each one especially interesting? When you've gathered a few ideas, review your notes and choose a topic.

. . . an observation:

OBSERVE THE ANIMAL WORLD

Have you ever watched a cat wrestling with a ball of yarn or a hamster stuffing its cheek pouches with food? Take some time to observe the behavior of animals. As you watch, jot down notes about how it looks and what it does. Later, review your notes for possible writing topics.

Addressing Ability Levels

Challenge your **advanced students** to describe their topic from an unusual point of view, similar to the approach suggested in the *Writing Lab* CD-ROM. For example, a student describing the turtle's journey onto the beach can present the struggle as if from the perspective of another animal watching the event. Students can write their descriptions of ideas, people, and events as if from the point of view of a pet, a family member, or even a celebrity or a famous person from the past.

. . . a description of a person:

List Anyone You Can Think Of

List your friends, the people in your family, the people you see every day on your way to school, the characters on television shows—any people you can think of. Look over your list and choose the person you think would make the best subject for a description. It could be someone with a striking appearance, someone who's especially funny, or someone who's very important to you. Any of these types of people could be a great subject for a description.

. . . a description of an event:

Survey Your Family and Friends

Get ideas about interesting events by taking a survey of your family and friends. Ask them to name interesting or amusing events they have recently witnessed. They might recall a great basketball game they saw, the first steps of a baby cousin, or a family reunion. Take notes as you ask questions about the event. Review your notes for possible writing ideas.

. . . an observation:

Group Activity

Create a Grab Bag

With a group of classmates, create a grab bag. Have each group member bring in from home an item that has an interesting shape, texture, or other sensory quality. Fill up a large bag with the items. (Don't peek while others put their items in.) One by one, let each person in the group select an item from the bag and, without looking at it, describe its shape and texture. One person in the group should record the observations and comments of the group members. When everyone has had a turn, review the notes for possible writing topics.

Cross-Curricular Connection: *Social Studies*

Provide interested students with "before and after" photos of a former president—one from the beginning of his tenure and one from the end—that show the effects of four or more years of stress on the job. They can write to describe the differences in appearance the photos show. Some can even suggest reasons for it. The photos of Lincoln at the beginning and end of his first term are the first and perhaps the best examples of how the demands of the office can age the officeholder.

Thematic Connection: Humor and Fun

Invite students to describe an event they witnessed that they thought was memorable because of how funny it was. Encourage students interested in this idea to talk with family members, who often can be counted on to recall a particularly humorous family incident—perhaps one the student has forgotten from his or her early childhood.

Irises *Vincent van Gogh*
Sotheby's, London

Inspirations for Description

The following are some writing topics for description:

A Description of Flowers

The painting above by Vincent van Gogh shows blue irises growing in a garden. Van Gogh captured the irises in paint. How would you describe these flowers using words? Write a description using clear, precise language to capture the look of these irises or any other flowers you especially enjoy. Use precise words and phrases to describe vividly the colors and shapes of the flowers.

A Description of a Creature

For centuries, people believed there were dragons—even though dragons do not actually exist. Today, some people still believe there exist creatures like the Loch Ness Monster and Bigfoot. There is no proof that these creatures exist, but there are many descriptions of them. What have you heard about these modern mysteries? How do you picture them? Describe Bigfoot, the Loch Ness Monster, or some other modern mystery creature that you know of or one you make up.

Writing Lab CD-ROM

Using the Inspirations for Description in the *Writing Lab* is an excellent way to stimulate creativity and to have students explore possible topics for descriptive writing. Students can browse individually or in small groups through the Inspirations. They can choose their own writing topics or you may prefer to assign topics.

The following is a list of the descriptive writing options included in the Inspirations, but not provided in the *Sourcebook*:

Observation of
- Animal behavior

Description of an event
- From a plant's viewpoint
- Seen in a photo

Description of a person
- From fiction to whom you would like to be related
- You know and admire
- With a heart of gold
- An ideal friend
- Via a character sketch
- Who is you as a writer might see you
- With figurative language
- That includes using original metaphors or similes
- From the viewpoint of a pet

Description of a place
- A habitat
- An urban intersection
- A real place
- A garden
- A setting in a story
- A fantasy setting
- An imaginary land

Description of an idea
- That is a goal you hope to achieve
- For a newcomer's dictionary for a sport
- For a new animal
- For a new amusement park ride
- For an imaginary landmark
- For a fantasy amusement park ride
- From a character's point of view

Description of
- Stonehenge video
- An imaginary invention
- Something large
- An animal in a story
- A dinosaur toy
- A mammal or any other class of animal
- An animal in a photo
- An animal's special features
- A machine
- A diagram

A Description of a Famous Athlete

Choose a famous athlete you look up to. Then write a description of this athlete. How does he or she look? What is special about his or her playing? Which of this athlete's accomplishments stand out in your memory?

A Description of a Story Character

Think of an unforgettable fictional character from a book that you especially enjoyed. Write a description of this character. Include details about his or her appearance, behavior, and personality.

A Description of an Imaginary Animal

Believe it or not, a few of the world's animals were just discovered in this century—for example, the megamouth shark, the giant muntjac deer, and the zebralike okapi. Imagine that you have just discovered a new animal. Where did you discover it? What does it look like? What characteristics make your new animal unique? Write a description of this newly discovered animal.

A Description of a Landmark

Many states and communities across the United States have famous landmarks—monuments, unusual stones or trees, or historic buildings. Landmarks such as the Statue of Liberty in New York harbor are visited each year by people from all over the world. Think about a local, state, or national landmark that interests you. What are the unique features, layout, and other important qualities of this place? Why do people come to see this place? Write a description of this landmark.

A Description of an Outing

The school year often features events such as a museum trip, a roller-skating party, or a field day. Think of a special outing or class trip that you have enjoyed with friends or classmates. Where did you go? What did you experience there? What made the event memorable for you? Write a description of the outing. Include details about such things as the sights and sounds of the outing and your thoughts, feelings, and sensations during the event.

Writing Strategy

Encourage your students who choose to write a description of a creature (p. 42) or an imaginary animal (p. 43) to browse through books about dinosaurs and other exotic and unique animals in order to get ideas for what their creature might look like, how it will move, what it could sound like, and what its surroundings might look like.

Thematic Connection: Imagination

Suggest to students who choose to write about a famous athlete that they may wish to create an imaginary "composite" athlete by combining in her or him the admirable qualities of several athletes they know and admire.

Alternative Activity

Students who choose to write a description of an outing can watch a travel video or a video about a scientific expedition such as one involving an archeological dig or one in which biologists observe animals in the wild. Students should watch the video *without* sound. They should write observations based only on what they see, as opposed to what the narrator is saying.

Cultural Connection

Students who choose to write a description of a landmark might focus their attention on a monument that reflects the cultural diversity of their community. In addition to describing the spatial and aesthetic details of the work, students may want to find out about the sculptor and history of the landmark itself.

Writing Lab CD-ROM

The Inspirations for Description in the *Writing Lab* also include the following Group Projects and Group Discussions. The Group Discussions encourage small groups of students to share their thoughts about an Inspiration and to generate possible writing topics. The Group Projects are structured activities in which students assume different roles.

Group Projects

- Making generalizations about mythical characters
- Describing family relationships
- Creating a bulletin board display of role models
- Imagining a rainbow world
- Educating people about problems facing sea turtles
- Creating a description for a time capsule
- Creating illustrations of descriptions—for example, drawing an animal you've never seen, solely from a written description of that animal
- Participating in a sensory scavenger hunt
- Creating science and math lessons that focus on amusement park rides
- Creating a friendship collage
- Assembling a wall display representative of different cultures

Group Discussions

- Sharing images of dinosaurs that are factual and images that are fanciful
- Sharing knowledge of another culture
- Sharing first impressions using characters from books and movies
- Discussing city life
- Evaluating advances in science and technology
- Talking about how animals in cartoon strips behave like humans

Writing Strategy

Suggest to students who are interested in describing a special person that they browse through a family photo album to get ideas for writing about a special person from their past.

MORE *Inspirations* for Description

Group Project: Compile a Friendship Book

Compile a book about friendship with a group of your classmates. Begin by brainstorming for a list of qualities that describe a good friend. Each of you should then collect quotations, photos, and magazine pictures that convey friendship. Meet again as a team to discuss what you've gathered. Choose the best pieces to be included in your book. Each of you should then create a page for the book. Each page should consist of a photo or an illustration and a brief paragraph describing a good friend. Bind the pages to create a book. Share it with the rest of the class.

A Description of a Special Person From Your Past

Write a description of a special person from your past. You might describe a friend or a relative who moved away to another town or a teacher you had in an earlier grade. Describe how the person looked and acted, and tell what made him or her special to you.

A Description of a Fantasy Setting

Fairy tales are often set in magical realms. Think of the setting of a fairy tale or fantasy story that you heard or read as a young child. What features of this place made it memorable to you? Write a description of this fantasy setting. You can invent sights or sounds to fill out your description of this imaginary place.

Group Project: Create a Time Capsule

Suppose that you and a group of your classmates have been asked to write a description of your classroom or schoolyard to be placed in a time capsule. Centuries from now, readers will use your description to form a picture in their minds and possibly even reconstruct the area you describe. As a team, decide which are the most significant features of the area. Break up into pairs to gather measurements and other details to be included in the description. Meet to share your findings. Then have each team member describe a specific part of your classroom or schoolyard. Finally, work together to assemble the individual descriptions into one complete description of the room or schoolyard.

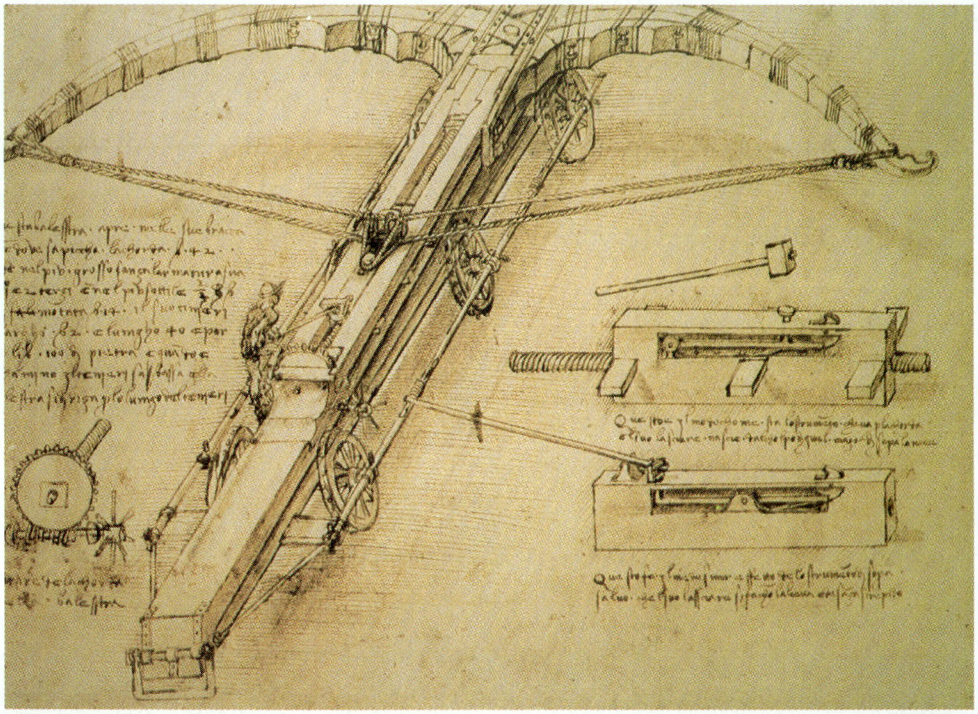

Giant Catapult *Leonardo da Vinci, Biblioteca Ambrosiana*

A Description of an Invention

The machines that Leonardo da Vinci drew, such as armored tanks and flying contraptions, were imaginary. He never actually constructed them, but they were visions of the future. Today, armored tanks and flying machines really exist. What kind of machine would you like to invent? What are its moving parts? Where does it get its energy? What is its purpose? Describe your invention. Include details describing how it works and how it looks and sounds.

A Description of the Features of a City

Millions of Americans live in cities. Millions of other people visit cities—to sightsee, to visit relatives, and to shop. Think about the characteristics of cities you have learned about from your own experience or from books, movies, or television shows. Imagine meeting someone who has never seen a city. How would you describe a city? Write a description, beginning with your strongest impressions. Include details that would help someone else imagine what a city is like.

Language Acquisition/ ESL Teaching Strategy

The Description of the Features of a City writing topic can be adapted to meet the needs of all your ESL students. Your basic ESL students have a limited vocabulary and lack experience with a range of grammatical forms. As a result, they will benefit from as much structure as possible. Show them a picture of a city, preferably from the perspective of a street corner. Have the students describe what they see, using the simple present and the present continuous tenses—for example, *The cars speed by. A lady yells for a cab. People are eating hot dogs.* Ask the students to write these descriptions on the board or in their notebooks. The students can then use these notes to write their own compositions.

Your intermediate ESL students have a more extensive vocabulary and experience with a wider range of grammatical structures. As preparation for their descriptions, have them complete a brainstorming activity in which they list words and phrases that describe the cities they have visited. Assign a student to write down the words and phrases for later reference by the group.

In preparing your advanced ESL students to write a description of a city, lead them into a discussion of their personal experiences. Ask them to describe a unique or scary experience, or the first time they were ever in a city. Because of their more advanced vocabulary and greater fluency, they should be able to help each other express themselves with relative ease.

Addressing Ability Levels

Challenge your **advanced students** to switch their point of view to write the description for the time capsule (p. 44) as if from the perspective of an animal. Examples might include a pet dog creating a time capsule for dogs of the future to find.

Cross-Curricular Connection: *Science*

Invite interested students to make up their own imaginative invention designed to be useful in their own lives. For example, students could describe a device that does homework, or one that cleans a room or does another household chore.

Writing Lab CD-ROM

The Narrowing Your Topic section of the tutorial includes the following options to help students come up with their own topics:

- **Video clip of topic ideas** Students play a video to get ideas for a place to write about in a short description.
- **Annotated instruction** Students choose questions for hints about whether a topic is narrow enough for a description.
- **Annotated examples of narrowed topics** Students choose narrow topics to see how each can be narrowed further.
- **Cluster Map** Students use a Cluster Map to obtain suggestions for a more narrowly focused topic.

Working individually or in small groups, students can experiment with these activities to find the ones that work best for them.

Language Lab CD-ROM

If students need additional guidance in determining how best to narrow their topic, you may want them to complete the part about narrowing a topic from the Considering Audience and Purpose lesson in the Composing unit of the *Language Lab*. It may be useful to set up brief conferences with these students to talk through some of the possibilities.

Narrowing Your Topic

Is your topic narrow enough to describe fully in a brief paper? If you're not sure, ask yourself the questions that follow. Your answers will help you decide whether you need to narrow your topic.

Questions for Narrowing Your Topic

- How long will your description be? Is your description limited to two pages? Three pages?
- In an essay this long, will you be able to describe your topic in detail?
- Can your topic be divided into subtopics? Can you use one of the subtopics to write your essay?

Use a Cluster Map to Narrow Your Topic

If you think your topic is too broad, you can narrow it by creating a Cluster Map. Start by writing your broad topic in the center of a sheet of paper. Circle this topic. Then, in the spaces around your topic, write in subtopics of this topic. Circle each subtopic. Then in the areas surrounding each subtopic, write ideas you have about each subtopic. Circle these ideas. Connect the circles, as shown below. Review your subtopics and ideas to see if any can stand alone as a topic. The following model of a Cluster Map shows some of the many subtopics of food.

Writing Model: Cluster Ma

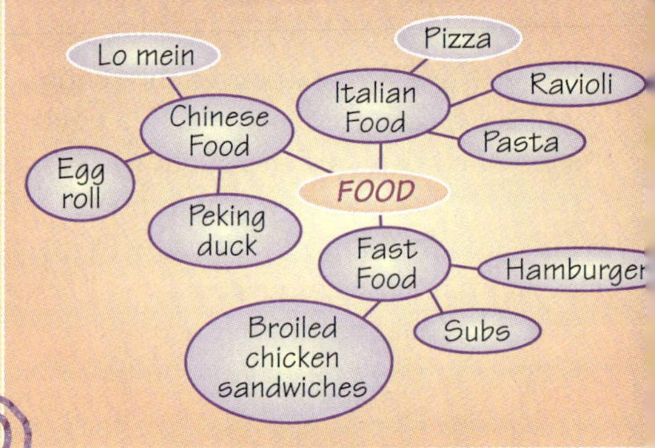

Considering Your Audience

Who will read your description? How much do they know about your subject? Identify your audience and decide on the kinds of details and language to use. If your audience has never seen what you're describing, include the basic details. If they're familiar with your subject, eliminate basic details and include unusual details.

Considering Your Purpose

What is the purpose for your description? Your purpose might be to amaze your audience by capturing the power of a tornado. Or to amuse your audience by describing the playfulness of a kitten. Identify your purpose and keep it in mind as you develop and draft your description. Choose words and details that fit your purpose. For example, use strong verbs to describe the power of a tornado.

Writing Models: Your Audience

The following paragraphs are from two descriptions of the same school gymnasium. In the first version, the details are geared to the interests of students. The language is informal and the tone is friendly. In the second version, the language is more formal and the vocabulary is sophisticated. The details are intended to appeal to an adult audience.

INTENDED AUDIENCE: STUDENTS

The new gym is finally complete, and it's a major improvement over the old one. It's much bigger than the old gym, for starters. There's a pool, a basketball court, a track, and a weight room. The gymnastics team will finally have tumbling space and room for its equipment. The skylights help to brighten the place. And we now have brand-new benches and lockers that actually work! It's a great place!

INTENDED AUDIENCE: PARENTS

The new $500,000 Memorial Athletic Center—featuring a pool, basketball court, track, and weight room—has recently been completed. Square footage is triple that of the old gym, and skylights brighten this state-of-the-art facility. The spacious locker rooms are gleaming with new hardware and benches. This new athletic center will vastly enhance the morale of students at Tagertown Junior High.

Language Lab CD-ROM

If students need additional guidance with the issues of audience and purpose, they may complete the Considering Audience and Purpose lesson in the Composing unit.

Writers at Work Videodisc

Play the videodisc segment in which Debbie Behler talks about her writing purpose and her audience. Ask:

- What does Debbie Behler say about the goal of her articles? How does knowing her audience affect the nature and style of what she writes?

Play frames 16680 to 17925

Writing Lab CD-ROM

The Considering Audience and Purpose section includes the following options to help students explore ways to gear their writing to the intended audience:

- **Video clip about audience and purpose** Students play a video about an advertisement for a house to hear how the writer's choice of details suits his intended audience.
- **Audience Profile** Students answer questions that help them focus on their intended audience.
- **Models From Literature, with audio annotations** Students choose passages from descriptions written for different audiences to hear about how the choice of audience affected the writing.
- **Video clips about writing purpose** Students play videos to hear how two writers considered their topics and came up with their writing purposes.
- **Interactive models with audio annotations** Students choose passages from descriptions written for different purposes to hear about the ways that they are different.
- **Interactive instruction on choosing details** Students select a writing purpose to see the kinds of details that will help them accomplish it.

Working individually or in small groups, students can experiment with these activities to find the ones that work best for them.

Writing Lab CD-ROM

The Gathering Details section includes the following options designed to help students come up with vivid sensory details for their descriptions:

- **Video clip of radio broadcast** Students play the video to hear examples of how Orson Welles used vivid details in his description of invaders from Mars.
- **Sensory Word Bin** Students choose from a menu to see lists of sensory images—one list for each of the five senses. To save images for later use, they can drag each one into their writing notebook.
- **Interactive writing instruction about using precise words** Students replace weak words or phrases with more vivid ones.

Writers at Work Videodisc

Play the videodisc segment in which Debbie Behler talks about how she gathers her details. Ask:

- Why do you think Behler believes that observing the animals is her most important source for gathering details?

Play frames 14072 to 16532

Encourage students to supplement descriptive details gathered from firsthand experience with others they find through research. For example, a student planning to describe the school gymnasium to a parent may gather information about older gyms to use for comparison.

Gathering Sensory Details

Sensory details tell how your subject looks, smells, tastes, sounds, or feels. Using sensory details in your description will help bring your subject to life. Before you start to write, list some vivid sensory details that you can use in your description. Create a chart like the one below to help you come up with sensory details.

Writing Model: Sensory Details

TOPIC: NEW PIZZA RESTAURANT

Sights	Sounds	Smells	Tastes	Touch
Checked cloths	Chef singing opera	Tomato sauce	Spicy	Gooey
Murals from Italy	Cheerful hubbub from diners	Garlic	Fresh	Hot
Colorful menus		Onions	Zesty	

Organizing Details

Arrange the details you've gathered in an order that readers can follow. Three methods of organization used for descriptions are chronological order, spatial order, and order of importance.

Chronological Order

Use chronological order to describe events or to show how a person, place, or object changes over time. Start with the event that happened first, then describe the next event that happened, and so on.

Writing Model

The details in this passage about the development of a tadpole into a frog are arranged in chronological order.

At first, the tadpole has a long tail and no legs. After a few weeks, little bumps appear. Next, the bumps begin to look like legs. While the legs are growing, the tail is shrinking. Finally, the tail disappears completely.

Writing Strategy

Emphasize to students that when describing something using sensory details, they should try to use more than one sense, and they should make an effort to *show* details rather than *tell* them to readers. For example, showing readers that "A cool breeeze rustled through the open window and made me shiver all over" is a more powerful description than telling readers that "There was a cool breeze."

Teaching Strategy

To help students appreciate how using sensory language makes descriptions more effective, invite volunteers to describe animals in much th same way Debbie Behler does—for example, by explaining what their skin feels like to the touch. Othe students can then try to gues which animal is being described.

Order of Importance

Use order of importance to show the most important characteristics of your topic. You might begin with the least important ideas and finish with the most important or begin with the most important and finish with the least important.

Writing Model

The details in this passage are arranged in order of importance—from least important to most important.

Swimming in the swamp is not recommended. The damp, humid air of the swamp is a magnet for mosquitoes. Snakes slither through the slimy mud. The oily, smooth water looks calm and almost peaceful, but those "logs" resting still and silent are really alligators with jaws that slam harder than a car door.

Spatial Order

Use spatial organization when the location of the parts of your subject is important. For instance, tell where a detail is located: top or bottom, left or right, east or west. This type of organization is useful when describing things with many parts or features.

Writing Model

The details in this passage are arranged spatially, according to their location.

The Greenditch Swamp has a lot to offer if you only know where to look. When approached from Stump Road, the first thing you see is the south shore. Moss-covered rocks and a cypress tree mark the southernmost point. To the east, a clump of tall reeds hugs the shore. Toward the north end of the swamp, a colony of frogs keeps busy croaking a nightly lullaby. The western shore is dominated by enormous lily pads that seem big enough for an elephant to sit on!

Writing Lab CD-ROM

The Organizing Details section includes the following options designed to help students come up with a reasonable way to organize the details they've gathered:

- **Video clip of details organized spatially** Students play the video to learn more about spatial organization.
- **Writing Model with audio annotation** Students choose passages to hear how the details in the description are organized spatially.
- **Topic Web** Students type their writing topic, use the web to help them identify spatial areas, and then fill in appropriate details.
- **Video clip of details organized chronologically** Students play the video to see events ordered by time.
- **Interactive Writing Model** Students choose passages to learn why a writer arranged details in a description chronologically.
- **Chain of Events Chart** Students move information about until details are placed in correct chronological order.
- **Video clip of an order of importance organization** Students play the video to learn more about ordering details according to their significance.
- **Interactive Writing Model** Students choose passages to learn why a writer arranged details in a description according to their importance.
- **Outliner** Students use this organizing tool to create an outline of topics, subtopics, and supporting details.

Working individually or in small groups, students can experiment with these activities to find the ones that work best for them.

Writing Strategies

Help students understand that when they arrange details in spatial order, they need to keep in mind how they want the reader to envision the scene they are describing. Point out that the order need not be from a two-dimensional perspective, such as from left to right, but may indicate depth, such as an inside-outside order or a far-away-to-close-up order.

Writing Lab CD-ROM

The Drafting section includes the following options designed to help students write the first draft of their description:

- **Video clip of writer** Students play the video to obtain drafting tips from Debbie Behler.
- **Interactive models, each showing a different approach to drafting** Students see examples of how to begin a description with a striking detail and how to start one with a general idea.
- **Transition Word Bin** Students can use this activity to come up with transitional words for their drafts.
- **Student model with audio annotations** Students read a draft of a description. They can play an audio recording to hear explanations of choices the writer made.

Writing Strategy

Discuss with students the tips of beginning a piece with a striking detail or with a comparison or an exaggeration. Ask them to tell what the two approaches have in common. Then remind students to think about how they intend to *conclude* their compositions. Here, as elsewhere in the writing process, students should focus on showing rather than telling the reader the conclusions they have drawn.

Literature Connection

Suggest that students study examples of descriptive writing in *Prentice Hall Literature, Copper*, to see how each begins. See the list of selections on page 30b.

Drafting

When you have a detailed picture of your subject and an idea of how to describe it, start drafting your description. Keep your audience and purpose in mind as you draft. It's also a good idea to keep your notes, graphic organizers, and any other prewriting materials close by in case you need to refer to them.

Beginning Your Description

Sometimes deciding how to begin your description is the hardest part of writing it. Here are a few ideas to help you begin:

Begin With a Striking Detail

Start with a striking detail that will capture your readers' interest. Notice how the powerful verbs in these sentences immediately grab your attention:

> Mary exploded into the room where I was waiting to interview her. Her coat swirled around her as she flew through the door.

Begin With a Comparison or an Exaggeration

Start by making a general comparison between your subject and something your readers will recognize. Or compare your subject to something your readers can only imagine. For example, begin with an exaggerated comparison that makes your readers want to read more:

> If you want to know what it's like to be in the middle of a hurricane, come to our house some morning when five late risers try to get out the door by 7:38 A.M.

Writing Hints: Sketching Details

If you're having trouble organizing the details, try sketching your subject. Use a pencil and paper to draw a picture. Then jot down the words and phrases that describe the details next to the appropriate places on your drawing. The organization of your details will be displayed before your eyes!

Establishing Assessment Criteria

As students begin drafting their descriptive writing, you may want to share with them the criteria you will use to evaluate their work. The following guidelines are from the tutorial on descriptive writing. You can use them as given, or modify them to suit your needs.

- Do you have a narrow, focused topic?
- Is the information in your description appropriate for your audience and your purpose?
- Have you used precise language and vivid sensory details?
- Have you followed a consistent, logical organizatic throughout your description?
- Have you used transition words to connect ideas?
- Have you focused your description on a few mair impressions?
- Is your composition free from errors in spelling,

Revising and Editing

Revising Your Work

How can you make your description better? If possible, take a break before you revise your draft so that you approach it with "fresh eyes." Then review it carefully, trying to improve it. Use the following checklist to guide your revision.

FROM a WRITER

"I would say I spend about sixty percent of my time editing and probably forty percent writing."

—Deborah Behler

Revision Checklist

1. In what ways have you considered your audience? What changes can you make to enhance your appeal to those readers?
2. What sensory details have you used? How can you strengthen your sensory details?
3. Which words can be replaced with more precise words?
4. How have you organized your description? How can you improve your organization plan?

Having a Peer Review Your Work

Work with a classmate as you revise your work. A second set of eyes and another point of view will help you pinpoint areas that need work. Ask a classmate to read your description using the following questions as a guide. Then review the suggestions and change your draft where necessary.

Peer Review Checklist

1. What is the strongest part of the description? How can the writer strengthen other parts of the description?
2. What parts are confusing, vague, or unclear? What can the writer do to make the writing clearer?
3. Are there enough sensory details? What details could be added?
4. Which nouns, adjectives, and adverbs could be more precise?
5. Is the organization of details effective? If not, how can it be improved?

grammar, and punctuation?

Writing Lab CD-ROM

The Revising and Editing section provides strategies for self-revision. It includes the following options to help students revise their first draft:

- **Video clip on revising** Students play a video to hear suggestions from Debbie Behler on revising descriptions.
- **Revision checker for vague adjectives** Students use this tool to help them replace adjectives in their draft with stronger descriptive words.
- **Self-Revision Checklist** Students answer questions to help them evaluate their draft for considering audience and purpose, word choice, and organization.
- **Student Model with audio annotation** Students read to see and hear how one student has revised her draft.
- **Featured Senses Bin** Students can choose words from the senses lists to replace vague or weak words in their descriptions.
- **Transition Word Bin** Students view categories of transition words. They can choose words from the list that fit their organization to insert in the appropriate places in their drafts.

Writers at Work Videodisc

Play the videodisc segment in which Debbie Behler talks about revising her work. Ask:

- What do you think about Behler's contention that she spends about sixty percent of her time revising? How does that compare with the time that you'll probably need to spend revising?

Play frames 18132 to 19161

Debbie Behler also says that she often makes the mistake of repeating words. Ask:

- What kinds of errors or features of your writing style will you fix in the revision stage? What resources can you use to help you make improvements? Explain.

Writing Lab CD-ROM

The Revising and Editing section includes the following options to help students develop strategies for proofreading their descriptive writing:

- **Proofreading Checklist** This checklist supplements the one provided in the *Sourcebook* (p. 52).
- **Student Model with audio annotations** Students can play an audio recording to hear an explanation of how the writer made proofreading corrections.
- **Interactive instruction on using adjectives and adverbs** To learn more about how adjectives and adverbs are used, students read sentences and then choose the modifier in each.

Working individually or in small groups, students can experiment with these activities to find the ones that work best.

Teaching Strategy

You may find it useful to have students proofread with a different peer than the one with whom they revised and edited their work. This way, students will have a fresh eye detecting errors that might have been missed earlier.

Proofreading

Writing that contains errors is distracting to the reader. Proofread your description for errors in spelling, punctuation, and grammar. Use the following questions as a guide while proofreading.

Proofreading Checklist

1. Are all your sentences complete?
2. Does each sentence start with a capital letter and end with the correct punctuation mark?
3. Are all the words spelled correctly?
4. Have you used adverbs and adjectives correctly?
5. Is your description neatly printed or typed?

Student Model: Revised Draft

Look at this passage from a revised draft of a description written by Keri Schadler, a student at Deerpark Middle School in Austin, Texas. Notice how she added details to make the description more vivid.

"Hey, guys! What's up?" Mrs. Mincho always greeted us ~~in a cheery way.~~ cheerfully when she came into class. Her bright smile and welcoming tone went perfectly with her overall appearance and attitude toward life. You wouldn't know it from her energy and young face, but she was in her forties. ~~but she didn't look it.~~

Portfolio Assessment

Have students write an evaluative statement that addresses some of the questions posed on page 53 of the *Sourcebook*. If students decide to include the completed descriptive piece in their portfolio, they might attach this statement to it. Otherwise, the statement itself can go into the

Publishing and Presenting

Now that you have finished proofreading your description, decide how you would like to publish or present your work. There are many ways to share your description. Following are a few ideas:

Post Your Description on an Electronic Bulletin Board Work with your school's technical adviser to gain access to a suitable bulletin board. Post your description there for others to read.

Mail Your Description to a Friend or a Relative Share your description by sending it to someone in the form of a letter or a postcard.

Videotape a Reading of Your Description Work with a classmate or a family member to videotape your description. Rehearse ahead of time. Then choose an interesting locale for the shoot. Arrange to show the finished tape to your class.

Compile a Booklet of Descriptions Work with a group of classmates to compile a booklet of descriptions. Choose photos and illustrations to accompany each description. Give your booklet a title and a table of contents.

Reflecting on Your Writing

What did you learn while writing your description? The following questions will help you think about your writing:

- What did you learn about the subject of your description? What else would you have liked to learn?
- If you were starting over, would you approach the assignment differently? Why or why not?
- How can you apply what you've learned to other writing assignments?

Writing Lab CD-ROM

The Publishing and Presenting section includes the following options to help students present their completed works to a wider audience:

- **Interactive model for giving a description a title** Students read a paragraph and choose titles to hear how effective each is.
- **Tips for creating a title** Students are presented with ideas for formulating a title for their description. Some suggestions involve using metaphors or using contradictions.

Students working individually or in small groups can use the ideas in the tutorial on descriptive writing to help in the publishing and presenting phase.

The Multimedia Workshop

Students can use the templates in the Writing Workshop component of *The Multimedia Workshop* to word-process and present their final descriptive pieces. For instance, a student writing an observation can use the field notes template or the lab report template. Students may choose to include the field or lab notes in their portfolio.

portfolio as a record of self-evaluation.

The following questions can be used to supplement the questions in the *Sourcebook*:

- What part of the descriptive-writing process did you find most satisfying? Most challenging?
- How do you feel about writing a descriptive piece, as compared with writing other kinds of pieces? Which type of descriptive writing would you like to try next time? Why?
- In what ways has your writing shown the most improvement?

After students have evaluated their work, confer with them to decide what to include in their portfolio. Students can select the completed piece and/or earlier drafts they think reflect growth and progress. Remind students to date all the work they add to their portfolio.

Teaching From the Model

Draw students' attention to how Keri Schadler's composition includes the elements of descriptive writing.

- *It has a catchy beginning.* By starting with an excited greeting, Schadler captures the reader's attention from the outset.
- *It uses precise language and sensory details.* Schadler uses descriptive language such as "welcoming tone" and "beaming happiness" to describe the teacher's overall appearance and demeanor. She refers to her "curly, dark-blond hair" that "bounced lightly" and her "pale complexion speckled with brown freckles" to describe precisely what she looked like.
- *It contains vivid images.* The writer uses descriptions such as "happiness spilled over everyone in the room" and "looked me in the eye and talked to me like an adult" to show rather than tell what Mrs. Mincho was like as a person.
- *It is organized effectively.* The details of the piece are organized according to an order of importance, culminating in a sweeping conclusion about the impact the teacher has on her students.
- *It conveys a main impression.* By this description, it is clear that Mrs. Mincho is a teacher anyone would like to have.

Student Model

Here is a complete, final draft of Keri Schadler's description of her favorite teacher.

The Wonderful Mrs. Mincho

by Keri Schadler

"Hey, guys! What's up?" Mrs. Mincho always greeted us cheerfully when she came into class. Her bright smile and welcoming tone went perfectly with her overall appearance and attitude toward life. You wouldn't know it from her energy and young face, but she was in her forties.

I began my description of Mrs. Mincho with one of her typical greetings to give readers an idea of her personality right away.

Curly, dark-blond hair bounced lightly as she moved about. Although she usually wore it down, sometimes she wore it in a bun or a twist. Her pale complexion speckled with brown freckles really set off her blue eyes. She hardly ever wore lipstick.

Here I described Mrs. Mincho's physical appearance. I used vivid adjectives to create a picture of her.

Although her perky appearance was memorable, I will always remember her best for her personality. She made kids feel good. Her beaming happiness spilled over everyone in the room, and she treated her students like adults.

One time in third grade, I had to interview her for an assignment. She looked me in the eye and talked to me like an adult. It really made me feel good.

After I described Mrs. Mincho's personality, I gave an example to support that description.

Everyone should have the opportunity to meet a wonderful teacher like Mrs. Mincho.

My conclusion sums up my attitude toward Mrs. Mincho.

Technology Note: Networking

After your class has read the Student Model, they may be interested in sharing their own descriptive efforts, including any photos or video they create as accompaniments, with students across the country via CompuServe, America Online, or the Internet by connecting to Prentice Hall's Internet home page. Look for special events, contests, as well as bulletin boards and pointers to student publications at http://www.prenhall.com. Request that other classrooms exchange similar descriptive pieces so students can compare them and also learn something about another part of the country. For example, a student living in the Midwest might find a description of a beach sand-sculpture contest interesting to read about. Another student could be intrigued by a description of a Cajun chef or a Zydeco musician from southern Louisiana.

Developing Your Style 1

Using Vivid Adjectives and Adverbs

The writer of the following description of a train has done a fair job of describing the sights and sounds of the train. Yet the description could be stronger. What can the writer do to improve it?

> A whistle sounded. The engine appeared from the depths of the tunnel. As the train neared, fumes filled the air. Steam rushed from beneath the wheels.

One way to improve the paragraph is to add modifiers. A **modifier** is a word or a group of words that adds meaning to another word. Modifiers make the meaning clear by answering questions such as *What kind? How? How many? When?* and *Where?* Two main types of modifiers are **adjectives** and **adverbs**. Adjectives add meaning to nouns and pronouns. Adverbs describe verbs, adjectives, or other adverbs.

Now read an improved version of the paragraph. Notice that it contains adjectives and adverbs (underlined), bringing the scene to life for the reader.

> A <u>shrill</u> whistle sounded. The engine <u>suddenly</u> appeared from the <u>dark</u> depths of the tunnel. As the train neared, <u>oily</u> fumes filled the air. <u>Hot</u> steam rushed from beneath the wheels

Whenever you write, use modifiers that describe exactly how something looks, sounds, feels, tastes, or smells. Avoid vague modifiers—such as *some* or *many*—and empty modifiers that have lost their meaning from overuse—such as *nice, well,* or *great*. Compare the following sentences and notice how specific modifiers help create a more vivid word picture.

> **Vague, empty modifiers:** <u>Some</u> <u>nice</u> passengers boarded the train for a <u>great</u> trip through the western states.
>
> **Specific modifiers:** <u>Four</u> <u>smiling</u> passengers boarded the train for a week-long <u>sightseeing</u> trip through the western states.

55

Teaching Strategy

The model passage that begins "A whistle sounded..." is somewhat dull because it lacks adjectives and adverbs. As is, the action is neither precise nor vivid. Before students read the revised version, ask volunteers to indicate which nouns and verbs in the original version could be brought to life with the addition of modifiers. If any students have themselves witnessed a train emerging from a tunnel, invite them to describe their recollection of the experience.

After students have read both versions, ask them to tell what kind of descriptive writing the passages typify and to explain their choice.

Integrating Skills With Writing

Teaching Strategy

To connect the skills lessons to the students' writing, explain that one important feature of descriptive writing is the use of vivid adjectives and adverbs that help to create sensory images.

Another important aspect of descriptive writing is clarity that results from the use of well-written, complete sentences.

Management Strategy

You can have students work through one or both of the skills lessons either before or after they write their descriptive pieces. If you use the lessons *before*, remind students to incorporate the techniques in their writing. If you address skills *after* students write their compositions, have them include a section on skills improvement in the self-assessment document they prepare for their portfolios. The next time they write, their work can be evaluated in terms of their mastery of these skills.

You may want to give students these lessons as take-home assignments to be completed prior to the drafting, revising, or proofreading stages—wherever you see the greatest need. Or you may choose to assign the skills lessons only to those students whose drafts indicate a need for direct instruction in these particular skills.

Writing Strategy

Emphasize the value to writers of avoiding the use of empty modifiers. Point out that although these words may be useful in speech, in writing they can deprive passages of their vividness and strength.

Technology Note: Word Processing

Guide students who use word processors to take advantage of the computer's thesaurus. Encourage students who are not word-processing to refer to a print thesaurus as a resource for finding vivid modifiers.

Writer's Companion

To provide students with additional support and reinforcement in using modifiers, direct them to the sections on identifying and using adjectives and adverbs beginning on page 284. Students might focus in particular on the sections entitled "Position of Adjectives," "Using Precise Adjectives," and "Comparative and Superlative Forms."

Remember these tips when you write and revise:

- Adjectives and adverbs help to make your meaning clear. They create specific pictures of what you are describing.
- Use modifiers that describe specifically how something looks, sounds, feels, tastes, or smells.
- Avoid vague modifiers, such as *some* or *many*, that don't help to make the meaning clear.
- Avoid empty modifiers—such as *nice*, *good*, *terrible*, and *excellent*—that have lost their meaning from overuse.

Practice Activities

1. Read each sentence carefully. Think of descriptive words you could add to make the sentence more clear and meaningful. Choose your words carefully. The sentences must make sense!
   a. The Japanese are known for their (adjective) trains.
   b. (Adjective) people ride these trains daily.
   c. In the railway station, there are (adjective) shops and restaurants.
   d. At rush hour, people crowd (adverb) into the train cars.
   e. Trains travel (adverb) through the countryside of Japan.
   f. When the train arrives at the station, riders exit (adverb).

2. Following is a description of a school event. Rewrite this paragraph, inserting vivid adjectives and adverbs where appropriate.

   Kinnetown Middle School's annual play was good. The costumes were nice. People sang their songs well. The sets were pretty and the acting was fine. At intermission, juice and carrot cake were served. The end of the play was interesting. At curtain call, everyone took a bow.

Practice Activities: Suggested Answers

1. Descriptive words will vary. Here are some suggestions:
   a. swift
   b. Countless
   c. attractive
   d. rapidly
   e. quietly
   f. promptly
2. Paragraphs will vary, but should contain vivid adjectives and adverbs like those underlined in this version:

   Kinnetown Middle School's annual <u>spring</u> play was <u>spellbinding</u>. The costumes were <u>colorful</u>. People sang <u>melodious</u> songs <u>zestfully</u>. The <u>stage</u> sets were <u>realistic</u> and the acting was <u>lifelike</u>. At intermission, <u>refreshingly</u> <u>chilled</u> juice and <u>sweet</u> carrot cake were served. The <u>climactic</u> end of the play was <u>surprising</u>. At curtain call, everyone took a <u>gracious</u> bow.

Developing Your Style 2

Avoiding Sentence Errors

Sentence errors can make it difficult for readers to follow your writing. Try to avoid the following common sentence errors.

Run-On Sentences

A **run-on sentence** consists of two or more complete sentences separated only by a comma or not separated at all. Run-on sentences make it difficult for a reader to tell where one thought stops and another starts. Look at the following sentences about a team that played in the Negro Baseball Leagues.

Run-on: The Pittsburgh Crawfords' owner built an expensive new stadium in 1931, the owner was determined to form the best team in African American baseball.

Corrected: The Pittsburgh Crawfords' owner built an expensive new stadium in 1931. The owner was determined to form the best team in African American baseball.

Fragments

A **sentence fragment** is a group of words punctuated as a sentence but not expressing a complete thought. Fragments usually lack a subject or a verb. A fragment cannot stand alone as a sentence.

The first group of words below is an example of a sentence fragment. The second group of words forms a complete sentence because it includes a subject and a verb and expresses a complete thought.

Sentence Fragments	Complete Sentences
• Because fans crowded the stadium.	• Because fans crowded the stadium, owners raised ticket prices.
• Pitchers warming up in the bull pen.	• Pitchers began warming up in the bull pen.
• Gloved the ball and threw home.	• The shortstop gloved the ball and threw home.

Integrating Skills With Writing

Teaching Strategy

Point out to students the importance of writing sentences that contain a subject and a verb and that express a complete thought. Mention that although when speaking we commonly do not use complete sentences because we can use gestures and inflection in our voice to make ourselves understood, we need to write only complete, correct sentences to make our writing understandable to readers.

Writing Strategy

Point out to students that run-ons can be corrected in ways other than breaking them into two shorter sentences. Invite volunteers to correct the sample by inserting a coordinating conjunction between the two ideas.

Teaching Strategy

Ask students to tell what is missing in each sentence fragment. Invite volunteers to suggest other ways to correct each of these fragments.

Teaching Strategy

Have students give two possible meanings for each sentence containing a misplaced modifier, and tell why one of the two makes more sense.

Language Lab CD-ROM

For additional practice avoiding common problems with sentences, students can refer to the following lessons in the Sentence Errors unit: Sentence Fragments, Run-On Sentences, and Misplaced Modifiers.

Teaching Strategy

Point out to students that there is more than one way to revise the passage in the first practice activity. Have students share and explain their revisions with the whole class.

Writer's Companion

To provide students with additional support and reinforcement in correcting misplaced modifiers, direct them to "Misplaced or Dangling Modifiers," beginning on page 277.

Language Acquisition/ ESL Teaching Strategy

For these practice activities, you can pair your advanced students and intermediate students. Then have them study each modifier in the paragraph, asking, *What does this refer to?* For example, in the first sentence, *What does "essentially a parallel universe" refer to?* The students can then move the modifiers closer to the words they modify. After the paragraph and the four examples that follow are completed, the students may write their own sentences and correct each other's work if necessary.

Misplaced Modifiers

A **misplaced modifier** is any word, phrase, or clause serving as a modifier but placed so far away from the word it modifies that it seems to modify something else. Using misplaced modifiers in your writing will confuse your readers. To make the meaning of your sentences clear, place the modifier as close as possible to the word it modifies.

Misplaced modifier: Sliding into home, the tag missed Cool Papa Bell by a hair.

Corrected sentence: The tag missed by a hair as Cool Papa Bell slid into home.

Misplaced modifier: The pitcher ran to the bull pen with ill-concealed fury.

Corrected sentence: With ill-concealed fury, the pitcher ran to the bull pen.

Practice Activities

1. Rewrite the following paragraph about the Negro Baseball Leagues. Fix any fragments and run-ons you see.

   The Negro Leagues began in the early twentieth century, essentially a parallel universe. The Negro Leagues played in the same stadiums as the major leaguers, but for far less money than the major leaguers. The breaking of the color barrier when Jackie Robinson joined the Brooklyn Dodgers. This helped to bring about the end of the Negro Leagues, black fans began flocking to see their favorite stars play in major league games. Attendance dwindled, and eventually, in the 1950's, the Negro Leagues ceased to be.

2. Rewrite each of the following sentences, correcting misplaced modifiers.
   - **a.** Hanging from the locker, the catcher removed his mitt.
   - **b.** The third baseman yelled at the umpire with a loud voice.
   - **c.** Satchel got on the bus with a long face.
   - **d.** The batter missed the ball, swinging hard.

Practice Activities: Suggested Answers

1. Paragraphs will vary. Here is a suggested version:

   The Negro Leagues began in the early twentieth century, essentially a parallel universe. The Negro Leagues played in the same stadiums as the major leaguers, but for far less money. The breaking of the color barrier when Jackie Robinson joined the Brooklyn Dodgers helped to bring about the end of the Negro Leagues. Black fans began flocking to see their favorite stars play in major league games. Attendance dwindled, and eventually, in the 1950's, the Negro Leagues ceased to be.

2. **a.** The catcher removed his mitt hanging from th locker.

   b. The third baseman yelled with a loud voice the umpire.

   c. With a long face, Satchel got on the bus.

   d. Swinging hard, the ba ter missed the ball.

Literature Model

Descriptive writing uses vivid words that let readers know how something looks, feels, sounds, tastes, or smells. In this essay, Jeanne K. Hanson and Deane Morrison describe the pangolin, a strange animal that lives in Africa and Asia. As you read, notice how Hanson and Morrison use sensory details to bring the pangolin to life for readers.

An Artichoke on Legs

by Jeanne K. Hanson and Deane Morrison

Hanson and Morrison use a humorous, descriptive title to give readers a chance to picture the creature.

It eats ants and termites—about 20,000 a day—but may not be related to the anteater. It has a foot-long tongue that darts out and probes like a length of sticky flypaper, then folds up for storage in a pocket in its throat. It has good claws for digging and no teeth. Its body is shingled with tough, sharp scales that can open and shut quickly, a body covering unique among mammals. When threatened, it can lash out with its tail, spray a smell worse than a skunk's, or roll up into an armored ball. It sleeps all rolled up too. As a species, it may well be as old as the last of the dinosaurs. It is the pangolin.

The authors use specific sensory details to describe how this unusual animal looks, acts, and smells. By the time they identify the creature by name, the reader has a good picture of it.

This odd, well-designed, usually nocturnal creature lives in Africa and Asia, where its seven species range in size from a house cat to a large dog and hardly make a sound. No one knows its life span, but naturalists worry about its survival, since its scales and hide are considered medicinal, lucky, and good for boots.

Hanson and Morrison compare the pangolin's size with the size of animals familiar to readers.

Integrating Literature With Writing

Management Strategy

You can have students read this model of descriptive writing either before or after they have written their own piece. If they read it *before*, you can draw their attention to techniques or ideas they can apply to their own writing. If they read it *after*, have them compare and contrast the selection with their own descriptive composition.

Activating Prior Knowledge

Invite students to tell what they know about the pangolin or about another animal it reminds them of.

Purpose-Setting Question

How do the elements of descriptive writing work to create a vivid picture of what a pangolin looks like?

Reading Strategy

You can help guide reading by asking students to look for and jot down words and phrases from the text that give precise details, descriptions, and images that appeal to the senses.

Teaching Strategy

Hanson and Morrison employ comparisons in their description, using precise details and vivid language to compare the actions, appearance, and size of the pangolin to other animals. Ask students to tell why they think using comparisons is or isn't an effective strategy.

Language Acquisition/ESL Teaching Strategy

Reading as a large group, your upper basic and intermediate ESL students can underline or copy words and phrases used to describe the pangolin. If time permits, ask an artistically inclined student to draw a picture of the animal for classroom display. The students can then write sentence strips to describe the appearance and behavior of the animal, such as *It has a foot-long tongue*, or *It has tough, sharp scales*. The sentence strips can then be posted along with the picture.

Closure and Extension

To complete the lesson, you can ask students to sum up what they have learned about descriptive writing by examining this description of an animal few know about.

Then invite students to share in small group discussions or through brief journal entries what points they would like to keep in mind for future descriptive writing.

3 Narration
CLASSROOM MANAGER

Writer's Solution *Materials for Teaching Narration*

The *Writer's Solution* includes a wide range of materials for teaching narration. You can pick and choose from among these materials to create a lesson plan that suits your classroom needs, teaching style, and equipment situation. In the pages that follow, you'll find lesson plans suggesting some of the most effective ways of using these materials. You do not have to use all the program components or all its features to use it effectively. Just use what works for you. For a detailed description of each of the components of the *Writer's Solution*, see pages T4–T6.

Below is a detailed list of the *Writer's Solution* materials for Narration.

Writers at Work Videodisc

Featured Writer: Virginia Hamilton, Fiction Writer

Videodisc Segments

About Narration
The Art of Storytelling
Writing Tips
- Showing, Not Telling
- Building Paragraphs
- Perfecting a Story

Interactive CD-ROMs

WRITING LAB

Tutorial on Narration

About Narration
- Includes annotated Models From Literature and Evaluation Checklist

Choosing Your Topic
- Includes Inspirations for Narration and a video about writing from memory

Considering Audience and Purpose
- Includes *Star Trek* video clip about identifying your audience and purpose

Developing Narrative Elements
- Includes Character Trait and Setting Details Word Bins and videos about developing characters, using details to describe the setting, and developing the plot

Drafting
- Includes a video tip from Virginia Hamilton, a Transition Word Bin, and a Student Model

Revising and Editing
- Includes a video tip from Virginia Hamilton, a revision checker for language variety, and Self-Evaluation and Peer Review Checklists

Proofreading
- Includes grammar instruction on pronouns and antecedents and a Student Model

Publishing and Presenting
- Includes tips for creating a class anthology, and a video about creating an audiotape

Writer's Tool Kit

Suggested Activities: Topic Wheel; Storyboard Activity; Audience Profile; Sunburst Diagram; Story Profile Activity; Self-Evaluation Checklist

LANGUAGE LAB

Related Lessons: Vivid and Precise Verbs (Choosing Words unit); Transitional Words (Building Paragraphs unit); Point of View, Considering Audience and Purpose (Composing unit); Pronouns and Antecedents (Using Pronouns unit)

Sourcebook

About Narration (pp. 64–70)
Guided Lesson on Narration (pp. 71–88)
Developing Your Style
- Using Vivid Verbs (pp. 91–93)
- Using Transitions (pp. 94–95)

Literature Model
- From *The Bells of Christmas* by Virginia Hamilton (pp. 96–97)

Below is a list of materials from Prentice Hall's student writing handbook that you can integrate with this lesson on narrative writing.

Writer's Companion

Mini-Lesson on Personal Narrative, p. 126
Mini-Lesson on Humorous Anecdote, p. 133
Transitional Words, p. 64
Precise, Vivid Verbs, p. 412

Teaching Integrated Language Arts Using the Writer's Solution*—Starting With Literature*

Have students read and respond to anecdotes, personal narratives, autobiographical incidents, firsthand biographies, short stories, and other types of narrative writing. When discussing the selections, draw students' attention to elements of narration such as choosing a point of view, describing characters, and developing a suspenseful plot in which a conflict of some kind is resolved. Point out that students can use the examples of narration they read as models for writing their own narratives. Lead into having students complete narrative writing assignments using the components of the *Writer's Solution*.

CONNECTIONS TO *PRENTICE HALL LITERATURE, COPPER,* SELECTIONS

Short Story	2E	3E
"Zlateh the Goat," Isaac Bashevis Singer	■	▲
"Dragon, Dragon," John Gardner	■	▲
"The King of Mazy May," Jack London	■	▲
"Greyling," Jane Yolen	■	▲
"Sarah Tops," Isaac Asimov	■	▲
"Lob's Girl," Joan Aiken	■	
"Becky and the Wheels-and-Brake Boys," James Berry		▲
"Auntie," Philippa Pearce	■	▲
"The Scribe," Kristen Hunter	■	▲
"Eleven," Sandra Cisneros	■	▲
"Aaron's Gift," Myron Levoy	■	▲
"Mowgli's Brothers," Rudyard Kipling	■	▲

Short Story/Anecdote/Personal Narrative/ Autobiographical Incident/Firsthand Biography	2E	3E
"The Dog of Pompeii," Louis Untermeyer	■	▲
"Thunder Butte," Virginia Driving Hawk Sneve	■	▲
"Breaker's Bridge," Laurence Yep	■	▲
"The Circuit," Francisco Jimenez	■	▲
"The Stone," Lloyd Alexander	■	▲
"The All-American Slurp," Lensey Namioka	■	▲
"Power," Jack Cope	■	▲
"The Sound of Summer Running," Ray Bradbury	■	▲
"The Platoon System," Beverly Cleary	■	▲
"Old Ben," Jesse Stuart	■	▲
Tuck Everlasting, Natalie Babbitt	■	▲

You can also use the *Writer's Solution* materials on narration to guide students through writing activities in response to works of literature.

CONNECTIONS TO *PRENTICE HALL LITERATURE, COPPER,* WRITING ACTIVITIES

Thinking and Writing Activities	2E	3E
Extending the Plot—Follows **"Dragon, Dragon,"** John Gardner	■	▲
Writing as a Story Character—Follows		
"Greyling," Jane Yolen,	■	▲
"Mowgli's Brothers," Rudyard Kipling,	■	▲
and **"The Circuit,"** Francisco Jimenez	■	▲
Extending the Story—Follows **"Becky and the Wheels-and-Brake Boys,"** James Berry	■	▲
Writing About an Experience in School—Follows **"Eleven,"** Sandra Cisneros	■	▲
Predicting Future Actions—Follows **"Thunder Butte,"** Virginia Driving Hawk Sneve	■	▲
Describing an Emotion—Follows **"The Sound of Summer Running,"** Ray Bradbury	■	▲
Writing a Biographical Narrative—Follows from ***Between the Devil and the Sea***, Brenda A. Johnston	■	▲
Writing an Autobiographical Sketch—Follows **"The Platoon System,"** Beverly Cleary	■	▲
Writing a Narrative Essay—Follows **"Old Ben,"** Jesse Stuart	■	▲
Writing a Tale—Follows **"He Lion, Bruh Bear, and Bruh Rabbit,"** Virginia Hamilton	■	▲

Handbook of Writing About Literature / Your Writing Process	2E	3E
Writing a Narrative—Includes activities and assignments		▲
Developing Characters Through Dialogue—Includes activities and assignments		▲
Writing From Personal Experience—Includes activities and assignments		▲

■ **(2E)** *Prentice Hall Literature, Copper,* Second Edition

▲ **(3E)** *Prentice Hall Literature, Copper,* Paramount Edition

CONNECTIONS BETWEEN INSPIRATIONS FOR NARRATION AND *PRENTICE HALL LITERATURE, COPPER*

You can use the multimedia Inspirations for Narration to motivate student reading as well as student writing. Many of the Inspirations are audio recordings or video adaptations of selections from *Prentice Hall Literature, Copper*. Have students work in small groups to look at and discuss an appropriate Inspiration before reading the corresponding selection. Then, after reading the selection, students can replay the Inspiration and select one of the accompanying writing options (see pp. 74–77). The following selections from *Prentice Hall Literature, Copper*, are included in the Inspirations for Narration:

- ***Tuck Everlasting***, Natalie Babbitt
- **"Dragon, Dragon,"** John Gardner
- **"He Lion, Bruh Bear, and Bruh Rabbit,"** Virginia Hamilton

Recommended Lesson Plan

The following lesson plan is recommended for providing students with thorough, comprehensive instructions in narrative writing. Because you may not have all the components of the *Writer's Solution* or may have limited access to equipment, the plan provides a number of options. Choose the options that best suit your teaching style and equipment situation. You may want to add a few days to the lesson plan to allow students time to publish their work and to hold conferences with students to discuss your assessment of their work.

FIVE-DAY LESSON PLAN		
Lesson Outcome:		**Each student writes a complete narrative.**
DAY 1		**Introduce your students to narrative writing.** Show the *Writers at Work Videodisc* segment featuring Virginia Hamilton. Use the segment as a springboard for class discussion or group activities.
DAY 2	 	**Have students choose a writing topic and plan their narratives.** OPTION 1 Have students work either individually or in small groups to look at About Narration and to choose a topic by browsing through the Inspirations for Narration. Then have students work individually to develop their narratives by completing the rest of the Prewriting stage of the tutorial on Narration. At the end of the period, have students print out their Prewriting notes. OPTION 2 Have students review the Models From Literature in the About Narration section of the *Sourcebook*. Then have them choose from the topic suggestions and begin developing their narrative by completing the rest of the Prewriting stage of the Guided Lesson (pp. 72–81).
DAY 3	 	**Have students draft their narratives.** OPTION 1 Have students write their drafts on the computer following the instructions and using the activities provided in the Drafting section of the tutorial on Narration. Have students print out their narratives at the end of the period. OPTION 2 Have students write their drafts on paper following the instructions in the Guided Lesson (pp. 82–84).

FIVE-DAY LESSON PLAN (continued)

DAY 4

Have students revise their narratives.

OPTION 1 Have students revise their narratives on the computer using the revision checkers, activities, and suggestions in the Revising and Editing section of the tutorial on Narration.

OPTION 2 Have students revise their narratives following the suggestions in the Guided Lesson (pp. 85–86).

DAY 5

Have students work in peer groups to make final revisions.

OPTION 1 Have pairs of students review each other's work following the guidelines in the peer revision section of the tutorial on Narration. The pairs should then hold conferences before each student makes final revisions. Students should then proofread and print out their final drafts.

OPTION 2 Have pairs of students review each other's work following the guidelines in the Guided Lesson (p. 86). The pairs should then hold conferences before each student makes final revisions.

Condensed Lesson Plans

Use the following lesson plans if you don't have a full week to devote to teaching Narration:

Four- and Three-Day Plans: Adapt the Five-Day Plan by having students learn about narration, choose a topic, and develop ideas for their narratives all during Day 1. As in the Five-Day Plan, have students spend a day writing their drafts. For a Four-Day Plan, follow the last two days of the Five-Day Plan; for a Three-Day Plan, simply condense these two days into a single day of revision and forgo the option of working in peer groups.

TWO-DAY LESSON PLAN

Lesson Outcome: **Each student writes a complete narrative.**

DAY 4

Have students choose a topic and write their first drafts.

OPTION 1 Have students work in the open-ended environment in the *Writing Lab*. Working individually, students should choose a topic by browsing through the Inspirations for Narration. Then they should write their narratives in the Writing Notebook using the available prewriting tools as needed.

OPTION 2 Using the suggestions and instructions in the *Sourcebook*, students should choose a topic and write a first draft of their narratives.

DAY 5

Have students revise and edit their work.

OPTION 1 Have students revise on the computer using the tools, activities, and instructions in the tutorial on Narration.

OPTION 2 Have students revise their narratives following the suggestions in the *Sourcebook*.

One-Day Lesson Plan: Students can work individually in the open-ended environment in the *Writing Lab* by browsing through the Inspirations for Narration to choose a topic, using the Prewriting tools as needed, then completing a quick-write draft of a narrative in their on-line Notebooks. Students may also use the *Sourcebook* to choose a topic and write a brief narrative.

Preparing to Teach

Lesson Objectives

Students will

1. Explore types and elements of narratives
2. Select an appropriate topic for a narrative
3. Write a narrative involving well-developed characters, a well-developed plot, and a clearly described setting
4. Revise their narratives to strengthen the characters, plot, and setting
5. Proofread their narratives for errors in spelling, grammar, and punctuation
6. Publish completed narratives

Activating Prior Knowledge

Tell students that narration is the process of telling a story. Invite volunteers to orally present summaries of stories, either based on their own experiences, true or made-up tales they can recall, or stories they make up right on the spot. Ask the class: *What makes a good story? What makes some stories better than others? What is the hardest part about writing a story?*

CHAPTER 3

An Elder Wearing Otuogwu Cloth Talking to a Teen Boy *John Mainga, LAMU, The Gallery of Contemporary African Art*

Narration

"We all tell stories, and of course we all have our own stories."

—Virginia Hamilton
Fiction Writer and Biographer

Humanities Note

The fine art is a painting called *An Elder Wearing Otuogwu Cloth Talking to a Teen Boy*, by John Mainga (1954–). African artist John Mainga gained a fine reputation as a clothing and textile designer in the city of Nairobi, Kenya. His cotton batik patterns are unusual in their depth of feeling and imaginative character. This exceptional quality is evident in his leather paintings on traditional African themes.

At first glance the painting *An Elder Wearing Otuogwu Cloth Talking to a Teen Boy* seems to be a complex design rather than a scene. Upon closer examination, the blending of subtly colored patterns becomes two figures inside a Nigerian dwelling. The richness of the pattern in this work speaks of John Mainga's experience in textile design.

The outside world seen through the doorway on the right is also stylized, but in contrast to the inside of the dwelling seems simple, almost plain. This may symbolize how human beings elaborate on nature's design. You might use the following questions as a basis for class discussion:

- Describe what is happening in this scene. What might the elder be telling the boy who has come to see him?
- The artist chose to paint this scene in a patterned style. What does this style add to the story told in the painting?
- How could you use the technique of patterning in telling a story? What kind of an effect would patterning have?

Addressing Your Classroom Situation

This chapter includes a variety of Models From Literature, writing topics, writing process strategies, and Student Models, along with two integrated skills lessons. Feel free to pick and choose from this material to create a customized lesson on narration that matches your classroom needs.

The following are some of the key features of the chapter:

- The chapter begins with a section introducing narration. This section includes thoughts about narration from writer Virginia Hamilton, group discussion questions, and Models From Literature for the following types of narration: autobiographical incident, anecdote, personal narrative, firsthand biography, short story.
- The Prewriting section includes an assortment of idea-generating activities to help students choose a type of narration, select a topic, and develop their characters, setting, and plot, along with some suggested topics from which they can select. This section also provides instruction and activities to help students consider their audience and purpose. Writing Models guide them through the process of developing all elements of their narratives, writing to their audience, and through other stages of the narration process.
- The Drafting section addresses the issues of how to begin a narrative, how to choose a point of view for a narrative, and suggests tips for sequencing events in the story and dealing with writer's block.
- The Revising and Editing section provides a checklist for self-evaluation and one for peer review, a tool for checking language variety, revising and proofreading tips, and strategies for working with a peer editor.
- The guided writing instruction is followed by a Student Model and then skills lessons on using precise and vivid verbs and using transitions.
- The chapter ends with a Model From Literature, a partial chapter excerpt from *The Bells of Christmas*, a novel by Virginia Hamilton.

Chapter Contents

About Narration

Guided Lesson

Student Model

Developing Your Style 1

Developing Your Style 2

Literature Model

"I grew up in a family of storytellers. Both my mother and father told wonderful stories. They could make them up on the spot."

"Narration is the accounting or telling of events through time. The march of words across the page takes us where we want to go."

—Virginia Hamilton
Fiction Writer and Biographer

"I begin every book with character. When you write a character, you're placing that character in time and place."

More About the Writer

Virginia Hamilton grew up in Ohio, where her grandfather settled after escaping from slavery. Most of her work has been fiction for young adults.

Virginia Hamilton has said that she "grew up in a family of storytellers." Talk with your students about what they think are the qualities of a good storyteller. Ask them to tell which quality is the most important one to have. Invite students to share personal anecdotes about storytelling experiences.

ech Prep Note

oint out that not only writ-
rs like Virginia Hamilton use
arration. Workers in other
elds write on the job.
)octors, nurses, and others in
ne medical field frequently
rite anecdotal records. So
o teachers and auto mechan-
:s. Some workers even con-
ibute anecdotes or short stories to company or industry-wide publications. Ask: *Think about the adults you know and the jobs they have. How do they use their narrative skills at work?*

Introducing Narration

Teaching Options

There are a variety of ways you can introduce narration using the components of the *Writer's Solution:*

- You can show the Narration segment from the *Writers at Work Videodisc.* Use this segment as a springboard for a class discussion on narration.
- You can have students work individually or in small groups to go through the About Narration section of the Narration tutorial in the *Writing Lab* CD-ROM.
- You can work through the About Narration section of the *Sourcebook* with the class.
- You can have students read the About Narration section of the *Sourcebook* before class starts, so that as a group you can concentrate on the videodisc or CD-ROM lesson.

Sourcebook

Have students read aloud and discuss the About Narration section of the *Sourcebook.* Use the following questions to guide the discussion:

- How can you recognize narration? Where might you find examples of narrative writing?
- Why would people seek out narrative writing?
- What makes narrative writing important?
- How is writing to tell a story different from writing a report or writing a description of something? How is it similar?

About Narration

What Is Narration?

Every time you tell a friend what you did over the weekend or describe a family vacation, you are using narration. **Narration** is the process of telling a story. Narratives can be true-life stories based on actual events or they can be made up. Usually, you meet the main characters near the beginning of the story, follow them as events unfold, and learn what happens to them at the end.

Group Discussion What stories have you told in the last few days? What kinds of stories have you heard? With a group of your classmates, talk about the plots of some recent movies or television shows you've seen or some books you've read. What was it about them that you liked or disliked? Then discuss some interesting events in which you've participated. What happened? Who was involved? As you relate these stories, think about the details that interest you and make you eager to hear more.

New York Historical Society

64 • Narration

Following the class discussion, divide your students into groups of three to five to engage in the group discussion on this page.

Writers at Work Videodisc

Use the Narration section of the videodisc, featuring writer Virginia Hamilton, as a springboard into a class discussion on narration. Play the chapter in its entirety, pausing as needed. Then feel free to use the bar codes to replay any segment to reinforce an important idea.

After students have viewed the video, have them take turns sharing their responses. Then move into a discussion of the writing techniques and personal insights that Hamilton share Ask:

- Why do you think that to Virginia Hamilton, writin a narrative is just like telling a story?
- What does Hamilton say about the element of time in narration? How can yo

How a Professional Writer Uses Narration

Writers use narration to weave stories for their readers. In creating her narratives—whether mysteries, folk tales, or biographies—award-winning writer Virginia Hamilton thinks about three things: what she knows, what she remembers, and what she can imagine. Here she tells us how they contribute to her narratives:

> "The *known* is all of the facts, past and present, that you need to know in order to write a story. The *remembered* is what you take from your past experiences. And the *imagined* is the imagination that puts together all those facts and all those memories into a new idea for a story.
>
> For instance, [the idea for M. C. *Higgins the Great*] started with the image of a boy running through the woods with a lettuce leaf attached to his wrist. So I started writing down what I saw. . . . All these ideas pop into your mind. Where is he going? Why is he running? Where does he live? Oh, I see, this is a mountain. This is a mountain path. There's somebody off the path that's shadowing him. He's running to his rabbit traps; that's why he has a lettuce leaf. Before you know it, there is a story working."

How Narration Fits Into Your Life

"The game was so boring!" "The trip was so exciting!" Statements like these are often the beginning of narratives—stories you tell every day to your friends, your teachers, your family. When you tell a story, you speak about the people involved in an event or situation and the outcome. In the same way, when you write a narrative, you weave a story about characters and their experiences.

show the passage of time when telling a story?

Play frames 22007 to 31109

Writing Lab CD-ROM

The About Narration section of the tutorial on Narration includes the following options to help students understand what narration is:

- **Author video clip** Students play a video to hear Virginia Hamilton's thoughts about narration.
- **Models of narration, with audio annotations** Students gain insights about the elements of different types of narratives.
- **Self-Evaluation Checklist** These guidelines can be presented to students either before or after they draft their narratives.

Writing Lab CD-ROM

Students can work individually or in small groups to complete the tutorial on Narration. Or, if you have access to a projection panel, you can work through the About Narration section with the entire class, discussing each part as you go.

Writers at Work Videodisc

Discuss with students what Virginia Hamilton means by the three things she says she thinks about when she writes. Invite volunteers to tell which of the three they think would be the most significant to someone writing a narrative—what the person knows, what the person remembers, or what the person can imagine.

Play frames 23551 to 24577

Real-World Writing

Help students identify people in your community who write narratives. These people might be local radio personalities, storytellers, or newspaper columnists.

Have students look for examples of narrative writing. They'll find them in posters, and in creative ads in bus and train stations. As students share their findings, ask:

- What common features, if any, do you notice among the different examples you saw?

Integrating Literature With Writing

Starting From Literature

You can use the models on pages 66–70 to illustrate the various elements of each type of narration. Or you can use the content or devices used in these pieces to inspire writing on any of the topics they address. For example, have students use their reactions to Beverly Cleary's autobiographical incident to write their own autobiographical incident recalling events leading to a discovery they made.

Teaching Strategy

You may wish to briefly introduce and define the type of writing each selection models. You might invite a student to read each piece aloud to the class. Follow up with discussion to reinforce students' understanding of each type of narration.

Clarification

Some students may be confused by all the different kinds of narratives presented here. Guide them to appreciate that each kind is simply a story, whether made up or true. Tell them that if it's a story, then it is a narrative.

Teaching From the Model

Guide students to analyze this excerpt from Beverly Cleary's book to understand the characteristics of an autobiographical incident:

- *It is a true story of an event in the writer's life.* This excerpt recalls an experience the writer had one Sunday evening.
- *It describes a significant incident in the writer's life.* Cleary discovered the pleasure of writing that rainy evening. She says that since then, she feels the urge to write whenever it rains.

Types of Narration

Virginia Hamilton says that narration is "the march of words across the page [that] takes us where we want to go, from the beginning to the logical end." Narration takes many forms, such as novels, short stories, anecdotes, biographies, and autobiographical incidents. Following are examples of different kinds of narratives:

1 Autobiographical Incident

- An autobiography is a writer's first-person account of his or her own life.
- An autobiographical incident is the true story of one event or occurrence in the writer's life.

Model From Literature

In this excerpt from *A Girl from Yamhill*, Beverly Cleary sets the scene for an autobiographical incident—her discovery of the pleasure of writing. Notice that Cleary provides specific details that help readers share the experience. She ends her account by explaining the importance of the incident.

That weekend, Mother happened to be visiting her parents in Banks, where Grandpa Atlee had bought back his store. . . . After I put together a Sunday dinner for my father, who gamely ate it and was enjoying his pipe and the Sunday paper, I sat down to write the essay. Which favorite character when I had so many? . . . I finally solved this problem by writing about a girl who went to Bookland and talked to several of my favorite characters. I wrote on and on, inventing conversations that the characters might have had with a strange girl. As rain beat against the windows, a feeling of peace came over me as I wrote far beyond the required length of the essay. I had discovered the pleasure of writing, and to this day, whenever it rains, I feel the urge to write.

Clarification

You may wish to discuss with students the distinction between an autobiographical incident and a personal narrative. Point out that whereas both are retellings of true stories in the writer's life, and both include some of the writer's thoughts and feelings, an autobiographical incident always relates a time when the writer gained an important insight. On the other hand, a personal narrative need not be about a significant moment in the writer's life.

2 Anecdote

- An anecdote is a short entertaining story that can be written or told aloud.
- It usually relates an interesting or amusing experience that happened to the storyteller.

Model From Literature

In the following anecdote from "Creature Design," Carlo Rambaldi tells about his first experience working for movie director and producer Steven Spielberg. His job was to design the alien that appears at the end of the movie *Close Encounters of the Third Kind.* Notice that Rambaldi presents background information informally and narrates events in the order in which they occurred:

After working on the film *White Buffalo*, I went back to Italy, where Steven Spielberg contacted me. I did not know Spielberg at all, but apparently he had seen King Kong and wanted me to design an extraterrestrial for his completed movie *Close Encounters of the Third Kind*. All he was missing was the alien that appears at the end of the picture.

I drew my idea of what the being should look like and sent it to him. By phone, Steven told me he liked the drawing. . . . I sculpted and built the extraterrestrial being in Italy and sent it over here. During the shooting, once in a while, Steven Spielberg would yell out to the others on the set, "Okay, everybody, pay attention! Here comes the extraterrestrial from Italy!"

Teaching From the Model

Guide students to recognize that the Carlo Rambaldi excerpt is an example of the type of narration known as an anecdote:

- *It relates an interesting and entertaining experience the storyteller had.* The writer describes the high-interest experience he had designing the alien for the hugely popular film by director Steven Spielberg. Theatergoers sat at the edges of their seats awaiting what the alien would look like.
- *It is an informal retelling of events in the order in which they occurred.* Rambaldi describes what happened in time order, from initial phone contacts with the director to events on the set.

Cross-Curricular Connection: *Art and Science*

Some students might be interested in writing an anecdote—about an amusing experience they had creating, inventing, or building something—that focuses on reactions to their efforts.

Teaching From the Model

Guide students to understand the characteristics of this type of narration by reading and discussing the excerpt from *Nadja on My Way:*

- *It is a story about a significant event that happened to the writer in the past.* In this excerpt, Salerno-Sonnenberg tells about the time her family decided to move from Italy to the United States.
- *It includes some of the writer's thoughts and feelings.* Salerno-Sonnenberg expresses her excitement about going to America and learning English.

Thematic Connection: Turning Points/Transitions

Have students recall a time in their lives just prior to a significant move or life change. Ask them to describe the situation they faced and how it made them feel. Students may choose to develop one of their remembrances as the topic for their narration.

3 Personal Narrative

- A personal narrative is a story about something that happened to you.
- It could be a story about events long past or a recent occurrence.

Model From Literature

In the following excerpt from *Nadja on My Way*, concert violinist Nadja Salerno-Sonnenberg writes about a significant event in her childhood. Salerno begins by summarizing the events that led up to her move to America. Because this is a personal narrative, Salerno includes some of her thoughts and feelings.

By the time I was eight, I had gotten better and better at the violin. Signore Marchetti told my mother and grandparents, "Nadja has promise, and I've taught her everything I can."

If they were interested, and if they were serious, he said, America was the place for a violinist to study. They thought it over, discussed it, and in the end, we started packing. . . . I must say I was more excited about going to America than sad to leave Italy. Even the language was exciting. Everyone in my family spoke English, and they taught me my first words: "Yankees," "America," and "hot dog."

4 Firsthand Biography

- A firsthand biography is a story about someone the writer knows personally.
- It might tell the story of the subject's life or it might relate just one event or episode.
- The writer usually plays a part in a firsthand biography but is not the main character.

Model From Literature

In the following excerpt from "Virginia Hamilton," the writer Lee Bennett Hopkins reveals what he had observed firsthand about Hamilton's personality. Notice that he includes himself in the description, making it clear that he knows Hamilton personally.

She is the kind of person one loves to be around. . . . I know her as being bubbly and bouncy, with a never-stand-still way about her that makes one quickly perceive her sparkling, contagious enthusiasm for life.

Miss Hamilton grew up in Yellow Springs, an Ohio village that had been a station on the Underground Railroad. The rural community, about sixty miles north of the Ohio River, is the home of Antioch College. The population includes descendants of abolitionists and fugitive slaves.

Underground Railroad
1982, Oberlin Seniors,
Courtesy of the artists

Teaching From the Model

Guide students to analyze this excerpt to understand how it exemplifies the characteristics of a firsthand biography:

- *It is about someone the writer knows personally.* Lee Bennett Hopkins knows Virginia Hamilton well enough to describe her as being ". . . bubbly and bouncy, with a never-stand-still way about her. . . ."
- *The writer plays a part in the story, but not the leading role.* Hopkins includes himself in the description when he writes that he has been around her and knows her.

Teaching From the Model

Guide students to analyze this passage from a John Gardner story to understand how it is an effective opening for a short story:

- *It is fictional.* Kingdoms are not and never were plagued by dragons, except in the imagination of storytellers.
- *The characters have a problem or conflict to solve.* The king and his wizard are at wits' end over their efforts to rid the realm of the dragon.

Thematic Connection: Imagination

Challenge students to brainstorm story ideas involving modern-day efforts to save your community from a fearsome dragon. Invite students who choose this writing option to select one of these topics for their short story.

Exploring Related Literature

For additional examples of short stories about fantastic characters, settings, or plots, invite students to read "Mowgli's Brothers," by Rudyard Kipling, and "Greyling," by Jane Yolen, in *Prentice Hall Literature, Copper.*

5 Short Story

- A short story is a brief fictional narrative.
- The characters in the story usually have a problem or a conflict that is resolved by the end of the story.
- The characters, setting, and problem can seem realistic or they can be completely fantastic.

Model From Literature

The following passage is from the opening of "Dragon, Dragon," a short story by John Gardner. Notice that Gardner reveals what his characters are like by making direct statements about them and by describing their actions.

> There was once a king whose kingdom was plagued by a dragon. The king did not know which way to turn. The king's knights were all cowards who hid under their beds whenever the dragon came in sight, so they were of no use to the king at all. And the king's wizard could not help either because, being old, he had forgotten his magic spells. Nor could the wizard look up the spells that had slipped his mind, for he had unfortunately misplaced his wizard's book many years before. The king was at his wit's end.

Language Acquisition/ ESL Teaching Strategy

The *Writing Lab* offers a variety of options that can be adapted to meet the needs of ESL students. The following are some examples of such adaptations.

- The Developing Narrative

Guided Lesson

Now that you have learned about different types of narration, you're ready to begin working on your own narrative writing. This lesson will help guide you through the process of writing your story. You may not want to start at the beginning of the lesson, however. Consider any ideas you have in mind for your narrative writing. Then use this chart to decide where to begin.

	START WITH
• If you **do not have a topic**	Choosing Your Topic
• If you **have narrowed your topic but need to determine the appropriate language and content for your readers**	Considering Audience and Purpose
• If you are **ready to plan the structure of your narrative and the details you will include**	Developing Narrative Elements
• If you **have a topic for your narrative and enough details to work with**	Drafting

Guiding Student Writing

Elements section includes a video clip from *The Jungle Book* in which students are told how to develop a character through direct description. Working in pairs, your upper basic and intermediate ESL students play the video and take notes on how to use direct description and record examples of how it is done in the excerpt. The students then write short descriptions of characters from *The Jungle Book* or characters from their own stories.

- The Drafting section offers Models From Literature, each showing a different way to begin a narrative. This option can be adapted to meet the needs of your advanced ESL students. As the students review the different passages, they jot down their ideas on why the authors may have chosen a particular way to begin their narratives—for example, with a description of a character, action, or setting. They write ideas on the advantages and disadvantages of using one type of introduction over another. Based on their notes, they decide on the best format for beginning their own narratives.
- The Revising and Editing section offers a Peer Review Checklist that can be used with your intermediate and advanced ESL students. The students take notes on the pointers that the checklist provides; they then use those notes when reading a classmate's narrative. It is suggested that an intermediate student be paired with an advanced student. Emphasis should be placed on discussion of the pointers and their application to ensure that all students understand the rationale involved in the evaluation.

Addressing Your Classroom Situation

- If you choose to assign topics or types of narration, allow time for students to narrow the topic to suit their interests or find an appealing focus to pursue.
- You may wish to have students work in pairs. If so, brainstorm ways partners might collaborate usefully and fairly. One way, for example, for two students to write a short story together is to come up with the characters, setting, and plot as a team, and then have one begin the story and the other finish it.

Writing Lab CD-ROM

The Choosing Your Topic section includes the following options to help students come up with their own topics:

- **Topic Wheel** Students generate story ideas by combining characters and situations until they find a combination that sparks their interest.
- **Instruction in freewriting, with audio annotations** Students choose words to hear insights about freewriting.
- **Storyboard activity** Students look through photographs to find a few they can arrange in a sequence that suggests a story.

Working individually or in small groups, students can experiment with these activities to find the ones that work best.

Writers at Work Videodisc

Play the videodisc segment in which Virginia Hamilton discusses getting topics for stories. Ask:

- What do you think about Hamilton's contention that ideas for her stories can come from a single image or scene? Have you ever had a similar experience? Explain.

Play frames 24578 to 25743

Prewriting

Choosing Your Topic

What will your narrative be about? Will you write a short story or a personal narrative based on real-life incidents? Decide on the type of narration you'd like to write. Then either choose from the selection of suggested writing options (see pages 74–77) or experiment with the following techniques to come up with your own topic.

If you're considering

. . . a firsthand biography:

TALK TO PEOPLE YOU ADMIRE

In your journal, list several people you admire—relatives, friends, teachers, your doctor or dentist, a classmate—noting their most admirable qualities. Then arrange to talk with three or four of them. Write down some questions to ask them about their lives—their childhoods, educations, career goals, joys, and disappointments. As you interview each person, take careful notes. Then review your notes to find inspiration for a firsthand biography.

. . . a personal narrative or an autobiographical incident:

TAKE A WALK IN YOUR NEIGHBORHOOD

You can find many memories close to home. Take a walk around your neighborhood. Who lives in the nearby houses or apartments? Who are the shopkeepers? What experiences have you had with these people? Where do you go with your friends? What parks did you play in? What events have occurred in these places that made an impression on you? Take a notebook with you on your walk and jot down your memories of people and places. Then review your notes to find topics for a personal narrative or an autobiographical incident.

Cultural Connection

Students interested in writing a firsthand biography can take this opportunity to talk with a person who is actively researching, celebrating, or in some other way advancing aspects of the cultural connections in their community. They can interview poets and novelists, artists, politicians, theatrical performers, entertainers, community activists, and others. Advise students who have access to tape recorders to use them and then transcribe their notes after the interview.

Teaching Strategy

Suggest to students that they keep a notebook to use exclusively for jotting down story ideas and other writing ideas. Suggest that the notebook should be small enough to carry around conveniently. It should also be chosen for its appeal or decorated as the student likes, so that he or she will treat it with care. Guide students, as they walk in the neighborhood, to record incidents and events they witness—as well as things they overhear or read—as inspirations for future writing.

. . . a fantastic story:

GIVE OBJECTS MAGICAL QUALITIES

One type of short story is a fantasy, in which magical things occur. Look around your house or neighborhood and imagine what would happen if furniture, buildings, or vehicles suddenly came to life. A chair talks, a house groans, and your bicycle takes flight. Think about magical qualities that inanimate objects might have. Take notes as you survey your surroundings. Then review your notes to find a fantastic tale to tell.

. . . an anecdote:

LOOK THROUGH PHOTOGRAPHS OR YOUR SCRAPBOOK

Photographs of celebrations and souvenirs from vacations or local events will help you remember amusing situations. Look through your scrapbooks and family albums. Think about the people, places, and activities. What happened that was unusual, funny, or outrageous? Take notes on your most interesting memories. Then review your notes to find a topic for an entertaining anecdote.

. . . a short story:

Group Activity

USE MAGAZINES AND YOUR IMAGINATION

Gather with a group of your classmates and go through several magazines. They may be news, sports, fashion, nature, or entertainment magazines. As you leaf through the pages, stop whenever pictures of people, animals, or situations catch your eye. As a group, discuss the kinds of lives the people might lead, the adventures the animals might have, or the outcomes of the situations depicted. Write down the most interesting ideas. Then review your notes to find a topic for a short story.

Thematic Connection: Humor

Suggest to students interested in writing an anecdote about a family event that they interview family members to hear remembrances of times past and get ideas for writing. Students can take notes during the interview or even tape-record the discussion.

Writing Lab CD-ROM

Using the Inspirations for Narration in the *Writing Lab* is an excellent way to stimulate creativity and to have students explore possible topics for narration. Students can browse individually or in small groups through the Inspirations. They can choose their own writing topics or you may prefer to assign topics.

The following is a list of the narration options included in the Inspirations, but not provided in the *Sourcebook*:

Anecdote

- About similar qualities

Personal Narrative About

- Animals in nature
- Nature
- Something suspenseful
- A turning point
- Taking a risk
- Letting something go
- A decision
- Getting along with others
- A personal celebration
- A family or community celebration
- Yourself
- A shared experience
- Friendship
- A helpful friend

Autobiographical Incident

- About change
- About a good-bye
- That shows your individuality
- About an achievement
- About disappointment
- Practicing hard

Firsthand Biography

- About turning points
- Of a special person you parted from
- About an older person

Short Story That

- Is suspenseful and about a sporting event
- Is a tale about regaining youth
- Is a tale about an animal feature
- Is set among buttes
- Is about a frightening encounter
- Has a surprise ending
- Solves a problem
- Has a humorous conflict
- Is about a magical creature
- Is about a familiar story
- Is about facing something frightening
- Is about nature
- Is about a unicorn
- Is about owls
- Is an adventure story about yourself
- Is about a race
- Is about a wish
- Is a tale about birds in flocks

The Village Dance *by Javran*

Inspirations for Narration

The following are some writing topics for narration:

An Anecdote About a Wish

What are some things people wish for in real life? For example, some people might wish to win a contest or become famous. When these wishes come true, what kinds of unexpected problems arise? Write an anecdote about a time when you or someone you know had a wish come true that didn't turn out as expected. Your anecdote should show how it isn't always good to get what you wish for.

An Anecdote About a Celebration

Many of the villagers in the painting above seem to be laughing as they celebrate. Someone must have said or done something funny to make so many people laugh. Think about large celebrations you have attended. Then write an anecdote that tells something humorous that took place at one of these gatherings.

A Firsthand Biography of an Adult

Most adults have fond memories of important events from their youth, and they often relive these experiences by recalling their past. Interview a parent or another adult about his or her youth. Use the information from your interview to write a firsthand biography about an important experience in this person's life.

Group Project

Assemble Autobiographical Incidents Involving Animals

Some animals seem vicious and aggressive when in fact they are not. Other animals have reputations for being cute and cuddly when in fact they can be dangerous. As a group, brainstorm about your encounters with animals that turned out to be different from what they first appeared. Then have each group member write an autobiographical incident describing an experience with such an animal. Each narrative should contrast the animal's appearance or reputation with its true nature. Assemble the narratives in a classroom display with drawings or photographs.

An Autobiographical Incident About an Experience You'd Like to Relive

If you could choose one experience in your life that you could relive, what would it be? Think about the most memorable experiences in your life—the good ones and the bad. Was there a particularly exciting or joyful event that you would love to experience again? Was there an experience or decision that you wish you could change—a situation that you would handle differently if only you could live through it again? Write an autobiographical incident about the experience and tell why you want a second chance.

An Autobiographical Incident About a Helpful Friend

Although most people enjoy sharing happy moments with their friends, a good friend is also someone with whom you can share your problems too. Think of a time when a friend of yours helped you through a difficult time. Write an autobiographical incident about it. What problem did you face? How did your friend help? What was the outcome? What might have happened without your friend's help? Use details and vivid language to express how you felt as well as what actually happened.

Teaching Strategy

Guide students who wish to write a firsthand biography of an adult to be sensitive to the needs and privacy of the adults they interview. Tell them that not all adults will be comfortable sharing difficult or painful experiences with them. Advise students to show respect for this reticence, and to interview others, as needed.

Writing Lab CD-ROM

The Inspirations for Narration in the *Writing Lab* also include the following Group Projects and Group Discussions. The Group Discussions encourage small groups of students to share their thoughts about an Inspiration and to generate possible writing topics. The Group Projects are structured activities in which students assume different roles.

Group Projects

- Making timelines about flight
- Creating a storybook
- Correcting animal reputations
- Sportscasting a decision
- Creating a dragon mural
- Creating a modern folk tale
- Creating a holiday display
- Creating an anthology of stories with related themes
- Creating a book of biographies of artists
- Writing jokes

Group Discussions

- Discussing contact sports
- Discussing eternal youth
- Working for change
- Discussing conflict and compromise
- Discussing how to eliminate prejudice
- Discussing winning and losing
- Appreciating different generations

MORE *Inspirations* for Narration

A Personal Narrative About a Sports Event

Basketball and hockey games, figure-skating competitions, and tennis matches can be exciting, action-packed events. What sports do you enjoy? Think about sports events you have either participated in or watched. Choose an event that was especially exciting or had a surprise ending. Then write a personal narrative about that event. Use details to create an accurate and lively picture of what happened.

A Tale About a Mythical Creature

Throughout the ages, mythical creatures—such as unicorns, dragons, trolls, elves, mermaids, and mermen—have been the subject of fascinating narratives in stories, poems, and works of art. Choose a mythical creature and write a tale, or story, about it. You might want to write from the point of view of a human encountering the creature or you might want to write from the point of view of the creature. How and where did the creature live? What adventures did it have? What caused its disappearance? You may include some historical facts in your story or make it completely fictional.

A Personal Narrative About a Lesson You've Learned

Older people pass down skills and knowledge to younger generations. Can you think of one thing you learned from an older friend or relative? How did you learn it? Write a personal narrative about this experience. In addition to telling what you learned, include details of how you felt about the experience and the person.

Group Project: Compile a Book of Stories Based on a Common Setting

Imagine that you are part of a team assigned to create a series of stories to film in a particular location—say, in the buttes or mesas of the Southwest or the streets of a large city in the Northeast. Using one of these locations or another of your choice, decide what kinds of stories might be appropriate. Keeping in mind that the stories are to be filmed, discuss how the location might affect the action of the story. Then each team member should write a story set in that location. Compile the narratives into a book. Add illustrations that convey the physical characteristics and the atmosphere of the setting.

Collaborative Learning

Within each story-creating group, students compiling the book of stories can share the tasks of recording locations, listing ways the locations might affect story topics, writing and editing the stories themselves, and assembling an anthology of these locale-centered stories. One member of the group can collect photos to accompany the collection. Another can find music appropriate for the stories. For example, Native American flute music might work well with stories to be filmed among mesas. If students present the stories orally, music and photos might enhance the presentation.

Bergheuer *by Ernst Ludwig Kirchner, Christie's, London*

A Firsthand Biography of a Person Who Helped You Grow

Which person in your life has helped you become an individual or more mature? Was the person a relative, a teacher, or a coach? Write a firsthand biographical account about this person. Relate incidents that reveal the person's character and how he or she enriched your life.

A Tale About a Figure in a Painting

You can see one woman talking to three men and another woman in the painting above. Imagine that the woman has just returned from a frightening experience. What happened? What did she see or hear? Write the tale that you imagine this woman is revealing. Use the first-person point of view and include vivid details to describe the setting and events.

Cross-Curricular Connection: *Art*

Invite students interested in writing a narrative based on what they see in a painting (p. 77) to browse through art books in the school or public library for inspirations. If students have access to an art museum or a local gallery, suggest that pairs pay a visit. You may wish to challenge your advanced students to attempt a story based on an abstract painting.

Writing Lab CD-ROM

The Considering Audience and Purpose section of the tutorial on Narration includes the following options to help students gear their writing to an intended audience:

- **Video clip from a *Star Trek* episode** Students play a video to see and hear what happens when language is used that an audience won't understand.
- **Audience Profile** Students answer questions that help them focus on how best to write for their intended audience.
- **Interactive instruction with audio annotations** Students read two versions of the same story, one written for a general audience and one for photography enthusiasts, then hear about how the choice of audience affected the writing (same models appear in *Sourcebook*, page 78).

Working individually or in small groups, students can experiment with these activities to find the ones that work best for them.

Writing Strategy

Guide students to think carefully about their intended audience in order to try to predict their reactions. Encourage them to respond in writing to the following questions, and to attach the answers to their drafts: *How much does your audience know about your topic? Will it be as meaningful to them as it is to you? If not, what can you do to hold their interest?*

Prewriting

Considering Your Audience

Who will be the readers of your narrative? Ask yourself what type of language and details will appeal to them. If you're writing for young children, for example, you'll want to use simple language. If you're writing for friends and classmates, you'll want the conflict and characters to be meaningful and interesting to people in your age group. To see how different audiences can affect your writing, look at these Writing Models about San Francisco. The first version was written for a general audience, and the second one was written for readers of a photography magazine.

Writing Models

GENERAL AUDIENCE

In this version written for a general audience, the writer focuses on giving details of San Francisco's spectacular scenery. This is the kind of information that would appeal to everyone.

VIEW FROM A SAN FRANCISCO HILLTOP

As I reached the top of the hill, the view that greeted me took my breath away. I was glad I had walked instead of taking the cable car, because I felt I had earned the reward of this spectacular view. As I gazed out at the bay, I could see all the way from the Golden Gate Bridge to a distant range of hills north of the bay.

READERS OF A PHOTOGRAPHY MAGAZINE

Although the writer of this version also enjoys the scenery, he is mainly interested in photography. His narrative contains the kinds of technical details that would appeal to readers of a photography magazine.

VIEW FROM A SAN FRANCISCO HILLTOP

As I reached the top of the hill, I was completely out of breath. I was carrying 35 pounds of cameras, lenses, and film in my pack, and I was sorry I had walked instead of taking the cable car. I stopped to get out my Nikon 35-millimeter single-lens reflex camera. I wanted to get a shot of the Golden Gate Bridge, and from this distance I needed my telephoto lens.

Teaching Strategy

Read the two models about San Francisco to the class. To reinforce how these models reflect writing for different audiences, invite a pair of volunteers to work together to present two brief oral passages on a topic about which they are knowledgeable. One of the passages should be for a general audience, and the other aimed at people who are well acquainted with the topic. For example, the pair can talk about an obscure television program or computer game that has hooked them both. One student can speak to the group assuming that classmates are familiar with the show's or game's characters, plot lines, and specific terminology, and th other can address the group assuming no such prior knowledge. Have the pair present their narratives to t class. Ask students to descri differences between them.

Considering Your Purpose

A narrative could have many purposes. You may want to inform your readers, entertain your readers, or praise a friend or relative. In fact, a single narrative may have more than one purpose.

If you're having trouble deciding on your purpose, start by considering the form of your narrative. At right is a list of types of narratives and their possible purposes.

Writing Model

TYPE OF NARRATIVE	POSSIBLE PURPOSE
Personal Narrative	To share a childhood experience; to examine an important event in your life
Autobiographical Incident	To relive an experience; to get a new perspective on a past event
Anecdote	To share a funny story about yourself; to amuse readers with a true-life story; to share an interesting experience
Firsthand Biography	To praise a friend or relative; to draw a picture of a person you admire using words
Short Story	To send a message; to examine the nature of human life; to create a fantasy world

Developing Narrative Elements

What are the elements of a narrative? A good narrative places the **characters** in a **setting**, or a time and a place. As the **plot**, or sequence of events, unfolds, readers get to know the characters. Before you begin drafting, gather details for each of these important elements of your narrative.

Writing Lab CD-ROM

The Considering Audience and Purpose section of the tutorial on Narration includes the following options to help students explore ways to focus the purpose of their writing:

- **Interactive instruction—tips for accomplishing a writing purpose** Students choose different purposes for writing to get pointers for accomplishing each one.
- **Model From Literature, with audio annotations** Students read an excerpt from "The Dog of Pompeii," then choose passages from it to hear about how each was written for a specific purpose.
- **Interactive instruction—tips for choosing a writing purpose** Students choose different forms of narratives to see some possible writing purposes for each.

Working individually or in small groups, students can experiment with these activities to find the ones that work best for them.

Language Lab CD-ROM

If students need dditional guidance in deternining how best to deal with he issues of audience and urpose, you may want them o complete the Considering Audience and Purpose lesson n the Composing unit.

Writing Strategies

Guide students to make their narratives more powerful by making their writing purpose more specific. Tell them that the more specific their purpose is, the more focused their writing will be. For example, *to write a tale about a mythical creature in order to entertain the reader and to share an observation about life* is a more specific writing purpose than simply *to tell a tale about a mythical creature in order to entertain*.

Point out to students that part of a writer's purpose in a narrative, particularly in a short story, is often to communicate to readers a feeling, an idea, or a belief. This intended message about life is known as the *theme* of the narrative. Guide students to consider keeping a theme in mind when they write their narratives.

Writing Lab CD-ROM

The Developing Narrative Elements section includes the following options designed to help students develop their characters, setting, and plot:

- **Video clip from *The Jungle Book*** Students play the video to hear one way of developing a character—by direct description.
- **Video clip from *Tuck Everlasting*** Students play the video to hear how author Natalie Babbitt reveals a character through that character's actions and dialogue.
- **Character Trait Word Bin** Students choose details from different categories to describe a character.
- **Model From Literature, with audio annotations** Students read an excerpt from Virginia Hamilton's story "He Lion, Bruh Bear, and Bruh Rabbit." They hear about how the characters' actions reveal a lot about them.
- **Slide show of Stonehenge, with audio narration** Students view slides while hearing about how a setting can have several moods, depending on changes in details.
- **Word Bin for setting** Students choose words and add words to help them develop a setting.
- **Sunburst Diagram with photographs** Students use photos that interest them to create details about a setting.
- **Story Line activity** Students use a diagram to record events that bring characters to a turning point and to record the resolution of the conflict.
- **Model From Literature, with audio annotations** Students read a summary of the events in the plot of Jane Yolen's story "Greyling." They choose portions to hear explanations of the elements of the conflict, climax, and resolution.
- **Story Profile activity** Students answer questions to create a profile of all the elements of their story.

Literature Connection

Point out to students that some short stories can be driven by descriptions of characters, others by their plot, and still others by their setting. Suggest that students read examples of each kind of story in *Prentice Hall Literature, Copper*. For example, they can read, respectively, "Auntie" by Philippa Pearce, "Dragon, Dragon" by John Gardner, and "Thunder Butte" by Virginia Driving Hawk Sneve.

Prewriting

FROM a WRITER

"I don't write just the way the character looks. I write what the character imagines, what the character sees and believes."

—Virginia Hamilton

Developing Your Characters

As you identify the people or animals in your narrative, think about how each one looks and acts. Consider each character's attitude toward the others and the attitude of others toward the main character. Do one or more of the following:

- Describe the character directly.
- Let the words of the other characters describe the character.
- Let the character describe himself or herself.
- Let information about the character come out through dialogue or descriptions of the character's actions.

Model From Literature

HOW TO DESCRIBE A CHARACTER'S ACTIONS

You can reveal a lot about your characters by describing their actions. In the following excerpt from Virginia Hamilton's story "He Lion, Bruh Bear and Bruh Rabbit," He Lion's roaring about himself shows that he is self-centered. Notice that in describing their actions, Hamilton reveals that the little animals are frightened, Squirrel is nervous and excited, and Possum is passive.

Say that He Lion would get up each and every mornin. Stretch and walk around. He'd roar, "ME AND MYSELF. ME AND MYSELF," like that. Scare all the little animals so they were afraid to come outside in the sunshine. Afraid to go huntin or fishin or whatever the little animals wanted to do.

"What we gone do about it?" they asked one another. Squirrel leapin from branch to branch, just scared. Possum playin dead, couldn't hardly move him.

He Lion just went on, stickin out his chest and roarin, "ME AND MYSELF. ME AND MYSELF."

Gathering Details for the Setting

A setting is much more than a time and a place. It helps your readers picture what is happening. Use details of time, place, weather, and historical period to create your setting. In your mind, picture the setting or settings where your story will take place. Then use vivid words to help your readers picture the setting.

Gathering Details for the Plot

A plot is a sequence of events with a shape, as in the diagram below. It usually begins with the exposition, in which characters become involved in a problem, or conflict. The action then rises until it reaches a climax, or turning point. The climax is followed by the conclusion, called the resolution, in which the conflict is resolved.

Write down your plot ideas for each point in the diagram. Then refer back to your diagram as you develop your story.

Plot Diagram

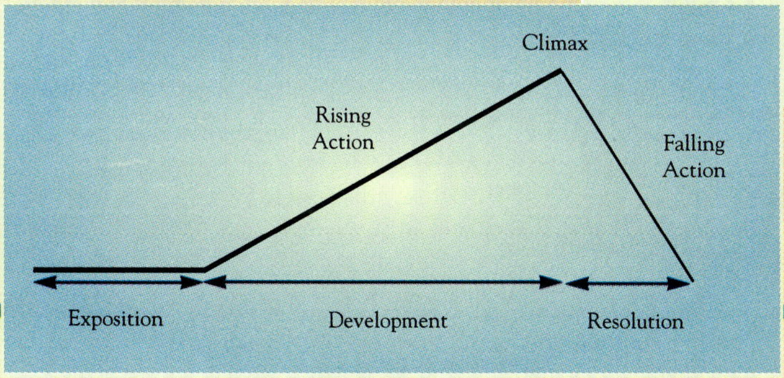

Model From Literature

This summary gives the beginning, middle, and end events in the plot of Jane Yolen's story "Greyling."

EXPOSITION

A fisherman and his wife have no child. He finds a *selchie*—human on land, a seal in water.

If the boy ever goes in the water, he will become a seal again and the couple will lose the child they love.

They decide never to let it return to the water.

DEVELOPMENT

The boy grows up. On Greyling's fifteenth birthday, the fisherman is thrown from his boat in a storm.

Greyling dives into the water to save the fisherman.

Greyling turns back into a seal.

RESOLUTION

The fisherman is saved, but the boy is gone.

The fisherman and his wife decide that it's best for Greyling to live as he was meant to live.

Once a year, Greyling returns to visit them.

Addressing Ability Levels

Challenge your **more-advanced students** to try these twists on the usual ways of developing narrative elements:

- Have a minor character tell the story.
- Set the story in a very unusual location. For example, have a figure-skating event on a moon of Jupiter, rather than in an Olympic skating rink.
- Don't reveal the conflict of the story until the middle. This way, readers will be wondering why the characters are acting as they are, and they'll be surprised when they learn the reasons.

Writing Strategy

Guide students to write narratives in which *one of the main characters* changes as a result of experiences in the story.

Writing Lab CD-ROM

The Drafting section of the tutorial on Narration includes the following options designed to help students write the first draft of their narration:

- **Video clips with drafting tips** Students play one video to hear a tip on drafting from Virginia Hamilton and another to hear how I. B. Singer begins one of his stories.
- **Models From Literature, each showing a different way to begin a narrative; with audio annotations** Students choose passages to see an example of how Jack London begins a short story with a character description, how Isaac Asimov begins one by jumping right into the action, and how Jack Cope begins one with a description of the setting.
- **Transition Word Bin** Students can find words and phrases they can use to indicate relationships of time.
- **Model From Literature showing a way to use transition words** Students choose words and phrases to see how writer John Gardner connects events in his short story "Dragon, Dragon."
- **Video clip about choosing a point of view** Students play a video to see how the same event can be viewed from different perspectives.
- **Models From Literature providing explanations of features of different points of view** Students choose passages from two different narratives to learn more about first-person and third-person narration. In the first story, one of the characters tells the story. In the second, the person who narrates the action doesn't participate in it.
- **Student Model with audio annotations** Students read a draft of a narration. They can play an audio recording to hear explanations of choices the writer made.
- **Video clip about overcoming writer's block** Students play a video to get suggestions for dealing with writer's block.

Working individually or in small groups, students can experiment with these activities to find the ones that work best for them.

Drafting

When you have decided on the type of story you will write, developed your narrative details, and identified your purpose and audience, you are ready to write your first draft. Remember to refer back to your prewriting notes as you write. For help as you draft, use one or more of the following strategies:

Starting Your Narrative

How will you start your narrative? Do you want to begin by describing the main character? By describing the setting? By plunging into the action? Choose the approach you find most interesting and best suited to your topic. Remember that it is important to grab the reader's attention right away.

Model From Literature

BEGINNING WITH THE MAIN CHARACTER

Writer Jack London begins his short story "The King of Mazy May" with a description of the main character, Walt Masters. Notice how London grabs the reader's attention by suggesting that Walt knows all kinds of things other people don't. He also describes the things Walt does not know. Then London tells why Walt is so special—and the reader wants to learn more, not only about the character Walt but also about Walt's world.

Walt Masters is not a very large boy, but there is a manliness in his make-up, and he himself, although he does not know a great deal that most boys know, knows much that other boys do not know. He has never seen a train of cars nor an elevator in his life, and for that matter he has never once looked upon a cornfield, a plow, a cow, or even a chicken. He has never had a pair of shoes on his feet, nor gone to a picnic or a party, nor talked to a girl. But he has seen the sun at midnight, watched the ice jams on one of the mightiest of rivers, and played beneath the northern lights, the one white child in thousands of square miles of frozen wilderness.

Language Lab CD-ROM

Students who need more help composing their drafts may benefit from work ing on the Point of View les son of the Composing unit, and also on the Transitional Words lesson of the Building Paragraphs unit. Direct students who would benefit fro

Model From Literature

BEGINNING WITH THE SETTING

Writer Jack Cope begins his short story "Power" with a description of the setting—a vast open space in a remote area of South Africa. Notice how Cope conveys a feeling of loneliness with his use of the words *nothing, unchanging*, and *empty*. Cope also suggests exotic qualities by using South African terms such as *veld*, an open grassy country, and *koppie*, a small hill.

From the gum tree at the corner he looked out over, well—nothing. There was nothing more after his father's place, only the veld, so flat and unchanging that the single shadowy koppie away towards the skyline made it look more empty still. It was a lonely koppie like himself.

Model From Literature

BEGINNING WITH ACTION

Isaac Asimov begins his short story "Sarah Tops" with an action episode that is almost guaranteed to spark the interest of the reader. Asimov grabs the reader's interest by jumping right into the action. You can't help wanting to know what has happened.

I came out of the Museum of Natural History and was crossing the street on my way to the subway, when I saw the crowd about halfway down the block; and the police cars, too. I could hear the whine of an approaching ambulance.

Writing Strategies

Discuss with students the importance of hooking their readers right from the start. Talk about ways to do this. You may wish to point out that O. Henry began his story "The Gift of the Magi" with the sentence fragment "One dollar and eighty-seven cents." Ask students how a beginning like this makes readers want to read further. Invite students to suggest other engaging ways to begin.

Remind students of the importance of using transitions to link ideas in their narratives. Discuss why words and phrases indicating a chronological order make the most sense for narratives.

Literature Connection

Suggest that students study examples of narration in *Prentice Hall Literature, Copper*, to get ideas from seeing how the short stories and other kinds of narratives begin. See the list of selections on page 606.

practice using quotations when writing citations to the Quotation Marks lesson in the Punctuation unit.

Writers at Work Videodisc

Play the videodisc segment in which Virginia Hamilton talks about developing characters, setting, and plot. Ask:

- What are the advantages of starting a narrative with character, as Hamilton says she always does?
- How does setting affect the way characters behave? Specifically, how *can* you "tell a city character from a suburban and a town character"?

Invite students to tell about other stories they've read or television shows or movies they've seen in which the result is told at the outset. Ask them to share their responses, as readers and viewers, to this writing technique.

Play frames 25968 to 28030

Group Discussion

After students read the models showing third-person and first-person points of view (p. 84), ask them to talk about the strengths and weaknesses of each approach. Students may say that when you write using a first-person narrator, you cannot reveal things that the character would not know. Others may say that a third-person narrator can express the thoughts of many characters, but may not provide the personal approach a first-person narrator does.

Teaching From the Model

Discuss the advantages of using first-person and third-person points of view.

- Point out that first-person narration gives the reader a ringside seat, making him or her an active participant in the story. You may wish to mention that another appeal of first-person narration is that it may make some parts of the writing easier, since characters cannot appear in the story until the main character meets up with them.
- Discuss with students that when using third-person narration, an advantage is that the writer can give readers a bird's-eye view of events—they can get inside other characters' heads and can know things the main character doesn't know.
- Invite students to suggest other reasons for choosing one viewpoint or the other. Suggest that they look through some of their favorite books or stories to see what viewpoint the authors use.

Choosing a Point of View

As you know, the same event can be viewed from different perspectives. Similarly, a narrative can be told from different points of view. Point of view refers to who tells your narrative and where that character is in relation to the action.

You can use either a first-person point of view or a third-person point of view. A narrative written from the first-person point of view is told through the eyes of one of the characters. A narrative written from the third-person point of view is told by a person who does not participate in the action.

Model From Literature

FIRST-PERSON POINT OF VIEW

This excerpt from James Berry's short story "Becky and the Wheels-and-Brake Boys" is told from the first-person point of view. The person may not be the author but a character in the story. Here it is a girl named Becky. Notice that Berry describes the action through Becky's eyes.

> I walked up to Nat, Aldo, Jimmy, and Ben and said, "Can somebody teach me to ride?"
>
> "Why don't you stay indoors and learn to cook and sew and wash clothes?" Jimmy said.
>
> I grinned. "I know all that already," I said. . . . "Can you cook and sew and wash clothes, Jimmy? All I want is to learn to ride. I want you to teach me." . . .

Model From Literature

THIRD-PERSON POINT OF VIEW

The following excerpt is from Jack Cope's "Power," a short story told from the third-person point of view. Notice how Cope describes the action from outside the story, as if he and his readers were invisible. When you write in the third person, the narrator knows more than any one character. You as the author decide whether or not you want the narrator to include the thoughts and feelings of any, all, or none of the characters.

> After school, André did not catch the bus home. Instead he took a bus the other way, into town. . . . When he got to the power station he was faced with an enormous high fence of iron staves with spiked tops and a tall steel gate, locked fast. . . .
>
> André's heart was pounding good and fast. He could hear the humming sound strongly and it seemed to come from everywhere, not so much a sound as a feeling under his feet.

Establishing Assessment Criteria

As students begin drafting their narratives, you may want to share with them the criteria you will use to evaluate their work. The following guidelines are included in the tutorial on Narration in the *Writing Lab* CD-ROM. You can use them as given, or modify them to suit your needs.

- Do you have a clear, focused story idea involving a conflict or problem?
- Have you used language and details appropriate for your audience and purpose?
- Is your plot well organized and easy to follow?
- Are your characters brought to life through dialogue and description?
- Have you described your settings so that the reader can picture them?
- Is your narrative free of errors in spelling, grammar, and punctuation?

Revising and Editing

Revising Your Work

When you have completed the draft of your narrative, read it over, looking for ways to improve it. The checklist below will help you evaluate and revise your narrative. As you go through your draft and answer the questions, strengthen your story where possible.

Revision Checklist

1. Who will be reading your narrative? What language and details can you add that will appeal to this audience?
2. What is your purpose? Have you accomplished your purpose?
3. How have you developed the characters? What can you add to strengthen them?
4. What is the setting? What details would strengthen the setting?
5. What would heighten the conflict?

Student Model: Revised Draft

Below is a revised paragraph from a short story by Jenny Huang, a student from Deerpark Middle School in Austin, Texas. Notice that Jenny strengthens her opening by introducing her main character right at the beginning. She also rewords her last sentence to improve its logic.

~~A setting sun lay, hazily on top of the dark horizon. Luscious green hills lined up next to each other, forming a landscape that seemed to go on forever.~~ Gazing at the ~~scene before her~~ setting sun above the far end of the lake, Jenny swung her paddle along the side of the canoe, helplessly. *It was no use*, she reflected, frustrated. They were never going to get back to shore. *How did I get myself into this*, she asked, sighing. Little did she know that Rebecca ~~had~~ was an impulsive ~~mind that would do things before~~ girl who acted without thinking.

Technology Note/ Writing Strategy

To help students avoid repeating the same words, guide them to use a thesaurus to help them choose effective, active verbs; precise nouns; and vivid modifiers, as needed. Direct students who are word-processing to use the computer's thesaurus.

Writers at Work Videodisc

Play the videodisc segment in which Virginia Hamilton talks about what she calls "constant revision," and in which she says that she always writes more than she will eventually use. Ask:

- What do you think about Hamilton's writing strategy of revising constantly? What are the advantages of this approach? Are there any disadvantages? Explain.
- What does Virginia Hamilton mean when she says, "I look for dead sentences that I can throw away"?
- What advantages does Hamilton get from having her husband read her work?

Play frames 28228 to 29442

Writing Lab CD-ROM

The Revising and Editing section provides the following strategies for self revision:

- **Video clip of a writer** Students play a video to hear suggestions from Virginia Hamilton on revising a story.
- **Self-Evaluation Checklist** Students answer questions to help them evaluate their drafts for considering audience and purpose, and for developing their characters, the setting, and the conflict.
- **Revision checker for language variety** Students use this tool to help them avoid the pitfall of using the same words over and over again.
- **Student Model, with audio annotation** Students read to see and hear how one student has revised her draft.
- **Video clip about peer review** Students can play the video to hear what writer Jane Yolen has to say about the advantages of having a fresh eye look over one's work.
- **Peer Review Checklist** Students get pointers to help them evaluate a classmate's writing.
- **Strategies for working with a peer editor** Students get advice about taking and giving constructive criticism.

Teaching Strategy

Work with students to establish a class environment that fosters mutual respect between writers and readers. You may wish to brainstorm additional guidelines students can observe for peer editing.

In addition to discussing the questions presented in the *Sourcebook*, you might invite students to ask others, such as:

- Does my opening make you want to read on? If not, what suggestions can you make as to how I might revise it?
- Can you picture the setting clearly? If not, what details or descriptions might I add?
- Does my story need a better conclusion? If so, what would you suggest I try to do to resolve the conflict?

Writing Lab CD-ROM

The Revising and Editing section includes the following options to help students develop strategies for proofreading their narratives:

- **Proofreading Checklist** This checklist is the same as the one provided in the *Sourcebook*, except that it addresses the possibility that a writer may choose to have characters not always speak in complete sentences.
- **Interactive instruction on having pronouns and antecedents agree in number and gender, and in punctuating dialogue** In the first activity, students choose pronouns that best complete sentences. In the second, they get tips for when and how to use quotation marks, commas, question marks, exclamation marks, and periods.
- **Student Model, with audio annotations** Students can play an audio recording to hear an explanation of how the writer made proofreading corrections.

Working individually or in small groups, students can experiment with these activities to find the ones that work best.

Language Lab CD-ROM

Students who need more practice working with pronouns and antecedents may benefit from working through the Pronouns and Antecedents lesson in the Using Pronouns unit. Those who could benefit from more practice punctuating dialogue can review the pertinent lessons in the Punctuation unit.

Portfolio Assessment

Have students write an evaluative statement that addresses some of the questions posed

FROM a WRITER

"What you want to do is make sure the story is going forward, so you cut and revise to make that happen. . . . No one starts out with a perfect story. You work a story into being perfect by revising it."

—Virginia Hamilton

Having a Peer Review Your Work

A fresh pair of eyes may notice weak spots in your work that you may have missed. After you've reread your narrative and made your revisions, have a classmate review your work and offer suggestions. Use the following questions to guide you and your classmate.

Peer Review Checklist

1. How are the characters introduced, and how well are they developed? Are they believable? How can they be improved?
2. Is the story entertaining? How can it be made more interesting?
3. Is the main conflict presented clearly? How can it be made more clear?
4. How realistic is the dialogue? How can it be improved?

Proofreading

Proofread your narrative, correcting errors in spelling, punctuation, capitalization, and grammar. Here is a checklist of things to look for when proofreading your narrative. You should be able to answer yes to the following questions:

Proofreading Checklist

1. Are all your sentences complete?
2. Have you punctuated dialogue correctly?
3. Have you spelled each word correctly? Have you double-checked the correct spelling of names and places?
4. Do all your subjects and verbs agree?
5. Do all your pronouns have clear antecedents?

Publishing and Presenting

When you have completed your narrative, think about ways to publish it so that others can enjoy it. Find a format that interests you and present your story for others to listen to or read. Here are several suggestions for publishing and presenting your narrative:

Choose a Title A catchy title will grab your readers' attention, give them an idea of what your narrative is about, and make them want to read it. Try one or more of these suggestions:

- Use a word or phrase from something that the main character says during the climax or the resolution of the story.
- Choose a word or phrase that sums up the theme.
- Use a phrase from your description of the setting.

Share Your Narrative With Family and Friends You might enjoy sharing your narrative with your family and friends to find out how they respond to your work. You might read the story aloud to them, let them read the story, or record it on an audiocassette so they can play it at their leisure.

Reflecting on Your Writing

What can you learn from the process you went through while writing your narrative? Here are some questions to help you reflect on your writing:

- What did you learn about your subject from your narrative? What else would you have liked to learn?
- If you were starting over, would you approach the assignment differently? Why or why not? What would you do differently?
- How can you apply what you have learned to other writing assignments?

Writing Lab CD-ROM

The Publishing and Presenting section includes the following options, both of which are also presented in the *Sourcebook*, to help students present their completed works to a wider audience:

- **Tips for choosing a title and for creating a class anthology** Students get suggestions for coming up with an engaging title that gives readers an idea about what the narrative is about, and for compiling their work into a single book.
- **Video clip of one student's audiotape recording session** Students play a video to learn how to create a particular tone when recording a narrative.

The Multimedia Workshop

Students can use the templates in the Writing Workshop component of *The Multimedia Workshop* to word-process and present their final narratives. For instance, a student writing an anecdote or a piece about an incident may wish to use the memo or messages template. One writing a short story might choose one of the magazines templates.

in the *Sourcebook*. If students decide to include the completed narrative in their portfolio, they might attach this statement to it. Otherwise, the statement itself can go into the portfolio as a record of self-evaluation.

The following questions can be used to supplement the questions in the *Sourcebook*:

- What part of the narrative-writing process did you find most satisfying? Most challenging?
- How do you feel about writing a story, as compared with writing other kinds of pieces? Which type of narrative writing would you like to try next time? Why?

After students have evaluated their work, confer with them to decide what to include in their portfolio. Students can select the completed piece and/or earlier drafts they think reflect growth and progress.

Teaching From the Model

Draw students' attention to how Jenny Huang's story includes the elements of narration.

- *It grabs the reader's attention right from the start.* The story begins with a brief description of the setting and then immediately presents the problem the characters face.
- *It has a point of view and a purpose.* Huang's story about the pitfalls of impulsiveness is told in a third-person point of view.
- *It presents conflicts that need to be resolved.* The conflicts are between the two girls, and between the girls and their physical predicament. Readers are kept in suspense right up until the resolution.
- *It has a climax.* Suspense builds until Rebecca's father shows up in the nick of time and helps the girls to safety.

Technology Note: Networking

After your class has read the Student Model, it may be interested in sharing narrative efforts with students across the country via the Internet or commercial on-line services such as Prodigy or America Online. Students can learn more about how their peers feel about similar problems and incidents in their lives. For example, students all over the country may be facing the conflict of how to deal with peer pressure, and will have different incidents or personal narratives to share about it. Your students may be surprised to discover how much they have in common with their peers around the country. Students can exchange narrative pieces with other students, including those using *Writer's Solution*, by connecting to Prentice Hall's Internet home page. Look for special events, contests, as well as bulletin boards and pointers to student publications at http://www.phschool.com.

Student Model

Here is the complete, final draft of Jenny Huang's story:

The Canoe Trip

by Jenny Huang

I started with a short description of the setting.

I presented the main problem here instead of in the middle of the story to grab the reader's attention. Also, as you can see, I wrote my story from a third-person point of view.

This is where the story actually begins. Once the readers are involved, they'll want to know how the problem develops.

Gazing at the setting sun above the far end of the lake, Jenny swung her paddle along the side of the canoe, helplessly. *It was no use*, she reflected, frustrated. They were never going to get back to shore. *How did I get myself into this*, she asked, sighing. Little did she know that Rebecca was an impulsive girl who acted without thinking.

When Rebecca had seen the two paddles and canoe, she had thought that they could paddle out on the lake and have some fun. It sounded great . . . except that they didn't know how to canoe.

"Oh, it's easy!" Rebecca had exclaimed as she stepped onto the canoe. "Just follow what I do."

The current carried them away from shore. When Jenny and Rebecca tried to paddle, the canoe started rotating in circles. So they stopped paddling and drifted for a while. When Jenny looked up, she saw that the shore was far off in the distance.

"We have to go back," she had muttered nervously to Rebecca.

"Okay," Rebecca replied.

They tried paddling again, but this time they began to

88 • *Narration*

move backwards, farther away from shore. "We should never have come out here," said Jenny, angrily.

"Well, if you didn't think it was a good idea, why did you come with me?" snapped Rebecca.

At this point, the problem is turning into a conflict between the two girls. The action is beginning to build toward a climax.

As the two argued, Rebecca didn't notice her paddle on her lap tipping dangerously into the water. Suddenly, with a *splash*, the paddle flopped into the water and slowly floated out of reach. Jenny groaned. Now they had only one paddle—hers. Jenny tried to paddle, but they went around in circles again. It really was no use. Jenny stopped paddling.

The sun set, and it started to get dark. The two of them just sat there, angry and scared. A cold breeze began to blow over the lake. Jenny shivered.

"Hey, girls!" A voice came from the distance. Looking toward the shore, Jenny saw a figure frantically swimming toward them.

This is the climax of the story—the main problem is about to be resolved.

"Dad?" Rebecca looked uncertainly at the thrashing figure.

Rebecca's dad swam up.

"C'mon, Rebecca, get out and help me pull this canoe back!" he panted, grabbing the side of the canoe.

"D-a-d!" Rebecca whined pitifully, "Do I have to?" She looked pleadingly at Jenny.

"Fine, I'll do it!" Jenny got up, hesitated briefly, and jumped into the cold water. It only took a few minutes to get back to shore, since Rebecca's dad did most of the work, but for Jenny, it seemed like years.

Jenny's mom met them at the shore. "Jenny, are you okay?" she asked.

"Yeah," said Jenny. "You know, I might try it again."

Her mom looked at her, alarmed.

"Just kidding." Jenny grinned sheepishly.

By showing that Jenny has not lost her sense of humor, I indicated the relief she felt at the way things turned out.

Language Acquisition/ ESL Teaching Strategy

The Student Model can be adapted to meet the needs of your upper basic and lower intermediate ESL students. Read the story, "The Canoe Trip," together with your students. Lead the students in a discussion of vocabulary, phrases, and the structure of the story—for example, setting, problem, climax. Ask the students to retell the story to you, being careful to provide details and to maintain the proper sequence of the story. On a sheet of paper, write the story as it is dictated to you. Cut the story apart by paragraphs or sentences, mix the pieces, and have the students put the story back together in the proper sequence. Before cutting the paper, you may wish to make photocopies of the dictated story so that different groups can work on it at the same time.

Integrating Skills With Writing

Management Strategy

You can have students work through one or both of the skills lessons either before or after they write their narratives. If you use the lessons *before*, remind students to incorporate the techniques in their writing. If you address skills *after* students write their stories, have them include a section on skills improvement in the self-assessment document they prepare for their portfolios. The next time they write, their work can be evaluated in terms of their mastery of these skills.

You may want to give students these lessons as take-home assignments to be completed prior to the drafting, revising, or proofreading stages—wherever you see the greatest need. Or you may choose to assign the skills lessons only to those students whose drafts indicate a need for direct instruction in these particular skills.

Teaching Strategy

To connect the skills lessons to the students' writing, explain that one important feature of narrative writing is to make sure to use precise and vivid verbs.

Tell them that another important aspect of narration is to indicate to readers how one idea is linked to another. To this end, writers need to use transitional words and phrases. This lesson focuses on three kinds of transitions: transitions showing time relationships, those showing spatial relationships, and those indicating an order of importance.

Developing Your Style 1

Using Vivid Verbs

Read the following account of the approach of a hurricane. Does it make you want to take shelter—or take a nap?

> Last week, Hurricane George was a slow-moving tropical depression in the Atlantic Ocean east of Bermuda. Suddenly, its winds grew stronger and George moved more rapidly northward. It went inland across southern Florida, damaging trees, bridges, and buildings before it changed direction again and headed back out to sea. Then the storm turned back again and took a northerly direction along the Carolina coast.

The writer wanted to show the violent, unpredictable force of the hurricane. But his verbs—*moved, went, became, was, took*—don't do the job. They are too general to create clear pictures. They are not lively enough to make the reader feel the hurricane's power. Read this revision of the hurricane's history. Now vivid and precise verbs (underlined) tell a story worth reading:

> Last week, Hurricane George <u>crept</u> around the Atlantic Ocean, a mere tropical depression east of Bermuda. Suddenly, its winds <u>whipped</u> themselves up, and George <u>hurtled</u> northward. It <u>tore</u> inland across southern Florida, <u>smashing</u> trees, bridges, and buildings before it <u>swung</u> about and <u>charged</u> back out to sea. Then the hurricane <u>veered</u> again and <u>flung</u> itself northward along the Carolina coast.

Teaching Strategy

Have volunteers read the two passages about Hurricane George aloud. Ask students to describe the differences between them. Ask them to describe how each replacement verb helps to paint a better picture of the storm.

Invite students to suggest other ways to revise the second version of the hurricane paragraph on this page by replacing the underlined words with other vivid verbs. You may wish to also challenge students to replace some of the nouns with other, more precise, nouns. For example, a student might suggest replacing *southern Florida* with "the Everglades," or *buildings* with "trailers, apartments, and small homes with screened-in porches."

Action Versus Linking Verbs

Verbs are parts of speech that show either an action or a state of being. **Action verbs**—such as *hop, sail, remember, chew,* or *whisper*—give the subject of the sentence a physical or mental activity to perform:

> Emma hopped on board the boat and grabbed the wheel.

In this sentence, both *hopped* and *grabbed* are action verbs, telling what the subject, *Emma*, did.

Linking verbs—such as *be, become, feel, appear,* and *seem*—do not show action. They are called linking verbs because they connect the subject to another word that identifies or describes it:

> Emma has become skilled at boating and is now a good sailor.

In this sentence, the linking verbs, *become* and *is*, connect the subject, *Emma*, to a predicate adjective, *skilled*, and a predicate noun, *sailor*. Because they don't add actions to your sentences, too many linking verbs can drain your writing of vitality. So make a special effort to substitute action verbs for linking verbs when you write, as in this example:

> **Linking verb:** Its winds grew stronger.
>
> **Action verb:** Its winds whipped up.

You will not be able to avoid linking verbs altogether, of course. But your writing will carry more punch if you make a conscious effort to use action verbs when you can.

Writing Strategy

Guide students to use action verbs instead of linking verbs wherever possible in their writing. Direct them to revise their narratives with this idea in mind. Remind students that they can use a thesaurus to help them make the replacements.

Language Lab CD-ROM

For additional practice using vivid and precise verbs, students can refer to the Vivid and Precise Verbs lesson in the Choosing Words unit.

Teaching Strategy

Point out to students that there is more than one way to revise each sentence in Practice Activity 1. Remind them to make sure not to change the meaning of the sentences when they improve them. Have students share and explain their revisions with the whole class. You might find it useful to have some new sentences read aloud.

Thematic Connection: Imagination

Invite students who have not personally experienced the wrath of nature to brainstorm descriptions of what they imagine it's like during hurricanes, tornadoes, snowstorms, earthquakes, floods, and other natural disasters. Then ask them to write their paragraphs using vivid and precise verbs.

Writer's Companion

To provide students with additional reinforcement in using vivid verbs and action verbs, direct them to "Action Verbs and Linking Verbs" on page 403, and "Using Precise, Vivid Verbs" on page 412.

Practice Activities: Suggested Answers

1. Answers will vary. Possible answers follow.
   - a. Raindrops streamed down the window.
   - b. The house shook whenever the wind howled.
   - c. We ran down to the basement when the worst part of the storm raged.
   - d. The hurricane blasted at its height for three hours.
   - e. The day after the storm, branches littered the ground.
2. Paragraphs will vary.

Vivid and Precise Verbs Enliven Writing

Using action verbs is a first step to strong writing, but you need to do more. You need to search out action verbs that are vivid and precise, as in the following examples:

General, dull verbs: It went inland across southern Florida, damaging trees, bridges, and buildings before it changed direction again and headed back out to sea.

Vivid, precise verbs: It tore inland across southern Florida, smashing trees, bridges, and buildings before it swung about and charged back out to sea.

See how *charged* paints a much clearer and livelier picture than *headed* does? *Headed* is another neutral way of saying *went*; *charged* tells you in forceful terms just *how* the hurricane went. Other good possibilities are *roared*, *thundered*, or *lurched*.

Practice Activities

1. Rewrite the sentences below. Replace linking verbs with action verbs, and replace dull, general verbs with vivid, precise verbs. You may use more than one verb per sentence.
   - a. Raindrops ran down the window.
   - b. The house seemed to move whenever the wind increased.
   - c. We went down to the basement when the worst part of the storm came near.
   - d. The hurricane was at its height for three hours.
   - e. The day after the storm, branches were all over the ground.
2. Write a paragraph describing a storm or other powerful natural force that you have experienced. Try to avoid linking verbs. Use at least one vivid, precise verb in each sentence.

Developing Your Style 2

Using Transitions

Transitions are words and groups of words that show relationships between ideas. Use transitions to tell your readers how one idea is connected to another—in time, in space, or in other ways. Transitions can show relationships of time, space, comparison, contrast, classification, cause-effect, and order of importance. Without transitions, writing seems jumpy, unconnected, and unclear.

How to Use Time Transitions

When you write a narrative, you need to let your readers know the time order in which the events occur. You also need to show when time is passing or if you are talking about something that happened earlier. In the following sentence, the underlined transitional words show the passage of time:

> Then after lunch, we moved across the street to join a large crowd at the Academy of Natural Science. . . .

Here are some transitions that you can use to express time order:

after	during	last week (month, and so on)	previously
ago	earlier	later	simultaneously
already	finally	next	then
at the same time	in the meantime	now	when
before	in the past	once	while

Writing Strategy

Ask students to explain why using transitions that signal time relationships is a sensible organizational strategy to employ when writing stories.

Teaching Strategy

To help students understand how each of these three kinds of transitions can be used effectively in a narrative, invite them to select passages from their own stories that use transitions, and share why it was essential to have used the transitions they did.

Writing Strategy

Suggest to students that the revision phase of their writing process is a good time to look for opportunities to add transitions to their narratives to make relationships between ideas more clear.

Writer's Companion

To provide students with additional practice in using transitional words, and to show them other transitional words they can use, direct them to "How Do I Follow an Orderly Plan?" starting on page 64 and "Transitional Words in Essays" beginning on page 68.

How to Use Space Transitions

Other transitions show spatial relationships between parts of things. Spatial transitions are helpful when you describe things: your town, your uncle's house, a friend's face, the Liberty Bell. In the following sentence, the underlined transitional words tell us *where* the Academy is.

> Then after lunch, we moved <u>across the street</u> to join a large crowd at the Academy of Natural Science. . . .

The following list includes some of the most common spatial transitions:

above	back	east (west, and so on)	middle
across	behind	in	there
around	below	into	under
at	down	left (right)	up

How to Use Order-of-Importance Transitions

You can use transitions to set priorities—to show order of importance. For instance, the underlined transitions in the following sentence tell you what the writer enjoyed most about her trip to Philadelphia:

> <u>The most memorable of all these sights</u> was the Liberty Bell.

Here is a list of some order-of-importance transitions:

as much as	greatest	less	of all
best	highest	main	more
finally	last	mainly	moreover
first	least	most (important, unforgettable, and so on)	worst

Transitions make your writing flow better and increase understanding. Look for opportunities to add transitions when your writing seems disconnected or when relationships between ideas are unclear.

Practice Activity: Suggested Answers

Revised paragraphs will vary. A possible revision follows.

I always wanted to visit New York City <u>more than anyplace else in America</u>. I got my chance on a class trip <u>last month</u>. <u>First</u>, we climbed to the top of the Statue of Liberty <u>in New York Harbor</u>.

Practice Activity

Revise the following paragraph by adding transitional words and phrases to answer the underlined questions in parentheses. Choose transitions from the previous lists of time relationships, spatial relationships, and order of importance. Use the fact list below the paragraph to help you answer some of the questions. Use your imagination to answer others.

I have always wanted to visit New York City (how important was this wish?). I got my chance on a class trip (when?). We climbed to the top of the Statue of Liberty (when? where?). We visited the World Trade Center (when? where?), twin giants that have replaced the Empire State Building as the tallest structure in New York. We could see all of the city—and beyond (from where?). We moved on to a show at the Radio City Music Hall (when? where?). We had just enough energy left for a quick look around the Central Park Zoo (when? where?). We all got a big kick out of the polar bear doing a lazy backstroke around his arctic pool. (Which part of the trip did you like best?)

Facts About New York:

- Radio City is in Rockefeller Center, in midtown Manhattan.
- The Statue of Liberty is in New York harbor, just off lower Manhattan.
- The Central Park Zoo is near the lower end of Central Park, less than a mile north of Rockefeller Center.
- The World Trade Center is a pair of 110-story buildings in lower Manhattan. One of the buildings has an observation tower.

Then, we traveled to lower Manhattan and visited the World Trade Center, twin 110-story giants that have replaced the Empire State Building as the tallest structure in New York. From the observation deck we could see all of the city—and beyond. Later that day, we moved on to a show at the Radio City Music Hall, which is located in Rockefeller Center in midtown Manhattan. At the end of the day, we had just enough energy left for a quick look around the Central Park Zoo, which is near the lower end of Central Park, less than a mile north of the World Trade Center. We all got a big kick out of the polar bear doing a lazy backstroke around his arctic pool. I liked our visit to the Statue of Liberty best. I can't believe that I actually climbed inside one of the most famous symbols of America.

Teaching Strategies

To ascertain whether they have made the passage more clear without altering its meaning, students can swap revisions with classmates to get a second read.

Ask students to tell the kind of narration this passage in Practice Activities exemplifies.

Language Acquisition/ ESL Teaching Strategy

Ask your intermediate ESL students to read through the paragraph and think about how to answer the questions. Lead them in a discussion of the different ways the questions can be answered. Ask them if they have ever been to New York City or if they would like to visit the city. Ask them what they know about the city's attractions. Read through the paragraph with your students and ask them to respond to the questions. After the discussion, ask the students to rewrite the paragraph, including the answers to the questions. Have the students take turns reading their completed paragraphs.

Alternate Assessments

You may wish to invite city students to demonstrate their understanding of the use of transitions by writing a one-paragraph narrative about a one-day trip to a country setting.

You might want to challenge your more-advanced students to swap papers with a classmate and rewrite each other's paragraph using different transitions that make sense.

Integrating Literature With Writing

Management Strategy

You can have students read this model of narration either before or after they have written their own narrative. If you choose to have them read it *before*, use it to draw their attention to techniques or ideas they can apply to their own writing. If you use it *after*, have students compare and contrast some of the elements of the piece with elements of their own narrative.

Activating Prior Knowledge

Invite students to tell anecdotes about times they were the only ones who did not know or notice something new or different. Discuss common features of each situation.

Purpose-Setting Question

How do the elements of narration work to create a clear picture of the scene in the parlor, the characters in the story, and the dinner that followed?

Reading Strategy

You can help guide reading by asking students to notice the point of view Virginia Hamilton uses to tell the story, how she uses details to create a vivid picture of the scene in the house and the characters involved, how she keeps the readers in suspense, and how she reveals the gift the father received. When they finish reading, students can work as a whole class or in small discussion groups to compare their responses to the piece.

Literature Model

As you read the following excerpt, notice that the events follow each other in the order in which they occurred. Also pay close attention to the way the characters are described and how they relate to each other.

The Bells of Christmas

by Virginia Hamilton

This example of narrative writing begins with the first-person narrator introducing most of the characters and giving information about the setting and the situation.

When Papa and Uncle Levi made their appearance, we were all back in the parlor. Mama had herded us there to sing carols. We had finished a sweet "Silent Night" when in came Papa, empty-handed. I couldn't see the present. It had been wrapped in a big box, too. Uncle Levi didn't have it either. What had happened to it?

Everybody stared at the two of them. Papa cut quite a figure in his Christmas suit. As he walked toward all of us and the tree, he held onto Uncle Levi's shoulder.

"Well, I declare," said Aunt Etta Bell. "Lou Rhetta, it sure is a wonder!" And she smiled brightly at Mama and all around. Mama looked Papa up and down, and then she, too, broke into a smile. "It's a wonder, indeed!" she said.

"And takes some getting used to, I'll wager," said cousin Chester Bell.

My brother Bob nodded agreement. "Papa will get used to it as quick as you please, if I know him," he said.

Well, I wondered! I gazed at my papa and he looked just like my papa, which he was. It

Christmas *Palmer Hayden, Michael Rosenfeld Gallery, NYC*

Teaching Strategies

- Discuss with students how Hamilton begins the chapter. Ask them to explain the strategies she uses to introduce and describe the characters and to give information about the setting and situation. Students should give examples to support their ideas.
- Hamilton uses a first-person point of view to tell the story. Have students discuss the effectiveness of this approach.
- Have students talk about how Hamilton uses specific details and precise verbs and nouns to describe the gift and the reactions to it, and to create a vivid scene for the reader.
- Point out that the excerpt is organized chronologically. Ask students to tell why they think Hamilton used this approach.
- Guide students to notice how often Hamilton uses dialogue in the story. Ask them to describe the

was Christmas, with everybody and Tisha and oh, so many new things and goings on. That was the wonder, that I could see anything atall.

"What in the world is everybody talking about?" I asked.

"Yes, what are you all talking . . ." Lissy began.

I cut her off. "Hush up!" I said. I did not like being left out of things.

Papa smiled at me and said, "Calm down, son." He took his hand from Uncle Levi's shoulder.

"Now," said Papa, "come see what your Uncle Levi made me."

There was silence as I came up close to Papa. Lissy was right behind me with her walking doll. Everybody else crowded around. To my surprise, Papa raised his pant leg.

"Just look," said Papa. "Two true feet!"

I bent near with my hands on my knees. Well, it was a shock! Sure enough, where once there had been only the tip of a peg leg, there was now a shoe. And I hadn't noticed atall. And in Papa's stocking in the shoe was a foot. It matched the foot he'd always had. Attached to the foot was an ankle and then a leg. Not a peg leg atall. It was a wonder, all right.

"Knock on it, Jason," said Papa. And I did. I knocked on the leg, and it was wood. Very gently, I touched it with my fingers, and it was smooth oak, turned and made perfect by a master carver. It looked true, like the one that was real.

I shook my head, it was so hard to believe. "Is it a mechanical thing?" I asked Uncle Levi, for I knew he had made it.

"In some ways it is," said he. "There are wonders going on in mechanics."

"The foot moves up and down, like any foot," said Papa, "and it walks comfortable. For now, I will wear Levi's fine 'mechanical thing' on special occasions, such as this Great Day."

We all applauded wildly.

"You should both take a bow," said brother Bob. And they did. Uncle Levi and Papa bowed, holding onto each other for support. Each swept his free arm back in a grand gesture. They gave us a swell stage bow.

"It's a great wonder," I said, "to have a mechanical leg and foot. Papa, you look just like everybody!" . . .

Everybody seems to know what Papa's Christmas present is except the narrator. The suspense builds, as the narrator is still in the dark. Building and maintaining suspense in a narrative is a good way to hold the reader's interest.

Hamilton gives enough specific sensory details about the amazing Christmas gift that the reader can easily picture it.

Hamilton has her characters speak and act in a realistic way, which helps create the narrative's happy mood.

mood of the chapter, and to tell how the dialogue helps to set that mood. Have them cite examples to support their ideas.

Thematic Connection: Turning Points/Transitions

Invite students to tell about a time that a special gift was given or received, or a surprise event or announcement set a particular tone for a memorable family gathering.

Language Acquisition/ ESL Teaching Strategy

Ask your upper-intermediate and advanced ESL students to read *The Bells of Christmas* to themselves, noting words and phrases that are troublesome. After a short discussion of vocabulary, put the students in pairs and ask them to summarize the story in writing, paying close attention to the sequence of events. You may suggest that they use the simple past, past continuous, and past perfect tenses. For example, *Papa and Uncle Levi made their appearance. We were singing Christmas carols. We had just finished a song.* Referring to their written summaries, the students verbally answer questions about the events and characters of the story.

Closure and Extension

To complete the lesson, you can ask students to sum up how this excerpt describing a family holiday event exemplifies what they have learned about narrative writing.

Then invite students to share in small group discussions or through brief journal entries what they learned about themselves as writers and what points they would like to keep in mind for future writing efforts. Also ask what topics they would consider for future narrative writing. You might keep some of the topics in an idea file for later use.

4

Exposition: Giving Information

CLASSROOM MANAGER

Writer's Solution *Materials for Teaching Exposition*

The *Writer's Solution* includes a wide range of materials for teaching expository writing that gives information. You can pick and choose from among these materials. In the pages that follow, you'll find lesson plans suggesting effective ways of using them. You do not have to use all the program components to use it effectively. For a detailed description of each of the components of the *Writer's Solution*, see pages T4–T6.

Below is a detailed list of the *Writer's Solution* materials for expository writing.

Writers at Work Videodisc

Featured Writer: Charles Tsang, Police Officer

Videodisc Segments

About Exposition: Giving Information

Writing on the Beat

Writing Tips:

Knowing Your ABC's

Recording the Facts

Interactive CD-ROMs

WRITING LAB

Tutorial on Exposition: Giving Information

About Exposition: Giving Information
- Includes annotated Models From Literature and Evaluation Checklist

Choosing Your Topic
- Includes Inspirations for Exposition and an Idea Wheel for gathering ideas

Narrowing Your Topic
- Includes a video clip showing broad and narrow topics relating to the newspaper business

Considering Audience and Purpose
- Includes Audience Profile

Gathering Details
- Includes a video clip of Officer Charles Tsang on gathering information

Organizing Details
- Includes a Cluster Diagram, a Chain of Events Activity, and a Notecard Activity

Drafting
- Includes a Student Model

Revising and Editing
- Includes a revision checker for transitional words and a Peer Revision Checklist

Proofreading
- Includes integrated grammar instruction on avoiding sentence fragments

Publishing and Presenting
- Includes tips for a class dictionary, an audio anthology, and a do-it-yourself magazine

Writer's Tool Kit

Suggested Activities: Idea Wheel, Topic Web, Audience Profile, Cluster Diagram, Transition Word Bin, Peer Revision Checklist

LANGUAGE LAB

Related Lessons: Exact Nouns, Vivid and Precise Verbs, Vivid Adjectives and Adverbs (Choosing Words unit); Considering Audience and Purpose (Composing unit); Sentence Fragments (Problems With Sentences unit); Agreement in Number, Agreement With Compound Subjects, Intervening Phrases (Subject-Verb Agreement unit)

Sourcebook

About Exposition: Giving Information (pp. 102–108)

Guided Lesson on Expository Writing (pp. 109–124)

Developing Your Style

Using Exact Nouns (pp. 126–127)

Using Correct Subject-Verb Agreement (pp. 128–129)

Literature Model

"My Life's Work: Crime Lab Scientist," by Jeff Saviano (pp. 130–131)

Below is a list of materials from Prentice Hall's student writing handbook that you can integrate with this lesson on expository writing.

Writer's Companion

Mini-Lesson on Choosing Specific Nouns, p. 345

Mini-Lesson on Writing to Inform: Extended Definition, p. 153

Teaching Integrated Language Arts Using the Writer's Solution—*Starting With Literature*

Have students read and respond to definitions, classifications, summaries of books and media programs, written instructions, and other types of expository writing. In discussing the selections, draw students' attention to expository elements, such as providing accurate information and details and using precise language. Point out that students can use the expositions they read as models for writing their own expository pieces. Lead into having students complete expository writing projects using the components of the *Writer's Solution*.

CONNECTIONS TO *PRENTICE HALL LITERATURE, COPPER,* SELECTIONS

Definition/Classification	2E	3E
"The Truth About Dragons," Rhoda Blumberg	■	▲
"Space Stations of the Mind," Neil McAleer	■	▲
"Thunder Butte," Virginia Driving Hawk Sneve	■	▲

Summary/Written Instructions	2E	3E
"How to Read Faster," Bill Cosby	■	▲
"Aaron's Gift," Myron Levoy	■	▲
"The Fly," Mai Vo Dinh	■	▲

You can also use the *Writer's Solution* materials on exposition to support any of the following writing activities in *Prentice Hall Literature, Copper*.

CONNECTIONS TO *PRENTICE HALL LITERATURE, COPPER,* WRITING ACTIVITIES

Thinking and Writing Activities	2E	3E
Writing an Explanatory Essay—Follows **"The Truth About Dragons,"** Rhoda Blumberg	■	▲
Writing About Spiders—Follows **"Arachne,"** Olivia Coolidge	■	
Summarizing a Folk Tale—Follows **"The Fly,"** Mai Vo Dinh	■	▲
Summarizing a Story in a Letter—Follows **"Aaron's Gift,"** Myron Levoy	■	▲
Explaining How—Follows **"How to Read Faster,"** Bill Cosby	■	▲

Handbook of Writing About Literature / Your Writing Process	2E	3E
Writing to Inform—Includes activities and assignments	■	▲
Preparing a Class News Publication—Includes activities and assignments	■	▲
Preparing a Collection of Folk Tales—Includes activities and assignments	■	▲
Writing About a Novel—Includes activities and assignments	■	▲

■ **(2E)** *Prentice Hall Literature, Copper,* Second Edition

▲ **(3E)** *Prentice Hall Literature, Copper,* Paramount Edition

CONNECTIONS BETWEEN INSPIRATIONS FOR EXPOSITION AND *PRENTICE HALL LITERATURE, COPPER*

You can use the multimedia Inspirations for Exposition to motivate student reading as well as student writing. Many of the Inspirations are audio recordings or video adaptations of selections from *Prentice Hall Literature, Copper*. Have students work in small groups to look at and discuss an appropriate Inspiration before reading the corresponding selection. Then, after reading the selection, students can replay the Inspiration and select one of the accompanying writing options (see pages 796–797). The following selection from *Prentice Hall Literature, Copper*, is included in the Inspirations for Exposition:

- **"Thunder Butte,"** Virginia Driving Hawk Sneve

Recommended Lesson Plan

The following lesson plan is recommended for providing students with thorough, comprehensive instructions in expository writing. Because you may not have all the components of the *Writer's Solution* or may have limited access to equipment, the plan provides a number of options. Choose the options that best suit your teaching style and equipment situation.

You may want to add a few days to the lesson plan to allow students time to publish their work and to hold conferences with students to discuss your assessment of their work.

FIVE-DAY LESSON PLAN	
Lesson Outcome:	**Each student writes a complete expository piece.**
DAY 1	**Introduce your students to expository writing.** Show the *Writers at Work Videodisc* segment featuring Charles Tsang. Use the segment as a springboard for class discussion or group activities.
DAY 2	**Have students choose a writing topic and plan their expository writing.** OPTION 1 Have students work either individually or in small groups to look at About Exposition and to choose a topic by browsing through the Inspirations for Exposition. Then have students work individually to develop their ideas by completing the rest of the Prewriting stage of the tutorial on Exposition. At the end of the period, have students print out their prewriting notes. OPTION 2 Have students review the Models From Literature in the About Exposition section of the *Sourcebook*. Then have them choose from the topic suggestions and begin developing their expository writing by completing the rest of the Prewriting stage of the Guided Lesson (pp. 110–119).
DAY 3	**Have students draft their expositions.** OPTION 1 Have students write their drafts on the computer following the instructions and using the activities provided in the Drafting section of the tutorial on Exposition. Have students print out their expository writing efforts at the end of the period. OPTION 2 Have students write their drafts on paper following the instructions in the Guided Lesson (pp. 120–121).
DAY 4	**Have students revise their expository writing.** OPTION 1 Have students revise their expository writing on the computer using the revision checkers, activities, and suggestions in the Revising and Editing section of the tutorial on Exposition. OPTION 2 Have students revise their expository writing following the suggestions in the Guided Lesson (pp. 122–123).

FIVE-DAY LESSON PLAN (continued)

DAY 5

Have students make final revisions.

OPTION 1 Have students review and revise their own work following the guidelines in the revising and editing section of the tutorial on Exposition. Students should then proofread and print out their final drafts.

OPTION 2 Have students revise and edit their work following the guidelines in the Guided Lesson (pp. 122–123).

Condensed Lesson Plans

Use the following lesson plans if you don't have a full week to devote to teaching expository writing.

Four- and Three-Day Plans: Adapt the Five-Day Plan by having students learn about expository writing, choose a topic, and develop ideas for their expositions all during Day 1. As in the Five-Day Plan, have students spend a day writing their drafts. For a Four-Day Plan, follow the last two days of the Five-Day Plan; for a Three-Day Plan, simply condense these two days into a single day of revision and forgo the option of working in peer groups.

TWO-DAY LESSON PLAN

Lesson Outcome: **Each student writes a complete expository piece.**

DAY 1

Have students choose a topic and write their first drafts.

OPTION 1 Have students work in the open-ended environment in the *Writing Lab*. Working individually, students should choose a topic by browsing through the Inspirations for Exposition. Then they should write their expositions in their on-line Notebooks using the available prewriting tools as needed.

OPTION 2 Using the suggestions and instructions in the *Sourcebook*, students should choose a topic and write a first draft of their expository pieces.

DAY 2

Have students revise and edit their work.

OPTION 1 Have students revise on the computer using the tools, activities, and instructions in the tutorial on Exposition.

OPTION 2 Have students revise their expositions following the suggestions in the *Sourcebook*.

If you only have one day to devote to teaching expository writing, students can work individually in the open-ended environment in the *Writing Lab* by browsing through the Inspirations for Exposition to choose a topic, using the prewriting tools as needed, and then complete a quick-write draft of an exposition in their on-line Notebook. Students may also use the *Sourcebook* to choose a topic and write a brief exposition.

Preparing to Teach

Lesson Objectives

Students will

1. Select an appropriate topic for a composition that defines or classifies a subject, summarizes information, or explains a process or gives instructions
2. Narrow the topic
3. Decide on purpose and audience
4. Gather and organize details
5. Complete an exposition in which they
   - include an introduction, a body, and a conclusion
   - include enough facts, examples, or other details to make the subject clear
   - arrange details in a logical order
6. Revise the writing for content, structure, and mechanics
7. Publish their finished work

Activating Prior Knowledge

Ask students to cite examples of times they have written to provide someone with information. Some may recall having left careful instructions for family members to follow when caring for pets or other belongings while they were away. Others may mention having written a summary of a movie, book, or play to a pen pal. Ask: *How did you help your readers understand the information you wanted to get across?*

CHAPTER 4

City Expanding *1989, Roger Brown, Phyllis Kind Art Gallery, New York*

Exposition: Giving Information

> "The important skills for writing good reports are accuracy, [brevity], and completeness."
>
> —Charles Tsang
> *New York City Police Officer*

Humanities Note

The fine art is a painting titled *City Expanding*, by Roger Brown (1941–). Roger Brown studied at the School of the Art Institute of Chicago and later became a leading painter in the "Chicago Imagist" movement—a group of painters who based the subject matter of their works on urban themes and then painted them in a modern folk-art style that is colorful, stylized, and often humorous.

This city view displays multiple high-rise buildings interwoven with crowded roadways. The silhouette of a different person appears in each lit window. The sky's red glow sprinkled with streaky white bands suggests smog. The cheerful pattern of the glowing windows and the evenly spaced buildings set against the looping curves of the sky and road suggests the bustling energy of city life.

Artists have always been inspired to paint their surroundings. A landscape artist takes inspiration from nature, combining its colors, forms, and lines to evoke a feeling or mood. This painting might be called a "cityscape." You might use the following questions for discussion:

- Notice the colors, forms, and lines used to portray this city setting. What do you think the artist is trying to say about city life?
- Imagine painting the city, town, or area you live in. What would you want to communicate about this setting? What would you paint and what colors, style, and so on would you use?

Addressing Your Classroom Situation

This chapter includes a variety of Models From Literature, topic ideas, writing process strategies, and Student Models, along with two integrated skills lessons. Feel free to pick and choose from this material to create a customized lesson on expository writing that matches your classroom needs.

The following are some of the key features of the chapter:

- The chapter begins with a section introducing expository writing. This section includes thoughts about expository writing from New York City Police Officer Charles Tsang, group discussion questions, and Models From Literature and Workplace Writing Models for the following types of expository writing: definitions, classifications, summaries, and written instructions.
- The Prewriting section includes an assortment of idea-generating activities to help students choose a type of expository writing, select a topic, and narrow the topic, along with some suggested topics from which they can select. This section also provides instruction and activities to help students consider their audience and purpose, and to gather evidence and organize details. A Topic Web helps students to narrow topics. Writing Models guide them through the process of writing to their audience and through other stages of the expository writing process.
- The Drafting section provides tips for writing different kinds of exposition and presents Writing Models for each type.
- The Revising and Editing section focuses on making sure that an exposition is well organized, easy to understand, and that it includes only pertinent information.
- The Guided Lesson is followed by a Student Model and then skills lessons on using exact nouns and on subject-verb agreement.
- The chapter ends with a complete Literature Model, an article entitled “My Life’s Work: Crime Lab Scientist,” by Jeff Saviano.

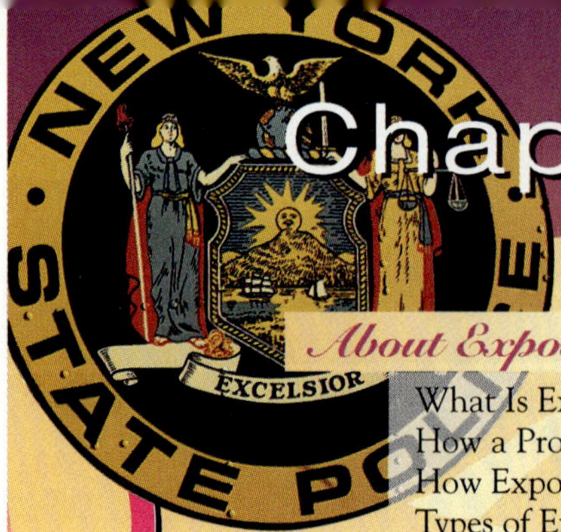

Chapter Contents

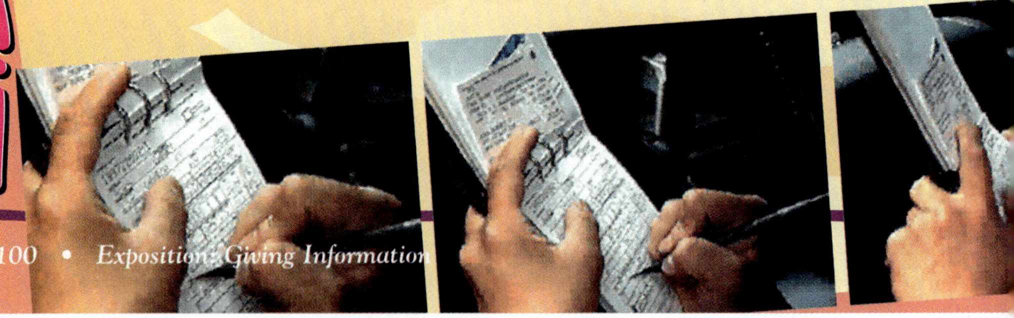

"If a person was robbed, you would write a complaint report, and if a person was the subject of an accident, you would write a police accident report."

"When you're summarizing a report, you have to be brief, but be as complete as possible without stating unimportant facts."

—Charles Tsang
New York City Police Officer

"Certainly, note-taking is very important in our job. . . . We would use those notes to refresh our memory when we're in court."

More About the Writer

Officer Charles Tsang walks a beat in New York City's Chinatown. He deals with many people and events during the course of a busy day in the neighborhood and in the precinct. In order to keep track of exactly what happens, Tsang takes careful notes. He uses the notes to write reports that summarize what happened. Talk with your students about how they think note taking and report writing help a police officer enforce law, preserve the peace, and deter crime.

Tech Prep Note

Point out that not only police officers like Charles Tsang use expository writing. Workers in other fields write expositions on the job. Architects and engineers write building and home inspection expository reports. Toy and game designers write instruction manuals for setting up and using their products, as do manufacturers of electronic equipment, cameras, and cars. Anthropologists, archaeologists, and other museum workers define and classify when they write copy for the exhibits and shows. Ask: *Think about the adults you know and the jobs they have. How do they use their expository writing skills at work?*

About Exposition: Giving Information

What Is Exposition?

If you've ever struggled through instructions explaining how to put a bicycle together, you're familiar with exposition. **Exposition**, or expository writing, is writing that informs or explains. It provides facts—rather than opinions—about a given subject. Examples of exposition include instructions on how to grow tomatoes, a definition of a type of music, and a summary of the plot of a movie.

Group Discussion You'll run into exposition almost everywhere. An encyclopedia article about birds and cooking instructions printed on boxes of frozen vegetables are both examples of expository writing.

What other examples of expository writing have you encountered? With a group of your classmates, share some examples of exposition that you've read. Give the source of each example—dictionary, encyclopedia, model airplane instructions—and tell why the piece was easy or difficult to understand. Then decide if some kinds of exposition—such as magazine articles—are easier to understand than others.

How a Professional Uses Exposition

People in many professions use expository writing. Newspaper reporters, movie critics, travel writers, biographers, and advertising copy writers are just some of the professional writers who write expository pieces. However, expository writing isn't limited to professional writers. People in many other professions—such as teachers, scientists, lawyers, physicians, and police officers—use exposition on the job.

Charles Tsang is a police officer in New York City. An important part of his job is writing accurate reports about crimes, accidents, and other types of incidents he deals with every day. As Officer Tsang explains, his police reports must include specific types of important information:

> "The features that we include in our reports are taught when we're in the [Police] Academy: First, stating when it happened and where it happened, who . . . was involved, what happened, how did it happen, and why it happened. So, when you have all of those items in a report, there is really no chance that you will make a mistake or that you will omit any important information."

How Exposition Fits Into Your Life

"Go about six blocks and make a left at the traffic light. Then go about four blocks until you see a gas station on the right. The store is just ahead on the left side of the street." Have you ever given someone directions to your home or anywhere else? If you have, you've used exposition, a form of speaking and writing that you probably use every day without realizing it. Any time you explain how to do something, give directions, or define or summarize something, you're using expository skills. This chapter will show you how to sharpen those skills so that you will be able to present information effectively in writing.

Integrating Literature With Writing

Starting From Literature

You can use the models on pages 104–108 to illustrate the various elements of each type of expository writing. Or you can use the content or devices found in these pieces to inspire writing on any of the topics they address. For example, have students use their reactions to the excerpt from "The Truth About Dragons" (p. 107) to write a definition of a favorite pet, real or imagined, by providing several precise and vivid details that show how it differs from other pets.

Teaching Strategy

Briefly introduce and define the type of writing each selection models. You might invite a student to read each piece aloud to the class. Follow up with discussion to reinforce students' understanding of each type of expository writing.

Teaching From the Model

Guide students to analyze Powell's summary of Scott O'Dell's *My Name Is Not Angelica* to understand the characteristics of a summary of a book:

- *It identifies the setting and main characters.* In the very beginning of the summary, Powell clearly introduces the prince and princess and succinctly describes what has happened to them.
- *It gives a brief description of the plot, without giving anything away.* Powell's summary tells the reader something about the plot without revealing any surprises the story has in store for them.

Types of Exposition

There are many kinds of expository writing. This chapter focuses on expository writing that gives information on a single subject. Included in this kind of writing are definitions, classifications, summaries, and instructions. Here are examples of each of these types of expository writing:

1 Summary of a Book

- A summary of a book—either fiction or nonfiction—highlights for readers the main points of the book.
- A summary of a novel gives readers a brief description of the setting, characters, and plot, without giving away any surprises or the ending of the story.
- A summary of a nonfiction work presents the most important facts and the organization of the content.

Workplace Writing Model

The following is Faye A. Powell's summary of *My Name Is Not Angelica,* a novel by Scott O'Dell. Notice that Powell identifies the setting and the main characters and tells us something about the plot, without giving away any of the story's surprises.

Raisha was going to become an African princess, because she was going to marry her love, Prince Konji. But instead, both were captured, torn from their African homes, brought to the West Indies, and enslaved. They were renamed Angelica and Apollo by the man who bought them.

The royal Konji became a common field hand, while Raisha forced the smile she had learned on the slave ship and became a house servant.

However, it wasn't long before Konji escaped and became the leader of 300 runaways. He began to plan a great revolt against the few rich plantation owners, a revolt that would eventually make Raisha fear for her own life. Yet it would also make her brave and rebellious enough to declare to the world, "My name is *not* Angelica!"

2 Classification

- When you classify, you group items into categories based on the things they have in common.
- An example of classifying is grouping plants into categories, such as flowers, trees, fruits, and vegetables.

Model From Literature

The following classification is an excerpt from the book *Gorillas* by Paul Hermann Bürgel and Manfred Hartwig. In this passage, the authors first name the group and then tell what characteristics all members of the group have in common.

One of the reasons that people are fascinated by gorillas may be the special connection that exists between humans and gorillas. Both belong to the same scientific group of animals. Like people, gorillas are classified as primates (prī«māts). Monkeys and chimpanzees are other members of this group.

Primates have many different physical features, but they have some important things in common. One is a large brain and often a high degree of intelligence. Other features common to many primates are flexible hands able to hold and grasp things.

Within the group of primates, gorillas are most closely related to chimpanzees, orangutans, and gibbons. All these animals are known as apes.

Teaching From the Model

Guide students to understand the characteristics of this type of expository writing by reading and discussing the excerpt from *Gorillas*, by Bürgel and Hartwig:

- *It groups items into categories based on common properties*. In this passage from a book, the authors discuss the special connection between humans and gorillas and cite the reasons that both humans and gorillas, as well as monkeys and chimpanzees, can be classified as primates.

Cross-Curricular Connection: *Science*

In recent years, scientists have come to believe that many dinosaurs did not die out, but have evolved into birds. Have interested students do research to find out more about the connection between birds and dinosaurs. Guide them to find out about common features and habits. Students may choose to develop this classification as the topic for their expository piece.

Teaching From the Model

Guide students to analyze this excerpt from *M*A*S*H: The Exclusive, Inside Story of TV's Most Popular Show* to understand how it exemplifies a summary of a media program:

- *The summary gives only basic information, telling who was involved and what happened.* Point out how David S. Reiss describes only the main events of an episode and names only the two main characters, Radar O'Reilly and Klinger.
- *Events are presented factually, and only the most important details are given.* Although it is very likely that other characters appeared in the episode and that there may have been subplots as well as some twists in plot, the reviewer sticks to the key details—the crisis created by the absence of the experienced Radar and the inability of Klinger to fill his shoes.

Clarification

Discuss with students that in addition to writing about books and television programs, publicists and reviewers write summaries of movies, shows, plays, and dance performances, as well as of tapes and compact discs.

3 Summary of a Media Program

- A summary of a media program gives the reader basic information without all the details.
- When you write a summary, tell the reader who was involved and what happened.
- Present events as factually as possible, giving only the most important details.

Workplace Writing Model

In the following excerpt from *M*A*S*H: The Exclusive, Inside Story of TV's Most Popular Show*, David S. Reiss briefly describes only the main events of a "M*A*S*H" episode.

GOODBYE RADAR

Company clerk Radar O'Reilly (Gary Burghoff), on leave in Tokyo, is desperately needed back at the crisis-stricken 4077th, but his return is delayed by outside events. While casualties continue to pour in from the front, the 4077th's generator conks out, depriving the medical unit of all electrical power. But Klinger, filling in for the vacationing Radar, lacks the expertise and experience to wheel and deal for a new machine.

Guest Cast: Marilyn Jones, Johnny Haymer, Michael O'Dwyer, Richard Lee-Sung, Tony Cristino, Arell Blanton.

Written by: Ken Levine and David Isaacs

Directed by: Charles S. Dubin

4 Definition

- A definition explains something by describing its main features.
- A definition may tell what category or group something belongs to. For example, a definition of a dog might state that a dog is a mammal.

Model From Literature

In this passage from *The Truth About Dragons*, Rhoda Blumberg defines a fictional type of dragon by providing details that show how it differs from other types of these imaginary creatures.

The smallest and most fearsome of all dragons was the basilisk. This mini-monster, ranging in size from six inches to two feet, had the head of a rooster, the warts of a toad, and the body of a snake. It hid in wells and in cellars. The basilisk's death-ray eyes killed with a look. Anyone it glared at dropped dead. Once common in Europe, basilisks were killed off by clever people who used mirrors as shields. The monsters died of fright when they saw their own horrid reflections.

Teaching From the Model

Guide students to recognize that the Rhoda Blumberg excerpt is an example of the type of expository writing known as a definition:

- *It explains something by describing its main features*. The writer describes the size, body, skin, and eyes of the dragon. She also points out its habitat and, of importance to all dragon fighters, its weapons as well as its weaknesses.
- *It explains how a thing differs from others like it*. The details Blumberg provides distinguish the basilisk from other dragons, many of which we envision as being much larger and fire-breathing.

Cultural Connection

Some students might be interested in learning more about dragons. They might find out, for instance, that dragons are seen differently in Eastern and Western cultures. Invite interested students to find out more about these different perceptions and share findings with the class.

Exploring Related Literature

Students who choose this kind of expository writing may wish to read "The Truth About Dragons," by Rhoda Blumberg, which can be found in *Prentice Hall Literature, Copper.*

Teaching From the Model

Guide students to analyze this excerpt from *Creative Kids* to understand how it exemplifies written instructions:

- *It describes the steps needed to do something.* The writer lists all necessary steps, in a logical order, in the process of making a rain gauge.

5 Written Instructions

- Written instructions describe the steps needed to make something or to get somewhere.
- Giving someone written instructions on how to get from your school to your home is an example.

Workplace Writing Model

The following excerpt from *Kids Discover* explains how to build and use a rain gauge. Notice that the writer lists all necessary materials and presents, in logical order, the steps for making a rain gauge.

Just how much RAIN has it RAINED? Without a rain gauge, it's not easy to tell!

A brief, sudden thunderstorm that looks very fierce may actually result in very little rain accumulation.

To see how much rain has fallen, make a rain gauge. You will need: a funnel; a heavy, straight-sided bottle; a piece of masking tape; and a waterproof marker.

Stick 3 inches of masking tape on the side of the bottle, then mark off quarter inches using a waterproof marker.

Place the funnel inside the bottle; then measure how much water accumulates every time it rains.

Guided Lesson

Now that you've learned about the different types of exposition, you're ready to start developing your expository paper. This lesson will help guide you through the writing process. You may not want to start at the beginning of the lesson, however. Decide what help you will need in writing your paper. Then use this chart to determine where to begin.

	START WITH
• If you **do not have a topic**	Choosing Your Topic
• If you **have a topic that seems too general** (such as Different Kinds of Animals)	Narrowing Your Topic
• If you **have a specific topic but aren't sure what details to include**	Gathering Information
• If you **have a topic and enough information to work with**	Drafting

Guiding Student Writing

Addressing Your Classroom Situation

- If you choose to assign topics or types of expository writing, allow time for students to narrow the topic to suit their interests or find an appealing focus to pursue.
- You may wish to have students work in pairs. If so, brainstorm ways partners might collaborate usefully and fairly. One way is for pairs to separate their chosen topic into parts so that one student begins the exposition and the other continues it. For example, to describe how to make a rain gauge, one might discuss the materials needed, telling what each is used for, and then begin the setup instructions. The other could then complete these instructions and describe how to use the finished product. The partners can discuss, in advance, what information each will cover.

Language Acquisition/ESL Teaching Strategy

The *Writing Lab* offers a variety of options that can be adapted to meet the needs of ESL students. The following are some examples of such adaptations.

- The Revising and Editing section provides an interactive writing model that can be used with your advanced ESL students. As the students read the two drafts, they take notes about why the author decided to remove certain details. They then refer to these notes when revising their own drafts.
- The Choosing Your Topic section offers an Idea Wheel that can be adapted for use with your upper-basic and intermediate ESL students. Working in pairs, the students spin the wheel and discuss each topic idea as it arises. Each student makes a list of the ideas for reference when writing a first draft.

Writing Lab CD-ROM

The Choosing Your Topic section of the tutorial on expository writing includes the following options to help students come up with their own topics:

- **Idea Wheel** In this activity, students spin a wheel to get topic ideas for each type of expository writing.
- **Self-interview** Students ask themselves questions that help them find out what their interests are.

Working individually or in small groups, students can experiment with these activities to find the ones that work best.

Writers at Work Videodisc

Play the videodisc segment in which Officer Tsang discusses his sources for topics. Tsang says that he talks with the people on his beat to find out about their problems, whether they are "crimes or quality of life" problems. Ask:

- How might you classify the kinds of reports a police officer writes?
- How else might Tsang get his topics and data for reports?

Play frames 35109 to 36099

Prewriting

Choosing Your Topic

What kind of expository paper would you like to write? You can write a definition, a classification, a summary, or instructions. To help you decide, you can choose from among the suggested writing options (see pages 112–115) or use one or more of the following techniques to discover a topic of your own.

If you're considering

. . . a definition, a summary, or written instructions:

CONDUCT A SELF-INTERVIEW

What kinds of exposition have you used recently? Conduct a self-interview to find out. Ask yourself the following questions and jot down your answers. One of those answers might include the writing topic you're looking for:

- What kinds of things have I defined, or explained recently?
- What movies or television shows have I summarized for someone who hadn't seen them?
- What instructions or procedures have I explained to someone?

. . . a classification or written instructions:

Group Activity

HOLD A HOBBY CONVENTION

What's your favorite hobby? Reading? Drawing? Chess? Basketball? Rock collecting? Hold a Hobby Convention with a group of your classmates and share your hobbies. Take turns describing your hobby and explaining exactly what you do. Do you follow any special procedures? Do you use any special tools or equipment? If possible, show examples related to your hobby, such as a flintstone collection or special brushes you use to paint watercolors. Jot down important points about each hobby mentioned. Then review your notes later for possible writing topics.

. . . a definition or a classification:

MAKE UP YOUR OWN CLASSIFICATIONS

Without realizing it, you probably already classify things in your mind. For example, you might divide desserts into classes, such as cookies, ice cream, cakes, pies, and so on. You might prefer a certain class of pet, such as tropical fish. Make a list of foods, activities, animals, objects, and events that interest you. Then sort your list into categories, such as winter sports, airplanes, or fast-food restaurants. Look over your notes for possible writing topics.

. . . a definition or written instructions:

START A HOW-TO HOT LINE

Do you know how to program a VCR? Can you prepare a grilled-cheese sandwich, sew on a button, plant flowers, fly a kite, or operate a microwave oven? If you can, you can help those who don't know how to do them by giving instructions over a how-to hot line. Jot down some of the things that you know how to do. Then review your notes to find procedures that you would like to explain step by step on a how-to hot line. You just might find a hot topic.

. . . a classification or a summary:

Group Activity

PRESENT ACADEMY AWARDS

What's your favorite recent movie? Which older movie have you seen several times? Honor these movies by presenting them with awards for excellence. With a group of your classmates, hold an Academy Awards ceremony. Take turns sharing the movies you would nominate for an award. For each movie, give its title as well as the category to which it belongs—such as adventure, comedy, or mystery. Then explain why you think the motion picture deserves an award. Jot down the names of all the nominated movies for possible writing topics.

Thematic Connection: Humor

Groups of students who are interested in the Academy Awards activity may enjoy the comedy challenge of presenting this year's crop of bad movies with awards for poor quality. They can hold a "Pie in the Face" ceremony honoring the worst movies of the year by category—the dullest adventure, the least-funny comedy, the least-scary science fiction, the least-dramatic drama, the driest underwater movie, and so on. Students can use the results of this activity to generate ideas for a definition or a classification.

Cross-Curricular Connection: *Math*

Students interested in the Start a How-To Hot Line activity can work together to generate a set of instructions for programming a VCR or for operating or setting up another appliance. However, they should purposely list the steps *out of order.* Another student, who will write operation or set-up instructions based on this data, must first rearrange the steps into a sensible order.

Writing Lab CD-ROM

Using the Inspirations for Exposition is an excellent way to stimulate creativity and have students explore possible topics for expository writing. Students can browse individually or in small groups through the Inspirations. They can choose their own writing topics or you may prefer to assign topics.

The following is a list of the expository writing options included in the Inspirations, but not provided in the *Sourcebook:*

Summary of

- An article or media program about becoming a writer
- A news event about a person overcoming defeat
- A story about a helpful animal
- A true story about a person and animal
- A movie or television show with elements of fantasy
- A hobby magazine
- A media program about sports
- A media program about a successful underdog
- A story about a conflict between the weak and strong
- Events that led to a sculpture
- A story about conflicts with tradition
- An event
- A favorite magazine

Classification of

- How spiders help or hurt humans
- Animals in cold climates
- Traditions in a culture
- Tokens of friendship
- A Starship Captain's duties
- Starship jobs
- Newspaper articles
- Events as types of newspaper articles
- Penguins

Instructions for

- How to be a happy baby
- A first officer

Definition of

- A desert
- Spiders
- Friendship
- A newspaper department

Speculation about

- Reasons for painting the *Mona Lisa*
- Reasons for the smile of the *Mona Lisa*
- Reasons for a person's unexpected behavior
- Causes for the fear of spiders
- Causes and effects of story characters
- Effects of a positive attitude

Prewriting

The Sleeping Gypsy *Henri Rousseau*

Inspirations for Exposition

Here are some writing topics for exposition:

A Definition of a Desert

When you think of a desert, what comes to mind—dry, sandy ground with an occasional cactus? Look at the painting above, *The Sleeping Gypsy*, for inspiration. Then write a short definition of a desert. To help you write your definition, check a reference work, such as an encyclopedia, to find facts about deserts. In your definition, you might want to compare the desert to another type of region, such as a jungle, a forest, or a beach.

A Classification of Cars

Hundreds of cars probably pass by you every week without your even noticing them. Take some time to look at the cars that travel your local streets and highways. What kinds of cars do you see? Write an expository paper in which you classify cars. You can categorize cars by type of vehicle, size, make, or even color. Some sample categories include compact, station wagon, convertible, hatchback, and van. Be sure to explain the chief elements of each car category that you list. You might want to record the number of each kind of car that passes your home over a given period of time.

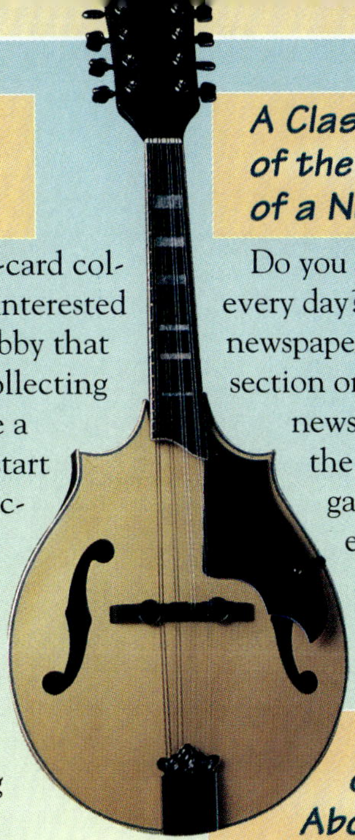

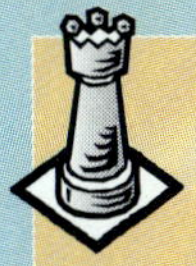

Instructions for Starting a Hobby

How do you start a baseball-card collection? How do you become interested in playing chess? Choose a hobby that interests you, such as stamp collecting or building model ships. Write a set of instructions for how to start the hobby. Present your instructions in the order in which they should be followed. You can write them in either a numbered list or in paragraph form. Be specific and include details so that readers will have no trouble following your instructions.

Group Project

Create a Television Viewing Guide

Imagine that you are a group of writers who prepare summaries of television programs for a daily television guide. As a group, create a nightly television schedule that lists your favorite shows. Then have each group member write a brief summary of an upcoming episode of a favorite show. What you'll actually do is summarize a memorable *past* episode and write about the episode as if it were an upcoming one. Make sure each summary includes exciting details about the characters, plot, and setting to capture the reader's interest.

A Classification of the Sections of a Newspaper

Do you browse through a newspaper every day? The different sections of a newspaper—such as an entertainment section or a sports section—categorize news and other information. Study the way a local newspaper is organized. Write a short paper that explains the paper's sections, or categories. Explain what kinds of information and articles are contained in each category.

A Summary of a News Story About Overcoming an Obstacle

Overcoming difficulties is often the theme of news stories. Think of a news story you have seen on television or read in a newspaper or magazine about a person who overcame an obstacle. Then write a summary of this story. Identify the person and explain the obstacle that he or she had to overcome.

Instructions for Becoming a Best Friend

Is there someone who is your best friend or whom you would like to be your best friend? With that person in mind, write a set of instructions for becoming a best friend. You might want to include in your instructions the attitude and behavior that would enable someone to become a good friend.

Addressing Ability Levels

Challenge your **more-advanced students** who choose to classify the sections of a newspaper to first list, then explain through classification, the sections of what they would consider the ideal newspaper for middle-school students. You may wish to have students collaborate to come up with the different sections.

Alternate Activity/ Thematic Connection: Social Responsibility

Suggest to students who choose to write instructions for becoming a best friend to consider instead writing instructions for becoming a caring, socially responsible citizen. These students may wish to interview someone they think of as being socially responsible in order to get ideas for their writing.

Writing Tip

Suggest to students who are interested in writing summaries of television shows that they browse through a few different guides to get a sense of the kinds of information given in these concise synopses. Remind students to avoid revealing any plot turns or surprising outcomes.

Thematic Connection: Exploring the Past

Suggest to students who choose to write a classification of cars (page 112) to consider writing about the earliest cars or cars of the past. Guide these students to visit the school library or to browse in a bookstore to get ideas and see photos of vintage cars.

Writing Strategy

Encourage students who choose to write about deserts to browse through books about deserts or to watch desert videos in order to get ideas for their definition. Point out that although all deserts may look different from one another, they have similar characteristics. Definitions should focus on these common features.

Writing Lab CD-ROM

The Inspirations for Exposition also include the following Group Projects and Group Discussions. The Group Discussions encourage small groups of students to share their thoughts about an Inspiration and to generate possible writing topics. The Group Projects are structured activities in which students assume different roles.

Group Projects

- Developing a guide for young writers
- Writing a book of quotations for a good life
- Creating a sequel for the sculpture
- Creating a cat poster
- Making a chart about baby development
- Developing a class newspaper

Group Discussions

- Giving an award for Best Animal in a Painting
- Choosing a favorite insect or spider
- Speculating about the effects of having a penguin as a pet
- Identifying a favorite sport
- Explaining dreams in fiction
- Identifying a favorite portrait
- Talking about how to enjoy reading a newspaper or magazine

MORE *Inspirations* for Exposition

A Definition of a Bird

What are the unique characteristics of birds? Think about all the different types of birds you are familiar with—for example, chickens, ostriches, canaries, penguins, peacocks, flamingos, and eagles. Even though these birds are quite different from each other, they have certain characteristics in common. Using your own personal observations and facts from reference books, write a definition of a bird. Point out the features that all or most birds share, which set them apart from other animals.

A Summary of a Personal Triumph

The ability to keep up an effort—instead of giving up—often helps people overcome great obstacles. Think of a movie or television program in which a person or character overcomes a major obstacle. Write a summary of the movie or program. Present a brief description of the character and the obstacle that he or she faced. Then write a clear, precise explanation of how the person has overcome the challenge. Be sure to tell what actions or personality traits led to the person's success.

Instructions on How to Feed a Baby

Because babies are totally dependent on other people for their survival, it is especially important that care be taken to feed them properly. In a short paper, give a set of instructions that explain how to feed a baby. Use library resources—or the manual your mother used—to find out the "dos" and "don'ts." Be sure to include information on foods that are nutritious and safe for babies to eat. You could write the instructions in a numbered list or in paragraph form, but arrange them in the order of their importance.

Group Project

Dream Up a Poster

Do you ever find yourself thinking about what your life will be like in the future? What are your hopes and dreams? How can thinking about your future help you plan for it? As a group, define several categories of hopes and dreams, such as educational or career goals, or places where you would like to live, and give examples of each. Then have each group member choose one of their hopes for the future and write a brief paragraph about making that dream come true. Collect the paragraphs and use them to create a poster entitled "Dreams for Tomorrow." Illustrate the poster for greater visual impact.

Judge and Dog *© Orlando R. Cuevas, Courtesy of the artist*

A Summary of Criminal Events

Look at the sculpture in the photograph above. Why is the dog before the judge? What crime do you think the dog committed? Perhaps the dog ran off with someone's towel at the beach or chewed on a piece of furniture. The dog may even have bitten someone. Do you think the little animal deserves to be punished? Imagine the events that led to the scene shown in the sculpture. Then write a short paper summarizing what happened.

Define Qualities of Heroic Leaders

Civil rights leader Martin Luther King, Jr., women's suffrage leader Susan B. Anthony, and Mahatma Gandhi, who led India's nonviolent struggle for independence, are heroes to millions of people. Think of other historical figures who have been admired around the world. What qualities do these people share? In a short essay, explain what you think makes these people outstanding. Feel free to use the library and other resources.

Language Acquisition/ ESL Teaching Strategy

Put your upper-basic and intermediate ESL students into multilevel groups of three to complete the Instructions on How to Feed a Baby. Ask them first to list the steps in the process, using personal experience and library resources. Then ask them to list the steps in order of importance. The upper-basic students can use the list to make an oral presentation to the other ESL students. The intermediate students should describe the feeding process in paragraph form.

You can use the Dream Up a Poster idea as a large Group Project for ESL students of all levels. After a discussion of the students' dreams for the future, ask them to write a short paragraph describing their desires. Encourage the students to use the verbs *will*, *would*, and *would like*. Each student then draws a small picture of his or her dream, and the group as a whole makes a collage of their paragraphs and drawings to be posted in the classroom.

Writing Lab CD-ROM

The Narrowing Your Topic section of the tutorial on Exposition includes the following options to help students come up with their own topics:

- **Video clip of topic ideas** Students play a video to see broad and narrow topic ideas related to the newspaper business.
- **Annotated instruction** Students learn about whether a topic is narrow enough for an exposition and can see examples of how broad topics have been narrowed. Additionally, they learn how to use tools such as a Timeline, a Topic Web, a Chain of Events Chart, and a Cluster Diagram to narrow their topics.

Working individually or in small groups, students can experiment with these activities to find the ones that work best for them.

Alternate Activity

As an alternative to the Cluster Diagram activity in the *Writing Lab* CD-ROM, pairs or individuals can create Cluster Diagrams on drawing paper.

Writers at Work Videodisc

Play the videodisc segment in which Officer Charles Tsang talks about the strategy he uses to narrow the topics of his reports. Ask:

- What does Tsang say about how he determines the kind of report he is going to file? What skills do you think are important for police officers to have in order to write competent, effective reports?

Prewriting

Narrowing Your Topic

Is your topic narrow enough to cover thoroughly in a brief expository paper? For example, you'd probably have to write a book to classify all the different kinds of plants growing throughout the world. In contrast, you could easily classify in a short paper the different kinds of pines that grow in your region. If you're not sure whether your topic is narrow enough, ask yourself the following questions:

Questions for Narrowing Your Topic

- How long will your paper be?
- Within that length, can you include all the important details, steps, or parts of your topic?
- Can you divide your topic into subtopics or stages and cover one of them more fully in your paper?

Use a Topic Web

If you decide your topic is too broad, use a topic web to narrow it. First, draw a line at the top of your paper and write your topic on that line. Next, write subtopics on lines beneath your topic. Use a line to connect each subtopic to your topic. Then write subtopics of your subtopics, connecting them with lines to the related subtopic. Look through your topic web for subtopics that interest you and choose one of them as the topic for your expository paper. A sample topic web follows.

Writing Model: Topic Web

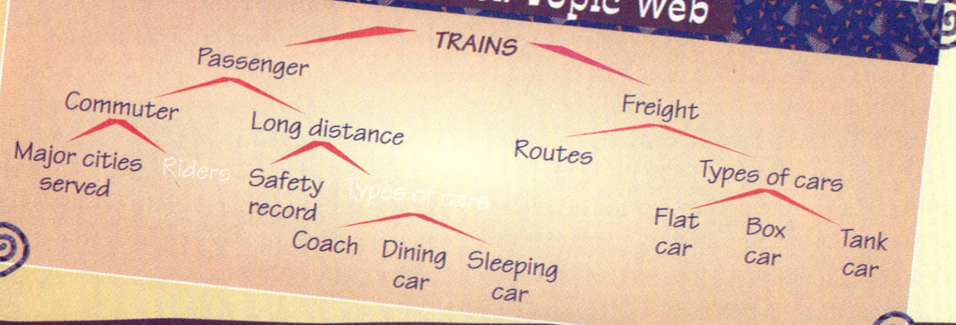

Play frames 33609 to 33984

Language Lab CD-ROM

If students need additional guidance in determining how best to narrow their topic, you may want them to complete the narrowing-a-topic lesson in the Composing unit of the *Language Lab*. It may be useful to set up brief conferences with these students to talk through some of the possibilities.

Writers at Work Videodisc

Play the videodisc segment in which Officer Tsang talks about making his reports "applicable to" the several people who will be reading his reports. Ask:

Considering Your Audience

As Officer Tsang indicates, there are many possible audiences for your expository writing. Your audience will influence what you write. For example, if your readers know little about your topic, you will have to include many details to help them understand it. On the other hand, if your readers know something about your topic, you can leave out the basics and present the latest information or little-known facts. Identify your audience and consider its age, interests, and knowledge of your subject.

FROM a WRITER

"Many people read a police officer's writings . . . a defense lawyer, a district attorney, a judge, insurance companies, private citizens."

—Charles Tsang

The two examples of expository writing below are about the same subject, baseball, but are written for two different audiences: experienced players and inexperienced players. Notice that the words *box*, *ump*, and *deliver* are used only in the example for experienced players. What other differences do you notice?

Writing Models: Considering Your Audience

INTENDED AUDIENCE: EXPERIENCED PLAYERS

Before you step into the box, you should always check with the third-base coach. Put your right foot in the box first, in the position you want it. Signal the ump for time out if you need it. Place your left foot in the box and adjust your stance. Finally, look up at the pitcher in the place where he will deliver, not at the hand that is holding the ball.

INTENDED AUDIENCE: INEXPERIENCED PLAYERS

Before you step into the batter's box on either side of home plate, always check with the third-base coach. Put your right foot in the box first, in the position you want it. Signal the umpire for time out by raising your right hand and saying "time please" if you need it. Place your left foot in the box and adjust your stance. Finally, look up at the pitcher in the place where he will release the ball, not at the hand that is holding the ball.

Writing Lab CD-ROM

The Considering Audience and Purpose section of the tutorial on expository writing includes the following options to help students explore ways to gear their writing to the intended audience and to choose their writing purpose:

- **Video clip about writing for a particular audience** Students play a video to hear how the writer's choice of details suits her intended audience.
- **Audio-annotated Student Models** Students choose passages from expositions written for different audiences to hear about how the choice of audience affected the writing.
- **Audience Profile** Students answer questions that help them focus on their intended audience.
- **Audio-annotated Models From Literature** Students choose passages from expositions written for different purposes to hear about how the choice of purpose affected the writing.
- **Purpose-statement activity** Students answer questions that help them define their writing purpose.

Working individually or in small groups, students can experiment with these activities to find the ones that work best for them.

- How can you make sure your readers will understand and appreciate your exposition?

Play frames 39958 to 40471

Language Lab CD-ROM

If students need additional guidance regarding audience and purpose, you can refer them to the Considering Audience and Purpose lesson in the Composing unit of the *Language Lab*.

Prewriting

Considering Your Purpose

Decide on the purpose for writing your exposition. Although your general purpose is to provide information, you should also have a more specific purpose in mind. Your purpose will affect your choice of language and details. Use the following questions to help you find your purpose:

- Why is it important for you to explain your subject?
- What makes your subject special or different from others of its kind?
- How will your audience use the information you're giving?
- What aspects of your subject are most important to emphasize?

FROM a WRITER

"[Write] as many important details as you can when you take notes. You might not have to use them all, but it's very important to list them all. . . ."

—Charles Tsang

Gathering Information

Follow Officer Tsang's advice and gather as much information as you can about your topic. Your information may be in the form of facts, examples, statistics, definitions, or categories. Here are some tips to help you gather information:

Tips for Gathering Information

- For a definition, take notes about the main features or details of what you are defining.
- For a classification, gather details that show the similarities of the members of the category.
- For a summary, list the main points of what you are summarizing. For example, note the main events in the plot of a movie.
- For written instructions, gather details relating to each step in the process you are explaining.

Writing Lab CD-ROM

The Gathering Information section of the tutorial on expository writing includes the following options designed to help students come up with details for their expositions:

- **Video clip on gathering information** Students play the video to see tips from Officer Charles Tsang.
- **Video clip on gathering details for a classification** Students play the video to hear suggestions for gathering details for their own classification.
- **Interactive model focusing on using details in a classification** Students choose the passage to learn more about how to use details to show that one group, whales, is part of a larger group, mammals.
- **Descriptive Word Bin** Students select their topic and choose from a menu of words that describe their topic or parts of it. To save descriptive words for later use, they can drag each one into their on-line notebook.
- **Interactive writing instruction about using details in a summary** Students learn about the kinds of information that will be necessary to include for different types of summaries, and use a Timeline Activity to help them decide which details in their own summary are most important to include.
- **Interactive instruction for giving written instructions** Students examine a model to see an example of using details, and use a Cluster Diagram to help them come up with details for their own instructions.

Working individually or in small groups, students can experiment with these activities to find the ones that work best for them.

Writers at Work Videodisc

Play the videodisc segment in which Officer Charles Tsang talks about the strategy he uses to pull together the details of his reports. Ask:

- What does Tsang say about how he determines what information to include in his reports and what to leave out?
- What do you think of his NEOTWY method? Can you apply a version of it to your prewriting phase? How?

Play frames 37680 to 38726

Writing Strategies

Encourage students to supplement details gathered from

CHALLENGE

For a challenge, you might try defining your topic by what it is *not*, rather than what it *is*. This works well for things that people mistake for other things. If you use this method, choose details to show that your topic doesn't fit into the class in which many people try to put it. Here are some possibilities:

- A whale is not a fish.
- A tomato is not a vegetable.
- The moon is not a planet.
- A peanut is not a nut.

Organizing Details

Now that you've finished gathering information, your next task is to organize it. A well-organized paper will be easier for your readers to follow and understand. You can organize your information spatially, chronologically, or by order of importance.

Spatial Organization

Use spatial organization to show the relationship of different parts of something to the other parts. For example, if you were explaining the parts of a car, you might start with the grille, headlights, and front bumper and work your way to the back. Spatial organization is often used for a definition.

Chronological Organization

Use chronological order when you want to summarize events or give step-by-step instructions. When you use chronological order, you simply present events in the order in which they occur.

Order of Importance

When you want to place extra emphasis on certain details or points, use an order-of-importance organization plan. List the most important information first and end with less important details, or vice versa.

You can organize a definition or a classification by order of importance.

esearch with others they find hrough firsthand experience. For example, a student planning to give written instructions for using certain functions on a calculator might nclude different but equally effective procedures, as well as shortcuts, learned through rial and error.

Language Lab CD-ROM

Students who need more practice using vivid language may benefit from working on the first three lessons from the Choosing Words unit of the *Language Lab:* Exact Nouns, Vivid and Precise Words, and Vivid Adjectives and Adverbs.

Clarification

Point out to students that although certain ways to order information may work best for certain kinds of expositions, these orders are not necessarily the only ones that make sense. Emphasize that it may be equally effective to use other types of organization. In addition, a given type of organization can be used in various ways. For example, when arranging details in spatial order, students needn't confine the order to a two-dimensional perspective, such as from left to right, but may indicate depth, such as an inside/outside order or a far-away-to-close-up order. Students should keep in mind how they want the reader to envision what they are describing.

Writing Lab CD-ROM

The Organizing Details section includes the following options designed to help students come up with an effective way to organize the details they've gathered:

- **Video clip of an unorganized passage** Students play the video to learn what happens when details are unorganized.
- **Cluster Diagram** Students use a Cluster Diagram to help them organize details spatially.
- **Chain of Events Activity** Students use this activity to help them place details in chronological order.
- **Notecard Activity** Students complete this activity to help them organize the details of their summary in order of importance. They can choose to see an example of how to use the note cards.

Working individually or in small groups, students can experiment with these activities to find the ones that work best for them.

Writing Lab CD-ROM

The Drafting section includes the following options designed to help students write the first draft of their exposition:

- **Video clip** Students play the video to obtain drafting tips from Officer Tsang.
- **Interactive models of classifications and definitions** Students see examples of approaches to and features of drafts of these two kinds of expositions.
- **Writing Tips** Students get pointers for writing a summary.
- **Interactive model of a written definition** Students can get pointers for how to write this kind of exposition.
- **Transition Word Bin** Students see transitional words they can use for different logical orders. They can drag helpful words into appropriate spots in their expositions.
- **Audio-annotated Student Models** Students read a draft of a definition. They can choose passages to hear explanations of choices the writer made.

Working individually or in small groups, students can experiment with these activities to find the ones that work best for them.

Drafting

Using your prewriting notes, begin drafting your paper. As you write, sort through your details, including the most important and leaving out the unimportant ones. Don't expect your first draft to be perfect. Correct the flaws in your paper just as professional writers do—later, during the revision stage. Here are some tips to guide you as you draft:

Tips for Drafting a Definition or a Classification

- Explain the main features of each subject you define.
- Define each group or class by telling what the members have in common and naming the categories within the group.

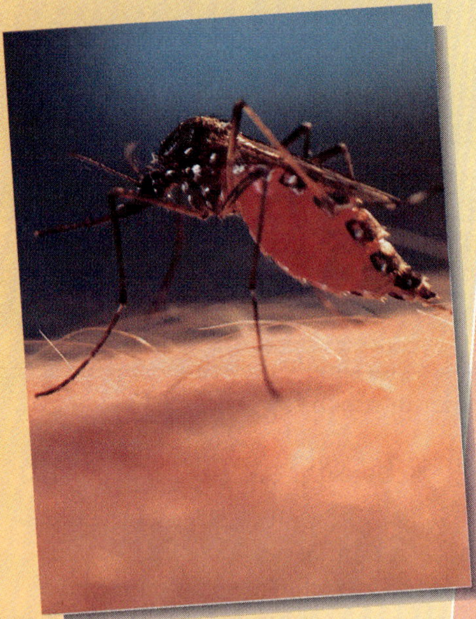

Writing Model: A Definition

In the following model of a definition of mosquitoes, the writer first gives a general definition of a mosquito and then defines three categories of the insect:

A mosquito is an annoying little insect related to the fly. Three kinds are especially annoying because they can spread serious diseases. These are the Anopheles, the Aedes, and the Culex.

Not all mosquitoes bite. Only the females do. The males drink fruit juice, but the females drink blood. When female mosquitoes are feeding from a person, germs on the mosquito can get into the person's bloodstream.

Anopheles mosquitoes carry parasites that breed malaria. Aedes mosquitoes carry viruses that cause yellow fever. Culex mosquitoes carry viruses that cause encephalitis, or inflammation of the brain.

Language Lab CD-ROM

Students who need more practice using transitional words to help organize their expositions may benefit from working on the Transitional Words lesson of the Building Paragraphs unit of the *Language Lab*.

Writers at Work Videodisc

Play the videodisc segment in which Officer Charles Tsang talks about tips for writing a good report. Ask:

- What does Tsang say about the important features of a well-prepared report?
- How does what Tsang says about skills used in drafting a report apply to drafting definitions, classifications, summaries of books and media, and instructions?

Play frames 41103 to 42006

Teaching Strategy/ Clarification

Discuss with students that this excerpt about mosquitoe shows that a composition car include elements of more than one kind of exposition. Point out that when writing a definition, it may be unavoidable or even very effective to categorize information. Guid

Tips for Drafting a Summary

- Write each point of information on a separate index card. Then arrange the cards in their order of importance.
- Identify the literary work or media program you're summarizing.
- Discuss each of the main characters and events.
- Be brief.

Writing Model: A Summary

The following model is the introduction to a summary of a book. Notice that the writer includes the most important points, including the title, author, main character, setting, and situation.

The book is Bridge to Teribithia by Katherine Paterson, a Newbery award winner. Jess Aarons, the main character, was a poor boy living in northern Virginia. He wanted to be the fastest runner in the fifth grade, so all summer he'd been practicing.

Tips for Drafting Written Instructions

- Tell what the activity is and why it is worth doing.
- Explain each step in the process in the order in which it occurs.
- Show how the steps are related.
- Explain the outcome.

Writing Model: Written Instructions

The following model of written instructions is part of a recipe for preparing pasta with peas. Notice that each step is described in detail and that words such as *meanwhile*, *then*, and *finally* help to signal when the steps are to be performed.

Blanch, or scald, the peas. Then drain and cool them. In a saucepan, heat 3/4 cup cream and the butter for two to three minutes, until the cream thickens slightly. Set the mixture aside. Meanwhile, boil the pasta in salted water until it is just barely tender. Drain the pasta and toss it with the cream-and-butter mixture over low heat. Next, add the remaining cream, cheese, and peas. Lightly season with salt, pepper, and nutmeg. Finally, toss until the sauce becomes thick. (Serves 4 to 6)

Establishing Assessment Criteria

Before students begin drafting their expositions, you may want to share with them the criteria you will use to evaluate their work. The following guidelines are included in the tutorial on expository writing. You can use them as given, or modify them to suit your needs.

- Did you identify your subject clearly?
- If you're writing a definition, did you use specific facts and details to help define your subject?
- If you're writing a summary, did you include only important information?
- If you're writing instructions, did you include every important detail?
- Is your writing well organized?
- Did you include an introduction, a body, and a conclusion?
- Did you use transitions effectively?
- Did you check for errors in grammar, spelling, and punctuation?

students to understand that it is more important for an exposition to be informative, clearly written, and well organized than for it to be precisely identified as either a definition or a classification.

Writing Strategy

Discuss with students how this writing model about *Bridge to Teribithia* begins by identifying the work and characters. Talk about why this is an effective way to begin a summary (it is informational and it entices readers to read on, for example). Invite suggestions for starting summaries in other ways.

Literature Connection

Talk with students about how this model of written instructions is organized. Have them suggest other ways to arrange the ideas in the piece. Then suggest that students study examples of expository writing in *Prentice Hall Literature, Copper*, to see how each is organized. See the list of selections on pages 796–797.

Revising and Editing

Revising Your Work

Does your draft contain information that is not pertinent, or connected with, the main ideas of your expository paper? Is any important information missing from your paper? Is your paper well organized and easy to understand? Carefully review your draft to see how you can improve it. Use the questions in the checklist to guide you.

FROM a WRITER

"When I revise a report, I have to make sure certain things which are not pertinent to the case are not included, such as a person's feelings about an incident."

—Charles Tsang

Revision Checklist

1. Did you identify your subject?
2. Did you use facts in your writing?
3. Did you include an introduction, body, and conclusion?
4. Did you leave out any important details?
5. Have you included unnecessary details?
6. What can you do to improve your organization?
7. Have you clearly shown the relationships between the steps, actions, or methods?

Student Model: Revised Draft

Here is a revised passage from a classification by Jessica Lee, a student at Tomball Junior High School in Tomball, Texas. Notice that Jessica added some additional details that make her paper more interesting.

Dogs are one of the most popular domesticated animals in the ~~United States.~~ world. They are kept as pets, companions, and many even work for a living. There are many breeds of dogs, and they are classified into groups by their characteristics.

One of the groups is the Toy group, which includes the Chihuahua, the Pekingese, the Pomeranian, and the Maltese. All of these dogs remain small and are kept by their owners as pets.

Writing Lab CD-ROM

The Revising and Editing section provides strategies for self-revision. It includes the following options to help students develop strategies to revise the first draft of their expositions:

- **Self-Evaluation Checklists** Students can answer questions in these checklists—one list of questions for each type of exposition—to help them make revisions to strengthen their drafts.
- **Revision checker for transition words** Students can use this tool to help them determine they've used transitional words that help readers follow the ideas in their exposition.
- **Interactive writing model** Students read sections of a first draft and a second draft of the same passage to hear why the writer decided to take out certain details.
- **Audio-annotated Student Model** Students read to see and hear how one student has revised her draft.
- **Video clip about peer revision** Students get pointers on how to work with classmates in the revision process.
- **Peer Revision Checklist** Peer reviewers read each other's drafts and then use responses to questions in this Evaluation Checklist to guide their revisions.

Working individually or in small groups, students can experiment with these activities to find the ones that work best.

Writers at Work Videodisc

Play the videodisc segment in which Charles Tsang talks about revising his reports. Ask:

- What do you think about Tsang's contention that personal feelings of a participant are not pertinent to a case and, if included in the draft, should be omitted during the revision process? Do you agree or disagree? Why? What do you think about the role of personal feelings in the kind of exposition you are writing?

Play frames 39289 to 39802

Having a Peer Review Your Work

After making revisions on your own, have a classmate help you make further revisions. Another person might see problems that you've missed. Choose one of your classmates as a revising partner. First, let your partner read your paper and make suggestions to improve it. Then read your partner's paper and find ways to improve it. Use the questions in the following checklist to guide you.

Peer Review Checklist

1. What is the main idea of the paper? Has the writer included enough information to develop the main idea?
2. Is the paper organized effectively? How can the writer improve the organization?
3. What ideas or events did the writer include that could be left out? Explain.
4. What did you learn about the subject? What parts of the writing did you find most interesting? Why? What parts did you find least interesting? Why?
5. How effective is the ending? How can the writer improve it?

Proofreading

Did you spell all the words correctly? Did you use the correct punctuation marks at the ends of sentences? Now that you've finished revising your paper, check it carefully for errors in spelling, punctuation, and grammar. Such errors can distract your readers from the information you're trying to present and make your paper difficult to understand.

Proofreading Checklist

Use these questions as you proofread your revised draft. If your answer to any of them is no, look through your draft and make the necessary changes.

1. Are your sentences complete?
2. Did you use commas, periods, and other punctuation marks correctly?
3. Have you avoided sentence fragments?
4. Is each word spelled correctly? Did you double-check the spelling of technical terms?
5. Did you use capital letters correctly?
6. Is each paragraph indented?

Language Lab CD-ROM

Students who need more practice identifying and correcting sentence fragments may benefit from working on the Sentence Fragments lesson in the Problems With Sentences unit.

Teaching Strategy

You may find it useful to have students proofread with a different peer than the one with whom they revised and edited their work. This way, students can have a fresh eye detecting errors that might have been missed earlier.

Teaching Strategies

- Work with students to establish a class environment that fosters mutual respect between writers and readers. You may wish to brainstorm guidelines students can observe for peer editing.
- Discuss the Peer Review Checklist presented in the *Sourcebook*. Ask students to compare it to other revision checklists they may have used to help revise their own work as well as that of classmates.
- You may want to make a large version of the checklist to post in your room for students to refer to as they revise their expositions. Feel free to adapt the list to include additional questions or techniques your students suggest for addressing each question. For example, when reviewing a summary, a peer reviewer might ask, "Has the writer kept it clear and brief?" or "Has the writer given away too much information about the plot?" When reviewing written instructions, a peer reviewer might ask, "Are there any gaps in the piece? If so, what must be done to complete the instructions?"

Writing Lab CD-ROM

The Revising and Editing section includes the following options to help students develop strategies for proofreading their expository compositions:

- **Proofreading Checklist**
- **Interactive instruction on avoiding sentence fragments** Students learn more about how to identify and correct sentence fragments.

Working individually or in small groups, students can experiment with these activities to find the ones that work best.

Publishing and Presenting

Now that you've finished your expository paper, it's time to share your work with your audience. Here are a few suggestions:

Compile a Class Dictionary If you and your classmates have written definitions, compile a class dictionary. Work with your classmates and follow these steps:

- Gather all the definitions.
- Arrange them in alphabetical order.
- Add appropriate illustrations.
- Design and make covers.

Create an Audio Anthology Have you and your classmates written summaries? If so, work with your classmates to create an audio guide to books, plays, movies, CDs, and television shows. First, group your summaries by type. Then have each student record his or her summary.

Construct a Class Do-It-Yourself Magazine If you and your classmates have written instructions, publish the work of the entire group in a class do-it-yourself magazine. Here are the tasks: First, design the pages. Next, illustrate the steps and the cover. Then write titles, subtitles, and captions. Finally, duplicate the pages and cover and bind the magazines.

Reflecting on Your Writing

The process of writing is a learning experience through which you can find out more about your subject and yourself. Reflect on how you wrote your expository paper, using the following questions:

- What do you enjoy most about expository writing? What do you enjoy least?
- What did you learn about your topic?
- If you could start the assignment over again, what would you do differently?
- How can you apply what you've learned to other assignments?

Writing Lab CD-ROM

The Publishing and Presenting section includes the following options to help students present their completed works to a wider audience:

- **Compile a class dictionary** Students follow directions to compile a dictionary of their written definitions.
- **Create an audio anthology** Students follow steps to create an audio guide that contains their summaries of books, records, movies, and shows.
- **Create a do-it-yourself magazine** Students work cooperatively to put together and publish all written instructions in a magazine.

Students working individually or in small groups can use the ideas in the tutorial on expository writing to help in the publishing and presenting phase.

Teaching Strategy

Invite students to make illustrations to accompany their definitions in the class dictionary and their written instructions in the do-it-yourself magazine. Students may wish to include in their portfolios a copy of the page of the class dictionary or magazine that includes their exposition and any pictures that accompany it.

The Multimedia Workshop

Students can use the templates in the Writing Workshop component of *The Multimedia Workshop* to word-process and present their final expository pieces. For instance, a student writing instructions can use the timeline template, and one writing a summary might use one of the magazine templates.

Portfolio Assessment

Have students write an evaluative statement that addresses some of the questions posed on page 124 of the *Sourcebook*. If students decide to include the completed expository piece in their portfolio, they might attach this statement to it. Otherwise, the statement itself can go into the portfolio as a record of self-evaluation.

The following questions can be used to supplement the questions in the *Sourcebook:*

- What part of the expository-writing process did I find most challenging? Most useful?
- How do I feel about writing an expository composition, as compared with writing other kinds of compositions? Which type of exposition would I like to write next time? Why?

Student Model

Here is the complete, final draft of Jessica Lee's expository composition on dogs.

The World of Dogs

by Jessica Lee

Dogs are one of the most popular domesticated animals in the world. They are kept as pets, companions, and many even work for a living. There are many breeds of dogs, and they are classified in groups by their characteristics.

One of the groups is the Toy group, which includes the Chihuahua, the Pekingese, the Pomeranian, and the Maltese. All of these dogs remain small and are kept by their owners as pets.

Another group is the Hound group. The Hound group includes the Irish Wolfhound, the Afghan Hound, the Borzoi, the Bloodhound, the Dachshund, the Basset Hound, and the Beagle. All of these dogs are good for hunting furred game. They chase after game that they track by sight or scent.

The Sporting group is a group that includes the Irish Setter, the English Setter, the Pointer, the Labrador Retriever, the American Water Spaniel, and the English Springer Spaniel. The dogs in this group are hunting dogs. They use their keen eyesight and sense of smell to locate game and either point to it or retrieve it.

A group that includes the Lhasa Apso, the Boston Terrier, the Poodle, the Bulldog, the Chow Chow, and the Dalmatian is called the Nonsporting group. As the group name suggests, these dogs are owned mainly as pets.

The Working group consists of the St. Bernard, the Doberman Pinscher, the Alaskan Malamute, the Pembroke Welsh Corgi, and the Collie. The Working group is generally heavy boned and rugged. Some of these dogs serve as police dogs, guard dogs, and sled dogs.

There are many types of dogs in the world. Dogs come in many sizes and shapes. It is difficult to imagine how the world would be without them.

I began my composition by briefly defining my subject and by identifying the type of expository writing as classification into categories.

In the body of my composition, I discussed five categories of dogs and the characteristics of each.

I included only facts in my writing because the purpose of my paper is to give information, not opinions.

For this group, I gave a physical characteristic these dogs share.

I concluded with a general statement emphasizing the great variety of dogs.

- In what ways has my writing shown the most improvement?

After students have evaluated their work, confer with them to decide what to include in their portfolio. Students can select the completed piece and/or earlier drafts they think reflect growth and progress. Remind students to date all the work they add to their portfolio.

Teaching From the Model

Draw students' attention to how Jessica Lee's composition includes the elements of exposition.

- *It has a succinct introduction that states the topic of this classification clearly.* Lee quickly introduces the topic of her piece and, also in the first paragraph, presents the main idea: that there are many breeds of dogs, each categorized by common characteristics.
- *It is organized effectively.* Lee's purpose is to show how many different kinds of dogs there are and how they can be classified by group. Following the opening paragraph, each successive paragraph prior to the concluding paragraph is about a different group of dogs. The order might best be described as an examples-of-groups order.
- *It contains clear descriptions of what the items in each category have in common.* The dogs are classified by breed: the Toy group, the Hound group, the Sporting group, the Nonsporting group, and the Working group. Lee provides the distinguishing characteristics of each group. She provides facts only.
- *It has an effective conclusion.* Lee concludes by summarizing what her composition implies: There are many types, sizes, and shapes of dogs.

Technology Note: Networking

After your class has read the Student Model, they may be interested in sharing creative efforts with students across the country via the Internet or commercial on-line services such as Prodigy or America Online. Students can exchange expository compositions with other students, including those using *Writer's Solution,* by connecting to Prentice Hall's Internet home page. Look for special events, contests, as well as bulletin boards and pointers

Integrating Skills With Writing

Management Strategy

You can have students work through one or both of the skills lessons either before or after they write their expositions. If you use the lessons *before*, remind students to incorporate the techniques in their writing. If you address skills *after* students write their compositions, have them include a section on "skills improvement" in the self-assessment document they prepare for their portfolios. The next time they write, their work can be evaluated in terms of their mastery of these skills.

You may want to give students these lessons as take-home assignments to be completed prior to the drafting, revising, or proofreading stages—wherever you see the greatest need. Or you may choose to assign the skills lessons only to those students whose drafts indicate a need for direct instruction in these particular skills.

Teaching Strategy

To connect the skills lessons to the students' writing, explain that one important feature of expository writing is to use exact nouns in order to create a clearer picture in the readers' minds.

Another important aspect of expository writing—or any other kind of writing—is to write sentences that are clear and precise because of correct subject-verb agreement.

Teaching Strategies

- The first version of the excerpt from a summary is unclear because it lacks exact nouns. The reader doesn't know one boat from another and cannot tell which boat is sailing and where it is sailing to. Before students read the revised version, ask volunteers to indicate which nouns in the original version could be made more specific if replaced by an exact noun.
- Ask students to explain how the second version improves upon the first with the substitution of exact nouns. If any students are familiar with kinds of boats, invite them to describe another way to revise the passage by inserting different exact nouns.

Developing Your Style 1

Using Exact Nouns

One challenge that writers face is using words to create a clear image of a scene. Can you explain why the following excerpt from a summary does not create a clear image?

> At the beginning of the movie, a boat moves slowly through the area, passing other boats that are moored there. Suddenly, a person jumps overboard and swims toward an authority's boat. As soon as the person jumps, the boat picks up speed and races out of the place into open water. In the next scene, the boat is sailing somewhere in the middle of the water.

Can you figure out what kind of boat was sailing and where it was sailing? The reason why you can't is that the excerpt lacks exact nouns. Look at the following revision.

> At the beginning of the movie "The Chase," a yacht moves slowly through the marina, passing other yachts that are moored there. Suddenly, a passenger jumps overboard and swims toward a Coast Guard cutter. As soon as the passenger jumps, the yacht picks up speed and races out of the marina into open water. In the next scene, the yacht is sailing somewhere in the middle of the Atlantic Ocean.

The revised paragraph creates a clearer image because it contains exact nouns. A **noun** is a word that names a person, place, or thing. An **exact noun** names a *specific* person, place, or thing. Exact nouns can create clear images, or word pictures, in the reader's mind. Whenever you write, use exact nouns to help the reader *picture* what you describe. Now choose the most exact noun to complete the following sentence:

> Jill and I crossed the pond in a __________, a boat that is powered by pedaling.
>
> a. boat   b. pedal boat   c. pleasure boat

The most exact noun is *pedal boat*, the name of a specific kind of boat. *Pleasure boat* is less exact, naming a class of boats. The word *boat* is the least exact noun. Boat is a general noun that includes all small water craft.

Practice Activities

1. Choose the most exact noun to complete each of the following sentences.

a. __________ are anchored floating objects—sometimes with a light or a bell—that mark safe channels for boats.
(1) Markers   (2) Buoys   (3) Structures

b. If we rent a rowboat, we can row to the other side of the __________.
(1) water   (2) area   (3) lake

c. As we boarded the fishing boat, numerous gray-and-white __________ flew past us.
(1) birds   (2) seagulls   (3) animals

d. The huge waves caused by the __________ tossed many small boats onto the docks.
(1) storm   (2) weather   (3) hurricane

e. A __________ is a craft that can rise out of the water on winglike structures and skim along at high speed.
(1) hydrofoil   (2) boat   (3) vessel

2. Write a summary of a real or imaginary adventure that occurred on a boat. Use exact nouns to create vivid word pictures for your readers.

Technology Note: Word Processing

Guide students who use word processors to take advantage of the computer's thesaurus whenever they write. As needed, invite peer tutors to help others use this tool. Encourage students who are not word processing to refer to a print thesaurus as a resource for finding specific nouns. Have students show one another how to use one, as needed.

Teaching Strategy

Challenge your **more-advanced students** to substitute exact nouns within each sentence in Practice Activity 1 in places other than those indicated.

Suggest to students that for Practice Activity 2 they use the strategy of first writing a rough draft of their summary and then going back and editing to replace general nouns with more-specific ones. Guide students to try to use precise verbs and modifiers as well.

Alternate Assessments

Students can demonstrate their understanding of using exact nouns in two other ways:

- They can swap papers with a classmate and revise the other's work by replacing the exact nouns with other exact nouns, so that the meaning remains the same.
- They can write an expository passage, filled with exact nouns, to either precede or follow the one written by a classmate.

Practice Activities: Suggested Answers

1. **a.** (2)
   b. (3)
   c. (2)
   d. (3)
   e. (1)
2. Summaries will vary, but should feature exact nouns that create vivid word pictures.

Writer's Companion

To provide students with additional support and reinforcement in using exact nouns, direct them to the section entitled "Choosing Specific Nouns" beginning on page 345.

Teaching Strategy

Point out to students the importance of writing sentences in which the subject and the verb agree in number. Invite students to suggest other ways to revise the paragraph about bicycles.

Also point out to students that plural nouns are not simply singular nouns with an *s* added to the end of the word. You may wish to use this opportunity to discuss some of the rules for special plural forms, such as for nouns ending in *ch*, *s*, *sh*, *x*, *z*, *f*, *fe*, *o*, and *y*. You may also wish to talk about the plural forms that don't follow any rules and need to be memorized, such as *woman/women*, *foot/feet*, and *louse/lice*.

Language Acquisition/ ESL Teaching Strategy

Working in pairs, have your intermediate and advanced ESL students copy the paragraph as is on a large sheet of construction paper. They then make the necessary corrections and explain each correction in the margin. Finally, they present their work to the basic ESL students in the classroom. As a follow-up, ask all your ESL students to write a paragraph describing a specific activity, and have them exchange their papers for correction.

Developing Your Style

Using Correct Subject-Verb Agreement

As a writer, you want to present clear, accurate information to the reader. What makes the following passage from a definition of a bicycle awkward?

> A bicycle are a two-wheeled vehicle powered by turning two pedals with the feet. Many people ride bicycles for recreation, but some people rides them to school or work. Bicycles comes in many sizes: 12, 16, 20, 24, 26, and 27 inches. The number of inches refer to the diameter of the wheel.

Did you notice something wrong with the paragraph? The paragraph is unclear because it contains subjects and verbs that do not agree in number. They clash because sometimes a singular verb is used with a plural subject and a singular subject is used with a plural verb. Here is the revised paragraph:

> A bicycle is a two-wheeled vehicle powered by turning two pedals with the feet. Many people ride bicycles for recreation, but some people ride them to school or work. Bicycles come in many sizes: 12, 16, 20, 24, 26, and 27 inches. The number of inches refers to the diameter of the wheel.

- Subjects and verbs must agree in **number**. A *singular* subject uses a *singular* verb, and a *plural* subject uses a *plural* verb.

Singular: Linda rides her bike to and from school every day.
Plural: They wear bicycle helmets for safety.

- Note that the verb *be* has special forms:

Singular:	I am, was	You are, were	He/She/It is, was
Plural:	We are, were	You are, were	They are, were

Singular: He is the bicyclist I see in the park on weekends.
Plural: My friends are happiest when riding their bikes.

- A **simple subject** is a noun or a pronoun that tells who or what the sentence is about.

  Example: My bicycle has twelve gears, hand brakes, and reflectors.

- A **compound subject** is two or more simple subjects joined by the word *and*, *or*, or *nor*. Use a plural verb with compound subjects joined by *and*.

  Example: A level street and a bicycle path are good places to ride a bike.

- When a compound subject is joined by *or* or *nor*, the verb agrees with the subject closer to it.

  Examples: Neither high winds nor heavy rain is likely during the bicycle race.
  A bumpy sidewalk or sharp stones are dangers that bike riders try to avoid.

- A **phrase** is a short group of words—such as *in the house* or *on the hill*—that does not contain a subject and a verb. When a phrase comes between a subject and a verb, it is called an **interrupting phrase**. The interrupting phrase does not affect the agreement.

  Examples: The bicycles *in this store* are expensive.
  A simple bicycle *with wide tires* is hard to find.

Practice Activities

1. Revise the following passage by making all subjects and verbs agree in number.

Bicycles come in a variety of styles. There are lightweight, middleweight, juvenile, and specialty bikes. Lightweight bicycles, in general, is built for speed and comfort. They weigh from 19 to 30 pounds and includes racing, touring, and mountain bikes. Each one of these three types have gears with 12 to 21 speeds to make pedaling easier. Racing bikes is used for racing, while touring bikes can be used for recreational riding. A mountain bike, with its wide tires, are built for travel on rough terrain.

2. Write instructions on how to perform a specific outdoor activity, such as riding a bicycle or flying a kite. Be sure that the subjects and verbs of all your sentences agree in number.

Teaching Strategy

Help students understand that even if a compound subject joined by *and* consists of two singular nouns, or a singular noun following a plural noun, it takes a plural verb. Provide examples such as these: *A man and a woman were riding bicycles. Two girls and a boy ride together.* Have students provide additional examples of each case.

Language Lab CD-ROM

For additional practice with subject-verb agreement, students can refer to all three lessons in the Subject-Verb Agreement unit.

Teaching Strategy

Point out to students that there is more than one way to revise the passage in Practice Activity 1. Have students share their revisions with the whole class by reading them aloud.

Addressing Ability Levels

For Practice Activity 2, challenge your **more-advanced students** to write instructions for an activity, focusing on things to be sure *not* to do and what to watch out for when performing the activity. Suggest to students that they consider using an importance order when writing this passage.

Writer's Companion

To provide students with additional support and reinforcement in detecting and correcting subject-verb agreement errors, direct them to Lack of Subject-Verb Agreement, beginning on page 271.

Practice Activities: Suggested Answers

1. Bicycles come in a variety of styles. There are lightweight, middleweight, juvenile, and specialty bikes. Lightweight bicycles, in general, are built for speed and comfort. They weigh from 19 to 30 pounds and include racing, touring, and mountain bikes. Each one of these three types has gears with from 12 to 21 speeds to make pedaling easier. Racing bikes are used for racing, while touring bikes can be used for recreational riding. A mountain bike, with its wide tires, is built for travel on rough terrain.
2. Instructions will vary but should feature sentences with correct subject-verb agreement.

Integrating Literature With Writing

Management Strategy

You can have students read this model of expository writing either before or after they have written their own piece. If you choose to have them read it *before*, use it to draw their attention to techniques or ideas they can apply to their own writing. If you use it *after*, have students compare and contrast some of the elements of the piece with elements of their own expository composition. Ask: *What can you learn from this essay that can help you the next time you use expository writing?*

Activating Prior Knowledge

Invite students to tell what they know about crime lab scientists. Ask them, in particular, to describe ways crime lab scientists might use expository writing in their work. Then ask: *Which types of job-related expositions are crime lab scientists and scientists in other fields likely to write?*

Purpose-Setting Question

What elements of expository writing in this model are used to inform readers about the work a crime lab scientist does?

Reading Strategy

You can help guide reading by asking students to jot down elements of expository writing as they read this essay. When they finish reading, students can work as a whole class or in small discussion groups to compare their responses to the piece.

Literature Model

Expository writing explains or gives information about a particular subject. In this essay, Jeff Saviano informs the reader about the work of a crime lab scientist. As you read, notice the factual details that Saviano provides in order to explain his subject.

My Life's Work: Crime Lab Scientist

by Jeff Saviano

Saviano defines his subject by giving the reader facts about the scope of his job. In expository writing, it is important to provide accurate information.

If a burglar were to break into your home while you and your family were on vacation, what kinds of clues might he leave behind? A fingerprint? A drop of blood? As a crime lab scientist at the sheriff's office in Colorado Springs, Colorado, it's my job to use science to help figure out who committed the crime.

Maybe the burglar broke a window to get into your house. In that case, it's likely that tiny pieces of glass became attached to his clothing. The crime lab may be able to match the glass in his clothes to the glass from your window.

Here Saviano gives examples of specific technical procedures to further explain the work of a crime lab scientist. One purpose of expository writing is to explain.

When someone touches an object, he often leaves behind fingerprints. By using certain scientific techniques, I can find fingerprints on a lot of different surfaces: Wood, glass, metal—even a piece of paper might have good fingerprints on it.

But what if your burglar was wearing gloves? Most people don't know this, but gloves can leave prints too. And those glove prints can be traced back to the glove that made them.

Saviano uses facts to inform readers about other methods for solving crimes.

The crime lab can help solve cases in other ways, including analyzing blood (maybe he cut himself while climbing

Teaching Strategies

- Discuss with students how Saviano provides specific information to help explain the work a crime lab scientist does. Ask them to cite examples.
- Saviano wrote this essay with a specific audience and purpose in mind. Have students discuss who they think Saviano wrote this piece for. Ask them to support their opinion with examples from the essay.

through the broken window) or comparing shoe prints and tire prints. Hairs and cloth fibers left at the scene can also be matched to the hair from the suspect's head or fibers from his clothing.

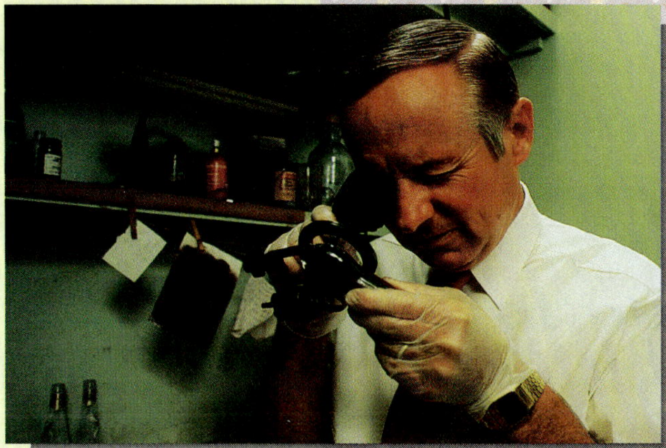

My tools range from magnifying glasses to microscopes, cameras to chemicals. Even lasers are used to examine evidence in the crime lab.

When I leave work at night, I never quite know what's going to be in store for me the next day. Tomorrow I might be called to look for evidence in a stolen car. . . .

Some days I dress in old clothes because I know I'm going to have to trudge through a field filled with weeds searching for a buried gun. Other days I'm a witness in the courtroom, so I have to wear a suit and tie.

In giving facts about what he wears to work, Saviano shows the relationship between specific tasks and appropriate clothing.

Working in a crime lab isn't always easy (try dragging yourself out of bed at 3 o'clock in the morning when your pager goes off), but there are a lot of rewards, and each day is different.

Here Saviano explains the pros and cons of his job.

If you think you might be interested in that type of work, you can start by getting acquainted with the sciences, especially biology and chemistry. Math will help too. And so will English (don't forget, you'll be writing reports and testifying in court).

Above all, you'll need to be honest about what you discover. Remember, everyone is innocent until proven guilty. The evidence you find as a crime lab scientist might help put a guilty man behind bars for years. It might also help an innocent person stay free like you and me.

Saviano concludes by giving factual information on the education and personal qualities required to become a crime lab scientist.

Closure and Extension

To complete the lesson, you can ask students to sum up what they have learned about expository writing by examining Jeff Saviano's definition of the work of a crime lab scientist.

Then invite students to share in small group discussions or through brief journal entries what they learned about themselves as writers and what points they would like to keep in mind for future expository writing. Also ask what topics they would consider for future writing. You might keep some of the topics in an idea file for later use.

Language Acquisition/ ESL Teaching Strategy

Lead your intermediate and advanced ESL students in a discussion of the facts the author provides in describing his job as a crime lab scientist. Ask questions that require the students to look at a particular paragraph for the answer. For example, *What tools does a crime lab scientist use?* You may wish to ask the more-advanced students to develop an outline of the facts provided in the essay.

5

Exposition: Making Connections
Classroom Manager

Writer's Solution *Materials for Teaching Exposition That Makes Connections*

The *Writer's Solution* includes a wide range of materials for teaching exposition that makes connections. You can pick and choose from among these materials. In the pages that follow, you'll find lesson plans suggesting effective ways to use them. You do not have to use all the program components to use it effectively. For a description of each of the components of the *Writer's Solution*, see pages T4–T6.

Below is a detailed list of the *Writer's Solution* materials for Exposition: Making Connections.

Writers at Work Videodisc

Featured Writer: Kevin Powell, Entertainment Critic

Videodisc Segments

About Exposition: Making Connections

"Bringing Events into Focus"

Writing Tips: Experiencing the World; Taking Notes; Breaking Writer's Block

Interactive CD-ROMs

WRITING LAB

Tutorial on Exposition: Making Connections

About Exposition
- Includes three Models From Literature and a video clip by Kevin Powell

Choosing Your Topic
- Includes Inspirations for Exposition, Topic Wheel, and Question and Answer forms

Narrowing a Topic
- Includes Cluster Diagram and a video tip

Considering Audience and Purpose
- Includes Audience Profile and a video tip

Gathering Information
- Includes a video tip from Kevin Powell

Organizing Details
- Includes Venn Diagram and Chain of Events

Drafting
- Includes audio and video tips

Revising and Editing
- Includes Evaluation Checklist, a video tip, revision checker, and Transition Word Bin

Proofreading
- Includes eliminating run-on sentences

Publishing and Presenting
- Includes tips for an activity guide and a problem-and-solution business letter

Writer's Tool Kit

Suggested Activities: Inspirations for Exposition, Topic Wheels, Cluster Diagram, Audience Profile, Evaluation Checklists, Peer Editing Worksheet, sentence variety checker

LANGUAGE LAB

Related Lessons: Correcting Stringy Sentences, Combining Sentences (Styling Sentences unit); Main Idea and Topic Sentence, Supporting and Concluding Sentences, Unity in Paragraphs, Transitional Words (Building Paragraphs unit); Narrowing a Topic, Considering Audience and Purpose (Composing unit); Forms of Comparison, Adjective or Adverb? (Using Modifiers unit); Run-on Sentences (Sentence Errors unit)

Sourcebook

About Exposition: Making Connections (pp. 136–140)

Guided Lesson on Exposition (pp. 141–159)

Inspirations for Exposition (pp. 144–147)

Developing Your Style

Using Prepositions and Conjunctions (pp.161–162)

Making Clear Comparisons (p. 163)

Literature Model

"Dad Just Got Traded!" by Susan Fornoff (pp. 164–165)

Writer's Companion

Mini-Lesson on Organizational Plans, p. 23

Mini-Lesson on Introductions, p. 27

Mini-Lesson on Elaboration, p. 31

Mini-Lesson on Conclusions, p. 37

Mini-Lesson on Paragraphs, p. 57

Mini-Lesson on Comparison-and-Contrast Essay, p. 156

Mini-Lesson on Problem-and-Solution Essay, p. 177

Mini-Lesson on Written Evaluation, p. 183

Teaching Integrated Language Arts Using the Writer's Solution*—Starting With Literature*

Have students read and respond to comparisons, evaluations, reviews, and other types of expository writing. In discussing the selections, draw students' attention to expository elements, such as presenting information through facts and supporting details and making comparisons and contrasts. Point out that students can use the expositions they've read as models for writing their own expositions. Lead into having students complete expository writing projects using the components of the *Writer's Solution*.

CONNECTIONS TO *PRENTICE HALL LITERATURE, COPPER,* SELECTIONS

Comparison and Contrast	2E	3E
"The All-American Slurp," Lensey Namioka	■	▲
"How to Read a Newspaper," Andrew A. Rooney	■	▲
"The Truth About Dragons," Rhoda Blumberg	■	▲

Review/Evaluation	2E	3E
"Space Stations of the Mind," Neil McAleer	■	▲
"Virginia Hamilton," Lee Bennett Hopkins	■	

You can also use the *Writer's Solution* material on Exposition: Making Connections to guide students through writing activities in response to works of literature.

CONNECTIONS TO *PRENTICE HALL LITERATURE, COPPER,* WRITING ACTIVITIES

Thinking and Writing Activities	2E	3E
Writing an Explanatory Essay—Follows **"The Truth About Dragons,"** Rhoda Blumberg	■	▲
Writing an Evaluation—Follows ***Tuck Everlasting,*** **Chapters 20–Epilogue,** Natalie Babbitt	■	▲
Comparing and Contrasting—Follows **"The Sound of Summer Running,"** Ray Bradbury	■	▲

Focus on Writing/ Your Writing Process	2E	3E
Focus on Writing: Writing to Inform	■	
Focus on Writing: Writing to Explore a Content Area	■	
Your Writing Process: Writing to Inform		▲
Your Writing Process: Writing to Explore a Content Area		▲
Your Writing Process: Writing About a Novel		▲

■ **(2E)** *Prentice Hall Literature*, Copper, Second Edition

▲ **(3E)** *Prentice Hall Literature*, Copper, Paramount Edition

CONNECTIONS BETWEEN INSPIRATIONS FOR EXPOSITION AND *PRENTICE HALL LITERATURE, COPPER*

You can use the multimedia Inspirations for Exposition: Making Connections to motivate student reading as well as student writing. Many of the Inspirations are audio recordings or video adaptations of selections from *Prentice Hall Literature*, *Copper*. Have students work in small groups to look at and discuss an appropriate Inspiration before reading the corresponding selection. Then, after reading the selection, students can replay the Inspiration and select one of the accompanying Topic Ideas (see pages 142–143). "The All-American Slurp," by Lensey Namioka, from *Prentice Hall Literature*, *Copper*, is included in the Inspirations for Exposition: Making Connections.

Recommended Lesson Plan

The following lesson plan is recommended for providing students with thorough, comprehensive instructions in expository writing to make connections. Because you may not have all the components of the *Writer's Solution* or may have limited access to equipment, the plan provides a number of options. Choose the options that best suit your teaching style and equipment situation.

You may want to add a few days to the lesson plan to allow students time to publish their work and to hold conferences with students to discuss your assessment of their work.

FIVE-DAY LESSON PLAN	
Lesson Outcome:	**Each student writes a complete exposition.**
DAY 1	**Introduce your students to expository writing.** Show the *Writers at Work Videodisc* segment featuring Kevin Powell. Use the segment as a springboard for class discussion or group activities.
DAY 2	**Have students choose a writing topic and plan their expositions.** OPTION 1 Have students work either individually or in small groups to look at About Exposition: Making Connections and to choose a topic by browsing through the Inspirations for Exposition. Then have students work individually to develop their expositions by completing the rest of the Prewriting stage of the tutorial on Exposition: Making Connections. At the end of the period, have students print out their prewriting notes. OPTION 2 Have students review the Models From Literature in the About Exposition: Making Connections section of the *Sourcebook*. Then have them choose from the topic suggestions and begin developing their expositions by completing the rest of the Prewriting stage of the Guided Lesson (pp. 148–154).
DAY 3	**Have students draft their expositions.** OPTION 1 Have students write their drafts on the computer following the instructions and using the activities provided in the Drafting section of the tutorial on Exposition. Have students print out their expositions at the end of the period. OPTION 2 Have students write their drafts on paper following the instructions in the Guided Lesson (pp. 155–156).
DAY 4	**Have students revise their expositions.** OPTION 1 Have students revise their expositions on the computer using the revision checkers, activities, and suggestions in the Revising and Editing section of the tutorial on Exposition. OPTION 2 Have students revise their expositions following the suggestions in the Guided Lesson (pp. 157–158).

FIVE-DAY LESSON PLAN (continued)

DAY 5	**Have students work in peer groups to make final revisions.** OPTION 1 Have pairs of students review each other's work following the guidelines in the peer revision section of the tutorial on Exposition. The pairs should then hold conferences before each student makes final revisions. Students should then proofread and print out their final drafts. OPTION 2 Have pairs of students review each other's work following the guidelines in the Guided Lesson (p. 158). The pairs should then hold conferences before each student makes final revisions.

Condensed Lesson Plans

Use the following lesson plans if you don't have a full week to devote to teaching expository writing.

Four- and Three-Day Plans: Adapt the Five-Day Plan by having students learn about exposition that makes connections, choose a topic, and develop ideas for their expositions all during Day 1. As in the Five-Day Plan, have students spend a day writing their drafts. For a Four-Day Plan, follow the last two days of the Five-Day Plan; for a Three-Day Plan, simply condense these two days into a single day of revision and forgo the option of working in peer groups.

TWO-DAY LESSON PLAN

Lesson Outcome:	**Each student writes a complete exposition.**
DAY 1	**Have students choose a topic and write their first drafts.** OPTION 1 Have students work in the open-ended environment in the *Writing Lab*. Working individually, students should choose a topic by browsing through the Inspirations for Exposition. Then they should write their expressions in their on-line Notebooks using the available prewriting tools as needed. OPTION 2 Using the suggestions and instructions in the *Sourcebook*, students should choose a topic and write a first draft of their expositions.
DAY 2	**Have students revise and edit their work.** OPTION 1 Have students revise on the computer using the tools, activities, and instructions in the tutorial on Exposition. OPTION 2 Have students revise their expositions following the suggestions in the *Sourcebook*.

One-Day Lesson Plan: Students can work individually in the open-ended environment in the *Writing Lab* by browsing through the Inspirations for Exposition to choose a topic, using the prewriting tools as needed, and then completing a quick-write draft of an exposition in their on-line Notebooks. Students may use the *Sourcebook* to choose a topic and write a brief exposition.

Preparing to Teach

Lesson Objectives

Students will

1. Select a topic for expository writing
2. Narrow their topic
3. Gather information
4. Select a method of organization
5. Write a composition that includes
   - an introduction
   - a body
   - a conclusion
6. Revise their writing for
   - content and structure
   - mechanics
7. Publish their finished composition

Activating Prior Knowledge

Ask students to give examples of expository writing they have done—writing that explains or presents ideas and information. Among other things, students may say that they have written reviews of concerts, movies, plays, or television shows; directions to a certain destination; procedures for a craft project or for cooking something; or essays that give opinions or suggestions on a current problem or topic of interest. Ask: *Based on your past experiences, what kind of expository writing have you enjoyed most? What features distinguish expository writing from other kinds of writing you have done? Explain your thinking.*

CHAPTER 5

Strike *Jacob Lawrence, The Howard University Gallery of Art, Washington, D.C.*

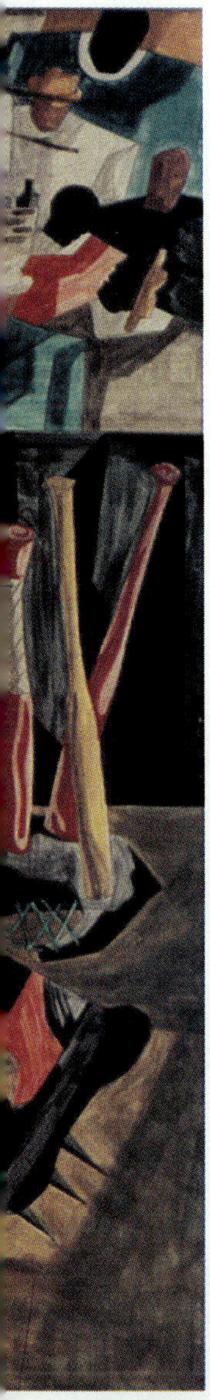

Exposition: *Making Connections*

"If you pay attention to the world, you'll be amazed at how much information you can accumulate."

—Kevin Powell,
Entertainment Critic

133

Humanities Note

Jacob Lawrence is one of the most acclaimed artists to come out of the Harlem Renaissance. Influenced by the bold forms of African art and the less realistic and more abstract forms of such painters as Picasso and Modigliani, Lawrence works in a cubist style. However, the human experience is at the heart of Lawrence's paintings. He once said that although his work is carefully designed and composed, it is not abstract in the sense of being without human content. "The human subject is the most important thing."

Notice what is unusual about this portrayal of a baseball game. The colors used in this painting are not the usual bright primary colors used to portray sports and crowd scenes. The onlookers are painted to communicate the feeling of a crowd rather than the uniqueness of individuals. The bold stances of the batter and catcher capture a split second of their movements.

In treating the subject of this painting, Lawrence has communicated a lot of information about the feeling of being at a baseball game. Clearly he chose to capture the feeling and action of the game rather than the realistic look of the setting or of individuals. You may want to use the following questions for class discussion:

- If you were going to write a description of going to a baseball game or some other sporting event, what information would you share?
- What sport would you like to learn more about?

Addressing Your Classroom Situation

This chapter, the second one on exposition, includes a variety of Models From Literature, writing topics, writing process strategies, and Student Models, along with two integrated skills lessons. Feel free to pick and choose from this material to create a customized lesson on exposition that matches your classroom needs.

Following are some of the key features of the chapter:

- The chapter begins with About Exposition: Making Connections. This section includes introductory statements about expository writing from entertainment critic Kevin Powell, a definition of exposition, group discussion questions, and Models From Literature of three types of expository writing: comparison-and-contrast essay, problem-and-solution essay, and evaluation or review.
- The Prewriting section includes an assortment of idea-generating activities to help students choose a topic, along with eleven topic ideas. This section also provides direct instruction and activities to help students narrow their topic, consider audience and purpose, and gather and organize details. Models From Literature, a Cluster Diagram on narrowing a topic, and a checklist for defining a purpose guide students through the steps of the expository writing process.
- The Drafting section addresses the importance of writing a strong introduction, body, and conclusion for the various types of expository writing, and provides models to illustrate each part.
- The Revising and Editing section offers techniques for both self-evaluation and peer evaluation to help students check that the exposition is well organized and includes the necessary facts and supporting details. There are also proofreading suggestions to remind students to check for errors in grammar, punctuation, or spelling.
- The Guided Lesson is followed by a Student Model and then skills lessons on using prepositions and conjunctions and making clear comparisons. You may want to address these skills before students draft their essays, or you may prefer t[o] focus on them during the revising/proofreading phase.
- The chapter ends with a complete Model From Literature, a comparison-and-contrast essay entitle[d] "Dad Just Got Traded!" b[y] Susan Fornoff.

Chapter Contents

"Writing is one of the freest things that you could ever do—to be able to express yourself on the written page."

"When I'm writing an article, I try to anticipate . . . what the audience would like to know about a particular subject."

—Kevin Powell
Entertainment Critic

"What's very important to me is the first paragraph, because it sets the tone. It also gives you a place to launch into the article you're writing."

More About the Writer

Kevin Powell is a staff writer for a national magazine about popular culture. As a critic, Powell may be assigned to review entertainment or media events, interview stars, or investigate what it's like behind the scenes as a performance or event takes shape. Talk with your students about how point of view and purpose can influence expository writing. Discuss how Powell's own interest in American youth culture can influence his work as an entertainment critic. Ask: *Do you think reviewers should be experts in the area they write about? Explain. How can writing an essay or review address the concerns of the audience that reads the article?*

Tech Prep Note

Point out that not only professional writers like Kevin Powell use exposition. Workers in many other fields use expository writing on the job. For example, a quality-control inspector may write a report to offer solutions to problems on the factory floor. An engineer might write an evaluation of a house to help a prospective buyer decide whether it would be a smart purchase, given its condition. Testers of consumer products often write comparison-and-contrast essays about items they evaluate. Ask: *Think about the adults you know and the work they do. How do they use expository writing on the job?*

About Exposition: Making Connecti

What Is Exposition That Makes Connections?

Exposition is writing that explains or presents information about a subject. Expository writing often makes connections by pointing out the similarities and differences between two things, exploring solutions to a problem, or by using facts to back up opinions.

Group Discussion When was the last time you told your friends whether you liked or disliked a new television show and why? What was the last problem you had to solve? Have you ever compared and contrasted two of your teachers? With a group of your classmates, discuss problems you have solved, comparisons you have made, or reviews you have given. Also think about types of expositions that you have read, heard on the radio, or seen on television. Discuss what makes these examples interesting and effective.

Introducing Expository Writing

Teaching Options

There are a variety of ways you can introduce exposition that makes connections by using the components of the *Writer's Solution:*

- You can show the expository writing segment from the *Writers at Work Videodisc*. Use this segment as a springboard for a class discussion on exposition.
- You can have students work individually or in small groups to go through the About Exposition: Making Connections section of the expository writing tutorial in the *Writing Lab* CD-ROM.
- You can work through the About Exposition: Making Connections section of the *Sourcebook* with the class.
- You can have students read the About Exposition: Making Connections section of the *Sourcebook* before class starts, so that, as a group, you can focus on the videodisc or CD-ROM lesson.

Sourcebook

Have students read aloud and discuss the About Exposition: Making Connections section in the *Sourcebook*. Use the following questions to guide the discussion:

- How does expository writing differ from other kinds of writing?
- Where and when might you expect to read examples of expository writing?
- What makes expository writing interesting to both the writer and the reader?
- How can expository writing help you expand your understanding of yourself or the world around you?

Following the class discussion, divide your students into groups of three to five to engage in the Group Discussion (p. 136).

Writers at Work Videodisc

Use the expository writing section of the videodisc featuring writer Kevin Powell to stimulate class discussion on exposition that makes connections. Play the chapter in its entirety, pausing as needed. Then feel free to use the bar codes to replay any segment to reinforce an important idea.

Before you play the first segment, ask students to listen for how Kevin Powell describes his approach to expository writing.

After viewing the segment, have students share their responses. Then discuss the writing techniques and insights that Powell shares.

How a Professional Writer Uses Exposition

Professional writers use exposition to explain their observations or discoveries about the world. For example, a science writer might share a discovery about the workings of the human brain, or a music critic might compare and contrast one CD with another. Kevin Powell is a staff writer for a national magazine about popular culture. He uses expository writing to evaluate events and provide information about film makers, rap artists, and television stars. Kevin explains how important it is to provide enough information so readers can then form their own opinions:

> "The kinds of things I look for when I put together an article—be it on a musical act or a media event—are as many details as possible. If it's a musical act, I want to know who they are, where they came from, what their background is, how the group got together, what kind of music they play, where do they want to go with their music. Those types of things are very important to me and, I think, very important to readers."

How Exposition Fits Into Your Life

Exposition is a big part of your life. Every time you evaluate a new pair of in-line skates, tell someone about a new movie, or compare two of your favorite computer games, you are practicing exposition. You also read exposition whenever you read an evaluation of a new product, a comparison of two movies or television shows, or a written solution to a problem. On the following pages, you'll learn how to use expository writing to explain your own observations and discoveries.

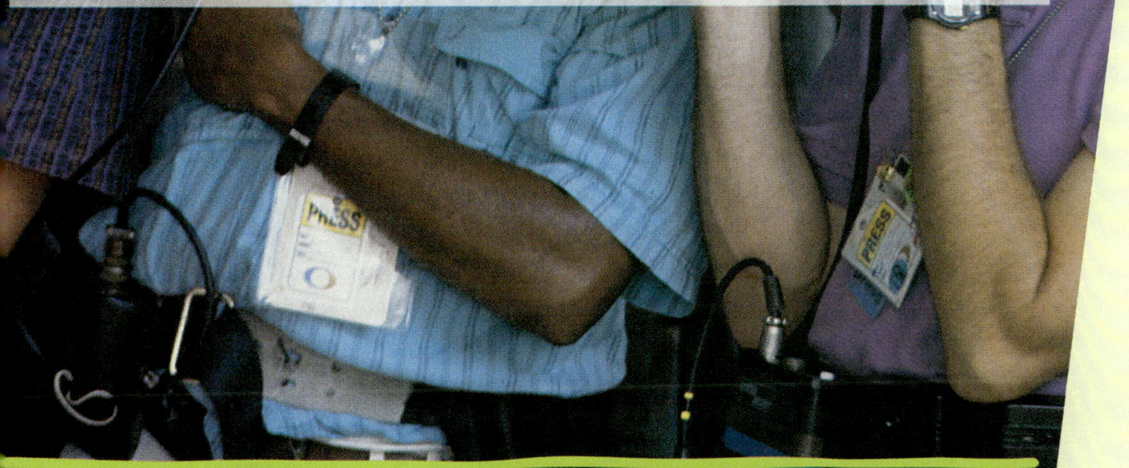

Ask:

- What does Powell say about the importance of details in an expository article?
- How does Powell use questioning to help him formulate an article?

Play frames 42884 to 51533

Real-World Writing

Help students identify people in your community who use expository writing in their work, such as film, music, or restaurant critics; technical writers of user manuals; or authors of how-to guides. Then have them find examples of expository writing in periodicals. For instance, students might see a review of a new film, an essay that compares and contrasts two schools, an evaluation of new software, or an essay that offers solutions to a health problem. As students share the examples, ask:

- What kind of exposition does the writer use? How does the writer support the information given?
- How do you think the writer gathered details for the piece?
- What features do these examples of expository writing include that differ from those found in other kinds of writing?

Writing Lab CD-ROM

The About Exposition: Making Connections section of the tutorial on expository writing includes the following options:

- **Author video** Entertainment critic Kevin Powell shares some insights about expository writing.
- **Audio-annotated literature models of expository writing** Comparison-and-Contrast essay, Problem-and-Solution essay, Review of a Media Program, and Evaluation of a Performance.
- **Evaluation checklist** You can present guidelines to students before they draft their expository pieces to serve as a checklist that directs their writing. The guidelines can also be used for self-assessment after writing. If so, students can incorporate the ideas into a reflective piece they may include in their portfolios.

Students can work individually or in small groups to complete the tutorial on exposition. Or, if you have access to a projection panel, you can work through the About Exposition: Making Connections section with the entire class, discussing each part as you go.

Integrating Literature With Writing

Starting From Literature

You can use the models on pages 138–140 to illustrate the various elements of each type of expository writing. Or you can highlight the content or techniques used in these pieces to inspire writing on any of the topics they address. For example, students can use their response to the excerpt from "Shark Attacks" by Jeanne K. Hanson and Deane Morrison to write a problem-and-solution essay about a similar problem between humans and wildlife in another ecosystem, such as wolves or bears harming livestock on ranches.

Briefly introduce and define the type of writing each selection models. You might invite a student to read each piece aloud to the class. Follow with discussion to reinforce students' understanding of each type of creative writing.

Teaching From the Model

Use the excerpt from "Shark Attacks" by Jeanne K. Hanson and Deane Morrison to help students recognize how a problem-and-solution essay exemplifies expository writing:

- *It clearly presents a problem and suggests a solution.* The authors give specific details in the first paragraph to describe where and why most shark attacks occur. Then they summarize simple precautions humans can take to avoid danger.
- *It explains why the solution would work.* The advice that Hanson and Morrison provide is clear and easy to follow. They include a basic tip for swimmers who are new to a swimming area: ". . . Ask local people if any swimming spots have been frequented by sharks—and if so, swim somewhere else."

Types of Exposition

You will use exposition when you are comparing and contrasting two people, places, or things; when you want to outline the solution to a problem; or when you are writing an evaluation or a review. Before choosing a topic, review the following writing models to learn more about the different types of expository writing.

1 A Problem-and-Solution Essay

- A problem-and-solution essay clearly defines and explains a problem and then provides possible solutions.
- When writing a problem-and-solution paper, back up all possible solutions with facts and explanations that tell why those solutions would work.

Model From Literature

In this excerpt from "Shark Attacks" by Jeanne K. Hanson and Deane Morrison, the authors describe a problem that sharks pose to humans and then present several practical solutions.

Most shark attacks occur in warm water, where bathers are more likely to be found. Many attacks may simply be cases of mistaken identity, in which the shark mistakes a bather for food. For example, a skin diver and a seal look a lot alike in profile, and a surfer paddling a small surfboard with head, hands, and feet dangling out, might resemble a giant sea turtle as seen from below. . . .

Precautions against shark attack include not swimming alone, at night, at dusk, near a fishing area, . . . [or] with an open wound; . . . not wearing bright objects, such as jewelry; and avoiding deep channels or shallow areas near a rapid drop-off. In an unfamiliar area, ask local people if any swimming spots have been frequented by sharks—and if so, swim somewhere else.

A Comparison-and-Contrast Essay

- A comparison-and-contrast essay explains the similarities and differences between two or more people, places, objects, or events.
- When you compare and contrast people, you might want to point out the similarities and differences in their backgrounds, physical appearance, and personalities.
- When you compare and contrast things, you might focus on how they look, what they're made of, and what they're used for.
- An interesting way to compare and contrast places or events is to list similarities and differences of the *same* place or event at two different times. For example, you might compare the appearance of a park in summer to the appearance of the same park in fall or winter.

Lincoln Boyhood National Memorial

Model From Literature

This passage from "A Backwoods Boy," by Russell Freedman, compares and contrasts the parents of Abraham Lincoln. Freedman begins and ends the passage with a trait they share but focuses on Lincoln's mother in the first paragraph and his father in the second.

Their parents couldn't read or write at all. Abraham's mother, Nancy, signed her name by making a shakily drawn mark. He would remember her as a thin, sad-eyed woman who labored beside her husband in the fields. She liked to gather the children around her in the evening to recite prayers and Bible stories she had memorized.

His father, Thomas, was a burly, barrel-chested farmer and carpenter who had worked hard at homesteading since marrying Nancy Hanks in 1806. A sociable fellow, his greatest pleasure was to crack jokes and swap stories with his chums. With painful effort, Thomas Lincoln could scrawl his name. Like his wife, he had grown up without education, but that wasn't unusual in those days.

Teaching From the Model

Guide students to recognize how the passage from "A Backwoods Boy," by Russell Freedman, exemplifies the comparison-and-contrast essay:

- *It points out similarities and differences between two subjects.* In this work, Freedman examines Abraham Lincoln's father and mother. He begins by discussing similarities they share, then contrasts them.
- *The author compares and contrasts the background, appearance, and personality of his subjects.* Freedman first points out a common trait—that Tom and Nancy Lincoln were uneducated. For contrast, he describes differences in their physical appearance by noting that Nancy was ". . . a thin, sad-eyed woman . . ." but Tom was ". . . burly [and] barrel-chested. . . ." Freedman also mentions the different ways the Lincolns chose to relax.

Clarification

The *Sourcebook* offers only one model of a comparison-and-contrast essay, but students can use this type of exposition to examine places, things, or events. The goal of any comparison-and-contrast essay remains the same, regardless of the subject: The writer presents similarities and differences so that readers can make connections. The specific details may vary to fit the subject. For instance, to compare and contrast two events, a writer might discuss settings and audiences.

Exploring Related Literature

Students who enjoyed this excerpt can find the full essay in *Prentice Hall Literature, Copper*. Students who are interested in this kind of exposition might consider an essay to compare and contrast characters in a myth. You can suggest that they read "Arachne" by Olivia Coolidge, in *Prentice Hall Literature, Copper*. They can write an essay to compare and contrast Arachne and Athene.

3 An Evaluation or a Review

- In an evaluation, you give an opinion about something and then support that opinion with evidence and examples. You can evaluate products, such as toothpastes, or performances, such as sports events.
- A review of a book, movie, or other form of entertainment mixes information about the work with opinions of it to create an overall impression of the work. Your overall impression may be negative—you were disappointed by the work and would not recommend it to others—or positive—you were pleased by the work and would recommend it.

Model From Literature

In the following excerpt from "Family Film Reviews," writer Joanne Bracco reviews the Disney film *Iron Will*. In the review, Bracco uses descriptive words—such as *exciting*, *fast-paced*, and *breathtaking*—as well as favorable opinions to convey a positive impression of the film.

> *Iron Will* is full of action and adventure. Mackenzie Astin is terrific as the young Will, a youth who will let nothing stop him from realizing his dream. The exciting scenes of fast-paced action as the dog sleds sail across the breathtaking, snow-covered mountain terrain plus a finely crafted story make this latest Disney release another splendid family classic film.

Teaching From the Model

Guide students to analyze this passage from Joanne Bracco's "Family Film Reviews" to understand how it exemplifies a review:

- *It mixes information and opinions about a work.* The author's subject is *Iron Will*, a new film. Bracco blends information about the film with her opinions of it. For example, she reveals that the action includes dog sledding. Her favorable opinion is clear in her description of *Iron Will* as ". . . another splendid family classic. . . ."
- *It conveys the reviewer's overall impression of the work.* Bracco must like the film because she uses positive language, such as "exciting scenes" and "finely crafted," to discuss it. These descriptive words and phrases support the reviewer's overall conclusion that the film is well worth seeing.

Teaching Strategy

To help students understand the key aspects of an evaluation, prepare an excerpt of a product report from a source such as *Consumer Reports*, *Macworld*, *Stereo Review*, *Road and Track*, or *Popular Mechanics*. Present it to students so they can see samples of information and facts on the product, and opinions or recommendations based on the evidence.

Clarification

Be sure students understand that a well-written evaluation or review should contain both fact and opinion. Some writers organize this type of essay by first presenting facts and then presenting conclusions based on the evidence. Other writers may weave fact and opinion together to create an overall impression of the product or work. Thus, reviews or evaluations of the same work or product may give objective facts that vary little, and subjective opinions that may differ among writers.

Language Acquisition/ESL Teaching Strategy

The *Writing Lab* offers a variety of options that can be adapted to meet the needs of your ESL students. The following are some examples of such adaptations.

- The Choosing Your Topic section offers a Question and Answer Checklist for product evaluations. Pair your upper-basic and intermediate students and have them answer the questions. The students then discuss how they are going to evaluate the product. Based on this discussion, the students write drafts of their expository compositions.

Guided Lesson

Now that you are familiar with different types of expository writing, it's time to begin mapping out your expository paper. This lesson will guide you through the process of developing your paper using each step of the writing process. You might not need to start at the beginning of the lesson, however. Think about the ideas that you have for your expository paper. Then use the following chart to decide where to begin.

	START WITH
If you **do not have a topic**	Choosing Your Topic
If you already **have a topic in mind but think it might be too broad to cover fully in a short paper**	Narrowing Your Topic
If you **have a specific topic but want to develop your ideas before you start writing**	Gathering Information
If you **have a topic and enough information to work with**	Drafting

Guiding Student Writing

Addressing Your Classroom Situation

- If you choose to assign topics or types of expository writing, allow time for students to narrow the topic to suit their interests or find an appealing focus to pursue.
- Some expositions, such as reviews or evaluations, are best suited for individual work so writers can express their opinions. However, you may have students work on comparison-and-contrast or problem-and-solution essays in pairs. If so, brainstorm with the class to determine fair ways for partners to collaborate.
- One way pairs can work together to write a comparison-and-contrast essay is for one student to focus on similarities while the other highlights differences. A team approach to the problem-and-solution essay might have students describe a problem together, then each propose a solution to it.

- The Gathering Information section provides a Venn Diagram that can be used with your basic and intermediate ESL students. Working individually or in pairs, your students organize information by differences and similarities. The students then decide how they might improve the organization of their own or each other's compositions.
- The Drafting section offers an audio tip from a student writer that can be used with your intermediate and advanced ESL students. Ask your students to take notes on the suggestions offered in the audio tip. Lead them in a discussion of what they learned. The students then use their notes and ideas from the discussion to write their drafts.

Prewriting

Choosing Your Topic

Do you want to compare and contrast two people, places, objects, or events? Would you rather write an evaluation of a product or a review of a movie? Maybe you'd like to write a solution to a problem you often encounter or observe others having trouble with? You can either choose from among the suggested writing options (see pages 144–147) or experiment with the following techniques to come up with your own topic:

If you're considering

. . . comparing and contrasting two people:

RECALL MEMORABLE CHARACTERS IN BOOKS OR MOVIES

Make a list of characters that stand out in your mind. They can be from books that you've read or from movies, plays, or television shows. What are your reasons for liking them or disliking them? Make a list of their differences and similarities—including a description of their appearances, personalities, and accomplishments. Then choose the two characters you liked best or least as a topic for your comparison-and-contrast paper.

. . . comparing and contrasting two places:

Group Activity

FORM AN EVENT-LOCATION COMMITTEE

With a group of your classmates, form an event-location committee. Your committee must find the ideal place for the next big event at your school. First, compile a list of events. They might include a school picnic, a concert, or a sports competition. Then suggest several places where each of the events could be held. Take turns describing the locations and giving the advantages and disadvantages of each. During the discussion, be sure to jot down notes. Later, review your notes and choose two places to compare and contrast.

Writing Lab CD-ROM

The Choosing Your Topic section of the tutorial on expository writing includes the following options to help students come up with their own topics:

- **Topic Wheels for generating ideas** Students can use three separate Topic Wheels to help them create ideas for their expository writing: comparing and contrasting people, comparing and contrasting places, and generating problems and solutions.
- **Question and Answer Checklist for product evaluations** Students answer five questions about a product and use the answers as the basis for an evaluation essay.
- **Sound pairs for comparison and contrast** Students play the audio to hear five pairs of related sounds, such as an electric guitar and an acoustic one, for ideas on comparing and contrasting subjects.

Working individually or in small groups, students can experiment with these activities to find the ones that work best.

Writers at Work Videodisc

Play the videodisc segment in which Kevin Powell discusses choosing a topic. Ask:

- Why do you think Powell makes a point of reading so many magazines and books and watching the news? How can you apply this technique to help you choose a topic for a piece of expository writing?

Suggest that students try Kevin Powell's strategy of gathering as much information as possible from many sources. Point out that in the drafting stage, more details may need to be obtained, but information gathered "up front" can often clarify a topic or spark a great idea.

Play frames 45181 to 45517

Collaborative Learning

Help students who choose the event-location committee Group Activity option to plan ways to facilitate the task. For instance, you might suggest that students visit and photograph the sites they plan to suggest. Students might work in pairs to investigate sites: One student focuses on positive aspects of using the site, while the other looks for drawbacks. When members report back to the group, the group facilitator can encourage presenters to give information as if they

. . . a solution to a problem:

OBSERVE THE WORLD OF PROBLEMS

We deal with problems every day: how to remove a food stain from a shirt, how to arrange a ride to soccer practice, where to obtain the right materials for a project, how to find time to finish your homework and see your friends. For three days, jot down the problems you have and the problems that others have. Include in your notes possible solutions. Review your notes and choose a problem as a topic for your problem-and-solution paper.

. . . an evaluation:

Group Activity

HOLD A MUSIC CONVENTION

Do you enjoy listening to a favorite kind of music, such as rock, pop, or rap? With a group of your classmates, hold a music convention in which you share the music that you love. Have each person listen at home to music on the radio or on a tape or CD and choose a favorite. Then hold a music convention in which each person names the musical piece and explains why he or she likes it. If possible, bring recordings of the music to class. Jot down the names of each piece and review your notes for a possible topic.

. . . a movie review:

BE A MOVIE CRITIC

What kinds of movies do you like? Comedies? Adventure stories? Science-fiction films? During the next week, be a movie critic. Watch a few movies—either rented or on television—and take detailed notes. For each movie, jot down the names of main characters and details about plot, setting, music, and special effects. After you have watched at least three movies, review your notes to find the movie you have the strongest opinion about—either positive or negative. Use that movie for your movie review.

Teaching Strategy

To help students who choose the movie critic option, show a short film or video to provide common ground for discussion. Have students take notes, and then ask volunteers to share the kinds of details they jotted down. Invite students to offer suggestions about what to look for and how best to record it. Discussions that arise from this exercise may lead to new topics for comparison-and-contrast essays or add insights students may use in reviews.

were making a comparison and contrast or presenting a problem and solution.

Prewriting

Inspirations for Exposition

Here are some writing topics for exposition:

A Comparison of Everyday Life With the Life of Astronauts

Do you hope to travel on board the space shuttle someday? What do you think life is like for the astronauts who explore space? Are their lives in any way similar when they're back on Earth? Write a paper that compares and contrasts the lives of astronauts in space with their lives on Earth. Support each comparison and contrast with examples. Include specific details that illustrate your ideas.

A Comparison of Two Pets

What kinds of pets are you familiar with? Cats? Dogs? Hamsters? Tropical fish? Choose two different kinds of pets. Then write a brief paper that compares and contrasts them. How are they alike? How are they different or unique? How easy or how difficult is it to care for each of these pets? What different or similar responsibilities are involved in their care? Use specific nouns, active verbs, and carefully selected modifiers to compare these pets. For each comparison, use examples or anecdotes as support.

Writing Lab CD-ROM

Using the Inspirations for Exposition in the *Writing Lab* is an excellent way to stimulate creativity and to have students explore possible topics for expository writing. Students can browse individually or in small groups through the Inspirations. They can choose their own writing topics or you may prefer to assign topics.

The following is a list of the expository writing options included in the Inspirations, but not provided in the *Sourcebook:*

Comparison and Contrast of

- The characters of the prince and the pauper
- Two people you know personally
- Two amusement park rides
- Two different age groups
- Two cheering crowds
- Birthday traditions
- Birthday celebrations in two families
- How two people or characters approach problems
- Written and spoken language
- Lifestyles of famous and ordinary people
- Elements of fame for two professions
- Two athletes
- Images in a photograph
- Contemporary and older cultures
- Traditional and contemporary clothes
- Children's learning
- City scenes
- Life in two city settings
- Two similar places in a community
- Two breeds of dogs

Problem-and-Solution Essay

- On how a newspaper reports the facts
- On how to enjoy an amusement park ride
- About throwing a birthday party
- For a troubleshooting guide about a physical activity
- On how explorers should act responsibly
- With suggestions for babysitting
- With suggestions for a toddler
- On urban problems
- With suggestions for a shopper
- With suggestions on training an animal

Evaluation of

- An imaginary performance
- The performance of the actor who plays both characters in *The Prince and the Pauper*
- A performance

A Solution to a Conflict Between Generations

Do you sometimes disagree with your parents? Young people and adults often do not see things the same way. It isn't uncommon for members of younger and older generations to see life differently or to have different dreams or goals. Think of a problem that can occur between young people and adults. Write a short paper that suggests one or more solutions to this kind of generation problem. Use specific examples that support your suggestions.

A Solution to the Problem of a Crying Toddler

Imagine that you are babysitting for a toddler who is crying loudly because her mother isn't there. What can you do to solve this problem? How do you make the toddler feel happy? Write a brief essay in which you explain how you solve the problem of the crying toddler. Use logic, as well as your imagination, to develop a good solution.

An Evaluation of an Athlete

What sports do you enjoy watching? Basketball? Baseball? Gymnastics? Think of an individual athlete you've seen perform. Did the athlete do well? What was it about the performance that stood out as excellent? What needed improvement? Write an evaluation of the performance.

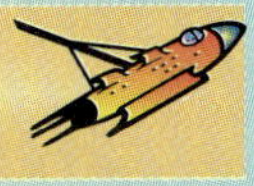

An Evaluation of an Amusement Park Ride

Have you ever been on a roller coaster? Would you want to take the ride again or would you prefer another ride instead? Write an evaluation of an amusement park ride. Include a clear, detailed description of the ride. State your opinion and feelings and make sure the details in the evaluation support that opinion.

Group Project: Develop a Booklet That Compares Different Cultures

As a group, look into the cultures of different peoples. *Culture* means the ideas, skills, arts, and ways of behaving of a certain group of people. Have each group member choose a unique group of people and find out about that group's traditional art, food, clothing, language, and customs. Each member should write a paragraph summarizing what he or she has learned. Then discuss how different cultures are alike and how they are different. Finally, put the paragraphs together in a book that shows all the cultures.

- A performance on a television program
- A musician's performance style
- A sports event

Review of

- A media program about a toddler

Writing Lab CD-ROM

The Inspirations for Exposition in the *Writing Lab* also include the following Group Projects and Group Discussions. The Group Discussions encourage small groups of students to share their thoughts about an Inspiration and to generate possible writing topics. The Group Projects are structured activities in which students assume different roles.

Group Projects

- Creating a declaration about toddlers
- Creating a language chart
- Creating image poems about human qualities

Group Discussions

- Comparing and contrasting news articles
- Creating a code of behavior for a prince
- Identifying stories with amusement park settings
- Nominating the best crowd for a school or community event
- Sharing ideas about the importance of birthday celebrations
- Providing advice for athletes in training
- Identifying highlights of space travel
- Developing guidelines for learning
- Planning a school market
- Nominating a best breed of dog

Cross-Curricular Connection: *Math*

Students who choose to review a television news show can conduct a statistical analysis of the show to generate data for their review. If possible, students should videotape the news show they plan to review. Then they can play back the tape with a stopwatch or other timing device (some VCRs have real-time counters) to determine how many minutes are devoted to various categories, such as human interest pieces, "hard" news, commercials, opening and closing credits, and so on. Students can present the findings in a graph or table, which they can include with their review.

Cultural Connection

Students who choose to write a solution to a problem a newcomer might face could interview someone who emigrated to the United States from another country to find out actual problems that person faced. As they conduct their research, students can ask about differences in language, culture, or customs that may have contributed to problems in the newcomer's adjustment. Students can also ask the newcomer to describe helpful solutions he or she found, as well as ideal solutions that might be helpful to others in similar situations.

Language Acquisition/ ESL Teaching Strategy

Your ESL students of all levels will be able to relate to the inspiration, A Solution to a Problem a Newcomer Might Face. Lead your students in a class discussion about the problems they faced when arriving in their new country. Draw a Topic Web on the chalkboard listing their ideas. Ask the students to choose a topic and list details describing the problem. The students then refer to these notes when writing their compositions.

MORE *Inspirations* for Exposition

A Review of a Television News Show

Do you think television news shows present facts in a clear way? Watch a television news show and jot down notes on the stories it covers. Then write a short review of the show. Were stories clearly told? Did they give enough information? Were there enough visual aids, such as photos, film clips, and charts? Present your ideas in the order of their importance. Be sure to support all your points with facts or examples from the telecast.

A Comparison of Two Famous People

As average people, we might think it would be wonderful to be famous. That may not actually be true. Think about famous people you've read about. How are they the same? How are they different? How have they handled their fame? What have they been able to accomplish in other ways because of their fame? What would you like to accomplish if you were famous? What might you like or dislike about being famous? Write a composition in which you compare and contrast the lifestyles of several famous people you admire. Support your comparison with examples, anecdotes, and other details.

A Solution to a Problem a Newcomer Might Face

Every year large numbers of people come to the United States either as immigrants or as tourists. What do you think it's like to arrive in a strange country for the very first time? What kinds of problems do you think a newcomer to the United States might face? Describe such a problem and suggest a possible solution. The problem may be based on a real-life or imagined experience. Use details to help readers picture the situation clearly and understand your solution.

Group Project: Create a Before-and-After Community Book

As a group, list categories that describe things that change in a community over time, such as shops, transportation, and recreation. Have each group member choose one item from the list and write one paragraph that describes the community from his or her earliest memories and another paragraph that describes it now. Newer community members can ask older members for details about how things used to be. Regroup and combine these paragraphs into a Before-and-After Community Book. If possible, illustrate your book with "then-and-now" photographs.

Marketplace, Guatemala *John Hollis Kaufman*

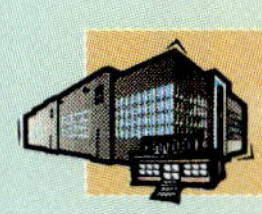

A Comparison of Two Places to Shop

What would it be like to shop in a marketplace like the one you see in the painting above? How would it be different from a shopping mall or another kind of shopping area in your community? How would it be the same? Write a composition in which you compare and contrast a marketplace to a shopping mall or another modern shopping area. Support each comparison with details. Base your ideas on what you see in the painting and what you know from your own experience.

A Review of a Musical Performance

Musical performances can be enjoyable and inspiring experiences. Have you ever performed in a school band or chorus? Have you ever attended a concert or seen a musical performance on television? Write a review of a musical performance that you have either seen or taken part in. Give your opinion of the performance and support that opinion with details and examples from the concert. You might focus on the type of music performed or point out outstanding performers.

Thematic Connection: Goals

Students who choose to review a musical performance can add another dimension to their review by exploring the goals performers set for themselves. For instance, is it enough for a performer to make no obvious mistakes? Is it important to develop rapport with the audience? Is it important to perform new works or to perform old familiar ones? Students can learn more about a performer's goals by interviewing someone who has performed, or someone who typically evaluates performers, such as a band leader or drama coach. The information students gather can help them create a more insightful review.

Writing Lab CD-ROM

The Narrowing Your Topic section of the tutorial on Exposition includes the following options:

- **Video tip on narrowing a topic** Students see football photographs and hear various ways to narrow the broad topic of football.
- **Interactive checklist** Students answer questions designed to help them decide whether a topic is too broad. Some of the questions appear on page 148 of the *Sourcebook*.
- **Cluster Diagram** Students use this graphic organizer to divide a broad topic into subtopics.
- **Audio-annotated examples of ways to narrow topics** Students choose a broad topic to hear how it could be narrowed.

Writers at Work Videodisc

Play the videodisc segment in which Kevin Powell discusses narrowing his topic. Ask:

- How does Powell justify his decision to narrow his topic to a piece about the two stars?
- Do you think Powell might have to narrow his topic again? Explain.

Play frames 46841 to 47458

Narrowing Your Topic

If you have chosen a topic but think it is too broad to be covered fully in a short paper, narrow your topic by considering the following questions:

Questions for Narrowing a Topic

- If you're writing a comparison-and-contrast essay, does your topic have only a few important parts to compare and contrast?
- If you're writing a problem-and-solution paper, is the problem you're explaining focused enough to solve in a short paper?
- If you're writing a review or an evaluation, can you cover your subject effectively in a short paper?
- Can you divide your topic into smaller subtopics?

Use a Cluster Diagram to Narrow a Topic

Use a cluster diagram to narrow your topic. Write your general topic in the center of a piece of paper. Next, write subtopics in circles surrounding the general topic. Then divide those subtopics into even narrower subtopics. Look through your narrowed topics and choose one to write about.

Varying the Writing Process

Have students collaborate with a peer editor to make a Cluster Diagram. They can benefit from getting another opinion at this stage of the writing process. Or, after individuals have created Cluster Diagrams, they can show them to peer editors, who may offer comments or suggest other subtopics to consider.

Addressing Ability Levels

Narrowing a topic may be difficult for some of your **more-challenged** students. They may benefit from working with a partner who can ask focusing questions such as those given on this page. Students can also ask some of the questions journalists ask: *Who? What? When? Where? Why?*

Language Lab CD-ROM

Students who need more support to narrow a topic may benefit from doing the Narrowing a Topic lesson in the Composing unit of the *Language Lab*.

Considering Your Audience

Who will read your exposition? Shape your paper according to the audience you are trying to reach. When planning your paper, consider the needs of your readers. Know how familiar your audience is with your topic and include information that they will need to know as well as information that may be new to them. For example, if your audience is not familiar with your topic, you will need to include basic background information. If your audience is somewhat familiar with your topic, you can leave out basic information and focus on what makes your topic special.

It is also important to use appropriate language for your audience. For example, if you are writing for your classmates, you might use informal language. If, however, you're writing for your teacher or your school or local newspaper, you should use formal language. Remember to explain terms that might be unfamiliar to your readers.

Considering Your Purpose

All writers have a purpose for their writing. The general purpose of exposition is to explain or inform. You will also have a more specific purpose, such as evaluating a new video game or comparing and contrasting two clothing styles. To help you define your purpose clearly, consider the following questions:

Checklist for Defining a Purpose

- What do you want to accomplish by writing this paper? What are your goals?
- What makes your subject special or different from others?
- How will your audience use the information you're explaining?
- Which pieces of information are most useful?

Jot down your answers to these questions in your notes and refer back to them as you draft your paper.

Writing Lab CD-ROM

The Considering Audience and Purpose section of the tutorial on Exposition includes the following options to help students gear their writing to their intended audience and define their purpose:

- **Video clip on the importance of knowing your audience** Students see a humorous clip from *A Connecticut Yankee in King Arthur's Court* to hear the effect of using language inappropriate to an audience.
- **Audience Profile** Students answer questions to help them focus on their intended audience.
- **Audio-annotated models of passages written for different audiences** Students hear explanations of why the writers of each passage chose certain language or styles to address their audiences.
- **Checklist for defining purpose** Students refer to this list of questions to help them define their writing purpose. The same questions appear on page 149 of the *Sourcebook*.

Working individually or in small groups, students can experiment with these activities to find the ones that work best for them.

Writers at Work Videodisc

Play the videodisc segment in which Kevin Powell discusses the importance of knowing his audience. Ask:

- Why does Powell try to anticipate questions his readers might ask?
- How can you apply Powell's method of anticipating his audience's concerns to your own writing?

Play frames 47589 to 48305

Language Lab CD-ROM

Students who need guidance to determine audience and purpose can complete the Considering Audience and Purpose lesson in the Composing unit of the *Language Lab*.

Addressing Ability Levels

Some of your **more-challenged** students may have difficulty establishing a purpose for their expositions. It may be useful to set up brief conferences with them to discuss possibilities. Or, peer partners can use the checklist on page 149 of the *Sourcebook* to help each other set or focus their writing purpose.

Writing Lab CD-ROM

The Gathering Details section of the tutorial on Exposition includes the following options designed to help students gather details for their topics:

- **Video tip from a professional writer** Students can play a brief clip in which writer Kevin Powell offers advice about taking notes.
- **Venn Diagram** Students can organize similarities and differences to compare and contrast a topic.
- **Video clip on gathering details** Students watch a parrot detect similarities and differences between objects to suggest how they can do the same with details for their topic.
- **Audio-annotated writing models** Students hear how writers use similarities and differences in a comparison-and-contrast essay and pose a problem and offer remedies in a problem-and-solution paper.
- **Audio-annotated model of a negative evaluation** Students read a passage from Harold Schechter's *Kidvid* to learn how details support his opinions.
- **Question and Answer form** Students create a research outline by answering questions for a problem-and-solution paper.
- **Cluster Diagram** Students see how specific details in an evaluation are evidence to support a judgment.
- **Interactive Writing Hints for details to include in evaluations** Students can choose subjects they might evaluate to get a list of possible details to include regarding that subject.
- **Interactive tips for gathering details from experts** Students can get advice if they choose a recommended way to contact experts and ask them for information on a topic.

Working individually or in small groups, students can experiment with these activities to find the ones that work best for them.

Prewriting

Gathering Details

After you have chosen a topic, you will need to start gathering details. Expository writing is based on facts, so gather factual details that will communicate your message as clearly and accurately as possible. You can gather information through library research, interviews and conversations with other people, and by observation.

How to Gather Details to Compare and Contrast

When gathering details for a comparison-and-contrast paper, choose two subjects that are related closely enough to have both similarities and differences. Include precise details—such as descriptions, facts, examples, and reasons—that show the similarities and differences between the subjects.

FROM a WRITER

"Note taking is probably the most important skill you could have as a writer. . . . In my opinion, nothing is more important than you, the human note taker, being able to listen and gather information . . . and then transferring it onto the written page."

—Kevin Powell

Writing Model

DETAILS SHOWING SIMILARITIES AND DIFFERENCES

TOPIC: INVENTORS ELI WHITNEY AND ROBERT FULTON

Both Eli Whitney and Robert Fulton made major contributions to the advancement of technology. Whitney was an inventor. He invented the cotton gin and interchangeable parts, which increased the production of factories and plantations in the United States. Fulton did not invent the steam engine, but he did design and build the first commercial steamboat. This made accurate scheduling possible and also increased productivity of American companies. Both men began in different fields. Whitney was a tutor, and Fulton trained to be an artist.

Teaching From the Model

Discuss how the writing model about Eli Whitney and Robert Fulton gives details that help readers understand similarities and differences:

- *It identifies its two subjects in the opening sentence.* The paragraph's topic sentence names Eli Whitney and Robert Fulton as contributors to technology.
- *The writer presents similarities and differences supported by facts and details.* The writer used the word *both* to begin two sentences with comparisons. In the first case, *both* opens a statement about the similar effect Whitney and Fulton had on American productivity. In the second case, the writer says that neither

How to Gather Details for a Problem-and-Solution Essay

Choose details that define your problem and give factual information. List all possible solutions. Note how people are affected by the problem, obtain information from organizations concerned with the issue, and determine what needs improvement.

Then note how the situation could be improved, who could help solve the problem, and how your solutions compare with other similar solutions.

Writing Model

DETAILS OF A PROBLEM-AND-SOLUTION ESSAY

PROBLEM

A professional sports team goes on strike because the players think the owners make too much money

SOLUTIONS

- Make tickets cheaper
- Give a large percentage of profits to charity
- Increase the salaries of the "little people" who are important in getting the game to happen

How to Gather Details for an Evaluation or a Review

When writing an evaluation or a review, gather factual details that support your opinion. For movies, note details about the characters, plot, actors' performances, and special effects. For music, note the type of music, length of selections, and information about the musicians and their voices and/or instruments. For products, note the type of product, its appearance and usefulness, and the price.

Writing Model

DETAILS FOR A MOVIE REVIEW

This cartoon version of the Jules Verne classic *Around the World in Eighty Days* is so bad that it's hard to sit through. . . . One of the more irritating things about this cartoon is the way it equates humor with the mindless repetition of jokes that aren't funny to begin with. For example, whenever Fogg finds himself in a trap, he raises a finger and announces, "The motto of the wise is: Be prepared for surprises." Young children might find this little rhyme clever, but even the most good-natured six-year-old is likely to start searching for something to throw at the screen after hearing Fogg's motto repeated for the twelfth time in as many minutes.

—Harold Schechter, *Kidvid*

Technology Note: Networking

Students with access to on-line forums or services might utilize one or more of them as a way to gather details for an evaluation or review. Students can read professional reviews or evaluations of films or new products to see how writers included details. Talk with students or teachers who have had experience browsing the Internet or participating in "chat rooms" or bulletin boards on America Online, CompuServe, or Prodigy. Help students pair up to take advantage of this opportunity with a partner who has on-line capabilities and experience.

Teaching Strategy

Gathering facts and details for a comparison-and-contrast essay demands research skills. Expository writing usually does not require source citation, but the techniques of gathering information and organizing it for reports may be helpful. You might have students review parts of the Reports chapter in the *Sourcebook* (pp. 198–235), in the *Writing Lab* tutorial on Reports, or in sections of the *Writer's Companion*.

Writing Strategy

Discuss how Harold Schechter conveys his dislike for the cartoon he writes about. Emphasize that any opinion, whether positive or negative, is more clear to readers when it is supported by specific examples. Stress to students the importance of backing up any claim they make with details that reinforce their viewpoint.

man began in the field for which he later became known. By showing that both men made major contributions, though one did so as an inventor and the other as a designer and entrepreneur, the writer weaves contrast and comparison together.

Clarification

Be sure students realize that the problem-and-solution model does not represent a complete essay. Rather, it shows notes a writer can use to plan the essay. Point out that the writer should gather background facts about the problem and details on implementing solutions.

Writing Lab CD-ROM

The Organizing Details section of the tutorial on Exposition includes the following options designed to help students effectively make connections among the details they have gathered on their topic:

- **Methods of organization checklist** Students use brief guidelines to help them choose an effective organizational plan for the type of exposition they plan to write.
- **Audio Literature Model of subject-by-subject organization** Students hear writer Roald Dahl read a passage from a description of his two aunts to hear how subject-by-subject organization can be used to compare and contrast.
- **Audio-annotated Writing Models of different organizational plans** Students read models that have been organized by subject, by point, by chronological order, or by order of importance. Each model includes explanations of why its writer chose that particular plan of organization.
- **Venn Diagram for organizing details in a point-by-point plan** Students can organize notes for similarities and differences on a topic of comparison and contrast.
- **Chain of Events for chronological order** Students organize details for a problem-and-solution paper by entering events into boxes and moving the boxes into an order that reflects a clear sequence.
- **Chain of Events for order of importance** Students can organize details for a review or evaluation. They enter events into boxes, whose positions can be changed until the details show order of importance.

Working individually or in small groups, students can experiment with these activities to find the ones that work best for them.

Prewriting

Organizing Details

After you have finished gathering details, decide on a method of organization that will help you present your topic clearly. Remember your general and specific purposes and then choose the organization that is most appropriate. Use the following guidelines to help you decide on a type of organization.

- If you are writing a comparison-and-contrast paper, organize similarities and differences point by point or subject by subject.
- If you are writing a problem-and-solution essay, use order of importance or chronological order.
- If you are writing a review or an evaluation, use order of importance.

How to Organize a Comparison-and-Contrast Paper

You can organize a comparison-and-contrast essay in two ways. You can use the subject-by-subject method to discuss all the qualities of each subject separately. Or you can use the point-by-point method to discuss similarities and differences one at a time.

The following writing models—at right and on page 153—show you how to organize both ways.

Writing Model

SUBJECT-BY-SUBJECT ORGANIZATION

The writer separates the two subjects of the comparison-and-contrast paper into two separate paragraphs. In the first paragraph, the qualities and characteristics of Martin Luther King, Jr., are discussed. In the second paragraph, the qualities and characteristics of Robert Kennedy are described.

Martin Luther King, Jr., was one of this century's great heroes. King spent years trying to gain equal rights for all people. He organized many boycotts, demonstrations, and marches. In 1964, he won the Nobel Prize for Peace. Two years later, he was killed.

Robert Kennedy was also one of this century's heroes. Like King, he worked hard to get equal rights for everyone. However, Kennedy worked as Attorney General and later as a Senator. He wanted to be President, but he, too, was killed. In fact, he was killed in the same year King was killed.

Teaching From the Model

Help students recognize how the model that illustrates subject-by-subject organization gives details about both subjects in a parallel way:

- *The first paragraph discusses the qualities and characteristics of one subject.* The writer gives a brief introduction to Martin Luther King, Jr., as "... one of this century's greatest heroes."
- *The next paragraph presents the same kind of information in the same order about the other subject.* Now the writer describes similar attributes of Robert Kennedy, but makes contrasts to differentiate the two men.

Writing Model

POINT-BY-POINT ORGANIZATION

In the following model, the writer compares and contrasts Martin Luther King, Jr., and Robert Kennedy by moving back and forth between the two subjects and explaining points of similarity and difference.

During the 1960's, many people tried to get equal rights for all people. Two of the best-known people were Dr. Martin Luther King, Jr., and Robert Kennedy. Both of these men tried peaceful, legal methods to achieve their goals. King worked to organize boycotts, demonstrations, and marches, while Kennedy worked to get new laws passed. The two men were honored during their lifetimes. King won the Nobel Prize for Peace in 1964. Kennedy was U.S. Attorney General and later a Senator.

How to Organize a Problem-and-Solution Paper

When you want to re-create a series of events or give step-by-step instructions, organize your paper by using chronological, or time, order.

Writing Model

CHRONOLOGICAL ORDER

In this model, the writer first states his problem. He then uses chronological order to describe the steps he took to solve it.

When I first moved to Maine, I didn't know how to ski. I would stay home every weekend during the winter. Finally, I decided to learn how to ski. First, I rented equipment and signed up for a lesson. Then I learned how to move slowly down the hill by pointing the tips of my skis in. Finally, I learned how to turn. Now I practice every weekend.

Language Lab CD-ROM

Successful subject-by-subject organization requires paragraphs with a main idea stated in a topic sentence and supporting sentences that elaborate on it. Students who need help in this area may benefit from doing the Main Idea and Topic Sentence and Supporting Sentences lessons in the Building Paragraphs unit of the *Language Lab*.

Writing Strategy

As students examine the model that illustrates point-by-point organization, be sure they realize that in that plan of organization, facts and details about both subjects appear in the same paragraph. Such a paragraph needs a topic sentence to express the main idea by identifying both subjects and suggesting why they are being compared.

Addressing Ability Levels

Help your **more-challenged** students to organize details into chronological order by having them create a simple timeline. They can write each step they propose on a separate index card, then move the cards around into a logical, sequential order. Students can also use this technique to rank details by order of importance.

Have students study the model, sentence by sentence, to recognize the well-organized way details are given. For example, both paragraphs mention "heroes," "equal rights," and "was killed."

Clarification

Tell students that it is acceptable for them to use chronological order in an evaluation or review if sequence is a key factor. For instance, a movie review might examine how tension builds as scenes unfold. A product evaluation might give steps in time order to highlight the product's strength or weakness.

Language Lab CD-ROM

Writers who organize their work by chronological order or order of importance use transitional words to make the connections easy to follow. Students who need additional practice using transitional words effectively should work through the Transitional Words lesson in the Building Paragraphs unit of the *Language Lab*.

How to Organize an Evaluation or a Review

Use order-of-importance organization for your evaluation or review by either beginning with the most important details and ending with the least important details or beginning with the least important details and ending with the most important details.

Writing Model

ORDER OF IMPORTANCE

Using order of importance in an evaluation or a review can help to make your writing more convincing. In the following model, a review of a storyteller's performance is organized by order of importance.

Saturday's performance by storyteller Enid Wexner was not a great success. For one thing, Wexner's voice was too soft. Listeners at the edge of the crowd could not really hear her. What was more important, though, was how Wexner used her voice. She didn't use it well. Most of the characters she played sounded very much alike. The worst thing about the show were the stories themselves. They were poor choices. Older students were bored by such stories as "The Three Little Pigs." Younger students were scared by the spooky stories, especially "The Headless Horseman."

The Headless Horseman Pursuing Ichabod Crane *1858, John Quidor, National Museum of American Art, Washington, D.C.*

Drafting

When you've gathered your details and decided on a method of organization, it's time to begin drafting your paper. As you draft, refer back to your notes for guidance. Keep writing without worrying about making grammatical or spelling errors. You'll be able to correct any mistakes when you proofread your paper.

Your paper will consist of three parts: an introduction, a body, and a conclusion. Read on to find out exactly what each part does.

Writing the Introduction

Your introduction begins your paper, so it's the first thing your audience will read. Grab your readers' interest so they will want to read on. Your introduction should do the following:

- Capture your reader's interest.
- Identify your subject and its main categories.
- Lead smoothly into the body.

Writing Model

THE INTRODUCTION

In this introduction to an evaluation, the writer opens with a vivid and unusual description that captures the reader's attention.

It smiles at me and says hello every time I turn it on. My new computer Rex 5000 is the most user-friendly computer available. Even my six-year-old brother can use it without any additional instruction.

Writing Hint

To attract your readers' attention and hold their interest, retell an amusing anecdote or an interesting story, or begin your introduction with a question that will get your audience thinking.

Writing Lab CD-ROM

The Drafting section of the tutorial on Exposition includes the following options to help students write their first draft, using details to convey the connections they wish to make:

- **Audio tips from a student writer** Students hear how one student begins to draft an exposition.
- **Audio-annotated Writing Models** Students hear writers' comments regarding their decisions as they drafted expository pieces.
- **Transition Word Bin** Students select transition words or phrases that work best with comparison and contrast, chronological order, and order of importance.
- **Audio-annotated Student Model** Students see a draft of a student's comparison-and-contrast paper and hear comments about the choices made in drafting it.
- **Video tips from an author** Students can hear Kevin Powell's comments about overcoming writer's block.

Working individually or in small groups, students can experiment with these activities to find the ones that work best for them.

Writers at Work Videodisc

Play the videodisc egment in which Kevin 'owell talks about beginning is draft. He says that the irst paragraph is very imporant to him. Ask:

- Why do you think Powell considers the opening paragraph of an exposition so important?
- How can the opening of your essay help to direct your audience?

Play frames 48460 to 48826

Writing Strategy

Discuss how the introduction to an exposition should make a good "first impression" on readers. A strong introduction acquaints readers with the subject and piques their interest to read on. Encourage students to experiment with their introduction to make it engaging.

Establishing Assessment Criteria

As students draft their expositions, you may want to share with them the criteria you will use to evaluate their work. The following guidelines are included in the tutorial on Exposition: Making Connections. Use them as given, or modify them to suit your needs:

- Does your writing have a narrow and focused topic?
- For a comparison-and-contrast paper, did you include details that show similarities and differences?
- For a problem-and-solution essay, did you identify a specific problem and provide a clear solution, including details to support your solution?
- For an evaluation, did you clearly summarize your subject and include enough details to support your opinion?
- Is your writing well organized?
- Did you check for errors in spelling, grammar, capitalization, and punctuation?

Addressing Ability Levels

To help your **more-challenged** students write better conclusions, have them verbalize the main point to a peer partner or to you. Saying ideas aloud can clarify them and make them easier to write. For reviews or evaluations, students can state what they recommend based on the details they gathered.

Language Lab CD-ROM

If students need additional guidance in writing concluding sentences, refer them to the Concluding Sentence lesson in the Building Paragraphs unit of the *Language Lab*.

Writing the Body

A body provides the bulk of information on the topic presented in the introduction. The body should

- Develop the main idea of your paper.
- Support your opinions with facts and examples.

Writing Model

THE BODY

The body of the evaluation of a computer explains why the computer is easy to use. Notice how the example about symbols supports the writer's main idea.

My computer talks to you and tells you what to do. My brother can follow the directions that the computer gives him. It is colorful and uses symbols that are the same as the operation, such as a pair of scissors that when clicked cut out the words.

Writing the Conclusion

The conclusion of your paper should restate the main idea. To make the conclusion more effective, try one of these:

- End with an informative or entertaining quotation.
- Make a recommendation.
- Tell a personal anecdote related to your subject.
- Ask a question that makes your audience stop and think.

Writing Model

THE CONCLUSION

The conclusion of the computer evaluation begins with an unusual question and ends with a recommendation.

Did you know that someday we will be able to put a microchip in anything to make it talk to us? Can you imagine talking to your furniture! For now, I'm happy talking to my Rex 5000, and I think you will be too.

Revising and Editing

Revising Your Work

After you've completed your draft, put it aside for a while. Then read through your draft, looking for ways to improve it. Use the following checklist to guide you.

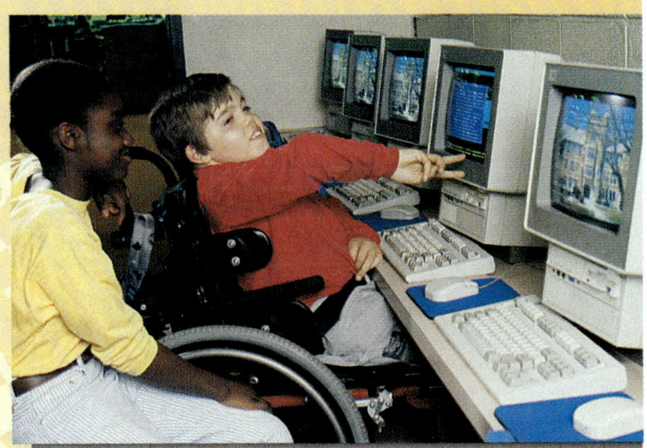

Revision Checklist

1. Did you identify your subject?
2. In what ways have you considered your audience? What can you do to make your paper easier to understand?
3. What kinds of details did you use? How can you improve your choice of details?
4. In what ways have you considered your purpose? How can you make your purpose more clear?
5. What kind of organization plan did you choose? How can you improve your organization of details?
6. Did you include an introduction, body, and conclusion?

Student Model: Revised Draft

Here is a revised passage of a comparison-and-contrast paper by Becky Hernandez, a student at Hale Middle School in Woodland Hills, California. Notice that Becky replaces the word *very* with *equally* to signal a comparison.

Billy, a character from *Where the Red Fern Grows*, is similar to Piggy, a character from *Lord of the Flies*. ~~First,~~ Billy and Piggy are [equally] ~~very~~ intelligent. Billy finds a way to hunt raccoons, and Piggy has an idea to get off the deserted island. [Also] ~~Secondly~~, Billy looks up to his grandfather because he teaches him [important and interesting] ~~neat~~ things. ~~and~~ Piggy always talks about his wonderful aunt.

Writers at Work Videodisc

Play the videodisc egment in which Kevin 'owell discusses his views on evising and editing. Ask:

- What is your view of Powell never taking for granted that his first draft is good? How does his view fit the writing process?
- What is your reaction to knowing that Powell often makes five or six drafts of a piece, if not more?
- How can you keep your purpose and focus in mind as you revise?

Play frames 48996 to 49866

Writing Lab CD-ROM

The Revising and Editing section of the tutorial on Exposition provides strategies for self-revision. It includes the following options to help students revise first drafts:

- **Self-Evaluation Checklists** Students answer questions on a general checklist, then move to a more specific list for the type of exposition they wrote.
- **Sentence openers variety checker** Students use a tool that highlights the start of each sentence in a draft so it can be checked for variety.
- **Transition Word Bin** Students select transition words or phrases to add to their drafts.
- **Audio-annotated Student Model** Students match the first draft of a comparison-and-contrast essay with a revised draft to learn how and why revisions were made.
- **Interactive hints for varying sentence openings** Students see examples of three ways to vary the start of a sentence.
- **Sentence-length checker** Students use this tool to see whether their draft includes sentences of varying lengths.
- **Video tips on peer revision** Students get suggestions for improving the peer editing process.
- **Peer Editing Worksheet** Peer partners use guiding questions to help them edit early drafts.

Working individually or in small groups, students can experiment with these activities to find the ones that work best.

Having a Peer Review Your Work

Work with a classmate to improve your writing. A peer might spot mistakes that you missed when you were revising. Read your draft aloud to your partner. Have him or her answer the following questions about your work and offer helpful suggestions. Then reverse roles and evaluate your partner's draft.

Peer Review Checklist

1. Is the topic clearly identified in the introduction? What is the purpose for writing?
2. What are the main points? Are they clearly stated?
3. What details support the main points? Should any details be added?
4. What parts of the writing did you find most interesting? Were any parts of the paper confusing?

> **FROM a WRITER**
>
> "It's very important to have a second person look at your work, your writing. Editors help me see things I didn't see when I was writing the article . . . or when I was revising the article. They can say, 'Hey, Kevin, you missed something here.' "
>
> —Kevin Powell

Proofreading

When you've completed your revision, check your paper for grammatical, spelling, punctuation, and capitalization errors. Use the following checklist to help you pinpoint errors in your draft. If your answer to any of the questions is no, make the necessary corrections.

Proofreading Checklist

1. Are your sentences complete?
2. Did you avoid using run-on sentences?
3. Did you use punctuation marks and capital letters correctly?
4. Did you use pronouns correctly in comparisons?
5. Did you use adjectives and adverbs correctly in comparisons?
6. Did you double-check the spelling of technical words?

Writers at Work Videodisc

Play the videodisc segment in which Kevin Powell talks about showing his work to different editors. Ask:

- How can the questions an editor asks help a writer revise a work that may have seemed finished?
- Why is another person's viewpoint valid if that person hasn't done the background work the writer did?

Discuss the advantages of peer review and of stepping away from a work for a time before trying to revise it.

Play frames 49867 to 50800

Peer Revision

Reading a piece aloud is a good way for writers or editors to notice disjointed sentences or paragraphs, overused words, or other errors. This approach works well for partners. The peer editor can read a draft aloud as the writer listens for places where revisions are needed.

Writing Lab CD-ROM

The Revising and Editing section of the tutorial on Exposition includes the following options to help students develop proofreading strategies for their essays:

- **Proofreading Checklist** Students can follow this checklist, which also appears on page 158 of the *Sourcebook*, to help them pinpoint possible errors in their drafts.
- **Audio-annotated Student Model of a proofread essay** Students can hear how the student writer identified and corrected errors in spelling and punctuation, as well as run-on sentences.
- **Interactive instruction on eliminating run-on sentences** Students see two possible ways to correct a run-on sentence, and learn why one way is better than the other.

Language Lab CD-ROM

Direct students who need additional work finding and correcting errors in pronoun usage in comparisons, or in comparative and superlative forms of adjectiv and adverbs, to the Pronoun Case and Special Problems with Pronouns lessons from the Using Pronouns unit of the *Language Lab*. They may also benefit from the Forms Comparison and Adjective Adverb? lessons in the Usin Modifiers unit.

Publishing and Presenting

Now that you've finished your paper, it's time to share it with your audience. Here are a couple of suggestions:

Publish a Troubleshooter's Guide If you and your classmates have written problem-and-solution papers, put them together to create a troubleshooter's guide. First, gather all the papers. Next, create covers from cardboard or construction paper. Finally, bind the book with string or staples. You might want to illustrate the cover.

Review and Evaluate With Class Gather all the reviews and evaluations done by your classmates. Work together to classify the papers according to their subject matter—*movies, books, products, foods*, and so on. Put together Review and Evaluation pamphlets. Make covers out of construction paper for each pamphlet. Then illustrate the covers, writing the appropriate category on each.

Reflecting on Your Writing

Writing is a learning experience. Here are some questions to help you reflect on your expository paper and discover what you've learned while you were writing it.

- What do you like best about expository writing? What do you like least?
- Did you find that you use exposition often in your daily life?
- What did you learn about your subject from writing your expository paper? What else would you have liked to learn?
- If you could start the assignment over again, what would you do differently?
- How can you apply what you have learned to other writing assignments?

Portfolio Assessment

Have students write an evaluative statement that addresses the questions posed on page 159 of the *Sourcebook*. If students decide to include the completed exposition in their portfolio, they might attach this statement to it. Otherwise, the statement itself can be included as a record of self-evaluation.

The following questions can be used to supplement the questions in the *Sourcebook:*

- What part of the expository writing process did you find most satisfying? Most challenging?
- In what ways has your writing improved the most?

Writing Lab CD-ROM

The Publishing and Presenting section of the tutorial on Exposition includes the following suggestions on how students might present their completed works to a wider audience:

- **Tips for creating an activity guide** Students use a checklist of suggested features for an activity guide for their town.
- **Form for writing a business letter** Students fill in parts of a business letter with information that offers a solution to a problem.
- **Tips for creating a consumer guide** Students see "job descriptions" for different members of their group to help them break down the tasks of creating a guide of products that would interest the class.

Students working individually or in small groups can use the ideas in the tutorial on Exposition to guide the publishing and presenting phase.

The Multimedia Workshop

Students who wish to make video presentations for an activity guide, collection of problem and solution letters, shopper's guide, or for individual expositions can use the Video Workshop Scene Maker and Sequencer. They select images from the Scene Maker and put them in order with the Sequencer. The Sequencer also lets students add narration, music, or sound effects. Students may choose to include the finished tape in their portfolio as an audiovisual selection.

Student Model

Here is the complete, final draft of Becky Hernandez's comparison-and-contrast paper of two literary characters:

A Comparison of Billy and Piggy

by Becky Hernandez

I stated the subjects of my comparison-and-contrast paper in the first sentence.

I used point-by-point organization, moving back and forth between the two characters to discuss each similarity and difference one at a time. This paragraph explained similarities.

Billy, a character from *Where the Red Fern Grows*, is similar to Piggy, a character from *Lord of the Flies*. Billy and Piggy are equally intelligent. Billy finds a way to hunt raccoons, and Piggy has an idea to get off the deserted island. Also, Billy looks up to his grandfather because he teaches him important and interesting things. Piggy always talks about his wonderful aunt. Last, Piggy and Billy got teased by other boys. For instance, Billy got teased about his dogs, and Piggy got teased about his weight.

In this paragraph, I described differences between the two characters.

On the other hand, they have many differences. First, Billy has loving and caring parents, but Piggy only has an aunt that he adores. Secondly, there are a lot of physical differences. Piggy is overweight, and Billy is skinny. Last, Piggy died in *Lord of the Flies*, and Billy is still alive in the story *Where the Red Fern Grows*.

160 • *Exposition: Making Connections*

Teaching From the Model

Discuss how Becky Hernandez's comparison-and-contrast essay on two literary characters includes the key elements of exposition:

- *It presents information that makes connections.* Hernandez has chosen to explore two characters from literature—Billy from *Where the Red Fern Grows* and Piggy from *Lord of the Flies*—as subjects of her essay.
- *It compares and contrasts the two subjects.* Hernandez gives similarities between the subjects, such as being intelligent, having influential relatives, and getting teased by others. She describes differences in their families, physical appearance, and in their status at the end of the story in which they appear.
- *It provides specific details organized to help readers make connections.* Hernandez organizes her supporting information in a point-by-point manner. Her first paragraph offers similarities between the subjects; her second paragraph presents differences.

Technology Note: Making a Database

One way to organize your class's expository writing is to create a database of their work. Ask the school computer teacher for help in creating the database, given the available software. Design it so students can search for exposition by type (comparison-and-contrast essay, review, problem-and-solution paper, evaluation), by subject (media, title, product, character), by organizational plan (point-by-point, subject-by-subject, chronological order, order of importance), or any other way that would be useful. You can enter the expositions or simply index the titles and authors.

Technology Note: Networking

After reading the Student Model, your class may be interested in sharing their writing efforts with students across the country via the Internet or commercial on-line services such as Prodigy or America Online. Students can exchange expositions with students, including those using *Writer's Solution*, by connecting to Prentice Hall's Internet home page. Look for special events, contests, as well as bulletin boards and pointers to student publications at http://www.phschoo com.

Developing Your Style 1

Using Prepositions and Conjunctions

This passage is from a student's report about stingrays. As a peer editor, what advice would you give to the student?

> Stingrays are beautiful to watch. These fish can be dangerous. Their long tails have poisonous spikes. If attacked, the stingray lashes its tail. It stings its attacker. That sting can be as deadly as a rattlesnake's bite.

You might say that there are too many short sentences that make the piece of writing sound choppy. You can avoid choppy writing by combining sentences. In this lesson, you will practice using prepositions and conjunctions to combine sentences.

How to Use Prepositions to Combine Sentences

One way to combine sentences is to use prepositions:

Two choppy sentences: We visited the aquarium. We saw two beautiful stingrays.

One combined sentence: <u>At the aquarium,</u> we saw two beautiful stingrays.

The sentence above was created by changing the first sentence into a prepositional phrase. The combined sentence does not change the meaning of the original sentence pair. Prepositions—such as *at*, *after*, *by*, *into*, *of*, and *with*—show relationships between one person, thing, or idea and another word in the sentence. A preposition begins a prepositional phrase. The phrase also contains modifiers and ends with a noun or a pronoun.

Example: The stingray disappeared <u>into the dark, dense seaweed</u>. (Prep.: into; Modifiers: the dark, dense; Object: seaweed)

Integrating Skills With Writing

Management Strategy

You can have students work through one or both of the skills lessons either before or after they write their expositions. If you use the lessons *before*, remind students to incorporate the techniques in their writing. If you address skills *after* students write their essays, have them include a section on "skills improvement" in the self-assessment document they prepare for their portfolios. The next time they write, their work can be evaluated in terms of their mastery of these skills.

Teaching Strategy

To connect the skills lessons to the students' writing, explain that good expository writing makes connections between ideas, topics, details, and conclusions. Proper use of prepositions and conjunctions makes these expository connections clearer to the writer's audience.

Another common aspect of expository writing is the use of comparisons. Using the correct comparative and superlative forms of adjectives or adverbs can improve an exposition.

Teaching Strategy

Ask a volunteer to read the passage about stingrays aloud so students can readily hear the choppiness. Discuss the effect of reading so many short sentences in a row. Talk about ways the writer might adjust the piece to make it more appealing to read.

Language Lab CD-ROM

Direct students who need help to combine sentences with prepositional phrases to the Combining Sentences lesson in the Styling Sentences unit of the *Language Lab*.

Addressing Ability Levels

To help your **more-challenged** students use prepositional phrases to show relationships, have them invent prepositional phrases that might begin a sentence, such as "*during* our dive," "*through* the sea," or "*in* the bay." Then have students use the phrases to begin sentences that express a complete thought, such as: "*In the bay*, we saw two dolphins."

How to Use Conjunctions to Combine Sentences

If two sentences contain ideas of equal importance, they can be combined to form a compound sentence. A compound sentence is formed when two independent clauses are joined by a comma and a coordinating conjunction, such as *and, or, but, yet,* or *nor.* An independent clause is a group of words that has a subject and a verb and can stand alone as a sentence. In the following example, two independent clauses are joined by the conjunction *and:*

Two simple sentences: The stingray lashes its tail. It stings its attacker.

One compound sentence: The stingray lashes its tail, and it stings its attacker.

Practice Activities

1. Combine the following sentences using prepositional phrases.
   - **a.** Seahorses cling to seaweed. They use their tails.
   - **b.** Stingrays often hide partially buried. The ocean floor is where stingrays hide.
2. Combine the following sentences using conjunctions.
   - **a.** Baleen whales have a reduced sense of smell. Their hearing is well developed.
   - **b.** Seahorses live in shallow water. Seahorses eat small animals.
   - **c.** Seahorses live in tropical seas. They are also found in temperate waters.
3. Write a paragraph about your last encounter with a fish or another kind of marine life—either at an aquarium or at the seashore. After you've written a first draft, use prepositions and conjunctions to combine sentences where appropriate.

Language Lab CD-ROM

For help combining short sentences with conjunctions, direct students to the Varying Sentence Structure lesson in the Styling Sentences unit of the *Language Lab*.

Language Acquisition/ ESL Teaching Strategy

Provide your basic and intermediate ESL students with pairs of sentence strips to be combined using prepositions and conjunctions. The sentences should be simple so that they can be easily combined. Also, you might consider limiting the number of prepositions and conjunctions so as to avoid confusing the students.

Writer's Companion

To give students additional support and reinforcement in how to combine sentences with conjunctions or prepositional phrases, direct them to the sections on Sentence Problems (pp. 72–77) and Sentence Combining (pp. 78–85).

Alternative Assessment

Students can demonstrate their ability to use prepositions and conjunctions to avoid short, choppy sentences by quick-writing a brief exposition on any topic of their choice. They should attempt to use smooth, flowing sentences that reflect the variety of techniques presented in this lesson.

Practice Activities: Suggested Answers

1. **a.** With their tails, seahorses cling to seaweed.
   b. Stingrays often lie partially buried on the ocean floor.
2. **a.** Baleen whales have a reduced sense of smell, but their hearing is well developed.
   b. Seahorses live in shallow water and eat small animals.
   c. Seahorses live in tropical seas and temperate waters.
3. Paragraph will vary.

Developing Your Style 2

Making Clear Comparisons

Adjectives and adverbs have different forms to show comparison. The **comparative form** of an adjective or adverb is used to compare one person, thing, or action with another person, thing, or action. It expresses *more* or *more than*.

> Railroad passengers in Japan reach their destinations sooner by riding in bullet trains. Among travelers in a hurry, the bullet train is more popular than conventional railroad passenger service.

The **superlative form** of an adjective or adverb is used to compare one person, thing, or action with two or more other people, things, or actions. It expresses the highest degree, or *most*.

> The most experienced bullet-train riders have been racing down the tracks since 1964. The Tokyo-Osaka stretch has the greatest number of riders.

Practice Activity

Revise the following paragraph by correcting any incorrect comparative and superlative forms of adjectives and adverbs.

At one time, the steam locomotive was more popularer than any other type of railroad locomotive. It was most importantest in its ability to pull heavy freight trains. The most greatest problem of the steam locomotive was that it burned too much fuel. During the 1930's, diesel-electric locomotives became more numerouser, while steam locomotives became less commoner.

Practice Activity: Suggested Answer

At one time, the steam locomotive was more popular than any other type of railroad locomotive. It was most important in its ability to pull heavy freight trains. The greatest problem of the steam locomotive was that it burned too much fuel. During the 1930's, diesel-electric locomotives became more numerous, while steam locomotives became less common.

Teaching Strategy

- Tell students that because it is so common in expository writing to compare and contrast subjects, it is particularly important in this type of writing to make comparisons clearly and correctly.
- Have students describe in their own words how they can remember the difference between the comparative and superlative forms of adjectives or adverbs.
- Students can use the "ear test" to determine whether to add *-er* or *more* to form a comparative adjective or adverb. For instance, if they want the comparative form of beautiful, they can say *beautifuler* and *more beautiful* to hear which sounds correct. The ear test can also be used to check the superlative form of adjectives or adverbs.

Clarification

Be sure students understand that it is incorrect to use double comparisons, such as *most longest* or *more faster*. Irregular forms, such as *good/better/best* or *bad/worse/worst*, must be learned case by case.

Language Lab CD-ROM

Students who need help making clear comparisons can benefit from working through the Forms of Comparison lesson in the Using Modifiers unit of the *Language Lab*.

Writer's Companion

Students who need practice in the correct usage of the comparative and superlative forms of adjectives and adverbs can find support on pages 285–287 and 291.

Integrating Literature With Writing

Management Strategy

You can have students read this model of expository writing either before or after they have written their own piece. If you choose to have them read it *before*, use it to draw their attention to techniques or ideas they can apply to their own writing. If you use it *after*, have students compare and contrast some elements of this piece with elements of their own exposition. Ask: *What can you learn from this piece that can help you the next time you use expository writing?*

Activating Prior Knowledge

Before students read the exposition by Susan Fornoff, invite them to share experiences they may have had moving to a new community. Encourage students to describe advantages as well as disadvantages. Jot down their ideas in a two-column chart.

Purpose-Setting Question

How does the author of this excerpt from a comparison-and-contrast essay present information to help her audience make connections?

Reading Strategy

You can help guide reading by asking students to identify key elements of exposition that makes connections: identifying subjects; kinds of information to compare and contrast; similarities and differences; supporting facts, ideas, and opinions; conclusions that fit the given information. When they finish reading, students can work as a whole class or in small groups to share and compare responses to the piece.

Writing Strategy

Help students examine the structure of the exposition: its introduction, its body, and its conclusion. Invite students' comments on how Fornoff began the piece. The anecdote about the Jones family grabs the reader. In the body, Fornoff compares and contrasts experiences of different baseball families. She concludes by suggesting that while many baseball kids are used to moving, they have mixed feelings about their frequent moves.

Help students analyze the essay to determine whether the body uses subject-by-subject or point-by-point organization. Ask them to identify transition words the writer used to move the piece along.

Literature Model

In the following excerpt, Susan Fornoff compares and contrasts the experiences of children of professional baseball players. Notice how Fornoff informs the reader about each child's feelings about having to move so often.

Dad Just Got Traded!

by Susan Fornoff

Fornoff defines her subject by using facts about Doug Jones's history of frequent moves and by showing the response of Doug's son, Dustin, to the latest move.

Dustin Jones didn't think that he had done anything wrong. So he was curious when his father and mother sat him down for a chat last December 2.

"I've just been traded," said Dustin's dad, Doug Jones, a four-time All-Star relief pitcher for the Houston Astros.

Doug had been sent to the Philadelphia Phillies (along with another player) for relief pitcher Mitch Williams. It was the fourteenth time in Doug's 15-year pro career that he had changed teams.

Dustin was excited. After all, the Phillies were the 1993 National League champs!

A few months later, the Jones family packed up and moved to Moorestown, New Jersey, near Philadelphia, Pennsylvania. Dustin had to leave his old school and say good-bye to his friends.

This quotation from Dustin further explains his emotional response to having to move. Appropriate use of quotations is a good way to make a point clear to your readers.

The move wasn't so bad, Dustin says, "because I didn't have to live in humid weather anymore." The hard part, he says, was having to meet new people. He also missed Houston's Astrodome, where he never had to worry about rainouts!

Dustin has lived in ten cities because of his dad's career. But you have to get used to moving if your dad plays baseball or any other pro team sport. Few players spend their whole career with just one team. When Dad gets traded, you have to make new friends, enter new schools, and adjust to new cities. . . .

No matter where you move, or how often, Dad is away a lot during the season. A big-leaguer spends at least three months a year playing away games, and he is at spring training for a month or more.

Some players will do anything to keep their kids nearby. San Francisco Giant second baseman Robby Thompson used to enroll his two oldest kids, Kristeena and Drew, in three different schools each year. In September, the Thompson kids would start school in California and stay until the season ended. In October, the Thompsons would move to their off-season home, in Florida, and the kids would go to school there. In late February, Kristeena and Drew would switch to a school in Arizona, where their dad was in spring training. In April, the season would open and the Thompson kids would return to their California school. Sound crazy? It was.

"We'd be doing multiplication in Florida," says Kristeena, 12. "Then we'd get to Arizona and do fractions, and I wouldn't have a clue what to do."

Now, Kristeena and Drew attend school in Florida all year. During the summer, the Thompson kids and their mom live with Robby in California. . . .

Baseball kids learn to roll with the punches when Dad gets traded or signs with a different team. Sometimes, though, they wish that they could just visit a place and not have to move there.

"I really want to go to Canada," says Dustin Jones. "But I don't want to get traded there. I'd have to learn a new national anthem."

Fornoff explains the reason for the constant moves. Remember that one purpose of expository writing is to explain.

Here Fornoff gives a major disadvantage of being the child of a professional baseball player.

In this example, Fornoff uses facts to explain the negative experiences of Kristeena and Drew Thompson.

After comparing and contrasting the experiences of baseball kids, Fornoff concludes by expressing the general reaction they share.

This final quotation from Dustin Jones leaves readers with an example of the mixed feelings about moving shared by baseball kids.

Cross-Curricular Connection: *Social Studies/Geography*

Have students indicate on a map the locations of the twenty-eight major league baseball teams. They can check a newspaper sports section for a list of teams. Have students pick two baseball cities and imagine moving from one to the other. Help them find out key characteristics of each place, such as climate, population, time zone, or proximity to areas of interest. They can use this information in an essay about life in the two cities.

Language Acquisition/ ESL Teaching Strategy

Ask your basic and intermediate ESL students to identify the states mentioned in the excerpt by Susan Fornoff. Using an atlas and an almanac, the students locate the states and take notes on the climate and other characteristics for use in brief oral presentations to other ESL students. Note that some ESL students will be intimately familiar with baseball and others will have no knowledge of the sport.

Closure and Extension

To complete the lesson you can ask students to summarize what they learned about expository writing by examining this comparison-and-contrast essay. Then have students share, through brief journal entries or in discussion groups, what they learned about themselves as writers and what points they would like to keep in mind for future writing. Also ask what related topics they might consider for upcoming writing, and what modes or types of writing would best explore their ideas.

6

Persuasion

Classroom Manager

Writer's Solution *Materials for Teaching Persuasion*

The *Writer's Solution* includes a wide range of materials for teaching persuasion. You can pick and choose from among these materials to create a lesson plan that suits your class needs. You do not have to use all the program components to use it effectively. For a detailed description of each of the components of the *Writer's Solution*, see pages T4–T6.

Below is a detailed list of the *Writer's Solution* materials for Persuasion.

Writers at Work Videodisc

Featured Writer: Doug Raboy, Advertising Copywriter

Videodisc Segments

About Persuasion

Persuading With Passion

Writing Tips:

Supporting Your Position

Putting Your Ideas on Paper

Interactive CD-ROMs

Writing Lab

Tutorial on Persuasion

About Persuasion
- Includes four Models From Literature and a video clip by copywriter Doug Raboy

Choosing Your Topic
- Includes Inspirations for Persuasion and Issues Wheels

Considering Audience and Purpose
- Includes Audience Profile and annotated Writing Models

Gathering Details
- Includes Pros and Cons Chart and video clip from Doug Raboy

Organizing Information
- Includes Notecard Activity

Drafting
- Includes Writing Models and Transition Word Bins

Revising and Editing
- Includes Self-Evaluation Checklist, sentence openers variety checker, and Peer Revision Checklist

Proofreading
- Includes instruction on using proper pronouns, checklist, and Student Model

Publishing and Presenting
- Includes tips for presenting a speech or other oral presentation and creating posters

Writer's Tool Kit

Suggested Activities: Inspirations for Persuasion, Evaluation Checklist, brainstormer, Issues Wheels, Pros and Cons Chart, Notecard Activity, Transition Word Bin, sentence openers variety checker

Language Lab

Related Lessons: Correcting Stringy Sentences, Combining Sentences (Styling Sentences unit); Narrowing a Topic, Considering Audience and Purpose (Composing unit); Pronoun Case (Using Pronouns unit); Commas (Punctuation unit)

Sourcebook

About Persuasion (pp. 170–174)

Guided Lesson on Persuasion (pp. 175–191)

Inspirations for Persuasion (pp. 178–181)

Developing Your Style

Using Commas (pp. 192–193)

Varying Sentence Length (pp. 194–195)

Literature Model

"All Together Now" by Barbara Jordan (pp. 196–197)

Below is a list of materials from Prentice Hall's student writing handbook that you can integrate with this lesson on persuasive writing.

Writer's Companion

Mini-Lesson on Introductions, p. 27

Mini-Lesson on Elaboration, p. 31

Mini-Lesson on Conclusions, p. 37

Mini-Lesson on Sentence Problems, p. 72

Mini-Lesson on Sentence Combining, p. 78

Mini-Lesson on Sentence Variety, p. 86

Mini-Lesson on Persuasion, p. 210

Teaching Integrated Language Arts Using the Writer's Solution—Starting With Literature

Have students read and respond to letters of advice, editorials, advertisements, public service announcements, opinion essays, and other types of persuasive writing. In discussing the selections, draw students' attention to elements of persuasion, such as stating a position clearly and supporting an opinion with evidence. Point out that students can use the persuasive writing they have read as models for writing their own persuasive pieces. Lead into having students complete persuasive writing projects using the components of the *Writer's Solution*.

CONNECTIONS TO *PRENTICE HALL LITERATURE, COPPER,* SELECTIONS

Written Advice/Advertisement

	2E	3E
"How to Read a Newspaper," Andrew A. Rooney	■	▲
"How to Write a Letter," Garrison Keillor	■	▲
"How to Read Faster," Bill Cosby	■	▲
"Letter to Scottie," F. Scott Fitzgerald	■	▲

Recommendation/Persuasive Essay

	2E	3E
"Letter to the U.S. Government," Chief Seattle	■	▲
"Letter to Joan," C.S. Lewis	■	▲

You can also use the *Writer's Solution* materials on persuasive writing to guide students through writing activities in response to works of literature.

CONNECTIONS TO *PRENTICE HALL LITERATURE, COPPER,* WRITING ACTIVITIES

Thinking and Writing Activities

	2E	3E
Supporting an Opinion—Follows **"Sarah Tops,"** Isaac Asimov	■	▲
Supporting an Opinion—Follows **"Breaker's Bridge,"** Lawrence Yep	■	▲
Writing a Persuasive Letter—Follows ***The Phantom Tollbooth***, Susan Nanus	■	▲
Writing a Persuasive Letter—Follows **"The Drive-In Movies,"** Gary Soto		▲
Writing a Letter of Advice—Follows **"How the Flamingoes Got Their Stockings,"** Horacio Quiroga	■	▲
Writing a Letter to Persuade—Follows **"The Riddling Youngster,"** Vivian L. Thompson	■	▲

Focus on Writing/Your Writing Process

	2E	3E
Focus on Writing: Writing to Influence—Includes activities and assignments	■	
Your Writing Process: Writing to Influence—Includes activities and assignments		▲

■ **(2E)** *Prentice Hall Literature, Copper,* Second Edition

▲ **(3E)** *Prentice Hall Literature, Copper,* Paramount Edition

CONNECTIONS BETWEEN INSPIRATIONS FOR PERSUASION AND *PRENTICE HALL LITERATURE, COPPER*

You can use the multimedia Inspirations for Persuasion to motivate student reading as well as student writing. Many of the Inspirations are audio recordings or video adaptations of selections from *Prentice Hall Literature, Copper*. Have students work in small groups to look at and discuss an appropriate Inspiration before reading the corresponding selection. Then, after reading the selection, students can replay the Inspiration and select one of the accompanying Topic Ideas (pp. 178–181). The following selections from *Prentice Hall Literature, Copper*, are included in the Inspirations for Persuasion.

- **"The Wise Old Woman,"** Yoshiko Uchida
- ***The Phantom Tollbooth***, Susan Nanus, based on the book by Norton Juster
- ***Tuck Everlasting***, Natalie Babbitt

Recommended Lesson Plan

The following lesson plan is recommended for providing students with thorough, comprehensive instructions in persuasive writing. Because you may not have all the components of the *Writer's Solution* or may have limited access to equipment, the plan provides a number of options. Choose the options that best suit your teaching style and equipment situation.

You may want to add a few days to the lesson plan to allow students time to publish their work and to hold conferences with students to discuss your assessment of their work.

FIVE-DAY LESSON PLAN

Lesson Outcome: **Each student writes a complete persuasive composition.**

DAY 1

Introduce your students to persuasive writing and have them choose and narrow their topic.
Show the *Writers at Work Videodisc* segment featuring Doug Raboy. Use the segment as a springboard for class discussion or group activities. Then choose one of the following options:

OPTION 1 Have students working individually or in small groups choose a topic by browsing through the Inspirations for Persuasion. Then have students work individually to develop a plan for their persuasive compositions by completing the Prewriting phase of the tutorial, which includes narrowing the topic and considering audience and purpose. At the end of the class, have students print out their prewriting notes.

OPTION 2 Have students working individually or in small groups read the Prewriting section of the *Sourcebook* (pp. 176–185) to help them choose a topic. They can get ideas by browsing through the Inspirations for Persuasion (pp. 178–181). Have students work individually to develop a plan for their persuasive compositions by completing the Prewriting section, which includes narrowing the topic and considering audience and purpose.

DAY 2

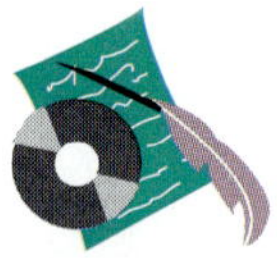

Have students gather evidence and organize details.
OPTION 1 Have students work individually or in small groups through the Gathering Evidence and Organizing Information section and provide time for them to conduct research.

OPTION 2 Have students work through the Gathering Evidence and Organizing Information section of the *Sourcebook* (pp. 183–185) and provide time for them to conduct research.

DAY 3

Have students organize evidence for their arguments and write a first draft of their persuasive compositions.

OPTION 1 Have students work through the Drafting section of the tutorial on Persuasion to help them decide on the focus and arrangement of ideas for their composition. Then have them write their drafts on the computer, following the instruction and using the activities provided in the Drafting section of the tutorial on Persuasion. Have students print out their compositions upon completion.

OPTION 2 Have students read the instructions in the Drafting section of the guided lesson (pp. 186–187) to help them decide on an arrangement of ideas for their compositions and to guide them as they write their drafts on paper.

DAY 4

Have students complete their drafts, then work in peer groups to revise their persuasive compositions.

OPTION 1 When drafts are completed, have peer partners revise their compositions on the computer, using the guidelines and suggestions in the Revising and Editing section of the tutorial on Persuasion.

OPTION 2 Have peer partners revise their compositions, following the suggestions in the Revising and Editing section of the guided lesson (pp. 188–189).

DAY 5

Have students make final revisions and proofread their persuasive compositions.

OPTION 1 Have pairs of students review each other's work, following the guidelines in the proofreading checklist in the Proofreading section of the tutorial on Persuasion. Students should then proofread and print out their final drafts.

OPTION 2 Have pairs of students review each other's work, following the guidelines in the Proofreading section of the *Sourcebook* (p. 189). Students should then proofread and make their final drafts.

Use the following lesson plans if you don't have a full week to devote to teaching persuasion.

Four- and Three-Day Lesson Plans: Adapt the Five-Day Plan by having students learn about persuasion, choose and narrow a topic, and gather evidence all during day 1. As in the Five-Day Plan, have students spend a day organizing ideas and writing their drafts. For a Four-Day Plan, follow the last two days of the Five-Day Plan; for a Three-Day Plan, simply condense these two days into a single day of revision and forgo the option of working in peer groups.

Two-Day Lesson Plan: If you have only two days to devote to teaching persuasion, on the first day have students choose a topic and write their first drafts, using the appropriate sections of the *Writing Lab* or the *Sourcebook*. On the second day, have students revise and edit their work.

One-Day Lesson Plan: Students can work individually in the open-ended environment in the *Writing Lab* by browsing through the Inspirations for Persuasion to choose a topic, using the prewriting tools as needed, and completing a quick-write draft of a persuasive composition in their on-line Notebooks. Students may also use the *Sourcebook* to choose a topic and write a brief persuasive composition.

Preparing to Teach

CHAPTER 6

Lesson Objectives

Students will

1. Explore different types of persuasive writing
2. Select an appropriate topic for persuasive writing
3. Write a persuasive piece that
   - follows a logical organization
   - is supported by research
   - includes facts to support an opinion
   - includes ideas that are linked and flow smoothly together
4. Revise their persuasive work for content, organization, and style
5. Participate in peer review
6. Proofread for errors in spelling, grammar, and punctuation
7. Publish their finished persuasive compositions

Activating Prior Knowledge

Ask students to share instances when they have written to persuade someone about something. Some may recall writing a speech to give in a debate; making a poster advertising a small business, such as a dog-walking service; giving advice to a friend in a personal letter; or making a recommendation in a book report. Ask: *How did you try to convince your reader of the value of your opinion or the validity of your viewpoint?*

Tech Prep Note

Not only professional writers like Doug Raboy use persuasive writing in their work. Workers in other fields write to persuade. A secretary may write to the office manager to make a case for buying new equipment. A car dealer may write an ad to attract new customers. A plumber may write a recommendation for certain types of fixtures for a kitchen repair. A security officer may write to a building supervisor to urge the installation of an alarm system. Ask: *Think about the adults you know and the work they do. How do they use persuasive writing on the job?*

The Much Resounding Sea *(detail) 1884, Thomas Moran, National Gallery of Art, Washington, D.C.*

Persuasion

"Persuasion is the art of breaking down barriers."

—Doug Raboy
Ad Copywriter

167

Humanities Note

The work of art is a painting by Thomas Moran (1837–1926) titled *The Much Resounding Sea*. Thomas Moran was an American landscape painter. He went on an early expedition down the Colorado River and illustrated the report made by the explorers.

The Much Resounding Sea is painted to capture the details of a natural setting. The movement of the sea is shown in the many waves rolling in toward the beach and their spray as they come to shore. Notice the details Moran took time to re-create. He even painted little pebbles and shells on the beach in the left-hand corner of the painting.

This painting may communicate information to supplement a written account of what the sea looks like. Moran's attention to detail persuades the viewer that he is portraying a setting as it really exists. Often details make a presentation—whether visual or written—more convincing. Point out to your students how information can be an important part of making an argument. You might want to use the following questions:

- What details in this painting give you a sense of the ocean?
- Think of a natural resource you feel strongly about protecting. What details would you use to make an argument about protecting the air, water, and so on?

Addressing Your Classroom Situation

This chapter includes a variety of Models From Literature, topic ideas, writing process strategies, and Student Models, along with two integrated skills lessons. Feel free to pick and choose from this material to create a customized lesson on persuasive writing that matches your classroom needs.

The following are some of the key features of the chapter:

- The chapter begins with a section About Persuasion, which includes opening statements about persuasion from ad copywriter Doug Raboy, a definition of persuasion, Group Discussion questions, and Models From Literature of three types of persuasion: written advice, advertisement, and persuasive essay.
- The Prewriting section includes an assortment of idea-generating activities to help students choose a topic. It also offers ten topic ideas and direct instruction and activities to help students consider audience and purpose, gather evidence, and organize information.
- The Drafting section addresses the issues of how to begin a persuasive paper and suggests focusing points into three parts: an introduction, a body, and a conclusion. It stresses developing and supporting a strong argument with facts, statistics, and reasons.
- The Revising and Editing section offers techniques for both self-evaluation and peer review to help students check that each persuasive piece is well organized and strongly supports the writer's position. Proofreading suggestions remind students to check for errors in grammar, punctuation, and spelling.
- The Guided Lesson is followed by a Student Model and then skills lessons on using commas and varying sentence lengths. You may want to address these skills before students draft their essays, or you may prefer to focus on them during the revising/proofreading phase.
- The chapter ends with a complete Literature Model, an excerpt from a persuasive essay by former Texas Congresswoman Barbara Jordan, entitled "All Together Now."

Chapter Contents

About Persuasion

Guided Lesson

Student Model

Developing Your Style 1

Developing Your Style 2

Literature Model

"Writing is about passion. If you can feel a passion for what you're writing about, your writing is going to be a lot better."

"The opportunity to influence an incredible number of people is just amazing to me and almost overwhelming."

—Doug Raboy
Ad Copywriter

"I know I've written too little when I don't feel I've persuaded myself with the message. . . . I haven't given people enough information."

More About the Writer

Doug Raboy owns his own advertising agency. There, he creates and writes many forms of advertising: radio and TV commercials, print ads for magazines and newspapers, and outdoor ads on billboards. Raboy developed an interest in this field by observing his father at work in advertising. Raboy was impressed by the humor and creativity in his father's work.

Doug Raboy says, "Persuasion is the art of breaking down barriers." Talk with students about different approaches a writer can try in order to make others see his or her point of view. Discuss how a person's beliefs, world view, or experience can influence the arguments he or she makes to persuade. Ask: *What are some elements of any persuasive work? How do those elements help a work to persuade? How can a strongly held opinion fail to persuade?*

Introducing Persuasive Writing

Teaching Options

There are a variety of ways you can introduce persuasive writing by using the components of the *Writer's Solution:*

- You can show the Persuasion segment from the *Writers at Work Videodisc.* Use the segment as a springboard for class discussion on persuasive writing.
- You can have students work individually or in small groups to go through the About Persuasion section of the tutorial in the *Writing Lab* CD-ROM.
- You can work through About Persuasion in the *Sourcebook* with the class.
- You can have students read the About Persuasion section of the *Sourcebook* before class starts so that, as a group, you can focus on the videodisc or CD-ROM lesson.

Sourcebook

Have students read and discuss the About Persuasion section in the *Sourcebook.* Then ask:

- How can you recognize persuasive writing? Where might you find examples?
- Do you think it's possible to use different approaches to writing persuasively about the same topic?
- Why would people seek out persuasive writing?

Following the discussion, divide your students into groups to engage in the Group Discussion (p. 170).

About Persuasion

What Is Persuasion?

What do advertisements and political speeches have in common? They're both examples of persuasion. **Persuasion** is writing or speaking that tries to influence people. Effective persuasion can change the way people think or convince people to take an action.

Group Discussion Whenever you turn on the television, open a magazine, or even ride down a highway, you see advertisements attempting to persuade you to buy a product or a service. Gather with a group of your classmates and brainstorm for a list of especially effective television commercials, magazine ads, and billboard displays. Then list advertisements that are not effective. Look over the lists. What do the effective advertisements have in common? What do the ineffective advertisements have in common? Share your observations with the rest of the class.

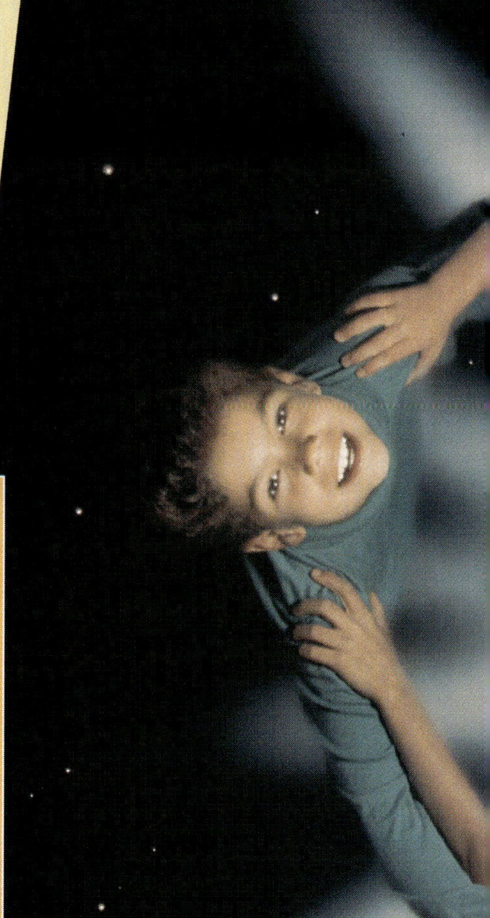

Writers at Work Videodisc

Use the Persuasion section of the videodisc featuring Doug Raboy to spark class discussion. Play the chapter in its entirety, pausing as needed. Then feel free to use the bar codes to replay any segment to reinforce an important idea. Before you play the first segment, ask students to listen for how Raboy describes the art of persuasion.

After students view the segment, have them share their responses, then discuss the techniques Raboy shares. Ask:

- What does Raboy say about how a writer makes people look for the message?
- How does Raboy attempt to reach the audience he wants to persuade?
- How do long persuasive works differ from short, dramatic "grabbers," such as the posters Raboy created for the Racial Harmony campaign?

Play frames 4 to 8981

How a Professional Writer Uses Persuasion

Before an advertisement can appear on television or in a magazine, someone must write it. Ad copywriters are the people who make a living by writing advertisements. Doug Raboy is a successful ad copywriter. He has written for radio, television, and magazines. As Raboy has discovered, it's not easy to convince people to believe in an advertiser's message:

> "People aren't looking to believe what you're writing. They aren't looking for your message. You have to make them look for it and believe it. So you break down the barriers. You speak to them in their own voice, in their own tone, and in their own language—and you start to get them to believe in the message."

How Persuasion Fits Into Your Life

Which baseball team has the best pitcher? Which television show is the best this season? Whose pet is the smartest? What kind of sneakers are best for running? If you have ever discussed questions like these, you have used persuasion. You have tried to convince others to agree with your opinion or to take a certain action. When you write persuasively, you have the same goals. For example, a letter that tries to convince the mayor to install lights on the community baseball field is a call to action. How can you use persuasive writing effectively to achieve your particular goals? This chapter will show you how.

Writing Lab CD-ROM

The About Persuasion section of the tutorial on Persuasion includes the following options:

- **Author video** Ad copywriter Doug Raboy shares some of his views on convincing people to listen to his message.
- **Audio-annotated Student Models of persuasive writing** Students can see excerpts from four kinds of persuasive compositions: written advice, written recommendation, advertisement, essay supporting an opinion.
- **Evaluation Checklist** Students can use these guidelines before they draft their persuasive pieces to direct their writing. They can also use the guidelines for self-assessment after writing. If so, students can incorporate the ideas into a reflective piece they may include in their portfolios.

Students can work individually or in small groups to complete the tutorial on persuasion. Or, if you have access to a projection panel, you can work through the About Persuasion section with the entire class, discussing each part as you go.

Real-World Writing

Tell students that people in your community routinely write persuasively. Have students find examples of persuasive writing in broadcast and print media. For example, they might find a letter to the editor that argues for better lighting in public areas. A radio public service announcement might urge cyclists to wear safety helmets. Students can also find persuasive writing in posters on telephone poles, billboards, or walls, as well as on moving vehicles. As students share their examples, ask:

- What does the persuasive piece try to convince its audience to do or think? How is the persuasive argument supported?
- What common features, if any, do you notice among the different persuasive writing examples you saw?
- What features do these examples of persuasion share that differ from features you see in other kinds of writing?

Thematic Connection: Social Responsibility

Many opportunities to persuade begin when a person decides that "something must be done!" Talk with the class about social action issues, such as efforts to help the needy or to elect a political candidate. Have students recall speeches they have heard and posters or letters they have read. Discuss the value of combining personal goals with persuasive writing to effect change.

Integrating Literature With Writing

Starting From Literature

You can use the models on pages 172–174 to illustrate the various elements of each type of persuasion. Or highlight the content or technique used in these pieces to inspire writing on any of the themes they address. For example, the persuasive essay about Paul Klee might inspire students to write a persuasive essay about an artist whose work they'd like to convince others to appreciate.

Clarification

Be sure students realize that speeches and commercials, although presented orally, are written and revised before they are given.

Teaching From the Model

Guide students to recognize how the passage from "How to Write a Letter" by Garrison Keillor is an example of one type of persuasive writing:

- *It gives suggestions about how to deal with an issue and solve a problem.* Garrison Keillor addresses the issue of shy people who feel, as he has, unappreciated or ignored. He suggests that shy people write, ". . . otherwise nobody will know who we are." Every paragraph in his essay includes support for his view that writing a letter can be a way to ". . . express the music of our souls. . . ."
- *It gives advice on a related issue.* Keillor recognizes that people may feel guilty for *not* writing as often as they might. He advises, "You don't 'owe' anybody a letter. Letters are a gift."

Types of Persuasion

There are many types of persuasion. Some, such as commercials and political speeches, are spoken or read aloud. Others, like newspaper editorials and advice columns, are written. Following are some examples of different types of persuasion.

1 Written Advice

- Written advice gives readers suggestions about how to deal with issues and solve problems.
- You'll find examples of written advice in the editorials and advice columns of newspapers and magazines.

Model From Literature

In this excerpt from "How to Write a Letter," Garrison Keillor gives advice to a specific audience—shy people. Notice that Keillor gives reasons to support his advice.

We shy persons need to write a letter now and then, or else we'll dry up and blow away. It's true. And I speak as one who loves to reach for the phone, dial the number, and talk. . . .

We need to write, otherwise nobody will know who we are. They will only have a vague impression of us as A Nice Person, because, frankly, we don't shine at conversation, we lack the confidence to thrust our faces forward and say, "Hi, I'm Heather Hooten: let me tell you about my week." Mostly we say "Uh-huh" and "Oh, really." People smile and look over our shoulder, looking for someone else to meet.

So a shy person sits down and writes a letter. To be known by another person—to meet and talk freely on the page—to be close despite distance. To escape from anonymity and . . . express the music of our soul. . . .

The first step in writing letters is to get over the guilt of not writing. You don't "owe" anybody a letter. Letters are a gift.

Exploring Related Literature

Students who enjoy this brief passage may enjoy reading the entire excerpt, which comes from the introduction of Keillor's book *We Are Still Married*. "How to Write a Letter" appears in *Prentice Hall Literature, Copper*.

Thematic Connection: Turning Points/Transitions

Ask students to recall a time they or someone they know faced a problem for which they received helpful advice in an article or column. For example, they may have found a useful approach to a family problem in a personal advice column or an article about managing family stress. Invite volunteers to describe the situation they faced and how that article or column guided them to a solution by presenting useful alternatives. Students might use this experience as a topic for their persuasive piece.

2 Advertisement

- An advertisement is a paid message that tries to persuade people to do something.
- An advertisement might try to convince people to buy a product, vote for a person, or support a cause.
- Advertisements appear in newspapers and magazines, on television, and on radio.

Writing Model

This newspaper advertisement tries to persuade people to attend a benefit concert. The first line of the ad grabs the reader's attention while appealing to two audiences: those who want to help others and those who want to have fun. Note also that the ad ends with a catchy, easy-to-remember slogan.

HELP THE HUNGRY WHILE YOU HAVE SOME FUN!

Come to the Battle of the Bands on Saturday, October 10, at Washington Middle School.

Admission is two cans or jars of food and ten food coupons.

A new toothbrush counts as a jar of food.

The Battle of the Bands is sponsored by local businesses and other volunteers. It features the best local groups, which were chosen by ballot. All proceeds go to Our Food Pantry, which distributes free food to local families.

Come to enjoy wonderful music, see your friends and neighbors, and help a worthy cause.

Show you care—be there!

Teaching From the Model

Use the newspaper advertisement for a benefit concert to analyze this very familiar type of persuasive writing:

- *It tries to persuade people to do something.* The sponsors of the Battle of the Bands paid to print this advertisement in a newspaper, where it could be seen by a wide audience that might attend. The ad includes statements to convince people to participate.
- *It attempts to involve people in a worthy cause.* The headline "Help the Hungry While You Have Some Fun!" is meant to catch readers' interest and persuade them that the event serves a dual purpose: People can be entertained while supporting an organization that the sponsors believe is worthy. This view is presented in the statement, "All proceeds go to Our Food Pantry, which distributes free food to local families."
- *It is written for the newspaper.* This advertisement opens with a headline, ends with a "tag line" or concluding slogan, and presents key facts about the event, such as *What? Where? When? How?* and *Why?* The sponsors of the event might reuse the same ad in a magazine, have it read on radio, or rework it to be part of a TV commercial.

Teaching From the Model

Help students analyze the excerpt from Hattie Clark's essay about the painter Paul Klee to understand how it models a type of persuasion:

- *It is a short piece of writing that tries to convince an audience to accept an opinion.* Hattie Clark presents details to advance her argument that artist Paul Klee "was a master at line drawing and painting." She gives details that support her view of Klee's talents.
- *It was written for a magazine.* Persuasive essays are commonly found in newspapers and magazines. The complete essay "Paul Klee" originally appeared in *Highlights*, a magazine for children.

Writing Strategy

Guide students to notice the informal way in which Clark begins her persuasive essay. Explain that while the goal of a persuasive essay is to convince an audience to accept an opinion or take an action, it need not present points in a heavy-handed way. Clark engages readers by suggesting that they draw a certain conclusion about a work of art, and then gently points out that this conclusion is wrong. The technique of anticipating an audience's response and then elaborating upon it can be effective in persuasions that must instruct in order to convince.

Exploring Related Literature

You may want students to read Hattie Clark's entire persuasive essay about Paul Klee, which can be found in *Prentice Hall Literature, Copper.*

Cat and Bird *(detail) 1928, Paul Klee, Museum of Modern Art, New York*

Puppet *Paul Klee*

3 Persuasive Essay

- A persuasive essay is a short piece of writing that tries to convince an audience to accept an opinion or to take some action.
- Editorials found in newspapers and magazines are examples of persuasive essays.

Model From Literature

In this passage from "Paul Klee," Hattie Clark tries to convince the reader that the painter Paul Klee was an outstanding artist. Notice that Clark begins by anticipating how some people might react to the artist's work. Clark then explains what makes the artist's work great.

Take a long look at the painting and the puppet. . . .

Ah, they were done by a little kid, you say.

Your guess couldn't be more wrong. These works are the creative products of Paul Klee. This artist, who spent much of his life in Switzerland, lived from 1879 to 1940.

Klee was a master at line drawing and painting. Sometimes his lines were slender as a spider's web, sometimes as thick as a little finger. He made his lines slide, skitter, and squiggle across the canvas. But he never let them go too far. He never stopped them too soon. Nor did he let his lines stray. Klee made both his lines and his colors the servants of his ideas.

Cross-Curricular Connection: *Art*

Students who are interested in art may enjoy doing a persuasive essay about a favorite artist or particular work of art. Invite students to browse through art books or visit local galleries or museums to select an artist or a work as a topic for a persuasive essay.

As an alternative, students might enjoy writing a persuasive essay about a well-known work they dislike to convey their contrary point of view.

Guided Lesson

Now that you've learned about several types of persuasion, you're ready to begin developing your own piece of persuasive writing. This lesson will help guide you through the process of writing your paper. You may not want to start at the beginning of the lesson, however. Decide what help you'll need to write your persuasive paper. Then use this chart to decide where to begin.

	START WITH
• If you **do not have a topic**	Choosing Your Topic
• If you **have a topic but aren't sure what evidence you'll use to support your opinion**	Gathering Evidence
• If you **have a topic and enough evidence to support it**	Drafting

Guiding Student Writing

Language Acquisition/ ESL Teaching Strategy

The *Writing Lab* offers a variety of options that can be adapted for use with ESL students of all levels. The following are examples of such adaptations.

- The Choosing Your Topic section offers a brainstormer for topic ideas that is particularly useful for your upper-basic and intermediate ESL students. Working in pairs, the students browse through the images and discuss possibilities for topics. When a pair has found a topic of mutual interest, they discuss it in greater detail and brainstorm persuasive points that can be used in their drafts. Encourage the students to take notes.
- The Drafting section offers an option on interactive instruction to avoid unreasonable arguments. This option can be used with your advanced ESL students. Working individually, the students list the examples of unreasonable arguments and provide short explanations for each. You may lead a short discussion and review of what the students have learned. Then direct the students to apply these principles in revising their drafts.

Addressing Your Classroom Situation

- If you choose to assign topics or types of persuasive writing, allow time for students to narrow the topic to suit their interests or find an appealing focus to pursue.
- It may work best when students work independently on persuasive essays so that they can express opinions freely. However, you may wish to have students work in pairs. If so, brainstorm ways partners might collaborate effectively and fairly. One way is for partners to take opposing views on a single topic. They can write simultaneously, or one can write in response to what the other has already written.

Writing Lab CD-ROM

The Choosing Your Topic section of the tutorial on Persuasion includes the following options to help students come up with their own topics:

- **Newspaper Headline Bins for topic ideas** Students can browse through a list of headlines they might see in newspapers that can spark ideas for persuasive writing.
- **Brainstormer for topic ideas** Students can browse through words and images that may spark ideas for persuasive writing.

Working individually or in small groups, students can experiment with these activities to find the ones that work best.

Alternative Activity

Instead of using the Newspaper Headline Bins in the CD-ROM lesson, students can browse through actual newspapers and magazines to see if any headlines or images stimulate ideas for persuasive pieces.

Writers at Work Videodisc

Play the videodisc segment in which Doug Raboy discusses choosing a topic for persuasive writing. Ask:

- What does Raboy mean by saying that "writing is about passion"?
- Why does Raboy believe that better writing happens when writers write about something they care about?

Suggest that students try Raboy's approach and select a topic about which they have strong feelings.

Prewriting

Choosing Your Topic

What kind of persuasive paper would you like to write? You can write a persuasive essay, an advertisement, or written advice. After you make your decision, either choose from among the suggested writing options (see pages 178–181) or use one or more of the following techniques to come up with a topic of your own.

If you're considering

. . . written advice or a persuasive essay:

CHECK THE HEADLINES FOR IMPORTANT TOPICS

How would you react to each of the following newspaper headlines? "Twelve-Month School Year Considered," "Group Names Ten Most Dangerous Toys," "Space Probe Finds Alien Life on Saturn," "Two Students Win Heroism Awards." Look through newspapers and magazines for headlines and article titles that interest you. Jot down any that you have strong feelings about. Then review your notes to see if you would like to use one as a writing topic.

. . . written advice or a persuasive essay:

Group Activity

HOLD A PRESS CONFERENCE

With a group of your classmates, hold a mayor's press conference. Take turns being either the mayor or the members of the press. As members of the press, ask the mayor five questions about issues that matter to you. For example, the press might ask such questions as "What can be done to clean up water and air pollution?" "Should skateboards be allowed on sidewalks?" "Should schools have longer lunch periods?" Ask the mayor different questions and jot down the key points of each answer. Later, review your notes for possible topics.

Play frames 2265 to 3154

Collaborative Learning

Help students who choose to hold a press conference plan how to make the conference stimulating. For instance, groups might prepare for the conference by browsing through the newspaper for questions on issues of current interest or concern in your state. Some students can jot down questions while others jot down the kinds of responses a governor might give. One student can serve as moderator to move the conference along, while other students jot down notes as if they were members of the press. Encourage students to share and trade roles.

. . . written advice, a persuasive essay, or an advertisement:

CONDUCT A SELF-INTERVIEW

What is important to you? What do you have strong opinions about? Ask yourself these two questions and jot down your answers. Perhaps you're concerned about how much allowance you get, the need for recycling, or the violence in video games. Maybe you feel that something should be done to help the homeless or the people who can't find jobs. Anything you care about—from fast food to scary movies—can be a topic for your persuasive writing. Review your self-interview notes for topic ideas.

. . . written advice or a persuasive essay:

THINK ABOUT WHAT BOTHERS YOU

What's bothering you? Does your little brother drop his food at every meal? Does your older sister get to choose the television programs you watch? Does your best friend usually forget what time you're supposed to meet? Jot down some of the typical day-to-day problems that you have. Also note how you can help solve each problem. Later, review your notes for possible persuasive writing topics.

. . . an advertisement or a persuasive essay:

Group Activity

PUT TOGETHER A NEW-PRODUCT FAIR

Would you like to invent something? A new mode of transportation faster than the space shuttle? An unbelievably different and delicious ice-cream flavor? A toothpaste that dissolves decay and fills cavities while you brush your teeth? A new video game that isn't violent? Now is your chance! With a group of your classmates, hold a new-product fair. First, decide what your pet gripes are that need fixing. Then decide what you need to invent. Take turns describing each new product in detail, using pictures and diagrams if you wish. Jot down notes about each product mentioned. Later, review your notes for possible topic ideas.

Writing Strategy

Students who want to conduct a self-interview might try the technique of freewriting or "freespeaking" (giving a monologue to a partner or talking into a tape recorder) to generate ideas for a persuasive piece.

Addressing Ability Levels

Have your **more-advanced** students of those who choose to hold a new-product fair brainstorm not only new products they can imagine inventing, but also the audience for the products and the advertising approaches that would suit the products. Challenge them to select a media celebrity to be an effective spokesperson for each product, and a slogan and catch phrase that would grab the attention of potential customers or users.

Writing Lab CD-ROM

Using the Inspirations for Persuasion in the *Writing Lab* is an excellent way to stimulate creativity and to have students explore possible topics for persuasive pieces. Students can browse individually or in small groups through the Inspirations. They can choose their own writing topics or you may prefer to assign topics.

The following is a list of the topics for writing responses to literature included in the Inspirations, but not provided in the *Sourcebook:*

Written Advice to

- Avoid dental problems
- A story character
- A young ruler
- Encourage acting on a problem
- A man who wonders whether to drink water that could make a person immortal
- The boy in "The Medicine Bag"

Advertisement for

- Good dental care
- Your neighborhood
- Dictionopolis, from *The Phantom Tollbooth*
- Students to think for themselves
- Wildlife conservation
- Voting for a historical figure
- An endangered species
- Water that makes people immortal

Persuasive Essay About

- A situation that needs change
- Age discrimination
- Attitude
- Your opinion of the Gatekeeper's solution in *The Phantom Tollbooth*
- Growing older
- Drinking from the Fountain of Youth
- Youth
- Winnie drinking the water in *Tuck Everlasting*
- Ownership of water
- A movie
- Your opinion on hunting
- A needed law
- Standards that public servants should uphold
- Your vision for the future
- Endangered species
- Immortality

Written Recommendation for

- A book for your peers
- A book to parents of young children
- A community issue
- Change in your school or community
- Another national anthem
- Dealing with stereotypes

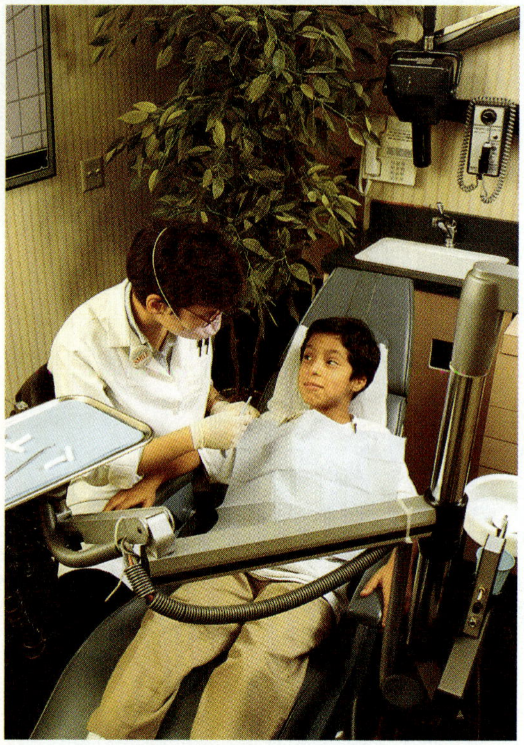

Inspirations for Persuasion

Here are some possible topics for persuasive papers:

An Advertisement for the Ideal Dentist

Do you think the boy in the photograph above has found his ideal dentist? What characteristics would your ideal dentist have? What would his or her personality be like? How would the office be equipped, and what would you find in the waiting room? How would those characteristics affect the way you feel about visiting the dentist? Use your ideas to create a humorous advertisement for the ideal dentist. Support your claims with facts and observations.

An Advertisement for a Book for Your Peers

For many people, there's nothing more pleasurable than reading a good book. What books have you read recently that you think your classmates would like? Write an advertisement for a book you think your classmates would enjoy. Along with a summary, present details about the characters, setting, and plot. Be sure your ad gives the reasons why you recommend the book to your classmates.

An Advertisement for a Movie

Suppose that you open your newspaper and find a full-page ad for a new movie. The ad features an enticing headline, a large picture, and several rave quotations from critics. Ads like this try to persuade people to see a particular film. Think of a movie you have enjoyed. Why was it special? What details do you remember? Use those ideas to develop a movie advertisement. Use vivid language to grab your readers' attention and persuade them to see the movie.

A Persuasive Essay About Being Young

Some people your age can't wait until they're older, while others enjoy being young. Do you think that being your age has advantages over being older? What, in your opinion, are the benefits of youth? Write an essay about the advantages of being young. Include a statement of your opinion, along with observations and facts to support it.

Written Advice About Solving an Environmental Problem

Air and water pollution can damage the environment and harm plants, animals, and people. What environmental problems does your community face? Perhaps factory smoke is polluting the air or litter dirties the streets. Choose a problem and give written advice on how to solve it. What steps can private citizens take to solve the problem? What can government officials do? Write your advice and support it with observations and facts.

A Letter to the Editor About Public Transportation

Before the invention of the automobile, trains were the preferred mode of transportation. As people become more concerned with the environment, public transportation is again becoming popular. Consider arguments for different modes of public transportation in your area. Then write a letter to the editor of a local newspaper, calling for better transportation services.

A Public Service Announcement in Support of Reading

There are television and radio programs, as well as campaigns sponsored by schools and libraries, that advocate reading. What reasons might you give to the public to promote reading? Create a public service announcement encouraging people to read more often instead of watching television.

Group Project

Assemble a Class Newsletter

A newsletter presents to its readers information and opinions on current topics. With a group of classmates, plan a newsletter for other students at your school. Brainstorm for a list of subjects and events for which you can present information and opinions. These can include such topics as books, movies, after-school activities or clubs, sports events, performances, and school issues. Each of you should choose one topic about which to write a brief review or persuasive article. When you've each finished your article, work together to assemble the newsletter. If possible, include photographs and illustrations.

Writing Lab CD-ROM

The Inspirations for Persuasion also include the following Group Projects and Group Discussions. The Group Discussions encourage small groups of students to share their thoughts about an Inspiration and to generate possible writing topics. The Group Projects are structured activities in which students assume different roles.

Group Projects

- Creating a dental hygiene poster
- Collecting essays on changing school policy
- Creating a persuasive argument for Milo of *The Phantom Tollbooth*
- Writing a public service announcement about water

Group Discussions

- Reading recommendations for a cat
- Describing how art can enrich everyday life
- Talking about how students would like older people to view them
- Examining the purpose of national anthems
- Describing laws that relate to animals
- Giving advice for people running for public office
- Examining the importance of animals for people
- Determining the ideal age
- Sharing recommendations for impressing friends
- Talking about drinking from the Fountain of Youth

Cultural Connection

Many nations, associations, or other kinds of groups have a special flag or other symbol to represent them. Students who choose to write a persuasive essay recommending a new national symbol may be interested to learn more about the origins of these diverse symbols. For instance, they might not know that the colors of the five Olympic rings were chosen to include at least one color from the flag of every nation of the world. Invite students to research the origins of some national symbols and present their findings in a piece of persuasive writing.

Thematic Connection: Turning Points

Students who choose to develop an advertisement for voting might like to advertise one of the major turning points in American voting history. They could feature the Fifteenth Amendment to the U.S. Constitution (ratified in 1870), which says that no one can be denied the right to vote based on race; the Nineteenth Amendment (1920), which gave women the right to vote; or the Twenty-Sixth Amendment (1971), which gave the right to vote to any citizen eighteen years of age or older.

MORE *Inspirations* for Persuasion

A Persuasive Essay Recommending a New National Symbol

The American flag, with its thirteen stripes and fifty stars, is a symbol of the United States. Another American symbol is the bald eagle. What else do you think would make a good symbol for the United States? Write a persuasive essay in which you recommend a new national symbol. Clearly state the reasons why you think your choice for a new national symbol is appropriate. Include observations and facts to support those reasons.

A Persuasive Essay About a Family Member or a Friend

Some people make a lasting impression on us because of their good qualities. These qualities might be unselfishness, the willingness to help others, a great sense of humor, loyalty to a friend, or the ability to stay calm in a crisis. Which family member or friend do you especially admire? What personality traits, accomplishments, and actions make this person special? If appropriate, you might want to direct your essay toward anyone you know who disagrees with you.

An Advertisement for Voting

In our democratic society, we hold elections to vote for officials at all levels—from members of our town council to President of the United States. Think of reasons why it is important to vote. What can you tell people that will make them want to go out and exercise this right? Try to develop an original slogan about voting that will catch people's attention. Use this slogan, along with facts and detailed observations, to create an advertisement encouraging people to vote.

Group Project: Create an Advertisement About Magical Water

Imagine that the water in one fountain in your school has extraordinary powers, such as the ability to make someone grow taller or understand any math problem. As a group, brainstorm for amazing qualities the water could have. Then choose one of these qualities and create an advertisement about it for your school. Have each group member write one or two sentences about the water, including personal observations and made-up facts that relate to its magical qualities. You might present the advertisement in poster form, with each person contributing appropriate art.

Hollywood Hills, California *(detail) Fred C. Czufin, Private Collection*

A Persuasive Essay About the Construction of New Housing

What would it be like to live on the hill shown in the painting if more houses were built there? How do people in your community feel about the construction of additional housing? Some people might oppose it because it can endanger local wildlife. Others might favor it because the construction provides new jobs. What is your opinion about whether additional housing should be built in your community? Write an essay in which you clearly state your opinion and support it with facts and observations.

Written Advice About Cooperation Between Two Groups

Two groups of people working together can accomplish tremendous things. Two groups of people arguing with each other, however, can accomplish nothing. Name two groups that can have a conflict—such as fans of opposing sports teams, two sides in a political debate, two groups of friends in a school. How could cooperation benefit both of the groups? Give written advice to the two conflicting groups about the benefits of cooperation. State your opinion and support your views with observations, details, and facts.

Language Acquisition/ ESL Teaching Strategy

Your upper-basic and intermediate ESL students will benefit from an adaptation of the Inspiration titled Create an Advertisement About Magical Water. The students brainstorm the qualities that such water might have. A more advanced student lists the ideas on a large sheet of paper and the group decides which to write about. Ask the students to write two or three observations attesting to the magical quality of the water. You may wish to have the students write in the simple past tense. The students then use these statements to create their group poster.

Writing Lab CD-ROM

The Considering Audience and Purpose section of the tutorial on Persuasion includes the following options to help students explore ways to determine their purpose and to gear their writing to their intended audience:

- **Audience Profile** Students can answer questions to help them focus on their intended audience.
- **Audio-annotated Writing Models that consider audience** Students compare two persuasive pieces, each giving advice about the same subject but targeted to different audiences.
- **Interactive examples of ways to define purpose** Students can select a broad purpose for persuasion to see how it can be more specific.
- **Audio-annotated Writing Models for different purposes** Students can compare two passages written about a neglected playing field that accomplish different purposes: to scare people into action or to appeal to community pride.

Working individually or in small groups, students can experiment with these activities to find the ones that work best for them.

Prewriting

Considering Your Audience

Before you begin writing, ask yourself these questions to help identify and consider your audience: Who will read your persuasive paper? Do you think they already have an opinion about your topic? What type of language will appeal to them? As you develop and write your paper, try to make your writing fit your audience. For example, if your intended audience is your class, use the same informal language you use every day. However, if your teacher or a newspaper editor is your audience, your language should be more formal.

Considering Your Purpose

What is the purpose of your persuasive paper? Of course, your general purpose is to persuade. You should also, however, have a more specific purpose in mind. For instance, you might want to persuade your classmates to join a club.

Your purpose will affect the words and details you use in your writing. For example, if you want to convince people not to see a certain movie, you'll tell them all the negative things about the movie.

The two paragraphs that follow are written about the same topic, but they have different purposes. What differences do you notice between the two models?

Writing Models: Considering the Purpose

INTENDED PURPOSE: TO SCARE PEOPLE INTO ACTION

This playing field must be rebuilt. It is a menace to our community. Our children play soccer and baseball on this field. Yet the field is full of rocks and holes. It is an accident waiting to happen. Just imagine a child hitting one of those while running. The result could be a broken leg and a lawsuit that the town would surely lose. We can't afford to wait until trouble strikes. We have to fix it now.

INTENDED PURPOSE: TO APPEAL TO PEOPLE'S PRIDE IN THEIR COMMUNITY

This playing field must be fixed. We have a beautiful community and caring citizens. Yet the field does not reflect this. It looks neglected and not well cared for. Each week, our sports teams compete with teams from other communities. The parents from those communities must think we don't care about our town or our children. We do care and we should show it. Let's make this field a showplace and not an embarrassment.

Writers at Work Videodisc

Play the videodisc segment in which Doug Raboy talks about knowing his audience. Ask:

- Why is it so important to identify your audience before you can persuade them to do anything?

Discuss with the class how a strong argument aimed at the wrong audience can be as ineffective as a poorly supported or disorganized one.

Play frames 3446 to 4408

Writing Strategy

Encourage students to consider their audience to predict its reactions. Encourage them to think about these questions: *How much does the audience know about your topic? How likely are they to agree with you?* Students may want to prepare an audience profile prior to drafting their persuasive pieces so they can refer to it as they write to check for suitable content and language.

Addressing Ability Levels

Challenge your **more-advanced** students to write a pair of persuasive pieces that

FROM a WRITER

"If you don't have a good argument, . . . people are going to see right through you."

—Doug Raboy

Gathering Evidence

How can you persuade your audience to agree with your position? The best way is to back up your argument with facts, reasons, statistics, and other supporting materials. Gather evidence you can use to support your argument. List as many facts as you can. Then look over your notes and decide whether you should gather additional evidence through research. Following are some suggestions to guide you as you gather evidence:

Gather Different Types of Evidence

Three types of evidence that you can use in your persuasive writing are facts, statistics, and quotes.

- **Facts** are statements of truth.

  Example: Kangaroos are native to Australia.

- **Statistics** are numerical facts.

  Example: Seventy-four inches of snow fell last winter in our town.

- **Quotations** are exact statements about your topic made by authorities.

  Example: The mayor said, "The new recycling law will help us reduce our waste-management costs by twenty percent."

CHALLENGE

For a challenge, discuss your opinions with someone who has a view different from your own. By working with someone who disagrees with you, you can be prepared for questions that your audience might have. Write down the opposing views that your partner expresses. Then try to appeal to those views in your own persuasive paper.

xplore the same topic but re each intended for a differnt purpose. Help them xamine the two Writing Models about the playing eld to understand the effect hat adjusting the purpose an have on a persuasive iece.

Language Lab CD-ROM

Students who need guidance dealing with the issues of audience and purpose can complete the Considering Audience and Purpose lesson in the Composing unit of the *Language Lab*.

Writing Lab CD-ROM

The Gathering Evidence section of the tutorial on Persuasion includes the following options designed to help students efficiently obtain information to support an opinion:

- **Video tips from Doug Raboy on gathering information** Students can hear Raboy's advice on the need to have facts to support your message.
- **Interactive instruction on separating fact from opinion** Students compare an opinion statement with a related statement that presents a verifiable fact.
- **Pros and Cons Chart** Students complete a chart in which they sort opposing ideas to build a strong argument.
- **Audio-annotated examples of types of supporting information** Students learn how facts, statistics, and quotes can add support to a persuasive piece.
- **Audio-annotated slide show with tips on gathering information from a library** Students get useful tips on using various library resources, such as a CD-ROM, an encyclopedia, microfilm, or on-line resources.

Working individually or in small groups, students can experiment with these activities to find the ones that work best for them.

Cross-Curricular Connection: *Math*

Students may view statistics as fact, but wily persuaders can use accurate statistics to mislead. For instance, an ad may claim that "100% of all doctors surveyed use Brand X" without saying that only one doctor was surveyed! Have students discuss in their math class how statistics can mislead and how to ensure that statistics add valid and reliable support to an argument.

Teaching Strategy

Students who need additional help doing library research may benefit from working through parts of the tutorial on Reports in the *Writing Lab* CD-ROM or in the related *Sourcebook* chapter.

Addressing Ability Levels

To help your **more-challenged** students distinguish fact from opinion, tell them that an opinion cannot be proven or researched in reference materials, while a fact can be verified in one or more sources. Even if a majority holds a certain opinion, if it cannot be verified by an objective source, it is not a fact. Make some factual statements and ask students how they might confirm them. Then make some opinion statements and discuss the difficulty of trying to confirm them.

Technology Note: Library Tools

If possible, arrange a time when the school librarian can instruct students to use the available library technology, such as CD-ROMs, computer databases, on-line services, or microfilm and microfiche readers. Allow time for students to explore and investigate on their own.

Separate Facts From Opinions

A good argument is based on facts. As you gather information, be sure to separate facts from opinions. **Facts** are statements that can be proved in some way. They are true. **Opinions** can't be proved. They are just someone's ideas or feelings. Here is an example of an opinion and a fact about a camera:

Opinion: This is an expensive camera.

Fact: This camera costs $69.99.

Use Library Resources

If you decide it's necessary, use the library to gather additional evidence for your persuasive composition. Before visiting the library, jot down what you are looking for and where you might find it. You can use a variety of sources, including encyclopedias, nonfiction books, magazines, newspapers, CD-ROM references, and on-line information services. If you don't know how to use any of these sources, ask the librarian for help.

If you're looking for information on a currently popular subject, you may find information in a recent issue of a magazine. Start with the *Reader's Guide to Periodical Literature*. This book lists magazine articles. To use the *Reader's Guide:*

- Decide which key words will lead to information about your topic.
- Look up those key words and skim the listings.
- Jot down the name of the magazine in which an article appeared, the date of the issue, and the page numbers.

Organizing Information

After you've gathered evidence to support your position, take some time to organize your ideas before you begin writing. First decide what type of organization you'll use. Two possibilities are pro-and-con organization and order-of-importance organization.

Pro-and-Con Organization

In pro-and-con organization, you weigh reasons for and against your position. The "pros" are details that support your position. The "cons" are details that oppose or contradict your position. When you present the reasons in favor of your opinion, explain why they are better than the opposing ones. Pro-and-con organization produces a balanced argument. It helps show your readers that you're being fair to the other side.

Writing Model

Voters will soon decide if the city should close its library branch in West Centerville. Those who favor the closing say that the city does not need three library branches. They also point out how much money would be saved. It costs about $50,000 a year to run each branch. But a city this size needs all three libraries. People can't easily go to other branches because there are no direct buses. The city could also cut back the hours of all three branches or could close each branch two days a week. This would keep a branch library in each neighborhood.

When you've decided which organization you'll use, arrange your evidence in that order. Go through your notes and number each piece of evidence or work up an outline.

Order-of-Importance Organization

Use order-of-importance organization to emphasize the strongest point of your argument. In this type of organization, present your argument so that you move from the weakest point to the strongest or from the strongest point to the weakest. This organization plan works best when it's clear that one point of your argument is more important than the others.

Writing Model

Each member of the family should be involved with fire safety—checking smoke detectors, planning fire drills, and choosing an outdoor meeting place. Some day these steps could save your life. Taking charge of your safety is not hard to do. Even young children can check a smoke detector and change its battery. Also, it takes only about ten minutes each month to perform a routine safety check.

Writing Lab CD-ROM

The Organizing Information section of the tutorial on Persuasion includes the following options designed to help students find an effective way to organize the supporting details they gathered:

- **Audio-annotated Writing Model to show pro-and-con organization** Students can see how a writer weighs reasons for and against a position to produce a balanced argument.
- **Audio-annotated Writing Model to show order-of-importance organization** Students can see how a writer presents points of an argument from the strongest to the weakest. The Notecard Activity that follows the model allows students to arrange supporting details in order from strongest to weakest, or from weakest to strongest.

Working individually or in small groups, students can experiment with these activities to find the ones that work best for them.

Clarification

Point out to students that no matter which way they organize details in their persuasive piece, they must state their opinion and support it with facts, statistics, and other kinds of evidence that suits their topic, audience, and purpose.

Writing Strategy

Help students recognize that while a strong argument for a position is appropriate in some persuasive works, an argument that is too one-sided may lack credibility. For this reason, many writers use a balanced argument that gives both supporting and opposing views. Transition words such as *however, on the other hand, although,* or *yet* are especially useful in this plan. A pro-and-con paper needs a clear conclusion in which the writer, who has shown both sides, finally presents his or her own opinion.

Drafting

Using your notes, begin drafting your paper. Focus on supporting your points with facts, statistics, and reasons. If you're writing a long persuasion paper, your draft will most likely include an introduction, a body, and a conclusion. Each of these three parts performs a specific job in helping to present your persuasive argument. The following tips and examples will help you write each section.

FROM a WRITER

"Sitting with a blank page in front of you is one of the scariest things in the world . . . which is why it's important to put down whatever comes into your head when you start to write. . . . Don't worry about getting it right the first time."

—Doug Raboy

Writing the Introduction

The **introduction** begins your persuasive paper. Begin your introduction with a statement about the issue. Then clearly state your opinion.

Writing Model

In this introduction, the writer first explains the issue in detail. Then he clearly states an opinion about the best way to solve the problem.

Some dogs are pests. They bark at your guests and jump up on your furniture. They chew your shoes, and they bother you when you're eating. Maybe these dogs were born this way, but that's unlikely. They probably became pests because their owners never trained them. Dogs need to be taught how to behave. They need to learn the family's rules, such as when it's okay to bark. A good obedience class can provide this education. Every pet dog should be required to attend such a class.

Writing Lab CD-ROM

The Drafting section of the tutorial on Persuasion includes the following options to help students effectively organize and present details for their essay:

- **Video tip from Doug Raboy about drafting** Students can hear Raboy's advice on how to overcome the fear of beginning a first draft.
- **Audio-annotated Writing Models of the parts of a persuasive essay** Students can see sample drafts of an introduction, a body, and a conclusion of a persuasive essay, and hear how each part advances the writer's argument.
- **Interactive instruction on avoiding unreasonable arguments** Students learn to recognize the problems of overgeneralization, bandwagon appeals, and loaded language, and get tips on why and how to avoid them.
- **Transition Word Bin** Students can select transitional words or phrases that help readers see connections among ideas in a persuasive argument.
- **Audio-annotated Student Model** Students see a first draft of a student writer's persuasive essay. Comments by the writer explain the choices she made in drafting the piece.

Working individually or in small groups, students can experiment with these activities to find the ones that work best for them.

Writers at Work Videodisc

Play the videodisc segment in which Doug Raboy talks about getting started on his draft. He finds it important to put down whatever comes into his head when he starts. Ask:

- Why would Raboy intentionally write more than he knows he can use in a first draft?
- Why do you think he advises writers not to "worry about getting it right the first time"?

Discuss the various methods students use to start drafting. Encourage them to consider alternatives to starting with the opening paragraph, such as drafting a strong closing statement they want to make.

Play frames 9524 to 10319

Writing the Body

The **body** is the main portion of your persuasive paper. In the body, develop a strong argument for your position. Each paragraph within the body should focus on a separate subpoint of your argument.

Writing Model

Below is a paragraph from the persuasive paper about pesky dogs. The writer begins with a humorous—though true—statement and then gives many reasons that support that statement.

Most importantly, obedience school trains the owner as well as the animal. This is crucial, because the owner must know how to control the dog. Otherwise, the dog will forget its training. In a few months, it will be a pest again. Owners that learn with their pets are rewarded in several ways. Their families and pets are happier because everyone is following the same rules. And their guests feel more relaxed because they don't have to worry about getting dog hair all over their clothes.

Writing the Conclusion

The **conclusion** is the final section. In the conclusion, restate the issue and your position and drive your point home.

Writing Model

In this conclusion, the writer restates his position and gives final words of support.

All dog owners should take their dogs to obedience school. Although you may love your pesky pooch, you would lose your patience in time. Obedience school can train almost any dog to behave.

Writing Hints

USE AN ATTENTION-GETTING INTRODUCTION

If you're not sure how to begin your persuasive paper, try an attention-getting introduction. Here are four ways:

- Begin with a **question.**
  Example: What kind of world do you want to live in?
- Begin with an **exaggeration.**
  Example: Some people have grown so used to their remote controls that they can't change channels without them.
- Begin with an **anecdote,** or brief story.
  Example: Last week my brother and I went fishing. Within an hour, we had caught two plastic bags, a candy wrapper, and part of a ball-point pen.
- Begin with a startling **fact.**
  Example: Even experts can be wrong. In 1901, Wilbur Wright predicted that humans wouldn't fly for fifty years.

Writing Strategy

Discuss with students some of the "hooks" a writer can use to introduce a persuasive piece. In the Writing Model of an introduction, the writer makes a terse statement about dogs that will likely get readers' attention. Some introductions begin with a quotation or example that will summarize or state the case the writer wants to make. Encourage students to use whatever style of introduction they think will best suit their audience and purpose and will also reflect their own writing style.

Varying the Writing Process

Because a strong introduction is such a crucial part of any well-crafted piece, it can be a daunting place to begin. Some writers prefer to work first on the body of an essay. This should be considered as an acceptable plan, especially when the writer knows the focus of the piece. When the body is done or well under way, the writer can back up to draft an effective introduction.

Clarification

Be sure students understand that although the Writing Model of a body has only one paragraph, the body of a complete work often contains many more body paragraphs. Encourage students to write as many unified paragraphs as they need to present their argument effectively.

Establishing Assessment Criteria

As students begin drafting their persuasive pieces, you may want to share with them the criteria you will use to evaluate their work. The following guidelines are included in the tutorial on Persuasion. Use the guidelines as given, or modify them to suit your needs.

- Have you kept your audience in mind?
- Does your essay state a focused opinion?
- Have you used facts, examples, reasons, or other evidence to support your opinion?
- Have you considered possible opposing ideas?
- Is your composition well organized?
- Have you used transitions between ideas?
- Did you check for errors in spelling, punctuation, and grammar?

Revising and Editing

Revising Your Work

Now that you've finished your first draft, start looking for ways to improve it. Have you made a strong, well-organized argument for your position? Review your draft, using the questions in the following checklist as a guide. Let your answers help you decide which aspects of your persuasive paper need improvement.

Revision Checklist

1. What is the main point of your persuasive paper? How can you make your main point more clear?
2. Did you use facts, statistics, examples, reasons, or other evidence to support the opinion? What can you add to make your position stronger?
3. What method of organization did you use? How can you improve your organization?
4. How have you linked ideas in your paper? Could your paper use words like *therefore*, *because*, and *finally* to help one idea flow smoothly into the next?
5. How did you end your persuasive paper? How can you make the ending stronger?

Student Model: Revised Draft

Here is a revised passage from a persuasive paper by Jamie Zalkus, a student at Conrady Junior High School in Hickory Hills, Illinois. Notice that in his revision, Jamie adds reasons that make his argument in favor of gym-class uniforms stronger.

We should wear uniforms in Physical Education^ for several reasons. They keep our clothes clean. They help tell us apart when we are on teams.^ In addition, we can wear them for other school-related activities.

To begin with, they keep our clothes clean. We don't have to wear our own clothes in gym class, so they do not become sweaty.^ Also, if we have class outside, our clothes don't get covered with grass and dirt.

Another reason for wearing uniforms is that during games we are able to tell the teams apart. The uniforms are reversible, so one team can wear one color and the other team can wear another color.^ This makes it safer for us as we play games.

Writing Lab CD-ROM

The Revising and Editing section of the tutorial on Persuasion provides strategies for self-revision, with the following options to help students revise their first drafts:

- **Interactive Self-Evaluation Checklist** Students enter responses to questions into a form that helps them judge the effectiveness of their persuasive essay.
- **Audio-annotated Writing Models of revised paragraphs** Students can compare before-and-after versions of drafts to show revisions made to add supporting details and to substitute more persuasive words.
- **Sentence openers variety checker** Students use a revision tool that highlights the first two words of every sentence so students can see whether they need to vary the beginnings.
- **Audio-annotated Student Model** Students can compare the first draft of a persuasive essay with a revised draft to learn how and why revisions were made.

Working individually or in small groups, students can experiment with these activities to find the ones that work best.

Writers at Work Videodisc

Play the videodisc segment in which Doug Raboy discusses his views on revising and editing. He says, "When you're close to your work, it's hard to see the difference sometimes in what will work and what won't." Ask:

- What does Raboy mean by being "close to your work"? How can another person help you step back from it?
- Raboy checks each idea he has written to check whether it is "doing anything" for the argument. Why is this especially important in a persuasive essay?

Play frames 6056 to 7651

Writing Strategy

Some students may benefit from having a pocket-sized copy of the Revision Checklist to refer to for self-revision. Feel free to add other questions to the list, such as *Does your opening gra[b] readers' attention? If not, what could improve it?*

Writing Lab CD-ROM

The Revising and Editing section of the tutorial on Persuasion provides strategies for peer

Having a Peer Review Your Work

Sometimes another person can give you ideas for improving your paper that you wouldn't think of yourself. Choose one of your classmates as a partner to help you revise your work. Let your partner read your paper and make suggestions to help you improve it. Then switch roles and read your partner's paper. See if you can think of ways to improve it. Use the questions in the following checklist to guide you.

Peer Review Checklist

1. Did the writer choose an appropriate topic for a persuasive composition?
2. How convincing is the paper? What can be done to make it more convincing?
3. What parts of the paper are most convincing? Why? What parts are least convincing? Why?
4. What, if any, unnecessary or unrelated ideas are included that could be cut?
5. What, if any, additional evidence is needed?
6. What have you learned about the topic? Was anything vague or hard to understand? Can you see the reasons for the writer's position?

Proofreading

Check your paper carefully for errors in spelling, punctuation, and grammar. Such errors can distract your audience's attention from the points you're trying to make. Use the following questions to help guide you as you proofread.

Proofreading Checklist

1. Are you sure of the meanings of all the words you used? Can you define them all?
2. Have you used modifiers—adjectives and adverbs—correctly?
3. Does every sentence end with the correct punctuation mark?
4. Have you used commas and other punctuation marks correctly?
5. Is each word spelled correctly?

effectiveness of the writing. Urge peer editors to identify specific problems in content or form objectively and clearly. Guide them to ask whether opinions are supported by details, even if the editor disagrees with the writer's view.

Writing Lab CD-ROM

The Revising and Editing section of the tutorial on Persuasion includes the following options to help students develop proofreading strategies for their persuasive essays:

- **Video clip that illustrates a grammar problem** Students can hear how double negatives detract from the effectiveness of the argument.
- **Proofreading Checklist** Students can follow this checklist, which also appears on page 189 of the *Sourcebook*, to help them pinpoint possible errors in their drafts.
- **Interactive instruction on using pronouns** Students can identify and correct errors in pronoun cases.
- **Annotated Student Model of a proofread persuasive essay** Students can compare "before" and "after" drafts to see how a student writer identified and corrected errors in spelling and pronoun agreement.

Working individually or in small groups, students can experiment with these activities to find the ones that work best.

evision, with the following ptions to help peer editors vork together effectively:

- **Peer Revision Checklist** Students can use an interactive peer-editing questionnaire to help them focus on what to look for when editing early drafts. The checklist is followed by suggestions for turning negative comments into positive ones.

Peer Revision

- Reading a piece aloud often helps writers or editors to notice choppy sentences, disjointed paragraphs, overused words, or other errors. This approach works well for peer partners. The peer editor can read a draft aloud as the writer listens for places where revisions are needed; roles can be reversed.
- Some students may feel ill at ease with peer editors, especially when sharing personal views or opinions. Peer editors may debate opinions rather than the

Writing Lab CD-ROM

The Publishing and Presenting section of the tutorial on Persuasion includes the following suggestions on how students might present their completed works to a wider audience:

- **Audio-annotated slide show on presenting persuasive pieces** Students can get ideas on ways to present their persuasive pieces, such as by creating a multimedia presentation, presenting pictures, or submitting the piece to a newspaper.
- **Tips for making a poster** Students can explore a list of suggestions designed to help them create a poster that gives a persuasive message and fits their audience and purpose.

Students working individually or in small groups can use these ideas to guide the publishing and presenting phase.

The Multimedia Workshop

Students can use the storyboard, magazine, or newsletter templates in the Writing Workshop component of *The Multimedia Workshop* to present their final persuasive piece. Students may want to print it and hand it out as a visual aid to the audience when they deliver their persuasive speeches.

Students who wish to make video presentations can use the Scene Maker and Sequencer of the Video Workshop. They select music and sound effects to enhance a recording of their own piece.

Publishing and Presenting

You've finished your persuasive paper! Now you can decide how to present it to your audience. You can create a multimedia presentation on a computer or send your paper to your school paper or the local newspaper. Here are some other publishing ideas:

Create a Bulletin-Board Display Work together with your classmates to create a bulletin-board display featuring your persuasive papers. If possible, find photographs or draw pictures to make the display eye-catching.

Deliver a Persuasive Speech With a little reworking, you can transform your paper into a persuasive speech. Follow these steps to make an inspiring presentation:

- Reread your composition. Transfer all important details onto note cards.
- Include charts, graphs, or other visual aids to make your points clear and to keep your audience interested.
- Practice your speech at home a few times, so you'll know the best way to express your ideas.
- Speak slowly and clearly when you present your speech.

Reflecting on Your Writing

By taking some time to think back on how you went about writing something, you help yourself improve as a writer. Here are some questions to help you reflect on the persuasive paper you've just finished.

- What do you like best about persuasive writing? What do you like least?
- What did you learn about your topic by writing your persuasive paper? What else do you wish you had learned?
- If you could start the assignment over again, would you do anything differently? Why or why not? Exactly what would you do differently?
- How can you apply what you've learned to other writing assignments?

Portfolio Assessment

Have students write an evaluative statement that addresses some of the questions posed on page 190 of the *Sourcebook*. If students decide to include the completed persuasive composition in their portfolio, they might attach this statement to it. Otherwise, the statement itself can go into the portfolio as a self-evaluation piece.

The following questions can be used to supplement the questions in the *Sourcebook:*

- What part of the process of persuasive writing did you find most satisfying? Most challenging?
- How do you feel about writing a persuasive composition, as compared wit writing other kinds of pieces?
- In what ways has your writing shown the most improvement? In which areas should you focus yo attention in future assign ments?

Student Model

Here is the complete, final draft of Jamie Zalkus's persuasive composition in favor of gym-class uniforms.

Uniforms Make Sense

by Jamie Zalkus

We should wear uniforms in Physical Education for several reasons. They keep our clothes clean. They help tell us apart when we are on teams. In addition, we can wear them for other school-related activities.

To begin with, they keep our clothes clean. We don't have to wear our own clothes in gym class, so they do not become sweaty. Also, if we have class outside, our clothes don't get covered with grass and dirt.

Another reason for wearing uniforms is that during games we are able to tell the teams apart. The uniforms are reversible, so one team can wear one color and the other team can wear another color. This makes it safer for us as we play games.

Finally, we can wear them for other school activities. For example, I wear my uniform to track meets and other sports events. This saves money, because there is no need to purchase a uniform for each team. The uniforms have our names on them, and this helps the teachers and coaches to remember our names.

For all these reasons, students at our school should continue to wear Physical Education uniforms. They keep our clothes clean and encourage school spirit.

I began my persuasive essay by stating three reasons for my opinion in favor of wearing Physical Education uniforms.

In each of the next three paragraphs, I explained in detail one of my reasons for wanting to continue to wear uniforms.

I mentioned a bonus that results from being able to tell teams apart by the color of their uniforms: It makes playing safer.

In my conclusion, I restated my opinion to drive it home. I also introduced a new idea, team spirit, for readers to think about.

After students have evaluated their work, confer with them to decide what to include in their portfolio. Students can select the completed piece and/or earlier drafts they think reflect growth and progress. Remind students to date all the work they add to their portfolio.

Teaching From the Model

Draw students' attention to how Jamie Zalkus's composition supporting gym-class uniforms includes the key elements of a persuasive essay:

- *It is a short piece of writing that tries to convince an audience to accept an opinion.* Zalkus builds a case to show her support for wearing gym uniforms. She begins her essay by clearly stating her position: "We should wear uniforms in Physical Education for several reasons."
- *It presents examples and details to support the opinion.* Zalkus builds her case in a point-by-point way. She states three main points in her introduction, and then expands upon each point in the subsequent body paragraphs of the essay.
- *It ends with a concluding paragraph that restates the writer's position and key arguments.* Zalkus signals her conclusion by writing "For all these reasons . . ." to remind readers of the case she made. This kind of transition also prepares them for a final restatement of her position that will drive home her point.

Technology Note: Networking

After your class has read the Student Model, students may be interested in sharing creative efforts with students across the country via the Internet or commercial online services such as Prodigy or America Online. Students can exchange persuasive pieces with other students, including those using *Writer's Solution*, by connecting to Prentice Hall's Internet home page. Look for special events, contests, as well as bulletin boards and pointers to student publications, at http://www.phschool.com.

Integrating Skills With Writing

Management Strategy

You can have students work through one or both of the skills lessons either before or after they write their persuasive pieces. If you use the lessons *before*, remind students to incorporate the techniques in their writing. If you address skills *after* students write their essays, have them include a section on "skills improvement" in the self-assessment document they prepare for their portfolios. The next time they write, their work can be evaluated in terms of their mastery of these skills.

You may want to give students these lessons as take-home assignments to be completed prior to the drafting, revising, or proofreading stages—wherever you see the greatest need. Or you may choose to assign the skills lessons only to those students whose drafts indicate a need for direct instruction in the particular skills.

Teaching Strategy

To connect the skills lessons to the students' writing, explain that a key feature of persuasive writing is the use of supporting details. Commas can help to separate ideas in a series to make them clear to readers. Also, commas must be used correctly in addresses, greetings, and closings of letters written to persuade.

Also point out that in order to make persuasive writing more compelling to read, it is a good idea to vary sentence lengths. This can be done by combining short, choppy sentences into longer ones, or by breaking long sentences into short ones linked by a transition word.

Developing Your Style

Using Commas

Whenever you speak, you pause between ideas to make your meaning easier to understand. Whenever you write, use a comma to show a pause between important ideas. **Commas** separate ideas and keep your reader from becoming confused. The following examples will show you when to use commas in your writing.

- **Use commas to separate items in a series.**
  A series is made up of three or more items. Use commas to separate those items. Don't use a comma after the last item:

> I've used watercolors, oils, acrylics, and pastels to paint.

- **Use commas to set off introductory words.**
  Words such as *yes, no, well, oh,* and *why* are sometimes used at the beginning of a sentence for emphasis or in response to a question in which an explanation follows. Set off such words with commas:

> Yes, that beautiful sculpture is by Michelangelo.

- **Use commas to set off nouns of direct address.**
  Commas are used to set off a noun of direct address, or the person to whom you are speaking. When such a noun appears in the middle of a sentence, place a comma both before and after it:

> When you go to the museum, Ashley, look at the colorful masks from Africa.
>
> Michael, these masks are truly beautiful.

- **Use commas in dates and addresses.**
  Use a comma to separate the day from the year:

> October 14, 1973

Teaching Strategy

Help students determine where commas belong by demonstrating how to apply the "pause test." Reading a sentence aloud while paying close attention to the natural pauses in their voice often signals where commas must go. Demonstrate this idea by first reading aloud a series of items with no discernible break between them, or by reading a direct address, greeting, or closing of a letter without pausing. Then read aloud the same examples, this time pausing where appropriate.

Exploring Related Literature

Have students browse through *Prentice Hall Literature, Copper,* to find selections that include examples of commas used in each case presented in the lesson. For example, "Letter to Scottie," by F. Scott Fitzgerald, shows commas in

Use a comma to separate the city from the state or country:

> Ms. Marie Samuels
> 15 Ellen Drive
> San Diego, California 92128

Use a comma after the last part of a date or address when they are included in a sentence:

> Keep May 12, 1996, open because on that day the Fredericks Gallery at 1562 15th Avenue, New York City, will hold a special art auction to benefit the homeless.

- **Use commas in the greetings and closings of letters.**

> Dear Amy,
>
> Sincerely,
> Manuel Sanchez

Practice Activity

Revise this persuasive letter by adding commas where necessary:

May 28 1996

Dear Billy

I'm so glad you asked me for advice about a hobby you could take up on weekends to relax. Honestly I can't think of a more enjoyable way to relax than to paint. My cares just melt away as I set up my paints brushes and canvas. Usually I begin to work on a painting at about nine in the morning. My favorites are rural landscapes flowers and animals. I can truthfully say Billy that I am happiest when I paint.

Billy I'm sure you could learn the basics of painting in no time because I know you like to draw. Get a book on painting from your library. Write me soon to tell me how you're doing.

Oh I almost forgot to tell you that we'll be on vacation in Miami Florida from July 16 1996 through July 22 1996. I'll write you as soon as we get back Billy.

Sincerely
Wendy

Practice Activity Answer

Dear Billy,

I'm so glad you asked me for advice about a hobby you could take up on weekends to relax. Honestly, I can't think of a more enjoyable way to relax than to paint. My cares just melt away as I set up my paints, brushes, and canvas. Usually, I begin to work on a painting at about nine in the morning. My favorites are rural landscapes, flowers, and animals. I can truthfully say, Billy, that I am happiest when I paint.

Billy, I'm sure you could learn the basics of painting in no time because I know you like to draw. Get a book on painting from your library. Write me soon to tell me how you're doing.

Oh, I almost forgot to tell you that we'll be on vacation in Miami, Florida, from July 16, 1996, through July 22, 1996. I'll write you as soon as we get back, Billy.

Sincerely,
Wendy

ne address, the date, the reeting, and the closing of a etter. "The Naming of Cats," y T. S. Eliot, shows commas eparating a series of items.

Language Lab CD-ROM

For additional help n using commas, students an work through the Commas lesson in the Punctuation unit.

Writer's Companion

To provide additional support and reinforcement in the correct use of commas, assign students the section on Comma (pp. 309–314).

Alternative Assessment

Students can demonstrate their grasp of the correct use of commas by writing a letter of advice to a friend. Have them feature the use of commas in each kind of case presented in the lesson.

Integrating Skills With Writing

Teaching Strategy

Discuss with students how variety influences their enjoyment of a work of art, literature, or any form of entertainment. Elicit the notion that too much "sameness" can feel dull and may eventually cause an audience to lose interest. Explain that this idea also applies to writing. Varying the length and style of sentences helps make writing more interesting.

Clarification

Point out that when combining two short sentences into a compound or complex sentence, writers should use the conjunction that best conveys the relationship between the sentences.

Language Lab CD-ROM

Students who need more practice in varying sentence length may benefit from working through the Correcting Stringy Sentences and Combining Sentences lessons in the Styling Sentences unit.

Portfolio Activity

Have students look through their writing for examples of sameness in sentence length and style. Encourage them to find ways to vary sentence length without losing meaning or clarity.

Developing Your Style

Varying Sentence Length

To make your writing more interesting and expressive, vary the length and structure of your sentences. Combine short, choppy sentences and break up long, stringy sentences.

How to Combine Short Sentences

Too many short sentences can make your writing sound choppy. If your writing includes many short sentences, look for ways to combine these sentences. Following are some ways to combine short, simple sentences that present related ideas. Note that a **simple sentence** is one that contains only one complete idea.

- **Form a compound sentence.**
  A **compound sentence** contains two or more complete ideas in one sentence. Use the words *and, but, or,* or a semicolon to combine two simple sentences into a compound sentence.

> **Simple sentences:** Some stones make a circle. Other stones form an oval.
>
> **Compound sentence:** Some stones make a circle, and other stones form an oval.

- **Form a complex sentence.**
  A **complex sentence** expresses one main idea and one or more less important ideas. The main idea in a complex sentence is called an **independent clause** because it can stand alone. The less important idea is called a **subordinate clause.** Subordinate clauses are introduced by special words called conjunctions, such as *because*, *although*, *before*, *since*, and *while*.

> **Simple sentences:** Scientists have been studying Stonehenge for a long time. They don't know its purpose.
>
> **Complex sentence:** Although scientists have been studying Stonehenge for a long time, they don't know its purpose.

Writer's Companion

Students who need additional practice in varying sentence length can find support in the sections on Sentence Problems (pp. 72–73), Sentence Combining (pp. 78–85), and Sentence Variety (pp. 86–88).

How to Revise Long Sentences

Too many long sentences can be just as boring as too many short sentences. If you've used too many long sentences, break up some of these sentences into shorter sentences. Use a **linking word**—such as *next*, *then*, or *finally*—to connect the ideas.

> **Long sentence:** We visited Stonehenge in the morning and then drove to London.
>
> **Two sentences with a linking word:** We visited Stonehenge in the morning. Then we drove to London.

The linking word *then* shows the relationship between the ideas. The drive to London occurred *after* visiting Stonehenge.

Practice Activities

1. Revise the following excerpt from a persuasive essay. Try to improve the variety of the sentence lengths.

   How could the stones of Stonehenge be transported so long ago? How could they be lifted into place? Thousands of years ago there were no cranes. Scientists have wondered about this. Most say that the builders made ramps of soil. They made rollers from logs. They pushed the stones. They dragged the stones. They got the stones up the ramps and into position.

   What was the purpose of Stonehenge? It might have been a place of worship. It might have been a giant calendar. It might have been both. No one knows. There is evidence for the calendar theory. The structure aligns with the position of the sun. This happens at certain times of the year. The stones align with the sun at the summer solstice. I have read much about Stonehenge. I think the calendar theory makes sense. In my opinion, Stonehenge was the largest calendar ever made.

2. Write a persuasive paragraph to convince a vacationer to visit a destination of your choice. Include reasons that make this location a great place for tourists. Use sentences of varying lengths.

Teaching Strategy

Tell students that there are many ways to revise the excerpt about Stonehenge in the Practice Activities. You might have students share and discuss their revisions with peer partners. You might also have some revisions read aloud or put on transparencies to be shown on an overhead projector.

Alternative Assessment

Students can demonstrate their ability to vary sentence length by taking an early draft of a piece they have in their portfolio and revising it specifically for sentence variety. Or they can take a passage from a piece in *Prentice Hall Literature*, *Copper*, and revise it for sentence variety.

Language Acquisition/ ESL Teaching Strategy

Put your intermediate students to work in pairs and rewrite the Stonehenge paragraph by varying sentence length. You may wish to assign the students roles—for example, Writer, Reader, or Checker. You may wish to lead your basic ESL students in a similar activity. Take sentences from the paragraph and write them on long strips of paper to be posted in the classroom near the chalkboard. Ask the students for suggestions on how to shorten or lengthen the sentences. The students take turns writing the new sentences on the chalkboard.

Practice Activities: Suggested Answers

1. Revised excerpts will vary. A possible revision follows:

   How could the stones of Stonehenge be transported and lifted into place so long ago? Scientists have wondered about this. Thousands of years ago there were no cranes. Perhaps the builders made ramps of soil and rollers from logs. They got the stones up the ramps and into position by pushing or dragging them.

   What was the purpose of Stonehenge? It might have been a place of worship, a giant calendar, or both. No one knows. There is evidence for the calendar theory because the structure aligns with the position of the sun at certain times of the year, such as at the summer solstice. After reading much about Stonehenge, I think the calendar theory makes sense. In my opinion, Stonehenge was perhaps the largest calendar ever made.
2. Persuasive paragraphs will vary, but should include sentences of varying lengths.

Integrating Literature With Writing

Literature Model

Racial Harmony Poster *Doug Raboy*

Barbara Jordan (1936–) was the first African American woman from a southern state to serve in the U.S. Congress. In the following excerpt, she writes about the need for further improvement in race relations in America. As you read, notice how Jordan makes her writing more persuasive by offering specific steps people can take.

All Together Now

by Barbara Jordan

When I look at race relations today, I can see that some positive changes have come about. But much remains to be done, and the answer does not lie in more legislation. We have the legislation we need; we have the laws. Frankly, I don't believe that the task of bringing us all together can be accomplished by government. What we need now is soul force—the efforts of people working on a small scale to build a truly tolerant, harmonious society. And parents can do a great deal to create that tolerant society. . . .

Jordan starts by letting readers know her opinion. A strong statement of your point of view is an effective way to start a persuasive essay.

How do we create a harmonious society out of so many kinds of people? The key is tolerance—the one value that is indispensable in creating community.

Jordan speaks to all Americans. It is important to know who your audience is when writing a persuasive essay.

If we are concerned about community, if it is important to us that people not feel excluded, then we have to do something. Each of us can decide to have one friend of a different race or background in our mix of friends. If we do this, we'll be working together to push things forward.

Management Strategy

You can have students read this model of persuasive writing either before or after they have written their own piece. If you have them read it *before,* use it to draw their attention to techniques or ideas they can apply to their own writing. If you use it *after,* have students compare and contrast some elements of this piece with elements of their own work. Ask: *What can you learn from this piece that can help you the next time you write a persuasive paper?*

Language Acquisition/ ESL Teaching Strategy

Put your intermediate and advanced ESL students into multilevel groups of four or five. Ask them to read the excerpt by Barbara Jordan, discussing troublesome vocabulary words and phrases. Then ask the students to identify the points Jordan makes in order to persuade her audience of the need for tolerance. You may wish to provide some questions to help the students organize their discussions, for example, *Why is tolerance so important to the writer? What points does Jordan make in favor of tolerance?* Ask the students to describe what they have learned from their discussion.

Activating Prior Knowledge

Before students read the excerpt from Barbara Jordan's persuasive essay, invite them to share their beliefs regarding the state of race relations today. Guide them to consider this issue as it is reflected in their community and in light of information from news media. Ask if they have ever read about the issue of race relations, and if so, what kind of writing it was.

Purpose-Setting Question

What techniques does the author of this essay use to persuade readers to accept her opinion?

Reading Strategy

You can help students to appreciate the style and structure of Jordan's essay by having them identify the features they would associate with any piece of persuasive writing. Ask:

- How does Jordan make her position clear to her audience?
- What evidence does Jordan present to support her opinions?
- How does Jordan conclude her piece to drive her point home?

After students finish reading, they can work as a whole class or in small groups to compare their responses.

One thing is clear to me: We, as human beings, must be willing to accept people who are different from ourselves. I must be willing to accept people who don't look as I do and don't talk as I do. It is crucial that I am open to their feelings, their inner reality.

Jordan offers one step that all people can take. Showing that it is possible to take some specific action can make your essay more persuasive.

What can parents do? We can put our faith in young people as a positive force. I have yet to find a racist baby. Babies come into the world as blank slates and, with their beautiful innocence, see others not as different but as enjoyable companions. Children learn ideas and attitudes from the adults who nurture them. I absolutely believe that children do not adopt prejudices unless they absorb them from their parents or teachers.

Jordan states that babies are not racists, and she argues persuasively why this is so. When writing persuasively, discussing what seems to be an obvious fact can be effective because the particular fact may not be obvious to all people.

The best way to get this country faithful to the American dream of tolerance and equality is to start small. Parents can actively encourage their children to be in the company of people who are of other racial and ethnic backgrounds. If a child thinks, "Well, that person's color is not the same as mine, but she must be okay because she likes to play with the same things I like to play with," that child will grow up with a broader view of humanity.

Here Jordan offers practical advice, which can be persuasive when you show people how they can benefit from it.

I'm an incurable optimist. For the rest of the time that I have left on this planet I want to bring people together. You might think of this as a labor of love. Now, I know that love means different things to different people. But what I mean is this: I care about you because you are a fellow human being and I find it okay in my mind, in my heart, to simply say to you, I love you. And maybe that would encourage you to love me in return.

Here it becomes clear that Jordan is writing from her heart. When trying to persuade others, it always helps if your opinion is something you feel strongly about.

It is possible for all of us to work on this—at home, in our schools, at our jobs. It is possible to work on human relationships in every area of our lives.

Jordan closes with a strong restatement of her opinion. An effective way to conclude your persuasive essay is to restate your main point concisely.

Teaching From the Model

Discuss "All Together Now" by Barbara Jordan with the class to help students understand how effectively it works as a persuasive essay:

- *Jordan states her personal view in the opening paragraph.* Jordan begins by acknowledging that race relations have improved over time, but contrasts this view by stating "But much remains to be done. . . ." As a former elected official, she is in a knowledgeable position to say "Frankly, I don't believe that the task of bringing us all together can be accomplished by government." Rather, she sees the need for "soul force," or the moral actions of individuals to effect change.
- *Jordan has determined an audience and purpose for her essay, and has taken an approach that suits them.* Jordan has chosen to make her case to individuals, especially parents, suggesting that improved race relations begin with individual actions and attitudes. "The best way to get this country faithful to the American dream of tolerance and equality is to start small."
- *Jordan provides evidence to support her views.* Jordan offers anecdotes and examples to strengthen her position that tolerance and equality begin at home. She states, "I have yet to find a racist baby. . . . Children learn ideas and attitudes from the adults who nurture them."

Thematic Connection: Social Responsibility

Renowned as a dynamic and moving speaker, Barbara Jordan has had a long career with a strong focus on civil rights. She was the first African American student at Boston University Law School in the 1950's, and served as a consultant to President Lyndon Johnson on civil rights legislation. In 1994, Jordan won the Medal of Freedom, the highest honor a United States civilian can receive. Invite students to learn more about Barbara Jordan and the roots of her beliefs in civil rights and social responsibility.

Closure and Extension

To complete the lesson, you can ask students to summarize what they learned about persuasive writing by examining this essay about race relations. Then have students share, through brief journal entries or in discussion groups, what they learned about themselves as writers and what points they would like to keep in mind for future writing.

Reports
Classroom Manager

Writer's Solution *Materials for Teaching Report Writing*

The *Writer's Solution* includes a wide range of materials for teaching report writing. You can pick and choose from among these materials to create a lesson plan that suits your classroom needs, teaching style, and equipment situation. In the pages that follow, you'll find lesson plans suggesting some of the most effective ways of using these materials. You do not have to use all the program components or all its features to use it effectively. Just use what works for you. For a detailed description of each of the components of the *Writer's Solution,* see pages T4–T6.

Below is a detailed list of the *Writer's Solution* materials for report writing.

Writers at Work Videodiscs

Featured Writer: Jean Craighead George, Novelist and Nature Writer

Videodisc Segments:

About Report Writing
Writing From Nature
Writing Tips:
Keep It Simple
If It's Hard to Start, Then Start Somewhere Else

Interactive CD-ROMs

Writing Lab

Tutorial on Reports

About Reports
- Includes five Models From Literature and a video clip featuring Jean Craighead George

Choosing Your Topic
- Includes Inspirations for Reports and an Idea Wheel activity

Narrowing Your Topic
- Includes an animated example, a Topic Web activity, and a narrowing checklist

Considering Audience and Purpose
- Includes *Star Trek* video clip, interactive annotated models, and Audience Profile activity

Gathering Information
- Includes *Star Trek* video clip, a video explaining library resources, a K-W-L Chart, and interactive models of note and source cards

Organizing Information
- Includes a video example, a Notecard Activity, instructions on different methods of organization, a Branching Outline organizer activity, and a Keyhole organizer activity

Drafting
- Includes *Jungle Book* video clip, a video clip with Jean Craighead George, a Transition Word Bin, interactive models, and a complete Student Model

Revising and Editing
- Includes Language Variety Revision Checker, a Student Model, and guided self-revision and peer-revision activities

Proofreading
- Includes integrated grammar instruction on capitalization

Publishing and Presenting
- Includes suggestions for presenting reports to wider and smaller audiences

Writer's Tool Kit

Suggested Activities: Inspirations for Reports, Topic Web, Purpose Checklist, Timeline, K-W-L Chart

Language Lab CD-ROM

Related Lessons: Main Idea and Topic Sentence, Supporting Sentences, Concluding Sentences, Unity in Paragraphs (Building Paragraphs unit); Narrowing a Topic, Considering Audience and Purpose (Composing unit); Capitalization, Quotation Marks (Punctuation unit)

Sourcebook

About Reports (pp. 202–208)
Guided Lesson (pp. 209–227)
Inspirations for Reports (pp. 212–214)
Developing Your Style
Citing Sources (p. 229)
Using Coordination and Subordination (pp. 230–231)
Literature Model
"Pandas," a research report by Gillian Standring, Nature Writer (pp. 232–235)

Below is a list of materials from Prentice Hall's student writing handbook that you can integrate with this lesson on report writing.

Writer's Companion

Mini-Lesson on Narrowing Your Topic p. 12
Mini-Lesson on Organizational Plans p. 23
Mini-Lesson on Biographical Sketch p. 111
Mini-Lesson on Observation Reports p. 123
Mini-Lesson on Book Reports p. 218
Mini-Lesson on Research Reports p. 224
Mini-Lesson on I-Search Reports p. 234
Mini-Lesson on Interviews p. 245
Capitalization p. 297
Conjunctions p. 323
Quotations p. 376

Teaching Integrated Language Arts Using the Writer's Solution*—Starting With Literature*

Have students read and respond to biographical sketches, research reports, interviews, and other types of reports. In discussing the selections, draw students' attention to organizational elements, such as chronological order or order of importance. Point out that students can use the reports they've read as models for writing their own reports. Lead into having students complete reports using the components of the *Writer's Solution*.

CONNECTIONS TO *PRENTICE HALL LITERATURE,COPPER,* SELECTIONS

Biographical Sketches/ Interviews	2E	3E	Library Research Reports	2E	3E
"Virginia Hamilton," Lee Bennett Hopkins	■	▲	**"Space Stations of the Mind,"** Neil McAleer	■	▲
"My Papa, Mark Twain," Susy Clemens	■	▲	**"The Strange Geometry of Stonehenge,"** Katherine B. Shippen	■	▲
"A Backwoods Boy," Russell Freedman	■	▲	**"The Giants of Easter Island,"** Carrol Alice Stout	■	▲
			"The Hatchling Turtles," Jean Craighead George	■	▲

You can also use the *Writer's Solution* material on reports to guide students through writing activities in response to works of literature.

CONNECTIONS TO *PRENTICE HALL LITERATURE, COPPER,*WRITING ACTIVITIES

Thinking and Writing Activities	2E	3E	Your Writing Process	2E	3E
Writing an Interview—Follows **"Virginia Hamilton,"** Lee Bennett Hopkins	■	▲	**Your Writing Process: Writing From Observation**	■	▲
Writing a Biographical Sketch—Follows **"A Backwoods Boy,"** Russell Freedman	■	▲	**Your Writing Process: Writing to Explore a Content Area**	■	▲
Writing an Anthropological Report—Follows **"The Giants of Easter Island,"** Carrol Alice Stout	■	▲			
Describing a Natural Occurrence—Follows **"The Hatchling Turtles,"** Jean Craighead George	■	▲			

■ **(2E)** *Prentice Hall Literature, Copper,* Second Edition

▲ **(3E)** *Prentice Hall Literature, Copper,* Paramount Edition

CONNECTIONS BETWEEN INSPIRATIONS FOR REPORTS AND *PRENTICE HALL LITERATURE, COPPER*

You can use the multimedia Inspirations for Reports to motivate student reading as well as student writing. Many of the Inspirations are audio recordings or video adaptations of selections from *Prentice Hall Literature, Copper.* Have students work in small groups to look at and discuss an appropriate Inspiration before reading the corresponding selection. Then after reading the selection, students can replay the Inspiration and select one of the accompanying topic ideas. The following is a list of selections from *Prentice Hall Literature, Copper,* included in the Inspirations for Reports.

- **"Space Stations of the Mind,"** Neil McAleer
- **"Light and Water/Luz y Agua,"** Juan Ramón Jiménez
- **"The Naming of Cats,"** T. S. Eliot

Recommended Lesson Plan

The following lesson plan is recommended for providing students with thorough, comprehensive instruction in writing reports. Because you may not have all the components of the *Writer's Solution* or may have limited access to equipment, the plan provides a number of options. Choose the options that best suit your teaching style and equipment situation.

You may want to add a couple of days to the lesson plan to allow students time to publish their work and to hold conferences with students to discuss your assessment of their work.

TEN-DAY LESSON PLAN	
Lesson Outcome:	**Each student writes a complete report.**
DAY 1  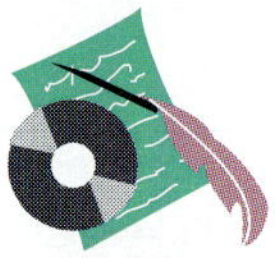 	**Introduce your students to report writing.** Show the *Writers at Work Videodisc* segment featuring Jean Craighead George. Use the segment as a springboard for class discussion or group activities. Then choose one of the following options: OPTION 1 Have students work either individually or in small groups to look at the About Reports section. Ask students to think about the type of report they wish to write. OPTION 2 Have students working in pairs or small groups read and discuss the About Reports (pp. 202–208 and Types of Reports (pp. 204–208) sections of the *Sourcebook.* Ask them to think about the type of report they wish to write.
DAYS 2 and 3  	**Have students choose a writing option and choose and narrow their topic.** OPTION 1 Have students working individually or in small groups choose a topic by browsing through the Inspirations for Reports. Then have students work individually to develop a plan for their reports by completing the rest of the Prewriting phase of the tutorial, which includes narrowing the topic and considering audience and purpose. At the end of the class, have students print their prewriting notes. OPTION 2 Have students working individually or in small groups read the Prewriting section of the *Sourcebook* (pp. 210–221) to help them choose a topic. They can get ideas by browsing through the Inspirations for Reports (pp. 212–214). Have students work individually to develop a plan for their reports by completing the rest of the Prewriting section, which includes narrowing the topic and considering audience and purpose.

TEN-DAY LESSON PLAN (continued)

DAYS 4 and 5	**Have students gather information.** OPTION 1 Have students working individually or in small groups work through the Gathering Information section of the tutorial on Reports. Then set aside time for them to conduct their research. OPTION 2 Have students work through the Gathering Information section of the *Sourcebook* (pp. 218–219) to help them decide on the focus and arrangement of ideas for their report.
DAY 6	**Have students organize their information to prepare for writing their first draft.** OPTION 1 Have students work through the Organizing Information section of the tutorial on Reports to help them decide on the focus and arrangement of ideas for their report. Then have them arrange their note cards to prepare for drafting. OPTION 2 Have students read the Organizing Your Information section of the *Sourcebook* (pp. 220–221) to help them decide on the focus and arrangement of ideas for their report. Then have them arrange their note cards to prepare for drafting.
DAYS 7 and 8	**Have students draft their reports.** OPTION 1 Have students write their drafts on the computer, following the instructions and using the activities provided in the Drafting section of the tutorial on Reports. Have students print out their reports at the end of these two days. OPTION 2 Have students write their drafts on paper, following instructions on Drafting in the guided lesson on Reports (pp. 222–224).
DAY 9	**Have students work in peer groups to revise their reports.** OPTION 1 Have peer partners revise their reports on the computer, using the guidelines and suggestions in the Revising and Editing section of the tutorial on Reports. OPTION 2 Have peer partners revise their reports, following the suggestions in the Revising and Editing section of the guided lesson (pp. 225–226).
DAY 10	**Have students make final revisions and proofread.** OPTION 1 Have pairs of students review each other's work, following the guidelines in the proofreading checklist in the Proofreading section of the tutorial on Reports. Students should then proofread and print out their final drafts. OPTION 2 Have pairs of students review each other's work, following the guidelines in the Proofreading section of the *Sourcebook* (p. 226). Students should then proofread and make their final drafts.

CONDENSED FIVE-DAY LESSON PLAN

On day 1, introduce your students to report writing by showing the *Writers at Work Videodisc* segment featuring Jean Craighead George. Then have students choose and narrow their topics using either the *Writing Lab* tutorial or the *Sourcebook*. On days 2 and 3, have your students gather and organize their formation; if time permits, they may begin drafting. Use day 4 to finish drafting and day 5 for revising, editing, and proofreading.

Preparing to Teach

Lesson Objectives

Students will

1. Select an appropriate topic for a report
2. Narrow their topic
3. Adapt their writing to suit audience and purpose
4. Organize facts and details logically
5. State the main idea in an introduction
6. Support the main idea in body paragraphs
7. Restate the main idea and summarize the key points in the conclusion
8. Credit sources of information

Activating Prior Knowledge

Ask students to explain how they have located information to learn about topics that were unfamiliar to them. They may say that they have read books or magazine articles, done library research, asked an adult or older student, consulted reference materials, conducted interviews, watched videos, and so on. Ask: *What are some ways you like to get new information?*

The Critic *The Inland Printer, After Original Japanese, The Free Library of Philadelphia*

Reports

"The wonderful thing about nature writing... is that wherever I go, a book happens in my head."

—Jean Craighead George
Nature Writer and Novelist

Humanities Note

The Critic is the title of this Japanese print by an anonymous artist. Among the most popular subjects for prints were landscapes, pictures of well-known theatre personalities, and character pieces like this one.

When the color print process was developed, it enabled many people to buy art for the first time. Prints appeared on walls, on calendars, in books, and as illustrations for familiar literary works. Part of the appeal of the print was its depiction of familiar, everyday happenings—particularly those with a humorous or witty theme. In this print, a well-dressed monkey is reading an article. He has already finished other reading material on the floor.

As the artist titles his print "The Critic," we assume that the monkey will make a profound judgment about the article. If, on the other hand, he cannot read, what is he doing? Use the following questions as a basis for class discussion:

- Why do you think the monkey is dressed up and placed among these objects that suggest an elegant home?
- Why do you think the artist called this picture "The Critic"? How do you think he feels about critics? Why do you suppose he chose a monkey to be the critic?
- Do reviews help you decide whether you want to read a book or see a movie?

Addressing Your Classroom Situation

This chapter includes a variety of Models From Literature, writing topics, writing process strategies, and a Student Model, along with two integrated skills lessons. Feel free to pick and choose from this material to create a customized lesson on reports that matches your classroom needs.

The following are some of the key features of the chapter:

- The chapter begins with a section introducing reports. This section includes a definition of reports from writer Jean Craighead George, group discussion questions, and models from Literature of the following five types of reports: biographical sketch, "I-search" report, nonfiction book report, library research report, and report on an experiment.
- The Prewriting section includes an assortment of idea-generating activities to help students choose a topic, along with some suggested topics from which they can select. This section also provides instructions and activities to help students narrow a topic, consider audience and purpose, and gather and organize information. Models of topic webs, idea lists, note and source cards, and outlines guide students through the steps of the process of planning to write their reports.
- The Drafting section addresses the issues of writing body paragraphs with a clear main idea supported by facts and examples, writing conclusions, and crediting sources.
- The Guided Lesson instruction is followed by skills lessons on citing sources and using coordination and subordination. You may want to address these skills before students draft their reports, or you may prefer to focus on them during the revising and editing or proofreading phases.
- The chapter ends with a complete Literature Model, a report entitled "Pandas," by nature writer Gillian Standring.

CONTENTS

About Reports

Guided Lesson

Student Model

Developing Your Style 1

Developing Your Style 2

Literature Model

"If you're looking for a theme, . . . be very simple: Look at your shoe. You can write pages about your shoe. Where it's been, or what it's made of. I think we try too hard to find subjects and themes to write about. And the more simplicity, the better."

"I was brought up in a family of naturalists, and I began to write—nature writing, natural history stories—things I knew about. . . ."

Jean Craighead George
Nature Writer and Novelist

"I have two hundred and fifty million species to write about. And it's sometimes very difficult to decide which one."

More About the Writer

Jean Craighead George grew up in a family of naturalists. Her deep interest in and respect for nature began at an early age and never abated. George has written more than thirty fiction and nonfiction books, including such acclaimed works as *My Side of the Mountain*, *Julie of the Wolves*, and the *Thirteen Moons* series. She calls her fiction works "documentary novels" because the investigations into nature within them are so carefully researched and scientifically accurate.

Group Discussion

Discuss with your students how and why a personal interest in a particular area, such as nature, often leads to research about specific topics within that area. Discuss the similarities and differences between "field research," such as interviews, and research from books or other print material. What do these sources have in common? What is unique about each kind of resource? How might a researcher approach a topic differently, depending on what resources are available? What are some ideas that are unlikely to emerge from researching books or articles?

Tech Prep Note

Not only professional writers like Jean Craighead George write reports in their work. Many workers in other fields use report writing on the job. For example, a large part of the work of mayors, governors, members of Congress, and political aides is to prepare research reports on topics of importance to their constituents. Insurance claims adjusters prepare reports specifying observed damages and costs to cover losses.

Report writing occurs in fields where it may be less apparent. Chefs and food-service staff may write nonliterary book reports to restaurant owners suggesting new menu items to try. Electronics or mechanical engineers may write I-search reports about new technologies. Ask: *What jobs do you know about that involve report writing? Why do the workers present information based on research?*

Introducing Reports

Teaching Options

There are a variety of ways you can introduce reports using the components of the *Writer's Solution:*

- You can show the Reports segment from the *Writers at Work Videodisc*. Use the videodisc segment as a springboard for a class discussion on reports.
- You can have students work individually or in small groups to go through the About Reports section of the Reports tutorial in the *Writing Lab* CD-ROM.
- You can work through the About Reports section of the *Sourcebook* with the class.
- You can have students read the About Reports section of the *Sourcebook* before class starts, so that, as a group, you can concentrate on the videodisc or CD-ROM lesson.

Sourcebook

Have students read aloud and discuss the About Reports section in the *Sourcebook*. Use the following questions to guide the discussion:

- In what sources have you found reports?
- What makes a report important?
- When and why do people seek out reports? What kinds of reports might they want to read?
- How can reports on the same topic be quite different, even when they are both based on the same facts?

Following the class discussion, divide your students into groups of three to five to engage in the group discussion (p. 202).

Writers at Work Videodisc

Use the Reports section of the videodisc featuring writer Jean Craighead George as a springboard for a class discussion on reports. Before you play the first segment, ask students to listen for the way Jean Craighead George describes her attitude toward report writing.

After students have viewed the segment, have them take turns sharing their responses. Then move into a discussion of the writing techniques and personal insights that George shares. Ask:

- What does George mean when she says that anything you're interested in can be a good topic for a report?
- What techniques does George use to prepare for writing a report?

Play frames 10322 to 19222

About Reports

What Is a Report?

A **report** is a piece of writing based on outside research. As a student, you will have to write reports in almost every school subject. As an adult, you will likely be expected to write reports as part of your work. People write reports in a wide range of occupations—from business to police work.

Group Discussion Think about the reports you have seen or read recently. Perhaps you have watched a news report on a sports figure, a scientific discovery, or an international incident. Or you may have read a magazine article about a favorite recording artist or a new fashion trend. Get together with a group of your classmates and discuss some articles or reports that have caught your attention recently. Explain what it was about these subjects that interested you. Did any of the reports inspire you to learn more about the subject? As you discuss these reports, suggest related topics that you might like to investigate. Ask questions about these new topics and think about ways you would search for the answers.

How a Professional Writer Uses Report-Writing Techniques

The techniques of report writing are used by many kinds of professional writers—journalists, biographers, historians, book reviewers, nature writers. In order to research and gather information, these writers may read numerous publications, perform experiments, interview people, or even travel into the wilderness. Indeed, writing a report can be a real adventure, as nature writer Jean Craighead George tells us:

> "I have gone up into the Arctic and stayed out on the sea ice at thirty-five below zero to understand the whales. I've climbed mountains to see the Rocky Mountain goats. I've slept out in the world of owls, so I know what they do at night. I travel all over the continent to write my stories. But it doesn't have to be that. It can be right on your own front porch. It's what you put into it that makes it a piece of writing."

How Reports Fit Into Your Life

Whenever you read a newspaper or a magazine or tune your TV to the news, a nature show, or a documentary, you are looking at a kind of report. The articles you read and the shows you watch are all the result of research and reporting—sometimes by an individual and sometimes by a team of reporters. Similarly, whenever you strive to learn more about a subject that interests you, you are conducting research that could lead to a report.

Real-World Writing

Help students identify a person who writes reports that affect your community. This person might be a member of the school board, a store manager, a doctor, a local historian, an environmental scientist, a social worker, or a police officer.

As an enrichment activity, have students find examples of reports about local issues or people. For instance, they might locate a newspaper report that explores the possibility of building a new park; a report concerning a public health issue; or a report on a new restaurant, play, or film. As students share these reports, ask:

- In what ways does the report show that the writer did research?
- How do you think the writer collected information?
- What features does the report include that differ from features you see in other kinds of writing?

Thematic Connection: Nature

Jean Craighead George incorporates her deep interest in nature into most of her books, even works of fiction such as *Julie of the Wolves*. Have students brainstorm for a list of interesting topics that involve nature. Some of these ideas may evolve into topics for their reports.

Writing Lab CD-ROM

The About Reports section includes the following options:

- Author video—Jean Craighead George on reports.
- Models of reports—Biographical Sketch, I-Search Report, Nonfiction Book Report, Library Research Report, and Report on an Experiment. Students can interact with these models to gain additional insights.
- Evaluation guidelines can be used by students before they draft their reports to serve as a checklist to guide their writing.

If you have access to a projection panel, you can work through the About Reports section with the entire class.

Integrating Literature With Writing

Starting From Literature

You can use the models on pages 204–208 to illustrate the various elements of each type of report. Or you can use the content of any of these reports to inspire writing on any of the themes they address. For example, you could use the biographical sketch about Abraham Lincoln to inspire students to research and write a biographical sketch about another historical figure they admire.

Briefly introduce and define the type of writing that each selection models. You might invite a student to read each report aloud to the class. Follow up with a discussion to reinforce students' understanding of each type of report.

Teaching From the Model

Guide students to analyze this work by Mebane and Rybolt to understand how it fulfills the requirements for a report on an experiment:

- *It begins with a question, the answer to which is the goal of the experiment.* Some reports on experiments begin with a statement of purpose and may or may not predict the outcome.
- *It lists the materials used in the experiment.* Point out that it is helpful to list materials in the order used and to give measurements, quantities, or other key characteristics, as appropriate.
- *It describes the procedure briefly but clearly.* This is important so that readers can understand what took place. It also allows the experiment to be repeated.
- *It gives objective observations of the experiment's outcome.* Such observations describe what really did happen, not just what the experimenters hoped would happen.
- *It presents a conclusion based on those observations.* Again, the conclusion must follow from the observations.

Cross-Curricular Connection: *Science*

Regardless of the scientific principle under investigation, any report on an experiment should include the steps of "scientific" or "experimental" methodology. Have students consult a science textbook or interview a scientist or science teacher to learn what these steps are.

Types of Reports

At this point in your life, most of the reports you write will be for your classes—a book report for language arts, a lab report for science, or a current events report for social studies. Occasionally, you may also write a report for a club you belong to, your school newspaper, or a local newspaper. In each case, your report writing will involve researching, organizing, and presenting information. Here are some examples of different types of reports:

1 Report on an Experiment

- A report on an experiment states a problem or a question that the experiment investigates and may include a prediction of the outcome.
- The report describes the materials used so that others will know what they'll need if they want to perform the experiment. It also tells how the experiment was set up, so that readers will know what procedures were followed.
- Finally, the report carefully records what was observed and states the conclusion that was reached based on the observations.

Model From Literature

In this excerpt from *Adventures With Atoms and Molecules* by Robert C. Mebane and Thomas R. Rybolt, the authors report on an experiment involving hot and cold molecules. Notice that their report begins with a question. It then lists materials, describes the authors' procedure and observations, and ends with their conclusion.

Problem: Do hot molecules move faster than cold molecules?

Materials: food coloring, a glass of hot water, a glass of cold water

Procedure: . . . Add one drop of food coloring to each glass of water. Do not cover the glasses. Watch the color in each glass.

Observations: . . . The hot water becomes colored faster than the cold water.

Conclusion: Hot molecules move faster than cold molecules.

Model From Literature

2 Biographical Sketch

- A biographical sketch gives a brief account of a person's life. It is based on actual facts about the person's experiences.

This excerpt is from "A Backwoods Boy," a biographical sketch of Abraham Lincoln written by Russell Freedman. Notice that Freedman includes dates, places, and facts about his subject's life—all important in a biography. Freedman tells us something about Lincoln's personality, where he grew up, and some key events from his boyhood.

> Abraham Lincoln never liked to talk much about his early life. A poor backwoods farm boy, he grew up swinging an ax on frontier homesteads in Kentucky, Indiana, and Illinois. He was born near Hodgenville, Kentucky, on February 12, 1809, in a log cabin with one window, one door, a chimney, and a hard-packed dirt floor.

Peculiarsome Abe *N. C. Wyeth, The Free Library of Philadelphia*

Thematic Connection: Exploring the Past

Russell Freedman's report offers information about Lincoln's early life to help readers learn more about a man who went on to become one of America's greatest presidents. Have students recall the circumstances of other famous figures whose early lives differed from their later lives. Ask them to explain how knowing the details of a person's early life can reveal something about the kind of person he or she becomes. If students choose to write a biographical sketch, they may wish to focus on the early life of a famous historical figure.

Exploring Related Literature

Refer to *Prentice Hall Literature, Copper*, for Freedman's complete biographical sketch of Lincoln. The following are other examples of biographical sketches included in *Prentice Hall Literature, Copper*: "Virginia Hamilton," by Lee Bennett Hopkins, and "My Papa, Mark Twain," by Susy Clemens.

Teaching From the Model

Guide students to recognize that the Russell Freedman excerpt is an example of the type of report known as a biographical sketch:

- *It provides facts about the subject's life.* A reader could verify the date and place of Lincoln's birth.
- *It reveals something about the subject's personality through the personal experiences described.* For example, Freedman says that Lincoln "never liked to talk much about his early life," then goes on to explain why this might be so: We learn he was so poor that he lived in a log cabin with only a "dirt floor."
- *It gives a brief account of Lincoln's early life.* To describe Lincoln "swinging an ax on frontier homesteads in Kentucky, Indiana, and Illinois" efficiently sums up an entire period in his life.

Teaching From the Model

Guide students to evaluate the model to understand how Patrick Jones's report on *Rock, Rap, and Rad* effectively fulfills the requirements of a nonfiction book report:

- *It gives the author, title, publisher, and copyright date of the book being reviewed.* In this model, this information appears as the opening line.
- *It provides a brief summary of the book.* Jones's first sentence expands upon the title and subtitle of the book.
- *It evaluates how effectively the book addresses its topic.* This information can help readers decide whether this is the book to consult if they are interested in its topic.
- *It gives the reviewer's opinion of the strengths and weaknesses of the book.* Jones provides evidence to support his conclusions.
- *It concludes with the reviewer's recommendation of a potential audience for the book.* This is another way for Jones to give a personal response to the book.

Writing Strategy

Although most students have had experience writing book reports based on fiction, the focus in this chapter is reporting on nonfiction books. Guide students to discuss some distinctions between fiction and nonfiction books and how these distinctions might affect the way a book is evaluated. For example, setting, character development, and plot are key factors to examine in a work of fiction. By contrast, a nonfiction book should be evaluated on how thoroughly, accurately, and clearly it presents information and on how well it reaches its intended audience.

3 Nonfiction Book Report

- When you write a report on a nonfiction book, you tell your audience what is in the book and discuss how thoroughly or accurately the subject is covered.
- You also offer your opinion about the book and explain the reasons why you did or did not like it.

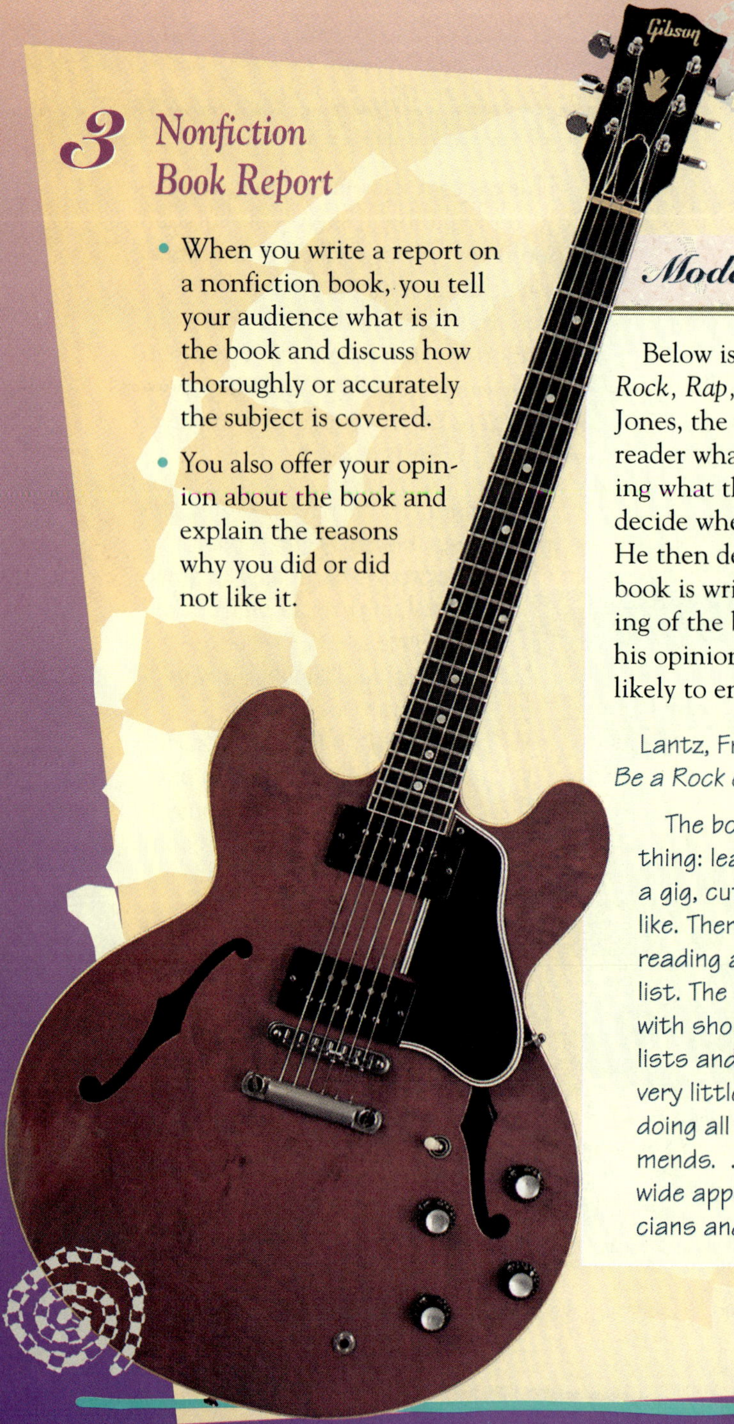

Model From Literature

Below is a book report on Fran Lantz's *Rock, Rap, and Rad.* Notice that Patrick Jones, the writer of the report, tells the reader what to expect. Jones starts by listing what the book includes, so readers can decide whether or not it interests them. He then describes the style in which the book is written and points out a shortcoming of the book. In the end, Jones sums up his opinion of the book and tells who is likely to enjoy it.

Lantz, Fran. *Rock, Rap, and Rad: How to Be a Rock or Rap Star.* Avon Flare, 1992.

The book covers just about everything: learning an instrument, landing a gig, cutting demo tapes, and the like. There's both a recommended reading and a recommended listening list. The book is very easy to read, with short paragraphs and the use of lists and other techniques. There is very little emphasis on the expense of doing all the things Lantz recommends. . . . Still, this should have a wide appeal with both aspiring musicians and air-guitar stars too.

Clarification

Be sure students realize that a reviewer does not have to like a book, but *does* have to read with a critical eye. Also, discuss that the reviewer of a nonfiction book may need to read more than one book on the same topic to be able to judge a book's effectiveness.

Library Research Report

- A library research report can be about almost any topic.
- Information for this type of report is gathered from the many sources available in libraries.
- Source materials are credited within the report and also in a bibliography.

Model From Literature

This excerpt from *Polluting for Pleasure* by Andre Mele presents facts, ideas, and quotations that come from a variety of library resources. Notice that Mele begins by stating the main idea of his report. He then supports his main idea with facts and quotations. The footnote at the end shows the source of the quoted words. Readers can look in the bibliography to find more sources on this topic.

Boatbuilding companies were started, for the most part, by enthusiasts, tinkerers, and inventors with precious little business sense. . . . Many a life's savings was wasted in pursuit of . . . the perfect pleasure boat. . . .

Both Henry Ford and Horace Dodge, highly successful as carmakers, foundered on the rocks of boatbuilding, and Ford is said to have commented after losing millions of dollars at it, "Boatbuilding was a little more difficult than I anticipated." *

---

* Fostle, 1988

Teaching From the Model

Focus on the excerpt from Andrew Mele's report on boatbuilding to help students understand how it exemplifies a library research report:

- *It is based on information from one or more sources.* This passage includes a footnote that refers to a 1988 work by Fostle. Explain that the complete bibliographical information for this source would appear at the end of the report.
- *It presents a main idea with supporting sentences.* In this report about the difficulties of successful boatbuilding, the author supports his point with facts and direct quotations.

Thematic Connection: Social Responsibility

This excerpt comes from Andrew Mele's report *Polluting for Pleasure*, which investigates some of the negative effects of pleasure boating. Discuss with students other kinds of hobbies or sports that people pursue that can harm the environment, such as mountain biking, snowmobiling, or off-road racing. Students may choose to investigate one of these as a topic for a library research report.

Exploring Related Literature

The following are examples of library research reports included in *Prentice Hall Literature, Copper:* "The Strange Geometry of Stonehenge," by Katherine B. Shippen, and "The Giants of Easter Island," by Carrol Alice Stout.

Teaching From the Model

Guide students to understand the characteristics of an I-search report by exploring John C. Lilly's report.

- *It presents a personal recollection about the author's initial interest in his topic.* The excerpt gives facts on how, when, and where Lilly's interest in seagoing mammals was first sparked.
- *It explains how the author decided to begin his research.* In this case, Lilly sought an acquaintance whom he knew was involved in that field.

Thematic Connection: Knowing Yourself/Identity

Tell students that some people develop interests that they pursue throughout their life. Working in small groups, students can list and discuss the interests they themselves have been pursuing. Invite them to tell how their interest began; who, if anyone, encouraged them; and how they locate information about their interest. Students may choose to develop one of their pursuits as the topic of an I-search report.

5 "I-Search" Report

- An I-search report is a personal, in-depth exploration of a topic that especially interests you. You gather as much information as you can in order to become more expert on the topic.
- When you write an I-search, you tell the story of how you became interested in the topic, how you went about exploring it, and what you learned during your exploration.
- You can begin an I-search by listing what you already know or by going to the library and locating books and articles about your topic.

Model From Literature

Man and Dolphin is an I-search about ocean mammals by John C. Lilly, M.D. In the following excerpt, the author tells us how he became interested in seagoing mammals. Notice that Lilly was first inspired by an item he read in the newspaper. Newspapers can be a good source of information for an I-search. Lilly was also fortunate to know an expert in his subject!

My interest in seagoing mammals began in 1949 after a tropical storm had struck New England. George Austin . . . and I were reading the *Boston Herald* in Woods Hole, Massachusetts, at breakfast. The last line of the account of the storm stated: "A whale was blown ashore at Biddeford Pool, Maine." . . . A former neighbor of mine in Swarthmore, Dr. Per Scholander, was working at the Marine Biological Laboratory in Woods Hole. He knows more about whales than anyone of my acquaintance.

Language Acquisition/ ESL Teaching Strategy

The *Writing Lab* offers a variety of options that can be easily adapted to meet the needs of all your ESL students.

- The Gathering Information section includes a slide show about library resources that will provide your basic and intermediate-level ESL students with an opportunity to see and hear information about library resources. As a follow-up, you may wish to take your ESL students to your school's library. Ask your students to identify and locate the references and materials that were discussed in the slide show.
- Since ESL students are often preoccupied with vocabulary and grammar, organizing their ideas becomes even more difficult. Your intermediate and advanced ESL students will find the Branching Organizer activity in the Organizing Information section useful because it helps them organize their

Guided Lesson

Now that you know what reports are, you're ready to begin working on your report. This lesson will help guide you through the process of writing your report. You may not want to start at the beginning of the lesson, however. Consider any ideas you have in mind for your report. Then use this chart to decide where to begin.

	START WITH
• If you **do not have a topic**	Choosing Your Topic
• If you already **have a general topic in mind but need to focus on one aspect of it for your report**	Narrowing Your Topic
• If you **have narrowed your topic but need to determine the appropriate language and content for your readers**	Considering Audience and Purpose
• If you **have established your audience and purpose**	Gathering Information
• If you **have planned the organization of your report and have enough information to work with**	Drafting Your Report

Guiding Student Writing

Addressing Your Classroom Situation

- If possible, arrange for class time in the library with the school librarian, who can help students to develop effective research skills. Anticipate that students may need time to become familiar with the materials and methods available to them.
- If you choose to assign topics or types of reports, allow time for students to narrow the topic to suit their interests or find an appealing angle to pursue.
- You may choose to have students work on reports in pairs. If so, brainstorm with the class to determine ways in which partners might collaborate fairly. For example, each partner could take notes independently from different sources, then combine them later.
- Partners can divide their chosen topic into subtopics that would work well together to form one unified report. Each partner would be responsible for one or more of the subtopics, including the research and writing.

ideas by type and results in a plan that resembles an outline. Have your ESL students work in pairs, helping each other organize their ideas to develop their outlines. Not only will discussion force the students to justify their decisions, but it will offer an important opportunity to develop their oral expression.

- The Drafting section offers many activities designed to help students write their first drafts. ESL students of all levels will benefit from the interactive writing model that compares the introduction and conclusion of the same library research report. You may lead your students in a discussion of what they learned from this activity and then have them work with their drafts. If your ESL students have not yet completed their drafts, ask them to apply the principles they learned from the model when writing.

Addressing Ability Levels

You may want to have your **advanced students** choose a topic by making a prediction about what will happen to a famous person, place, or thing. Students write the prediction as a single sentence. Then, using that statement, students gather facts to support the prediction.

Writers at Work Videodisc

Play the videodisc segment in which Jean Craighead George discusses choosing a topic. Have students notice some of the techniques she uses to observe nature, such as sniffing leaves, observing and listening to a bird, or collecting specimens on a nature walk. Ask:

- How do you think it helps George in her research to use such a variety of techniques?
- How does she record her observations?

Have students link some of George's observation techniques to the topics they are considering. For instance, a student who wants to write a biographical sketch of a hockey player might observe a hockey team at practice to learn more about what makes the subject stand out, or to discover an interesting angle to explore.

Play frames 10950 to 12227

Prewriting

Choosing Your Topic

What will your report be about? You can choose almost anything that interests you. Decide what type of report you'd like to write. Then either choose from a selection of suggested writing options (see pages 212–215) or experiment with the following techniques to come up with your own topic.

If you're considering

. . . a biographical sketch:

Conduct a Series of Interviews

Think about some of the people you know. What were their childhood experiences? What have they accomplished in their lives so far? Over a short period of time, interview several people. They might include family members, friends, a teacher, your doctor, or a shopkeeper. Ask your interviewees about their education, work, and hobbies. Ask them to describe their achievements and disappointments. Take careful notes as you interview each person. Then review your notes to find a topic.

. . . an I-search or a library research report:

Group Activity

Read Your Daily Newspaper

Any page of a newspaper may carry a subject to spark your interest and lead to a research report. A news story might inspire you to research a foreign culture or an aspect of government. The financial section might prompt you to research a new technology. The society pages might suggest a report on the latest wedding fashions. Together with a group of your classmates, explore your local newspaper. Assign each group member a page or a section of the paper in which to identify research topics. Be

Exploring Related Literature

Students who choose to write a biographical sketch may want to read Lee Bennett Hopkins's interview with Virginia Hamilton, which can be found in *Prentice Hall Literature, Copper.*

Collaborative Learning

Have those students who will be conducting interviews for a biographical sketch form a discussion group. Have them brainstorm for plans and strategies that will help them conduct effective interviews. For instance, students might discuss preparing questions in advance, making an appointment to ensure a set time for the interview, locating a quiet place for the interview, bringing a notebook or a video- or audiotape recorder and blank tape, and so on. The group might prepare a list of "Dos and Don'ts" for interviewing to refer to throughout the project.

sure to examine the ads as well as the news stories and special features. After several days, meet to review what each person has found. Keep clippings or lists of subjects to which you can refer when you need a research topic.

. . . report on an experiment:

Explore Your Library's Science Shelves

The shelves of your school or local library hold a number of books describing experiments that can be done by students your age. Check the card or computer catalog under "General Science, Experiments," or look under a specific branch of science, such as chemistry or ecology. If you need help or advice, talk to the librarian or a science teacher at your school. Find one or more books containing experiments in a branch of science that interests you. Then borrow the books or photocopy several experiments that you find interesting. If possible, perform several of the experiments. Remember to take careful notes on your problem (or question), materials, procedures, and results. Keep your notes as a source for your report.

. . . a report on a nonfiction book:

Explore Your Interests at the Library

In nonfiction books you can read about famous people and fascinating places, about nature, technology, and music. You can also learn how to do things—identify wildflowers or improve your soccer skills. Make a list of subjects that interest you. Then go to the library and explore the books that are available on those subjects. Start your search in the subject section of the card or computer catalog. For each of your subjects, list the title, author, and call number of several books. Then locate the books on the shelves and scan them to decide which ones you might like to read for a book report. For future reading, keep a list of the books that seem most interesting.

and nouns on separate sets of index cards, which they can use to make their own idea wheels.

Teaching Strategy

Another strategy that might help students select a topic for a nonfiction book report relies on the Dewey Decimal System. Display the broad breakdown of call numbers that represent nonfiction books: 300's are books on social sciences, 500's are science books, 600's are books on technology and applied science, and so on. After choosing a broad category, students roll a number cube to generate the other two digits. For example, a student who selects the 500's for science books, and then rolls a five and a one would be led to explore the 551's, or books about weather phenomena.

Cross-Curricular Connection: *Science*

You may wish to collaborate with a science teacher to provide a series of hands-on experiments that students can report on. Students conduct the experiments in science class, then use their experiences as the basis for their reports.

Writing Lab CD-ROM

The Choosing Your Topic section of the CD-ROM section includes the following options to help students come up with their own topics:

- **Video clip** Jean Craighead George discusses choosing a topic. She encourages students to choose a simple topic that they can find information about.
- **Idea Wheel activity** Students spin three wheels to generate random combinations of Who-What-Where questions, adjectives, and nouns to create possible ideas for reports.
- **Interactive free association activity** A student narrator describes a simple technique for generating ideas based on what is right in front of you.

Alternate Activity

As an alternative to the Idea Wheel activity in the *Writing Lab* CD-ROM, pairs or groups can list questions, adjectives,

Writing Lab CD-ROM

Using the Inspirations for Reports in the *Writing Lab* is an excellent way to stimulate creativity and to have students explore possible topics for report writing. Students can browse individually or in small groups through the Inspirations. You may let them choose their own writing topics or you may assign topics.

The following is a list of the topic ideas included in the Inspirations in addition to those appearing in the *Sourcebook:*

Biographical Sketch of

- A school athlete
- A writer from another culture
- A hero from the past
- George Washington Carver
- A medical pioneer
- Sir Isaac Newton
- A service professional or volunteer

I-Search Report About

- Space travel
- A Spanish-speaking country
- An Asian Country
- An Explorer
- The effects of weightlessness
- Popular indoor pets
- An honored person's achievements

Nonfiction Book Report on

- A book about an athlete
- An animal guide
- A book about farming
- A book about an island country
- A book about a transportation pioneer
- A book about George Washington Carver
- A book about Helen Keller

Library Research Report on

- The settlement of your state or area
- A sport
- Personal exercise goals
- An endangered species
- An animal in different environments
- Pet laws
- Wildlife protection
- Foods from other countries
- Transportation
- A search for a legendary place or object

Prewriting

Inspirations for Reports

The following are some writing topics for reports:

A Library Research Report on a Celebration From Another Culture

Cultures around the world celebrate special occasions in many different ways. Find out more about a celebration that takes place in a country or a culture other than your own. On what legends, traditions, or historical events is the celebration based? What kinds of music, dances, food, and special clothing are associated with the celebration? Write a research report on the celebration, using the library and other resources. Share your report with your classmates. Consider using photos, music, and other media to enhance your presentation.

A Biographical Sketch of a Famous Athlete

Jackie Joyner-Kersee was one of the most successful Olympic athletes of all time. Find out about Joyner-Kersee's life and achievements, or about those of another famous athlete, by exploring resources available in the library. Then write a biographical sketch of your subject. Focus on events and experiences that helped him or her succeed as an athlete. You may wish to use chronological order to organize your information.

A Biographical Sketch of a Contemporary Hero

Choose a living person—either someone famous or someone you know personally—whom you think of as a hero. Gather information about this person and write a biographical sketch describing your subject's heroic qualities. Be sure to support your statements about this person with examples from his or her life.

A Library Research Report on an Animal's Habitat

Every species of animal needs a particular habitat in which to live and survive. Choose an animal that interests you. Use library resources to find out about the animal's habitat. Take notes on the features of the habitat—landforms, climate, vegetation, and other animal life. How does the animal use the habitat to survive? Write a research report on your findings. If you wish, create a model habitat based on your findings to accompany your report.

A Library Research Report on an Experiment by a Famous Scientist

Marie Curie discovered radium, and Louis Pasteur found a cure for rabies. George Washington Carver's work with plants helped modernize the world of agriculture, and Jonas Salk developed a vaccine against polio. Use the library or other available resources to find out about an experiment performed by a famous scientist. Write a report about the experiment. In the report, identify the hypothesis of the experiment, or the prediction that the scientist was testing. Then list the materials used and the procedures followed. Write a description of what happened and explain the conclusion(s) the scientist reached.

A Library Research Report on a Nonfiction Book About Space Travel

Enormous progress has been made in space travel since the Soviet Union launched *Sputnik I* in 1957. Find a book about an aspect of space travel that interests you. It might be a history of space travel, an account of a particular event like the first moon walk, the story of America's space shuttle program, or a biography of an astronaut. Then write a report in which you discuss the book's content and its organization. Be sure to include what you liked and did not like about the book, and support your opinions with specific details. Mention also the kind of reader who is likely to enjoy the book.

- An endangered species
- An animal that lives in different environments
- A celebration in another culture
- The Dead Sea Scrolls

Cultural Connection

Students who choose to write about a celebration from another culture (page 212) might supplement their library research by interviewing someone in the class or community who is from that culture. This can offer a new dimension to the research. Interviewers can gather information they might not be able to locate through library research alone. Furthermore, the subject may be able to share family objects associated with the celebration—such as special garments, food, and customs—which can help the researcher develop a richer understanding of the celebration.

- Advances in agriculture
- Health risks
- The Dead Sea
- A country in the Middle East
- Land, air, and water pollution
- The history of Japan
- An aspect of Japanese culture
- A local environmental problem
- A celebration
- A foreign culture
- Severe weather safety precautions
- Education for the hearing and visually impaired
- A service occupation
- A service organization

Report on an Experiment

- By George Washington Carver
- About plants
- About weather and soil

Multimedia Presentation on

- Travel brochure
- Space travel
- How weather helps people

Writing Lab CD-ROM

The Inspirations for Reports in the *Writing Lab* also include the following Group Projects and Group Discussions. The Group Projects are structured activities in which students assume different roles. The Group Discussions encourage small groups of students to share their thoughts about an Inspiration and to generate possible writing topics.

Group Projects

- Creating a multimedia report about the Middle East
- Creating a poetry anthology
- Making recommendations for a children's zoo
- Creating a booklet about public services in your area
- Writing an evaluation report about your class
- Creating a multimedia health care display
- Creating a television newscast about a historical moment in space travel history
- Creating a television newscast about severe weather

Group Discussions

- Sharing favorite sports and activities
- Evaluating movie scenes
- Sharing knowledge about cultures as revealed in literature and the arts
- Brainstorming for a list of science and research-related occupations
- Brainstorming for problems caused by pollution and ways they could be solved or prevented
- Sharing knowledge about celebrations
- Exchanging ideas about service groups
- Brainstorming for local issues that need attention and service opportunities for solutions
- Sharing thoughts about the quest for youth

MORE *Inspirations* for Reports

A Library Research Report on the Common Cold

Over the centuries, scientists have made great advances in the treatment of many diseases. However, there is still no way of preventing or curing the common cold. How do you catch a cold? What happens to your body when you have a cold? How do you treat a cold? Use library resources to find out about colds. Then write a report on the common cold. Tell about its causes, symptoms, and treatments, and discuss the likelihood that a cure will be found. Remember to document your sources.

A Library Research Report on an Experiment About the Effects of Salt in Water

People can float like corks in very salty water, such as that of the Great Salt Lake in Utah or the Dead Sea, which lies between Israel and Jordan. How does salt affect the ease with which people and objects float in water? Make a prediction about the effect of salt. Think about a way you can test your prediction, or hypothesis, using materials that are readily available. Design an experiment, including a list of the materials needed; the procedure, or steps, to be followed; and an outline for observing and recording results. If possible, perform your experiment and report on the actual results you observe and the conclusions you draw.

Group Project: Report on the Effects of Pollution

Pollution of water, land, and air can seriously affect plant and animal life. Imagine that you are a citizens committee concerned about the effects of pollution on your community. As a group, discuss some of the problems that pollution causes. Share ideas about how these problems could be solved or prevented. Then have each group member pursue one type of pollution as the subject of an I-search report. Each report should discuss the causes and effects of the pollution and the pros and cons of various courses of action for stopping it. The reports should also describe how the information was found. Illustrate the reports with appropriate charts, graphs, and drawings, and gather them into a binder. Create a title page and a table of contents for your collection.

Commuters II *Diana Ong*

An I-Search Report on a Form of Transportation

This painting by Diana Ong focuses on the subway, one of the most popular forms of transportation in large cities. Think about a type of transportation that interests you. It might be a taxi, bus, ferry boat, helicopter—or the subway. Become expert on a particular form of transportation by completing an I-search on the topic. Start by listing some questions you have about your subject. Then find answers to the questions by using the library and other resources. In your report, explain why you chose your topic, how you researched it, and what you learned.

An I-Search Report on Food Distribution

What did you eat for breakfast this morning? Eggs and toast? A bowl of cereal with milk and fruit? Where did your food come from, and how did it reach you? There are many steps in the chain that transports food from its source to our dinner plates. Learn about how food gets to your table by completing an I-search on this topic. Choose one type of food. Then find out how it is raised, processed, shipped, and sold. When you write your report, remember to include how you researched the information.

Cross-Curricular Connection: *Science*

Those students interested in writing an I-search report on transportation might consider forms of space travel as a topic. One resource for them to use in answering their initial questions on this topic is their science teacher. Another good place to begin is Neil McCleer's report "Space Stations of the Mind," which can be found in *Prentice Hall Literature, Copper.*

Writing Lab CD-ROM

The Narrowing Your Topic section includes the following options to help students come up with their own topics:

- **An animated example of narrowed topics** allows students to see and hear ideas on how to narrow a topic.
- **A Topic Web activity** helps students narrow their topics.
- **Interactive models** show how a topic can be narrowed; for example, students see Astronomy, a broad topic, narrowed to Comets, then to Halley's Comet.
- **An interactive model of how to use *Who/What/When/Where/Why* questions to narrow a topic** allows students to see how answers to such questions can lead to a narrowed version of an interesting topic.

Working individually or in small groups, students can experiment with the activities to find those that work best.

Addressing Ability Levels

You may want to have your **more-challenged students** refer to the Writing Hints to help them narrow a topic. This screen poses three questions to guide students to narrow a topic more effectively:

- What are some examples of people, places, things, or events that fit into my topic?
- What's one part of the history of my topic?
- Why am I interested in my topic?

Narrowing Your Topic

Some topics are much broader than others. Some are best suited for a book. Others are just right for a brief article. To decide whether your topic is narrow enough to cover fully in your report, ask yourself these questions:

Questions for Narrowing Your Topic

- How long will your report be?
- Will you be able to include all the important information and necessary details within this length?
- Can your topic be divided into subtopics or sections? (If so, write them down and decide which aspect is most interesting.)
- Can the most interesting subtopic stand alone as a topic?

Use a Topic Web to Narrow Your Topic

One way to narrow your topic is to weave a topic web, such as the one below. Enter your broad topic on the top line; then divide it into subtopics. Next, divide your subtopics into subtopics, and so on. Look through your narrowed topics and decide which one would make the best topic for a report.

Student Model: Topic Web

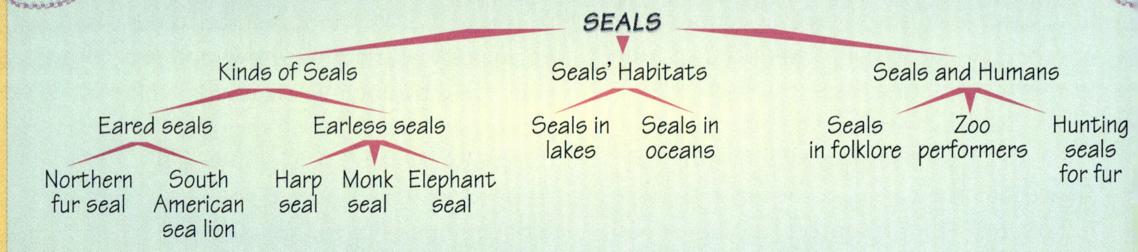

Language Lab CD-ROM

If students need additional guidance in narrowing their topics, have them complete the Narrowing Your Topic lesson in the Composing unit.

Considering Your Audience

Decide on the audience for your report. Your audience will determine the details you include in your report and the language you will use. Will your audience be your teacher, your friends, your family, or the readers of a local newspaper? How much do they already know about your topic? If your readers are familiar with your topic, do not include background information that they would already know. Instead, provide a fresh perspective on your topic and focus on the features that may be new to your audience. If your audience is not familiar with your topic, provide basic information and define all technical terms.

Considering Your Purpose

Decide on your purpose. One of the best ways to determine your purpose is to ask yourself these questions about possible purposes for your report:

- How do you want your audience to feel about your topic?
- What do you want them to know about your topic?
- What is the main idea you hope to communicate?

Look over your answers to these questions. Based on your answers, state your purpose in a single phrase or sentence.

Writing Hints

After you've identified your purpose, be sure to include the right information to help you accomplish it. Use the following chart as a guide.

If you want your audience to	
. . . have a favorable impression of your topic:	Include facts, details, and examples that show the strengths, advantages, and other favorable points.
. . . have a negative impression of your topic:	Include facts, details, and examples that show the weaknesses, disadvantages, and other unfavorable points.
. . . understand the significance of your topic:	Include cause-and-effect information that shows how your topic affects other events, ideas, or people.
. . . know the history of your topic:	Include details about dates, places, and events in chronological order.

Writing Lab CD-ROM

The Considering udience section includes the llowing options to help students explore ways to gear eir writing to the intended dience:

- **Interactive annotated models** Students explore excerpts that illustrate the effect of audience on a writer's choice of details.
- **Audience Profile activity** Students answer questions that help them focus on their intended audience.

Working individually or in small groups, students can experiment with the activities to find those that work best for them.

Addressing Ability Levels

Suggest that your **more-advanced students** who plan to write a report on a topic about which they know a great deal write for an audience who has little or no familiarity with or interest in the subject. For instance, a student with vast knowledge about rap music might write for people who have never heard rap music or who are more interested in other forms of music. Although any report should be clearly written and well organized, this approach presents writers with the challenge and opportunity to express to others why their interest is so compelling.

Writing Lab CD-ROM

The Considering Purpose section includes the following options to help students examine what part of their topic to emphasize, what information will be useful, how to present information, and the most appropriate style of language:

- **Video clip from *Star Trek*** Students see and hear Spock attempting to determine the specific purpose of a group of travelers.
- **Purpose Checklist** Students answer questions to help them focus their purpose.
- **Writing Hints** Students are given suggestions for accomplishing their purpose.

Working individually or in small groups, students can experiment with the activities to find those that work best for them.

Language Lab CD-ROM

If students need additional guidance in determining how best to deal with the issues of audience and purpose, you may want them to complete the Considering Audience and Purpose lesson in the Composing unit.

Writing Lab CD-ROM

The Gathering Information section includes the following options designed to help students learn methods for gathering information and developing a research plan:

- **Video clip from *Star Trek*** Students observe how Captain Kirk obtains information from a computer.
- **K-W-L Chart (Know-Want to know-Learn) activity** Students use this graphic organizer to plan and implement their research.
- **Slide show about library resources** Students see and hear information about library resources.
- **Guidelines for taking detailed, clear notes** Students can refer to this checklist of tips to guide their research.
- **Interactive models of notes taken from a book, an article, and an experiment** Students use these models to see how to take notes from a variety of sources.
- **Interactive models of source cards** Students are shown the proper way to cite sources when using an encyclopedia, a book, and a magazine article.
- **Writing Hints** Students are given tips to help them decide how to focus their research.

Working individually or in small groups, students can experiment with the activities to find those that work best for them. When they finish working through this section, students should have a research plan that they can implement using the library or other resources.

Prewriting

Gathering Information

Before you can write your report, you need to gather information on your topic. Through this process you will discover many things that you didn't know before. The following suggestions can help you plan your research:

List What You Know and What You Want to Find Out

Before you start your research, list some important things that you already know about your topic. Then list questions to which you want answers. Keep your lists with you as you gather information. New questions will surely arise during your research. Add the new questions to your list as you go along, and then look for the answers.

Begin at the Library

Your school or local library should provide you with almost everything you need to research your topic. When you begin your research, you may be overwhelmed by the amount of information that is available. If so, you may need to narrow your topic further. If you can't find enough information, however, you may need to choose another topic.

Following are some of the many types of resources you can explore in the library:

- **Encyclopedias** and other reference works provide basic facts about a topic.
- **Nonfiction books,** located in the card or computer catalog, supply more in-depth information.
- ***The Reader's Guide to Periodical Literature*** will help you locate recent magazine and newspaper articles for more up-to-date information on your topic.
- **On-line information services** may furnish the most recent information.

Ask your librarian for additional help in using these sources of information.

Take Detailed Notes

As you gather information, compile detailed notes that you'll be able to follow when you write your report. Use these tips to guide you:

- **Write your notes on 3" x 5" or 4" x 6" index cards.** Use one card for each note, and give each note a key word so you'll be able to sort the notes and organize them later.

Addressing Ability Levels

Challenge your **more-advanced students** to keep a research log that describes the adventure of searching for information. Remind them of the videodisc interview with Jean Craighead George, in which she kept a log of her observations with sketches and diagrams and notes from reference materials. Students may find that by keeping such a log they will jot down ideas for future projects.

Teaching Strategy

Students who may have limited access to a library may require help to refocus their ideas to benefit from the resources that are available to them. For example, if the only available resources are an encyclopedia and some content-area texts, students might find a topic in a textbook, then turn to the encyclopedia for more informatic to expand upon it.

- **Write each fact or idea clearly.** Always double-check the spelling of names and technical terms after you write them. It saves checking them later.
- **Use quotation marks if you copy exact words** from your source.
- **Record the title of the book or article and the page number** on each card.
- **Create a source card** for each resource, listing the author, the title, the publisher, and the place and date of publication.

Look at these examples of a note card and source cards:

Writing Models

SAMPLE NOTE CARD

Key word	Language
Note	As girls, Yoshiko and her sister spoke a mixture of English and Japanese
Book title	Invisible Thread (underlined)
Page number	p. 17

SAMPLE SOURCE CARD FOR A MAGAZINE ARTICLE

Author	Popkin, James (last name, first name)
Article title	"A Break for Wild Cockatoos" (in quotation marks)
Magazine title	U.S. News and World Report (underlined)
Publication date	November 9, 1992
Page number	p. 99

SAMPLE SOURCE CARD FOR A BOOK

Author	Uchida, Yoshiko (last name, first name)
Book title	The Invisible Thread: A Memoir (underlined)
Publisher	Julian Messner
Place of publication	Englewood Cliffs, NJ
Copyright date	1991

Language Lab CD-ROM

If students need additional practice in the use of quotation marks or capitalization to help them do their research, you may want them to complete the lessons on Quotation Marks and Proper Nouns in the Capitalization and Punctuation units of the *Language Lab*.

Writing Strategy

Help students understand the distinction between cards that contain facts and those that cite sources. It may help them to use different-colored pens to differentiate these two types of cards. Some students may use colored index cards for sources and white index cards for notes.

Tell students that they are likely to generate many note cards that correspond to one source card. Students may devise a code system to link note cards with their source card. Or they may clip or band note cards together behind the related source card until they are ready to organize their notes.

Group Discussion

An important point to emphasize to students as they do research is the value of using a variety of sources. An encyclopedia article, for instance, can provide a basic introduction to a topic. More detailed information should then be obtained from articles or books that focus on the topic. Point out that a variety of references can help the report writer make a balanced and thorough examination of a topic. Invite students to share examples of conflicting facts or differing points of view or conclusions among sources. Ask students why variations may occur and how they can be dealt with, as they gather information and later as they write.

Writing Lab CD-ROM

The Organizing Information section of the tutorial on Reports in the *Writing Lab* includes the following options designed to help students organize their information:

- **A technique for identifying a thesis** Students can follow a four-step process to decide on a focus or main idea for their report.
- **A Branching Organizer activity** Students arrange their facts and ideas by type, which results in a plan that resembles an outline students can refer to during the drafting phase.
- **Interactive models** Students examine groups of ideas that are organized either by type, by chronological order, or by importance.
- **Keyhole Organizer activity** Students arrange facts and ideas in order of importance.
- **Timeline activity** Students organize facts in time order.
- **Notecard activity** Students rearrange note cards until they hit upon an organizational plan they think works best.

Working individually or in small groups, students can experiment with the activities to find those that work best for them.

Alternate Activity

As an alternative to using the Timeline activity on the CD-ROM, students can organize notes in chronological order by creating a timeline on notebook paper or a long sheet of butcher paper.

Students can try a variation of the Notecard activity by using their own handwritten note cards.

Prewriting

Organizing Your Information

Well-organized writing helps your readers follow your thinking. To begin organizing, decide on the main idea, or focus, of your report. Then decide which key points you wish to make and how you'll arrange them. Follow these steps:

- First, **read your notes** to review the information you've found.
- Next, **identify the key point** or key words of each note.
- Then, **sort your note cards into groups** according to key points or key words. If a fact or a detail is not related to your main idea, eliminate it.
- Finally, **determine the one main idea** that the key points have in common.

Choose an Organization Plan

After you've grouped your notes, decide on a way to organize your report. You can organize your details in order of importance, in chronological order, or by type.

Order of Importance

- When some of the ideas related to your topic are more important than others, you can organize them by order of importance. You might start with the most important ideas and end with the least important, or you could start with the least important and end with the most important.

Writing Model

In the following, details are organized by order of importance, beginning with the most significant fact of Wilt Chamberlain's basketball career. Notice that the other two details support the writer's main idea but are not as important as the first.

Topic: Wilt Chamberlain

Main idea: Chamberlain is a basketball legend.

1. Holds the all-time scoring record
2. Led the league in scoring from 1960 through 1966
3. Only center to lead the league in assists

Writers at Work Videodisc

Review the videodisc segment in which Jean Craighead George discusses focusing her ideas by looking over her information until she notices a theme emerging. Point out that once students settle on a main idea they should use only the facts that pertain to and support that idea. Ask:

- Why do you think Jean Craighead George might change her focus after she has done her research?
- Why do you think she says that it's "much easier to pull your material together" when you see the theme that emerged?

Play frames 14772 to 15229

Ordering by Type

- When you organize information by type, you group related ideas together. This method of organization is especially useful for writing about topics that can be divided into parts of equal importance.

Writing Model

In the example below, notice that the writer grouped the information by type for a report on Japanese society.

Family Life	The Arts	Religions
1. Children study hard	1. Scroll painting	1. Shinto
2. Grandparents often live with family	2. Haiku	2. Buddhism
	3. Noh and Kabuki theater	3. Zen

Chronological Order

- Chronological order is the order in which the events occurred. Use chronological order when you're writing about a sequence of events.

Writing Model

Look at the following notes about the poet and fiction writer Langston Hughes. Notice that the writer has arranged the notes in the order in which the events occurred.

1. Langston Hughes was born in Joplin, Missouri, in 1902.
2. He grew up in Cleveland, Ohio.
3. He began writing when he was young.
4. His first poem was published while he was still in high school!

Langston Hughes *c. 1925, Winold Reiss, The National Portrait Gallery, Smithsonian Institution*

Clarification

Point out that although ordering by type is one plan students can choose, this method can be seen as an umbrella for other ways to organize ideas. For instance, the notes on Langston Hughes's life are given chronologically, yet they are also related by type—events of his early life. The next part of this report might provide information chronologically about another phase of his life, such as his experiences during the Harlem Renaissance.

Addressing Ability Levels

Your **more-challenged students** may work more effectively in pairs. This enables them to bounce ideas back and forth as they work, in order to find the best way to organize information for their report.

Clarification

Point out that information given in chronological order need not include specific dates. In the Writing Model on page 221 of the *Sourcebook*, the only date given is 1902, the year Langston Hughes was born. Readers infer the order of the other statements from clues that each one contains.

Establishing Assessment Criteria

Before students begin drafting their reports, you may want to share with them the criteria you will use to evaluate their work. The following guidelines are included in the tutorial on Reports in the *Writing Lab* CD-ROM. You can use them as given or modify them to suit your needs.

- Does your report have a narrow, focused topic?
- Does your report contain accurate facts and details from a variety of sources?
- Is your report well organized?
- Does your report have an introduction that states the main idea, a body that supports it, and a conclusion that summarizes it?
- Do you give credit to your sources of information?
- Is your report free of errors in spelling, punctuation, and capitalization?

Writing Lab CD-ROM

The Drafting section includes the following options to help students write the first draft of their reports:

- **Interactive models of introductions, body paragraphs, and conclusions** Students explore excerpts from different types of reports through annotations explaining the key features of each model.
- **Transition Word Bin activity** Students use transitional words to show connections between ideas that indicate organization by type, by chronological order, or by order of importance.
- **Comparison** Students see the introduction and conclusion of the same library research report side by side to demonstrate how these parts of the report work together.
- **Interactive Student Model of a completed draft** Students examine the first draft of a student's report, including an audio annotation by the author that explains her thinking.
- **Video clip** Students hear tips from Jean Craighead George on how to overcome writer's block.

Literature Connection

Suggest that students study examples of reports in *Prentice Hall Literature*, *Copper*, to see how each begins. See the list of selections on page 198b.

Drafting

If you have gathered all your information and organized your notes, you are ready to write your first draft. Refer back to your outline or your organized notes as you write. Also, remember to keep your audience and purpose in mind. Your draft should have an introduction, body paragraphs that support your main idea, and a conclusion. For help in writing each of these parts, look at the following suggestions.

Writing the Introduction

Begin your report with an introduction in which you present your main idea, grab your readers' interest, and make a transition to the body of the report. Here are some examples:

Writing Model

Introduction to a Biographical Sketch

Here is the first sentence of an introduction to a biographical sketch of George Washington Carver. Notice how the writer catches her readers' interest and indicates the focus of her report.

From peanuts to plastics, George Washington Carver used his knowledge and talents to improve the economy of the South.

Writing Model

Introduction to a Library Research Report

In this passage from an introduction to a library research report, the writer states the main idea, connects the topic to the audience's prior knowledge, and introduces the subtopics covered in the body of the report.

The area that is now Southern Mexico was once home to the Mayas, one of the most advanced civilizations in the Western Hemisphere. By AD 400, the Mayas had developed a complex system of writing and had made advances in science, mathematics, architecture, and the arts.

Writing the Body

In the body of your report, develop and support your main idea with facts and examples. Focus each paragraph on a single key point stated in a topic sentence. Make sure that all the sentences in a paragraph support the topic sentence. Looking at these model passages from the bodies of reports by other writers will help you write the body of your report.

Writing Model

Body of an I-Search Report

An I-search differs from that of other reports because it is told as a narrative, or a story. Notice that this body paragraph includes the details of the search as well as the information that was found.

While helping me locate books about the arts in West Africa, the librarian suggested that I also write to the consulates of some of the West African countries. I contacted the consulates of Senegal, Mali, and Burkina Faso. I was surprised to learn that several award-winning films have been produced in Senegal.

Writing Model

Body of a Library Research Report

In the body of a library research report, focus each paragraph on a single subtopic of your main point. Notice that this paragraph focuses entirely on the causes of erosion.

Erosion can occur in several ways. A sandy area that has few trees or plants can easily be eroded by the wind. Erosion can occur in hilly areas after a severe storm. The sudden rush of water can carry away soil and uproot plants. Canyons, such as the Grand Canyon, are the result of millions of years of erosion by strong, swift river currents.

Teaching Strategy

You may wish to copy the list of drafting tips from he CD-ROM lesson onto a oster and hang it in the lassroom for students to refer o as they work. These tips elate to the specific mode of eport writing, but they can lso prove valuable for other kinds of writing that students will do throughout the year.

Language Lab CD-ROM

Students who need more practice in writing introductions, body paragraphs, or conclusions may benefit from working on the following lessons from the Building Paragraphs unit of the *Language Lab* CD-ROM: Main Idea and Topic Sentence, Supporting Sentences, Concluding Sentences, Unity in Paragraphs, Transitional Words.

Varying the Writing Process

A well-structured report has three distinct sections—the introduction, the body, and the conclusion. Students may consider starting with whichever section they feel most comfortable, then going back to write the remaining ones. For example, a student might draft the introduction and conclusion together, because these sections often parallel each other.

Writers at Work Videodisc

Replay the videodisc segment in which Jean Craighead George discusses writing her first draft. Have students listen for techniques George uses, such as revising as she writes, rereading to make adjustments, and fleshing out sections that need more detail. Ask:

- Why would George revise as she writes? Do you find this a useful technique when you write?
- How does George justify leaving out information she so carefully gathered during the research phase of the report?

Play frames 15231 to 17392

Language Acquisition/ ESL Teaching Strategy

As a preparation to writing their conclusions, your intermediate and advanced ESL students can practice writing conclusions for reports already completed by others. Make copies of library research reports from your current or former students, being sure to cover the concluding paragraph. Give these reports to your ESL students and ask them to write a conclusion based on the information provided in the report. They should then compare their conclusions with that of the original. The students may work individually or in small groups. Lead your ESL students in a discussion of the elements of a conclusion and how it restates the main idea and the key points of the report. Your students are now ready to work on the conclusions of their own reports.

Writing Strategy

Suggest that as students draft their reports they consider using headings and/or subheadings. Headings can indicate the main idea of a section. Subheadings can signal the parts of that idea. This technique can help students organize as they write and can be useful if they wish to create a table of contents.

Writing Lab CD-ROM

The Drafting section of the tutorial on Reports includes the following options to help students credit their sources:

- **List of guidelines** Students receive direct instructions for when to indicate sources of information and why this is an important aspect of report writing.
- **Interactive models of methods of citing sources** Students see two ways to cite sources: footnotes and parentheses. They hear audio comments that explain guidelines for using each style.
- **Interactive model of a bibliography** Students see how to list sources in a bibliography, with comments that provide details of the citation.

Working individually or in small groups, students can experiment with the activities to find those that work best.

Writing the Conclusion

In your conclusion, restate your main idea and sum up your key points. Look at the following example from a library research report.

Writing Model

Conclusion to a Library Research Report

The introduction to this library research report stated that the Mayan culture was one of the most advanced in this part of the world. Notice that the conclusion restates the main idea. It also summarizes the key points that support the main idea.

The ancient Mayas show that a society does not have to be modern to be advanced. They made great achievements in mathematics, science, architecture, and the arts. The Mayas were one of the most advanced civilizations of their time.

Crediting Your Sources

Your report will probably include information from books, magazines, reference works, interviews, and other sources. You must indicate the source of your information whenever you use someone else's exact words, use a statistic that readers may want to check, or use little-known facts. Providing the source of the information tells your readers that the information came from someone else and allows your readers to check your facts. To see different methods for crediting your sources, turn to Developing Your Style 1 on page 229.

Revising and Editing

FROM a WRITER

"The first draft is a process of organizing in my head. I will change it many times before I get to the final. I rewrite five, six times."

—Jean Craighead George

Revising Your Work

Read through your draft looking for ways to improve it. Check to see that you have clearly stated and thoroughly supported your main idea. Each time you find something that doesn't seem quite right, work on revising it until you feel satisfied with it. To help you revise, use the following guidelines. You should be able to answer yes to all the questions. If your answers to any of the questions is no, work on improving those aspects of your writing.

Revision Checklist

- Does your report have a narrow, focused topic? If not, find one aspect of your topic that you can adequately cover in detail.
- Does your report contain sufficient facts and details from a variety of sources? If not, review your notes and, if necessary, check your original sources for additional facts and details.
- Is your report well organized? If not, rearrange your information so that it is presented in a logical order. Also check the coherence of your paragraphs, and eliminate or revise any sentences that do not focus on the paragraph's main idea.
- Does your report have an introduction that states the main idea, a body that supports it, and a conclusion that summarizes it? If not, strengthen the areas that are weak.
- Do you give credit to your sources of information? If not, add footnotes or credits in parentheses wherever you have used someone else's exact words, statistics, or little-known facts.

Writing Lab CD-ROM

The Revising and Editing section includes the following options to help students revise their first drafts:

- **Interactive models for self-revision** Students hear explanations of decisions made during one writer's revisions.
- **Interactive checklist** Students answer questions to help them evaluate and revise their reports.
- **Interactive word-replacement activity** Students choose from a list of informal words to see more formal words that could replace them.
- **Revision checker for coherence** This tool helps students check for coherence by highlighting the first and last sentences of each paragraph in their reports.
- **Revised student model with audio annotations** Students read the revision and hear the writer explain why she made specific changes to the first draft.

Working individually or in small groups, students can experiment with the activities to find those that work best.

Teaching Strategy

You may want to make a large version of the Revision Checklist on page 225 of the *Sourcebook* to post in your room so students can refer to it as they revise their work. Feel free to adapt the list to include ideas or techniques that students suggest to address each question or problem.

Writers at Work Videodisc

To emphasize the importance of the revision phase, replay the section of the videodisc in which Jean Craighead George discusses revision. Have students discuss what they learned. Ask:

- What technique does George use to replace a cliché or an ineffective word?
- How does George check for accuracy?
- Why would she add details after she finishes a first draft?

Play frames 17396 to 18648

Student Model: Revised Draft

Here is a revised paragraph from a library research report on elephant seals by Leisje Lindstedt, a student at Southport Middle School in Port St. Lucie, Florida. Notice that she reorganized the paragraph so that it begins with a topic sentence.

Having a Peer Review Your Work

Sometimes someone else can spot problems that you've missed. Work with a peer to get a fresh opinion of your report. Ask one of your classmates to read your draft. Have that person answer questions such as those below. Listen carefully to your peer editor's responses, and make appropriate changes to your draft.

Peer Review Checklist

- Did the writer choose an appropriate topic for the report? Was it narrow enough?
- What is the most interesting part of this draft? Why is it interesting?
- What is the least interesting part? Why isn't it interesting?
- What did you learn about the subject?
- Were you confused at any point? How can the writer make the report easier to understand?

Proofreading

After revising your work, check it carefully for errors in grammar, spelling, punctuation, and capitalization. For help in proofreading your writing, use the following guidelines:

Proofreading Checklist

- Are all the sentences complete?
- Does every sentence end with the correct punctuation?
- Are commas and other punctuation marks correct?
- Are direct quotations punctuated correctly?
- Are all the words spelled correctly? Check the spelling of any words you're not sure of.
- Does every sentence begin with a capital letter?
- Do all proper nouns and proper adjectives begin with capital letters?

Peer Revision

Some students have trouble working with a peer editor. One way to make this process more effective is to encourage peer editors to identify problems clearly and specifically and to offer constructive suggestions to the writer for addressing problems in the draft.

In addition to discussing questions presented in the *Sourcebook*, you might ask others, such as these:

- Does your introduction grab the reader's attention? If not, can you suggest how to revise it?
- Can you follow the topics and subtopics presented? Would it help to use headings?
- Do you notice a gap in the information presented? What should the writer do to fix this?
- Do the conclusions follow from the information presented? If not, how should the writer revise this?

Writing Lab CD-ROM

The Proofreading section includes the following options to help students develop strategies for proofreading their reports:

- **Proofreading Checklist** This checklist is also provided on page 226 of the *Sourcebook*.
- **Interactive student model with audio annotations** Students see and hear explanations of how the writer knew that changes were needed.
- **Capitalization hints** Students are reminded to check for correct capitalization and are given examples to guide them.

Working individually or in small groups, students can experiment with these activities to find those that work best.

Teaching Strategy

You may want to have students proofread with a different peer editor from the one who helped with revising and editing. A fresh eye may detect errors previously missed.

Publishing and Presenting

After you've finished revising and proofreading your report, you may want to share it with others. Following are a few ways you can publish your work:

Conduct a Critics' Corner Gather with three or four of your classmates who have reported on nonfiction books. You might form your group with classmates who reported on books with similar topics: animals, science, or biographies of athletes or heroes, for example. Form a "Critics' Corner," at which you discuss the books you reported on. Each member should present his or her book and give reasons for recommending—or not recommending—it. You might conduct your Critics' Corner as a panel discussion, giving the rest of the class a chance to ask the panel members questions about their books.

Present a Mini-Lesson on Your Topic You probably learned a lot about your topic as you researched and wrote your report. You might share what you've learned by using your report as the basis of a mini-lesson on your topic. Plan a lesson that includes an activity related to the topic of your report. Present your lesson to a group of classmates.

Create a Bulletin Board Display Give your teachers and fellow students a chance to read your reports by mounting them in an attractive bulletin board display. Arrange the reports either by topic or by type. Add any appropriate artwork, and create an interesting title for the display.

Reflecting on Your Writing

What can you learn from the process you went through while writing your report? The following questions will help you reflect on your writing:

- What did you learn about your subject while writing your report? What else would you have liked to learn?
- If you were starting over, would you approach the assignment differently? Why or why not? What would you do differently?
- How can you apply what you have learned to your other writing assignments?

Writing Lab CD-ROM

The Publishing and Presenting section of the tutorial on Reports in the *Writing Lab* includes the following options:

- **Suggested ideas for publishing and presenting reports**
- **Writing Hints** Students can consider ways to share completed reports with a more limited audience.

Teaching Strategies

Help students form critics groups if groups do not readily suggest themselves. You may allow some groups to present their reports to other classes.

Students who present a mini-lesson can videotape their presentation so it can be shared with other classes, or kept as an audiovisual selection for their portfolio.

Collaborative Learning

Assign a group the task of creating an attractive bulletin board display. Jobs may include making titles or headings, creating a background, finding or making illustrations, labeling displayed works, categorizing reports, and designing and preparing feedback forms that students can fill out after they read a posted report.

Portfolio Assessment

Have students write an evaluative statement that addresses some of the questions posed on page 227 of the *Sourcebook*. If students decide to include the finished report in their portfolio, they might attach this statement to it. Otherwise, the statement itself can go into the portfolio as a record of self-evaluation.

The following questions can be used to supplement the questions in the *Sourcebook:*

- What part of the report-writing process did you find most satisfying? Most challenging?
- How do you feel about writing a report, as compared with writing other kinds of compositions?
- Did your research spark a new interest or awaken an old one? Explain.
- In what ways has your writing shown the most improvement? In which areas should you focus your attention in future assignments?

After students have evaluated their work, confer with them to decide what to include in their portfolios. Students can select the completed report and/or earlier drafts, note cards, prewriting notes, outlines, or any other parts they think reflect growth and progress. Remind students to date all the work they add to their portfolios.

Technology Note Networking:

Share the reports your class created with other students across the country via CompuServe, America Online, or the Internet. Aside from organizing reports by topics, you could organize them by themes, such as Exploring the Past, Nature, or Heroes. Request that other classrooms exchange similar reports so that students can compare and contrast styles, approaches, and conclusions.

Teaching From the Model

Draw students' attention to how Leisje Lindstedt's library research report includes the major parts of a strong report:

- *It begins with an engaging opening sentence.* Leisje chose to open with a question to grab the reader's attention.
- *The introductory paragraph states the topic of the report and gives the writer's slant.* Leisje is writing about the elephant seal and how it had been an endangered animal.
- *The next three paragraphs are body paragraphs that support the main idea through subtopics.* Paragraph two is about the elephant seals' appearance; paragraph three is about their size; paragraph four is about their near extinction.
- *Sources are cited.* The writer has chosen to use parenthetical citations. This excerpt reflects information from at least two sources, although others may appear in the bibliography, which is not available here.
- *The concluding paragraph makes a smooth transition from the paragraph before it.* The writer thanks Mexico for its efforts to protect elephant seals. She also refers back to the introduction, where she stated that elephant seals nearly faced extinction.

Student Model

Here is the complete, final draft of Leisje Lindstedt's library research report on elephant seals.

Here I gave the main idea for my report, which is that elephant seals are big and odd looking and that they almost became extinct.

Here my topic sentence makes it clear that this paragraph will be about the seal's appearance.

I decided to use parentheses instead of footnotes to credit my sources.

In my conclusion I referred again to the seal's looks and to the fact that it was almost extinct.

Elephant Seals

by Leisje Lindstedt

What has no ears and a big snout and can be found living in oceans all around the world? Answer: the elephant seal. The elephant seal is known for its unusual appearance and size, but there was a time when it was in danger of not being known at all.

Elephant seals have a comical appearance that is revealed by their name. Male elephant seals have a long proboscis, or snout. Although this "trunk" is not as long as an elephant's, it is similar. The elephant seal's skin is coarse and wrinkled, with dull brown hair.

Also like elephants, elephant seals are very large. They grow to be 18 feet long and can weigh as much as 5 tons (*Macmillan Illustrated Animal Encyclopedia*, p. 110). Fortunately, they have 6 inches of blubber to keep them warm, since they spend much of their time swimming in the cold waters of the Atlantic and Pacific oceans. Even baby elephant seals are large. After they are born, they can gain up to 10 pounds a day!

The elephant seals almost became extinct. In the 1800's, they were hunted for their fat and oil, and by 1911 there were only a few left. They were surviving on Guadeloupe Island off the coast of Mexico. Then the Mexican government gave them protection, and today their numbers are increasing (*Collier's Encyclopedia*, Vol. 20, p. 559). Thanks to Mexico, these enormous strange-looking "elephants of the sea" can again be found in the world's oceans.

Developing Your Style 1

Citing Sources

When you write, give the sources for quotations, facts, and ideas that are not your own. You can credit a source by using either **parentheses** or **footnotes**. A citation in parentheses follows the information to which it refers. It includes the author's last name and the page number on which the information appeared.

"Armstrong, Aldrin, and the 10 astronauts who followed returned with samples that contain a fascinating history of the moon and the Earth." (Taylor, p. 40)

To use a footnote citation, place a number at the end of the quotation. Then at the bottom of the page, write the same number, followed by source information:

"Armstrong, Aldrin, and the 10 astronauts who followed returned with samples that contain a fascinating history of the moon and the Earth."[1]

1. Taylor, p. 40.

A bibliography is an alphabetical list of the sources you consulted for your report. Look at these examples to see the correct form:

Interview	Beamer, Emily. Interview. October 12, 1995.
Encyclopedia entry	"Moon." *Encyclopaedia Britannica*. Vol. 8, p. 299, 1990.
Full-length book	Sagan, Carl. *Cosmos*. New York: Random House, 1980.
Magazine article	Taylor, G. Jeffrey. "The Scientific Legacy of Apollo." *Scientific American*, July 1994, pp. 40–47.

Practice Activities

1. Write a parenthetical citation and a footnote for each source:
1. *History of Art* by H.W. Janson, page 40.
2. "Dream Machines" by Mark C. Timney, page 22

2. Write a bibliographical entry for this source:
Book title: *The Illustrated History of Magic;* author: Milton Christopher; publisher: Thomas Y. Crowell Company; place: New York; date: 1973

Writer's Companion

For additional support and reinforcement for preparing a bibliography, direct students to the section on research reports, which covers the forms for bibliography entries, along with other general information about report writing.

Practice Activities Answers

1. a. (Janson, p. 40); [1] Janson, p. 40.
b. (Timney, p. 22); [1] Timney, p. 22.

2. Christopher, Milton. *The Illustrated History of Magic*. New York: Thomas Y. Crowell Company, 1973.

Writing Strategy

Remind students that the entire bibliography is always listed in alphabetical order, based on the first word that appears. This can be confusing, because sometimes the first word is a person's name and other times it is the title of an article.

Integrating Skills With Writing

Management Strategy

You can have students work through these two lessons either before or after they write their reports. If you use the lessons *before*, remind students to use the techniques that follow in their writing. If you address skills *after* students have written their reports, have them include a section on "skills improvement" in their portfolios.

Teaching Strategy

To connect the skills lessons to the students' writing, explain that one important feature of report writing is to credit the sources from which the writer gathered information. Another important aspect of report writing is to develop an appealing, flowing writing style. One way to do this is to combine short, choppy sentences into longer, smoother ones.

Clarification

Explain that any material taken directly from another source should be cited.

- Either a footnote or a parenthetical citation is correct, although footnotes are considered more formal.
- Although the entire article from *Scientific American* runs from pages 40 to 47, the citation need only mention the particular page that has the quoted information. If the quotation began on page 40 and ended on page 41, the citation would say *Taylor*, pp. 40–41.

Teaching Strategy

Ask a volunteer to read the first model paragraph aloud to the class. Elicit students' comments on the writing style. If necessary, point to the abundance of choppy sentences. Ask: *How would you evaluate a report written with all sentences like these?* Then have another volunteer read the revised paragraph aloud. Ask for students' reactions. Guide them to compare the original paragraph to its revision, sentence by sentence, to see how the changes were made.

Group Discussion

To help show students why combining sentences is relevant to report writing, ask: *What hidden message can a writer give by combining sentences through coordination? Through subordination?* Discuss how coordination links ideas of equal importance, whereas subordination links a more-important idea with a less-important one. Encourage students to offer their own examples of these strategies.

Language Acquisition/ ESL Teaching Strategy

As ESL students develop fluency in English, they find it increasingly necessary to employ conjunctions, some of which are difficult to master, such as *yet*, *although*, *unless*. Prior to having your ESL students complete the Practice Activities on page 231, you may review the use of conjunctions by means of a sentence strip activity. Write a series of sentence pairs, for example: *Tommy likes cats. He's allergic to them.* Ask your students which coordinating conjunction can be used to connect the two sentences. A student responds, *Tommy likes cats but he's allergic to them.* You may wish to have the students come to the board and add conjunctions to the sentence pairs and/or copy the new sentences into their notebooks, being sure to use the correct punctuation. As a group activity, the students may also work with the sentence strips at their tables. When you're confident that your ESL students are familiar with the conjunctions, you have them complete the Practice Activities.

Developing Your Style

Using Coordination and Subordination

The following paragraph tells about the writer's experience as a beginning animator. However, her writing could use a little animation of its own. The paragraph contains a number of short, choppy sentences. As a result, it sounds as awkward and sluggish as the cartoon character Droopy Dawg. What can be done to improve it?

> I have always been interested in animation. I didn't know much about it. Then I went to my first animation class. The whole process sounded very complicated. I didn't expect to create a cartoon right away.

One technique the writer can use is called coordination. **Coordination** means combining two simple sentences into a new sentence that gives equal importance to each thought. When you join sentences in this way, use one of the following coordinating conjunctions:

and   or   but   nor   yet

Also, when you combine sentences in this way, you put a comma before the coordinating conjunction:

> **Original:** I have always been interested in animation. I didn't know much about it.
>
> **With coordination:** I have always been interested in animation, but I didn't know much about it.

Another technique the writer can use is called subordination. **Subordination** means combining two sentences in a way that gives more importance to one sentence than to the other. Use one of the connectors at the top of page 231 to combine sentences through subordination.

Relative pronouns: who, which, what, that

Subordinating conjunctions: after, although, as, because, before, if, since, so, so that, unless, until, when, whenever, where, wherever, while

When you combine sentences through subordination, the resulting longer sentence is called a complex sentence:

Original: The whole process sounded very complicated. I didn't expect to create a cartoon right away.

Revision: Because the whole process sounded very complicated, I didn't expect to create a cartoon right away.

Practice Activities

1. Use coordination to combine the following sentences. Combine each pair of sentences by using one of the coordinating conjunctions listed on page 230.
   1. My little brother loves to watch cartoons. Sometimes I join him.
   2. He loves cartoon superheros. My favorite characters are the funny ones.
   3. My sister used to like cartoons too. Now she prefers live-action shows.
   4. The drawing in cartoons is simple and lively. I often try to imitate it.
2. Use subordination to combine the following sentences. Combine each pair of sentences using one of the connectors listed above.
   1. My uncle is an actor. He specializes in cartoon voiceovers.
   2. He is a man of many voices. He reminds me of Robin Williams.
   3. My uncle does one of his cartoon voices. His face and body change too.
   4. I like all of his voices. My favorites are his high, squeaky rodent characters.
3. Write a paragraph of six or eight sentences about your all-time favorite animated movie. Be sure to vary your sentences by using coordination and subordination. Include at least two compound and two complex sentences.

Addressing Ability Levels

Have your **more-advanced students** write a complex sentence that uses subordination. Challenge them to revise it to switch the importance of the two ideas. Discuss how the revision changes the meaning the writer originally intended.

Writer's Companion

For additional support and reinforcement in combining sentences through coordination and subordination, direct students to the sections on coordinating and subordinating conjunctions. In each section, students will see examples of coordinating and subordinating conjunctions and the kinds of sentences that can be formed when these conjunctions are used.

Language Lab CD-ROM

For additional practice using coordination and subordination to revise sentences, have students use the Correcting Stringy Sentences and Combining Sentences lessons from the unit Styling Sentences.

Practice Activities Answers

1. **1.** My little brother loves to watch cartoons, and sometimes I join him.
   2. He loves cartoon superheroes, but my favorite characters are the funny ones.
   3. My sister used to like cartoons too, but now she prefers live-action shows.
   4. The drawing in cartoons is simple and lively, and I sometimes try to imitate it.
2. Order of clauses may vary in responses. Sample answers:
   1. My uncle is an actor who specializes in cartoon voiceovers.
   2. Because he is a man of many voices, he reminds me of Robin Williams.
   3. When my uncle does one of his cartoon voices, his face and body change too.
   4. I like all of his voices, although my favorites are his high, squeaky rodent characters.
3. Responses will vary. Make sure that students have written at least two compound and two complex sentences. Help students to spot short, choppy sentences and to combine them.

Integrating Literature With Writing

Management Strategy

You can have students read this model of a research report either before or after they have written their own reports. If you choose to have them read it *before*, use it to draw their attention to techniques or ideas they can apply to their own writing. If you use it *after*, have students compare and contrast some of the elements of this report with elements of their own reports. Ask: *What can you learn from this report that can help you the next time you write a report?*

Activating Prior Knowledge

Invite students to share what they know about pandas. Jot down their ideas in brief form on the board or on chart paper. Guide students to examine the list they generated to suggest how the ideas might be grouped to create questions to investigate in a report on pandas. Ask:

- What questions about pandas would you want a report to answer?
- How might the report be organized?
- What parts and features should this report, or a report on any other topic, have?

Plan to refer back to the students' ideas after they read Standring's report. Discuss whether Standring included any of the facts that students knew or any of the parts and features they suggested. Talk about how she expanded upon what they knew or clarified information about or added new insights into their understanding of pandas.

Literature Model

This report by nature writer Gillian Standring offers a wealth of information about one of the world's endangered species, the panda. As you read, pay attention to how Standring has grouped and organized her information. Notice that each paragraph focuses on one main idea. Also take note of how Standring offers facts and details to support each of her main points.

Pandas

by Gillian Standring

Introducing Pandas

Standring labels each section of her report. She begins with a section introducing pandas.

In her first paragraph, Standring establishes her thesis, or central point—that pandas are an extremely rare and special animal that must be preserved.

Standring presents statistics to support her claim that pandas are one of the rarest animals in the world.

The giant panda is one of the best-known animals in the world. It is also one of the rarest. In 1990 there were only about one thousand giant pandas living wild in China, and only fifteen in zoos outside China. So if you have seen pandas in a zoo, you are very lucky.

Pandas have lived in China for thousands of years, but there have never been many of them. They were highly valued by the ancient Chinese emperors. Few travelers from Europe visited China until the late nineteenth century. In 1869 a French priest, Father Armand David, discovered the fabulous "black and white bear" and brought its skin and bones back from China to be studied by scientists in Paris. The first living pandas outside China were brought to the United States in 1936 and to Britain in 1938.

Ever since, the giant panda has been of great interest to scientists, zookeepers, and all animal lovers. Because it is so popular and so unusual, it was chosen as the symbol of the World Wildlife Fund (WWF), the world's best-known conservation organization.

Purpose-Setting Question

What are some of the organizational techniques the writer uses to present the facts and details she wants to share about pandas?

Reading Strategy

Before students read the entire report, point out the headings that divide it into sections. Ask students to read just the headings, then predict the slant on pandas that the report will have. Students may say that the report focuses on conservation issues regarding pandas rather than the biology or natural history of pandas.

You can help guide reading by asking students to jot down questions that arise or reactions they have as they read Standring's report. Also, ask them to determine the main idea of each paragraph. When they finish reading, students can work as a whole class or in small discussion groups to compare their responses to the report.

Teaching Strategy

Read the opening paragraph together. Ask students whether they agree with the writer's

Life in the Wild

Pandas, unlike people, prefer to be cool and damp. Hot, dry weather is bad for them. High up in the mountains of Sichuan in southwest China, there are thick, misty forests where it is always cool and damp. Pandas spend most of the year in these forests. In winter they come down to the lower slopes to get away from the deep snow and freezing cold. There are few people living in this part of China.

Notice that each paragraph focuses on a single main idea. This one tells about the pandas' habitat.

Pandas are famous for eating bamboo. Their food grows all around them in the bamboo forests, so they never have to hunt for it. However, they like to eat only a few kinds of bamboo, and their digestion is not very good, so they spend almost all the day just eating. Pandas also eat grasses, roots, bulbs, and tree bark. Sometimes they catch little cane rats and fish. They often take long drinks from mountain streams and rivers.

Why Are Pandas So Rare?

DISAPPEARING BAMBOO

Giant pandas have probably never been common anywhere. There are several reasons for this. They do not produce many babies. As we have seen, they can live only in cool bamboo forests. Each panda needs a big area of forest to itself, and even large areas of suitable mountain forest have room for only a few pandas.

After establishing that pandas are rare and telling about their habitat and eating habits, Standring explains why pandas are endangered.

Pandas also need plenty of their favorite bamboo. This plant has a very unusual way of growing. For perhaps a hundred years, bamboo plants spread by underground branches. Then suddenly, all the bamboo plants over a wide area flower, make seeds, and die. This leaves no food for the pandas until new plants grow from the seeds. Many pandas die of starvation when this happens, as it did in 1975–6.

For thousands of years, the giant panda's homeland in southwest China was very hard for people to reach, so it was left undisturbed for pandas and other wildlife. Now the millions of Chinese people need more land for their farms and villages. Modern roads help them to reach even the farthest mountains of Sichuan. As the people cut down the mountain forests, the pandas have fewer unspoiled bamboo groves to live in.

Cross-Curricular Connection: *Social Studies*

Display a map of China so students can locate the province of Sichuan. (Note: Some maps may use alternate spellings, such as Szechwan.) Ask them to describe the approximate location of the panda's natural habitat.

Teaching Strategy

To help students recognize some features of a well-structured report, have them find examples of how the writer creates coherence through connections she makes within and between sections. For instance, the phrase "As we have seen" in the first paragraph of "Why Are Pandas So Rare?" reminds the readers that earlier in the report they read about the panda's habitat. In the last paragraph of this section, the writer repeats the fact that pandas live in southwest China, then goes on to say how that area has changed. The opening sentence of the next section, "Another reason why pandas are rare...," reminds readers of the main point of the report—to show why the panda is endangered. Discuss other examples students find to highlight this technique.

opening statement. Have them identify details the writer provides to support her claim.

Point out that the second paragraph uses chronological order as a way to organize the information presented. Students may notice the transitional phrase "Ever since," which opens the following paragraph and continues the time-order connection.

Teaching Strategy

Discuss the main idea and supporting details the writer uses in each of the three paragraphs of the section called "The Panda Trade." Have students identify the topic sentence and evaluate the other sentences to understand how they support the main idea.

Thematic Connection: Global Responsibility

The writer refers to the World Wildlife Fund (WWF), a conservation organization that uses the giant panda as its symbol. This and other like-minded groups have pooled their efforts and resources with the Chinese government and people to save the panda and its habitat. Students interested in finding out more about the World Wildlife Fund and its work to save the panda may write to the group's headquarters at 1250 24th Street NW, Washington, D.C. 20037. [From p. 131 of the book *For Kids Who Love Animals: A Guide to Sharing the Planet*, by Linda Koebner, Living Planet Press, © 1991; also p. 566 of 1994 *World Almanac*.]

Encourage students to read other reports or articles that address the theme of global responsibility through efforts to save other endangered animals or habitats.

Group Discussion

For her report, Gillian Standring chose to organize information by type. Discuss how this plan made the report easy to follow and understand.

Another decision Standring made was to determine her audience and purpose. Have students state who the audience is and what the purpose of the report is. Challenge them to review the report to find examples to support their ideas about audience and purpose.

The Panda Trade

Another reason why pandas are rare is that people have captured them from the wild. Since pandas were first brought out of China, zoos around the world have wanted to have their own pandas to attract crowds of visitors. In the past, expensive expeditions were sent to China to catch and bring back wild pandas. Fortunately, those days are now over. The People's Republic of China banned the hunting of pandas in 1962. Now zoos can obtain pandas only as a gift from the Chinese people or from other zoos.

Here Standring presents the reason why people risk their lives to hunt pandas—they are motivated by greed.

However, panda-hunting still goes on in spite of the ban. The pandas are not captured to be taken to zoos but are killed for their skins. Panda fur is too coarse to use for fur coats, but some people like to have a panda skin to decorate their home. In Japan people will pay a great deal (over $200,000) to have a black-and-white panda skin rug on the floor.

Of course, this hunting is against the law, and if the hunters are caught they are imprisoned for life or even sentenced to death. However, the hunters still manage to smuggle a few panda skins out of China. They take the risk because they are well paid by the people who want the panda skins.

Saving the Panda

Panda Reserves

Although pandas are in danger from hunting, the main threat to them is the loss of their bamboo forests. There is some good news for pandas, however. The Chinese people and international conservation organizations are working hard to protect them.

After explaining why the panda is endangered, Standring describes what can be done to save it.

Now there are 12 special panda reserves in China, where some 450 pandas are living in safety. The reserves were created to protect the pandas and the bamboo forests they need. The cutting down of bamboo and felling of trees by people is strictly controlled. Armed guards patrol the reserves to protect the pandas from hunters and to ensure that local people do not destroy the trees.

Besides protecting the pandas, it is important to tell the local people why these animals are so special. So the peo-

Language Acquisition/ ESL Teaching Strategy

The report, *Pandas*, by Gillian Standring, can offer your basic and intermediate ESL students an opportunity to review the structure of a research report. Begin by reading the story with the entire class. On the side, discuss vocabulary and unusual phrases with your ESL students. Elicit the meaning of words from your students through the use of description, examples, mime, and gestures. Try to avoid dictionary definitions and translations, since English learners are likely to forget the meaning and use of words. Once the ESL students are familiar with the vocabulary, pair them with English-speaking students. Have the pairs read the report together and identify how the author has grouped and organized her information. Ask the students to write an outline or summary of the report, with a listing of the main ideas and pertinent points.

ple from 5,000 villages in Sichuan are taught about the need to protect pandas and how to care for starving pandas. They are told why they should not cut down trees and bamboo. If a panda causes damage to the local people's farm crops, the people are paid to cover the damage.

The largest reserve, at Wolong, was created in 1975. In 1980, the Chinese government and WWF built a special panda-breeding and research center there.

The Future for Pandas

The giant panda is a strange and wonderful animal. Perhaps we like it because it reminds us of ourselves, with its flat face, big eyes, cuddliness, and playful ways. It sits up to eat, as we do. It has a simple black-and-white pattern and an easy name. It is rare and mysterious and very valuable. Sad to say, we have helped to make pandas even rarer, and we will have to work hard to save them.

On the brighter side, the giant panda's urgent need for help has brought together conservation workers, vets, scientists, zookeepers and animal lovers from all over the world. The Chinese people and conservation organizations have managed to protect large areas of bamboo forest and guard the pandas that live in them. We have already found some ways of helping pandas to survive, by studying them in the wild and in captivity.

If we can give enough support to the efforts to save pandas, perhaps in the next century there will be more pandas in the world than now. Then the panda on the WWF badge will be the symbol of a success story in wildlife conservation.

Standring ends her report by reinforcing her central point. She reminds readers of the qualities that make pandas special and makes a plea for help in preserving this special animal.

Closure and Extension

To complete the lesson, you can ask students to sum up what they have learned about report writing through examining this report on pandas. Ask them what aspects of report writing the model does *not* show: citation of sources through footnotes, parentheses, or bibliography.

Invite students to share in small group discussions or through brief journal entries what they learned about themselves as writers and what points they would like to keep in mind for future writing. Also ask what topics they might consider researching for future reports. You might keep some of the topics in an idea file for future use.

Teaching Strategy

Draw students' attention to the concluding section of the report. Discuss how the information and details in the section echo the statements the writer made in her introduction and in subsequent body paragraphs of the report. Ask:

- How does the conclusion involve the reader in the plight of the panda?
- How does the conclusion convey optimism in spite of the writer's concern?
- How does the concluding sentence end the report effectively?

Cultural Connection

A recurring theme in the environmental debate is the problem of balancing the needs of endangered animals or habitats with the often conflicting needs of local residents. Discuss how the report addresses this issue. Explore how the situation for pandas and bamboo groves in China parallels the situation for rain forest plants and animals in many tropical regions of the world, especially along the Amazon River of Brazil. Invite students who come from other cultures, as well as those who have lived in other areas of the United States, to share their experiences with this issue. You may want students to research and hold a debate in which one side takes the viewpoint of local farmers and the other takes the viewpoint of environmentalists.

8

Creative Writing
Classroom Manager

Writer's Solution *Materials for Teaching Creative Writing*

The *Writer's Solution* includes a wide range of materials for teaching creative writing. You can pick and choose from among these materials to create a lesson plan that suits your classroom needs, teaching style, and equipment situation. In the pages that follow, you'll find lesson plans suggesting some of the most effective ways of using these materials. You do not have to use all the program components or all its features to use it effectively. Just use what works for you. For a detailed description of each of the components of the *Writer's Solution*, see pages T4–T6.

Below is a detailed list of the *Writer's Solution* materials for Creative Writing.

Writers at Work Videodisc

Featured Writer: Gary Soto, Poet and Fiction Writer

Videodisc Segments

About Creative Writing

Writing Tips:

- Creating Pictures With Words
- Using Active Verbs

Interactive CD-ROMs

Writing Lab

Tutorial on Creative Writing

About Creative Writing
- Includes four annotated Models From Literature

Choosing Your Topic
- Includes Inspirations for Creative Writing and Photo Storyboard

Considering Audience and Purpose
- Includes Audience Profile activity, interactive Models From Literature, and a slide show

Gathering Details
- Includes Sensory Image Bin, Character Trait Word Bin, and Cluster Diagram

Drafting
- Includes video tip about poetry from writer Gary Soto, video example of the use of dialogue for character development, interactive Models From Literature, and Student Models

Revising and Editing
- Includes video tip, Word Bin for revising vague images, and vague adjectives checker

Proofreading
- Includes integrated grammar instruction on possessive nouns, Proofreading Checklists for poems and plays, and Student Model

Publishing and Presenting
- Includes suggestions for presenting a staged performance of a play and holding a class poetry festival

Writer's Tool Kit

Suggested Activities: Revising and Editing Checklists, Sunburst Diagram, Photo Storyboard, Word Bins for sensory images and character traits, Cluster Diagram

Language Lab

Related Lessons: Vivid and Precise Verbs, Vivid Adjectives and Adverbs (Choosing Words unit); Considering Audience and Purpose, Writing Dialogue (Composing unit); Possessive Nouns (Using Nouns unit); Possessive Pronouns and Contractions (Using Pronouns unit); Quotation Marks, Apostrophes and Hyphens (Punctuation unit)

Sourcebook

About Creative Writing (pp. 240–244)

Guided Lesson on Creative Writing (pp. 245–261)

Developing Your Style
- Punctuating and Formatting Dialogue (p. 263)
- Using Contractions (p. 264)

Literature Model
- "Ode to Weightlifting" by Gary Soto (p. 265)

Below is a list of materials from Prentice Hall's student writing handbook that you can integrate with this lesson on creative writing.

Writer's Companion

Mini-Lesson on Word Choice, p. 89

Mini-Lesson on Figurative Language, p. 95

Mini-Lesson on Creative Writing: Poem, p. 145

Missing or Misplaced Possessive Apostrophes, p. 279

Teaching Integrated Language Arts Using the Writer's Solution—*Starting With Literature*

Have students read and respond to poems, song lyrics, monologues, dialogues, and other types of creative writing. Draw students' attention to creative elements, such as using imagination, using natural speech and language to express thoughts and emotions and to advance plot, using sensory images and concrete and figurative language, and using sound devices. Point out that students can use the creative writing they read as models for writing their own creative pieces. Lead into having students complete creative writing projects using the components of the *Writer's Solution.*

CONNECTIONS TO *PRENTICE HALL LITERATURE, COPPER,* SELECTIONS

Poems/Song Lyrics

Poems/Song Lyrics	1E	2E
"Abuelito Who," Sandra Cisneros		■
"Cat and the Weather," May Swenson	●	
"The Geese," Richard Peck	●	■
"Dust of Snow," Robert Frost	●	■
"Adventures of Isabel," Ogden Nash	●	■
"The Shark," John Ciardi	●	■
"Door Number Four," Charlotte Pomerantz	●	■
"Books Fall Open," David McCord	●	■
"Simile: Willow and Ginkgo," Eve Merriam	●	■
"Sun," Valerie Worth	●	■
"Ankylosaurus," Jack Prelutsky	●	■
"Cumulus Clouds," Sheryl L. Nelms	●	
"How to Write a Poem About the Sky," Leslie Marmon Silko		■
"April Rain Song," Langston Hughes	●	■
"Winter Poem," Nikki Giovanni	●	■
"Fireflies," Paul Fleischman	●	■
"The Fairies' Lullaby," William Shakespeare	●	■
"hist whist," E.E. Cummings	●	■
"Arithmetic," Carl Sandburg	●	■
"The Sidewalk Racer," Lillian Morrison	●	■
"Two Riddles," Ian Serraillier and Mary Austin	●	■

Poems/Song Lyrics (continued)

Poems/Song Lyrics (continued)	1E	2E
"The Walrus and the Carpenter," Lewis Carroll	●	■
"Alone in the Nets," Arnold Adoff	●	■
"Light and Water/Luz y Agua," Juan Ramon Jimenez	●	■
"How soft a Caterpillar Steps—," Emily Dickinson	●	■
"Beauty," E-Yeh-Shure	●	■
"Two Limericks," Anonymous	●	■
"Two Haiku," Bash and Soseki	●	■
"Wilderness Rivers," Elizabeth Coatsworth	●	
"One," James Berry		■
"Sea Songs," Myra Cohn Livingston	●	■
"If I Were in Charge of the World," Judith Viorst	●	■
"Change," Charlotte Zolotow	●	■
"Daydreamers," Eloise Greenfield	●	■
"Whatif," Shel Silverstein	●	■
"The Naming of Cats," T. S. Eliot	●	■

Monologues/Dialogues

Monologues/Dialogues	1E	2E
***The Phantom Tollbooth,* Acts I and II,** Norton Juster, adapted by Susan Nanus	●	■

You can use the *Writer's Solution* material on creative writing to guide students through writing activities in response to works of literature.

CONNECTIONS TO *PRENTICE HALL LITERATURE, COPPER,* WRITING ACTIVITIES

Thinking and Writing Activities

Thinking and Writing Activities	1E	2E
Writing a Script—Follows ***The Phantom Tollbooth***, Norton Juster, adapted by Susan Nanus	●	■
Using Images to Describe People—Follows **"Abuelito Who,"** Sandra Cisneros		■
Writing Another Stanza—Follows **"Adventures of Isabel,"** Ogden Nash	●	■
Writing a Poem of Contrast—Follows **"Sun,"** Valerie Worth	●	■
Writing Metaphors—Follows **"How to Write a Poem About the Sky,"** Leslie Marmon Silko		■
Writing a Dream Poem—Follows **"Winter Poem,"** Nikki Giovanni	●	■
Modernizing a Poem—Follows **"The Fairies' Lullaby,"** William Shakespeare	●	■
Writing a List Poem—Follows **"Arithmetic,"** Carl Sandburg	●	■
Writing a Concrete Poem—Follows **"The Sidewalk Racer,"** Lillian Morrison	●	■

Thinking and Writing Activities (continued)

Thinking and Writing Activities (continued)	1E	2E
Writing Another Ending—Follows **"The Walrus and the Carpenter,"** Lewis Carroll	●	■
Writing a Monologue—Follows **"Alone in the Nets,"** Arnold Adoff	●	■
Writing a Dialogue—Follows **"Señor Coyote and the Tricked Trickster,"** I. G. Edmonds	●	■
Writing Lyrics—Follows **"Orpheus,"** Alice Low	●	■

Handbook of Writing About Literature / Your Writing Process

Handbook of Writing About Literature / Your Writing Process	1E	2E
Developing Characters Through Dialogue	●	■
Writing a Readers Theater	●	■
Playing With Words	●	■
Playing With Images	●	■
Playing With Forms	●	■
Compiling a Poetry Anthology	●	■

● **(1E)** *Prentice Hall Literature, Copper,* First Edition

■ **(2E)** *Prentice Hall Literature, Copper,* Paramount Edition

CONNECTIONS BETWEEN INSPIRATIONS FOR CREATIVE WRITING AND *PRENTICE HALL LITERATURE, COPPER*

You can use the multimedia Inspirations for Creative Writing to motivate student reading as well as student writing. Many of the Inspirations are audio recordings or video adaptations of selections from *Prentice Hall Literature, Copper*. Have students work in small groups to look at and discuss an appropriate Inspiration before reading the corresponding selection. Then, after reading the selection, students can replay the Inspiration and select one of the accompanying writing options (see pages 248–251). The following is a list of selections from *Prentice Hall Literature, Copper*, included in the Inspirations for Creative Writing:

- **"Sea Songs,"** Myra Cohn Livingston
- Excerpt from ***The Jungle Book***, Rudyard Kipling
- **"Beauty,"** E-Yeh-Shure
- **"The Sidewalk Racer,"** Lillian Morrison
- **"Whatif,"** Shel Silverstein

Recommended Lesson Plan

The following lesson plan is recommended for providing students with thorough, comprehensive instructions in creative writing. Because you may not have all the components of the *Writer's Solution* or may have limited access to equipment, the plan provides a number of options. Choose the options that best suit your teaching style and equipment situation.

You may want to add a few days to the lesson plan to allow students time to publish their work and to hold conferences with students to discuss your assessment of their work.

FIVE-DAY LESSON PLAN	
Lesson Outcome:	**Each student writes a complete poem, song lyrics, monologue, or dialogue.**
DAY 1	**Introduce your students to creative writing.** Show the *Writers at Work Videodisc* segment featuring Gary Soto. Use the segment as a springboard for class discussion or group activities.
DAY 2	**Have students choose a writing topic and plan their creative writing.** OPTION 1 Have students work either individually or in small groups to look at About Creative Writing and to choose a topic by browsing through the Inspirations for Creative Writing. Then have students work individually to develop their ideas by completing the rest of the Prewriting stage of the tutorial on Creative Writing. At the end of the period, have students print out their prewriting notes. OPTION 2 Have students review the Models From Literature in the About Creative Writing section of the *Sourcebook*. Then have them choose from the topic suggestions and begin developing their creative writing by completing the rest of the Prewriting stage of the Guided Lesson (pp. 246–255).
DAY 3	**Have students draft their creative writing pieces.** OPTION 1 Have students write their drafts on the computer following the instructions and using the activities in the Drafting section of the tutorial on Creative Writing. Have students print out their creative writing at the end of the period. OPTION 2 Have students write their drafts on paper following the instructions in the Guided Lesson (pp. 256–258).
DAY 4	**Have students revise their creative writing.** OPTION 1 Have students revise their creative writing on the computer using the revision checkers, activities, and suggestions in the Revising and Editing section of the tutorial on Creative Writing. OPTION 2 Have students revise their creative writing following the suggestions in the Guided Lesson (pp. 259–260).

FIVE-DAY LESSON PLAN (continued)

DAY 5	**Have students make final revisions.** OPTION 1 Have students review and revise their own work following the guidelines in the Revising and Editing section of the tutorial on Creative Writing. Students should then proofread and print out their final drafts. OPTION 2 Have students proofread their work following the guidelines in the Guided Lesson (p. 260).

Condensed Lesson Plans

Use the following lesson plans if you don't have a full week to devote to teaching creative writing.

Four- and Three-Day Plans: Adapt the Five-Day Plan by having students learn about creative writing, choose a topic, and develop ideas for their creative writing pieces all during Day 1. As in the Five-Day Plan, have students spend a day writing their drafts. For a Four-Day Plan, follow the last two days of the Five-Day Plan; for a Three-Day Plan, simply condense these two days into a single day of revision and forgo the option of working in peer groups.

TWO-DAY LESSON PLAN

Lesson Outcome:	**Each student writes a complete poem, song lyrics, monologue, or dialogue.**
DAY 1	**Have students choose a topic and write their first drafts.** OPTION 1 Have students work in the open-ended environment in the *Writing Lab*. Working individually, students should choose a topic by browsing through the Inspirations for Creative Writing. Then they should write their creative pieces in their on-line Notebooks using the available prewriting tools as needed. OPTION 2 Using the suggestions and instructions in the *Sourcebook*, students should choose a topic and write a first draft of their creative pieces.
DAY 2	**Have students revise and edit their work.** OPTION 1 Have students revise on the computer using the tools, activities, and instructions in the tutorial on Creative Writing. OPTION 2 Have students revise their creative writing following the suggestions in the *Sourcebook*.

If you have only one day to devote to teaching creative writing, students can work individually in the open-ended environment in the *Writing Lab* by browsing through the Inspirations for Creative Writing to choose a topic, using the prewriting tools as needed, and completing a quick-write draft of a creative piece in their on-line Notebooks. Students may also use the *Sourcebook* to choose a topic and write a brief creative piece.

Preparing to Teach

CHAPTER 8

Lesson Objectives

Students will

1. Select an appropriate subject for a poem, song lyrics, monologue, or dialogue
2. Gather specific details
3. Write a poem or song lyrics in which they
   - express their ideas or feelings
   - use vivid imagery
   - use sound devices

   Or, write a monologue or dialogue in which they
   - express their ideas or feelings
   - use dialogue and actions that bring the character(s) to life
   - write stage directions
4. Revise their work for content, structure, and mechanics
5. Publish their finished creative piece

Activating Prior Knowledge

Ask students to recall poems they have read, song lyrics they know, or plays they have performed, seen, or read. Invite them to share their impressions, telling what they liked and disliked about these creative pieces. You might have volunteers read aloud a few lines of a poem or song lyric they enjoy or, with a partner, read a scene from a play. Ask: *How is creative writing—such as plays, song lyrics, and poetry—like other kinds of writing? How do you think it differs? Based on what you've read, which of these examples of creative writing do you enjoy the most? The least? Explain.*

Against the Enamel of a Background Rhythmic With Beats and Angles, Tones, Tints, Portrait of M. Felix Feneon in 1890

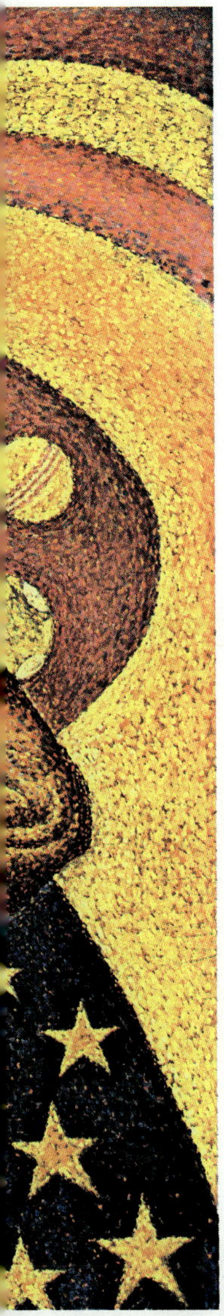

ignac, Private Collection

Creative Writing

"My ideas come from a mixture of imagination and . . . memory."

—Gary Soto
Poet and Fiction Writer

Humanities Note

The work of art is a painting by Paul Signac (1863–1935) with the lengthy title *Against the Beats and Angles, Tones, Tints, Portrait of M. Felix Feneon in 1890*. French artist Paul Signac lived and worked in Paris. He collaborated with his friend, the painter Georges Seurat, to develop the neo-impressionist technique called *divisionism*. This technique applied scientific formulas of color theory to painting. Tiny dots of several pure colors were used to make up large areas of a different color, allowing the viewer's eye to blend them.

If you look closely, you'll see that the hat in this painting is actually many different colors but, from a distance, it appears to be satiny black. Here Signac used his system of painting to eliminate "muddy mixtures" and create true, luminous colors that were naturally harmonious.

There are details that make it clear that this is a portrait of a magician. His eyes focus on the flower he holds at arm's length, leading our eyes to this same focal point. Notice the swirling shapes and colors behind him that seem to represent the world around him. You might use the following questions as a basis for class discussion:

- What did the painter do in this portrait to communicate that his subject is a magician? How does a magician change the way we see the world around us?
- Imagine painting a portrait of someone magical in your life. How would you communicate the magic in your painting? How would you write about the magical qualities of your subject?

Addressing Your Classroom Situation

This chapter includes a variety of Models From Literature, writing topics, writing process strategies, and Student Models, along with two integrated skills lessons. Feel free to pick and choose from this material to create a customized lesson on creative writing that matches your classroom needs.

The following are some of the key features of the chapter:

- The chapter begins with a section introducing creative writing. This section includes thoughts about creative writing from poet and fiction writer Gary Soto, group discussion questions, and Models From Literature for the following types of creative writing: poems, song lyrics, monologues, dialogues.
- The Prewriting section includes an assortment of idea-generating activities to help students choose a type of creative writing, along with ten topic ideas. This section also provides direct instruction and activities to help students consider their audience and purpose and gather details. Professional and student Models From Literature; a chart of sensory images; a Cluster Diagram on poetic details; and tips for developing character, plot, and setting guide students through the steps of the creative-writing process.
- The Drafting section addresses the key issue of *showing* rather than *telling* feelings the writer wants to express. It introduces the importance of using sound devices to enhance the mood and meaning of a poem or song lyric, as well as tips for writing stage directions to enhance monologues and dialogues.
- The Revising and Editing section focuses on helping students revisit their creative writing to check that their images, feelings, and ideas are presented clearly and in fresh, vivid ways. Students are given pointers about reading their work aloud as a way to revise it. A Proofreading Checklist guides them to find and correct any errors in spelling, capitalization, punctuation, and spacing.
- The Guided Lesson is followed by a Student Model and then skills lessons on punctuating and formatting dialogue and on using contractions. You may want to address these skills before students draft their creative writing pieces, or you may prefer to focus on them during the revising/proofreading phase.

Chapter Contents

About Creative Writing

Guided Lesson

Student Model

Developing Your Style 1

Developing Your Style 2

Literature Model

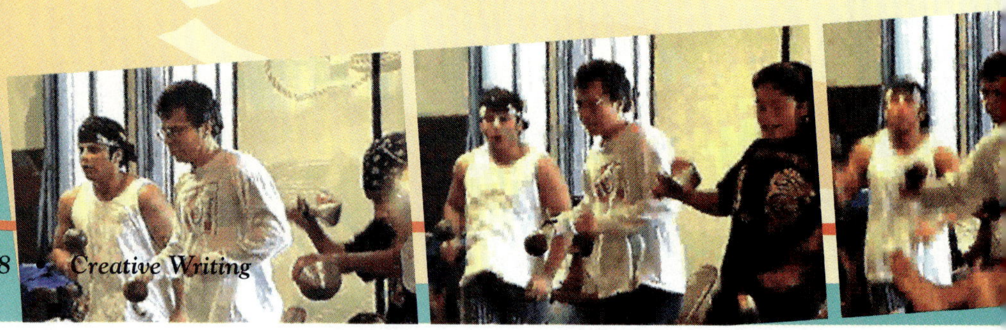

"I read a little bit of the newspaper, and . . . I'll try to get some kind of energy from other writers. And then something comes up and I'm off. I will write for probably two or three hours."

"No poet works alone. He or she must have a sounding board. I get feedback and I give feedback."

—Gary Soto
Poet and Fiction Writer

"When you write poetry, you have to show me the world that you live in or the world that you want to present. You can't just tell me about it."

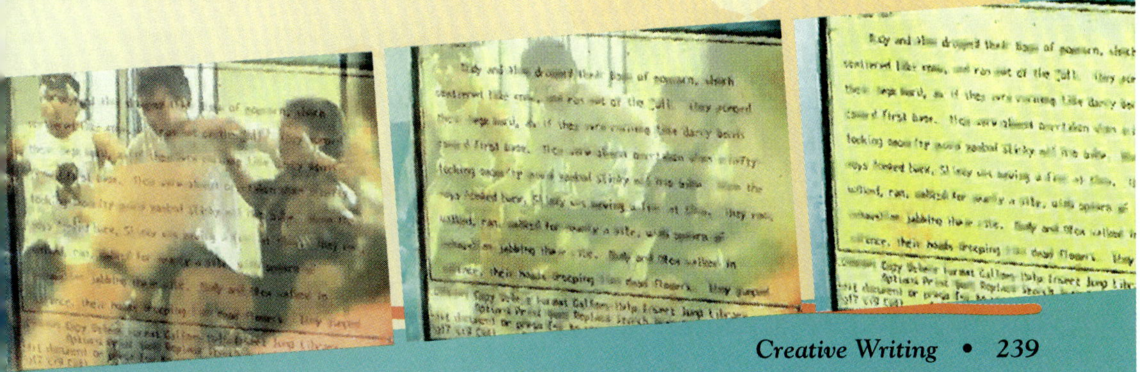

- The chapter ends with a complete Literature Model, a poem by Gary Soto entitled "Ode to Weightlifting."

More About the Writer

Gary Soto once worked as a migrant laborer in the San Joaquin Valley of central California. Today, he is an acclaimed poet and fiction writer who lives and teaches in Berkeley, California. Many of Soto's poems and prose works reflect his personal experiences and interests. In his first book of poetry, *The Elements of San Joaquin*, Soto expressed his thoughts about people and places of his youth. *Living Up the Street* presents his personal recollections in prose. Gary Soto has written four collections of essays, several poetry collections, and a well-known book for young adults entitled *Baseball in April and Other Stories*.

Gary Soto has advised young poets to "look to your own lives" to find inspirations for their poems. Talk with your students about what they think Soto means by this statement. Ask: *How can a person's ordinary experiences evolve into a piece of creative writing with broad appeal? How would such a work differ from a narrative or expository piece about the same experience?*

Tech Prep Note

Point out that not only professional writers like Gary Soto use creative writing. Workers in other fields may have opportunities for creative writing on the job. For example, workers may find themselves writing or collaborating on a script for a short play, lyrics for a song, or words to a poem or monologue to be performed at a company-wide gathering or party to honor a co-worker. Also, workers in large companies may contribute their creative writing for publication in a company newsletter or industry-wide publication. Ask: *Think about the adults you know and the work they do. How do they use creative-writing skills on the job?*

Introducing Creative Writing

Teaching Options

There is a variety of ways you can introduce creative writing using the components of the *Writer's Solution:*

- You can show the creative-writing segment from the *Writers at Work Videodisc*. Use this segment as a springboard for a class discussion on creative writing.
- You can have students work individually or in small groups to go through the About Creative Writing section of the tutorial in the *Writing Lab* CD-ROM.
- You can work through the About Creative Writing section of the *Sourcebook* with the class.
- You can have students read the About Creative Writing section of the *Sourcebook* before class starts so that, as a group, you can concentrate on the videodisc or CD-ROM lesson.

Sourcebook

Have students read aloud and discuss the About Creative Writing section in the *Sourcebook*. Use the following questions to guide the discussion:

- How can you recognize creative writing?
- Where might you find examples of creative writing?
- What makes creative writing appeal to both the writer and the reader?
- How can creative writing help you discover more about yourself?

About Creative Writing

What Is Creative Writing?

In **creative writing** you can let your imagination run free. You can create your own world and the people who live there. You can blend your fantasies with events from your real life. There are many types of creative writing—poems, plays, stories, and television programs. In this chapter, you'll learn about writing poetry and drama.

Group Discussion Did you realize that song lyrics are a type of creative writing? With a group of classmates, brainstorm for a list of your favorite songs. Discuss the lyrics of each. What makes the lyrics fun to listen to? Do the lyrics have a certain rhythm, or beat? Do they rhyme? Do they tell a story? What is the message the songwriter is presenting?

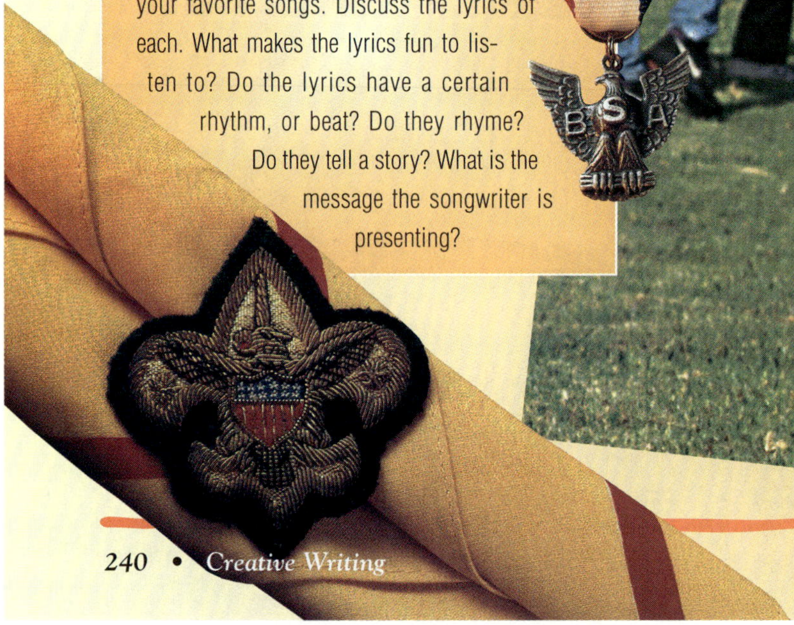

Following the class discussion, divide your students into groups of three to five to engage in the group discussion (p. 240).

Writers at Work Videodisc

Use the Creative Writing section of the videodisc featuring writer Gary Soto as a springboard into a class discussion on creative writing. Play the chapter in its entirety, pausing as needed. Then feel free to use the bar codes to replay any segment to reinforce an important idea.

Before you play the first segment, ask students to listen for how Soto describes his feelings about creative writing as a test of his inner self. After students have seen the segment, have them take turns responding to it. Then move into a discussion of the motivations and personal insights that Gary Soto shares. Ask:

- What does Soto say about where his ideas come from
- What does Soto mean by

How a Professional Writer Uses Creative Writing

Some people devote their lives to creative writing. One such person is Gary Soto. Soto writes poems, stories, and personal essays based on his experiences growing up in Fresno, California. Using his imagination, Soto transforms his childhood experiences into successful pieces of creative writing. Here Soto describes the process of creative writing:

> "Creative writing tests your inner self. It tests your ability to come up with phrases and language that are fresh. One of the tasks of a poet or a short story writer or a playwright is to provide real, fresh, vibrant language, with characters that are interesting but also accessible, that are known to us."

How Creative Writing Fits Into Your Life

Just about every day you probably use your imagination to invent new ideas. You might make up a scary story or dream up your own episode for your favorite television program. Or you might imagine what your own life will be like ten years from now. To become a creative writer, all you have to do is capture your imaginative ideas on paper.

the creative writer's "luxury to present a world that's . . . just slightly different"?

Play frames 20877 to 29643

Writing Lab CD-ROM

The About Creative Writing section of the tutorial includes the following options:

- **Author video** Gary Soto discusses his belief that creative writing is a mix of imagination and memory.
- **Audio-annotated Models From Literature of four kinds of creative writing** Poetry, song lyrics, monologue, dialogue.
- **Evaluation Guidelines** These guidelines—one set for poetry, another for drama—can be presented to students before they draft their creative pieces to serve as a checklist that directs their writing. The guidelines can also be used for self-assessment after writing. If so, students can incorporate the ideas into a reflective piece they may choose to include in their portfolios.

Students can work individually or in small groups to complete the tutorial on Creative Writing. Or, if you have access to a projection panel, you can work through the About Creative Writing section with the entire class, discussing each part as you go.

Real-World Writing

Help students identify people in your community in whose lives creative writing plays an important role. These people might be singers, storytellers, performing artists, comedians, television writers, composers, stage and film directors, set designers, columnists, broadcast journalists, and advertising copywriters.

Have students look for examples of creative writing in unexpected places, such as in store window displays, in product descriptions, and in posters on buses, trains, and billboards. As students share their findings, ask:

- What are some of the more surprising places in which you found examples of creative writing?
- What common features, if any, do you notice among the different pieces of creative writing you saw?
- What impact does a vivid word, phrase, or image have on the reader of a piece of creative writing?

Integrating Literature With Writing

Starting From Literature

You can use the models on pages 242–244 to illustrate the various elements of each type of creative writing. Or you can highlight the content or devices used in these pieces to inspire writing on any of the topics they address. For example, students can use their response to the lyrics of "Buttermilk Hill" to write lyrics for a new antiwar song. Challenge students to apply the devices of rhyme, rhythm, and repetition, as the original lyricist did, to create a poignant mood.

Briefly introduce and define the type of writing each selection models. Follow with discussion to reinforce students' understanding of each type of creative writing.

Teaching From the Model

Help students analyze this excerpt from the play *The Phantom Tollbooth* to understand the characteristics of a monologue:

- *It is a dramatic speech spoken by a single character.* This excerpt from the stage adaptation of Norton Juster's classic fantasy could be part of a stand-up comedian's routine or an aside to the audience during the play. It is clear that Clock is speaking directly to the audience, not to another character.
- *Though part of a longer drama, it can stand alone.* Some monologues serve a specific function in a staged drama, such as to allow time for a change of scenery or costume. However, any good monologue can stand alone, as if it were a speech, and needs no particular response.
- *It blends opinion and observation with a touch of wry humor.* As in many fantasies, an inanimate object speaks, philosophizing and giving its opinion to the audience. This monologue mixes seriousness and whimsy. Monologues can be funny, scary, poignant, or foreboding.

Teaching From the Model

Focus on the excerpt from *The Phantom Tollbooth* to help students appreciate how a dialogue exemplifies creative writing:

- *It is a conversation between two characters.* One character—a boy named Milo—talks with another character, named Watchdog. Following the typical format of a written drama, each line is preceded by the name of the character speaking it.

Types of Creative Writing

There are many types of creative writing—poems, stories, plays. Here are the types of creative writing you'll explore in this chapter:

1 Monologue and Dialogue

- A monologue is a dramatic speech that's spoken by one character.
- Some monologues are part of longer dramas. Others are written to stand alone.
- A monologue can be funny, serious, scary, or educational.
- A dialogue is a conversation between characters in a drama.
- Dialogue helps to further the action in a drama and develops the characters' personalities by expressing their ideas.

Model From Literature

This monologue is from the play *The Phantom Tollbooth*, which has been adapted for the stage by Susan Nanus, based on the book by Norton Juster. Notice that the monologue sounds like the speech of a real person and that Clock is speaking to "you," the audience.

CLOCK: . . . Time is important, but it's what you do with it that makes it so. So my advice to you is to use it. Keep your eyes open and your ears perked. Otherwise, it will pass before you know it, and you'll certainly have missed something!

Later in the play, this dialogue takes place between Milo, a boy, and Watchdog, a character that is part dog and part clock.

MILO: I think I was on my way to Dictionopolis when I got stuck here. Can you help me?

WATCHDOG: Help you! You've got to help yourself. I suppose you know why you got stuck.

MILO: I guess I just wasn't thinking.

WATCHDOG: Precisely. Now you're on your way.

MILO: I am?

WATCHDOG: Of course. Since you got here by not thinking, it seems reasonable that in order to get you out, you must start thinking.

2 Poem

- A poem is writing that uses language in a special way.
- In most poems, language is compressed—many ideas are expressed in a few words.
- The sound of most poems is just as important as the meaning.
- Many poems use sound devices like rhyme and rhythm to create a musical quality.
- Many poems contain images, or word pictures, that have an emotional effect on the reader.

Model From Literature

In this poem, "Change" by Charlotte Zolotow, notice the imagery of the seasons and the gentle effect created by the repetition of the phrase "as it did last year."

The summer
still hangs
heavy and sweet
with sunlight
as it did last year.

The autumn
still comes
showering gold and crimson
as it did last year.

The winter
still stings
clean and cold and white
as it did last year.

The spring
still comes
like a whisper in the dark night.

It is only I
who have changed.

- *It helps to further the action in a drama.* Through dialogue, readers learn that Milo is on a journey and Watchdog plans to join him. The dialogue establishes a relationship between two characters in the play.
- *It furthers character development as the characters express their ideas.* This excerpt reveals that Milo is modest, curious, and reflective, while Watchdog is very logical, assertive, and arrogant. The differences between them can add humor or tension to the drama. Point out the stage directions, which give additional hints into the personality and motivation of each character.

Clarification

Be sure that students grasp the distinction between a monologue and a dialogue. Point out that plays, movies, and TV shows often have monologues *and* dialogues. Ask a volunteer to look up the prefixes *di-* and *mono-* in a dictionary. Invite students to compare other words with those prefixes.

Teaching From the Model

Guide students to understand the characteristics of poetry by discussing the poem "Change" by Charlotte Zolotow:

- *It vividly expresses the poet's experience.* The feeling throughout most of this poem is gentle, yet Zolotow concludes with a strong statement: "It is only I/who have changed." The poem's dramatic change of mood helps the poet express the impact of her own experience by contrasting it with the constancy of the seasons.
- *It uses few words to express many ideas.* By saying that the summer ". . . hangs/heavy and sweet/with sunlight . . ." the poet gives readers a sharp image in very few words.
- *It uses the sound devices of repetition and rhythm to create a musical quality.* Zolotow ends each of the first three stanzas by repeating the words "as it did last year." She uses the same rhythmic beginning of naming a season in all stanzas but one. The last two lines break the pattern of repetition and rhythm, thus emphasizing the poet's concluding statement.
- *It includes imagery that produces an emotional effect in the reader.* Most readers will respond to the familiarity of the seasons, each of whose characteristics Zolotow compresses into one strong image. However, the image of spring, so often described in terms of renewal and optimism, is more sober here, perhaps to foreshadow the strong ending.

Teaching From the Model

Guide students to recognize how the excerpt from the folk song exemplifies the type of creative writing in which a writer creates song lyrics:

- *It uses sound devices similar to those of poetry.* The stanzas share a similar pattern of stressed and unstressed syllables, which gives the lyrics a musical rhythm. The lyricist used melodious phrases. For instance, the phrase "Me oh my, I loved him so" conveys the moaning quality of a lament. The word *gone* in the line "Johnny has gone for a soldier" has an explosive consonant sound like a drumbeat, emphasizing the finality of Johnny's departure.
- *Like poetry, it uses rhyme and repetition.* The first three lines of each stanza end with words that rhyme: "hill/fill/mill" and "so/go/woe." In addition to using end rhymes and strong imagery, the lyricist ends each verse with the words "Johnny has gone for a soldier." Beyond concluding the stanza, this phrase echoes the singer's deep sadness.

3 Song Lyrics

- Song lyrics contain many of the sound devices that poetry uses.
- Like poetry, song lyrics often use rhythm, rhyme, and repetition.

Model From Literature

The following is a popular old song. Notice that the lyrics of the song contain rhyme, rhythm, and repetition.

There I sat on Buttermilk Hill,
Who could blame me, cry my fill;
And ev'ry tear would turn a mill:
Johnny has gone for a soldier.

Me oh my, I loved him so,
Broke my heart to see him go,
And only time will heal my woe:
Johnny has gone for a soldier.

Language Acquisition/ ESL Teaching Strategy

The *Writing Lab* offers a number of options that can be adapted for use with ESL students of all levels. The following are examples of such adaptations.

- The Gathering Details sec tion offers a Cluster Diagram for feelings and ideas that can be used by your intermediate ESL stu dents. Working in pairs, the students choose a feel ing they want to express and then list people and places that suggest the fee ing. They should be encouraged to discuss thei

Guided Lesson

Publishing and Presenting · Prewriting · Revising and Editing

Now that you know what creative writing is, you're ready to start developing your own piece of creative writing. This lesson will help guide you through the process of writing it. You may find that you do not want to start at the beginning of the lesson, however. Think about the ideas you have in mind for your writing, then use this chart to decide where to begin.

	START WITH
• If you **do not have a topic**	**Choosing Your Topic**
• If you already **have a topic in mind but aren't sure what details to include**	**Gathering Details**
• If you **have a topic and enough details to work with**	**Drafting**

Guiding Student Writing

Addressing Your Classroom Situation

- If you choose to assign topics or types of creative writing, allow time for students to narrow the topic to suit their interests or find an appealing focus to pursue.
- You may wish to have students work in pairs. If so, brainstorm with the class to determine ways partners might collaborate fairly. For example, one way for a team to write dialogue is for each student to write the lines for one of the characters. To write a poem or song lyrics as a team, partners can begin by discussing audience and purpose and choosing a rhythm and rhyme. The pair can take turns writing lines and then revise the piece together, polishing it by adding poetic devices such as repetition and onomatopoeia.

ideas and help each other elaborate upon ways of expressing the feeling in the poem. Have the students take notes on phrases and images they like.

- The Drafting section offers audio-annotated professional Writing Models that can be used with your intermediate and advanced ESL students. Ask the students to take notes on the examples of effective dialogue they see in the option. Referring to these notes, the students write their drafts and then read and discuss what they have written with others in the ESL group. The students should feel free to offer suggestions.
- The Revising and Editing section provides an interactive Self-Evaluation Checklist for poetry that can be used with your upper-intermediate and advanced ESL students. Upon completing the checklist, the students revise their poems and then exchange their "before" and "after" drafts with each other. The students read each other's drafts to see how they improved focus and used sound devices.

Writing Lab CD-ROM

The Choosing a Topic section of the tutorial on Creative Writing includes the following options to help students come up with their own topics:

- **Sunburst Diagram with a wheel for exploring topic ideas** Students browse a random assortment of sounds, words, and images to spark topic ideas. They enter their choices into a Sunburst Diagram.
- **Photo Storyboard for generating ideas** Students see a series of photographs, which they can arrange into any order they wish to suggest a writing topic.

Working individually or in small groups, students can experiment with these activities to find the ones that work best.

Writers at Work Videodisc

Play the videodisc segment in which Gary Soto discusses how he finds ideas for his poetry. Soto says he doesn't know how poems actually take shape, but that he is ". . . willing to be involved in the writing, willing to be foolish." Ask:

- What does Soto mean by saying that he's "willing to be foolish"? How can being foolish relate to creativity and imagination?
- How can you begin to transform personal feelings and experiences into a poem or other kind of creative writing?

Play frames 23498 to 24524

Prewriting

Choosing Your Topic

Although we don't know how the imagination works, we do know that exploring different ideas can trigger the imagination. To spark your imagination and help you come up with a topic, experiment with any of the following techniques. Or you can choose from the suggested writing topics on pages 248 through 251.

If you're considering

. . . song lyrics:

LISTEN TO POPULAR SONGS

Listen to the radio for an hour or so. As each song comes on, jot down its title and its theme, or what it's about. Also pay attention to the sound of the lyrics. Do the lines rhyme? Are certain lines or words repeated? How would you describe the rhythm? When you've finished, look over your notes. What topic ideas do you see? What techniques have you learned that you can use in your own song lyrics?

. . . a poem:

GET INSPIRATION FROM NATURE

Through the ages, nature has been a source of inspiration for artists and writers. Many poets have responded to the powerful forces of hurricanes, blizzards, thunder and lightning storms, and waves breaking on the shore. Others have been moved by tiny details of nature, such as a glistening drop of water on a blade of grass or a pattern on a butterfly's wings. Think about your own responses to nature. For example, how does a thunderstorm make you feel? Does it frighten you or excite you? Does a rainbow stir your imagination? Jot down your thoughts. Then look through your notes for possible topics for a poem.

Teaching Strategy

Have students share techniques they have found effective when trying to select a creative-writing topic. You may want to set up a communal idea file in your classroom. It can take the form of ideas jotted on index cards, files of pictures or articles, evocative excerpts, or word or name lists. Invite students to use the file to get an idea or to contribute ideas others might use.

Cultural Connection

Suggest that students interested in writing song lyrics listen to music associated with their own culture or another that interests them. Obtain a variety of CDs or tapes of music from around the world so stu dents can have a choice. Students who may, for instance, be unfamiliar with Native American flute music Hindu *ragas*, or Indonesian *gamelan* music may discover that this music evokes feelings of harmony with nature. Music without lyrics, or with lyrics in other languages, can

. . . a monologue:

Group Activity

NAME THAT CHARACTER!

With a group of classmates, discuss famous people known for their unique personalities. Discuss with the group what makes each one special and how that person could be brought to life through a monologue. Take notes during the discussion. Then review your notes and choose one of the personalities as the subject for a monologue.

. . . a poem, song lyrics, a monologue or dialogue:

KEEP A JOURNAL

What unusual people have you met? What memorable places have you visited? Is there one special place that you would like to see again? Capture the most important people, places, and moments from your everyday life by keeping a journal. Start by writing a journal entry in which you respond to the previous questions. Then look over your entry for possible writing topics. Begin writing regularly in your journal—once a day, once a week, or as important events occur. Use your journal as a source of future writing ideas.

. . . a dialogue:

Group Activity

INTRODUCING PAST AND PRESENT

With a group of classmates, brainstorm for a list of famous people from the past and a list of famous people from the present. Then pair the people, one from each list. Discuss what these people would say to each other if they could meet. For instance, imagine a conversation between explorer Christopher Columbus and actor Tom Hanks. Would they like each other? Would they have difficulty understanding each other? Go through the possibilities and change the settings of the dialogues as appropriate. Review the group's ideas for possible writing topics for a dialogue.

Group Activity

If students participating in the Name That Character group activity have trouble identifying people with unique personalities, suggest that they browse through current news magazines for ideas or consult the listings of guests who appear on talk shows. You might also suggest that students focus on unique personalities closer to home, such as well-known local political figures or members of the school community.

Thematic Connection: Exploring the Past

Invite students to pretend that they were witnesses—up close and personal—to an event of historical significance, such as the signing of the Declaration of Independence or the first moon walk. Have students read about an event that interests them to get ideas for an imaginary dialogue between themselves and a principal participant in the event. They can write dialogue that reveals the participant's hopes and fears to contrast with the witness's questions and impressions. They might include stage directions, as needed, to provide key background details.

till evoke emotional respons-
es that may lead to creative
writing ideas.

Writing Lab CD-ROM

Using the Inspirations for Creative Writing in the *Writing Lab* is an excellent way to stimulate creativity and to have students explore possible topics for creative writing. Students can browse individually or in small groups through the Inspirations. They can choose their own writing topics or you may prefer to assign topics.

The following is a list of the creative-writing options included in the Inspirations, but not provided in the *Sourcebook:*

Song Lyrics

- About friendship
- For the nightingale's song
- About a quality you admire
- About a special relationship
- With strong feelings
- For an already-familiar song

A Poem

- With personification
- About a force in nature
- About children playing
- That is a haiku about a city
- About feeling safe
- About beauty
- With the point of view of something in nature
- About the value of nature
- Of metaphors about activities
- That is a haiku about motion
- That is a concrete poem about transportation
- That is a haiku about a motorcycle
- That compares one form of transportation with another
- That is a narrative poem about a celebration
- About a pet
- About a particular age
- About a list of "Howdo's" (using Shel Silverstein's poem "Whatif" as a model)

A Monologue

- By a woman standing by the ocean
- About a friend
- By a child playing in the mud
- About beautiful things
- For Shere Khan (from *The Jungle Book*)
- In which a character explains his or her qualities
- By Earth
- By a boy or a man
- By a cat
- About a humorous birthday experience
- About worries
- About becoming younger

A Dialogue

- About children playing
- Between Raksha and Akela about Mowgli (fror *The Jungle Book*)
- About reliving youth
- Between a young boy and an old man
- About "what if" question

Prewriting

Boys in the City *Diana Ong, Private Collection*

Inspirations for Creative Writing

Here are some creative writing ideas:

A Monologue by a Boy in a Painting

Many city dwellers live in apartment buildings, such as the one in the painting above. Notice the boys in the painting. What impression do you think city life has on them? Write a monologue that voices the thoughts of one of the boys. How does he feel about living in an apartment in the city? What are some of his experiences? Use your imagination, but base your ideas on the details of the painting.

Song Lyrics About an Emotion

Songwriters compose lyrics that express a variety of emotions. To what topics do you have a strong emotional response? Choose a topic that makes you feel an emotion—such as sadness, happiness, or anger—and write song lyrics about it. When writing the lyrics, include a repeating line or group of lines that emphasize the emotion you want to convey.

Song Lyrics About the Forces of Nature

The forces of nature can be quite powerful. During a hurricane, mountainous ocean waves can wash away coastal beaches, while battering winds can uproot trees and damage houses. Think about some other powerful forces of nature—earthquakes, tornadoes, and lightning storms, for example. Write lyrics to a song that describes a force in nature. Try to develop a refrain, or group of repeating lines, to communicate the main idea of your song lyrics.

A Dialogue About Friendship

Think about your definition of a friend. You might say a friend is someone you enjoy being with. You can have fun with a friend. A friend is someone who will be there for you when you need help. However, the road of friendship isn't always a smooth one. Even the best of friends have arguments and disagreements. Recall a situation from a story you've read—or make up a situation—in which two friends have a serious disagreement that threatens to end their friendship. Write a dialogue in which they reach a compromise that saves their friendship.

A Poem About a Special Place

Is there a special place where you really like to be? Perhaps a room in your home, a park or playground in your community, the seaside, or a hidden spot in the woods is special to you. Write a poem in which you use images, or word pictures, to capture what this place looks like and to share what makes the place special.

Group Project: Write a Poem About Musical Instruments

Do you like music? Do you like the sounds of some musical instruments more than others? As a group, list the names of different kinds of musical instruments. Have each group member choose one or two of these instruments and think of a verb for each to describe the sound it makes. (For example, you might say that a trumpet *screams.*) Each individual should use that verb to write a line of poetry about the sound of that instrument. As a group, combine these lines into a group poem that captures the sounds of a band.

A Monologue About Impossible Things

Everyone has special hopes and dreams. For example, someone might hope to be a doctor, a writer, or a movie star. Some hopes and dreams, however, will never or could never happen. Nothing can make an older person young again or change the outcome of events that have already occurred. What are some other things that people hope for that cannot really happen? Write a monologue in which you present some options for dealing with an impossible dream.

A Song for an Ad

Some songs, called jingles, are written to persuade people to buy a product. Think of a product you find especially appealing and write a jingle for it. Try to use humorous lyrics with a catchy rhythm and rhyme. If possible, base your lyrics on a familiar tune or on one you make up yourself.

Writing Lab CD-ROM

The Inspirations for Creative Writing in the *Writing Lab* also include the following Group Projects and Group Discussions. The Group Discussions encourage small groups of students to share their thoughts about an Inspiration and to generate possible writing topics. The Group Projects are structured activities in which students assume different roles.

Group Projects

- Creating a poem web about friendship
- Writing monologues by the boys in the painting "Boys in the City" by Diana Ong
- Writing a dialogue between the emperor and the nightingale
- Writing a narrative poem about a skateboard adventure
- Writing motorcycle riddles
- Writing a collaborative poem about aging
- Creating a carnival dialogue
- Developing a dialogue between earth and people

Group Discussions

- Talking about the power of the ocean
- Creating dreams for Mowgli in the jungle
- Thinking about age
- Identifying images of beauty
- Identifying qualities of favorite pets
- Choosing the best birthday celebrations
- Comparing serious and humorous poems
- Discussing the best and worst moments of childhood

Thematic Connection: Knowing Yourself/Identity

Students who choose to write a poem about a person's inner beauty might enjoy putting a personal spin on it by writing about their own inner beauty. Suggest that they write a poem about themselves, about that private person inside who most others have not met or might not recognize.

Exploring Related Literature

Provide students who choose to write a concrete poem about city life with an example of a concrete poem by directing them to read "The Sidewalk Racer" by Lillian Morrison, which can be found in *Prentice Hall Literature, Copper*.

Language Acquisition/ ESL Teaching Strategy

The Group Project, Develop a Dialogue Between Animals and People, can be adapted for use with ESL students of all levels. Multilevel groups of four or five students brainstorm the types of animals found in the wild and what their concerns might be. When they have decided on a particular animal, they create a short dialogue between the animal and a human being. As students write their dialogues, it may be useful to assign roles, such as *writer, grammar checker, editor*. When each group finishes composing a dialogue, group members read the dialogue for other ESL groups or for the class at large.

MORE *Inspirations* for Creative Writing

A Poem About a Person's Inner Beauty

Beauty comes in many forms. There is the beauty we see in a colorful flower or a smiling face. Then there is the kind of beauty that we don't see with our eyes—inner beauty. We often "see" inner beauty in the good things that someone does for others. Choose someone whom you feel possesses inner beauty—a friend, a relative, or a public person you admire. Write a poem in which you describe this person and capture what makes him or her so special.

A Humorous Monologue by a Skateboard, Bike, or Other Object

Do you ever go skateboarding or bike riding? Do you find the experience enjoyable and exciting? If the skateboard or bike could talk, would it find the experience as thrilling or as much fun as you do? Pretend that the skateboard or bike could feel. Write a humorous monologue from the point of view of a skateboard, bike, or any other object—such as a tennis racquet or a basketball—that you use to have fun. Picture yourself as the object and try to imagine what the object feels.

A Concrete Poem About City Life

Millions of people live in cities. How do you feel about cities, and why do you feel the way you do? Express your feelings about cities in a concrete poem. A concrete poem is one with a shape that suggests its subject. The lines of the poem are arranged to create a picture on the page. Write your concrete poem in the shape of a city building. Determine the line lengths and line placement necessary to write a poem that resembles a building.

Group Project: Develop a Dialogue Between Animals and People

What images come to mind when you think of nature? Mountains and waterfalls? Rivers and seas? Creatures of the forests and the mountains? Nature is both beautiful and vital. Imagine that several animals want to question us to find out if we are taking good care of the natural world. As a group, create a dialogue between you and the animals. First, develop questions that the animals might ask you—about growing industries, farmlands, spreading populations, and pollution controls, for example. Next, each of you should write answers to at least one of the questions. As a group, arrange the questions and answers into a dialogue. Act out your dialogue for the class.

A Dialogue Between You and a Cat

What do you think the cat in the photograph above is thinking about? What is it feeling? What have been its most interesting experiences? Think of questions you would like to ask the cat. First, try to determine the kind of *purr*sonality you think the cat has by studying its expression in the photograph. Next, create questions that you think are appropriate to ask that cat. Answer the questions in the way you think the cat would. Use your questions and answers to create a dialogue between you and the cat. You can make the dialogue a humorous one if you wish.

A Poem Created From Magazines and Catalogs

Do you receive magazines or catalogs in the mail? Have you seen any interesting ones lately? Look through magazines and catalogs at home or in your school or local library. You might choose gardening catalogs, travel magazines, or sports publications. As you leaf through the paper, note any photographs or headlines that grab your attention and jot down any ideas or feelings they inspire in you. Then write a poem about the photograph or headline that makes the strongest impression upon you.

Thematic Connection: Imagination

Invite students who choose to write a dialogue between themselves and a cat to consider writing a dialogue between themselves and any pet or animal with which they are familiar. For example, a student might write a dialogue between him- or herself and a spider who creates an intricate web outside his or her bedroom window. Or a student might create a humorous dialogue with a cow that grazes near his or her schoolbus stop.

Writing Lab CD-ROM

The Considering Audience and Purpose section of the tutorial on Creative Writing includes the following options to help students explore ways to gear their writing to their intended audience:

- **Audience Profile activity** Students answer questions that help them focus on their intended audience.
- **Audio-annotated slide show about audience** Students see images of different audiences to help them grasp the importance of considering their audience as they write.
- **Audio-annotated models of two poems written for different purposes** Students compare two poems about night. The purpose of one is to frighten; the other attempts to excite. Audio annotations explain how the poets accomplished their purposes.

Language Lab CD-ROM

If students need additional guidance dealing with the issues of audience and purpose, you may want them to complete the Considering Audience and Purpose lesson in the Composing unit of the *Language Lab*. It may be useful to set up brief conferences with these students to talk through some possibilities they can consider.

Writing Strategy

Emphasize to students that whatever the purpose of their piece of creative writing, it will be more effective if they use vivid and exciting language wherever possible.

Considering Your Audience

Who will read your creative writing? Are you writing for yourself, your classmates, your teacher, or someone else? Decide on your audience and think about how it will affect your writing. For example, in a poem written for a first-grader, you'd use very simple language and include details that a young child might enjoy. Keep your audience in mind as you develop and draft your paper.

Considering Your Purpose

Your purpose will also affect your writing. Think of what you want your writing to accomplish. Do you want to make your audience laugh or do you want to make them cry? Obviously, the answer to that question will have a major impact on the way you write. The type of language you use and your choice of words depend to a great extent upon your purpose. For example, if your purpose in a poem about the planet Mercury is to amaze your readers, you might include words that convey its intense temperatures.

To see how purpose affects creative writing, look at the following poems. Both are written about the same subject, but each has a different purpose. Find words in each passage that help achieve the desired purpose.

Writing Models: Considering Purpose

INTENDED PURPOSE:
TO FRIGHTEN

The night is a blanket of
darkness
Filled with danger and fright
So stay in your home
When at night you're alone
Or you might be snatched
out of sight.

INTENDED PURPOSE:
TO EXCITE

At night there's a world of
excitement
Cool things can come out of
the dark
If your eyes can get right
and adjust to the light
You can have a nighttime lark.

Draw attention to the figurative language used in the Writing Models. Point out the opening metaphor, "The night is a blanket of darkness," and then highlight its impact by substituting commonplace words, such as "The night is very dark."

Writing Lab CD-ROM

The Gathering Details section of the tutorial on Creative Writing includes the following options designed to help students efficiently gather sensory images and poetic details for a poem or for song lyrics, or details about charac

Gathering Details

Before you begin drafting your poem, song lyrics, monologue, or dialogue, gather the details that you will use. The following sections will help you gather details for the particular type of creative writing that you've chosen.

FROM a WRITER

"When I come up with an idea, it might be based on memory. But then the imagination takes over, and no one knows how the imagination works."

—Gary Soto

How to Gather Details for a Poem or Song Lyrics

If you're writing a poem or song lyrics, use details that create pictures, or images, with words.

Gather Sensory Images When collecting details for a poem or song lyrics, gather sensory images, or word pictures that appeal to the five senses. Describe how your subject looks, sounds, feels, tastes, and smells. For example, if you were to list details about how a kitten feels, you might jot down the words *soft, velvety, warm,* and *cuddly.* For details about how a storm sounds, you might include *rumbling thunder, cracking lightning, whistling wind,* and *pounding rain.* The following chart contains other examples of sensory images. Try creating your own sensory image chart.

SENSORY IMAGES				
EYES	EARS	NOSE	MOUTH	FINGERS
Setting sun	Crackling fire	Sea spray	Lemon juice	Frosty window
Red stoplight	Shrieking siren	Smoky fire	Apple	Prickly stems
Sparkling waves	Purring cat	Gasoline	Honey	Sandpaper
Wrinkled wet fingertips	Thumping heart	Garlic bread	Jalapeño pepper	Suntan oil
Full moon	Giggling	Musty attic	Cinnamon	Slimy algae
Dandelion	Roaring engine	Wet dog	Salt water	Hand squeeze

er, setting, and plot for monologues and dialogues:

- **Dramatic video reading of a poem** Poet Valerie Worth reads her poem "Sun" to demonstrate how vivid imagery can bring creative writing to life.
- **Sensory Image Word Bin** Students choose from a menu to see lists of sensory images, one list for each of the five senses. They can save images they like in their on-line Notebook for later use.
- **Cluster Diagram for feelings and ideas** Students choose a feeling or idea they want to express in a poem and write it in the center of the diagram. Then they list specific people, places, objects, or actions that suggest the feeling or idea.
- **Character Trait Word Bins** Students choose words from various bins to determine significant traits for each character in their writing. They can consider details such as goals, personality, habits, abilities, and physical appearance.
- **Video clip about developing character through monologue** Students play a clip from *Star Trek* that demonstrates how the character of Spock is revealed through the words he says.
- **Interactive instruction on using dialogue to develop character** Students choose each character trait listed to see a model of dialogue that expresses that trait.
- **Interactive instruction on adding details through stage directions** Students compare two drafts of setting notes to see the effect of adding vivid details through stage directions.

Working individually or in small groups, students can experiment with these activities to find the ones that work best for them.

Writers at Work Videodisc

Play the videodisc segment in which Gary Soto talks about embellishing the truth to create a poem. Ask:

- What does Gary Soto mean when he says that the experience was "really almost true"?
- What strategies can you use to help you gather words and images for a poem or for another kind of creative writing?

Play frames 24540 to 25950

Prewriting

Use a Cluster Diagram Completing a Cluster Diagram is another good way to gather details for a poem. First, decide what feeling or idea you want to express in your poem and write it in the center of a circle. Around that main circle, list specific people, places, objects, and actions that suggest the feeling or idea. Then use lines to connect related items to each other. Refer to your Cluster Diagram when you draft your poem.

Here is a sample Cluster Diagram for the feeling *coziness*.

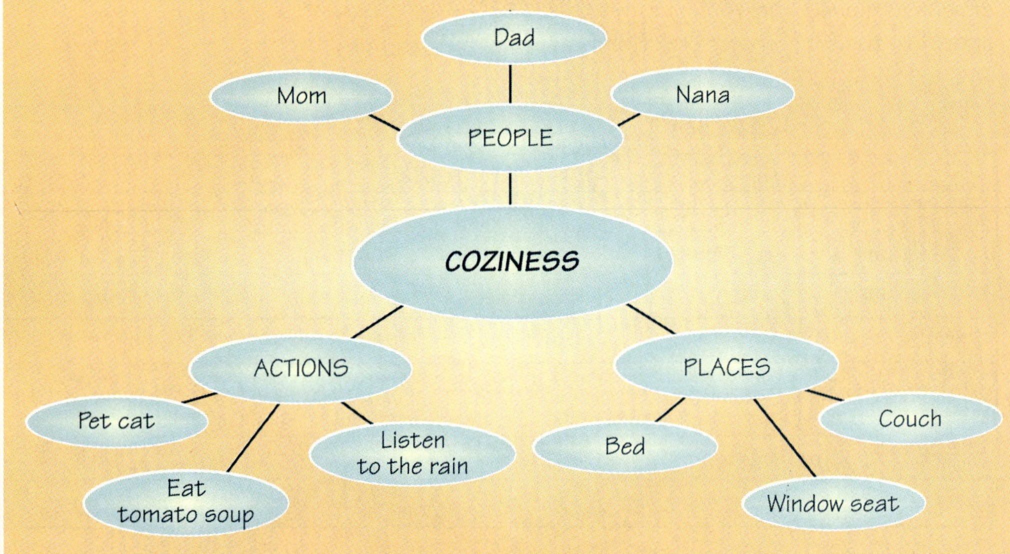

How to Gather Details for a Monologue or Dialogue

If you're writing a monologue or dialogue, gather details about the setting, plot, and characters. The **setting** is the time and place where the action occurs. The **plot** is the sequence of events in the monologue or dialogue. The **characters** are the persons or animals that take part in the action. Think about the characters you plan to include. Consider each character's habits, likes, and dislikes, and then jot down the character's traits. Here are some examples: angry, nosy, unhappy, suspicious, greedy, jealous, cheerful, brave, cautious, shy, and generous.

Then decide where and when your monologue or dialogue will be set. Sometimes a setting can add excitement and tension to a play. Think about specific details that can make the setting more exciting. Also, decide what props to include. Props are objects—such as pens, clocks, calculators, or fishing rods—that the characters use on stage. The right props can strengthen a setting by suggesting a specific time or place. Look at the following notes about a particular setting:

Writing Model

When and where play starts: National forest far from civilization during an unexpected April blizzard

What happens: Tony and Daryl get lost during a class trip to a national forest. At first the boys don't get along. When the storm strikes, however, they must quickly learn to cooperate in order to survive.

Addressing Ability Levels

You can help your **more-challenged students** focus on details of setting, plot, and character for a play by identifying and discussing these elements within the context of a well-known television show or film. Talk about how the audience learns about setting (by the scenery and props used) and plot (through action, monologue, and dialogue). Students are likely to be most attuned to characterization, which they can understand through what characters do and say, what they wear, where they live, who they associate with, and so on. Discuss how students can weave some of these ideas into their own creative pieces through dialogue and stage directions.

Clarification

Point out that when gathering specific details about setting, students need not list every possible prop or aspect of setting a director might include in a fully staged production of a play. However, they should indicate key props or details about setting that are essential to the plot or to specific events or characters.

Drafting

Good writers *show*; they don't merely *tell*. If you're writing a poem or a song, use images, or word pictures, to *show* the feelings you're expressing. If you're writing a monologue or dialogue, *show* how your characters feel through the way they speak and act. (*Example*: "I don't think I can take another step. My legs feel as if they have weights on them.") Don't just have your characters *tell* how they feel. (*Example*: "I'm very tired.")

As you draft your piece, concentrate on *showing* rather than *telling*. Use the following tips for additional guidance as you write.

Using Sound in a Poem or Song

Poetry and song have much in common. Both rely on the sounds of words to help set a mood, but a song adds the dimension of music. A song is, in effect, poetry set to music.

As you draft your poem or song, concentrate on sound as well as meaning. Depending on the sounds you choose, a poem or a song can seem bouncy and cheerful or slow and mournful. Here are some ways you can use sound in your poem or song:

- **Rhyme** is the repetition of sounds at the ends of words. Many poems and songs use end rhymes, or rhyming words at the ends of lines.

Model From Literature

In the following excerpt from the poem "The Geese" by Richard Peck, the rhyming words are indicated by single and double underscores.

My father was the first to hear
The passage of the geese each fall,
Passing above the house so near
He'd hear within his heart their call.

Writing Lab CD-ROM

The Drafting section of the tutorial on Creative Writing includes the following options designed to help students write the first draft of their poem, song lyrics, monologue, or dialogue:

- **Video tip on drafting from professional writer Gary Soto** Students hear Soto's ideas about how a poem must *show* rather than *tell*.
- **Interactive direct instruction about using sound devices in poetry** Students see annotated examples to learn about the devices of rhyme, rhythm, and onomatopoeia.
- **Sensory Image Bins** Students refer to five bins of images—appropriate for each of the five senses—to help them draft their poems or song lyrics.
- **Audio-annotated student Writing Models** Students can hear writers' insights into the choices they made to create the first drafts of two poems: one that rhymes, and another without a regular rhyme scheme.
- **Audio-annotated professional Writing Models** Students see examples of how to write effective dialogue and how to add details through stage directions.
- **Video example of dialogue used to develop character** Students can play a video to see how dialogue is used to describe the thoughts, emotions, attitudes, and habits of characters.

Working individually or in small groups, students can experiment with these activities to find the ones that work best for them.

Teaching Strategy

Play the videodisc segment in which Gary Soto talks about the importance of *showing*, not just *telling* about the world you live in. Ask:

- What does Gary Soto mean by this distinction?
- How can the idea of showing rather than telling apply to writing a monologue or dialogue as well as to poetry?

Encourage students to read the drafts of their creative pieces aloud to check for language and imagery that shows rather than tells. Remind students that monologues or dialogues can show how characters feel through what the characters say and do.

Play frames 29646 to 30720

- **Rhythm** is the pattern of beats, or stresses, in language. In many poems and songs, you can count the number of beats in a line. Do you want your poem or song to have a regular rhythm? For example, you might alternate lines with four beats with lines with three beats.

Model From Literature

In the following excerpt from a riddle by Mary Austin, the obvious rhythm adds a playful mood to each line.

I come more softly than a bird, (4 beats)
And lovely as a flower; (3 beats)
I sometimes last from year to year (4 beats)
And sometimes but an hour. (3 beats)

(In case you're wondering, the answer to the riddle is "snow.")

- **Onomatopoeia** is the use of words that imitate sounds. The word *hiss* is an example. Do you want to use this device in your poem or song?

Model From Literature

In the following haiku by Bashō, notice how the word *splash* momentarily breaks the silence.

An old silent pond . . .
A frog jumps into the pond,
splash! Silence again.

Drafting • 257

Clarification

A rhyme scheme is named by the pattern the poet uses. For example, the poem "The Geese" (p. 256) has an ABAB pattern: the first and third lines end with one rhyme, and the second and fourth lines end with another. A poet can choose any rhyme scheme, but that scheme should remain consistent through the poem.

Teaching Strategy

Students may best recognize the impact of rhythm in poetry by hearing what happens when the rhythm is "off" or absent altogether. Invite students to alter the wording in Mary Austin's riddle to change its mood. For instance, changing the fourth line to "And sometimes I only last a short time" would destroy the rhyme and make the poem feel clumsy.

Writing Strategy

Have students brainstorm a list of onomatopoetic words, such as *sizzle*, *gurgle*, and *pop*. They may want to use some of these words in their drafts, or keep the list for later use when they revise their creative pieces.

Exploring Related Literature

Students who enjoy rhyme may wish to read and analyze the rhyme patterns in the following poems, all of which appear in *Prentice Hall Literature, Copper*: "Dust of Snow" by Robert Frost, "The Shark" by John Ciardi, "Books Fall Open" by David McCord, and "Adventures of Isabel" by Ogden Nash.

Writing Strategy

While students may equate poetry with rhyme, they should realize that words chosen simply *because* they rhyme can make a poem seem forced and dilute its emotional impact. Urge students who write rhymed poetry to include vivid language and fresh imagery so the poem avoids sounding sing-songy or trite. Students who use rhyme might try making a rhyme chain. To do so, they choose a word that appeals to their senses, such as *bell*, and then list several words that rhyme with it, such as *tell, fell, well, cell, propel, lapel, groundswell*. This technique can help them strive for surprising or less overused rhymes.

Some poets and lyricists consult a rhyming dictionary to help them find just the right rhyming word. You might make such a resource available to students while working on this unit.

Teaching Strategy

To help students understand how dialogue can reveal character, have each student write one line of dialogue they might say to show a key trait about themselves. For instance, to show impatience, a student might write, "How long do I have to wait to give my speech?"

Language Lab CD-ROM

Students who need additional help in understanding how dialogue can reveal character may benefit from doing the Writing Dialogue lesson in the Composing unit of the *Language Lab*.

Clarification

Emphasize to students that there is a different format used for dialogue in plays than in narrative writing. Scripts do not use quotation marks; rather, the name of the character who speaks precedes each line he or she says. Stage directions in monologues or dialogues appear in parentheses to set them apart from the actual words a character says. Stage directions, which are usually in the present tense, may be words, phrases, or complete sentences.

Developing Characters in a Monologue or Dialogue

When you write a monologue or dialogue, make sure your characters use language that clearly expresses their individual personalities. Think about the personalities of each of your characters. Consider their habits, likes, and dislikes. How can you convey their personalities through what they say and the way they speak?

Think about how you want your characters to act and then write dialogue to suit them. At right are some writing models that illustrate how spoken words reveal character traits. Notice how each character trait is clearly expressed through the corresponding passage.

Writing Hint

READ ALOUD TO GET THE RIGHT SOUND

Poems, songs, dialogues, and monologues are meant to be heard as well as read. As you draft, read your work aloud to hear how it sounds. If there is anything that could be made more clear, vivid, or dramatic, make the changes now.

Writing Model

USING DIALOGUE TO SHOW CHARACTER TRAITS

(Character traits are in italic type.)

- *Angry*: "I've had enough of you and your foolishness. Clean that up and don't ever touch my things again!"
- *Nosy*: "Who said she went to the movies with him? Tell me everything—every little detail."
- *Suspicious*: "I don't trust those kids from the other school. They just look like they're up to something."
- *Greedy*: "I want the whole bunch of grapes, and save me an apple and a banana, too."
- *Brave*: "Wait! I don't want to put you in danger, Steve. Let me go first."
- *Cautious*: "I'm not too sure about this. The last kids that tried it got hurt."
- *Shy*: "I don't want to say hello—I don't even know them. You speak to them first."
- *Generous*: "Oh, is it raining? Well, take my umbrella. I can wear my hood and we'll both stay dry."

Establishing Assessment Criteria

As students begin drafting their creative-writing pieces, you may want to share with them the criteria you will use to evaluate their work. The following guidelines are included in the tutorial on Creative Writing in the *Writing Lab* CD-ROM. Note that there is one set of questions for poetry, which can also be applied to song lyrics, and another set for drama, which applies to dialogue or monologue. Use guidelines as given, or modify them to suit your needs.

Evaluation Guidelines for Poetry

- Is the subject of your poem clear?
- What ideas or feelings does your poem express?
- Did you use imagery or word pictures in your poem?
- Did you use rhyme, rhythm, or other sound devices in your poem?
- Did you select a standard form for your poem?

Evaluation Guidelines for Drama

- Does your dialogue or monologue convey the personality of each character?
- Does the way each character speaks sound real?

Revising and Editing

FROM a WRITER

"When you revise a poem, what you have to look for is insincere writing or loose language—words that can be cut out. . . . I have to shave language so that it's concise and succinct and . . . a pleasure to the ear and to the eye."
—Gary Soto

Revising Your Work

Now that you've finished drafting, it's time to reread your writing to look for ways to improve it. Does your poem or song create a vivid image? Do the characters in your dialogue or monologue seem real? Use one of the following checklists to focus your revising process.

Revision Checklist for a Poem or a Song

1. What is the subject of your poem or song? How can you make the focus of your work more clear?
2. What vivid images, or word pictures, did you use? How can you improve your images? What images might you add?
3. What sound devices—such as rhyme, rhythm, or onomatopoeia—did you use? How can you improve your use of sound devices?

Revision Checklist for a Monologue or Dialogue

1. What is the main subject of your dialogue or monologue? How can you make that subject more clear?
2. How did you use the words spoken by the characters to reveal their personalities? What revisions can you make to capture their personalities even more effectively?
3. What kind of information do your stage directions provide? How can you improve them?

Writing Lab CD-ROM

The Revising and Editing section of the tutorial on Creative Writing provides strategies for self-revision. It includes the following options to help students develop strategies to revise the first draft of their creative pieces:

- **Video tip from a writer** Students hear suggestions from Gary Soto on revising poetry to include interesting verbs.
- **Interactive Self-Evaluation Checklist for poetry** Students answer questions to help them to evaluate their draft for focus, imagery, and sound devices used.
- **Interactive Self-Evaluation Checklist for drama** Students answer questions to help them to evaluate their draft for focus, use of dialogue, and stage directions.
- **Audio-annotated Student Models** Students can compare first drafts with revised drafts to understand how and why revisions were made to a rhyming poem and to a poem without a rhyme scheme.
- **Image Bin** Students use the words and phrases in five sensory bins to revise vague images.
- **Annotated models of revised dialogue** Students compare the first draft of dialogue with the revised version to see the writer's reason for revising.
- **Vague adjectives checker** Students use a revision checker that highlights any vague or overused adjectives in their draft.

Working individually or in small groups, students can experiment with these activities to find the ones that work best.

Writers at Work Videodisc

Play the videodisc segment in which Gary Soto discusses revising a poem. He says that it's important to look for "insincere writing or loose language." Ask:

- What does Soto mean by "insincere writing and loose language"? How can you recognize this kind of problem in your own writing?

Soto also discusses how he shares his poetry with others and the benefit he sees in peer editing. Ask:

- Why does Soto believe that a writer ". . . must have a sounding board"? What experiences with peer editors have helped you revise your work?

Play frames 26762 to 27580

Student Model: Revised Draft

Here is a revised stanza from a poem by Jimmy Pacheco, a student at Roncalli Middle School in Pueblo, Colorado. Notice how Jimmy's changes create more vivid images, or pictures with words.

The ^sandy beach is my favorite place to go
Because the ~~water~~ ^waves just flows.
Its sand is so ^lightning bright,
like flying a kite
The California sunshine
is better than ~~being in the~~ ^a wood of pine.

Having a Peer Review Your Work

After you've revised your own work, have one of your classmates review it. Your classmate's responses to the following questions can guide you in making final revisions.

Peer Review Checklist

1. Which images in the poem or song lyrics could be made stronger? How?
2. What could make the poem or song lyrics sound better?
3. How could the monologue or dialogue suit the characters' personalities better and sound more natural?

Proofreading

After you've revised your poem, song, dialogue, or monologue, check it carefully for errors in spelling, punctuation, and grammar. Such errors can detract from the image or scene you are trying to create and make your work difficult to read. Use the following checklist as a guide while you proofread your work.

Proofreading Checklist

1. Have you spelled each word correctly?
2. Have you used capital letters correctly, especially at the beginnings of lines of a poem or a song?
3. Have you used punctuation marks correctly?
4. Did you use indents or other kinds of spacing consistently?

Teaching Strategies

- Discuss the two Revision Checklists presented in the *Sourcebook*. Ask students to compare them to other revision checklists they have used.
- You may want to make large versions of the checklists to post in your room for students to refer to as they revise their plays, poems, or song lyrics. Feel free to adapt the lists to include techniques or ideas your students suggest in response to each question.

Alternate Activity

As an alternative to simply reading a creative piece aloud to hear how it sounds, students might read the piece into a tape recorder. Then they can play it back as often as necessary, listening carefully each time for rhythm, rhyme, or other sound devices, as well as for the realism or flow of the language used.

Writing Lab CD-ROM

The Revising and Editing section of the tutorial on Creative Writing includes the following options to help students develop strategies for proofreading their creative writing pieces:

- **Proofreading Checklists for poetry and drama** Students use the checklist that applies to the kind of writing they have done.
- **Audio-annotated Student Model of a proofread poem** Students hear explanations of how and why the writer made certain corrections.
- **Interactive instruction on possessive nouns** Students can choose from a list of singular and plural nouns to see each one change to the correct possessive form that shows ownership.

Working individually or in small groups, students can experiment with these activities to find the ones that work best.

Language Lab CD-ROM

Students who need additional practice using possessive nouns correctly may benefit from doing the Possessive Nouns lesson in the Using Nouns unit.

Peer Revision

You might suggest that students proofread with a different peer editor than the one who helped them revise and edit. A fresh eye often detects errors previously missed.

Publishing and Presenting

How will you present your creative writing to your audience? You can read a poem or song aloud or choose some artwork to accompany a printed version of it. If you have a melody in mind for song lyrics you've written, you can sing your song. You can even perform a dialogue (with a partner) or a monologue as a short play in front of the class. Here are a couple of other publishing ideas.

Hold a Poetry Festival A poetry festival provides an opportunity for many people to enjoy poetry. Each performer can read an original poem and a favorite published poem. Follow these suggestions to hold a poetry festival:

- Hold a group discussion to decide how many people will read, in what order they will read, and how the poems will be organized.
- Advertise the festival to attract a wide audience. Put up posters and write a news article about the festival for the local newspaper.
- Plan the actual poetry festival. Put someone in charge of organizing the readers, someone in charge of the location and seating, and someone in charge of preparing printed programs.

Present a Full Performance of a Monologue or Dialogue If you want to share your dialogue or monologue as a complete play, present a full performance of it. However, preparations for the performance will take time and effort. Here are some tips to get you started:

- If you want to put on a full performance, you'll probably need adult help. This person can reserve space for performing and rehearsing and can organize things in general.
- Start planning for your performance several weeks ahead of time. Pick a cast for the play and choose a director.
- Assemble or make costumes, a stage set, and props.
- Prepare programs for the audience.

Writing Lab CD-ROM

The Publishing and Presenting section of the tutorial on Creative Writing includes the following options to help students present their completed works:

- **Tips for presenting a play** Students get ideas on how to cast and perform a play for an audience.
- **Tips for holding a poetry festival** Students consult a list of guidelines for having a poetry reading to share creative works with a wider audience.

The Multimedia Workshop

Students can use the templates in the Writing Workshop component of *The Multimedia Workshop* to word-process and present their final creative-writing pieces. For instance, a student writing dialogue can use the script template. A student writing free verse might use the greeting card template and import a photo or clip art to accompany the poem.

Students who wish to make video presentations can use the Video Workshop Scene Maker and Sequencer. For example, a student writing a monologue can create a video performance of the speech, with music and sound effects to enhance it.

Alternate Activity

As an alternative to staging a full performance of a dialogue or monologue, students might present such works as radio plays. Actors or readers would present each part and an assistant would add simple sound effects. Students could make an audio tape of the presentation to include in their portfolio.

Portfolio Assessment

Have students write an evaluative statement that addresses questions such as the following:

- What part of the creative-writing process did you find most satisfying? Most challenging?
- How do you feel about writing a creative piece, as compared with writing other kinds of pieces? Which type of creative writing would you like to try next time? Why?
- In what ways has your writing shown the most improvement? In which areas should you focus your attention in future assignments?
- What did you learn while writing creatively that you can apply to other writing assignments?

If students decide to include the completed creative piece in their portfolio, they might attach this statement to it. Otherwise, the statement itself can go into the portfolio as a record of self-evaluation.

Student Model

Teaching From the Model

Discuss how "The Beach" by Jimmy Pacheco includes the essential elements of poetry.

- *It expresses the poet's experience.* Pacheco begins by saying that the beach is "my favorite place to go." Once he reveals his love for the beach, the details that follow support his feelings.
- *It expresses ideas in a few words.* At the end of the poem, Pacheco says, "I go home and eat pie." This brief statement conveys the celebratory mood the poet feels after spending time at the beach.
- *It uses sound devices.* Pacheco uses rhyme and onomatopoetic language to create vivid images and a melodic feeling. He used a pattern in which every two lines rhyme. His use of the onomatopoetic words *thrashing* and *shimmering* vividly suggests the sound and movement of the sea.
- *It includes sensory details and imagery that produces an emotional effect.* The simile that likens the ocean to a "sorcerer's potion" is an appealing comparison that gives emotional power to Pacheco's poem through the use of fresh imagery. By describing sand as "lightning bright," he makes readers imagine both warmth and nature's power.

Here is the complete, final draft of Jimmy Pacheco's poem about the beach.

The Beach

by Jimmy Pacheco

In this stanza, I expressed an opinion about the beach and supported my opinion with vivid images of the beach.

The sandy beach is my favorite
  place to go
Because the waves just flow.
Its sand is so lightning bright,
Like a flying kite.
The California sunshine
Is better than a wood of pine.

Here I used a simile to express the magical quality that the ocean holds for me.

The thrashing ocean is good to surf
But I'd rather run on turf.
The shimmering ocean
Is like a sorcerer's potion.
But when the tide is high,
I go home and eat pie.

Technology Note: Networking

After your class has read the Student Model, students may be interested in sharing creative efforts with students across the country via the Internet or commercial online services such as Prodigy or America Online. Students can exchange creative pieces with other students, including those using *Writer's Solution*, by connecting to Prentice Hall's Internet home page. Look for special events and contests, as well as bulletin boards and pointers to student publications at http://www.phschool.com.

Management Strategy

You can have students work through one or both of the skills lessons either before or after they write their creative pieces. If you use the lessons *before*, remind students to incorporate the techniques in their writing. If you address skills *after* students write their poems, lyrics, dialogues, or monologues, have them

Developing Your Style 1

Punctuating and Formatting Dialogue

When you write dialogue, you present the words that each person says. **Quotation marks** show where a speaker's words begin and end. A speaker's exact words, called a **direct quotation**, are enclosed in quotation marks.

- Begin a quotation with a capital letter and enclose the entire quotation in quotation marks. Remember to use a comma to separate a quotation from words that identify the speaker.

  Example:

  "The word *castle* comes from a Latin word that means *fortress.* I read that in a book about castles," said Andrew.

- Capitalize the first word of a quotation and begin a new paragraph each time a different person speaks.

  Example:

  "Castles were built during the Middle Ages," said Beth.
  "Most of them were built of stone," added Steve.

- Commas separate quotations from words that identify the speaker, no matter where those words appear in a sentence. Commas always appear before quotation marks.

  Example:

  "The walls of a castle were up to thirty-three feet thick," said Michael.
  Melissa added, "The walls were made thick for protection against enemies."

Practice Activity

Rewrite the following dialogue to correct the punctuation and capitalization. Make sure that each time a different person speaks, a new paragraph begins.

Wow! It must have been thrilling to tour an English castle said Tammy. Tell me all about it. Bob said It was exciting. Until our vacation in England, I had only seen pictures of castles in books. I was impressed by the thick stone walls. Linda chimed in, we were amazed that people hundreds of years ago, without modern machinery, could build such massive structures.

include a section on "skills improvement" in the self-assessment document they prepare for their portfolios.

You may want to give students these lessons as take-home assignments to be completed prior to the drafting, revising, or proofreading stages—wherever you see the greatest need. Or you may choose to assign the skills lessons only to those students whose drafts indicate a need for direct instruction in these particular skills.

Teaching Strategy

To connect the skills lessons to the students' writing, explain that one important feature of writing plays, or anything with dialogue, is to make sure that the dialogue is clear and easy to follow. One way to remove vagueness or confusion is to use the conventions of punctuating and formatting written dialogue.

Another aspect of effective dialogue writing is to use natural language that sounds realistic. One way to do this is to use contractions, which are commonly heard in informal speech.

Integrating Skills With Writing

Teaching Strategy

Review the conventions for writing dialogue in a play. Students should note the boldface type and the capital letters used to name each character that speaks, the lack of quotation marks, and the italicized stage directions set apart from the spoken words by parentheses. Point out that dialogue used in other forms of writing, such as a short story or novel, follows the conventions taught in this lesson.

Writer's Companion

To provide students with additional support and reinforcement in punctuating and formatting dialogue, direct them to the section on quotations, which begins on page 373. Students may also benefit from reading the section on using realistic dialogue (p. 142).

Practice Activity Answer

"Wow! It must have been thrilling to actually tour an English castle," said Tammy. "Tell me about it."

Bob said, "It was exciting. Until our vacation in England, I had only seen pictures of castles in books. I was impressed by the thick stone walls."

Linda chimed in, "We were amazed that people hundreds of years ago without modern machinery could build such massive structures."

Developing Your Style

Using Contractions

When you write creatively, you must also write clearly. Your audience must be able to understand you. Why is the following dialogue hard to understand?

> "Lets take you're insect book along with us and see how many different kinds of bugs will see in the park," said Dan.
> "Thats a great idea. Ill bet will see all kinds of bugs they're, especially when were near the pond," replied Justin.

The dialogue is littered with incorrect words that make its meaning puzzling. The puzzling dialogue is the result of the incorrect use of contractions. Now read the revision:

> "Let's take your insect book along with us and see how many different kinds of bugs we'll see in the park," said Dan.
> "That's a great idea. I'll bet we'll see all kinds of bugs there, especially when we're near the pond," replied Justin.

A **contraction** is a combination of two separate words written in a shortened form. An apostrophe shows where letters have been omitted. For example, the apostrophe in *we'll*—formed from *we will*—stands for the letters *w* and *i*, omitted from the word *will*. Here are some commonly used contractions:

I'll (I will)	he's (he is)	aren't (are not)	wasn't (was not)
she'll (she will)	couldn't (could not)	isn't (is not)	hasn't (has not)

Practice Activity

Write the contractions that can be used in place of the underlined words in the following sentences.

1. Who is going to see the new insect exhibit at the museum?
2. There is a beautiful orange-and-black butterfly on the rose.
3. You will be surprised when you first spot a Goliath beetle.
4. Is not that an insect that is four inches long when fully grown?
5. Who has got the magnifying glass that we are to use?

Teaching Strategy

After students read both excerpts, ask them why the revised version is so much better. Explain that because contractions are common in everyday speech, they are easy on the ear. However, they are used less often in formal writing, so they require some care to make them easy on the eye.

Brainstorm with the class to add to the list of contractions that appears on page 264. For each addition, write the two words and the contraction with an apostrophe to indicate the omitted letter(s).

Addressing Ability Levels

Challenge your **more-advanced students** to show their understanding of the difference between the troublesome word pairs *its/it's*, *theirs/there's*, *whose/who's*, and *your/you're* by writing sentences that contain both words correctly used. For instance: "*It's* about time the cat got *its* food" or "It's so noisy in the hall, I can't tell *who's* knocking at *whose* door!" Post the sentences in the classroom as resources to help students avoid usage errors with these troublesome pairs of words.

Language Lab CD-ROM

For more practice using contractions, students can work through the Possessive Pronouns and Contractions lesson in the Using Pronouns unit and the Apostrophes and Hyphens lesson in the Punctuation unit.

Language Acquisition/ ESL Teaching Strategy

The Practice Activity can be easily adapted for use with your basic ESL students. Use cards and a pocket chart to review and reinforce the use of contractions. For example, on one card, write *you;* on another card, write *will*. On the back of the card with *will* write *'ll*. Ask the students to write or say the contraction for *you will*. Then turn over the second card so that they can see if they were correct. Ask the students to read the sentences of the Practice Activity, using the appropriate contractions. As a follow-up, have them write their own sentences with contractions.

Writer's Companion

To provide students with additional support and reinforcement for using contractions correctly, direct them to the section on Contractions, which begins on page 330.

Practice Activity Answers

1. Who's
2. There's
3. You'll
4. Isn't; that's
5. Who's; we're

Literature Model

According to poet and novelist Gary Soto (1952–), creative writing is what happens when "the imagination takes over." It's up to the writer or poet to come up with new ideas and creative ways to use language. As you read Soto's poem "Ode to Weightlifting," notice the precise language he uses to express his idea about the linkage of apple eating and weightlifting.

Ode to Weightlifting

by Gary Soto

Tony eats apples
On Saturday morning,
Two for each arm,
And one for the backs
Of his calves.
He's twelve
And a weightlifter in his
garage.
He bites into an apple,
And, chewing,
He curls weights—
One, two, three . . .
His face reddens,
And a blue vein
Deepens on his neck—
Four, five, six . . .
Sweat inches down
His cheek. A curl of
Hair falls in his face—
Seven, eight, nine . . .
He grunts and strains—
Ten, eleven, twelve!
Tony curls his age,
And he would curl his weight
Of 83 pounds, but he
Would pull a muscle
In his arm.

Tony pulls off his T-shirt.
He flexes his biceps,
And apples show up in his arms.
"Pretty good," he says,
His fists clenched.
He takes another
Bite of apple,
And out of happiness
Bites the apples
In his biceps, tenderly
Of course. The teeth
Marks are pink,
His arms brown,
And his roar red as a lion's
With a paw swiping at air.

Soto uses precise language in order to give the reader a lot of information in a few words.

Soto uses lines of numbers to set up a rhythm. Between each of these lines, sensory details build on each other to create the vivid image of Tony straining with his weights.

Here Soto creates an original image of biceps transformed, in Tony's eyes, into apples. Soto succeeds in showing the reader a brand-new way of looking at the ordinary, everyday activity of weightlifting.

Soto uses a simile to compare Tony to a lion.

Integrating Literature With Writing

Teaching From the Model

Discuss Soto's work to help students see how it typifies a poem:

- *It is a vivid expression of an experience.* Although the audience may not know whether Soto himself lifts weights, the careful detail with which he presents the story of a boy who lifts weights in his garage demonstrates familiarity with the subject.
- *It uses compressed language to express ideas succinctly.* Soto conveys the effort Tony expends to lift weights in short, concise images, such as "His face reddens."
- *It uses rhythm and repetition.* Although Soto has chosen not to rhyme his poem, he does use rhythm. The counting in groups of three moves the middle part of the poem toward a climax of energy as Tony lifts his weights again and again. Soto uses repetitions in a subtle way. For example, he uses the word *curl* in two ways—as a form of lift and as a piece of hair.
- *It uses imagery that produces an emotional impact.* Soto ends the poem with the simile about Tony's roar, making it clear how proud the boy is of his efforts.

Closure and Extension

To complete the lesson, ask students to sum up what they have learned about creative writing through their examination of this poem.

Language Acquisition/ ESL Teaching Strategy

Read through the poem by Gary Soto with your intermediate and advanced ESL students and ask them to identify unfamiliar words and phrases such as *curls*, *flexes*, *grunts*. When discussing new vocabulary, use gestures, pictures, and examples in order to force the students to figure out the meaning on their own. Then lead the students in a discussion of the poem's interpretation. Ask the students, *How does the author link eating an apple with weightlifting? How do you think the weightlifter feels about his sport?* Ask the students to justify their answers.

Activating Prior Knowledge

Before students read Gary Soto's poem, invite them to share ideas, attitudes, or experiences about weightlifting.

Purpose-Setting Question

How does the poet use the elements of creative writing to create a vivid image of weightlifting?

9

Response to Literature

Classroom Manager

Writer's Solution *Materials for Teaching Response to Literature*

The *Writer's Solution* includes a wide range of materials for teaching response to literature. You can pick and choose from among these materials. In the pages that follow, you'll find lesson plans suggesting some of the most effective ways to use them. You do not have to use all the program components to use it effectively. For a description of each of the components of the *Writer's Solution*, see pages T4–T6.

Below is a detailed list of the *Writer's Solution* materials for Response to Literature.

Writers at Work Videodisc

Featured Writer: Joseph Bruchac, Writer and Editor

Videodisc Segments

About Response to Literature

Writing Tips:

Responding With an Open Mind

Finding the Balance

Interactive CD-ROMs

WRITING LAB

Tutorial on Response to Literature

About Response to Literature
- Includes seven Models From Literature

Choosing Your Topic
- Includes Inspirations and Idea Wheels

Focusing Your Response
- Includes Topic Web and a video tip from Joseph Bruchac on focusing a response

Considering Audience and Purpose
- Includes Audience Profile

Gathering Details
- Includes Chain of Events and Character Personality Profile

Drafting
- Includes Writing Models and Transition Word Bins

Revising and Editing
- Includes Self-Evaluation Checklist, revision checker, and tips for peer editors

Proofreading
- Includes integrated grammar instruction and a Proofreading Checklist

Publishing and Presenting
- Includes tips for creating a class publication

Writer's Tool Kit

Suggested Activities: Inspirations for Response to Literature, Topic Wheels, Audience Profile, Character Personality Profile, Sunburst Diagram, Self-Evaluation Checklist, revision checker, Peer Editing Worksheet, Proofreading Checklist

LANGUAGE LAB

Related Lessons: Eliminating Unnecessary Words (Styling Sentences unit); Main Idea and Topic Sentence, Supporting Sentences, Concluding Sentence (Building Paragraphs unit); Narrowing a Topic, Considering Audience and Purpose (Composing unit); Commas, Quotation Marks (Punctuation unit)

Sourcebook

About Response to Literature (pp. 270–276)

Guided Lesson on Response to Literature (pp. 277–290)

Inspirations for Response to Literature (pp. 280–283)

Developing Your Style

Using Quotation Marks and Underlining (p. 292)

Eliminating Unnecessary Words (p. 293)

Literature Model

"The Circle of Blessing: Joy Harjo's 'Eagle Poem' " by Joseph Bruchac (pp. 294–295)

Below is a list of materials from Prentice Hall's student writing handbook that you can integrate with this lesson on Response to Literature.

Writer's Companion

Mini-Lesson on Introductions, p. 27

Mini-Lesson on Elaboration, p. 31

Mini-Lesson on Conclusions, p. 37

Mini-Lesson on Figurative Language, p. 95

Mini-Lesson on Response to Literature, p. 210

Teaching Integrated Language Arts Using the Writer's Solution*—Starting With Literature*

Have students read and respond to reader's journals, literary reviews, letters to authors, and other types of responses to literature. In discussing the selections, draw students' attention to elements of response, such as including precise details or quotations and sharing personal thoughts and feelings. Point out that students can use the responses to literature they've read as models for writing their own response pieces. Lead into having students complete response writing projects using the components of the *Writer's Solution.*

While *Prentice Hall Literature*, *Copper*, contains no examples of responses to literature per se, the works listed here served as subjects for model responses that appear in the *Writing Lab* CD-ROM and the *Sourcebook.* You may want students to refer to them when reading the responses to literature.

CONNECTIONS TO *PRENTICE HALL LITERATURE, COPPER,* SELECTIONS

Short Stories/Novels	2E	3E
"The Dog of Pompeii," Louis Untermeyer	■	▲
"Dragon, Dragon," John Gardner	■	▲
"The King of Mazy May," Jack London	■	▲
"Eleven," Sandra Cisneros	■	▲
Tuck Everlasting, Natalie Babbitt	■	▲
"Zlateh the Goat," Isaac Bashevis Singer	■	▲
"The Circuit," Francisco Jimenez	■	▲
"The Stone," Lloyd Alexander	■	▲
"Mowgli's Brothers," Rudyard Kipling	■	▲
"Breaker's Bridge," Lawrence Yep	■	▲
"Sarah Tops," Isaac Asimov	■	▲
"Power," Jack Cope	■	▲
"Becky and the Wheels-and-Brake Boys," James Berry	■	▲

Journals/Poems/Essays/Drama	2E	3E
"My Papa, Mark Twain," Susy Clemens	■	▲
"Whatif," Shel Silverstein	■	▲
"Arithmetic," Carl Sandburg	■	▲
"The Naming of Cats," T. S. Eliot	■	▲
"The Shark," John Ciardi	■	▲
"Ankylosaurus," Jack Prelutsky	■	▲
"Adventures of Isabel," Ogden Nash	■	▲
"Dust of Snow," Robert Frost	■	▲
"Winter Poem," Nikki Giovanni	■	▲
"The Sidewalk Racer," Lillian Morrison	■	▲
"How to Read a Newspaper," Andrew A. Rooney	■	▲
The Phantom Tollbooth, Susan Nanus, based on the book by Norton Juster	■	▲

You can also use the *Writer's Solution* material on responding to literature to guide students through writing activities.

CONNECTIONS TO *PRENTICE HALL LITERATURE, COPPER,* WRITING ACTIVITIES

Thinking and Writing Activities	2E	3E
Supporting an Opinion—Follows **"Breaker's Bridge,"** Lawrence Yep	■	▲
Responding to the Theme—Follows **"The Stone,"** Lloyd Alexander	■	▲
Writing About a Novel—Follows ***Tuck Everlasting,*** Natalie Babbitt	■	▲
Writing About a Poem—Follows **"Stopping by Woods on a Snowy Evening,"** Robert Frost	■	▲

Focus on Writing/ Your Writing Process	2E	3E
Focus on Writing: Writing About Theme—Includes activities and assignments	■	
Focus on Writing: Reflective Writing—Includes activities and assignments	■	
Focus on Writing: Writing About a Novel—Includes activities and assignments	■	
Your Writing Process: Writing About Theme—Includes activities and assignments		▲
Your Writing Process: Reflective Writing—Includes activities and assignments		▲
Your Writing Process: Writing About a Novel—Includes activities and assignments		▲

■ **(2E)** *Prentice Hall Literature*, *Copper*, Second Edition

▲ **(3E)** *Prentice Hall Literature*, *Copper*, Paramount Edition

CONNECTIONS BETWEEN INSPIRATIONS FOR RESPONSE TO LITERATURE AND *PRENTICE HALL LITERATURE, COPPER*

You can use the multimedia Inspirations for Response to Literature to motivate student reading as well as student writing. Many of the Inspirations are audio recordings or video adaptations of selections from *Prentice Hall Literature*, *Copper*. Have students work in small groups to look at and discuss an appropriate Inspiration before reading the corresponding selection. Then, after reading the selection, students can replay the Inspiration and select one of the accompanying Topic Ideas (pp. 280–283). The following selections from *Prentice Hall Literature*, *Copper*, are included in the Inspirations for Response to Literature.

- **"Dragon, Dragon,"** John Gardner
- **"Adventures of Isabel,"** Ogden Nash
- **"Greyling,"** Jane Yolen
- **"He Lion, Bruh Bear, and Bruh Rabbit,"** Virginia Hamilton
- **"Winter Poem,"** Nikki Giovanni
- **"Eleven,"** Sandra Cisneros
- **"Thunder Butte,"** Virginia Driving Hawk Sneve
- ***Tuck Everlasting,*** Natalie Babbitt
- **"The King of Mazy May,"** Jack London
- **"Breaker's Bridge,"** Lawrence Yep
- **"Virginia Hamilton,"** Lee Bennett Hopkins

Recommended Lesson Plan

The following lesson plan is recommended for providing students with thorough, comprehensive instructions in responding to literature. Because you may not have all the components of the *Writer's Solution* or may have limited access to equipment, the plan provides a number of options. Choose the options that best suit your teaching style and equipment situation.

You may want to add a few days to the lesson plan to allow students time to publish their work and to hold conferences with students to discuss your assessment of their work.

FIVE-DAY LESSON PLAN

Lesson Outcome:	**Each student writes a complete response to literature.**
DAY 1	**Introduce your students to response to literature.** Show the *Writers at Work Videodisc* segment featuring Joseph Bruchac. Use the segment as a springboard for class discussion or group activities.
DAY 2	**Have students choose a writing topic and plan their responses to literature.** OPTION 1 Have students work either individually or in small groups to look at About Response to Literature and to choose a topic by browsing through the Inspirations for Response to Literature. Then have students work individually to develop their responses by completing the rest of the Prewriting stage of the tutorial on Response to Literature. At the end of the period, have students print out their prewriting notes. OPTION 2 Have students review the Inspirations from Literature in the About Response to Literature section of the *Sourcebook*. Then have them choose from the topic suggestions and begin developing their responses by completing the rest of the Prewriting stage of the Guided Lesson (pp. 278–286).
DAY 3	**Have students draft their responses to literature.** OPTION 1 Have students write their drafts on the computer following the instructions and using the activities provided in the Drafting section of the tutorial on Response to Literature. Have students print out their responses at the end of the period. OPTION 2 Have students write their drafts on paper following the instructions in the Guided Lesson (p. 287).

FIVE-DAY LESSON PLAN (continued)

DAY 4

Have students revise their responses.

OPTION 1 Have students revise their responses on the computer using the revision checkers, activities, and suggestions in the Revising and Editing section of the tutorial on Response to Literature.

OPTION 2 Have students revise their responses following the suggestions in the Guided Lesson (pp. 288–289).

DAY 5

Have students work in peer groups to make final revisions.

OPTION 1 Have pairs of students review each other's work following the guidelines in the peer revision section of the tutorial on Response to Literature. The pairs should then hold conferences before each student makes final revisions. Students should then proofread and print out their final drafts.

OPTION 2 Have pairs of students review each other's work following the guidelines in the Guided Lesson (p. 288). The pairs should then hold conferences before each student makes final revisions.

Condensed Lesson Plans

Use the following lesson plans if you don't have a full week to devote to teaching expository writing.

Four- and Three-Day Plans: Adapt the Five-Day Plan by having students learn about response to literature, choose a topic, and develop ideas for their responses all during Day 1. As in the Five-Day Plan, have students spend a day writing their drafts. For a Four-Day Plan, follow the last two days of the Five-Day Plan; for a Three-Day Plan, simply condense these two days into a single day of revision and forgo the option of working in peer groups.

TWO-DAY LESSON PLAN

Lesson Outcome: **Each student writes a complete response to literature.**

DAY 1

Have students choose a topic and write their first drafts.

OPTION 1 Have students work in the open-ended environment in the *Writing Lab*. Working individually, students should choose a topic by browsing through the Inspirations for Response to Literature. Then they should write their responses in their on-line Notebooks using the available prewriting tools as needed.

OPTION 2 Using the suggestions and instructions in the *Sourcebook*, students should choose a topic and write a first draft of their responses.

DAY 2

Have students revise and edit their work.

OPTION 1 Have students revise on the computer using the tools, activities, and instructions in the tutorial on Response to Literature.

OPTION 2 Have students revise their responses following the suggestions in the *Sourcebook*.

One-Day Lesson Plan: Students can work individually in the open-ended environment in the *Writing Lab* by browsing through the Inspirations for Response to Literature to choose a topic, using the prewriting tools as needed, then completing a quick-write draft of a response in their on-line Notebooks. Students may also use the *Sourcebook* to choose a topic and write a brief response.

Preparing to Teach

Lesson Objectives

Students will

1. Select an appropriate piece of literature, a focus, and a format for a written response
2. Respond to the piece of literature in the chosen format, taking into consideration
   - the audience and purpose for the writing
   - the use of specific details
   - a plan of organization that effectively presents the response
3. Revise work for content and structure, mechanics, and style
4. Participate in peer review
5. Proofread for errors in grammar and punctuation
6. Publish the finished work

Activating Prior Knowledge

Ask students for examples of the kinds of literature they have read and various ways they have responded to these works. Among other things, students might say they have written book reports or character sketches, designed book jackets, made timelines or plot diagrams, and kept reading logs. Ask: *Based on your experience, what kinds of responses to literature do you enjoy writing the most? Why? Are there other kinds of responses that you've considered but not yet tried? Explain.*

CHAPTER 9

Voices of the Clouds *Jessie Lee Geiszler, Courtesy of the artist*

Response to Literature

"I'm reading a manuscript [and] I suddenly find myself in the middle of someone else's entire world."

—Joseph Bruchac
Native American Writer and Editor

267

Humanities Note

The work of art is a painting by Jessie Lee Geiszler titled *Voices of the Clouds*. A study in curvilinear motion, *Voices of the Clouds* features soft mounds of sand-colored mountains flowing into the rhythmic upward sweep of clouds. This movement serves to lead the viewer's eye to the two figures silhouetted against the landscape.

The simple complementary color scheme of orange and blue creates an intensity that suggests the glow of sunset or sunrise. It also provides a striking contrast to the dark forms of the two figures. By including a few simple costume details, the artist indicates that the people observing the sky are Native Americans.

In this painting, the artist expresses a view of the natural world. The mountains and the sky are painted not as a static backdrop but almost as living things. You might wish to use the following questions for discussion:

- What feelings about nature and the connection between human beings and their surroundings does the artist express in this painting?
- Imagine yourself in what you consider to be a beautiful place: on a mountaintop or in a park or garden, for example. What feelings do you have about nature when you are in this setting?

Addressing Your Classroom Situation

This chapter includes a variety of Models From Literature, topic ideas, writing process strategies, and Student Models, along with two integrated skills lessons. Feel free to pick and choose from this material to create a customized lesson on Response to Literature that matches your classroom needs.

The following are some of the key features of the chapter:

- The chapter begins with a section introducing response to literature. This section includes introductory statements about responding to literature from writer and editor Joseph Bruchac, a definition of Response to Literature, group discussion questions, and Models From Literature of five types of response to literature: reader's response journal entry; response to a short story; response to a poem; letter to an author; letter to a character.
- The Prewriting section includes an assortment of idea-generating activities to help students choose a topic, along with many topic ideas. This section also provides direct instruction and activities to help students focus their response, consider audience and purpose, and gather details. Professional and student Writing Models and a series of checklists for gathering details on different kinds of literary works guide students through the steps of the response-writing process.
- The Drafting section addresses the importance of using quotations from a literary work to support the respondent's ideas and opinions about it, and provides a model to illustrate this technique.
- The Revising and Editing section offers techniques for both self-evaluation and peer review to help students check that their response is well organized and includes personal reactions and feelings supported by details from the work. There are proofreading suggestions to remind students to check for errors in grammar, punctuation, or spelling.
- The Guided Lesson is followed by a Student Model and then skills lessons on using quotation marks and underlining, as well as eliminating unnecessary words.
- The chapter ends with a complete Literature Model, an excerpt from Joseph Bruchac's response to a poem, entitled "The Circle of Blessing: Joy Harjo's 'Eagle Poem.'"

Chapter Contents

About Response to Literature

Guided Lesson

Student Model

Developing Your Style 1

Developing Your Style 2

Literature Model

"Responding to literature requires both a mechanical response—to the specifics of grammar and syntax and structure—and also a philosophical, a historical, and even perhaps a spiritual response."

"I think that as a reader of other people's work, I have a great responsibility."

—Joseph Bruchac
Native American Writer and Editor

"When I look at someone's piece of work, first of all, it was important to them or they would not have put it on paper. Secondly, there is always something good to be found in it."

Response to Literature • 269

More About the Writer

Storyteller, novelist, and poet Joseph Bruchac was born in the Adirondack Mountains of New York State. His writings reflect the lore of his birthplace and his Native American (Abenaki) heritage. Bruchac has won national awards for his writing. His poetry has appeared in many magazines and he has authored more than twenty books of poetry and fiction. An acknowledged expert on Native American tradition and founder and editor of the Greenfield Press Review, Bruchac often reviews works by other writers, especially those with Native American themes. Discuss with your students how a person's heritage, beliefs, or experience can influence an appreciation for certain themes or literary styles. Ask: *How can a response to literature vary from reader to reader? What are some elements common to any response to literature, regardless of the work or the respondent's background?*

Tech Prep Note

Not only professional writers like Joseph Bruchac respond to literature in their work; people in other kinds of work sometimes do so as well. However, occasions to respond to fiction on the job may be limited. Librarians and bookstore owners may respond to literature to make purchasing decisions. On-the-job responses to nonfiction may be more common. For example, scientists may respond to articles they read in professional journals by writing to the editor. Office managers who read a favorable review of software in a computer journal may write to the editor to refute claims if their experience with the software has been fraught with problems. Employees in any field may respond to evaluations written by their supervisors to offer details and examples that support or defend an alternate viewpoint. Ask: *Think about the adults you know and the work they do. How do they respond to literature on the job?*

About Response to Literatur

What Is Response to Literature?

Have you ever read an exciting novel or short story and then told a friend all about it? If so, you were responding to literature. You were expressing thoughts and feelings about a literary work. A **response to literature** is any spoken or written reaction to a work of literature. It can take the form of a recommendation, a critique, or simply an expression of feelings stirred by the work.

Group Discussion You have probably responded to literature more often than you think—and not just in homework assignments. Perhaps the most basic response has been a thought, such as "This book is great!" or "This story is boring." A more deliberate response occurs whenever you recommend a book to a friend. With your classmates, discuss the ways in which you have responded to literature. First, brainstorm for the kinds of literature you have responded to, such as novels, short stories, poems, and plays. Then discuss your responses. Have you described a novel to someone? Have you written a journal entry about how a short story made you feel? Describe your responses in detail.

Introducing Response to Literature

Teaching Options

There are a variety of ways you can introduce response to literature using the components of the *Writer's Solution:*

- You can show the Response to Literature segment from the *Writers at Work Videodisc*. Use the segment as a springboard for a class discussion on literary response.
- You can have students work individually or in small groups to go through the About Response to Literature section of the tutorial in the *Writing Lab* CD-ROM.
- You can work through the About Response to Literature section of the *Sourcebook* with the class.
- You can have students read the About Response to Literature section of the *Sourcebook* before class starts, so that, as a group, you can focus on the videodisc or CD-ROM lesson.

Sourcebook

Have students read and discuss the About Response to Literature section in the *Sourcebook*. Use the following questions to guide the discussion:

- What might prompt you to respond to literature?
- How can you recognize responses to literature?
- Where do you find examples of literary responses?
- How can a response to literature engage the reader?
- How can responding to literature help you discover more about yourself?

Following the class discussion, divide your students into groups of three to five to engage in the group discussion (p. 270).

Writers at Work Videodisc

Use the Response to Literature section of the videodisc featuring Joseph Bruchac to spark class discussion on responding to literature. Play the chapter in its entirety, pausing as needed. Then feel free to use the bar codes to replay any portion to reinforce an important idea. Before you play the first segment, ask students to listen for how Joseph Bruchac describes the responsibility h feels as someone who responds to literature.

After students have viewed the segment, have them take turns sharing thei responses. Then move into a discussion of the techniques

How a Professional Writer Uses Response to Literature

Believe it or not, responding to literature can be a full-time occupation. For example, book editors spend much of their work life reading and responding to manuscripts that have been submitted for publication. As a publisher as well as a writer, Joseph Bruchac often reads and evaluates manuscripts. He tries to approach each one with an open mind:

> "When you're responding to literature, I think you need to relax and give yourself to whatever it is that you are reading. Don't enter it with preconceptions. Understand that literature can make us grow, can make us understand ourselves and our world and other people better. It also can give you a great deal of wonderful experience."

How Response to Literature Fits Into Your Life

"You've just got to read this novel. It's so funny!" Recommending a book to a friend is a typical example of a response to literature used in everyday life. Whenever you describe the outlandish characters of a ghost story or recount the grueling hardships revealed in an Arctic explorer's biography, you are responding to literature. Have you ever shared a good laugh with a friend while reading a book of jokes? That, too, is a response to literature. In this chapter, you'll learn how to support your reactions to literature. You'll also learn how to express your responses to literature effectively in writing.

and insights Bruchac shares. Ask:

- What does Bruchac say about the different levels of response to literature he must consider?
- Why would other editors approach him to review literary works?

Play frames 31394 to 40818

Real-World Writing

Tell students that people in your community may routinely respond to literature in their work. Have students seek examples of responses in local newspapers or magazines. For example, they might find a letter to a magazine editor that discusses a recently published story or poem. A newspaper columnist might write about a recent drama. An editor might write an editorial in response to a work that tackled a controversial issue. As students share examples, ask:

- What does the response reveal about the writer's attitudes or feelings? How does the writer support his or her point of view?
- How do you think the writer gathered details for the piece?
- Did the writer cite the work? If so, how?
- What features do these examples of responses to literature share that differ from features you see in other kinds of writing?

Writing Lab CD-ROM

The About Response to Literature section of the tutorial includes the following options:

- **Author video** Writer and editor Joseph Bruchac shares some of his views on responding to literature.
- **Audio-annotated Models From Literature** Students can see seven kinds of responses to literature: Response to a Poem, Response to a Short Story, Reader's Response Journal Entry, Letter to an Author, Letter to a Character.
- **Evaluation Guidelines** You can present guidelines to students before they draft their responses to serve as a checklist that can direct their writing. The guidelines can also be used for self-assessment after writing. If so, students can incorporate the ideas into a reflective piece they may include in their portfolios.

Students can work individually or in small groups to complete the tutorial on Response to Literature. Or, if you have access to a projection panel, you can work through the About Response to Literature section with the class, discussing each part as you go.

Integrating Literature With Writing

Starting From Literature

You can use the models on pages 272–276 to illustrate the various elements of each type of response to literature. Or highlight the content or technique used in these pieces to inspire writing on any of the themes they address. For example, the reader's response journal entry (p. 274) might inspire students to write a response journal entry that conveys how they felt when they read a controversial work or one with strong parallels to their own life. Brainstorm with the class a list of evocative poems, stories, plays, or novels that would make good topics for a response to literature.

Briefly introduce and define the type of writing each selection models. You might invite a student to read each piece aloud to the class. Follow with discussion to reinforce students' understanding of each type of response to literature.

Exploring Related Literature

The goal of this *Sourcebook* chapter is to help students write effective responses to literature. In most cases, responses or ideas for writing refer to a particular work of literature, or an excerpt from it, that may be found in *Prentice Hall Literature, Copper.* Feel free to have students read any work that initiated the response to better understand the ideas discussed in the response.

Types of Responses to Literature

Responses to literature can take many forms—from personal journal entries to letters to authors. On the following pages are a few examples of the types of responses you might write.

1 Response to a Poem

- In a response to a poem, tell whether or not you liked the poem and how the poem made you feel.
- You might also explain what you think the poem was about, or its message.

Writing Model

The following passage is a response to the poem "Whatif" by Shel Silverstein. Notice that the writer discusses his feelings about the poem and gives details to explain these feelings.

When I first read "Whatif," I thought it was silly. I mean, "Whatifs" crawling inside your ear, and then a poem that goes on and on, each line beginning with "Whatif." But when I read the poem again, I noticed how every two lines rhyme. I like poems that rhyme, and I was beginning to enjoy this poem. So I read it another time, and now I noticed that a lot of the questions in the poem are about things that I've thought or worried about at one time or another. For example, what if a war starts? Or what if somebody beats me up? There are also some very funny images—for example, green hair growing on my chest or my head getting smaller. I think that any poem that can be serious, funny, and clever all at the same time has a lot going for it.

Teaching From the Model

Guide students to analyze this excerpt from an essay about the poem "Whatif" by Shel Silverstein to understand how it models a response to a poem:

- *It conveys the writer's attitude toward the poem.* The respondent's opening statement engages the reader by implying that at first reading, the poem seemed "silly." However, the writer explains that after several more readings, the poem grew more appealing and evoked broader reactions. The concluding sentence reveals the writer's appreciation for the poem because it is ". . . serious, funny, and clever all at the same time."
- *It offers a description of the poem's structure and its message.* The writer summarizes the structure of the poem by saying that every line begins with the word "Whatif" and that every

2 *Response to a Short Story*

- In a response to a short story, you can present your overall reactions to the story or focus on one element of the story that interests you.
- In your response, you might deal with only the characters, the plot, or the setting.

Writing Model

The following passage is from an essay about "The Dog of Pompeii," a short story by Louis Untermeyer. Notice that the writer focuses on the story's setting.

Louis Untermeyer's short story "The Dog of Pompeii" is about one of the greatest natural disasters in history—the destruction of the ancient Roman city of Pompeii by the catastrophic eruption of Mt. Vesuvius. Set against this backdrop is the story of the blind homeless boy Tito and his dog Bimbo. The author gives specific details about the setting—for example, about the streets and houses, and even the foods people ate—making it easy to imagine what daily life must have been like in Pompeii. Once the volcanic eruption begins, the author shows its effect on the characters through his use of sensory details. For example, the air had "turned to powder, a warm powder" that Tito could taste and "that stung his nostrils and burned his sightless eyes." The setting is so vividly pictured that as I read the story, I felt as if I too were running in terror through the streets of Pompeii along with Tito and Bimbo.

Teaching From the Model

Discuss how the passage from an essay about Louis Untermeyer's "The Dog of Pompeii" typifies a response to a short story:

- *It names the work and author and briefly states its theme*. The excerpt opens by identifying the literary work as a short story and naming its author and title. The writer continues with a summary of the theme of the short story and links that theme to the situation of its main character.
- *It focuses on narrative elements in the story*. The essayist responds to Untermeyer's effective description of setting: "The author gives specific details about the setting, for example about the streets and houses, and even the foods people ate. . . ." The essayist explains how sensory details enhance the vivid descriptions by citing two direct quotations from the work to support this view. The response discusses the effect of strong setting on the reader: "The setting is so vividly pictured that as I read the story, I felt as if I, too, were running in terror through the streets of Pompeii. . . ."

two lines rhyme. The essayist recognizes that the poem's questions, which range from funny imaginary situations to realistic fears, cleverly reflect the diversity of life. It is this balance between the silly and the serious that makes the poem appeal to the respondent.

Teaching From the Model

Guide students to recognize how the passage from the diary of Susy Clemens is an example of one type of literary response known as the reader's response journal entry:

- *It records the feelings or thoughts that a work of literature evoked.* Susy Clemens's comments refer to *The Prince and The Pauper*, a recent book written by her father. She is clearly moved by her father's new book: "unquestionably the best book he has ever written." Susy Clemens reveals her emotional response toward the work in the phrase ". . . oh and then what followed!"
- *It includes informal language.* Susy Clemens refers to her father informally when she says "One of *papa's* latest books. . . ." This style would be unsuitable in a formal response, where she might have written "One of *my father's* latest books . . ." or "One of *Mark Twain's* latest books. . . ."

3 Reader's Response Journal Entry

- A reader's response journal is a record of your thoughts and feelings about literature you have read.
- In a reader's response journal, you can use informal language and include thoughts and feelings you may not want to share with others.

Model From Literature

The following journal entry was written over a hundred years ago by thirteen-year-old Susy Clemens, the daughter of the famous writer Mark Twain. In this passage, she discusses her feelings and thoughts about a book her father wrote. Notice that she explores one episode from the book in depth to explain how the book makes her feel.

One of papa's latest books is "The Prince and the Pauper" and it is unquestionably the best book he has ever written. . . . I think that one of the most touching scenes in it is where the pauper is riding on horseback with his nobles in the "recognition procession" and he sees his mother oh and then what followed! How she runs to his side, when she sees him throw up his hand palm outward, and is rudely pushed off by one of the King's officers, and then how the little pauper's conscience troubles him when he remembers the shameful words that were falling from his lips when she was turned from his side "I know you not woman" and how his grandeurs were stricken valueless and his pride consumed to ashes.

Writing Model

The following passage is from a letter to author Judy Blume about her novel *Tiger Eyes*. Notice that the writer identifies with one of the characters of the book and goes on to explain how the book has helped her get through a similar situation.

Dear Ms. Blume:

I know how Davey, in the book *Tiger Eyes*, felt when her mother started seeing that man you called the Nerd, because my mom was recently married to a man. I try to like him but it's hard. I sometimes feel he might try to take the place of my father and no one could ever do that.

Your book has helped me understand my feelings and to know I have to be strong, if only for my mother's sake. I have gotten my mom to read it too and hope it helps her as much as it did me.

4 Letter to an Author

- In a letter to an author, you can express your appreciation for a literary work.
- A letter to an author is also your opportunity to ask questions, suggest topics for another book, or offer constructive criticism.

Teaching From the Model

Guide students to recognize how this excerpt from a letter to author Judy Blume exemplifies this type of response to literature:

- *It is a first-person response to a work, written directly to the author.* The letter writer names the particular work that prompted the response, and expresses personal reactions to it. The response is written in the style of a personal letter, although the letter writer probably has never met the author.
- *It describes a connection between the work and the respondent's life.* The letter writer tells that the situation in *Tiger Eyes* mirrors a similar situation in her own life, and this parallel made the book especially meaningful to her. Knowing about this connection can help Judy Blume know how her audience receives her books, and can inspire her in future works.

Clarification

Tell students that letters written to a living author can be sent to the publisher of the work, whose address may be found inside the book or at a library. Letters received are then forwarded to the author (or to the author's agent or publicist).

Writing Strategy

Many letters written to authors are filled with praise, but it is equally valid to write to an author to ask questions or offer constructive criticism. Suggest that students who choose this kind of response write to an author to express concerns or reservations about a literary work, such as misrepresentation of a region or culture or unrealistic description of a situation or character.

Teaching From the Model

Guide students to recognize how this excerpt from a letter written to a fictional character typifies this kind of response to literature:

- *It is written directly to the character.* The letter writer addresses "Larry" as if he were a real person, and discusses points about the story as if Larry could read the response.
- *It describes a connection between the character and the respondent.* The letter writer explains that he has ". . . been to that museum many times . . ." so he can admire the resourceful way Larry solved the mystery. The letter writer contrasts what he might have done in a similar situation, and sums up his feelings in the closing statement: "Anyway, I'm sure you have a brilliant career ahead of you as a detective."

Clarification

Explain that although the character to whom this letter was written appears in a short story, students who choose this type of response can select a character from any type of literary work, including poems, dramas, novels, or diaries.

5 Letter to a Character

- One interesting way to respond to literature is to write a letter to a character in the book.
- You can give your opinion about something the character did, describe the way the character made you feel, or ask questions or make suggestions.

Writing Model

The following passage is from a letter to Larry a character in the story "Sarah Tops" by Isaac Asimov. In the passage, the writer explains that he has something in common with the character. He then expresses his admiration for the wa the character has solved a mystery.

Dear Larry,

I enjoyed reading about your adventure in the Museum of Natural History in "Sarah Tops." I've been to that museum many times, but I don't think I would have been able to solve the mystery the way you did. I would really like to know how you figured it out. I would have thought Sarah Tops was a woman's name, and since it wasn't listed in the phone book, I would have figured she had an unlisted number. And that would have been the end of the story. Anyway, I'm sure you have a brilliant career ahead of you as a detective.

Guided Lesson

Now that you've learned about the different kinds of responses to literature, you're ready to write your own response. This lesson will help guide you through the process of writing your response. You may not want to start at the beginning of the lesson, however. Use this chart to help you decide where to begin.

	START WITH
• If you **do not have a topic**	Choosing Your Topic
• If you **have a topic but aren't sure what details to focus on**	Gathering Details
• If you **have a topic and know what you want to say**	Drafting

Guiding Student Writing

Language Acquisition/ ESL Teaching Strategy

The *Writing Lab* offers a variety of options that can be adapted to meet the needs of your ESL students. The following are examples of such adaptations.

- The Choosing a Topic section offers Idea Wheels for generating topics, an option that is particularly useful for your upper-basic and intermediate ESL students. Working in pairs, the students review the words and visual images while discussing any ideas that come to mind. The students take notes and later describe to you the ideas they have.
- The Gathering Details section provides an option, Chain of Events for plot, that can be used with your intermediate and advanced ESL students. As the students fill in their charts, ask them to be consistent with the tenses they use, such as the simple present or a combination of past tense forms. When their charts are finished, the students review them orally with their ESL classmates.
- The Revising and Editing section offers a language variety checker that is very useful for ESL students of all levels. After the students have identified repeated words in their drafts, they work in pairs or groups of three to look for replacement words. They may use a dictionary, thesaurus, and each other's suggestions in their revisions.

ddressing Your lassroom Situation

If you choose to assign topics or types of responses to literature, allow time for students to narrow the topic to suit their interests or find an appealing focus to pursue.

If you allow students to select the literary work for their written responses, set aside adequate time for them to browse, select a work, and perhaps discuss it with a peer partner.

- It may work best when students work independently to write a literary response so that they can freely express their thoughts and feelings. However, you may choose to have students work on responses in pairs. One way a team can do this is for both partners to read the same work, discuss it, and then write different forms of response to it, such as a letter to the author and a letter to a character in the work.

Prewriting

Choosing Your Topic

What kind of response to literature will you write? What work will you respond to? What elements of that work will you discuss in your response? The answers to these three questions are the keys to choosing your topic. For help in selecting a topic, either choose from among the suggested writing options (see pages 280–283) or use one or more of the following techniques to discover a topic of your own.

If you're considering

. . . a reader's response journal entry or a response to a short story or a poem:

USE PICTURES TO REFRESH YOUR MEMORY

Is a picture worth a thousand words? Perhaps. Certain pictures— either separately or in combination—may remind you of a short story, novel, play, or poem that you've read. Flip through magazines and newspapers, looking at the pictures. Jot down notes about any picture that makes you think of something you've read. Note any new ideas you may have about a literary work. Review your notes for possible topics.

. . . a response to a literary work or a letter to an author or a character in a drama:

TRY FREEWRITING

To come up with a topic, try a method called freewriting, which is simply writing down whatever comes into your mind. If you want to choose a novel, short story, drama, or poem to explore, simply freewrite about literary works that you've read. Don't worry about your sentence structure or your spelling. Just jot down *any* impressions about literature that come into your mind. Those impressions might be about plot, setting, theme, characters, or something else. Later, review your freewriting and choose a literary work or a specific part of a work to write about.

Writing Lab CD-ROM

The Choosing a Topic section of the tutorial on Response to Literature includes the following options to help students come up with their own topics:

- **Idea Wheels for generating topics** Students can use wheels that offer words and visual images to help suggest literary works they have recently read, which could become topics for a written response.
- **Audio-annotated example of using freewriting to discover topics** Students can read a model of freewriting and hear how the writer used this technique to find a topic for a response to literature.
- **Audio tips from a student on choosing literature that strongly affects you** Students can hear how a story that mirrored a student's own experiences prompted her to choose that work as a topic for a response to literature.
- **Audio tips from a student on using reader's response journals** Students can hear how one student referred to past entries in a reader's response journal to remind her of an appealing literary work she might otherwise have forgotten. Having this personalized reference tool provided her with a topic for a new response to literature.
- **Audio writing hints on another way to find a topic** Students hear a dialogue between a teacher and a student that models an effective way to discover a topic for a literary response.

Working individually or in small groups, students can experiment with these activities to find the ones that work best.

Writers at Work Videodisc

Play the videodisc segment in which Joseph Bruchac discusses responding to literature. Ask:

- What do you think Bruchac means by saying that literary response requires ". . . a philosophical, a historical, and even perhaps a spiritual response"?
- How can you apply this way of looking at a literary work to help you find a topic for your own response to literature?

Suggest that students try Bruchac's strategy of asking the question "Does [the worl have everything in it that yc need to understand it?" Poin out that the more questions respondents ask as they read, the greater can be the oppor tunities for response.

Play frames 32254 to 33610

. . . a response to a short story, a poem, or a play:

Group Activity

Hold a Literary Convention

What novels, short stories, plays, or poems have you read recently that had a strong effect on you? Hold a literary convention with a group of your classmates and take turns sharing your favorite stories, poems, or plays. How do your classmates' favorites compare with your own? Take notes during the discussion and refer to them later for possible writing topics.

. . . a reader's response journal entry:

Check Your Reader's Response Journal

A reader's response journal is a good place to record your thoughts about a work of literature while it's still fresh in your mind. If you keep a journal, look through it for possible topics for a response to literature. If you haven't been keeping a journal, now is a good time to start. In your journal, jot down the title of each work you read and your impressions of it. Your reader's response journal can be a great source for future writing topics!

. . . a response to a short story or a letter to an author or a character:

Group Activity

Bring the Literary Repair Crew to the Rescue

Perhaps you have read a novel that was great until the ending, then it just fizzled. If you've ever thought that about a book, don't just sit there and do nothing. Instead, fix it! Form a literary repair crew with a group of your classmates and replace the dull, predictable ending with a satisfying new one. With your repair crew, share elements of other literary works that you think need fixing. Perhaps you found the plot of a novel weak. Maybe you felt one or more of the characters in a short story didn't seem real. Whatever the problem, share it with your crew and suggest a way to fix it. Jot down notes for possible repair jobs—and topics.

Addressing Ability Levels

Your **more-challenged students** who choose the Try Freewriting option (p. 278)—and who have difficulty writing—might benefit from adapting this idea to "freespeaking." They can register impressions or ideas that come to mind about literature, but instead of writing them, they can say them into a tape recorder. Later, they can review the tape for ideas they might use to write a literary response.

Collaborative Learning

Help students who choose the "literary repair crew" option plan ways to facilitate the task. For instance, suggest that groups brainstorm new endings for a predictable work, or freewrite brief character sketches to inject life into dull or stereotyped characters. Partners might prefer to "take apart" a familiar work to find ways to make it even better. Some students might read professional reviews of novels or short stories to learn about points of weakness others may have found.

Writing Strategy

Students who choose the Use Pictures to Refresh Your Memory option (p. 278) to help them discover topics for a literary response may consider browsing through collections of photographs, art books, or picture books, especially folk tales, legends, or books with science themes.

The Council Rock *1913, Maurice and Edward Detmold, Donnell Library Center, The New York Public Library*

Inspirations for a Response to Literature

Here are some topic ideas for responses to literature:

Group Project

Interview an Unusual Character

"Mowgli's Brothers" by Rudyard Kipling is a short story about Mowgli, a human child raised by wolves. In the end, Mowgli leaves the jungle to meet "those mysterious things that are called men." Read or review "Mowgli's Brothers." Then, with a group of your classmates, imagine that Mowgli now lives in the city with humans as neighbors, not wolves. Imagine, too, that you are reporters who will interview Mowgli about his life in the jungle. As a group, brainstorm for questions to ask Mowgli during the interview. Each person should then write an answer that Mowgli might give to one of the questions. Publish the interview for your classmates to read and discuss.

Writing Lab CD-ROM

Using the Inspirations for Response to Literature in the *Writing Lab* is an excellent way to stimulate creativity and to have students explore possible topics for literary responses. Students can browse individually or in small groups through the Inspirations. They can choose their own writing topics or you may prefer to assign topics.

The following is a list of the topics for writing responses to literature included in the Inspirations, but not provided in the *Sourcebook:*

Reader's Response Journal Entry About

- "Dragon, Dragon" by John Gardner
- Isabel's character in "Adventures of Isabel" by Odgen Nash
- Three characters' reactions to the idea of being young again in *Dr. Heidegger's Experiment* by Nathaniel Hawthorne
- Walt's point of view of the chase in "The King of Mazy May" by Jack London
- Breaker's meeting with the emperor in "Breaker's Bridge" by Lawrence Yep
- Virginia Hamilton's statement that writers "tell more than one truth" from the article "Virginia Hamilton" by Lee Bennett Hopkins
- Dreams as a source of story ideas, based on the article "Virginia Hamilton" by Lee Bennett Hopkins

Response to a Short Story That Focuses on

- Characters' feelings evoked by "Dragon, Dragon" by John Gardner
- The reason for the King's invitation in "Dragon, Dragon" by John Gardner
- Expressing an opinion of "Greyling" by Jane Yolen
- The point of view of the selchie in "Greyling" by Jane Yolen
- The character of the lion in "He Lion, Bruh Bear, and Bruh Rabbit" by Virginia Hamilton
- Age in "Eleven" by Sandra Cisneros
- Your opinion of Norman's challenge in "Thunder Butte" by Virginia Driving Hawk Sneve
- Contrasts between traditional and modern ways in "Thunder Butte" by Virginia Driving Hawk Sneve

A Response to a Folk Tale

Read or review an African American folk tale told by Virginia Hamilton, or another folk tale. Then write a response to the tale. What is the lesson in this tale? What is your reaction to the characters? Do they remind you in any way of people you know? If so, how?

A Letter to a Character in a Short Story

In the short story "Eleven" by Sandra Cisneros, a girl named Rachel has an embarrassing experience on her eleventh birthday. Her teacher insists that an old, ugly sweater that's been in the coatroom for a month belongs to her. As the teacher puts the sweater on Rachel's desk, the eleven-year-old is so upset that she can't think of anything to say. Have you ever, like Rachel, found yourself speechless? What caused the situation? How did you handle it? Respond to Rachel's problem by writing her a letter in which you share your own experience.

A Letter to a Character from The Phantom Tollbooth

The play *The Phantom Tollbooth* is the story of a boy, Milo, and his magical journey to rescue a princess. Throughout the play, Milo finds himself in strange places. Read or review the play. Then write a letter to Milo in which you react to his adventures. Tell him about any experiences that you have had that remind you of his. Ask any questions you may have about his experiences.

A Response to a Poem That Rhymes

Read or review a poem that rhymes. Then think about what the poem would be like if it didn't rhyme. How would this change affect your response to the poem? Write a short paper in which you discuss the effect of rhyme in the poem you chose. Tell whether or not the rhyming words added to your enjoyment of the poem.

A Response to "Adventures of Isabel"

The humorous poem "Adventures of Isabel" by Ogden Nash is about a girl who does some incredible deeds, such as eating a bear. Read this poem or another humorous poem. Then write a journal entry in which you respond to the poem. Consider these questions: Why do you or don't you find it funny? What elements of the poem contribute to your reaction?

- Facing danger in "Thunder Butte" by Virginia Driving Hawk Sneve
- How Mowgli uses his intelligence in "Mowgli's Brothers" by Rudyard Kipling
- Relationships between Mowgli and the jungle animals in "Mowgli's Brothers" by Rudyard Kipling
- The effect of setting in "Mowgli's Brothers" by Rudyard Kipling
- The importance of courage in "The King of Mazy May" by Jack London
- Survival skills in "The King of Mazy May" by Jack London
- Breaker's personality in "Breaker's Bridge" by Lawrence Yep

Response to a Poem That Focuses on

- Ogden Nash's use of rhyme in "Adventures of Isabel"
- An image in "Winter Snow" by Nikki Giovanni
- The message of "Winter Snow" by Nikki Giovanni

Response to a Novel That Focuses on

- Winnie's reactions in *Tuck Everlasting* by Natalie Babbitt
- Character development in *Tuck Everlasting* by Natalie Babbitt
- The theme of becoming young again in *Dr. Heidegger's Experiment* by Nathaniel Hawthorne

Letter to the Author of

- "Winter Snow," the poem by Nikki Giovanni
- *Tuck Everlasting,* the novel by Natalie Babbitt
- "Breaker's Bridge," the short story by Lawrence Yep
- "He Lion, Bruh Bear, and Bruh Rabbit," a folk tale transcribed by Virginia Hamilton

Letter to the Character of

- "Greyling" in the short story by Jane Yolen
- The teacher in the short story "Eleven" by Sandra Cisneros
- Dr. Heidegger in *Dr. Heidegger's Experiment* by Nathaniel Hawthorne

Language Acquisition/ ESL Teaching Strategy

The Group Project, Interview an Unusual Character (p. 280), can be adapted for use with ESL students of all levels. Put your ESL students into multilevel groups of five or six. After reading "Mowgli's Brothers" and discussing vocabulary, the students think of several questions they would like to ask Mowgli about his life in a city. Each student chooses a question to answer that will become a part of the group's interview with Mowgli. The interview may be published or acted out.

Writing Lab CD-ROM

The Inspirations for Response to Literature in the *Writing Lab* also include the following Group Projects and Group Discussions. The Group Discussions encourage small groups of students to share their thoughts about an Inspiration and to generate possible writing topics. The Group Projects are structured activities in which students assume different roles.

Group Projects

- Creating a different version of the poem "Adventures of Isabel" by Ogden Nash
- Writing letters to Jane Yolen about "Greyling"
- Focusing on the final image in the poem "Winter Snow" by Nikki Giovanni and creating new endings for it
- Compiling a collection of character portraits of main characters from short stories

Group Discussions

- Identifying animals with character traits and personalities like yours
- Comparing traditions
- Responding to the elements of casting, acting, and costuming in a dramatization of the novel *Tuck Everlasting* by Natalie Babbitt
- Nominating a fictional character for an imaginary "Best Youth of the Year" award
- Showing how setting affects the story "The King of Mazy May" by Jack London
- Casting a movie version of Lawrence Yep's story "Breaker's Bridge"
- Identifying possible sources for stories

MORE *Inspirations* for a Response to Literature

Response to the Dialect in a Tale

The narrator and the characters in Virginia Hamilton's "He Lion, Bruh Bear, and Bruh Rabbit" speak in a dialect, a variation of English spoken in a particular region of the United States. Read this tale or another story that contains dialect. Did you find the dialogue difficult to understand? Would the tale have had the same effect if it had been told in standard English? Write a letter to the author expressing your thoughts about the use of dialect in this folk tale.

Group Project: Respond to Modern-Day "Dragons"

Stories about dragons are very popular. Also popular are stories about monsters and other creatures. As a group, brainstorm for a list of books, movies, or television shows about monsters, such as *Frankenstein, Godzilla,* or *Jurassic Park.* Next, have each group member choose an item on the list with which he or she is familiar and write a response to that story. Then, as a group, share written responses.

A Letter to an Author

What would you like to say to the author of the novel you've read most recently? Write a letter to the author of this novel and express your reactions to the work. Tell what you liked best about it and why. Also include any questions you'd like to ask.

A Response to an Adventure Story

What is your favorite adventure story? Imagine what it would have been like to be the main character in this story. Write a short paper telling how you would have felt if you were this character. What would you have done differently? Why?

A Letter to an Author of a Short Story

"Breaker's Bridge" by Laurence Yep is the story of a character who faces a difficult challenge. Read and review this story. Or read another story about a character who faces a challenge. Then write a letter to the author in which you express your reactions. What did you like about the story? What experiences of your own did it remind you of? What questions do you have for the author?

Group Project: Assemble a Collection of Scary Stories

What are your favorite scary stories? With a group of classmates, brainstorm for a list of your favorite scary stories. Then work together to create a collection of scary stories. Each of you should find at least one story. Then write an introduction that tells why you liked the story. Use vivid words to encourage others to read it. Work together to assemble the introductions and stories into a collection. If possible, find photographs and illustrations to accompany the stories.

A Letter to a Poet

Read "Winter Poem" by Nikki Giovanni or another poem about nature. Does the poem bring to mind any of your own experiences? How does the poem make you feel? Write a letter to the poet in which you express your feelings. Ask any questions you have about the poem.

A Reader's Response Journal Entry About "Dust of Snow"

Read or review "Dust of Snow" by Robert Frost. How do you think the poet feels about winter? Do you feel the same way about the season? Write a journal entry in which you discuss your reactions to the poem and tell how Frost's thoughts about winter compare with your own.

Writing Lab CD-ROM

The Focusing Your Response section of the tutorial on response to Literature includes the following options to help students decide what they want to say about their chosen work:

- **Video tip from Joseph Bruchac** Writer and editor Bruchac offers advice on how to approach a literary work with an open mind.
- **Topic Web** Students use this organizing tool to help them divide and subdivide topics.
- **Interactive examples of narrowed topics** Students see examples of how broad topics can be narrowed.

Working individually or in small groups, students can experiment with these activities to find the ones that work best for them.

Writers at Work Videodisc

Play the videodisc segment in which Joseph Bruchac discusses reading a work several times before writing a response to it. Ask:

- Why do you think Bruchac believes that ". . . there is always something good to be found in [a work of literature]"?
- How can the work itself help you to focus your response to it?

Invite students to share the focus of topics they are considering so they can get input from classmates about how to narrow that focus.

Play frames 35199 to 36330

Prewriting

Focusing Your Response

If you've chosen a literary work but aren't sure what to say about it, take some time to focus your response. What interests you most about the work? What experiences did it bring to mind? What feelings did it bring out? Answering these questions will help give direction to your writing. You might decide to focus on how you feel about one of the characters. Or you might tell how the setting reminded you of a place you know. Remember to keep an open mind. You may see things in the work of literature that didn't occur to you before.

Considering Your Audience

Who will read your response? Decide on your audience and think about how it might affect your writing. For example, if you're writing a letter to a young character in a short story or a novel, your language must be easy enough for this character to understand. If you're writing a letter to an author, you'll probably want to use more formal language.

Considering Your Purpose

What is your purpose for writing about the literary work? Is it to encourage someone else to read it? To explain the work? To evaluate it? Your choice of a purpose will affect your writing.

Tips for Accomplishing Your Purpose

- If you are writing to express your feelings, you might compare experiences you've had with those of a character in the literary work.
- If you are writing to explain a work of literature, you might mention some of the literary elements in the work. For example, you could explain a poem's structure and rhyme scheme.
- If you are writing to evaluate a literary work, give your opinions about it and support your opinions with specific examples.

Language Lab CD-ROM

Students who need more support to focus a topic may benefit from doing the Narrowing a Topic lesson in the Composing unit of the *Language Lab*.

Writing Lab CD-ROM

The Considering Audience and Purpose section of the tutorial on Response to Literature includes the following options to help students explore ways to decide on their purpose and to gear their writing to their intended audience:

- **Audience Profile** Students answer questions to help them focus on their intended audience.
- **Audio-annotated Writing Models that consider audience** Students compare two responses to the novel *The Lion, the Witch, and the Wardrobe*, one of which is a reader's response

Gathering Details

Before you begin writing, gather details that you can use to support your reaction to the work. Think about the elements of the work that stand out in your mind. If you're responding to a short story or a drama, did characters make a strong impression? What did they look like? How did they act? What was the setting? During what season or historical period did the story take place? Was the action indoors or outdoors? If you're responding to a poem, what images, or word pictures, affected you most? How did the sounds of the poem affect you? The following sections will help you gather details for the various types of literary works.

How to Gather Details About a Novel or a Short Story

What interests you most about the work? Is it the plot, the setting, or the main character? The following guidelines will help you gather details about whatever elements you want to explore.

Tips for Gathering Details About the Plot

- Include the events that you think are most important.
- Jot down how the events are influenced by the characters and the setting.

Tips for Gathering Details About the Setting

- Include details of the setting that you find most striking or important.
- Jot down how the setting affects the plot and the characters.

Tips for Gathering Details About the Characters

To help you gather details about a character, answer the following questions:

- What does the character look like? What are his or her distinguishing features?
- What are the characters likes and dislikes? What are his or her feelings?
- How does the character behave?
- How does the character change during the novel or short story?
- What do others say or think about the character? How do others react to him or her?
- What are your thoughts and feelings about the character?
- Does the character remind you of someone you know?

journal entry, the other an essay written for a teacher.

- **Audio-annotated Writing Models that consider purpose** Students examine passages from models that show and explain how writers accomplished various purposes.

Working individually or in small groups, students can experiment with these activities to find the ones that work best for them.

Writing Lab CD-ROM

The Gathering Details section of the tutorial on Response to Literature includes the following options designed to help students efficiently move through the process of gathering details for their topic:

- **Video tips on gathering details** Students can play an audio-annotated slide show about the importance of gathering details to support a literary response.
- **Chain of Events for plot** Students can complete a chart that presents a series of events to help them gather details about a novel or short story.
- **Character personality profile** Students can answer questions to help them gather details about character for a response to a novel or short story.
- **Audio-annotated Models From Literature that highlight poetic elements** Students can learn how similes and metaphors as well as rhythm and rhyme can influence response to poetry.
- **Video clip from a drama** Students hear a character in a dramatization of Nathaniel Hawthorne's story *Dr. Heidegger's Experiment* express his feelings in a monologue.
- **Audio-annotated Models From Literature of dramatic elements** Students can understand how to gather details about a drama from stage directions and dialogue.
- **Interactive writing hints for gathering details** Students can hear a student writer's strategy for using freewriting to develop the main point of a literary response.
- **Sunburst Diagram** Students use this tool to help them organize words and phrases that support a topic.

Working individually or in small groups, students can experiment with these activities to find the ones that work best for them.

Clarification

Be sure students realize that in a response to literature, they need not retell an entire plot or fully describe the characters. Rather, they should select pertinent details that support their opinions about the work and present them in a way that furthers their view.

Collaborative Learning

An effective way to help students gather details about poetry is to have them work in small groups. The group should choose a moderator and select a poem to explore and respond to. One student reads the chosen poem aloud as others listen for details about sound. The group can discuss details about the poem's meaning, which the group's recorder can jot down. The group's results can be used by individuals when they begin to draft their responses.

Language Lab CD-ROM

Students may benefit from reviewing the use of vivid and precise language as they gather details about a poem. If so, refer them to the lessons on Exact Nouns, Vivid and Precise Verbs, Vivid Adjectives and Adverbs, and Figurative Language in the Choosing Words unit of the *Language Lab*

How to Gather Details About a Poem

When gathering details from a poem, consider the meaning of the poem, the sound of the poem, or both.

Tips for Gathering Details About the Meaning

- What does the poem mean to you?
- What images, or word pictures, contribute to the meaning?
- What examples of figurative language, or language not meant to be interpreted literally, can you find?
- How does this language contribute to the poem's meaning?

Tips for Gathering Details About the Sound

- Is the rhythm of the poem fast or slow? How does it make you feel?
- Do any of the lines of the poem rhyme? Is there a pattern of rhyming lines?
- Are the rhyming words humorous or serious? How do the rhyming words make you feel?

How to Gather Details About a Drama

Even though drama has many of the same elements as short stories and novels—characters, setting, plot, and theme—there is one important difference: Drama is written to be performed. The whole story must unfold through the words and actions of the characters.

Answer the following questions as you gather details about a play.

- What actions do the characters take?
- What do these actions tell you about the characters?
- What passages of dialogue reveal the most about the characters?

How to Gather Details Related to Your Life

You will often come across elements in a work of literature that will remind you of people or situations in your own life. Making such connections can be helpful in gathering details about the work.

- Jot down any character or situation that you identify with, or connect with.
- Explain why a character is similar to you.
- Explain why a situation is similar to yours.
- Explain how the literary work has affected your life.

Establishing Assessment Criteria

As students begin drafting their responses to literature, you may want to share with them the criteria you will use to evaluate their work. The following guidelines are included in the tutorial on Response to Literature

Drafting

FROM a WRITER

"I sit down and start typing, and I keep writing until I feel I've said everything I have to say. It may be three or four pages that will be narrowed down to only a page or a half page. But in your first draft, put in everything."

—Joseph Bruchac

Using any details you've gathered, begin drafting your response. Take Joseph Bruchac's advice: Get all your thoughts down on paper. You can always revise your work later.

As you draft, support your main ideas and opinions with quotations from the literary work. Quotations provide evidence to back up what you say. They also give your readers a sample of what the literary work is really like.

Writing Hint: Getting Started

Sometimes the hardest part of writing a paper is getting started. If you are stuck, don't give up hope. Instead, try one or more of the following strategies designed to get your writing rolling.

- Jot down what interests you most about your topic, such as the setting or the characters.
- Write words and phrases related to the details of your topic.
- Jot down the one main idea you want to write about.
- Write an interesting quotation from the work.
- Write a question that your paper will answer.

Writing Model: Using Quotations for Support

The following two sentences from a response to a poem are shown separated to illustrate the impact quotations can have on a piece of writing. Pause after reading the first sentence. See if you feel as if something is missing from the response. Then read the second sentence, noting how the quotations clarify the main idea of the response.

In "The Sidewalk Racer," poet Lillian Morrison uses a metaphor to compare the act of riding a skateboard to something else to create a feeling of flowing movement in the poem.

For example, Morrison says, "Skimming an asphalt sea," and then continues the metaphor with "I'm the sailor and the sail."

in the *Writing Lab* CD-ROM. Use the guidelines as given, or modify them to suit your needs.

- Have you mentioned the title and author of the literary work?
- Does the response include your thoughts and feelings about the work?
- Have you supported your opinions with details from the work?
- Does your response include details about specific literary elements of the work?
- Is your writing in a format suitable for your audience and purpose?
- Is your writing organized in a way that will make sense to readers?

Writing Lab CD-ROM

The Drafting section of the tutorial on Response to Literature includes the following options to help students organize and present details for their response to effectively convey their feelings and reactions to a literary work:

- **Audio-annotated Student Models of the parts of a literary response** Students can see sample drafts of an introduction, body paragraphs, and a conclusion to a literary response, and hear the student writer discuss his various writing choices.
- **Transition Word Bin** Students select transition words or phrases that help readers see connections in order of importance, logical relationships, or time order.
- **Audio-annotated Student Model** Students see a first draft of a student's literary response. Comments by the student author explain the choices made in drafting the piece.

Working individually or in small groups, students can experiment with these activities to find the ones that work best for them.

Writers at Work Videodisc

Play the videodisc segment in which Joseph Bruchac talks about getting started on his draft. He says that he just sits down and starts to type. Ask:

- Why would Bruchac intentionally write in a first draft more than he knows he can use?
- Why do you think he advises writers not to be ". . . afraid to put in everything"?

Play frames 36346 to 37153

Revising and Editing

Revising Your Work

When you finish your first draft, it's time to find ways to improve it. Rarely, if ever, does anyone draft a finished piece of writing. In fact, professional writers often revise a work many times before publishing it.

Read through your first draft, searching for elements that need improvement. Use the following checklist to guide you.

Revision Checklist

1. Who will read your response? What language and details can you add to make it more appropriate for your audience?
2. Do you need to make your purpose clearer?
3. What personal reactions and feelings about the work have you included? What, if any, reactions would you like to add?
4. What details have you used to support your response? What details might you add?
5. Do you need to add more precise adjectives, adverbs, nouns, or verbs?
6. How did you organize your response? Can you improve your organization?
7. Does your draft include an introduction, a body, and a conclusion?

Having a Peer Review Your Work

A fresh pair of eyes may see areas for improvement that you've missed. After you've revised your paper on your own, exchange papers with a classmate.

When you review your classmate's work, you may read the paper out loud or silently or have the writer read it to you. You might want to read the paper through once just to get a general impression. Then read the paper a second time and take notes on your reaction to it. Tell the

Writing Lab CD-ROM

The Revising and Editing section of the tutorial on Response to Literature provides strategies for self-revision and peer revision. It includes the following options to help students revise their first drafts:

- **Interactive Self-Evaluation Checklist** Students enter responses to questions into a form that helps them judge the effectiveness of their literary response.
- **Language Variety Checker** Students use a revision tool that highlights words used four or more times so the draft can be revised to use fewer repeated words.
- **Audio-annotated Student Model** Students compare the first draft of a literary response with a revised draft to learn how and why revisions were made.
- **Video tip from Joseph Bruchac on peer review** Students can hear Bruchac's viewpoint on the value of working with a peer editor.
- **Tips for peer editors** Students can use a list of suggestions on improving the peer editing process.
- **Peer Revision Checklist** Peer partners use guiding questions to help them focus on what to look for when editing early drafts.

Working individually or in small groups, students can experiment with these activities to find the ones that work best.

Writers at Work Videodisc

Play the videodisc segment in which Joseph Bruchac discusses his views on revising and editing. Bruchac says that ". . . what you say the first time is not as precise as what you might say the second time." Ask:

- How does Bruchac approach the editing and revising part of the writing process? What is your own view of this part of the process?
- Bruchac checks the tone of his response as he revises. Why is this important in a literary response?

Play frames 37169 to 39444

Writing Strategy

Some students may benefit from having a notebook-sized copy of the Revision Checklist to refer to as they revise their work. Feel free to adapt the list to include additional questions, such as these:

- Have you included any direct quotations from the

writer what you like about the paper and ask any questions that the paper raised in your mind. Finally, offer suggestions for improvement. You can use the following checklist for guidance.

Peer Review Checklist

1. What part of the paper did you find most interesting? Why?
2. How clearly did the writer express his or her thoughts and feelings about the work?
3. Were the writer's thoughts and opinions supported by details from the work? What, if any, additional support is needed?
4. Was anything in the paper unclear to you? If so, what?

Proofreading

Now proofread your paper for any errors in spelling, punctuation, and grammar. These types of errors can draw your reader's attention away from your main ideas.

Proofreading Checklist

1. Does each sentence start with a capital letter and end with the correct end punctuation mark?
2. Are all titles of literary works written correctly?
3. Has all quoted material been copied and punctuated correctly?
4. Are all words spelled correctly?
5. Do all your subjects and verbs agree?

Student Model: Revised Draft

Here is a revised passage of a response to literature by Alison Basford, a student at Mark Twain Middle School in Brooklyn, New York. Alison's composition is a response to *Six Months to Live* by Lurlene McDaniel, a book about thirteen-year-old Dawn Rochelle's battle against leukemia. Notice that Alison's revisions add details about Dawn's teddy bears.

She uses her teddy bear collection to help her.

Dawn fights the disease with her mind. ~~One of her favorite things are~~

She has 103 teddy bears and has been collecting them since she was two years old.

~~teddy bears.~~ She imagines that her favorite teddy bear is fighting the leukemia, and it kills the disease. An important part of getting well is thinking that you will get well and that the drugs from chemotherapy are helping you, even if you feel really sick from them.

work? If so, are they in proper form?

- Does your introduction grab the reader's attention? How?

Peer Revision

- Reading a piece aloud can help writers or editors to hear overused words, choppy sentences, disjointed paragraphs, or other errors. This approach works well for partners. The peer editor can read a draft aloud as the writer listens for spots where revisions are needed; roles can be reversed.
- Some students may feel ill at ease with peer editors, especially when sharing personal opinions. Urge peer editors to identify specific problems in form or content objectively and clearly. Guide them to ask whether opinions are supported by details or quotations, even if the editor disagrees with the writer's view.

Writing Lab CD-ROM

The Revising and Editing section of the tutorial on Response to Literature includes the following options to help students develop proofreading strategies for their literary responses:

- **Proofreading Checklist** Students can follow this checklist, part of which appears on page 289 of the *Sourcebook*, to help them pinpoint possible errors in their drafts.
- **Audio-annotated Student Model of a proofread literary response** Students can compare "before" and "after" models and hear how the student writer identified and corrected errors in capitalization, spelling, and punctuation.
- **Interactive instruction on using commas** Students learn to identify and correct errors in the use of commas to separate items in a series.
- **Interactive instruction on punctuating titles of literary works** Students see models of the correct use of italics, quotation marks, or underlining to present the titles of books, short stories, poems, and plays.

Working individually or in small groups, students can experiment with these activities to find the ones that work best.

Language Lab CD-ROM

Direct students who need additional practice using commas correctly in a series to the Commas lesson in the Punctuation unit of the *Language Lab*.

Publishing and Presenting

Now that you've finished your response to literature, it's time to decide how to share it with an audience. Here are just a couple of the many possibilities:

Make a Library Display Work with a group of classmates and your school librarian to encourage other students to read books that you have enjoyed. Prepare a library display that features the books you have read along with your reports on them. Update the display periodically. For example, a monthly library display could feature "The Best Books of the Month."

Create a Terrific Title and a Colorful Cover Turn your main idea, theme, or opinion into a lively title. For example, if you're responding to a book about baseball that you enjoyed, you might use the title "It's a Grand Slam!" Conversely, if you didn't like the book, "Strike Three!" might be more appropriate.

An illustrated cover can bring your composition to life. Draw a picture relevant to the literary work. Then staple the picture to a piece of construction paper .

Reflecting on Your Writing

What did you learn from writing your response to literature? Here are some questions to help you reflect back on the process you used to write your response:

- What did you learn about the literary work and about yourself from writing your response to literature?
- If you could start the assignment over again, what would you do differently?
- How can you apply what you've learned to other writing assignments?

Writing Lab CD-ROM

The Publishing and Presenting section of the tutorial on Response to Literature includes the following suggestions on how students might present their completed works to a wider audience:

- **Tips for creating an interesting title** Students refer to suggestions and sample titles that indicate the theme with a catchy phrase, that suggest a personal response, or that hint at the main idea of the response.
- **Tips for making a class publication of literary reviews** Students explore a list of questions to help them break the large task into manageable parts.
- **Tips for making a library display** Students explore suggestions for ways to bring the literary works featured in the responses to the attention of a wider audience.
- **Audio clip of a student response** Students hear an example of a way to present a literary response to a wider audience.
- **Tips for creating a videotaped book discussion** Students read suggestions for how to use their literary responses as "notes" for a book discussion that can be videotaped.

Students working individually or in small groups can use the ideas in the tutorial to guide the publishing and presenting phase.

The Multimedia Workshop

Students can use the magazine or newsletter templates in the Writing Workshop component of *The Multimedia Workshop* to word-process and present their final responses to literature.

Students who wish to make video presentations can use the Video Workshop Scene Maker and Sequencer.

Portfolio Assessment

Have students write an evaluative statement to address some of the questions posed on page 290 of the *Sourcebook*. If students decide to include the completed literary response in their portfolio, they might attach this statement to it. Otherwise, the statement itself can go into the portfolio as a record of self-evaluation.

The following questions can be used to supplement the questions in the *Sourcebook:*

- What part of the process of responding to literature did you find most satisfying?
- In what ways has your writing shown the most growth? In which areas should you focus attention in future assignments?

Student Model

Here is the complete, final draft of Alison Basford's response to the book *Six Months to Live*.

Review of Six Months to Live

by Alison Basford

Six Months to Live, by Lurlene McDaniel, is about thirteen-year-old Dawn Rochelle and her battle with leukemia, a form of cancer. Most of the story takes place in Children's Hospital in Columbus, Ohio. Dawn shares a room with Sandy Chandler, another girl who has been diagnosed with leukemia. The room is filled with games, toys, projects, and video games. Even though the situation is pretty sad, I liked this story because there was a feeling of hope throughout the book. That's because Dawn is determined to fight the leukemia until it goes into remission, meaning the disease symptoms disappear.

I gave some details about the setting so that the reader will have a clear picture of where the action of the story unfolds.

Here I described my reaction to the story and gave a reason for it.

Dawn fights the disease with her mind. She uses her teddy bear collection to help her. She has 103 teddy bears and has been collecting them since she was two years old. She imagines that her favorite teddy bear is fighting the leukemia, and it kills the disease. An important part of getting well is thinking that you will get well and that the drugs from chemotherapy are helping you, even if you feel really sick from them.

I wanted readers to understand that it was Dawn's attitude that helped her.

The only thing I didn't like about the book was the ending. Dawn gets well and goes home from the hospital, but her roommate Sandy dies. I found that a very sad ending, and I prefer happy endings, although I loved the book. In a way, though, I thought the ending of the story was perfect because the author was trying to show that people are not always as lucky as Dawn in surviving leukemia.

Even though my reaction to the book was favorable, there was one thing I wasn't too happy about. I think it's important that I give readers my honest response to the book.

Technology Note: Networking

After your class has read the Student Model, students may be interested in sharing creative efforts with peers across the country via the Internet or commercial on-line services such as Prodigy or America Online. Students can exchange responses to literature with other students, including those using *Writer's Solution*, by connecting to Prentice Hall's Internet home page. Look for special events, contests, as well as bulletin boards and pointers to student publications at http://www.phschool.com.

Teaching From the Model

Draw students' attention to how Alison Basford's piece on the book *Six Months to Live* includes the key elements of a response to literature:

- *It gives a personal response to a literary work.* Basford chose to respond to a novel, which she identifies by title and author in her first sentence.
- *It conveys personal opinions of the work with supporting details.* Basford explains that despite the serious theme—the challenge of battling a grave illness—she loved *Six Months to Live* "because there was a feeling of hope throughout the book." The response provides evidence to support her opinion, not through direct quotations, but with details from the story.
- *It briefly summarizes parts of the work.* Without revealing the whole story, Basford's response discusses elements of plot, setting, and character. Basford gives general statements about plot, such as "Dawn is determined to fight the leukemia . . ." and "Dawn gets well and goes home. . . ." She describes the setting by saying that "Most of the story takes place in Children's Hospital in Columbus, Ohio." In the second paragraph, Basford provides readers with a feeling for Dawn's character by giving details from the story: "Dawn fights the disease with her mind. . . . She imagines her favorite teddy bear is fighting the leukemia. . . ."
- *It presents an honest criticism of the book.* In the final paragraph, Basford admits not liking the book's sad ending. Yet she is able to see that the author may have increased the impact of Dawn's story by creating such an ending: ". . . [T]he author was trying to show that people are not always as lucky as Dawn in surviving leukemia."

Integrating Skills With Writing

Management Strategy

You can have students work through one or both of the skills lessons either before or after they write their literary responses. If you use the lessons *before*, remind students to incorporate the techniques in their writing. If you address skills *after* students write their essays, have them include a section on "skills improvement" in the self-assessment document they prepare for their portfolios. The next time they write, they can evaluate the work in terms of mastery of these skills.

You may want to give students these lessons as take-home assignments to be completed before drafting, revising, or proofreading—wherever you see the greatest need. Or you may choose to assign the skills lessons only to those students whose drafts indicate a need for direct instruction in the particular skills.

Teaching Strategy

To connect the skills lessons to students' writing, explain that an important feature of a literary response is the use of direct or indirect quotations from the work to support a respondent's views.

The goal in writing a response to literature is to clearly communicate opinions and ideas. Learning to avoid empty modifiers, empty phrases, and redundant words and phrases can help streamline a response so the intended audience can readily follow it.

Developing Your Style

Using Quotation Marks and Underlining

In your responses to literature, you can use direct quotations or indirect quotations. A **direct quotation** provides the exact words of the work you are quoting. Use a comma to separate the quotation from your own writing, and use quotation marks to show where the quotation begins and ends. When you put someone else's thoughts or ideas in your own words, you are using an **indirect quotation**. Do not use quotation marks.

Direct quotation: Katherine B. Shippen states, "In 1918 Sir Cecil Chubb of Salisbury made a unique gift to the English government."

Indirect quotation: Katherine B. Shippen states that in 1918 Sir Cecil Chubb gave the English government a unique gift.

A response to literature must include the title of the literary work. Titles of short stories and poems are surrounded by quotation marks. Titles of books and plays are written in **italics**, or slanted type. So too are the titles of periodicals, films, television programs, and works of art.

If you use a personal computer, set words in italics. If you are writing by hand, **underline** any title that should be in italics.

Short story title: "Dragon, Dragon"

Book title: *The Phantom Tollbooth* or The Phantom Tollbooth

Practice Activity

Correct the following examples from a response to literature by placing quotation marks and other punctuation where needed. Underline any titles.

1. The play entitled The Phantom Tollbooth, written by Susan Nanus, is based on the book by Norton Juster.
2. When Milo says that he is just killing time, Watchdog replies Killing Time! It's bad enough wasting time without killing it.

Language Lab CD-ROM

For extra help with the use of quotation marks, students can do the Quotation Marks lesson in the Punctuation unit.

Writer's Companion

To provide reinforcement to punctuate direct and indirect quotations, assign students the pertinent pages within the sections on Capitalization (pp. 297–304), Commas (pp. 309–314), and Ellipses (p. 335). Students can refer to a chart on page 398, which shows the use of italics for certain titles.

Practice Activity Answers

1. The play entitled *The Phantom Tollbooth*, written by Susan Nanus, is based on the book by Norton Juster.
2. When Milo says that he is just killing time, Watchdog replies, "Killing Time! It's bad enough wasting time without killing it."

Developing Your Style 2

Eliminating Unnecessary Words

Writing should communicate a message or convey an image without wasting words. Make your sentences as simple and direct as possible. Avoid unnecessary words. Such words act like a thick fog, hiding what you're trying to say.

- **Avoid Empty Modifiers** **Empty modifiers** are adjectives and adverbs that take up space but add little or no meaning, such as *very*, *highly*, *truly*, and *really*. These words can usually be left out without changing the meaning of a sentence.

  Wordy: "Sarah Tops," written by author Isaac Asimov, is a truly fascinating story.

  Better: "Sarah Tops," by Isaac Asimov, is a fascinating story.

- **Avoid Empty Phrases** **Empty phrases** are those that add little or no meaning. Here are some examples to avoid:

  there is no doubt that, it is a fact that, due to the fact that, more or less, as a matter of fact, at this point in time, it is my opinion that, I believe that

- **Avoid Redundant Words and Phrases** **Redundant words and phrases,** such as *each and every*, restate other words or phrases in the sentence.

  Wordy: Various different rhyme schemes are used in all three poems.

  Better: Different rhyme schemes are used in the three poems.

Practice Activity

Revise the following paragraph, eliminating unnecessary words and phrases.

There is the essay by Andrew A. Rooney entitled "How to Read a Newspaper" that is truly quite entertaining. In the essay, Rooney really doesn't teach a method of reading a newspaper. Instead, he actually tells how he really reads a paper, and it is a fact that he admits he doesn't actually do a good job. As he really states, "There's nothing I do so much of that I do so badly."

Teaching Strategy

Write the statement "Less is more" on the chalkboard. Ask students what they think it means. Guide them to relate this idea to their writing by suggesting that it's better to avoid extra words when fewer words convey the same idea.

Challenge students to look through their writing for examples of empty modifiers and empty phrases. Point out that while it can sometimes be appealing to "pad" writing with empty modifiers or phrases, doing so adds little or no meaning.

Language Lab CD-ROM

Students who need practice to avoid empty or redundant words or phrases may benefit from doing the Eliminating Unnecessary Words lesson in the Styling Sentences unit of the *Language Lab*.

Language Acquisition/ ESL Teaching Strategy

Ask your upper-basic and intermediate ESL students to work in pairs to revise the paragraph. Have the students copy the paragraph onto a large sheet of colored paper and cross out unnecessary words with a red marker. In the margins around the paragraph, the students should indicate the reason why any words were eliminated. They can write *empty modifier*, *empty phrase*, and *redundant word*. The sheets can be hung in the classroom for reference.

Writer's Companion

Students who need additional practice to identify and eliminate unnecessary words can find support on page 74.

Teaching Strategy

Tell students that there are many ways to revise the Practice Activity paragraph. You might have students share and discuss their revisions with peer partners. You might also have some revisions read aloud or put on transparencies for the overhead projector.

Practice Activity: Suggested Answer

Revised paragraphs will vary. Here is a possible revision.

Andrew A. Rooney's essay "How to Read a Newspaper" is quite entertaining. In the essay, Rooney doesn't teach a method of reading a newspaper. Instead, he tells how he reads a paper, admitting that he doesn't do a good job at it! He states, "There's nothing I do so much of that I do so badly."

Integrating Literature With Writing

Literature Model

In the following excerpt, Native American writer Joseph Bruchac responds to Joy Harjo's poem by focusing on the meaning, or message. As you read, notice how Bruchac connects the ideas in the poem to Native American traditions and religious beliefs.

The Circle of Blessing: Joy Harjo's "Eagle Poem"

by Joseph Bruchac

Many years ago, I visited an elderly friend on the Onondaga Indian Reservation near Syracuse, New York. As soon as I walked into her house, she said, "Let me get you a glass of water." She walked to the sink and as she filled the glass I heard her say, in the Onondaga language, a prayer of thanks to the Creator. The lesson I learned that day remains an important one to me. Many things that we take for granted or even fail to notice—like a glass of cool water—are actually wonderful gifts. It does us good to remember those gifts and speak our thanks.

Bruchac begins his response with a brief personal narrative. This lets readers know that he feels a connection with the poem.

To understand Joy Harjo's poem, and most contemporary American Indian poetry, we need to understand the importance of spirit and prayer in everyday Native life. There are more than four hundred different Native languages and cultures in North America. However, the practice of giving thanks to the Creator is found in all of them. In all of those cultures, too, is found a deep belief in the sacred nature of life. All life is a great mystery. Everything around us in the

Bruchac gives the reader general information about Native American religion. If your response focuses on a work's meaning or message, you may need to give readers some background.

294 • *Response to Literature*

Management Strategy

You can have students read this model of a response to literature either before or after they have written their own piece. If you choose to have them read it *before*, use it to draw their attention to techniques or ideas they can apply to their own writing. If you use it *after*, have students compare and contrast some elements of this piece with elements of their own response. Ask: *What can you learn from this piece that can help you the next time you respond to a literary work?*

Activating Prior Knowledge

Before they read Joseph Bruchac's response to a poem by Joy Harjo, invite students to share experiences they have had being moved or inspired by something in nature. Ask if nature has ever motivated them to write, and if so, what kind of writing they did.

Purpose-Setting Question

How does the author of this response help his audience understand the message he finds in the poem?

Reading Strategy

Help students appreciate the style and structure of Bruchac's response by having them identify the features that they would associate with any response to literature:

- Does it tell whether or not Bruchac liked the poem and how the poem made him feel?
- Does it describe how the poem is presented and how it sounds?
- Does it offer personal opinions and supporting details from the poem?

After they finish reading, students can work as a whole class or in small groups to compare their responses.

Clarification

Note that this Literature Model offers a response to a poem without reprinting the whole poem. The intent is to have students focus on the effectiveness of the response rather than on the poem.

Teaching From the Model

Discuss "The Circle of Blessing: Joy Harjo's 'Eagle Poem'" by Joseph Bruchac to help students see how it typifies a response to poetry.

- *Bruchac shares his personal opinions about the poem.* Bruchac uses the poem as a springboard to discuss his views on ". . . the importance of spirit and prayer in everyday Native life." "Eagle Poem" caused Bruchac to reflect on his beliefs as they are mirrored in Harjo's imagery and language.

natural world is filled with spiritual energy because it was created by God. It is a proof of the existence of the Creator, who is often called "The Great Mystery" in various Native American languages.

Of course, this concept of God being in all things is found in other cultures. The nineteenth-century English poet Gerard Manley Hopkins saw God's presence in nature when he wrote his poem "The Windhover." Like Harjo, who focuses her poem around a circling eagle, Hopkins wrote his poem upon seeing a falcon (a "windhover") in flight.

Bruchac compares an image in Harjo's poem to an image in a poem by an English poet. Making such cross-cultural comparisons is one more way to clarify the ideas in a poem.

Because life is sacred, it is our responsibility as human beings to treat all life with respect and care. The modern science of ecology teaches us that all things are interdependent. Ecology is not an abstract scientific idea for Native Americans. It is a very old way of life. As Harjo puts it:

> . . . we must take the utmost care
> And kindness in all things.

Bruchac uses a quotation from the poem to point out a connection between traditional Native American culture and modern ideas of ecology. Quotations from a work can be used to make a point or to help explain an idea.

In Native American culture, it is understood that giving thanks is something human beings need to do. However, prayer is not just the speaking of memorized words. It is also the actions that go with those words. Moreover, prayer is something that is very personal. It must come from the depth of your own heart, and you must speak and act with an awareness of the sacredness that is all around you. As Harjo says in the very first lines of the poem:

> To pray you open your whole self
> To sky, to earth, to sun, to moon
> To one whole voice that is you.

Here Bruchac uses a quotation from the beginning of the poem that speaks directly about his main idea.

- *Bruchac offers explanations of the poem's meaning.* Bruchac says that it is common in Native American culture and religion to give thanks to the Creator. He discusses spiritual energy and interdependence as key beliefs that emerge as themes in Harjo's poem. The background information he provides about Native American beliefs can guide an audience unfamiliar with these ideas to grasp the poem's message.
- *Bruchac uses some elements of a literary review.* Point out that the response to "Eagle Poem" has a more formal tone than other literary responses students may have read. Details on Native American culture provide background for Bruchac's opinions and lend credibility to his evaluation. He compares "Eagle Poem" to "The Windhover," a poem by a nineteenth century English poet, to show that exploring the ". . . concept of God being in all things is found in other cultures."

Ask students to describe a possible audience for this type of response.

- *Bruchac includes quotations from the poem.* Discuss how the quotation ". . . we must take the utmost care/And kindness in all things" works in two ways: It gives a taste of Harjo's style and supports Bruchac's point that the poem is deeply rooted in Native American philosophy.

Language Acquisition/ ESL Teaching Strategy

Put your intermediate and advanced ESL students into groups of three or four. Ask them to read Joseph Bruchac's excerpt together, keeping the following questions in mind: *Does he like Joy Harjo's poem? Why does he believe it is an important poem? How does Harjo's poem reflect Native American culture?* After a student-led discussion, ask your students what they learned from Bruchac's response to Harjo's poem.

Closure and Extension

To complete the lesson you can ask students to summarize what they learned about responding to literature by examining this literary response. Then have students share, through brief journal entries or in discussion groups, what they learned about themselves as writers and what points they would like to keep in mind for future writing.

SUMMARY OF GRAMMAR

Nouns A **noun** is the name of a person, place, or thing. A **common noun** names any one of a class of people, places, or things. A **proper noun** names a specific person, place, or thing.

Common Nouns	**Proper Nouns**
poet	Eve Merriam, Nikki Giovanni
river	Missouri, Congo, Rio Grande

Pronouns A **pronoun** is a word that stands for a noun or for a word that takes the place of a noun.

A **personal pronoun** refers to (1) the person speaking, (2) the person spoken to, or (3) the person, place, or thing spoken about.

	Singular	**Plural**
First Person	I, me, my, mine	we, us, our, ours
Second Person	you, your, yours	you, your, yours
Third Person	he, him, his, she her, hers, it, its	they, them, their, theirs

I know *her* as being bubbly and bouncy, . . .
— "Virginia Hamilton," Lee Bennett Hopkins

How can *you* buy or sell the sky. . . ?
— "Letter to the U.S. Government," Chief Seattle

Demonstrative pronouns point out people, places, or things.

this is John *that* tastes good

Indefinite pronouns refer to people, places, or things, often without specifying which ones.

They did *much* of the work yesterday.
All of these apples are ripe.

Verbs A **verb** is a word that expresses the condition of a person, place, or thing. An **action verb** indicates the action of a person or thing. The action can be physical or mental.

The tiger's roar *filled* the cave with thunder.
— "Mowgli's Brothers," Rudyard Kipling

Tilted umbrellas *nod* in soft sand.
— "Sea Songs," Myra Cohn Livingston

A **linking verb** joins a noun or pronoun at or near the beginning of a sentence with a word at or near the end. The word at the end identifies or describes the noun or pronoun.

Arithmetic *is* numbers you squeeze from your head. . . .
— "Arithmetic," Carl Sandburg

Suddenly it *seemed* too late for Tito.
— "The Dog of Pompeii," Louis Untermeyer

Helping verbs are verbs that come before th main verb and add to its meaning.

We *had invited* Chinese friends to eat with us before, but this dinner was going to be differe
— "The All-American Slurp," Lensey Namioka

Adjectives An **adjective** is a word that describ something. Adjectives answer these questions:

What kind?	*silver* tray, *large* can
Which one?	*that* bus, *those* flowers
How many?	*eight* minutes, *many* people
How much?	*no* clouds, *heavy* traffic

The articles *the*, *a*, and *an* are adjectives. *An* is used before a word beginning with a vowel soun

Adverbs An **adverb** is a word that modifies a verb, an adjective, or another adverb. Adverbs answer the questions Where? When? In what ma ner? To what extent?

She *often* sang. (modifies verb *sang*)
He was *amazingly* tall. (modifies adjective *tall*)
We swim *rather* regularly. (modifies adverb *regularly*)

Prepositions A **preposition** relates a noun or a pronoun to another word in the sentence. Prepos tions are almost always followed by nouns or pro nouns.

before the end	*in* my room	*except* them
at sunset	*without* us	*behind* that ca

Conjunctions A **conjunction** connects words, groups of words, and whole sentences. **Coordin ing conjunctions** connect similar kinds or group of words.

trees *and* flowers faint *but* visible

Correlative conjunctions are used in pairs to connect words or word groups.

both Dad *and* Mom *either* she *or* I

Interjections An **interjection** is a word or phrase that expresses sudden excitement or strong feelin

"Psst," I said to each person who came in.
— "The Scribe," Kristin Hunter

"Ho! ho!" said Mowgli.
— "Mowgli's Brothers," Rudyard Kipling

Sentences A **sentence** is a group of words with two main parts: a complete subject and a comple predicate. Together these parts express a complete thought.

The first eight were given to Felix on his ninth birthday.
— "Paul Klee," Hattie Clark

Near the edge of the Liberian rain forest, on a hill overlooking the Cavally River, was the village of Kundi.

— "The Cow-Tail Switch," from *Liberia,* Harold Courlander and George Herzog

A **fragment** is a group of words that does not xpress a complete thought.

The Roman writers with whose work he was familiar

— "The Strange Geometry of Stonehenge," Katherine B. Shippen

whirled with the angry words his parents had spoken

— "Thunder Butte," from *When Thunders Spoke,* Virginia Driving Hawk Sneve

ubject-Verb Agreement To make a subject and rb agree, make sure that both are singular or oth are plural. Two or more singular subjects ined by *or* or *nor* must have a singular verb. hen singular and plural subjects are joined by *or nor,* the verb must agree with the closer subject.

They are here.

She is making sandwiches.

Neither the *road* nor the *paths are marked* here.

Many of the houses *need* painting.

hrases A **phrase** is a group of words, without a ubject and verb, that functions in a sentence as ne part of speech. A **prepositional phrase** is a roup of words that includes a preposition and a oun or pronoun.

during the play	*inside* that drawer
to school	*in* the neighborhood
by the lake	*with* her sister

An **adjective phrase** is a prepositional phrase at modifies a noun or pronoun.

Kai felt a chill *of dread.* Had he mistaken the look *of sympathy in Kelii's face?*

— "The Riddling Youngster," from *Hawaii,* Vivian L. Thompson

An **adverb phrase** is a prepositional phrase that odifies a verb, adjective, or adverb.

He broke a cookie *into small crumbs* and tossed some *toward the pigeon.*

— "Aaron's Gift," Myron Levoy

An **appositive phrase** renames, identifies, or xplains the noun with which it appears.

I pulled [the stinger] out quickly, ran water over the sting, and packed it with mud, *Grandmother's remedy.*

— "The Drive-In Movies," Gary Soto

A **participial phrase** is a participle modified by an adjective or adverb phrase or accompanied by a complement. The entire phrase acts as an adjective.

Looking at the fly on the pole, the boy said, "A fly is a good enough witness for me."

— "The Fly," from *Vietnam,* Mai Vo-Dinh

It was a fixed routine, a custom *understood between boy and dog since the beginning of their friendship,* and the way it worked was this: . . .

— "The Dog of Pompeii," Louis Untermeyer

Clauses A **clause** is a group of words that contains both a subject and a verb. An **independent clause** has a subject and a verb and can stand by itself as a complete sentence.

Abraham passed his eighth birthday in the lean-to.

— "A Backwoods Boy," Russell Freedman

He has never seen a train of cars nor an elevator in his life, and for that matter *he has never once looked upon a cornfield, a plow, a cow, or even a chicken.*

— "The King of Mazy May," Jack London

A **subordinate clause** has a subject and a verb but cannot stand on its own as a complete sentence.

Since I could not sleep, I decided to get up and join Papá and Roberto at breakfast.

— "The Circuit," Francisco Jiménez

Breaker kept hold of the pellets *until he reached the inn.*

— "Breaker's Bridge," Laurence Yep

SUMMARY OF CAPITALIZATION AND PUNCTUATION

CAPITALIZATION

Capitalize the first word of a sentence and the first word of a direct quotation when it is used as part of a longer sentence.

Once the snakes decided that they would give a costume ball; . . .

— "How the Flamingoes Got Their Stockings," from *Uruguay,* Horacio Quiroga

After I asked, Mom looked kind of funny and said, "He was in the museum at the very time."

— "Sarah Tops," Isaac Asimov

Capitalize all proper nouns and adjectives.

Jane Yolen	Stonehenge	Liberia
April	Chinese	Kentucky

Capitalize a person's title when it is followed by the person's name or when it is used in direct address.

Reverend   Chief Seattle   Miss Crawford

Capitalize titles showing family relationships when they refer to a specific person unless they are preceded by a possessive noun or pronoun.

Daddy   Auntie   her niece

Capitalize the first word and all other key words in the titles of books, periodicals, poems, stories, plays, paintings, and other works of art.

Tuck Everlasting   "The King of Mazy May"
"The Drive-In Movies"   *The Sleeping Gypsy*

Capitalize the first word and all nouns in letter salutations and the first word in letter closings.

Dear Mr. Cosby,   Sincerely yours,

PUNCTUATION

End Marks Use a **period** to end a declarative sentence, an imperative sentence, an indirect question, and most abbreviations.

The sun was just beginning to rise when John woke Norman the next morning.
— "Thunder Butte," from *When Thunders Spoke,* Virginia Driving Hawk Sneve

"Don't get any ideas into your head, and don't go near that pylon."
— "Power," Jack Cope

Use a **question mark** after an interrogative sentence or after a word or phrase that asks a question.

How did you do that?
— *Phantom Tollbooth,* Act II, based on the book by Norton Juster, Susan Nanus

But if you did get up, what then?
— "Power," Jack Cope

Use an **exclamation mark** after a statement showing strong emotion, an urgent imperative sentence, or an interjection expressing strong emotion.

"Mush! Hi! Mush on!"
— "The King of Mazy May," Jack London

"No, no!" cried Maibon.
— "The Stone," Lloyd Alexander

Commas Use a **comma** before the conjunction to separate two independent clauses in a compound sentence.

He could just make out the pale, murky shape of a mound, but that was all.
— "Breaker's Bridge," Laurence Yep

Use commas to separate three or more words, phrases, or clauses in a series.

The next day, Miss Smith read my letter to t class, praised me for using my imagination, and said everyone else in the class had to t again.
— "The Platoon System," from *A Girl Fro Yamhill,* Beverly Cleary

Use a comma after an introductory word or phrase.

"*First,* I know just what you want to buy," sai Mr. Sanderson.
— "The Sound of Summer Running," fron *Dandelion Wine,* Ray Bradbury

"*By the time I was seven,* I knew that life mu be freedom; . . ."
— "Virginia Hamilton," Lee Bennett Hopki

Use commas to set off interrupting words and phrases.

Well, *as anyone knew,* the hills around town were wild with friends putting cows to riot, . .
— "The Sound of Summer Running," from *Dandelion Wine,* Ray Bradbury

Use commas with places and dates made up o two or more parts.

Sandra Cisneros was born in Chicago, Illino
F. Scott Fitzgerald wrote to his daughter on August 8, 1933.

Use commas after items in addresses, after the salutation in a personal letter, after the closing in a letters, and in numbers of more than three digits.

The Kilns, Headington Quarry, Oxford
—"Letter to Joan," C. S. Lewis

Dear Josh,   Yours truly,   4,589

Use a comma to set off a direct quotation.

"Besides," he added, "my father dreamed of this happening."
— "Thunder Butte," from *When Thunders Spoke,* Virginia Driving Hawk Sneve

Semicolons Use a semicolon to connect two ind pendent clauses that are closely connected in meaning.

Last year they and several others had spent much toil and time on the Mazy May and endured great hardships; the creek, in turn, was just beginning to show up its richness ar to reward them for their heavy labor.
— "The King of Mazy May," Jack London

Colons Use a colon after an independent clause order to introduce a list of items.

298

Mrs. Gleason exclaimed at the beautifully arranged dishes of food: the colorful candied fruit in the sweet-and-sour pork dish, the noodle-thin shreds of chicken meat stir-fried with tiny peas, and the glistening pink prawns in a ginger sauce.

— "The All-American Slurp," Lensey Namioka

Jse a colon in numbers giving the time, in salu-
ons in business letters, and in labels used to sig-
important ideas.

From 9:00 to 9:30 we take our early midmorning nap. . . .

— *The Phantom Tollbooth,* based on the book by Norton Juster, Susan Nanus

Dear Mr. Rawls: Danger: Forest Fire Zone

otation Marks A **direct quotation** represents a
son's exact speech or thoughts and is enclosed
uotation marks.

Commenting on her childhood, she states: "I was born in a miserable corner of southern Ohio and dutifully raised there, . . ."

— "Virginia Hamilton," Lee Bennett Hopkins

An **indirect quotation** reports only the general
aning of what a person said or thought and does
require quotation marks.

They said that no man sentenced to the *Jersey* survived unless he was removed in a short time, but then, James thought, most prisoners were white.

— from *Between the Devil and the Sea,* Brenda A. Johnston

Always place a comma or a period inside the
l quotation mark.

"Louder," said Miss Harrington. "I can't hear you."

— "The Platoon System," from *A Girl From Yamhill,* Beverly Cleary

Place a question mark or exclamation mark
de the final quotation mark if the end mark is
t of the quotation; if it is not part of the quotation,
ce it outside the final quotation mark.

She looked back at him questioningly, as if to say, "Where are you taking me?"

— "Zlateh the Goat," Isaac Bashevis Singer

Did Lynette write her report on Carl Sandburg's "Arithmetic"?

Underline or italicize the titles of long written
rks, movies, television and radio series, paint-
s, sculpture, and specific vehicles.

The Phantom Tollbooth   *Star Trek*
Man Walking   the Enterprise

Use quotation marks around the titles of short written works and other short artistic works.

"Aaron's Gift" "The Shark" "Jingle Bells"

Hyphens Use a hyphen with certain numbers, after certain prefixes, and with some compound nouns.

eighty-nine mid-March six-year-old seven-thirty S-shaped curve

Apostrophes Add an apostrophe and *-s* to show the possessive case of most singular nouns.

Clemens's stories a mother's prayer

Add an apostrophe to show the possessive case of plural nouns ending in *-s* and *-es.*

the spectators' cheers the Martinezes' car

Add an apostrophe and *-s* to show the possessive case of plural nouns that do not end in *-s* or *-es.*

the men's store the deer's tails

Use an apostrophe in a contraction to indicate the position of the missing letter or letters.

It's as crunchy as a bone.

— *The Phantom Tollbooth,* based on the book by Norton Juster, Susan Nanus

GLOSSARY OF COMMON USAGE

accept, except

Accept is a verb that means "to receive" or "to agree to." *Except* is a preposition that means "other than" or "leaving out."

Aaron sadly *accepted* his father's decision to sell Zlateh.

Everyone *except* the fisherman and his wife had children.

affect, effect

Affect is normally a verb meaning "to influence" or "to bring about a change in." *Effect* is usually a noun, meaning "result."

The sight of the pigeon with a broken wing *affected* the boy, and he broke the cookie into small crumbs to feed the bird.

The wizard's spell had an immediate *effect* on the queen. She turned into a rosebush.

ain't

Ain't was originally a contraction of *am not.* It is not considered standard English. Avoid it in all writing and speaking.

"I *am not* impressed by Father's advice," said the eldest son to himself.

299

among, between
Among is always used with three or more items. *Between* is generally used with only two items.

"Arithmetic" was *among* the poems Jill liked best.

The conversation *between* Larry and his father shows that Larry must think for himself.

amount, number
Amount refers to quantity or a unit, while *number* refers to individual items that can be counted. Therefore, *amount* generally appears with a singular noun, and *number* appears with a plural noun.

A large *amount* of mathematical knowledge is not needed to appreciate *The Phantom Tollbooth.*

A *number* of letters were in the package.

any, all
Any should not be used in place of *any other* or *all.*

Santos thought "The All-American Slurp" was funnier than *any other* story he had read this year.

Of *all* the characters in "Mowgli's Brothers," I like Bagheera best.

around
In formal writing, *around* should not be used to mean *approximately* or *about.* These usages are allowable, however, in informal writing or in colloquial dialogue.

The turtle laid *approximately* a dozen eggs.

The rural community, *about* sixty miles north of the Ohio River, is the home of Antioch College.

as, because, like
The word *as* has several meanings and can function as several parts of speech. To avoid confusion, use *because* rather than *as* when you want to indicate cause and effect.

Because the excavator noticed a pattern on the stone, he looked more closely.

Do not use the preposition *like* to introduce a clause that requires the conjunction *as.*

C. S. Lewis advises Joan to write *as* an educated person would speak.

at
Do not use *at* after *where.*

Where is Stonehenge?

bad, badly
Use the predicate adjective *bad* after linking verbs such as *feel, look,* and *seem.* Use *badly* whenever an adverb is required.

Mouse does not feel *bad* about tricking Coyote.

In the myth, Athene treats Arachne *badly.*

because
Do not use *because* after *the reason.* Eliminate or the other.

The reason I began to hurry was that my arm were hurting and my stung foot looked like water balloon.

I began to hurry *because* my arms were hurti and my stung foot looked like a water ballo

because of, due to
Use *due to* if it can logically replace the phrase *caused by.* In introductory phrases, however, *because of* is better usage than *due to.*

The huge migration of fortune hunters was *d to* the discovery of gold in Alaska.

Because of the mayor's demonstration, Heyerdahl concluded that the statues had been carved with crude stone tools.

beside, besides
Beside means "at the side of" or "close to." *Besi* means "in addition to."

Sitting *beside* his parents, Greyling sings son of the wonders that lie beneath the sea.

Besides "Alone in the Nets," what other poem did you like this year?

bring, take
Bring means to carry something from a distant place to a nearer one. *Take* means the reverse: carry something from a near place to a more dis place.

The emperor commanded his servants to *brir* the clever builder to him.

Panchito's father *takes* his family to Fresno in search of work.

can, may
The verb *can* generally refers to the ability to do something. The verb *may* generally refers to permission to do something.

Maibon replies that he *can* still see the dwarf.

In Jack Cope's story, the officials tell Andre th they *may* not cut off the power, even for a minute.

compare, contrast
The verb *compare* can involve both similarities a differences. The verb *contrast* always involves d ferences. Use *to* or *with* after *compare.* Use *with* after *contrast.*

Rena *compared* Lewis's "Letter to Joan" *to* Fitzgerald's "Letter to Scottie."

In many works of science fiction, elements of fantasy *contrast with* the reality of the every day world.

300

erent from, different than
erent from is generally preferred over *different* *n.*
Fables are *different from* myths because fables usually involve animal characters.

ne
ne is the past participle of *do.* It should always ow a helping verb.
The director and his assistant thought that the dog *had done* something strange.

't
doesn't, not *don't,* with third-person singular noun subjects and singular noun subjects.
Norman *doesn't* agree with his grandfather about the cause of the thunder and lightning.

er, less
fewer for things that can be counted. Use *less* amounts or quantities that cannot be counted.
Which poem has *fewer* rhyming lines: "April Rain Song" or "Ankylosaurus"?
Because Walt had to harness the team quickly, he had *less* time than he needed to choose a good lead dog.

ne, went
ne is the past participle of *go.* It should be used a verb only with a helping verb. *Went* is the past se of *go* and is never used with a helping verb.
Her family thought that Auntie *had gone* to mail a letter.
When James *went* down to the docks, he took only his mother's Bible and a bag of marbles.

od, well
the predicate adjective *good* after linking verbs h as *feel, look, smell, taste,* and *seem.* Use *well* enever you need an adverb.
Most people feel *good* when they receive letters from friends.
n "The Dog of Pompeii," Louis Untermeyer describes the eruption of the volcano especially *well.*

into
efers to position and means "within" or "inside." suggests motion from outside to inside.
'Sarah Tops" takes place *in* New York City.
The swallow became caught when it flew *into* the pylon.

, it's
not confuse the possessive pronoun *its* with the ntraction *it's,* standing for "it is" or "it has."
The village of Kundi was well known for *its* rice and cassava fields.
The Mathemagician says that *it's* numbers that count.

kind of, sort of
Do not use *kind of* and *sort of* to mean "rather" or "somewhat."
Sandra thought that the fate of Orpheus was *rather* cruel.
In "Thunder Butte," the atmosphere at dinner is *somewhat* strained.

lay, lie
Lay is a transitive verb meaning "to set or put something down." Its principal parts are *lay, laying, laid, laid. Lie* is an intransitive verb meaning "to recline." Its principal parts are *lie, lying, lay, lain.*
Aaron *lays* some popcorn on the floor for Pidge.
The boy makes a pillow out of some hay and *lies* down to sleep.

learn, teach
Be careful not to use *learn* (meaning "to acquire knowledge") when your context requires *teach* (meaning "to give knowledge").
Did you *learn* a lot about hatching turtles from Jean Craighead George's essay?
For fifteen years, Emma Greig *taught* in a rural school.

leave, let
Leave means "to go away" or "to allow to remain." *Let* means "to permit."
When the volcano erupted, Bimbo did not want to *leave* Tito's side.
She opened the door and *let* the moth fly out.

like
Like is a preposition that usually means "similar to" or "in the same way as." *Like* should always be followed by an object. Do not use *like* before a subject and a verb. Use *as* or *that* instead.
Myths *like* "Arachne" explain the origins of things in nature.
Tuck Everlasting did not end *as* Alicia expected.

loose, lose
Loose can be either an adjective (meaning "unattached") or a verb (meaning "to untie"). *Lose* is always a verb (meaning "to fail to keep, have, or win").
Chief Seattle believes that the links between human beings and the land should be strong, not *loose.*
Auntie realized that to save Billy's life she would have to *lose* her own.

301

may be, maybe
Don't confuse the verb phrase *may be* with the adverb *maybe* (meaning "perhaps").

Conflicts *may be* external or internal.

Maybe the cobbler's first son would have succeeded if he had paid attention to his father's advice.

of, have
Do not use *of* in place of *have* after auxiliary verbs like *would, could, should, may, might,* or *must.*

Maibon realizes that he *should have* destroyed the stone.

raise, rise
Raise is a transitive verb that usually takes a direct object. *Rise* is intransitive and never takes a direct object.

The Mathemagician *raised* his staff.

When the bell rings for lunch and the other children *rise* to leave the classroom, Rachel sees Phyllis Lopez.

set, sit
Set is a transitive verb meaning "to put (something) in a certain place." Its principal parts are *set, setting, set, set. Sit* is an intransitive verb meaning "to be seated." Its principal parts are *sit, sitting, sat, sat.*

The Walrus *sets* a loaf of bread and some pepper and vinegar on the rocks.

I would like to read "Sea Songs" while I *sit* on a beautiful beach.

than, then
The conjunction *than* is used to connect the two parts of a comparison. Do not confuse *than* with the adverb *then,* which usually refers to time.

Rudyard Kipling lived longer *than* Jack London.

The water in the public fountains boils, and *then* the streets of Pompeii start to crumble.

that, which, who
Use the relative pronoun *that* to refer to things or people. Use *which* only for things and *who* only for people.

The ancient coup stick *that* Norman finds might have been buried with a dead warrior.

The theme, *which* is the central message of a literary work, is often not directly stated.

Robert Frost is a poet *who* writes vividly about nature.

their, there, they're
Their is a possessive adjective and always modifies a noun. *There* is usually used either at the beginning of a sentence or as an adverb. *They're* is a contraction for *they are.*

In Thurber's fable, some of the beasts did no[t] even know what *their* fight was about.

There was nothing that could frighten Isabel i[n] Ogden Nash's poem.

Limericks are short. *They're* usually also humorous.

to, too, two
To is a preposition that begins a prepositional phrase or an infinitive. *Too,* with two *o's,* is an adverb and modifies adjectives and other adverb[s]. *Two* is a number.

Mr. Lema spoke *to* Panchito about learning t[o] play the trumpet.

The weather was *too* cold for Old Ben, so he holed up for the winter in the hayloft.

Bruh Bear and Bruh Rabbit are *two* character[s] with strength and experience.

unique
Because *unique* means "one of a kind," you sho[uld] not use it carelessly instead of the words *interes[ting]* or *unusual.* Avoid such illogical expressions as "most unique," "very unique," and "extremely unique."

Billy gradually realized that Auntie was *uniqu[e]* and he never forgot her.

use to, used to
In formal writing, do not replace *used to* with the nonstandard phrase *use to,* which sounds very s[im]ilar in speech.

According to Russell Freedman in "A Backwo[ods] Boy," Abraham Lincoln never *used to* talk much about his early life.

when, where, why
Do not use *when, where,* or *why* directly after a [link]ing verb such as *is.* Reword the sentence.

An argument is a set of reasons that lead to a conclusion. (Rewording of: An argument is *when* a set of reasons lead to a conclusion

In a biography, a writer tells the life story of another person. (Rewording of: A biograph[y is] *where* a writer tells the life story of another person.)

The author wrote this essay to persuade the reader. (Rewording of: To persuade the rea[d]er is *why* the author wrote this essay.)

who, whom
In formal writing, remember to use *who* only as a subject in clauses and sentences and *whom* only as an object.

Nikki Giovanni, *who* wrote "Winter Poem," often expresses her concern for the black commun[ity]

One poet *whom* Cesar especially liked was Ju[an] Ramón Jiménez.

302

D

304

305

306

S

INDEX

307

308

ACKNOWLEDGMENTS (continued from page ii)

Paul S. Eriksson, Inc.
From "My Papa, Mark Twain" by Susy Clemens, from *small voices* by Josef and Dorothy Berger. Copyright © 1966 by Josef & Dorothy Berger. Used by permission of the publisher, Paul S. Eriksson, Inc.

Samuel French, Inc.
Reprinted by permission from *The Phantom Tollbooth* by Susan Nanus and Norton Juster. Copyright © 1977 by Susan Nanus and Norton Juster. CAUTION: Professionals and amateurs are hereby warned that "THE PHANTOM TOLLBOOTH," being fully protected under the copyright laws of the United States of America, the British Commonwealth countries, including Canada, and the other countries of the Copyright Union, is subject to a royalty. All rights, including professional, amateur, motion picture, recitation, public reading, radio, television and cable broadcasting, and the rights of translation into foreign languages, are strictly reserved. Any inquiry regarding the availability of performance rights, or the purchase of individual copies of the authorized acting edition, must be directed to Samuel French Inc., 45 West 25 Street, NY, NY 10010, with other locations in Hollywood and Toronto, Canada.

Harcourt Brace & Company
"Ode to Weightlifting" from *Neighborhood Odes,* copyright © 1992 by Gary Soto. Excerpt from *The Bells of Christmas,* copyright © 1989 by Virginia Hamilton. Reprinted by permission.

HarperCollins Publishers, Inc.
"An Artichoke on Legs" and "Shark Attacks" from *Of Kinkajous, Capybaras, Horned Beetles, Seladangs, and the Oddest and . . .* by Jeanne K. Hanson and Deane Morrison. Copyright © 1991 by Jeanne K. Hanson and Deane Morrison. From *Letters of E. B. White,* collected and edited by Dorothy Lobrano Guth. Copyright © 1976 by E. B. White. From "The Hatchling Turtles," from *Spring Comes to the Ocean* by Jean Craighead George. Copyright © 1965 by Jean Craighead George. Reprinted by permission of HarperCollins Publishers, Inc.

Highlights for Children, Inc.
From "Paul Klee" by Hattie Clark, from *Highlights for Children,* January 1986. Copyright © 1986. Used by permission of Highlights for Children, Inc., Columbus, Ohio.

Houghton Mifflin Company
"Rhyming Riddle #1," from *The Children Sing in the Far West* by Mary Austin. Copyright 1928 by Mary Austin, © renewed 1956 by Kenneth M. Chapman and Mary C. Wheelwright. Reprinted by permission of Houghton Mifflin Company. All rights reserved.

Barbara Jordan
From "All Together Now" by Barbara Jordan, originally published in *Sesame Street Parents,* July/August 1994. Used by permission.

Garrison Keillor and International Paper
From "How to Write a Letter," from *We Are Still Married* by Garrison Keillor. Copyright © 1987 by International Paper Company; copyright © Garrison Keillor 1989. Reprinted by permission of the author and International Paper Company.

Alfred A. Knopf, Inc.
From *The People Could Fly: American Black Folktales* by Virginia Hamilton. Text copyright © 1985 by Virginia Hamilton. Reprinted by permission.

Mark Levine, Publisher
From "Just how much Rain has it RAINED?" from *Kids Discover Magazine,* December 1992, Volume 2, Issue 10. Reprinted by permission of the publisher.

Estate of John C. Lilly
From *Man and Dolphin* by John C. Lilly, MD. Copyright © 1961. Published by Doubleday & Company, Inc.

Morrow Junior Books, a Division of William Morrow & Company
From *A Girl From Yamhill: a Memoir* by Beverly Cleary. Copyright © 1988 by Beverly Cleary. Reprinted by permission.

W. W. Norton & Company, Inc.
From *Polluting for Pleasure* by Andre Mele. Copyright © 1993 by Andre Mele. Reprinted by permission of W. W. Norton & Company, Inc.

Orchard Books, a Division of Franklin Watts, Inc. and Dieter Klein Associates
From "Becky and the Wheels-and-Brake Boys" from *A Thief in the Village and Other Stories* by James Berry. Copyright © 1987 by James Berry. Used by permission.

Pocket Books, a division of Simon & Schuster, Inc.
From "Around the World in 80 Days," from *Kidvid: A Parents' Guide to Children's Videos* by Harold Schechter. Copyright © 1986 by Harold Schechter. Reprinted by permission of Pocket Books, a division of Simon & Schuster, Inc.

The Putnam Publishing Group
Reprinted by permission of The Putnam Publishing Group from *Letters to Judy: What Kids Wish They Could Tell You* by Judy Blume. Copyright © 1986 by Kids Fund. From *Childhood* by Bill Cosby. Copyright © 1991 by William H. Cosby, Jr. Used by permission.

Marian Reiner
Japanese haiku by Bash from *Cricket Songs,* translated by Harry Behn. © 1964 Harry Behn, © Renewed 1992 Prescott Behn, Pamela Behn Adam, and Peter Behn. Reprinted by permission of Marian Reiner.

Jeff Saviano
From "My Life's Work: Crime Lab Scientist" by Jeff Saviano. Published in *Boy's Life* magazine, January 1992. Reprinted by permission of the author.

Scarecrow Press, Inc.
From a book review by Patrick Jones of Fran Lantz's *Rock, Rap, and Rad: How to Be a Rock or Rap Star,* from *Voya*/April 1993, Vol. 16, No. 1. Reprinted by permission of Scarecrow Press, Inc.

Scribner, an imprint of Simon & Schuster, Inc.
Excerpted with permission of Scribner, an imprint of Simon & Schuster, Inc., from "Letter to Scottie" 8/8/33, from *F. Scott Fitzgerald: A Life in Letters,* edited by Matthew J. Bruccoli. Copyright © 1994 by The Trustees Under Agreement Dated July 3, 1975, Created by Frances Scott Fitzgerald Smith.

Sports Illustrated For Kids
Excerpts are reprinted courtesy of *Sports Illustrated For Kids* from August 1994 issue. Copyright © 1994, Time Inc. From "Dad Just Got Traded!" by Susan Fornoff. All Rights Reserved.

Scott Treimel on behalf of Charlotte Zolotow
"Change" from *River Winding* by Charlotte Zolotow. Copyright © 1970 by Charlotte Zolotow. Reprinted by permission of Scott Treimel on behalf of the author.

Bess Morrison Unger for the author
From *M*A*S*H: The Exclusive, Inside Story of TV's Most Popular Show* by David Reiss. Copyright © 1980 Twentieth Century-Fox Film Corporation. Published by Bobbs-Merrill Company, Inc.

University Press of New England
From "The Drive-In Movies," from *A Summer Life* by Gary Soto, © 1990 University Press of New England. Reprinted by permission of University Press of New England.

Viking Penguin, a Division of Penguin Books USA Inc.
From *Zlata's Diary: A Child's Life in Sarajevo* by Zlata Filipovic, translated by Christina Pribichevich-Zoric. Translation copyright © Fixot et editions Robert Laffont, 1994. Used by permission.

Wayland (Publishers) Ltd.
From *Wildlife at Risk: Pandas* by Gillian Standring. Copyright © 1991 Wayland (Publishers) Ltd. Reprinted by permission of the publisher.

The H. W. Wilson Company
From Faye A. Powell's review of *My Name Is Not Angelica* by Scott O'Dell, from *Booktalk! 4,* copyright © 1992 by Joni Richards Bodart. Reprinted by arrangement with The H. W. Wilson Company.

Note: Every effort has been made to locate the copyright owner of material reprinted in this book. Omissions brought to our attention will be corrected in subsequent printings.

309

Photo Research: Brian Rohan, Catalina Gavilanes

Photo/Art Credits

iv (top to bottom) Johnny Johnson/Natural Selection Stock Photography, Inc.; Randy Wells/Tony Stone Images; ©The Stock Market/R. B. Sanchez 1995 **v** (top and center top) Anthony Mercieca/Natural Selection Stock Photography, Inc.; (center bottom) ©The Stock Market/Bill Benzen 1995; (bottom) ©Jeanne White/Photo Researchers, Inc. **vi** (top) Andre Jenny/International Stock Photography, Ltd.; (top center) ©1995 Mike Malyszko/FPG International Corp.; (bottom center and bottom) NASA **vii** (top and top center) Movie Still Archives; (bottom center) ©, New York; New York City Department of Mental Health, Mental Retardation and Alcoholism Services, 1994; (bottom) David W. Hamilton/The Image Bank **viii** (top and top center) Mike Yamashita/Woodfin Camp & Associates; (bottom center) ©George Holton/Photo Researchers, Inc.; (bottom) Uniphoto **ix** (top to bottom) Mark Heifner/Natural Selection Stock Photography, Inc.; Siqui Sanchez/The Image Bank; David Muench/Tony Stone Images; Tom Bean/Tony Stone Images **1** *Amanecer en la Montaña (Dawn on the Mountain)*, 1949, Dr. Atl, (Gerardo Murillo) Patrimonio de Jalisco, Reproduction authorized by the Instituto Nacional de Bellas Artes y Literatura, Photo by John Lei/Omni Photo Communications, Inc. **2** Akuma Takegami/International Stock Photography, Ltd. **4** (left) Wayne Aldridge/International Stock Photography, Ltd.; (right) Mimi Forsyth/Monkmeyer **7** AP/Wide World Photos **8** Michael Euler/AP/Wide World Photos **9** Culver Pictures, Inc. **10** Guy Marche/Tony Stone Images **11** ©The Stock Market/Mugshots 1995 **12** John Michael/International Stock Photography, Ltd. **13** Randy Wells/Tony Stone Images **14** David Young-Wolff/PhotoEdit **15** (top) Wayne Sproul/International Stock Photography, Ltd.; (bottom) Bill Stanton/International Stock Photography, Ltd. **17** *Shoe Series 1*, Marilee Whitehouse-Holm, Private Collection/Superstock **18** ©The Stock Market/Mugshots 1995 **20** ©Lawrence Migdale/Photo Researchers, Inc. **21** ©1995 Arthur Tilley/FPG International Corp. **23** Paul Conklin/Monkmeyer **24** John Warden/Tony Stone Images **28** Johnny Johnson/Natural Selection Stock Photography, Inc. **29** Anthony Mercieca/Natural Selection Stock Photography, Inc. **30** *Tintern Abbey*, J.M.W. Turner, Copyright British Museum **32** (top and bottom) Anthony Mercieca/Natural Selection Stock Photography, Inc. **33** ©Wildlife Conservation Society **34** (left) ©The Stock Market/R. B. Sanchez 1995; (right) ©The Stock Market/Tom Brakefield 1995 **36** ©Gregory Dimijian/Photo Researchers, Inc. **37** ©The Stock Market/Randy Ury 1995 **38** Jim Corwin/Tony Stone Images **39** ©The Stock Market/Mugshots 1995 **40** Paul Thompson/International Stock Photography, Ltd. **41** Donna Day/Tony Stone Images **42** *Irises*, Vincent van Gogh, Sotheby's, London/Superstock **43** Al Clayton/International Stock Photography, Ltd. **45** *Giant Catapult,* Leonardo da Vinci, Biblioteca Ambrosiana/Superstock **46** ©1995 Frank Cezus/FPG International Corp. **49** (top) Uniphoto; (bottom) Charles Mauzy/Natural Selection Stock Photography, Inc. **50** ©Blair Seitz/Photo Researchers, Inc. **52** Jay Wiley/Monkmeyer **53** Lynn Saville **54** ©The Stock Market/Don Mason 1995 **59** ©1995 Phil Agland/Oxford Scientific Films/Animals Animals **60** *An Elder Wearing Otuogwu Cloth Talking to a Teen Boy*, John Mainga, LAMU, The Gallery of Contemporary African Art, Photo by John Lei/Omni-Photo Communications, Inc. **64** (left) Jeffrey Dunn/Stock, Boston; (right) Photograph by H. P. Moore, Collection of The New-York Historical Society **67** Movie Still Archives **68** AP/Wide World Photos **69** *Underground Railroad*, 1982, Oberlin Seniors, Courtesy of the artists **70** Brian Rohan, Courtesy of the artist **71** Jeff Cadge/The Image Bank **72** ©The Stock Market/Mugshots 1995 **73** ©The Stock Market/Norbert Wu 1995 **74** *The Village Dance*, Javran/Superstock **75** ©Jeanne White/Photo Researchers **77** *Bergheuer*, Ernst Ludwig Kirchner, Christie's, London/The Bridgeman Art Library, London **78** ©Steve Elmore **79** ©The Stock Market/Jose L. Pelaez 1995 **80** ©The Stock Market/Zefa Germany 1995 **82** ©The Stock Market/Craig Tuttle 1995 **83** ©Bill Bachman/Photo Researchers, Inc. **84** Audrey Gottlieb/Monkmeyer **86** Sobel/Klonsky/The Image Bank **87** ©The Stock Market/Michal Heron 1995 **88** ©The Stock Market/Bill Benzen 1995 **96** *Christmas*, Palmer Hayden, Collection of Collette and Bernard King, Courtesy of Michael Rosenfeld Gallery, NYC **98** *City Expanding*, 1989, Roger Brown, Courtesy of Phyllis Kind Art Gallery, New York **100** Andre Jenny/International Stock Photography, Ltd. **102** (left) Robert Clay/Monkmeyer; (right) Debbie Hershkowitz/Monkmeyer **105** ©George Holton/Photo Researchers, Inc. **106** Movie Still Archives **107** Brian Rohan, Courtesy of the artist **108** Superstock **109** Yellow Dog Productions/The Image Bank **110** ©Richard Hutchings/Photo Researchers, Inc. **111** ©F. Stuart Westmorland/Photo Researchers, Inc. **112** *The Sleeping Gypsy*, Henri Rousseau/Superstock **113** ©The Stock Market/Richard Abarno 1995 **115** ©Orlando R. Cuevas, Courtesy of the artist **116** ©The Stock Market/Gabe Palmer 1995 **118** ©Renee Lynn/Photo Researchers, Inc. **119** J.P.H. Images/The Image Bank **120** ©Richard T. Nowitz/Photo Researchers, Inc. **123** Frank Siteman/Monkmeyer **124** Lynn Saville **125** ©1995 Mike Malyszko/FPG International Corp. **130** Peter Menzel/Stock, Boston **131** Bill Gallery/Stock, Boston **132** *Strike*, Jacob Lawrence, The Howard University Gallery of Art, Washington, D.C. **134** ©1995 Kent Knudson/FPG International Corp. **136** (left and right) Bob Daemmrich/Stock, Boston **138** ©Marty Snyderman/Planet Earth Pictures **139** Lincoln Boyhood National Memorial **140** Photo: John Bramley ©The Walt Disney Company **142** Superstock **143** Movie Still Archives **144, 145** NASA **147** *Market Place, Guatemala*, John Hollis Kaufman/Superstock **149** Jay Wiley/Monkmeyer **150** The Bettmann Archive **152** Dennis Brack/Black Star **153** (top) UPI/Bettmann; (bottom) William Johnson/Stock, Boston **154** *The Headless Horseman Pursuing Ichabod Crane*, 1858, John Quidor, National Museum of American Art, Washington, DC, Museum purchase made possible in part by the Catherine Walden Myer Endowment, the Julia D. Strong Endowment, and the Director's Discretionary Fund/Art Resource, NY **155** Nel DiGiacomo/The Image Bank **156** ©Bill Aron/Photo Researchers, Inc. **157, 159** Lynn Saville **160** (top and bottom) Movie Still Archives **164** AP/Wide World Photos **166** *The Much Resounding Sea*, 1884, Thomas Moran, Gift of the Avalon Foundation, © 1995 Board of Trustees, National Gallery of Art, Washington **168** ©, New York; New York City Department of Mental Health, Mental Retardation and Alcoholism Services, 1994 **170** (left) David W. Hamilton/The Image Bank; (right) Mike Agliolo/International Stock Photography, Ltd. **173** Grant LeDuc/Monkmeyer **174** (left) *Cat and Bird (Katze und Vogel)*, 1928, Paul Klee, Oil and ink on gessoed canvas, Mounted on wood, 15 x 21" (38.1 x 53.2 cm), The Museum of Modern Art, New York, Sidney and Harriet Janis Collection Fund and gift of Suzy Prudden and Joan H. Meijer in memory of F. H. Hirschland, Photograph ©1995 The Museum of Modern Art, New York; (right) Puppet, Paul Klee, Photo by Adriano Heitmann **175** Lynn Saville **176** ©B. Bardinet/Petit Format/Photo Researchers, Inc. **177** ©The Stock Market/DiMaggio/Kalish 1995 **178** Bill Aron/PhotoEdit **179** ©The Stock Market/Dick Frank Studio 1995 **181** *Hollywood Hills, California* (detail), Fred C. Czufin, Private Collection/Superstock **184** ©J. Gerard Smith/Photo Researchers, Inc. **185** ©The Stock Market/Chuck Savage 1995 **186** Ted Russell/The Image Bank **189** Patti McConville/The Image Bank **191** Bob Daemmrich/Stock, Boston **196** Doug Raboy, Courtesy of the artist **198** *The Critic*, The Inland Printer, After the original Japanese, The Free Library of Philadelphia/Scala/Art Resource, New York **200** Mike Yamashita/Woodfin Camp & Associates **202** (left) ©James R. Fisher/Photo Researchers, Inc.; (right) Harry Walker/Monkmeyer **205** *Peculiarsome Abe*, N. C. Wyeth, The Free Library of Philadelphia **206** ©Mandolin Brothers/Photo Researchers, Inc. **207** Dick Huffman/Monkmeyer **208** ©Francois Gohier/Photo Researchers, Inc. **209** Ian Shaw/Tony Stone Images **210** Ire Kirschenbaum/Stock, Boston **211** Ted Streshinsky/Photo 20-20 **212, 213** Steve Vidler/Leo de Wys, Inc. **215** *Commuters II*, Diana Ong/Superstock **216** Patti McConville/The Image Bank **218** Lew Merrim/Monkmeyer **220** UPI/Bettmann **221** *Langston Hughes*, c. 1925, Winold Reiss,The National Portrait Gallery, Smithsonian Institution, Gift of W. Tjark Reiss, in memory of his father, Winold Reiss, Art Resource, New York **223** ©David Muench 1995 **224** ©George Holton/Photo Researchers, Inc. **225** Grantpix/Monkmeyer **228** ©1995 Patti Murray/Animals Animals **232** ©Eric & David Hosking/Photo Researchers, Inc. **235** ©1995 Zig Leszczynski/Animals Animals **236** *Against the Enamel of a Background Rhythmic with Beats and Angles, Tones, Tints, Portrait of M. Felix Feneon in 1890*, Paul Signac, Private Collection, Photograph © Malcolm Varon **238** (top) George Zimbel/Monkmeyer; (bottom left) Frank Siteman/Monkmeyer; (bottom right) Donna Jernigan/Monkmeyer **239** Photo by Carolyn Soto **240** (left) ©1995 Brenner-Lennon Photo Product/FPG International Corp.; (right) Joseph Sohm/Tony Stone Images **243** ©Frank J. Miller/Photo Researchers, Inc. **244** Henryk Kaiser/Leo de Wys, Inc. **245** ©Jeff Greenberg/Photo Researchers, Inc. **246** Mark Heifner/Natural Selection Stock Photography, Inc. **247** AP/Wide World Photos **248** *Boys in the City*, Diana Ong, Private Collection/Superstock **249** Bob Firth/International Stock Photography, Ltd. **251** Superstock **252** ©The Stock Market/Michal Heron 1995 **254** Mel Digiacomo/The Image Bank **255** Steve McCutcheon/Monkmeyer **256** William Wright/Monkmeyer **257** Uniphoto **259** ©1995 John Terence Turner/FPG International Corp. **261** ©The Stock Market/Michal Heron 1995 **262** ©Rick Golt/Photo Researchers, Inc. **265** Maria Taglienti/The Image Bank **266** *Voices of the Clouds*, Jessie Lee Geiszler, Courtesy of the artist **268** David Muench/Tony Stone Images **270** (left) Tom Bean/Tony Stone Images; (right) Chris Noble/Tony Stone Images **273** Scala/Art Resource, NY **274** Brian Rohan, Courtesy of the artist **275** ©Will & Deni McIntyre/Photo Researchers, Inc. **276** Siqui Sanchez/The Image Bank **277** ©Bachmann/Photo Researchers, Inc. **278** Ric Ergenbright/Tony Stone Images **279** Hugh Rogers/Monkmeyer **280** *The Council Rock*, 1913, Illustration by Maurice and Edward Detmold from *The Jungle Book* by Rudyard Kipling, The Century Company, The Central Children's Room, Donnell Library Center, The New York Public Library **281** ©Stephen J. Krasemann/Photo Researchers, Inc. **283** Benn Mitchell/The Image Bank **284** ©The Stock Market/Michal Heron 1995 **285** Lynn Saville **286** Rhoda Sidney/Monkmeyer **288** ©Russell D. Curtis/Photo Researchers, Inc. **290** ©Blair Seitz/Photo Researchers, Inc. **291** ©Joseph Nettis/Photo Researchers, Inc. **294** Lon E. Lauber/Natural Selection Stock Photography, Inc.

310